Austen Chamberlain and Baldwin posing, at Baldwin's instigation, after Chamberlain had been told that he would not be in the government in May 1923.

THE IMPACT OF LABOUR
1920-1924

THE BEGINNING OF
MODERN BRITISH
POLITICS

MAURICE COWLING
Fellow of Peterhouse, Cambridge
University Lecturer in History

CAMBRIDGE
AT THE UNIVERSITY PRESS
1971

Published by the Syndics of the Cambridge University Press
Bentley House, 200 Euston Road, London N.W.1
American Branch: 32 East 57th Street, New York, N.Y.10022

© Cambridge University Press 1971

Library of Congress Catalogue Card Number: 73–127236

ISBN: 0 521 07969 1

Printed in Great Britain
at the University Press, Aberdeen

CONTENTS

CONTENTS

PREFACE

The core of this book is based on the letters and diaries written by politicians and preserved in the collections listed in the bibliography. No other material can bring us within comprehending distance of the working of the political system in the period under discussion. Without the care taken by owners and others to preserve it and make it available, historians would be unable to move beyond the desiccated contentions of political science or the formal pieties of official history.

The author therefore owes a central debt to the owners, custodians and archivists of these collections, and especially to Mr John MacCallum Scott for the loan of his father's diary, to Lords Ponsonby and Simon for lending their fathers' papers, to Lord Bridgeman for a copy of his father's diary, to Lady Davidson for access to her husband's papers, to Lord Salisbury, Mr Julian Amery, M.P. and Mr John Grigg for access to their fathers' papers and to Mrs Stephen Lloyd for kindness and hospitality in allowing access to the papers of her father, Neville Chamberlain, while they were in her possession. He is grateful also to owners of copy-right material who have given permission for it to be used and he apologises to any whom he has failed to approach. For their exertions in seeking, or facilitating, access to collections, he is indebted to Professor Douglas Johnson, Mr Michael Bates, Dr Anil Seal, Mr William Rees-Mogg, Mr Robert Rhodes James, Mr Robert Blake, Mr G. D. M. Block, Mr David Marquand, M.P., Mr Russell Lewis, Dr R. M. Hartwell, Sir Michael Fraser, Dom David Knowles, Mr Michael Wolff and Mr George Hutchinson.

He is grateful to Mr A. J. P. Taylor for allowing him to see a draft typescript of his *Beaverbrook* and to Lord Rothermere for conversation which he hopes will not seem ill-requited.

He is grateful to Mr Andrew Winckler of Christ's College for checking references and reading proofs, and to Mr F. Lipsius of Peterhouse, Cambridge for checking references. He is grateful to Professor Vincent of Peterhouse and Bristol for commenting on parts of the typescript, to Mr Alistair Cooke for supplying a quotation from the Carson papers and to Mr C. P. Cook, Mr E.

vii

David and Professor J. Gallagher for advice about particular points. He owes a particular debt to Professor J. R. Jones of Norwich for reading the typescript and making searching criticisms at two stages.

He owes a large debt to the staff of the Beaverbrook Library, and in particular to Miss Rosemary Brooks, not least for doing the major part of the reading of the proofs. He is grateful to Mr A. E. B. Owen and Miss J. B. Shiel, and to the staffs of the Royal Archives, Cambridge University Library, the British Museum, the Public Record Office, *The Spectator*, the Scottish Public Record Office, the House of Lords Record Office, the National Library of Scotland, the India Office Library, the National Register of Archives, the Bodleian and the Libraries of Churchill College, Cambridge, Trinity College, Cambridge, *The Times*, the London School of Economics and the Universities of Newcastle and Sheffield.

He is indebted to Mrs E. D. Beebe, Mrs O. G. Page, Miss Ann Parr, Miss E. D. Box and others for typing various parts of the drafts of the book, and to Mr E. E. Reynolds for making the index.

He owes a continuing debt to the Master and Fellows of Peterhouse for providing conditions in which historical work can be done.

November 1970   Maurice Cowling

'If you are good enough to afford me the opportunity I shall in the future in a final article attempt to state in a series of generalities the points which may serve as a rallying-ground for the national party of the future. . . The formation of such a party may easily be postponed. It may be postponed too long. It may be called a National Party, a Constitutional Party or a People's Party. But even if it be postponed: by whatever name it be called, all those who have criticized me, except those who belong to the Socialist party, will within five years – in office or in opposition – find themselves, as I shall, among the roll of its members.'

Birkenhead writing in Weekly Dispatch, January 25 1920

'The other man – "FE" – is disreputable and has been hitherto unfriendly to your government. I do not imagine he has got many political principles and most of what he has got are wrong . . . What . . . we have to consider is what effect the quasi-public reception of him may have amongst the leaders of thought in the democracy. They are panting after ideals which they are afraid may be slipping from them. They have no sympathy whatever with the hard-shelled defence of the Haves against the Have-Nots. I think FE – without ideals and with his crude attachment to the interests of wealth – would lose us more than Austen [Chamberlain] would gain us.'

Salisbury to Baldwin, January 26 1924, in protest against Birkenhead and Austen Chamberlain being asked to join the Conservative Shadow Cabinet

' "By the way", Mr Wickham Steed interjected, "how do you account for the curious circumstance that the word 'Socialism' has now become a scarecrow in British politics. Thirty years ago people in England talked of 'Socialism' without half the horror shown or affected now." "There are several reasons but the main, the real reason", said the Premier, "is because the older parties and some of the sections of the community which support them fear the moral fervour of the Labour party. They cannot match it, and they feel in their bones that when a party has an ideal and is devoted to it, it gathers a momentum that makes it dangerous to older and less vital organizations." '

MacDonald in interview with Wickham Steed, Manchester Guardian, October 7 1924

INTRODUCTION: THE CHARACTER OF HIGH POLITICS

Between 1920 and 1924 the Conservative party made three long-term decisions. The first was to remove Lloyd George from office. The second was to take up the rôle of 'defender of the social order'. The third was to make Labour the chief party of opposition. These decisions were attempts to contain the upheaval caused by the Labour party's arrival as a major force and to gain whatever advantage could be gained from it. They were deliberately made and strongly contested and were the cause of continuous dispute between the leaders. Their outcome, and the consequence of the general election of 1924, was that for the next phase of political activity Baldwin wore the mantle Lloyd George had worn in his last two years of office as leader of resistance to 'Socialism'.

'Resistance to Socialism' first became a possible programme when Labour won the Spen Valley by-election in January 1920. In this story Spen Valley was crucial. From Spen Valley onwards, the Labour party was the major problem. Whether by outbidding it, by detaching some Labour leaders from it or by rallying all forces against it, the attempt to deal with it was the central fact in political calculation in the years that followed. This was true of the Conservatives who admired Lloyd George. It was true of those who disliked him. It was true of the Conservatives who destroyed his Coalition. It was true of the Asquithean Liberals whom his Coalition had destroyed. Salisbury wanted to make the Conservative party the centre of resistance by detaching it from Lloyd George. Birkenhead, Austen Chamberlain and at times Churchill wanted to submerge it in a Centre party of resistance under his leadership. Lord Robert Cecil wanted a Centre party to ignore the Conservative Right, embrace the Asquitheans and the 'respectable' Labour leaders and avoid Lloyd George. Mond, Fisher and Hilton Young wanted resistance to be led by a progressive Liberal party with Lloyd George at its head. Gladstone, Cowdray and Maclean wanted much the same under Viscount Grey. At some points Rothermere wanted a Liberal-based Centre party under Lloyd George, Grey, Maclean or McKenna. At others he wanted it to be led by Derby, Birkenhead or Austen Chamberlain.

Just as these Liberals and Conservatives sought rôles as defenders against Socialism, so in the Liberal and Labour parties others sought scope for futures as leaders of progress against Conservative reaction. Despite instincts which were conservative in the post-war context, this is what Asquith wanted to do with the Liberal party. In Thomas's, Clynes's and Snowden's calculations, Lloyd George figured as a possible bridge between conventional Radicalism and a Centre party alliance to which Liberals and radical Conservatives could adhere. Haldane hoped for something of the kind with prominence for himself. So in some moods did Grey provided Lloyd George was not involved. In this they were distinguished from MacDonald whose object, from his election as Chairman of the Parliamentary Labour Party in 1922, was to make Labour the only party of progress. MacDonald's willingness to take office in 1924 once the Liberal party had decided that he should do so did not reduce his desire to supersede it.

The election of 1924 demolished the Liberal party and destroyed all hope of a Centre party. It established that there would be one party of change and one of resistance and that the Conservative party would for the moment be the party of resistance. Baldwin, Bridgeman, Salisbury, Amery, Wood, Hoare, Joynson-Hicks and Neville Chamberlain succeeded where nearly all other leading politicians failed. These failures should not conceal the fact that from the Spen Valley by-election to the day on which the election results were declared in October 1924, there was something resembling equality of opportunity for all the groups concerned.

One mythology, invented by Lloyd George and Birkenhead, implied that the overthrow of the Coalition in October 1922 and resistance to its revival involved replacing the modern government of an industrial nation by a recalcitrant group of reactionary Die Hards. Another, invented by Baldwin and his followers, was that their task was to prevent the escalation of class conflict promised by the personal immorality, opportunist cynicism and aggressive determination to do down the poor which were alleged to be the salient features of Coalition politics. Both were half-truths. The struggle which occurred in the Conservative party between 1920 and 1924 was a struggle about method rather than about policy. It was a struggle to decide what to say, and what tone to say it in, in attempting to construct a broad-based body of resistance to

'Socialism'. Baldwin was opposed to 'Socialism'. So was Salisbury. So were all the Conservative enemies of Lloyd George, all his Conservative supporters and all the advocates of a Centre party. About the damage it would do and the danger it would bring, if not resisted, there was agreement. But differences about method were inseparable from disputes about persons which centred around Birkenhead and Lloyd George on the one hand and first Salisbury and then Baldwin on the other. In this respect Baldwin was the beneficiary of the position established by Salisbury between 1920 and 1922 when Lloyd George's willingness to resist Labour did not stop criticisms of the justification he offered for resistance. Before the fall of the Coalition these involved rejection of Birkenhead's idea that 'resistance to Labour' was its raison d'être. When it fell, one thing that was thought to have fallen with it was the idea that 'Labour' was 'the common foe'. Between 1922 and 1924 the chief concern of the Conservative leaders was to find something to say which was not as bare. Until the election of 1924 it was not certain that 'resistance' would be successful electorally, that success was possible under Conservative leadership or that the accommodating style of resistance established on the fall of the Coalition could survive. The central theme of this book will be the process by which it was established that it could.

In following this process we shall concentrate on the high politics of the politicians who mattered. Back-benchers and party opinion will appear off-stage as malignant or beneficent forces with unknown natures and unpredictable wills. Civil servants will hardly appear at all except Thomas Jones as speech-writer, Hankey and Warren Fisher as wheel-oilers and others as possible Labour ministers in 1924. Issues of substance, except about the party system, will be considered so far as solutions, or failure to provide solutions, affected the standing of the governments or politicians concerned. Europe, Russia, Ireland, India and the Empire will be treated in the way politicians treated them – as incidents in the history of what was taken to be the central domestic problem.

This procedure will be followed because the first context in which high politics was played was the context in which politicians reacted to one another. The political system consisted of fifty or sixty politicians in conscious tension with one another whose accepted authority constituted political leadership. In this context significance arose from mutual recognition; not from office, but from a distinction between politicians, inside parliament and outside, whose actions were thought reciprocally important and those whose actions were not. It was from these politicians that almost all initiative came. The language they used, the images they formed, the myths they left had a profound effect on the objectives other politicians assumed could be achieved through the political system.

This procedure has been adopted, secondly, because it is necessary to understand what the ruling groups were doing before more general questions can be answered. A study of the impact of politicians on British public opinion would be an important extension of this book, but it is not what it is about. However desirable it may be to understand the Labour and Conservative movements as aspects of total social history, an essential preliminary is to understand the ignorance and eccentricity from which they were led. It was not because they were typical of the English people that the leaders were in a position to lead, though most of them, once in power, thought or pretended that they were. They were there because they had made their way to the top and used the opportunities this gave to say whatever they thought it suitable to say. They talked, both publicly and one to another, about public opinion as a factor by which they should be guided: in some respects their words and actions were affected by what they took it to be. But in these years there was more difficulty than usual in knowing what it was and almost insuperable difficulty in knowing what the electoral effects would be when a predominantly new electorate was faced with a choice between two Liberal parties, Labour in a strength which was in itself new and a Conservative party which constantly promised to be as divided as the Liberal party. In these circumstances, since they were playing in the dark, politicians either made up their tunes as they went along or replayed the tunes they had learnt before the lights went out in 1914.

We shall proceed in this way, thirdly, because it is the only way to understand the exact nature of the responsibility of which politicians were conscious when they exercised power. High politics was primarily a matter of rhetoric and manoeuvre. The predominating preoccupation of politicians at the top was the moral and mental vacuum they believed had been established by the destruction of the pre-war landmarks, by the arrival of the Labour party and by the newness and ignorance of the new electorate. Political rhetoric was an attempt to provide new land-marks for the electorate. Political manoeuvre was designed to ensure that the right people provided them. The essence of the politics of these years was a struggle to decide which rhetoric to use and which group was to use it in establishing the Labour party on the one hand or a body of resistance to it on the other. There were as many nostrums as there were political groups. It was the resolution of the conflicts between them which accounts for the time that elapsed between the first unfolding of the Labour problem in 1920 and the establishment of the Labour/Conservative polarisation in 1924.

The fourth reason for adopting this procedure is that the 'vacuum' of which politicians were conscious gave them a freedom they had not felt before. In this sense their actions were constructive: they were trying not merely to say what electors wanted to hear but to make electors want them to say what they wanted to say in the first place. Rhetoric was a form of exemplary utterance, an attempt at constructive teaching, an effort to persuade the new electorate to enter the thought-world inhabited by existing politicians. It was an attempt to secure acquiescence through words, a claim on the part of politicians who demanded it to speak for the people and persuade them that they had the keys of whatever kingdom they thought it desirable to enter. Which kingdom they claimed to be entering varied with the tactical occasion. Which intention they announced depended on calculation of the consequences. Out of all the moods the electorate could be persuaded to feel, the choice made by each politician on each occasion was affected by the choice made by his rivals as all fought for footholds in the patriotic, war-weary, peace-loving, moral, decent, idealistic, class-conscious, resentful public of their imaginations.

This method of proceeding has been adopted, finally, because it is necessary to understand the details of political manoeuvre in order to highlight the relationship between situational necessity and the intentions of politicians. In this respect one has to convey the involvement in the compulsions and uncertainties of the system

5

which was characteristic of the whole of a politician's public life. For this purpose biography is almost always misleading. Its refraction is partial in relation to the system. It abstracts a man whose public action should not be abstracted. It implies linear connections between one situation and the next. In fact connections were not linear. The system was a circular relationship: a shift in one element changed the position of all others in relation to the rest. The reactions of politicians were developed in full awareness of the relationship and in conscious knowledge of the need to move whenever it moved. Without understanding the perpetual nature of these motions, one can convey neither the powerlessness nor the impact of individual politicians nor understand the extent to which they were moved by antipathy towards their rivals. Antipathy, self-interest and mutual contempt were the strongest levers of action, the most powerful motives in conflict, and they were so because no one knew what the outcome of conflict would be. It was the fact that they knew that they were fighting for an unknown future which explains the heat of the politics we are discussing and justifies the weight given to factors which politicians in retrospect prefer to forget. This would be true of any historical period. It was particularly true when the future was as open, hope and fear as strong and the situation as new as the one we are discussing.

The question we have to ask is whether the procedures we have adopted are helpful in understanding the history of the Labour party which claimed to be more democratic than the parties it was attempting to replace. To this our answer is that they are, that in these years the Labour leaders committed themselves to the politics they found established and that in all important respects the politics of 1920/24 were continuous with the politics of the previous ninety years.

The salient feature of the political system since 1832 was not the attempt of popular feeling to make itself felt in parliament but the attempts of parliamentary politicians to find ways of securing support from extra-parliamentary opinion. In this respect the Reform Bill of 1832 introduced only a new factor into calculation. The need to manipulate the electorate instead of influencing it was increased by subsequent extensions of the franchise. But the parliamentary politicians who managed the system after 1832, 1867, 1884 or 1918 had as little intention as their predecessors of encouraging the electorate to enter into the high places of power. What they wanted the electorate to want was not participation but vicarious satisfaction at the leadership of the politicians who operated the system or claimed the right to operate it in the future.

This meant that, as the franchise was extended, there was not only increasing need to catch hold of working-class opinion where that differed, or could be made to differ, from the opinions of other classes, but also an increasing chance to do the same with all other sorts of opinion, including agrarian, industrial, bourgeois, anglican, nonconformist, celtic and anti-working-class opinion where these promised to be helpful. From 1832, and increasingly after 1867 and 1884, all these factors operated, often in the mind of the same politicians. In one respect, however, the polarisation of rhetoric did not produce a polarisation of action: social inequality was preserved by collusive collaboration to make rhetoric not action the centre of dispute. This was why 'conflict' was 'synthetic'. This was why parliamentary politics were 'ambiguous'.

The most important political leaders did not occupy small patches of rhetorical ground: they 'recognised the force' of all effective opinions and batted on all sides of whatever wicket they chose to make their own. This was so in general. It was so where relations between the classes were concerned. Even where the language was democratic, as with Bright, Joseph Chamberlain and Lloyd George, there was no expectation that the masses could dominate the classes and no real commitment to make them do so. Parliament was an arena for conflict between politicians from different classes. But politicians were leaders, not followers: they found in parliament a terminal beyond which conflict would not ride. In practice conflict divided parliamentary politicians far less than consciousness of the power of parliament united them. The social ambiguity of parliamentary Radicalism, agreement about the desirability of parliamentary government and the openness of the party situation in a parliament of patchwork groups and opinions put controlled, large-scale, predictable social change out of the question.

From this point of view party must be seen as protecting the classes by persuading the masses to support the parliamentary conflict through which inequality was sustained. As social institutions or cultural landmarks, parties embodied the will to preserve the virtues and inequalities of the landed and industrial hierarchies to which they were attached. In this respect they changed slowly. In parliament, and among the political leaders, the reality was not only continuity but also the possibility of disrupting it. In parliamentary terms party was subject to continuous review and the continuous possibility of disruption. In 1846, 1886, 1918, 1922 and 1931 major reviews were carried through in conditions of heat and anger. At almost all other times the possibility of disruption on the scale which occurred on these occasions was a major stimulator of events and a major creator of expectations among those who expected new rôles for themselves in the process of disruption. The idea of a Centre party, of Tory Democracy, of Liberal Unionism, of Liberal Imperialism, of a radicalism of the Left or a Die Hard party of the Right, of Lowe, Goschen, Harcourt, Northcote, Granville, Spencer, Carson, Birkenhead, both Churchills, two Devonshires, two Derbys, two Greys, two Chamberlains, two Halifaxes and innumerable others as Prime Minister suggested repetitions of what Disraeli had done in 1846 or the Peelites thereafter, even when they came to nothing. It was the tension between existing and possible party alignments which gave alternative leaders the chance to identify their futures with unexplored possibilities, gave every major politician the opportunity to exercise power without office and enabled figures like Baldwin and Campbell-Bannerman – both possible Speakers – to reach positions neither could expect until the hierarchy of dominant merit had been broken. It is this that makes context, tension and total situation central if major decisions are to be understood.

The centre of tension was continuous theorising about the next thing politicians claimed to wish to do with party, government or the constitution. Party politics issued in this sense in political theory, a rhetorical persuasion to adopt the language and expectations of the politician who used it, a succession of affirmations designed to sound resonantly in the ears of whatever audience was being addressed. These resonances, whether imitations of great social purposes or instruments of politicians on the make, bore little relation to politics as politicians experienced them or to life as electors led it. Politics was conceived as touching the hem of the garment of Truth. It was an area of Right and illuminated by Faith. Politicians, where not merely entertainers, were presented

8

as crusaders or philosophers. In a curious conjunction of myth and fantasy it seemed almost to be suggested that they were the unacknowledged poets of the time.

This was true not just of democratic, liberal or progressive politicians but of all. It was true of attempts to attract sympathy not just from working-class interests but from all interests. It applied to any use any politician made of whatever was available in the political spectrum, which was a rag-bag of opinions and feelings existing in the hearts of back-benchers or the minds of electors and explored according to necessity or instinctive preference.

Instinctive preference is a way of describing belief, but in asking whether politicians believed the opinions they explored, one is reaching for the limits of explanation. Opinions were believed without being thought suitable for expression: situations brought forth opinions which politicians did not previously know they had believed. Accumulation of material will not tell us whether conservative leaders *believed* there was a threat to the social order in 1867, 1885, 1910 or 1921. It will not tell us in what sense Bright, Gladstone, Joseph Chamberlain or Lloyd George *believed* in the attacks Conservatives may have believed they were making. Belief in these, and in all other cases, must be imputed not to an affirmation of the heart, but to public conduct, the tip of an iceberg we assume emerged from real humanity by courses too random and obscure to yield to the historical conventions.

The study of politics at the top is, therefore, not a simple matter. One is dealing with a problematical, high-level activity where the meaning of the material is not self-evident. At the core of each politician there was temperament which impregnated everything he did. That, however, was the chief continuity: the manifestations of temperament cannot be deduced from it. Speech was often designed to conceal: there was little correlation between what politicians said and the objective world about which they said it. At every point a politician can be found 'not wanting' office when it was clear to everyone else that he did. Almost every year produced a 'political crisis', a 'new situation' or a 'conflict of principle fundamental to the future of the country'. But not every 'new situation' was new nor every 'crisis' critical. Nor were many 'conflicts of principle' fundamental to the future of the country. The claim that they were shows not that nonsense was being talked but that there was a well-understood public language in which 'crisis', 'principle' and 'novelty' were conventional instruments for establishing positions in the monastic, or rotarian, world we are discussing.

The world of high politics was not, of course, entirely monastic or rotarian. But there were two reasons why it was untypical. In the first place, it was self-perpetuating. Secondly, changes in the social structure were not readily reflected in the character of the political power. Until 1916 the original 'workshop of the world' was governed by country gentlemen, dukes' relatives, rentiers, literary Radicals, educated intellectuals and professional politicians with occasional, and on the whole unwelcome, irruptions from Rochdale or Birmingham armed with monocle, orchid or stuffed shirt to preserve the necessary distance. The poor had no place in government. With rare exceptions whelk-stalls figured little in the experience of leading politicians whose function in relation to the public is best understood as something between corporate monarch, witch-doctor and bard. Incantations varied according to fashion and taste: they were made cynically or seriously according to temperament and education. They were made in the shadow of the fact that the involvement they encouraged electors to feel was negligible and that the reality they protected was a method of proceeding with the nation's business.

This is to say not that government by businessmen, trades unionists or anyone else would have been better than government by professional politicians, but that businessmen, trades unionists and anyone else who exercised power adopted the conventions of the system, that these conventions are intelligible only from within and that the contradiction between words and deeds, with which much innocent amusement can be had, will only be resolved by realising that the central political achievement was not represent-ation but rhetoric – the continuous process by which politicians created personalities for themselves in order to claim the right to play a part in reducing political problems to a form suitable for governmental decision.

Now the point in interpreting the political system in this way is to show how parliamentary politicians conceived their function, and the reason for putting the Labour party in this context is that this is how the Labour leaders saw themselves. Since they had no social distance to protect them, they had, more perhaps than other political leaders, to reflect the wishes of their followers. Since, like Joseph Chamberlain, their power rested on the electorate far more than on parliamentary performance, they had to represent its discontents. But even when they said the opposite, they assumed that the political and social system could not be overturned and that it was impossible to establish a hegemony of the poor over the rich. Not only Fabianism but the whole thought-world of the Labour party, including the Labour Left, testified, however wrongly, to the solidity of the structure and the pervasiveness of the conceptions that were the objects of attack. The Labour party might, as a consequence, have remained a party of propaganda or become a party of revolution. The leaders chose instead to aim at parliamentary success when it became possible after 1919, to convince themselves that the Labour party consisted of 'sober and moderate'[1] people, and to use the tactical situation of 1924 to show that they understood more than the distress of coal, steel and cotton and the unappeasable resentments which the poor could be made to feel against the rich.

This book, then, has been written in self-imposed limitation. It assumes that the crude picture politicians had of the electorate was a significant factor in determining their reaction to the problems it presented. It displays the connection between the guesses they made about its nature and the approaches they made to it. But it discusses neither the validity of the views they took of it nor the impact it felt as they faced up to the problems presented by its overwhelmingly working-class composition. Back-bench opinion, party feeling, the decisions of civil servants, the preferences of electors, the opinions of newspapers and the objective movements of social power all contribute to understanding. But the key lies in the minds of the politicians who exercised ostensible power and in the relationship they envisaged with the society they wished to rule. In this book we posit the existence of a network of plebiscitary demagogues whose chief way of understanding their impact was by understanding the reaction of other members of it and whose chief purpose was to jostle each other as they picked their way through the limitations imposed by all these forces to a position of creative sympathy with an unknown public. In 1920 this network consisted of the leaders of the Conservative and the two Liberal parties, the leaders of the Labour party and a handful of publicists of whom Bottomley, Rothermere, Lansbury and Northcliffe were the chief. This book uses letters, diaries and public speeches to display the impact each had upon the others as all, including the Labour leaders, made innumerable false starts in answering the questions, given that the Labour movement was the one new force that had emerged since the war, what politically could be done with it? what should be done about it?

PART I

I

THE THREAT FROM LABOUR

'The whole body of employers and the State, acting through Parliament, could do much to create the right spirit in the mind of Labour by understanding clearly that Labour would not long remain as a submissive victim to any system which it considered to be unfair. Even if Labour is wrong, it has the power of numbers and that quality for wealth production which is reposed in muscle that it could for a considerable time place the country at its mercy. But this is exactly what Labour should try to avoid, and in order that it should be avoided employers and the State should take every reasonable step to reconcile Labour to a just acceptance of a particular system rather than leave Labour in a temper of serious discontent or in actual revolt against a new system.'

Clynes at luncheon at National Liberal Club, *Daily Telegraph*, October 31 1918

'... there is no line to be drawn between profit-making and profiteering ... It is ... the system that is wrong. If the system continues, it means disaster for us all... We must have, whether by political or industrial means, an immediate and complete reversal of the system and the establishment of that national production and... distribution which only the workers believe in and which only the workers can achieve.'

Daily Herald, leading article, September 5 1919

'The great advantage which the Labour party possesses is that its policy is so framed as to permit it to adopt any form of Socialism at a moment's notice.'

Duke of Northumberland at meeting with H. M. Hyndman in House of Commons, June 8 1921, *Daily Herald*, June 9

(i)

Between Gladstone's arrival as a major leader in the 1860s and his retirement in 1894, the Liberal party spanned a wide range of popular support, embracing urban and rural Radicalism, English, Scotch and Welsh nonconformity and substantial parts of the professional classes in the English, Welsh and Scottish cities. It was led by a Liberal gentry, a Whig aristocracy and the owners of urban wealth who were held together by a self-perpetuating cadre of professional politicians. At the same time as they were held together, the leaders were tending constantly to fly apart. From the 1860s onwards, there was a stream of secessions to the

15

Conservative party over the franchise, Land, Ireland, the Church of England and the personal question of Gladstone's leadership. The Whig and Chamberlainite secessions of 1886 strengthened and deepened the process. They removed any threat that there might have been to Gladstone but greatly weakened the Liberal party.

Though Gladstone broke Whig predominance and drove some Whigs out of the Liberal party, the core of Liberal leadership was still provided by Whigs and the Liberal gentry whose object was to preserve power in safe hands while the forces of progress and discontent followed. As the Liberal working class and the working-class movement grew, the terms had to be raised. But the equilibrium, maintained throughout the nineties, became firmer as the Conservative party began to disintegrate during Balfour's premiership. Conservative disintegration and the Lib/Lab alliance at the 1906 election enabled Campbell-Bannerman and Asquith to continue the style of part-Whig, part-professional trimming leadership to which the party had become accustomed.

At the general election of 1906 the Liberal party had nearly 380 M.P.s and a majority of more than 80 over Labour, Conservatives and Irish Nationalists combined. Over the whole of Scotland and Wales, it was triumphant: in England it won victories where victories had never been won before. Its leaders arrived in office with no very exact programme. Its supporters could still be excused the illusion that a new era had dawned in which alliance with Labour, a restoration of relations with the Liberal Unionists and a steady trickle of fugitives from the Protectionism with which Joseph Chamberlain had divided the Conservative party had made the Liberal party not just the horse-trading reconciler of dissentient interests but more than usually the party of the nation.

The illusion did not last long. By 1908 the electoral advantage had begun to disappear. Under collectivist pressure from within and a formidable Labour by-election vote from without, the Liberal government proposed a social programme which was presented as proof that working-class political requirements could be met within the framework of the Liberal party. Under guidance from Lloyd George it developed a style of class conflict which forced some Whig and Liberal leaders to think of withdrawing. Over Ireland, the House of Lords, the Welsh Church, Temperance Reform, Women's Suffrage and Trades Unionism, tension was heightened as the government was faced by a formidable and effective opposition. In 1910 the Liberal majority was removed. By 1911 the Liberal party, dependent on Irish Nationalist support, was just one conflicting party within the State. By the time the war began in 1914, the authority of 1906 had disappeared.

In the next two years the Liberal régime was destroyed. Lloyd George, Simon, Beauchamp and Harcourt thought seriously of resigning when war was declared in August 1914: Trevelyan, Morley and Burns did so. Distrust of Churchill's influence with Asquith was one reason for the formation of the Asquith/Conservative/Labour Coalition in May 1915: Churchill was removed from office in November. Haldane was driven out as a condition of Conservative support. Beauchamp, Buckmaster, Harcourt and Emmott were removed, or removed themselves. Simon, Home Secretary in the Asquith Coalition, resigned over conscription in January 1916. Birrell resigned as a result of the Irish rebellion. Loss of public confidence, differences about policy and military defeat produced the displacement of Asquith by Lloyd George. In December 1916, without a general election, Lloyd George and his Conservative allies completed the removal of nearly all the leading Liberals who had held office when the war began.

As Prime Minister from December 1916 onwards Lloyd George created a new range of Liberal minister whose prominence depended on himself. Isaacs had left the Asquith government in 1913 to become Lord Chief Justice: he played a prominent part in the Lloyd George Coalition. Macnamara, Munro and Lewis made a smooth transition from one leader to another. So did Wimborne and Islington who were ex-Conservatives. Churchill – also an ex-Conservative – wished to make the transition and was eventually allowed to in 1917. Montagu made it in 1917: he would have made it in 1916 if he had been offered what he thought he had been promised.[1] McKenna did not try to make it. Haldane was not able to. The existence of two ministerial cadres within the party and the presence of Lloyd George, Addison, Fisher, Hewart, Cawley, Winfrey, Rhondda, Weir, Maclay, Compton-Rickett and Illingworth where Asquith, Runciman, Grey, Samuel, Buckmaster, Simon, Beauchamp, McKenna and Crewe had sat before was of great importance for the Liberal party's future.

1917 was a bad year for Lloyd George. There was no guarantee that his government would survive. He tried to bring back Asquith just as he had tried to keep him the previous December. Asquith did not see why Lloyd George should be rescued. He refused to come and would have stopped others coming if he had had the chance.[1] Lloyd George survived the difficulties of 1917: resolution, vigour and luck carried him from near defeat in March 1918 to an unforeseen pinnacle as the national hero in November.

When the second Coalition was formed in December 1916, it was an alliance between Lloyd George and the Conservative and Labour parties. The Labour party had Henderson and, on Henderson's resignation in 1917, Barnes in the War Cabinet. It had Hodge and later Roberts in the Cabinet and Barnes and later Clynes, Roberts and Hodge as ministers outside the Cabinet. It had Brace, Roberts and later Clynes, Parker, Wardle and Walsh as parliamentary secretaries. As Privy Councillors it had Bowerman and in 1917 Thomas who refused office in December 1916 despite pressing offers from Lloyd George. Apart from Lloyd George and the Labour ministers, there were seven non-Conservative ministers in the Cabinet[2] and seven more outside it.[3] But one of these – Morison – was a Scottish Law Officer who did not sit in the House of Commons. Another – Compton-Rickett, a prominent Free Churchman – was nearly seventy. Stanley was a business administrator. Fisher was Vice-Chancellor of Sheffield University: like Stanley and Maclay he had never sat in the House of Commons. Illingworth had been there for a year. Apart from Stanley, all fourteen of these ministers were Liberals, but none of them had been in the Cabinet. Maclay and Illingworth combined long business experience – in India in the one case, in Bradford in the other – with service on government committees. Apart from Rhondda, whom Lloyd George had defeated to the leadership of Welsh Liberalism ten years before,[4] none had political standing of their own. What weight Isaacs carried with Lloyd George he carried as Lord Chief Justice, not as a member of the Cabinet. Montagu was employed in 1917 because he had been close to Asquith, but neither he nor Churchill, in the circumstances in which Churchill took office in 1917, were more than dependents of Lloyd George. F. E. Guest, Lloyd George's Chief Whip from 1917, was an ex-Conservative. Seely – yet another ex-Conservative

– had resigned from the War Office after the Curragh mutiny in 1914. His eighteen months as an under-secretary from July 1918 after three years of Army service, Cowdray's, Rothermere's and Weir's brief passages as Presidents of the Air Board and Council and Smuts's identification with the Liberal party[1] did not alter the fact that the politically substantial members of the government during the war, apart from Lloyd George and Henderson in his brief period of office, were all Conservatives, politically inexperienced or instruments of Lloyd George.

This did not prevent Lloyd George rewarding Liberal and other contributors to his funds with peerages, baronetcies and so on. Fisher, Addison and Montagu were given considerable scope over India, Education and Reconstruction. Fisher was in a powerful position as chairman of the Home Affairs Committee of the Cabinet. The industrialists, millionaires and newspaper owners whom Lloyd George brought to Whitehall were more practical embodiments of Liberal Capitalism than the Whig-Asquithean élite they replaced. Maclay, Devonport, Rhondda, Cowdray, Weir, Rothermere, Northcliffe, Beaverbrook, Riddell and Dalziel in association with Barnes, Hodge and the Labour and trades union leaders constituted an effective version of the Radical nation. Through his private office, the 'Garden City' and his personal entourage, Lloyd George had a formidable body of informal advice most of which was Liberal or Welsh. Thomas Jones, David Davies, J. T. Davies, Adams, Curtis, Grigg, Sutherland, Ernest Evans and Kerr ensured as effectively as Liberal ministers would have done that policy was formulated, where necessary, in a liberal manner.

With the fall of Peel in 1846, the Conservative party became a party of opposition. From the death of Palmerston in 1865 and with increasing success after 1880, it restored itself to being the permanent party of government. In face of whatever threat was presented by the Irish and working-class sympathies which Gladstone affected and in face of the various sorts of social, religious and educational radicalism presented by Bright, Dilke, Forster and Joseph Chamberlain, it developed a position as the party of caution, responsibility, respectability and moderation which was heightened by the Liberal split of 1886 and the development of the 'New Unionism'.

The exodus of the Hartingtonian Whigs and Chamberlainite Radicals, though it damaged the Liberal party for the next two decades, eventually had a shattering effect on Conservatives. In the first decade of the twentieth century the conflicts which had divided the Liberal party in the eighties were repeated in the Conservative party – sometimes, as with Hartington and Joseph Chamberlain, under the same leaders and, between 1902 and 1905, with the same damage to its standing as the party of government.

Between 1903 and 1914 the Conservative party witnessed a prolonged effort to carry the party leadership screaming and struggling into the twentieth century. From Joseph Chamberlain's resignation and proclamation of a Tariff Reform campaign down to the encouragement of forcible resistance to Home Rule the olympian leadership offered by Salisbury in his prime and old age was replaced by a militant vigour which concerned itself with the expansion of British and Imperial power, the development of armed strength against Germany, the improvement of National Efficiency, forcible resistance in Ulster and the deliberate involvement of the Crown in crucial questions of party politics. The new rhetoric of these years was a rhetoric of revolt – against the predominance of the great landed families inside the Conservative party and against the hypocrisy and provocations of the Liberal party outside. It was a rhetoric of solidarity, antirevolutionary resistance and national regeneration which provided social cement between a Protectionist gentry, the chauvinistic leaders of urban industry, the Goschen tradition of banking and high thinking and the bureaucratic intellectuality of Milner's version of Liberal Unionism.

By 1910 the new rhetoric had captured the Conservative party as a whole: it had captured a large part of the Conservative party in parliament. It had not, however, been as successful in capturing the Conservative leaders whose opinions continued to reflect the deposits of the previous thirty years. Balfour did not reflect the new militancy: Law did. Like Balfour, Law had to resolve conflict among the leaders; he was helped by strains in the Liberal party as Asquith carried it further towards Irish and Labour positions than he may have wanted to. By 1914 Conservatism, as embodied in the Conservative party, meant a position of force and point.

From the outbreak of war in 1914 the Conservative party was a success story. As the largest party in the House of Commons, it held up the operation of Welsh Church Disestablishment and Home Rule. It expelled Churchill and Haldane. It was primarily responsible for the removal of Asquith and the destruction of the Liberal government. With Lloyd George as disreputable ally, its pre-war climate found secure fulfilment in a nation at arms. At the election of 1918 it was the party that had won the war.

Until after the election in 1918, the Conservative element in the Coalition was stable. Austen Chamberlain resigned in July 1917 because, as India Secretary, he was responsible for Mesopotamia: he was brought back to office the following year in order to forestall a Conservative Cave against the implementation of Home Rule. Three weeks after Austen Chamberlain's resignation, Neville Chamberlain was removed after nine months as Minister of National Service to become one of the earliest of Conservative irreconcilables where Lloyd George was concerned.[1] Carson resigned with Craig in January 1918 when consideration was given to establishing an all-Ireland parliament. Duke, the Conservative Irish Chief Secretary, resigned with Wimborne, the Lord Lieutenant, in May. On Austen Chamberlain's and Duke's resignations, Montagu and Shortt – both Liberals – took over Ireland and India. But Law, Curzon, Balfour, Crawford, Milner, Finlay, Cave, Prothero, Long, Smith, Talbot and Derby – until he went to Paris as ambassador in 1918 – were in office continuously. When Younger, Long and Law persuaded Conservatives to accept continued Coalition as the basis for an electoral platform in 1918, they were perpetuating an accomplished fact.

Their object was to gain a secure footing in the uncertainty created by the Reform Bill of 1918 at an election at which three potential electors out of four would not have voted at the general elections of 1910.[2] It was intended originally to seek a mandate for the next phase of war government against Asquith, Runciman and McKenna. The German collapse in November merely made the Coalition more desirable. In negotiating the terms, Lloyd George closed his bargain with the Conservative leaders and squared the Coalition Liberals afterwards.[3] The outcome was a transformation in the House of Commons. In the old parliament there were about 280 Conservatives, 260 Liberals, 25 Ulster Unionists and 40 Labour M.P.s. In the new House 360 Conservatives[1] had nearly three times as many seats as the 130 Lloyd George Liberals. They had an absolute majority over the 25 Ulster Unionists, 10 members of the National Democratic Party and the Lloyd George Liberals with whom they were allied, as well as the 30 or so anti-Coalition Liberals and 60 or so Labour members who, together with the Sinn Feiners, would have constituted an opposition of 160 if the Sinn Feiners had not refused to take their seats.

These changes were the result of the Liberal split, the war spirit, the loss of Irish support in England and Scotland and the assaults made by Labour on the Liberal party. They did not suggest that the Coalition should be destroyed. Lloyd George wanted Coalition because he expected a Conservative majority even if the Conservative party stood alone, but much of the Conservative majority was attributed by Conservatives to their association with him. The outlines of policy had been agreed by both sides before the election: the Conservative leaders felt no pressing need to abandon the hostages given to the Coalition Liberals. To Conservatives who had prospered with them and probably to Coalition Liberals also Lloyd George and Coalition were a barrier against the return of the 'old gang' and the pre-war controversies which ministerial success made them unwilling to revive.[2] Conservatives who disliked the alliance were neither powerful enough personally nor in a position to make an impact.

In agreeing to go to the election as part of a Coalition, the Lloyd George Liberals attached importance to support from Labour ministers and to the following Lloyd George was supposed to have among potential Labour voters. The National Democratic Party had developed out of the British Workers' League as a patriotic Labour party financed by Conservatives and Coalition Liberals and dedicated to supporting Lloyd George in fighting the war: ten of its candidates were returned as Coalitionist M.P.s including three who defeated Henderson, Jowett and MacDonald. On the other hand, four ministers – Hodge, Roberts, Walsh and Barnes – stood as Labour supporters of the Coalition and were opposed by Labour party candidates. Parker stood as a Labour supporter of the Coalition and had only an Asquithean against him. Clynes, Wardle and Brace were unopposed as Coalition ministers standing as Labour party candidates. The Labour party compelled Clynes, Brace, Hodge and Walsh to resign when the election was over. Only Parker – the ex-navvy – stayed in office until his defeat as a Lloyd George Liberal in October 1922[1] making money, if his account is to be believed, by investment on tips from millionaires.[2] By April 1920 Wardle and Barnes (his debts paid through subscription by Law)[3] had retired. On leaving office in 1920, Roberts returned as a director to the firm he had left as works manager on entering parliament in 1906. He sat on the Coalition back benches from which he retained his seat as a Lloyd George Liberal at the 1922 election, lost it as a Conservative in 1923 and spent the remaining five years of his life in the sugar-beet industry.[4]

The withdrawal of the Labour party before the 1918 election and of all but one of the Labour ministers in the eighteen months following damaged Lloyd George as a leader of safe progress, struck blows at the possibility of a Liberal revival and destroyed the raison d'être of the National Democratic Party which converted itself from being the party of the anti-pacifist working classes to being the 'enemy of class hatred and communism'.[5] Labour advances at the by-elections of 1919 created a new political situation.

(ii)

The question – what should be done about working-class political consciousness – was older than the first major working-class enfranchisement in 1867. The Reform Acts of 1867 and 1884 made it an immediate problem which was dealt with in the first place by stimulating working-class voters to support existing parties. There was no effective party or parliamentary organization dedicated to working-class interests. The working-class majority and the extension of organised trades unionism solidified potential class resistance among the richer supporters of both parties. Class consciousness formed part of the repertoire of many Radicals, but their practical reservations reflected an assumed conservatism in relation to working-class power.

Gladstone taught the Liberal and Radical working classes to want respect and regard but to live within the framework of the constitution. He did not envisage a class party organised on class lines which presented a threat to the Liberal party as he left it. The threat offered by the Labour Representation Committee was checked by the Gladstone/MacDonald pact of 1903 and the alliance between the Liberal and Labour parties at the election of 1906. In 1909 Lloyd George gave the first demonstration that government could be used as an instrument of this sort of class conflict. 'Limehouse', the People's Budget and the attack on the House of Lords, however, had no consequences and did no immediate damage to the control exercised over the Liberal party by the opportunist aristocracy of intellect and station which characterised Asquith's leadership.

Throughout the war the working-class question exercised politicians who contemplated the world after the war. 'Reconstruction' and the promise of a 'Land Fit for Heroes' reflected fears about what would happen if Heroes – especially Industrial Heroes – did not find England fit to live in. Lloyd George was expected by politicians who disliked him to encourage 'a dangerous spirit of class bitterness' by supporting working-class claims. In fact he did the opposite. In 1917 and 1918 he involved not only trades union leaders but also employers at the centre of government where neither had been in large numbers before except by reason of any standing individuals had had as parliamentary politicians.

At the election of 1910 less than one elector in twenty voted Labour. Fourteen candidates were defeated. Forty-two M.P.s were returned, nearly all on Liberal votes. At the election of 1918 the Labour party, standing by itself, received over two million votes. Over 300 candidates were defeated including all who stood in Ireland. The pacifist element was for the moment irrelevant. Solidarity was dented by Lloyd George's popularity, by the return of the ten members of the National Democratic Party and by the presence on Lloyd George's platforms of four out of the eight Labour members of his Coalition. When the Labour Conference decided that the Labour party should fight the election on its own, Hodge, Roberts, Walsh and Barnes refused to follow. Clynes conformed but thought membership of the Coalition the best guarantee of a Labour impact on post-war policy.[1] He expected decimation if the Labour party stood alone.[2] The worst he feared did not occur. But persistent dedication and intensive activity over the eight years of the old parliament produced a gain of only twenty seats in the new one.

Nevertheless, the situation in 1918 promised opportunities which Labour expected to be able to take. It was believed that the circumstances of 1918 were particularly unfavourable and that, when favourable circumstances returned, Labour's strength would be revealed. Just over half the electorate had voted. Lloyd George had gained an overwhelming majority in the House of Commons with less than 25% of the possible electors voting for him. The temporary advantage gained by the timing of the election was expected to disappear as voting became a habit among new electors and the country turned its attention to its peacetime prospects.[1]

These predictions were accurate. The Labour party made extensive advances between 1918 and 1921, succeeding in the process in consolidating its position as the chief opposition party in the country. There were difficulties about money and about candidates. There were many constituencies which the Labour party either did not fight or did badly in when it fought. Its strongholds remained areas of depressed industry. It made some effort, and with some success, as a party of agrarian and suburban grievance.[2] But the salient characteristic of the politics of 1919 and 1920 was that, in a period of high employment, all the hopes entertained in 1906 seemed closer to realisation than in 1918.

The first inroads on the Coalition majority, therefore, were made before the collapse of the economic boom in late 1920. They began in July 1919 with a marked increase in the Labour vote at Swansea East and a victory in a 1918 Coalition seat at Bothwell in Lanarkshire. They were followed by successes in the municipal elections of November 1919 and by a gain from the Conservative party at Widnes in September. Though Bothwell, Widnes, Spen Valley, Dartford and South Norfolk[3] were the only seats gained between the general election of 1918 and the Dudley by-election of March 1921, the Labour vote increased considerably at sixteen other by-elections in this period. It went down in hardly any.[4] At nearly all it was markedly higher than in 1918. Pontefract, Rusholme, the Isle of Thanet, St Albans, Bromley, The Wrekin, Argyllshire, Camberwell, Northampton, Nelson and Colne, Sunderland, Woodbridge and Dudley testified to the variety of seats in which something was promised for the future. Even if others did not promise much,[1] few of these promised anything for either of the Liberal parties which the Labour party aimed chiefly to replace.

These gains marked the beginning of a psephological earthquake which politicians recognised for what it was. It confirmed fears which had been felt extensively before the war. It showed that an independent working-class politics which had erupted on a large scale in a small electorate after 1907 had broken the dams which the Liberal party had built from the Unauthorised and Newcastle programmes onwards. The collectivist and class-conflict propaganda which had been carried on in the Liberal and Labour parties before and during the war was now freed from Liberal leadership. Some Liberals saw at once that the Labour party was the party of the future. Others saw that the Labour movement had to be captured and wanted a radical Liberal policy to enable Liberals to capture it. The obvious leader for a policy of this sort was Lloyd George but Lloyd George was in Conservative chains. The question was whether his place could be taken by the Asquithean mandarinate.

Between 1900 and 1914 the Labour party was a disjointed amalgamation between the Fabian Society, the Independent Labour Party and the Trades Union Congress. Its advance in 1906 was made possible by electoral alliance with the Liberal party: its recession coincided with the Liberal recession of 1910. War and conscription divided it. The crucial position of the trades unions in a State organised for war made Labour co-operation more desirable than its strength in parliament made necessary. Labour participation in both wartime Coalitions, and the presence of a Labour intelligentsia in various parts of the machinery of wartime government, was the outcome.

Labour support for the war and the presence of Labour ministers in office did not mean that industrial action ceased. Throughout the war industrial agitation continued. There were large-scale strikes in the South Wales coalfields and on the Clyde in 1915 and a nation-wide engineering strike in 1917. Alongside the popular rhetoric of patriotic sacrifice, class-conflict propaganda used 'war profits', 'conscription' and 'inequality of sacrifice' to preserve the Labour movement against the merging of identity which Coalition and 'national solidarity' might otherwise have effected. It produced a brand of social self-righteousness which later became prominent in the post-war assault on the materialism and hypocrisy imputed to the ruling classes' treatment of the people by whom they had been defended.

In addition there were striking assertions from the Independent Labour Party and the Union of Democratic Control of the belief that the war was wrong, immoral or unjust; that it had been produced by secret and incompetent diplomacy; and that efforts must be made to achieve a negotiated peace. Throughout the war this range of opinion was expressed by MacDonald, Wallhead, Snowden, Allen, Anderson, Morel, Richardson and Jowett among Labour leaders and by Trevelyan and Ponsonby among Liberals. With the kites flown by Lansdowne and Smuts for a negotiated peace in 1917/18, it received a fillip. With the German advance in March 1918, events seemed to show that it was right. The sudden German collapse in October and November destroyed its credibility, but dissension about the Peace Treaties, post-war disillusionment and the broad wave of League of Nations and liberal idealism which engulfed England between 1919 and 1922 made it more central than it had ever been before.

In the Labour party the war produced no truce. Not only did industrial and pacifist militancy continue: parts of the Labour intelligentsia saw in the replacement of Asquith by Lloyd George the promise of serious handling of power by themselves. The Tawneys, Zimmerns, Lloyds, Greenwoods, Webbs, Mallons and Joneses who looked to Lloyd George in the first moment of success in 1917 hoped to use the opportunity which State control in war provided to convert England into the society they wished it to become. They saw in the Lloyd George/Fisher/Montagu/Addison axis a basis for a progressive politics in the future.[1]

These expectations did not survive the first six months of the Lloyd George Coalition. With Henderson's forced resignation over the Stockholm Conference, they were broken. When Henderson began to organise the Labour party for the future, he had well-tilled soil and a variety of experience close to the centre of government to work with. The reorganisation of the party machinery, the adoption of a party programme and the publication of *Labour and the New Social Order* gave Labour a formidable potential. If there had been no Allied victory in 1918, Labour would have been a formidable force in fact. Comparative failure at that election did nothing to diminish expectations which had been established by forty years of propaganda and two false dawns in 1908 and 1917.

Like the pre-war Liberal party, the Labour movement in the early 1920s was a rag-bag of attitudes, purposes, programmes and intentions which were held together by a common language, a small number of common objectives and the Trades Union movement. Russell believed in the redistribution of wealth as a way to the reconstruction of civilisation. Shaw believed in a new élite and State ownership supported by State purchase of existing rights in property. Tawney was a Christian Socialist, a believer in State action to decrease inequality and an advocate of Education as the guarantee of human self-respect. The Webbs wanted moral revolution – an attempt to replace self-interested Capitalism by a civilisation based on altruism and public duty. Wedgwood was a Single-Taxer and a raw and ruthless believer in the rights of the oppressed nations and the inadequacy of the upper classes among whom he lived. Thomas's line was a 'bloodless and peaceful revolution' to create 'a ... healthy ... beautiful and ... enduring England' where there would be 'real partnership in industry', where 'the best ... education ... w[ould] be open to all whose talents show they can benefit' and where Labour 'would throw the door wide and lead the way into a era of progress and sanity'.[1] Snowden's 'New World Order' would

raise the workman from the condition of a 'wage slave' ... make ... machines ... the obedient instruments of social service ... eliminate the artificial frontiers which men ha[d] reared to separate people from people [and] ... bring under tribute for the benefit of all the resources of every country ... In working for a happier Order ... those who ... profit ... under the present immoral conditions ... would find a greater satisfaction than the possession of riches could ever give [as] humanity [was enabled] to reach the loftiest heights its vision can but dimly see today.[2]

The Fabians believed in State control, Guild Socialists in worker control. Strains of anti-plutocratic Anglicanism were present in Lansbury, Tawney, Slesser, the Buxtons and others. There was as much of Henry George, William Morris, Wells, Blatchford, Angell, Scott Holland, Lowes Dickinson, Hobson and Gore as there was of Marx. Trevelyan, Ponsonby and the Buxtons were brought in by dislike of Liberal foreign policy.[1] Some welcomed the Russian revolution: others attacked it.[2] Some supported the Temperance movement; some did not. Some who believed in the redistribution of wealth did not believe in the extension of State power. Some joined the Labour party when the Liberals would not have them: others did so after 'conversion'.[3] Henderson had been a Liberal agent. Some[4] were eccentric. Some could have succeeded in any conventional profession to which they had turned their minds. In some there was guilt. In some there was relentless certainty. In all, or nearly all, there was a high regard for education. Allen, Jowett, Wells, Shaw and Russell were free thinkers. Roden Buxton was an Anglican converted to Quakerism because of the Church of England's attitude to war.[5] Henderson was a Methodist preacher: so was Hodges. Pethick-Lawrence was a Unitarian. Ammon claimed that 'the best Socialist teaching [came] from the Bible'.[6] Thomas professed the religion of all sensible men.

In the Labour party there was little wealth and very few rich men. Ponsonby was brought up at Windsor. So, as the son of King George V's tutor, was Dalton. Trevelyan was heir to a medium-sized estate in Northumberland. H. Markwald, a Swiss-German merchant who had spent part of his business life in London, gave money to Morel, Snowden and MacDonald until he died in 1924 just before it became public knowledge that MacDonald had a motor-car subsidy from a Scottish biscuit king. Shaw had married a rich wife: by 1920 he was rich in his own right. Clifford Allen's father had a large drapery business in Newport: Mary Macarthur's was a store owner in Glasgow. Henderson and Clynes had no money. Thomas and MacDonald were both born illegitimate and poor. MacDonald married well, if not profitably. Snowden built a rather better house than might have been expected. Even in the twenties Thomas's style of living was thought surprising. Sidney Webb married, among other things, an income. Lansbury's firm came through his wife's father. The leaders of the large unions had large sums of money available for investment. But few of the Labour leaders had money or social position of their own: hardly any had experience of industrial management. Apart from the writers, teachers and trades unionists almost none had succeeded at anything before they became politicians.

There were variations of tone. There was a malicious tone which came chiefly from members of the upper classes who were sourer about the rich than those who had made their way.[1] There were tones of confident contempt, protesting innocence, resentful virtue, honest indignation and pious hopefulness. There was a restrained eloquence (from Clynes), second-rate poetry (from MacDonald), first-rate rant (from Lansbury), patriotic pastiche (from Thomas), ordinary cant (about springing from the 'loins of the common people'[2]) from Robert Williams – all touching existing, or creating fresh, cords of sentiment.

Despite these variations, there was a common assertion of the need to raise up the poor to equality with the rich and of the importance of political action in doing so. This implied equality of consideration for the working classes in relation to the classes which had exercised power in the past and a recognition that they had 'an elementary right' not just to food for subsistence but to 'good houses, leisure, art, literature and music'.[3] All the leaders of the Labour movement wanted to redistribute wealth, whether by confiscation, by trades union negotiation or by State purchase: the removal of poverty was an essential ingredient whether the mixture was socialist, Bolshevik or Christian. There was the usual amount of ambition, vanity and manoeuvre inseparable from political action.[4] Many trades union leaders reflected a range of opinions which had little to do with the interests of their members, and much to do with the indoctrination they received in the course of self-education. But the movement was the assertion of a claim that 'the workers were the governing class',[5] that they were as good as the upper classes and that working-class control of political power would be as beneficial to the nation as it would be to the working classes themselves. It was the assault on deference as much as the threat to property which made the Labour movement the danger it was understood to be by those who had hoped that deference would continue. It was the motivating political energy as much as the programme that mattered as this ill-defined but effective combination of patriotic, pacifist, revolutionary, socialist, syndicalist and Bolshevik feeling advanced over many fronts at once because it had the advantage of an unsuccessful régime to attack.

Between 1918 and 1922 the Labour movement was led by a variety of leaders who, though they were not moving in a common direction, left the impression that they were. The 1918 election removed Snowden, MacDonald and Jowett from the House of Commons, along with most of the pacifist and anti-war members of the ILP and UDC. It left a strong preponderance of trades unionists. Adamson was made leader while Labour was still in the Coalition in 1917: he remained leader until replaced by Clynes in 1921. Adamson was helped, and overshadowed, by Thomas, by Clynes after he left the Coalition, by Brace until he became a permanent official in the Ministry of Labour and by Henderson when he returned to the House of Commons after losing his seat in 1918. The party organisation was run by Henderson: its policies were made by Henderson, Clynes, Thomas and Webb. From 1918 until 1920 Snowden was chairman of the Independent Labour Party, a vigorous enemy of the Russian revolution and a productive propagandist. When he left the chairmanship in 1921 he was succeeded by MacDonald. Snowden's relations with the body of the ILP had been poor: they became poorer after his resignation. MacDonald's relations with the Parliamentary Party were as bad as his relations with Snowden: they became worse in the course of 1920/21. Webb was the author of the 1918 programme and a member of the National Executive: after serving on the Sankey Commission on the Coal Industry, he became candidate for Seaham. Smillie, Williams, Cramp, Gosling, Thomas, Bevin and Hodges were prominent by reason of their leadership of the Triple Alliance.

Smillie and Hodges were both members of the Sankey Commission, but it is not clear why at the last moment Lloyd George added Tawney, Webb and Chiozza Money, only one of whom knew about Coal at first hand. The spectacle of Smillie and Hodges civilly, and Tawney and Money uncivilly, subjecting some of the richest colliery and land owners to informed scrutiny was, nevertheless, a landmark in the development of the movement's status. The Commission's recommendation in favour of nationalisation lent respectability, even though the government rejected it.

Between 1919 and 1921 the increase in the Labour vote coincided with a systematic attempt to persuade the Labour movement to achieve political objectives by direct industrial action. At all crucial moments between 1919 and 1922, the claim that national policy could be changed by exerting industrial power was matched by success in the political field, even when the leaders of the Parliamentary Labour Party were opposed to the industrial action involved.

The growth of Labour support in its strongholds is the history of leadership in South Wales, Glasgow, West Yorkshire, Durham, Northumberland and East London where an impact was made on the expectations of politicians with interests in these areas. The impact of Labour on the political system depended as much on the creation of the belief that Labour was not just a class movement with a particular interest in mining and the declining industries but was a genuine, and dangerous, contribution to the improvement of mankind. This impact was made not just in South Wales, Glasgow, West Yorkshire, Durham, Northumberland or East London but by the tension which developed nationally between Clynes, Henderson, Thomas and Webb on the one hand and the movement for Direct Action under Smillie, Hodges, Williams and Lansbury on the other.

Smillie was an Ulsterman who came to Scotland as an orphan when he was fifteen. From the Lanarkshire coalfields he was the chief force behind the creation of a unified miners' union in Scotland and was then vice-chairman of the Miners' Federation of Great Britain in the 1890s.[1] He was a founder-member of the ILP. Between 1894 and 1910 he fought seven unsuccessful parliamentary elections. He opposed both the Boer War and the Great War: he was in part responsible for strikes in South Wales in 1915 and on the Clyde in 1917. In the same year he refused the Food Controllership from Lloyd George.[2] He was a member of the Sankey Commission but was seriously ill after it. He was a miners' hero, difficult, obstinate and moody – an admirer of William Morris who probably believed that there really

had been more conspiracy and plotting ... during the past few years within a hundred yards of the House of Commons than there had been in Labour circles [and] that scheming and plotting ... [had] gone on in the interests of the possessing classes who, prior to and especially during the war, had amassed additional capital out of the necessities of the people.[3]

In 1920 Hodges was thirty-two. He was born in England but grew up in Abertillery: he became a collier when he was thirteen.

In his teens he was a Primitive Methodist preacher and representative on the Miners' Federation. From Ruskin College, Oxford he helped to establish the Left Wing Central Labour College where he spent his last two years as an undergraduate. After a period in France learning French, he returned to Abertillery where he made a reputation as a trades union negotiator. The 1912 Coal Strike established his name throughout South Wales. He became General Secretary of the Miners' Federation of Great Britain in 1918. Like Smillie he was a member of the Sankey Commission. It is difficult to know how far this 'handsome, cultured, intelligent young man' – a fine platform speaker with a clear grasp of the most complicated commercial aspects of the Coal Industry – was a genuine revolutionary. Between 1918 and 1921 he made a national mark as a Welsh Bolshevik. In the same period he came to be thought of, among those close to events, as a man who had two faces one of which responded to the flesh pots.[1] His public position was that, unless there was 'National Ownership of the entire [Coal] industry with joint control by the full personnel of the industry and representatives of the whole community ... all our political and social superstructure [would] come crashing down'.[2]

Smillie disliked London and kept his home in Larkhall. Hodges was a fine flower of the Welsh yearning for advancement through education. Robert Williams was an ex-coal trimmer from Cardiff and secretary of the National Transport Workers' Federation. He was a Conscientious Objector during the war, a director of the *Daily Herald* and for a short time a member of the Communist party before being expelled for his part in Black Friday in 1921. Bevin's Transport and General Workers' Union deprived him of employment in 1925. He committed suicide in the thirties. Lansbury was an East End employer and son of an employer who, after emigrating to Australia in the 1880s, was given a partnership in his father-in-law's business in Bow. He began political life as a Liberal. As a member of the Social Democratic Federation, he was elected to the Poplar Board of Guardians from which he became a muck-raking councillor, alderman and mayor. He opposed the Gladstone/MacDonald pact of 1903 and in 1906 stood as a Socialist against Havelock Wilson at Middlesborough. In 1910 he won Bow and Bromley but lost it two years later on resigning to fight a by-election in defence of women's suffrage.

He was involved in campaigns against the Boer War and against the Great War. He signed the Minority Report of the Royal Commission on the Poor Law in 1909. In 1911 he founded the *Daily Herald* which, when converted into a daily newspaper, had a circulation of a quarter of a million. In 1920, as a Christian Socialist and follower of William Morris, he made a well-publicised visit to Russia.

The objectives of Direct Action varied as political opportunities occurred. In January 1919 Williams wanted a general strike to force Lloyd George to toe President Wilson's line at the Peace Conference.[1] In September the TUC agreed to co-operate with the Miners' Federation in compelling the government to nationalise the mines.[2] When the government refused to support nationalisation attempts were made to persuade the TUC to take action.[3] In March 1920 Shaw, Thomas and Clynes persuaded the TUC to take political action in favour of a general election instead of a general strike in favour of nationalisation.[4] In July it decided on a general strike if the government refused to withdraw troops from Ireland and Russia.[5] During the Russo-Polish crisis in August, the Labour Council of Action, urged on by Bevin and supported by the leaders of the Parliamentary Party, threatened a general strike against the supply of arms to Poland: when Lloyd George backed down, it claimed a victory which there is no reason to think that it had won.[6] This 'victory' stimulated a campaign to set up Councils of Action everywhere.[7] From the beginning of 1921 plans were made for a general strike to enforce Labour's views about unemployment and wages. In February, Thomas, Clynes and Henderson persuaded the TUC not to accept them.[8] In March the Triple Alliance decided that it had no authority to call a national conference on wages.[9] It was not until the Lock-Out, instituted by the colliery owners in the wake of the proposal to reduce wages and wind up the national wage negotiation machinery after the withdrawal of government control of the Coal Industry in March, that the Triple Alliance decided in favour of a general strike.[10]

The phase of optimism about the possibility of a general strike ended on Black Friday, April 15 1921, when the Triple Alliance suffered a mortal blow, not through the firmness or belligerence of the government but because of the lack of co-operation between the leaders of the unions involved. The general strike in support of the miners' claims about the wage level and the national negotiating machinery was not destroyed by the Emergency Powers Act of 1920. Nor was it destroyed by the government's determination to support the mine owners for whom ministers had a good deal of contempt. It was destroyed by Hodges's apparent abandonment of national wage negotiating machinery in his talk to House of Commons back-benchers a couple of days before Black Friday and by the refusal of the railway and transport leaders to support a strike after Hodges had compromised one of the main points for which the miners were supposed to be fighting.

The decision to call a general strike was not, strictly speaking, an example of Direct Action. It was made by the Triple Alliance in pursuit of the financial interests of its members and implied no claim to supersede parliament in determining the general policies of government. The general strike was abandoned because the issue had been fudged and the miners would not explain their position to the rest of the Triple Alliance: abandonment was the work of Bevin and Williams, who supported Direct Action, quite as much as of Thomas, who opposed it. Smillie resigned from the Miners' Federation because he thought the miners' belligerence would be unsuccessful. Hodges offered his resignation when the miners rejected the concession he had suggested. The effect, nevertheless, was to kill whatever life was left in Direct Action.

The practical effect of Direct Action was limited. It would have left little mark without the part played by the *Daily Herald* in systematising its insights and publicising its intentions. Under Lansbury, Ewer, Brailsford, Meynell, Williams and Mellor and with money from trades unions, the Soviet government and Zaghloul, the Egyptian nationalist leader, it presented a fundamental challenge. This challenge, the same in principle as the challenge of 1912, seemed vastly more threatening after the Russian experience of 1917 and the German experience of 1919 and when it was spelt out as clearly as the *Herald* spelt it at a time when the Labour party had become the chief party of opposition, when trades union leaders were frequent visitors to Downing Street and when its organisational possibilities had been greatly extended by the development of the shop stewards' movement.

The challenge was a demand to overthrow the existing order and replace Capitalism by a society based on Equality and Human Brotherhood. It took shape in the claim that the institutions of government were the creation of plutocratic capitalism, that compromise with them was immoral, and that workers who had seen through them would see that the only instruments likely to destroy them were those which had been created by forty years of working-class activity. These views emerged from an understanding of 'capitalistic society' which identified Lloyd George, Rothermere, Northcliffe, the Geddeses, Weir, the Conservative party and both Liberal parties as agents of Big Business whose business it was to ensure that Cabinet, parliament and press consecrated Capitalism's robbery of the worker. Britain was seen as a 'Junkerism'[1] – 'a Capitalistic Oligarchy'[2] where 'the employing class ... had no regard whatever ... for the well-being of the people',[3] where 'starvation [was] a favourite weapon'[4] and where a 'doctrine of hatred and blood lust' denied the people the opportunity for a 'wholesome life'.[5] The whole system was rotten and was perpetuated by the rottenness of its parts. The press was corrupt, parliament servile,[6] the government 'untruthful, a liar and a rogue to its backbone'.[7] Among the 'master-class ... there [was] a large element which ... intended to provoke a bloody revolution in order that the workers may be ... shot down like dogs'.[8] Against this framework constitutional methods would not be effective. If anything was to be achieved, the system had to be destroyed. No legality, it was suggested, and no concern for trades union stability should prevent Labour using the general strike to emulate the Russian attempt to 'get rid of the system of production for profit, substitute production for use, have done with market chasing [and] abolish the wage system'.[9]

This view of the political system, though dogmatic, was flexible: it was applied to problems as they arose. In 1919/20 it was used to explain the high cost of living, the treatment of ex-Service men, the decline in coal production, the harshness of the Peace Treaties, the attacks on Russia, the support of Poland, British involvement in Mesopotamia and the 'atmosphere of indolence, cynicism and patronage' which trades union leaders found when they made their way into that 'decadent Chinese doss-house' the Houses of Parliament.[10] It justified demands for the nationalisation of the mines, banks and railways as a prelude to the nationalisation of everything else, the Capital Levy and direct taxation of land as a prelude to more general redistribution of wealth and public campaigns against Profiteering and in favour of 'the restoration of land to the people'.[1]

These campaigns were a call to see the manifest truth, to draw lines clearly and 'convince ... even the most sceptical that present-day civilization is founded on a perpetual struggle of classes'.[2] They were an affirmation of the belief that the 'cleavage between the working class and the class which lives upon them [was] becoming ... acute',[3] that 'there exists within our nation a very large mass of people who are determined at all costs to maintain the social order founded on individual greed and pride of power'[4] and that the only answer to 'the solidarity of property and privilege' was 'working-class solidarity'.[5] No palliatives were acceptable. Joint worker/employer control of industry was an employers' trick.[6] So was the claim that wage reductions were needed to make production costs competitive in a world of falling prices. The 'impartiality of government' was an illusion: government would 'use all the powers of organized Capitalism backed by the material ... wealth of the whole nation' to destroy the Trades Union movement if it could.[7]

This line of rhetoric was laid down when unemployment was confined to limited areas. When unemployment became widespread it was applied more generally. In the year before Black Friday it ran through the whole range of accusations from the claim that 'the cause of unemployment ... is the ... inability of the capitalist system to supply the prime needs of mankind'[8] through 'Unemployment Pays Big Business'[9] to 'Capitalism *likes* unemployment as a means of forcing down the wages of the unemployed'.[10] Black Friday was a defeat, but the attitude to the Coalition was the same afterwards as it was before. The government's suggestion of short-time working to share employment was 'the last cry of cynicism' from the 'gentry who have fought every claim put up by the workers for a shorter working week'.[11] Mond's Bill to discontinue housing subsidies was 'a foul policy of saving money by leaving little children to be murdered through the evil conditions of slumdom'.[12] The government's refusal to pay unemployment relief for more than eight weeks at a stretch was

37

'utterly and insultingly inadequate'.[1] Its plans for relieving unemployment were an 'artificial rejuvenation of doomed private
enterprise ... a system of doles for Capitalists with ... higher
prices or lower wages'.[2] The Safeguarding of Industries Bill – a
Protectionist measure wrung out of Coalition Liberals by the
Conservative party – was not a way of *reviving* industry but 'a new
way of protecting the profiteer and fleecing the worker and con-
sumer'.[3] Lloyd George's announcement of his unemployment
plans in the House of Commons on October 19 was 'his familiar
bluff coupled with a very insidious incitement to the further
cutting of wages under guise of the phrase "Costs of production
must come down"'.[4] Even the decision not to build four new
destroyers, taken as a result of the Washington Conference, was
treated not as a move towards the limiting of armaments but
as an example of 'economy for the taxpayer but unemployment
for the worker'.[5]

What Lansbury was doing was to establish a body of prejudice.
It was not just a question of the worker having a right to work and
a right to maintenance if work was not available. It was that the
'claims of flesh and blood came before those of money' and 'if it
[was] necessary for suffering and misery to be endured for which
as individuals we are not responsible, then everybody of all classes,
from the highest to the lowest, should ration income and all be
put on one level so far as the means of life are concerned'.[6]

Lansbury did not expect this to happen. He probably did not
expect anything to happen. His achievement was the creation of
a framework in which politics could be understood and a mental
wound which sustained hope and hatred even in defeat after
Black Friday when 'Labour's army', compelled to 'give ground
before the tremendous onslaughts of organized capital', did so
'not as rabble [but] ... as an army, with its moral forces in
being'.[7] His incitements to wreck the Poor Law system by legal
action and his period in prison as a Poplar Guardian in 1922 did
nothing to reduce the tempo of the agitation to establish as a
received truth the fact that Lloyd George – 'the bondservant of
moneybags'[8] – and the Coalition – 'the dictatorship of the Capitalists'[9] – stood 'alongside the Capitalists against the working
classes'.[10]

At its most extensive Direct Action had a formidable following among trades unionists: it had little support in the House of Commons. It created a style of politics which no Labour leader could ignore, but the official Labour leaders kept their distance. They believed that repeated strikes or a general strike would involve a challenge to the existing régime which would not succeed, for which trades unionists were not prepared and which could 'inflict more damage on the Labour side than on any other'.[1] They thought that greater opportunities existed for themselves, for the trades unions and for the Labour party by operating as part of the existing system than by risking a confrontation with it, that an 'appeal to force' would produce 'an answer in terms of force'[2] and that Labour success in defeating the government at by-elections made action outside the parliamentary and collective bargaining system unnecessary. They made these positions plain in a succession of statements and actions from September 1919 onwards.[3] Though they were defeated on a number of occasions in 1919 and 1920, their victory in April 1921 was total and was used by them as proof that they were right.

It is not clear whether these views were expressed in order to meet the accusation that Labour was not fit to govern, whether they were expressed because rivals used contrary slogans as a challenge or whether they reflected the limits of the mental world in which the Labour leaders lived. They probably wrote few letters. Few of these have been preserved. They made speeches. Speeches do not reveal the relationship between belief and calculation. At street corners, in factories, in constituency associations and in the *Daily Herald*, 'class conflict' created an attitude towards government which made it difficult for trades union leaders to collaborate openly.[4] The result was a heightening of language even when they did not mean it. Yet at times there was something resembling co-operation between Lloyd George and Thomas who was not alone in combining leadership of one of the major constituents of the Triple Alliance, a public name as a 'concocter of extreme policies' and a reputation as a negotiator with whom ministers could work.[5] Walsh, Brace, Hartshorn, Hodges and others saw Lloyd George secretly at moments of tension.[6] In the period before Black Friday Walsh, McGurk and others lunched at Knowsley with Derby who found them searching for help

against 'the extremists' in the Miners' Federation.[1] They all left
the impression of pronounced dependence on government for the
maintenance of their own positions.[2]

Between 1918 and 1921 the official Labour leaders did not
anticipate breakdown in the working of the capitalist system:
they did not base their programme on the probability that it
would occur. They attacked Capitalism for producing 'a C3
nation' and the 'class which governed in this country and . . . on
the continent' for killing 'twenty millions of men . . . causing
millions to be crippled' and 'burden[ing] every country in Europe
. . . with an intolerable burden of debt'.[3] They based their claims
on the assertion that State power and monopoly Capitalism had
destroyed private enterprise, on the effectiveness of the class
hatred they were careful 'to recognize' but 'not' to 'preach'[4] and
on an idealism about the future which issued in the claim that
moral brotherhood would replace private profit as the socialist
aspect of the moral revolution they intended to create.[5]

What they would have done if economic collapse had occurred
in 1918 instead of 1920 it is difficult to know. Their inability, and
the inability of government, to propose measures to control it
within the framework of the existing system would have highlighted the question of the system itself. The need for a rhetoric,
the readiness of their 'extremists' and the example of the Russian
revolution might have compelled them to attack the system if they
were not to be pushed aside by those who were willing to do so.
By the time the collapse came in late 1920, they had not only
established a line of Labour policy which was ostentatiously
unrevolutionary but had electoral success to 'prove that Labour [was]
no longer viewed as a freakish interference in national politics'.[6]

As trades unionists they sought a larger share of the national
wealth through trade union negotiation. As leaders of the Labour
party they favoured the redistribution of wealth by taxation. They
used class slogans to discredit Lloyd George and the Conservatives
by whom he was surrounded. But they were neither syndicalists
nor revolutionaries. They neither wanted nor sought more than *co-
operation* between worker and management. They had no wish
to risk the defeat which large-scale industrial action might involve.
'There was no country', they claimed, 'less qualified to bear the
strain of continual internal disturbance than Britain.'[7] A 'bloody

revolution was not only unnecessary but would be ruinous to all sections of the people'.[1] It was absurd for Lloyd George to talk of Labour as the 'common foe'.[2]

Though buttressed by a movement of opinion which was not primarily parliamentary, the official Labour leaders were parliamentary politicians. They behaved according to the conventions of the party system, deployed a general political programme and used such opportunities as they could make to criticise other parties for failing within the objectives they had set themselves. They criticised the Coalition for botching the reconstruction it had promised in 1918[3] and for a policy of atrocity in Ireland.[4] They criticised it for 'fail[ing] to safeguard national finances at a time when every penny of State money should have been economically spent'[5] and for withdrawing 'unemployment benefit without making any alternative provision for unemployed persons'.[6] They criticised it for the level of the National Debt and for failure to impose a Capital Levy to reduce it.[7] They criticised it for 'high taxation and inflation of currency and credit', for its failure to bring down prices[8] and for continuing to use indirect taxation as a way of discriminating against the poor.[9] They criticised it for failing in consistency, principle and honour, for making the parliamentary system more contemptible than it had ever been before and for such deplorable misgovernment that even that falsely imputed to a socialist State could not possibly be worse.[10]

What they offered in its place was a combination of promises, idealism and common sense. From the body of opinions which had been diffused by forty years of Labour propaganda, they presented a businesslike edition for public consumption. They presented themselves as the party of financial rigour, the new diplomacy and a League of Nations which was not a 'League of Kings' or 'Cabinet Ministers' but 'a League of Free peoples who ... would use their influence and power to see that war was made impossible in the future'.[11] They castigated Labour neglect of foreign policy, the 'pathetic ... monument [to which] ... was the graves of ... 800,000 soldiers ... in the soil of foreign countries'.[12] They emphasised industrial co-operation and worker involvement in management.[13] They stressed the intimacy of the connection between increased production, working-class prosperity and the working of the economic system and offered Nationalisation as a 'patriot's' means of 'acquir[ing] property for the nation in order to advance the well-being of the community'.[1] They presented Syndicates, Trusts and Capitalistic Combines as destroyers of 'the small trader, the struggling little shopkeeper and overburdened middle-class man [who] knew better than the Prime Minister how completely private enterprise ha[d been] ... strangle[d]'.[2] They repeated Asquith's dictum that 'Taxation is a potent instrument of reform'. They accepted Hobson's that 'ability to pay' is the 'basic consideration'. They asserted that

the surplus of all individual incomes, after provision for ... efficiency ... comfort ... saving and ... expansion ... [was] available for taxation and pending such changes in the system of property-owning and the relations of capital and labour as will deprive individuals of the means to appropriate unearned wealth and incomes ... as a result of exploitation of the community ... may be usefully employed by the State to obtain a return of some portion of this exaction to be used for the purpose of improving the conditions of life of the dispossessed classes.[3]

These efforts at rhetorical plausibility were increased by the assertion that the Labour party had nothing in common with Bolshevism, by Thomas's and Clynes's attacks on Ca'Canny,[4] by Snowden's anticipation of 'national bankruptcy' if national indebtedness was not reduced and by repeated declarations that the only way to working-class prosperity was through full working of the economic system. The Labour leaders had a policy about poverty and the poor. They urged that the unemployment incidental to existing Capitalism should be made tolerable by supporting men who wanted work when work could not be made available. They 'had to take up unemployment' in early 1921[5] because it was a subject on which ' "Labour" [was] going to do well ... and the Government badly':[6] they made detailed proposals to extend the Trunk Road programme, the Trade Facilities Act and so on. But they had no positive policy for preventing long-term unemployment and no real conception of the need to have one. Trevelyan thought Labour had no real future in England unless there was a major economic crisis, but at one stage Henderson was 'gloomy' because the unemployment campaign 'clashe[d] with the campaign he had arranged on Ireland'.[7] Their economic policy – Cobdenite restoration of world markets – was honest in its vagueness and modesty.

These lines of argument were designed to discredit the Coalition and defeat the Asquithean Liberals on their traditional ground. They were intended to give an idealistic covering to the politics of material advancement, to persuade middle- and lower-middle-class support to identify with claims to working-class solidarity[1] and to enable the Labour party to replace the Liberal party as the party of progress and emancipation. Consciousness of equality between the Labour and Liberal leaders was not strong in 1918. It became very strong as a consequence of the election results of 1919.

In 1919 and 1920 the Labour party fought by itself: there was no thought of alliance with either Liberal group. The attempt to amalgamate the Conservative party and the Coalition Liberals in March 1920 after the TUC had decided against Direct Action was expected to give electors 'a fair opportunity of choosing between the class politics of Mr Lloyd George and the policy of public ownership and democratic administration of public enterprise for which Labour stands'.[2] The definitive breach between Asquith and Lloyd George in May 1920 was welcomed because it would 'forc[e] many of the Coalitionists to veer to the Right' and 'result in the more advanced Liberals coming over to [the Labour] ranks'.[3] The arrival in the Labour party of ex-Liberal ministers and M.P.s – Trevelyan, Noel and Roden Buxton, Wedgwood, Lees-Smith, Money, Alden, King, Outhwaite, Rutherford, Lambert and Ponsonby – and their articulateness at the expense of the Liberal party, lent weight to these claims.[4] Lloyd George's 'unprincipled dictatorship',[5] Churchill as the Liberal who 'wanted to split the progressive vote'[6] and Asquith as the 'incarnation of the old diplomacy' heightened the differences which were deepened by the moral and intellectual superiority affected by the Asquithean leaders. Maclean's attack on the proposal to exempt M.P.s salaries from income tax created particular bitterness.[7] The victory over Sir John Simon at the Spen Valley by-election in 1920 was a major achievement. The high-water-mark of equality was reached with discussions in June 1921 about the possibility of a Clynes government in the event of Lloyd George resigning over Ireland.[8]

By early 1921 the Labour party was established as a two-faced threat to the established order which was greater because it had two faces. It had the face of Thomas, Webb, Henderson and Clynes: it had the face of Lansbury, Smillie, Williams and Hodges. The first four were not mistaken for dangerous revolutionaries. Dangerous revolutionaries or not, they were leaders of a party which presented a threat to existing wealth, to the ownership of property and to the whole range of beliefs and institutions on which established, conservative and bourgeois England was supposed to rest. Whatever it might say about the economic system, the Labour party was committed to the establishment of a society in which inequality would be limited, educational opportunity extended, class rule abandoned and a new morality advanced. It was committed to support movements within the Empire against white predominance and Imperial control. It was committed to some measure of capital redistribution so as to take from the rich in order to give to the poor. Unless Clynes is regarded as its Whig, it had no Whig leader with proved capacity to restrain it. As the Labour vote grew, the dangers were apparent.

II

THE IMPORTANCE OF
HORATIO BOTTOMLEY

'I believe Mr Lloyd George could still carry the nation with him if . . .
discarding his present entanglements, [he] declared that henceforth he
would devote himself to the restoration of national solvency . . . But he
will never do it while he remains under the domination of a Conservative
Coalition.'
>> Rothermere writing in *Sunday Pictorial*, August 31 1919

'When *will* these politicians realize . . . that all the old Party cries are dead
and gone for ever.'
>> Bottomley discussing Salisbury's call to detach the Conservative
>> party from the Lloyd George Coalition, *John Bull*, July 2 1921

'As a political force . . . Mr Bonar Law . . . is as moth-eaten as Hatfield.'
>> *Sunday Pictorial*, leader column, discussing the possibility that
>> Law might replace Lloyd George as Prime Minister, June 26
>> 1921

The by-elections of 1919 were favourable to the Labour party but
produced no serious parliamentary attempt to unseat Lloyd George.
The evidence they gave of a Labour threat suggested, if anything,
that Lloyd George was indispensable. The first serious evidence
that he might not be was displayed in three by-elections between
February 1920 and January 1921 – two at The Wrekin, one at
Dover – at which large numbers of voters voted for anti-Coalition
Independents standing on various platforms hostile to party
politics, the high level of taxation and the extent of governmental
intervention in social and economic life. The atmosphere in which
these defections occurred was created by the Rothermere and
Northcliffe newspapers and by the interventions of Horatio
Bottomley.

Northcliffe and Rothermere were brothers, the joint bene-
ficiaries of the revolution in newspaper presentation which
Northcliffe had instituted in the 1880s and 1890s. Since his initial
successes with *Answers, Comic Cuts* and so on, Northcliffe had
extended his range and political importance. Though he stood as a
Conservative in Portsmouth in 1895, Northcliffe was not primarily

a politician. He was a newspaper proprietor of genius who was brought into politics, as he was brought into anything he touched, by production of vigorous and up-to-date newspapers. Once launched by his early thirties into the highest reaches of newspaper ownership, he was a figure whose opinions mattered in a political system in which newspapers were a major instrument of communication. Balfour made him a baronet and then, in 1905, a peer: he was probably the first newspaper proprietor to be honoured without performing public services outside newspaper management. By 1907 he owned among other newspapers the *Daily Mail*, the *Evening News*, the *Weekly Dispatch* and the *Observer*. With his purchase of *The Times* in 1908, he was the most important newspaper proprietor in England.

The political recipe in Northcliffe's newspapers was simple. They were capitalist and patriotic. So far as he had consistent political views, Northcliffe was a Chamberlainite and Tariff Reformer with Roseberyite overtones: his newspapers reflected this aspect of his mind. He was unsympathetic to Hatfield's high respectability. His opposition was matched, and stimulated, by Conservative criticism of his peerage. Before the war he was committed to the existence of a German menace: his newspapers predicted the war that occurred. When the war came, they supported it. Northcliffe was more immediately responsible than anyone else for creating the atmosphere in which Asquith was replaced by Lloyd George. In 1917 Lloyd George made him head of a major mission to the United States. In 1918 he became Director-General of Propaganda in Enemy Territories.

Northcliffe was dictatorial by temperament. At the point at which he bought *The Times*, he suffered a radical illness which Mr Cecil King, his nephew, says was syphilis.[1] The effect at first was confined to personal dealings with his staff and had little impact on his political activity. It was not until the later stages of the war that he began to show signs of political megalomania which operated chiefly through his direction of *The Times* and the *Daily Mail*. With the decision to replace Geoffrey Dawson by Wickham Steed as editor of *The Times* in early 1919, it had a major impact.

Northcliffe first met Lloyd George in 1909. He helped to make him in 1916. In 1919 Lloyd George refused to let him conduct

British propaganda at the Peace Conference. From 1919 he pursued Lloyd George with relentless denunciation, first over his reluctance to have a Carthaginian Peace Treaty, then over his refusal to get rid of the 'old Tory gang' who would 'blunder our country into something like a revolution',[1] finally, for damaging the Anglo-American alliance by failing to move towards a settlement to keep Ireland a united Dominion within the Commonwealth. From 1919 despite increasing tension between Northcliffe as proprietor and Steed as editor, *The Times* was the enemy of Lloyd George more even than it was the enemy of the Conservative party by whom he had been captured.

The assault from *The Times* mattered. But neither Northcliffe nor *The Times* put up candidates at by-elections. The first steps in this direction were taken by Rothermere and Bottomley.

Rothermere was Northcliffe's younger brother who had begun his working life as a clerk in the Inland Revenue. He had been brought into journalism by Northcliffe, had prospered with him and had broken from him financially before the war. In 1919 at the age of fifty-one he was one of the richest men in England for whom politics and newspapers were part of the process of arrival. In 1919 the *Daily Mirror* and the *Sunday Pictorial* were the chief vehicles of his political expression.

Rothermere had few social graces. He was kind, shy, human and at times abrupt. His private life was remarkable, and perhaps well-known. On those who disliked him he left an impression of social vulgarity and responsibility for a popular chauvinism for which Cecilian Conservatism had the greatest dislike. The *Daily Mirror* and the *Sunday Pictorial* supported the war and helped to create conditions in which Asquith was removed in 1916. Rothermere spent a brief period as President of the Air Council in 1917/18. His son Esmond went with Lloyd George to the Peace Conference in 1919.[2]

Rothermere believed in private enterprise, individual effort, national solidarity and individual national effort in relation to the rest of the world: his politics may best be described as the politics of capitalistic nationalism. In Lloyd George his newspapers created the image of a figure who had come up the hard way to embody the secular national will to 'destroy the Hun' and establish in post-war Britain a society in which neither rank nor education but only effort would open the highest places to those who worked within the framework of free capitalism.

Rothermere was not a Conservative, but many of his attitudes were reflected in the Conservative party. He was a Protectionist: in relation to Ireland he was a Unionist. But he had even less instinct than Northcliffe for the aristocratic, rural or ecclesiastical Conservatism represented in their differing ways by Salisbury, Long and Lord Hugh Cecil. So far as a millionaire could he embodied what he took to be the non-clerical average opinion of a nation which he wished to persuade to defer to no authority except that approved by the empire of political indoctrination he had at his disposal. His political attention was intermittent: he spent part of each year out of England. His attacks on the Coalition from 1919 to 1922, on the Conservative governments in 1922/23 and on the Labour party throughout were conducted with a confidence – sometimes comic and seldom just – in his ability to bring public success to any figure or cause he decided to support.

In 1918 Rothermere was a supporter of Lloyd George, but only on his own terms. He liked neither the Conservative alliance nor an Austen Chamberlain/Long/Salisbury-style Conservative party. He believed that neither Lloyd George nor 'the returning soldier' would 'get a square deal from these people' who would 'baulk and thwart all land legislation' without a 'most revolutionary' form of which it would be impossible to 'save the country from Bolshevism'.[1] He resented Conservative objections to newspaper proprietors' employment in high office recalling not just the comments in parliament but also a telephone call in which Law suggested that he should resign the Presidency of the Air Council 'because he feared the criticisms of Mr Austen Chamberlain and ... others'.[2] He did not like the Coalition platform at the 1918 election and would have preferred to support a Lloyd George/ Asquith/Runciman alliance. He disapproved of the Coupon arrangement[3] and demanded written guarantees – which he did not get – that the 'Old Gang' would not be returned to office after the election if he supported it.[4] For the first nine months after the election, his newspapers supported Lloyd George as the embodiment of the nation's achievements in war and its hopes for the future.

When Rothermere began to turn on the heat in August 1919,

it is not clear whether he was reflecting public feeling or trying to create it, whether he was acting as a newspaper owner trying to sell newspapers or as a publicist creating a climate of opinion; or whether he was a father trying to find a political platform for his son. His campaign to end the Coalition, begun on August 3 1919[1] in the wake of two Labour by-election successes,[2] developed out of an indictment of its financial policies into fundamental criticism of the whole range of its activity.

Rothermere's message was that parliament was failing the nation. Dominated by the Coalition, its debates were inert. Hampered by obsolete procedures, it could not control the bureaucracy. It had allowed the Coalition to entangle itself in Russia and the Caucasus and showed no sign of reducing the size of the Armed Forces which the destruction of German power had made possible.[3] Expenditure on education and subsidised housing was going to rise far more than was desirable.[4] The condition of agriculture was deplorable. It was difficult to credit the extent to which the British farmer was 'being harassed and badgered' by 'young inspectors in motor cars ... tearing about the countryside ... demanding to see farmers' wages sheets',[5] and this was paralleled in all parts of the governmental machine by a combination of the spending and the controlling habit which was destroying both the liberties and the finances of the nation.

What Rothermere was attacking was currency inflation. What he demanded was an end of Coalition and a restoration of party government based not on the pre-war slogans which were irrelevant to the modern world, but on the problems which faced a nation on the verge of bankruptcy. This meant reducing taxation, if necessary by making a special levy on war fortunes.[6] It meant 'an immediate and final evacuation of all our posts in French and Belgian territory' and 'clearing out of Russia ... the Caucasus ... Syria ... Asia Minor and Turkey-in-Europe'. It meant giving up 'the Bermudas, the Bahamas ... British Guiana and ... Honduras' in order to pay off the American Debt. It meant that 'any garrison left in Palestine should be cut down to a minimum ... the project for ... the occupation of Mesopotamia abandoned [and] the huge programme for [its] development ... indefinitely postponed'. In 1920 it included abandonment of the idea of Palestine as a Jewish State, removing the ring around Bolshevik Russia in order to 'let in the air' and the view that 'under no circumstances' could Britain go to war for the sake of Poland. In 1921 it meant a determined assault on Naval Expansion and a Naval Holiday with Japan and the United States. It meant recognising that there was a crisis to be faced, that national bankruptcy meant 'national starvation' and that there was only one way to avoid it. Every government department 'had to be put on the anvil and ... hammer[ed] ... down to proportions within the nation's means'. Britain must cease to be 'the policeman of the world'. Her policy must be 'to add not a single rood of land to [her] present overseas territories'. All subsidies 'should be stopped save perhaps the subsidy on bread'. Private enterprise should be given its head in relation to Housing: 'the occupants of all new houses should pay economic rents from the outset, except in needy areas'.[1] There had to be a 'gradual deflation of the currency' which would be 'almost automatic if ... national expenditure was reduced by one-third or one-half'.[2]

Rothermere was not demanding a Businessman's government. Rather he was making a statement of the belief that Britain was an economic rather than a military or administrative nation and that this was the most important fact about her. This situation, he claimed, demanded economic leadership which would not be supplied by Conservatives who were as closely linked with the military bureaucracy as Law and Austen Chamberlain and depended on the middle classes who were now 'threatened with extinction' by the policies of the government they were supposed to be supporting.[3] Apart from Lloyd George the Coalition Liberals had nothing to recommend them. Fisher and Addison did not understand Retrenchment: Churchill 'to all intents and purposes ... [had] become a member of the Conservative party in which, as an advocate of big armaments, he [would] find full play for his striking abilities'.[4] The time had come for 'the creation of a new "bloc" ' to reduce expenditure to the level it had reached in the late Victoria era on 'the principles which guided the economical administrations of the 60s and 70s of the last century ... a progressive party which [would] take real reconstruction for its watchword and ... do for this country what Lord Cromer did for Egypt when he found it bankrupt and derelict and made a little money go a long way'.[5]

The object in refashioning the party system was to find ways of reconciling the working classes to existing capitalism and to pre-empt the loyalties which revolutionary leaders would claim. Rothermere recognised working-class consciousness as a fact of life. He knew that the Reform Bill had created a new electorate without settled loyalties and that he was rich because some of his newspapers had a working-class readership. 'Economy without Exception' was designed to provide indoctrination, to explain the basis of British prosperity and to establish that neither Conservative/landed/military leadership nor the leadership of intellectual Socialism could guide Britain into the industrial/commercial future on which her material existence depended.

Rothermere was explaining the relevance of Capitalist Truth to working-class lives. In 1919/20 he offered it as a cure for inflation, in 1921 as a cure for unemployment. In both situations he made a distinction between the 'millions of industrial workers who wished to lead peaceful lives' and the trades union and Labour 'extremists' whose object was 'to ... throw the country into chaos'. He claimed that there need be no 'battle' between Capital and Labour and that 'defeat' and 'victory' were irrelevant. Labour, he was saying, must recognise the importance of 'serving the community': it would not even serve itself if it made wage demands the achievement of which would add to the inflation which all policy needed to remove.[1] For him, as for others, Smillie, Mann, Hodges and Williams provided convenient scapegoats.

Rothermere's object was to provide a doctrine and form a movement which offered these truths for the nation's education. He wanted Lloyd George to lead the movement. He intended at first to base it on Maclean's Liberals with the implied expectation that McKenna would play a part as well.[2] For a time he gave a platform to George Lambert.[3] He ran Worthington-Evans to succeed Austen Chamberlain as Chancellor. That, however, in 1919 and 1920 was all Rothermere did. His son, Esmond, aged twenty-one, was returned at the Isle of Thanet by-election in November 1919 as the official 'Stop-the-Waste' candidate of the Unionist association after an announcement that he would stand whether it supported him or not;[4] in the House of Commons he worked with Erskine when Erskine joined him on winning St George's, Westminster as an Anti-Waste candidate in 1921.[5] In 1919 and 1920 neither he nor Rothermere attempted to create a new party outside the House of Commons. Until the beginning of 1921 Rothermere confined himself to a newspaper campaign in which he was assisted by Horatio Bottomley.

In 1919 Bottomley was fifty-nine. He was the son of a Hackney tailor and nephew of George Jacob Holyoake: he claimed to be Bradlaugh's illegitimate son. Both his legal parents died when he was a child. At the age of ten Holyoake put him in an orphanage. He left at fourteen, worked in a solicitor's office in the City and as a shorthand writer in the Law Courts and finally set up as a suburban newspaper owner. At thirty-one he was bankrupt. At thirty-three he had successfully conducted his own defence against charges of conspiracy to defraud. At forty he was a slightly shady large-scale company promoter with a name which ranked among the leading speculative financiers in London.

Like most of the Bradlaugh/Holyoake circle, Bottomley was a Liberal. He stood first in Hornsey as a Gladstonian at a by-election in 1887 and then again in Hackney South at the general election of 1900. He was elected to parliament in 1906 against an Independent Liberal who received official support from the Liberal party. In the same year he founded *John Bull*, making it a paper of anti-party thinking and 'businesslike' methods in government and the centre of a popular political organisation – the John Bull League – whose main function turned out to be to support him in Hackney and whose chief success was the destruction for the moment of the career of Masterman for whom Bottomley had developed a deep personal hatred. By the time of Bottomley's second bankruptcy and resignation from parliament in 1912, the League had adopted a small number of parliamentary candidates, one of whom fought a by-election that year. By the beginning of the war in 1914, it had done nothing more spectacular, though bankruptcy and retirement from the House of Commons seem not to have prevented Bottomley living well and keeping up an acquaintance with the rich and politically successful.[1]

John Bull had been type-cast as the bible of the average, sensual man who did not believe in conventional politics, assumed that capitalism was right and was interested in horse-racing, boxing, drinking and so on. The war converted it from being the enemy of Serbia into being the enemy of Germany. Bottomley made it the patriotic recruiting agents' magazine, propagating his message with the same fervour as Bradlaugh and Holyoake had shown on behalf of their popular secularism two generations earlier. In doing so, he became a major public figure. He visited the Front, was fêted at public luncheons, had a well-publicised tea with Bishop Winnington-Ingram[1] and was received at Downing Street by Lloyd George. By 1918 he had gained the stature of a popular folk hero, despite a shady past and intermittent attacks on his honesty.

In addition to the John Bull League, Bottomley had founded the Business Government League which broke the electoral truce in 1915 by putting up a candidate against Herbert Samuel and supporting Pemberton Billing at the Mile End by-election. Neither candidate was successful. While the war lasted Bottomley had no representation in parliament. At the 1918 election he stood once more in Hackney as an Independent, the withdrawal of the Unionist candidate enabling him to inflict an overwhelming defeat on the Asquithean Liberal. In May 1919 he launched The People's League as the basis for 'a great Third Party' which would represent the body of 'the People' against organised Labour and organised Capital.[2] In 1919 he was not only the editor and proprietor of *John Bull* but was the chief columnist in the *Sunday Pictorial*, occupying most of page 4 of the paper, his weekly column being supported about once a month on the opposite page by a signed article on a major political question from Rother-mere.

Bottomley's capacity for self-advertisement was immense. His ambition was Napoleonic. His fall – when it came in 1922 – complete. His capacity and industry were enormous also. As a journalist he made a brilliant deployment of a broad-based secularism, spreading out from a dogmatic non-denominationalism through anti-temperance to defence of British liberty and the merits of the free market. If he had a humbug of his own, he made mincemeat of the humbug of others, excoriating the more extreme claims made on behalf of the League of Nations, dismissing most forces in international politics except those based on power and ridiculing the naïvest sorts of Labour claim to have discovered an inexhaustible supply of wealth and wages.

Bottomley presented himself as a secular patriot, anxious for the nation's good, undeceived by idealistic claptrap and concerned to create a Britain in which the poor and underprivileged, who had proved themselves in war, would enjoy the fruits of a sane, healthy, rich and powerful civilisation. As the promises of 1918 faded, he reflected dissatisfaction with their fading, excepting Lloyd George from criticism but not concealing the failure of the Coalition to give the people what it promised. At the same time he spoke as the defender of constitutional government against the Bolshevik extremism manifested by Smillie, Williams, Hodges and Mann.

Bottomley's attitude to the Labour movement was both hostile and accommodating. He believed in 'the patriotism of the British people', thought the working man neither a laggard nor a revolutionary and encouraged an attitude of give-and-take which would thwart the efforts of those who wished to plunge the nation into revolution. He asserted the merit of work and did not believe that the working man feared it. He asserted the possibility of a good life for all and welcomed the working man's attempt to get it. He distinguished between the leaders of the trades unions and the Labour movement on the one hand and their followers on the other: during the Coal disputes of 1919/21 he demanded secret ballots at each point at which strikes seemed likely to happen. Like Rothermere, Bottomley was an exponent of the merits of a free capitalism. Like Rothermere he attacked governmental waste and bureaucratic interference. He propagated a comprehensive gospel including a secular version of the religion of all good men which might 'convert what is now a mere sectarian body into a true Church of England – a Temple of Brotherhood broad as the bounds of man's eternal need'.[1]

Bottomley pursued Rothermere's policies – over Addison, Fisher, Nationalisation, Economy, Taxation, Reparations, the Near East, the Far East and Russia. He advocated co-operation between Unionists, Liberals and moderate Labour leaders and made a point of flattering Clynes, Thomas and G. H. Roberts.[2] He advocated a Round Table Conference on Industrial Peace after the failure of the Triple Alliance in 1921.[3] In addition, he deployed a pantechnicon of opinions in favour of the Prince of Wales as 'every man's pal', the Britisher's real liking for the Irish, the abolition of King's Proctor and ecclesiastical Courts and the liberalisation of Army discipline, the establishment of the Unknown

Warrior and Premium Bonds, control of the Anglo-Continental horse traffic, the improvement of transport facilities and the closure of obsolete railways, the Cinema as a place of 'wholesome entertainment', the superiority of 'Empire' to 'Commonwealth' Day, the desirability of a 'Merrie England' attitude to the Sabbath and the importance of restoring the Cat for brutal outrages against the person.[1]

Bottomley ceased to write for the *Sunday Pictorial* in June 1921. His main lines of argument there, in *John Bull* and in the *Sunday Illustrated* were formed before unemployment had become a major factor. His chief contributions to political understanding centred on inflation and the level of government spending, the hammering, through *John Bull*, of the details of bureaucratic incompetence, the possibility that a minority Bolshevik party would capture the Labour movement and the importance of responding to the desire he claimed was felt by most electors to vote independently of party. With Bottomley independence of party was a long-standing slogan. It was a major feature of his politics in 1919 and 1920.

Rothermere intended originally to found an Anti-Waste party in 1919 in order to fight elections against the Coalition. Perhaps because Esmond Harmsworth was adopted as official candidate of the Unionist association in the Isle of Thanet, this intention was abandoned. Rothermere refused to support proposals to amalgamate the Conservative and Lloyd George Liberal parties in early 1920 because he did not believe that Economy was being taken seriously.[2] The two anti-Coalition by-election victories in 1920 were won, however, not by himself and his son, but by Bottomley who, the day after the Labour victory at Spen Valley, announced that Charles Palmer – the assistant editor of *John Bull* – would be fighting The Wrekin. The Wrekin had become vacant by the death of the sitting Coalition Liberal for whom a well-known local successor had already been chosen. Bottomley and Palmer not only defeated him: when Palmer died later in the year, Bottomley persuaded General Townshend – heir to the Marquis Townshend and hero of Kut – to stand in his place and helped him to be returned with a larger vote. It was not until they ran a 'Ruthless Economy' candidate at the Dover by-election of January 1921 that Rothermere and Harmsworth conducted a by-election.

The Dover by-election was more important than either of the Wrekin ones. At The Wrekin there was no Conservative candidate in 1918 or at the by-election: The Wrekin had been a Liberal seat for a very long time. Its effect in any case was spoilt by an unsuccessful Bottomley campaign at Stockport in April. At Dover a Die Hard Conservative had been returned in 1918: the Coalition Conservative by-election candidate was J. J. Astor supported by all the clergy of the constituency. His defeat on Conservative votes by Sir Thomas Polson, a Director of the British Motor Trade Corporation whom Rothermere had known while Director-General of the Army Clothing Department, was a major blow to the Conservative party.[1] It suffered another with the success of Beaverbrook's campaign to defeat Griffith-Boscawen on re-election at Dudley after becoming Minister of Agriculture.[2] Dover was followed by the formation of the Anti-Waste League with Rothermere as president, Polson as treasurer and Esmond Harmsworth as chairman.[3] In the eight months after the Dover victory, Anti-Waste candidates were adopted in about twenty London constituencies and elsewhere in preparation for the next general election.[4]

Rothermere and Harmsworth worked with Bottomley over the Dover by-election but Bottomley had no office in the Anti-Waste League. The Anti-Waste victory at St George's, Westminster in June 1921 was the work of Rothermere and Harmsworth using Mesopotamia, Palestine and Economy to defeat Sir Herbert Jessel, a well-known London Jew.[5] Gee's victory over MacDonald at Woolwich in March and Sueter's victory at Hertford in June – on an Anti-War as well as an Anti-Waste platform – were the work of Bottomley.[6] When he founded the *Sunday Illustrated* at the end of June, Bottomley was replaced as chief columnist in the *Sunday Pictorial* by Lovat Fraser. In August there was a sharp quarrel over the Abbey by-election in Westminster where Bottomley supported one 'Anti-Waste' candidate, General Nicholson standing with support from the Conservative association, against Colonel Applin, the candidate of the Anti-Waste League, who was defeated decisively. At the West Lewisham by-election in September, Bottomley refused to support anyone,[7] the Rothermere candidate[8] being defeated by an official Conservative with an 'Anti-Waste' label. There were no further Anti-Waste League interventions at by-elections except, again unsuccessfully, at the City of London in May 1922.

At the height of their quarrel Rothermere accused Bottomley of putting too low a priority on reducing governmental expenditure.[1] Bottomley accused Rothermere of concentrating on Anti-Waste 'which [was] a mere negative cry involving, by its maxim of Economy without Exceptions, the cutting down of pensions and allowances' where Bottomley's party had the 'constructive and statesmanlike ... policy of Economy with Efficiency'.[2] Bottomley conducted the Wrekin by-elections on a programme which laid as much emphasis on being anti-party as on being anti-waste: his general propaganda covered a broader front than Rothermere's. The Independent party he led in parliament in 1921/22 had a more varied programme than Rothermere allowed the Anti-Waste League to deploy. For a time nevertheless Bottomley and Rothermere worked together. Between them they created a distinctive climate, made a recognisable assault, demonstrated the vulnerability of the Coalition and, while claiming to be rescuing Lloyd George from the Conservative party, greatly increased his dependence on it as the inroads they made on Conservative support increased Conservative dissatisfaction with him.

In parliament neither movement mattered. Esmond Harmsworth and Erskine did not have a party of their own; they made no impact except as symbols of newspaper power. The Rothermere newspapers' trumpeting of Harmsworth as leader of the Anti-Waste party[3] was as absurd as Bottomley's claim that his Independent party was the party of the future. Harmsworth's inclusion among the Conservative leaders who asked Law to lead them after the Carlton Club meeting in October 1922 had nothing to do with his achievements in the House of Commons. Bottomley's parliamentary speeches were uniformly ineffective. His Independent party had an office and a Whip of its own, but it was in sight neither of political respectability nor of widespread acceptance. At its largest it consisted of Bottomley, Townshend, Polson, Sueter, Nicholson and Sir Cecil Beck, an unemployed ex-Coalition Liberal Whip,[4] as well as two Lowthers – Christopher and Claude[5] – with, on Bottomley's part, a claim, substantiated only by the publication of his memoirs in the *Sunday Illustrated*, that they had support from Christopher Lowther's father,

Speaker Lowther – Lord Ullswater – after his retirement from the Speakership in April 1921. Despite Bottomley's repeated claim that they constituted a signpost towards more general independence in the future, the association of these figures with him testified merely to the strength of the reputation he had gained during the war, the skill with which he created an impression of financial genius, the naive way in which some of them accepted his assistance when it was offered at by-elections and the extent of the dissatisfaction electors in the South of England could be induced to feel at the policies of the Coalition and the increase which had occurred since 1914 in the amount of governmental intervention.

In June 1921 the Conservative leaders were so worried by Anti-Waste that they prosecuted the *Daily Mirror* for contravening the Corrupt and Illegal Practices Act at the Hertford by-election. By late 1921 they had taken its measure. Rothermere then sought more effective ways of damaging the Coalition by supporting the Die Hards over the Irish Treaty, Mesopotamia and German Reparations.[1] When Lloyd George failed to force the Conservative party into an election in January 1922, the *Sunday Pictorial* suggested that he should resign.[2] In the next couple of months Esmond Harmsworth demanded a general election while Rothermere ran Derby, McKenna, Maclean and Grey as possible Prime Ministers[3] and renewed support for the Asquithean Liberals. The Asquitheans, however, neither succeeded in making a mark electorally nor met Rothermere's requirements in relation to government spending.[4] The Die Hards disappointed him by failing to support his candidate in the City of London by-election.[5] In June 1922 the *Sunday Pictorial* resumed support for Lloyd George: in September his Greek policy made it withdraw.[6] When Northcliffe died in August Rothermere tried to buy *The Times*, first in order to support Lloyd George after he left office, then, after the Greek crisis, to help establish Law in office. In May 1922 Bottomley was convicted of fraudulent conversion: he was expelled from the House of Commons after being sentenced to seven years' penal servitude. The fact that the Coalition did not fall until October 1922 should not obscure the importance of the part played by Rothermere and Bottomley between 1919 and 1921 in stimulating respectable Anglican, Conservative politicians to do to Lloyd George and the Coalition what previously a plutocratic press lord on the one hand and an ex-bankrupt, adventurer, demogogue and free thinker on the other alone had done effectively.

III

THE CONSPIRACIES OF
LORD ROBERT CECIL

'I thought his long letter to the press dull, pompous and egotistical but his later pronouncement is much plainer for it merely says frankly that, as he thinks the Coalition doomed and the Tory party unlikely to get into power, he will join up with Grey and Asquith if necessary in order to get into power.'

> Sir George Lloyd to Austen Chamberlain, June 9 1922, discussing Lord Robert Cecil

'. . . you must remember that I was brought up to think that a class war, whether the class attacked be landowners or Labour, is the most insidious form of national disintegration.'

> Lord Robert Cecil to Austen Chamberlain, April 20 1921

'If only Bob Cecil were not Bob Cecil, I think there would be a great opportunity for him.'

> Neville Chamberlain to Hilda, January 18 1920

With the loss of public confidence of which Anti-Waste candidates were as significant a symptom as the increased Labour vote, the first person to attempt a reconstruction of parties was Lord Robert Cecil. Croft, Ampthill and Cooper formed the National party in 1917 and ran candidates against the Coalition at the 1918 election. Salisbury and Joynson-Hicks demanded an end to Coalition in 1920 in order to restore a Conservative government. Neville Chamberlain would have welcomed a chance to destroy the Coalition in 1920 but was restrained by modesty, indifference or unwillingness to quarrel with Austen Chamberlain and the body of Birmingham Coalitionists.[1] Rothermere had called for reconstruction but had done nothing to effect it. Cecil's was the first attempt to bring down Lloyd George by constructing a new progressive alliance between such anti-Coalition, anti-socialist forces as he found available.

Cecil was a devout, public-spirited, high-minded Anglican with some experience of foreign policy as Under-Secretary at the Foreign Office and Minister of Blockade but little knowledge of most domestic questions. As the third son of the third Marquis of

Salisbury, he felt himself part of the Conservative leadership which Joseph Chamberlain threatened from 1903 onwards. In the 1906 parliament he was an opponent of the Tariff Reform movement for 'being sordid and materialistic ... and the high road to corruption':[1] he had difficulty with, and had to leave, his constituency association and approached Asquith about an arrangement with the Liberal party.[2] He did not in fact make one: between 1909 and 1914 he developed strong commitments to the House of Lords, the Irish Union and the Welsh Church and a considerable aversion to Asquith as tension heightened in consequence of Asquith's conduct of these questions. He joined Asquith's Coalition in 1915. After trying to remove Lloyd George from office he joined Lloyd George's in 1916, but regarded Lloyd George as the most temporary and undesirable of allies.[3] He threatened to resign in June 1918 in protest against the Cabinet's failure to act decisively in Siberia.[4] He expected his resignation over Welsh Church Disestablishment at the end of 1918[5] to be more widely supported in the Conservative party than it was. It did not prevent him standing as a Coalitionist at the general election. In 1919 he voted against the financial settlement consequent on Disestablishment.[6]

For Lord Robert Cecil the war was a turning-point in British politics. He believed that the prominence given to organised Labour during the war and the part its leaders had played in office meant that post-war political problems would be novel in scale and content. The new politics Britain needed necessitated a reconstruction of the thought-world in which politicians moved. No less than Bertrand Russell and the Webbs, he felt obliged to initiate a reconstruction of civilisation. The central problem as he saw it was that 'the war ha[d] shattered the prestige of the European governing classes',[7] and that their disappearance had created a vacuum which needed to be filled if disaster was not to overtake the British. The central remedy in his mind was the construction of a European order which the Treaty of Versailles had failed to create – the establishment on the basis of 'Christian morality'[8] of a machinery of legal conciliation within which 'Junkerism and Chauvinism' would be destroyed[9] and economic activity restored to its pre-war level. He objected to intervention in Russia. He criticised the Upper Silesian and Saar clauses of the Versailles

Treaty because they would make a permanent peace impossible, opposed the Reparations clauses because they would hamper German economic recovery and feared that the treaty generally would divide Britain from the United States and delay the restoration of a stable European polity the 'lasting settlement' of which was 'the preponderating desire of the English people'.[1]

Cecil was a Free Trader in the widest and most elevated sense. The League of Nations as he conceived it was a political aspect of a Cobdenian vision of the world where trade, 'self-sacrifice' and international co-operation went hand in hand in the beneficent shadow of international ajudication and specific mutual guarantees of international peace. In his hands the League of Nations was not merely a remedy for war between nations. It was also the guarantee that civilisation would be preserved in each of the nations of the world including Britain, where 'the League point of view [ran] through all politics – Ireland, Industry, even Economy ... [involving] a new way of looking at things political – or rather a reversion to a very old way'.[2]

In this pious, misty but practical mind the League of Nations was not conceived as an instrument of democratic control. On the contrary it involved transposition into a new age of the manner and temper which had been effective in governing England in the nineteenth century. It lay at the root of all political problems because it involved a moralisation of politics parallel to the moralisation Disraeli had persuaded 'the old-fashioned country gentlemen' to achieve fifty years before. Cecil regarded himself as the heir to gentry Conservatism. Despite the fact that Grey was a Whig with little spontaneous interest in the League of Nations, he treated Viscount Grey as its exponent, regarding him as the embodiment of that reputation for 'justice' which he supposed was Britain's 'greatest National asset ... in foreign affairs ... for the last two generations'.[3] He treated Lloyd George as its enemy, the Versailles Treaty as evidence of 'moral bankruptcy' and reprisals in Ireland as objectionable because they would 'never be permitted in actual warfare by any civilized nation' and would have a disastrous ... effect ... on revolutionaries in England and ... other parts of the Empire'. His political objective from 1920 onwards was to overthrow Lloyd George.

His object was to ensure that, if Lloyd George was superseded, he would be superseded not by a 'reactionary' Conservative party but by some sort of 'progressive' one. These were the terms in which he thought: they were the terms on which he acted. He had no wish to dismantle the British Empire, grant self-government to Ireland, allow Germany to restore herself to the centre of the European scene or carry the demand for reductions in government spending to its logical conclusion by immediate withdrawal from Mesopotamia.[1] He believed that 'extra-legal proceedings' should be resisted whether in the form of 'direct action' in England or 'reprisals' in Ireland,[2] but part of his objection to Lloyd George's Irish policy was that it was damaging Britain's relations with the United States.[3] He believed that mere repetition of the claim that 'the only alternative to Lloyd George is Labour' would 'sooner or later' mean that the 'country [would] try Labour [for which he] did not know that he should blame them'.[4] He intuited in the 'non-political mass'[5] as well as in the Conservative party a liberal rather than a reactionary temper and a concern for 'clean and honest government':[6] he had no confidence in the ability of the Conservative party in the House of Commons to reflect it. Northumberland, though 'a charming fellow', he thought 'a confirmed militarist': the Gretton/Northumberland combination was unsuitable to the circumstances by which it was confronted.[7] His wife thought Lloyd George 'degraded' everything he touched.[8]

Lord Robert Cecil's dislike was shared by many Conservatives. The desire to avoid 'the wickedness of class hatred',[9] to damp down class conflict and to prevent a confrontation with organised Labour co-existed with a desire to resist. It did little to distinguish Cecil from Salisbury who in his terms was close to being 'reactionary'. It did not distinguish him from respectable Conservatives like Hartington, Hoare, Ormsby-Gore, Lytton, Mosley, Lord Hugh Cecil, Wood and Lord Eustace Percy who disliked both the businessman Conservatism they saw much of in the House of Commons and the jingoistic reaction of Northumberland and Gretton.[10] What distinguished Cecil and Mosley, who had been a supporter of a Lloyd George Centre party in 1919,[11] was their willingness to leave the Conservative party and the belief the others held that a new party was impossible or undesirable.

Lord Robert Cecil was a conspirator, the would-be constructor of a shifting body of high-minded persons whose independent influence would determine the course of any government that happened to be in office. Like the Webbs he believed in permeation: like the Webbs he had a strategy to effect it. He did not mind whether it was effected by working within the Conservative party or by detaching a body of Conservatives from it. If Conservative leaders had responded in 1921, he would not have tried to move elsewhere. If the most articulate opposition to Lloyd George in 1920 and 1921 had not been Die Hard, he would not have lost confidence in the Conservative party. Whereas Salisbury thought a decent alternative to the Coalition could be provided by the Conservative party acting on its own, Cecil decided from early 1920 that the only way to make himself effective was by producing a situation in which a government under Grey became a possibility.[1]

This had been in his mind before the Spen Valley by-election in January 1920.[2] It was strengthened by the result of that election and by Birkenhead's attempt to use it as a reason for converting the Coalition into a permanent anti-socialist party.[3] As much as Birkenhead, Lord Robert Cecil wanted to create an anti-socialist party of the Centre. He wanted much the same range of electors to support it. But he wanted it to have a gentry and intellectual tone as he conceived it, embracing the whole range of respectable opinion from Lansdowne, Salisbury or Lord Hugh Cecil on the one side to Hammond, Clynes, Massingham and Gilbert Murray on the other. He was insistent that it should neither be run by Lloyd George nor be ostentatiously anti-working class and that it should reject 'the autocratic theory of employment' which, though 'quite a good working hypothesis fifty or a hundred years ago ... will not ... and ought not to be ... accepted nowadays'.[4] He believed that 'the best of the Liberals and Labour people' would work with 'some of the old landowning Tories if [these] would only think their own instincts and not be led by solicitors and businessmen ...'.[5] It was with this object in view that he thought of sitting on the Opposition benches below the gangway in April 1920 and sent a letter of support to Asquith when Asquith stood at the Paisley by-election in February.[6] It was with this in mind that he put out feelers to Clynes four months later for an electoral arrangement between the Labour party and League of Nations candidates if Coalition Liberal and Conservative supporters of the League made of the government's coolness towards it the occasion for sitting on the Opposition front benches.[1] This was why, along with Lord Hugh Cecil, he resigned the Conservative Whip in February 1921 in order to sit on the Opposition front bench.[2]

For Lord Robert Cecil an appeal to progressive opinion meant a League of Nations appeal and a positive attempt to prevent the division of English parties on class lines; it did not involve a commitment to high taxation or a high level of government spending. Cecil was a prominent member of the People's Union for Economy which he helped Salisbury to manage. He thought it important that the Anti-Waste movement, which had taken hold of parts of the Conservative party, should be led by respectable politicians like himself instead of by Rothermere, Bottomley and Esmond Harmsworth. Up to the middle of 1921 Salisbury and Lord Robert Cecil worked closely together. The government's anxiety to halt public expenditure having by then become clear, the Union's original purpose had been fulfilled. Salisbury's attempt to amalgamate it thereafter with Askwith's Middle Class Union drove them to some extent apart because Lord Robert Cecil was not much pleased by the Middle Class Union which he saw as a strike-breaking body whose object was to persuade 'the smaller trading, propertied and professional classes [to] band themselves together to protect their interests ... and secure their property ... from revolution and extreme Labour demands'.[3]

The idea of Grey returning to public life had been in Cecil's mind since early 1920.[4] The idea of a Grey government became a major obsession from April 1921 onwards. The government's tendency 'to incite the possessing classes to band themselves together under their leadership for a fight against Labour' made it necessary:[5] the collapse of the Triple Alliance on Black Friday made it possible. The failure of the projected general strike, displaying, as he supposed, the uselessness of Direct Action provided the 'psychological' opportunity to involve the Labour leaders in a movement of this sort.[6] In July 1920 Clynes seems to have signed an appeal to Grey to return to public life.[7] There is nothing else to show that any of the Labour leaders would have followed Cecil into a reconstructed Liberal-based Centre party, even under Grey's leadership. Some of Cecil's natural allies among the Lib/Lab intelligentsia mistrusted his caution about Ireland or believed that 'in modern political conditions not much can be done by a man like Cecil, merely by the issue of manifestoes'.[1] Nor is it clear that any of the Conservatives who were approached had any intention of following him or Grey or anyone else. In mid-1922 Cecil thought he had brought Grey back 'under conditions which make success absolutely hopeless'.[2] In 1921, in a situation in which the Coalition had lost six by-elections since the beginning of the year, he and Steel-Maitland made the attempt.

Steel-Maitland was a Round Tabler, a Milnerite, a Protectionist and member for a seat in Birmingham. As Chairman of the Conservative party between 1911 and 1916, he had completed the absorption of the Liberal Unionists and amalgamated Central Office, the National Union and the Liberal Unionist Council into a single organisation under central control.[3] He was a junior minister in the 1915 Coalition: he gave up the party chairmanship to Younger on joining the Lloyd George Coalition in 1916. In 1919 he resigned because he had nothing to do. In February 1920, along with Salisbury, Selborne, Willoughby de Broke and Godfrey Locker-Lampson, he pressed Law for a statement of party principles before any step was taken towards fusion.[4] He opposed the attempt at fusion in March. Derby thought him 'shifty'[5] and an Empire-builder. Neville Chamberlain mistrusted him deeply. He worked closely with Cecil, Salisbury, Selborne and other of Lloyd George's critics from inside the National Union.[6]

After extensive discussion between Cecil and Gladstone, Asquith was persuaded to talk to Grey. At an interview on June 29 he told him that the Coalition's difficulties were the Liberal party's chance and that he wanted to establish co-operation between the Labour, Conservative and Liberal critics of Lloyd George. Asquith said nothing about a change of leader. Grey talked at length about his eyesight and suggested a further meeting to draft a policy declaration.[7] In the next five weeks there were four meetings at which Grey, Crewe, Runciman, Maclean, Asquith, Simon and Lord Robert Cecil discussed co-operation. Cecil and Steel-Maitland abandoned the attempt to insist on a new party, though they stopped Asquith making the first public approach to Grey on the ground that a Liberal approach would destroy the supra-party character of the operation.[8] The Liberal leaders in their turn agreed that Cecil need not declare himself a Liberal but should announce his interest in Grey's future as soon as Grey made a public move which he promised to do at Berwick on October 10.

Cecil and Steel-Maitland spent August and September preparing such newspapers as would listen for Grey's return to public life. To Spender, Garvin, Harris and Scott in particular they underlined the significance of Grey's speech, suggesting that Grey would make the Liberal party a more credible alternative government and more attractive to non-Liberals than it could be under Asquith's leadership.[1] Cecil had written a public letter to his constituency association in July 1921[2] attacking the Coalition. After Grey's Berwick speech in October he published a second in which he announced his desire to co-operate if a Grey government could be formed.[3] When the Irish question seemed likely to destroy the Coalition in November, he urged the King to make Grey Prime Minister instead of Clynes, Asquith or Law.[4] In early 1922 he was joined by Lord Henry Bentinck.

Bentinck was the half-brother of the sixth Duke of Portland. He had first been elected to parliament in 1886 and had been M.P. for South Nottingham with one brief break since 1895. He had never held office but had served in South Africa and the Dardanelles and had been a member of the London County Council. Before 1914 he belonged to a Conservative back-bench group which claimed special sympathy for the working classes. He had played a part in establishing the League of Nations Union. His *Tory Democracy*, published in 1918, was a call to resist the 'Plutocracy' through which 'Imperial financiers' supported by a 'servile Press' and the sale of Honours were planning to turn the British Empire into a 'bag-man's paradise' and, 'while everything generous, self-sacrificing and noble [was] shedding its blood on the fields of France and Flanders', was supplementing the hold it had gained on the pre-war Liberal party by splitting the Labour party and commercialising the Conservative party.[5] Bentinck was not a figure of consequence, but he shared in an off-beat way the dislike felt by all three Cecils for the threat presented to their style of politics by the Tariff Reform League and by Lloyd George's employment of the plutocracy in high places. In early 1918, when he published his book and left the Conservative party, Bentinck probably expected Labour to be stronger than it was at the general election. Between 1918 and 1922 he was a sort of unofficial Labour sympathiser. During the Coal Strike of 1921 he lead a Labour delegation to protest to the Home Secretary against the imprisonment of miners who had had brushes with the police. His co-operation with Lord Robert Cecil in 1922 was a recognition that there were Conservative stirrings which it was possible to think would be effective. On March 5 and April 15 he was host at meetings to which Cecil invited fifty peers, M.P.s and others.

These meetings were attended by about twenty people including Hartington, Lord Eustace Percy, Mosley, Ormsby-Gore, Aubrey Herbert, Godfrey Locker-Lampson and Cecil's constituency chairman[1] who regarded Cecil as a potential party leader.[2] Afterwards Cecil sent out a further constituency letter[3] in which he spelt out the importance of not being reactionary and, by implication, dissociated himself from the other anti-Coalition movements operating inside the Conservative party. In May 1922 he claimed that the dominant force in the Conservative party was a body of men who cared only for 'the preservation of its property', declared once more his willingness to serve under Grey than whom no man 'differs so completely both in his qualities and defects from the Prime Minister' and spelt out a programme based on industrial co-operation and the League of Nations.[4] On May 16 he was responsible for defeating the government on an amendment to its Teachers' Superannuation Bill.[5] In the course of the summer he developed a platform which included Proportional Representation, support for depressed industries and the restoration of Free Trade. At one stage he was supported by Rothermere. At another Northcliffe began to support him.[6] On October 9 Cecil formally asked Asquith to make clear his willingness to step down in favour of Grey which, as soon as it was certain that Lloyd George would be leaving office, Asquith formally refused to do.[7]

The significance of Lord Robert Cecil's line was not its success, for, except amongst the Asquithean leaders, it had none. Its significance lay in the fact that he said extravagantly in public what some Conservatives said in private and that, in constructing a movement against the day when the Conservative party split, he was contributing to that eventuality. The Liberal leaders knew that he was important as a leader of liberal opinion but showed no inclination to disturb the Liberal party in order to get him.

Maclean, Cowdray and Gladstone shared his desire to get rid of Asquith but did not know how to do it. Cecil objected to the treatment he received from the Liberal press after his response to Grey's Berwick speech.[1] He took exception to Grey's decision to appear on Asquith's platform as an ordinary Liberal in early 1922 when, by avoiding party connections, Grey might have left open the possibility of a supra-party platform.[2] In 1921 he was offered financial support by Cowdray who had already supported the League of Nations Union:[3] in early 1922 he decided not to take it because he had ceased to believe that the Liberal leaders wanted to reconstruct the party system.[4] Throughout the summer of 1922 Gladstone tried to tempt him into the Liberal party without advance insistence on Grey being Prime Minister in a Liberal government.[5] Cecil refused to come so long as Asquith remained leader.[6] In September he pointed out that he could not become a Liberal while sitting for his present constituency which was close to Hatfield, but hinted that he might do so if a safe seat could be found elsewhere. When Warrington, held by Birkenhead's brother, Harold, was suggested[7] with the apology that the Liberal party had no safe seats in England,[8] the idea was abandoned. The Conservative rejection of Lloyd George and the fall of the Coalition in October made its revival unnecessary. When Law became Prime Minister, Cecil promised support. He was not offered office. Nor was he offered it after the election in November. He dropped a hint to Law four months later[9] but received nothing until, in different circumstances in May 1923, Baldwin made him Lord Privy Seal in his first Cabinet.

IV

LORD SALISBURY'S CONNECTIONS

'You say we might "have conceivably a Mond-Montagu-Samuel-Sassoon government". Is that not very much what we *have* got? Jews have lost us India. A Jew has played the devil in Palestine. Who appointed these persons? How could they have attained immense power if the government was not of their complexion. And why are most important Conferences held at Lympne under Sassoon's auspices, if this is not the case.'

Sydenham to Strachey, June 18 1921

'I need not say that I hate the name of Diehard which has done us no good. But I do not regret the movement, for it is a genuine movement of honest men who have risked their political reputation in order if possible to rescue the Country, and however people may sneer such an effort always does good in the long run. And they are of course much more powerful in the country than they are in the House of Commons. Still I do not conceal from myself that their weakness in the House of Commons has been almost a fatal handicap.'

Salisbury to Law, March 4 1922

'Fix your imaginative eye on the late W. H. Smith as a representative figure.'

Lady Gwendolen Cecil to Salisbury, July 19 1922

Lord Robert Cecil was a political maverick who mattered because of the liberal grandeur of the reputation he had made as the force behind the League of Nations Union. He did not matter much, where he was not greatly disliked by the solid minds which sat with the Conservative party, in the House of Commons. Salisbury was as willing as Lord Robert Cecil to use the instruments available in a democratic system to advance the political causes to which he was committed, but he avoided the 'shiftiness'[1] and intellectual volatility which was at once his brother's strength and his greatest weakness. Salisbury was not by nature a 'man of action'.[2] During the period under discussion he was impulsive, edgy and nervously stretched.[3] His reputation as guardian of one of the Conservative faiths cost him mental exertion and nervous exhaustion. But where Lord Robert Cecil had 'the mind of a Jesuit', Salisbury had 'the mind of an Englishman' and a sure touch with the body of. the Conservative party. He was his father's son and used the authority this gave him – in the party, the newspapers and the House of Lords – to make the party what he thought it should be.

In 1920 Salisbury was fifty-nine. He had been brought up at Hatfield along with Lady Gwendolen Cecil, with his brothers, Hugh and Robert who became politicians and with William, who became Bishop of Exeter. He had been educated at Eton and Oxford and been a Member of Parliament, with one brief break, from 1885 until his father's death in 1903. In this period he made a reputation as an honest, industrious, uncompromising and tactless parliamentarian, as an impetuous defender of the Church of England and as the assailant of any erosion of the Irish Union and Irish landholding arrangements.[1] Along with Selborne, he was one of the founders of the Church Parliamentary Committee set up to fight the Charity clauses of the Parish Councils Bill in 1892. From 1893 he was a leading member of the Central Church Committee. In the South African War he commanded a battalion. From 1900 he was Lansdowne's Under-Secretary at the Foreign Office until he entered the Cabinet when Balfour – who was his cousin – allowed Devonshire, Ritchie and Joseph Chamberlain to resign simultaneously in 1903. Like his brothers he was a Free Trader to whom Joseph Chamberlain threatened more than a change of policy. Like Austen Chamberlain, he remained alongside Balfour until the government went out of office in 1905.

From then onwards Salisbury remained out of office. He was not involved in the Asquith Coalition. Despite Carson's request that he should be, he was not invited to join Lloyd George's. In relation to the House of Lords he was a ditcher. He supported Austen Chamberlain for the Conservative leadership in 1911. He agreed to support the Lloyd George Coalition when it became clear that Milner would be prominent in it.[2] He ran the Unionist War Committee. He was a member of the Committee on Post-War Reconstruction. He acquiesced in Lloyd George running the government and Law the Unionist party so long as war lasted, but probably shared Selborne's view that Austen Chamberlain should be put up to stop them if they tried to go on running it once the war was over.[3]

Salisbury's disapproval of the Coalition took shape in criticism of its policies in India and Mesopotamia. He criticised its reluctance to reform the House of Lords, its inability to hold down the level of government spending and its refusal to allow private building to display the social advantages of the free economy.[1] He opposed Welsh Church Disestablishment.[2] He had an irreducible commitment to keeping the whole of Ireland in the United Kingdom and was party to the creation of a body of resistance to an Irish settlement on federal – or indeed any lines – in 1918.[3] Though he served from February 1919 as chairman of the Munitions Ministry Advisory Council on the sale of government surplus property,[4] he did not expect Lloyd George to last and expected the unprincipled capitalist ethos generated by the Coalition to play into the Labour party's hands by heightening class tension when it ought to be reduced. He objected to all proposals to involve the Conservative party in a wider amalgamation. In March 1919 he revived the Association of Independent Unionist Peers. From January 1920 he was an open critic of the Coalition and its leaders.

Like Lord Robert Cecil, Salisbury regarded class conflict as the worst of political evils and the one subject about which discussion should be avoided. As Lloyd George, Birkenhead and Churchill made their mark on industrial relations, he anticipated a situation in which necessary efforts to deal with Direct Action would be turned by defects in tone into demonstrations of the power and arrogance of wealth.[5] Salisbury had no more desire than Birkenhead to capitulate to the trades unions. He was no less convinced of the need to preserve the economic and social order. He had no animus against Lloyd George, thinking him in some respects too accommodating, in other respects not accommodating enough. But he was troubled by the connection he made between the ostentatious vulgarity of Birkenhead's personal life, the provocations offered by his political rhetoric, the serviceless plutocracy he saw rewarded in the Honours system as Lloyd George operated it and what the working classes would do if they were not led by the right sort of politician.

Salisbury did not believe in the Coalition Liberal party which, in common with most Conservatives, he regarded as a lifeless rump. He did not believe that Lloyd George would recover from the electoral blows he had suffered: he believed that Labour would gain what the Coalition lost. From his first major assault in a letter to *The Times* six days after the Spen Valley by-election result right the way through 1920, 1921, and 1922 his message was a criticism of the 'opportunism' displayed by the Lloyd George/ Conservative combination, a warning that its want of principle would 'make the triumph of Mr Smillie's policy inevitable' and a call to ministers to re-establish the principle that government stood impartially between Capital and Labour.[1] At each point at which Coalition Conservatives suggested amalgamating the Conservative party with the Coalition Liberals, he criticised them.[2] It was their wish to keep amalgamation open as one possible line of advance which stimulated his first call in March 1920 to free the Conservative party from all connection with the Coalition if the Coalition continued to pursue policies of which Conservatives disapproved.

This demand struck few notes amongst Conservatives. Salisbury repeated it without effect during the Stockport by-election.[3] His speeches and letters up to the middle of 1921 assumed continued co-operation between the two wings of the Coalition because he did not believe that co-operation could be ended.[4] It was not until two Anti-Waste victories over Coalition Conservatives – one on his own doorstep in Hertford in June – that he replied to the defence Austen Chamberlain then made of the Coalition by calling on him to save himself from the 'morass' into which the party was sinking[5] and urged 'every Unionist association in the country ... to approach its Unionist member or candidate and request that henceforth he shall consider himself free from any binding obligation to support the Coalition government'.[6]

Salisbury's conception of the nation was not confined to the gentry and the working classes. His father had had to have 'villadom' pointed out to him. Salisbury had absorbed the lesson. He sensed not one need but two. He sensed the need to convince the working classes that the ruling class were not hostile to them. He sensed the need, which Anti-Waste pinpointed, to convince taxpayers that their difficulties had not been forgotten. The first took shape in the policy of 'Co-operation'. Co-operation was sold to Salisbury by Lord Robert Cecil as part of the fashionable furniture of Lord Robert's mind: it met Salisbury's desire to minimise class conflict which Right and Left, rightly or wrongly, were supposed to want. Co-operation meant replacing the 'hard commercial scientific ... relation ... of the present competitive system [by] a true relation of mutual responsibility'.[1] It involved the assertion that 'the greatest defenders of moderation in Church and State [were] to be found among the working class',[2] that 'there should be a policy of absolute confidence and sympathy towards Labour' and that they 'should be told everything and have their full share – but not more than their share – in the management of industry'.[3]

The second need was met by the People's Union for Economy.[4] The PUE was a respectable copy of Anti-Waste. It began as a committee to draw parliament's attention to opportunities for reductions in government spending and to carry on a campaign in the constituencies. Its members included Selborne, Midleton and Steel-Maitland, Lord Chalmers, the retired Permanent Secretary to the Treasury, Lord Inchcape, the Free Trade shipping magnate, Walter Leaf, the banker, and Cowdray who, in addition to being an Asquithean benefactor, was a major City figure.[5] Cowdray was not alone among its leaders in having been a Lloyd George minister who had suffered at Lloyd George's hands. The same could be said of Lord Emmott, of Lord Islington who had been removed from the India Office in 1918 to make way for Sinha and of Lord Askwith, the leader of the Middle Class Union and ex-Industrial Commissioner who, having been brought into the civil service by Lloyd George, resigned when his post was dismantled in the course of 1919.[6]

In February 1921 a parliamentary committee was set up. This consisted of about sixty members of both Houses of Parliament,[7] including Midleton and Emmott among peers, Godfrey Locker-Lampson, Steel-Maitland, Mosley and Lord Robert Cecil as leading M.P.s and Hore-Belisha, the Liberal ex-president of the Oxford Union, as administrative assistant until, misunderstanding the scope of his responsibilities, he had to resign a month later.[8] In the next few months the People's Union for Economy held parliamentary meetings and issued statements demanding control of rate expenditure. It fought no elections. In collaboration with the Middle Class Union it helped to create the atmosphere in which Addison was driven first from the Ministry of Health and then from office.[9] It annoyed Austen Chamberlain by persuading 150 or so M.P.s to sign a demand for control of government

74

spending when '87 [had] absented themselves' and 14 voted for a Labour party motion 'to add 15 millions to our pensions expenditure'.[1] Salisbury thought the PUE 'had a good share in impelling the government towards economy':[2] by the side of the Anti-Waste movement its impact was probably small. One of its members – Inchcape – was a member of the Geddes Committee.

In all this activity Salisbury had a random collection of allies. There was Lord Robert Cecil. There was Lord Midleton – Curzon's Brodrick – who refused the Lord Lieutenancy of Ireland in 1918 and, as spokesman for Southern Unionism, felt betrayed by Law's and Balfour's Ulster-orientated connivance at the division of Ireland.[3] There was Lord Selborne – Churchman, Tariff Reformer, ex-Liberal Unionist and ex-Governor-General of South Africa – who made a reputation on Agriculture and Ireland over which he had resigned from the Asquith Coalition in 1916: as a peer's son who had not been allowed to renounce his peerage on his father's death in 1895,[4] he made a strengthened House of Lords one of the chief objects of his political activity from 1918 onwards.[5] There was the Duke of Northumberland's Die Hard contingent: there was Colonel John Gretton's. There was the British Empire Union and about twenty similar organisations which it absorbed in England and Ireland.[6] There was the remnant of Ampthill's, Croft's and Cooper's National party.[7] There was J. R. Pretyman Newman – Irish landowner, Conservative M.P. for Finchley and Askwith's colleague in the Middle Class Union. There was Lord Sydenham, the seventy-year-old anti-Bolshevik ex-Governor of Madras and ex-Secretary of the Committee of Imperial Defence, whose brief experience of wartime politics as a member of the Air Board had ended with Asquith's fall in December 1916 and who combined a Liberal past, Unionist principles in Ireland, acute consciousness of the Jewish peril and unfailing ferocity towards democratisation in India. And there was Sir William Joynson-Hicks, the Conservative teetotal, sabbatarian solicitor-M.P. for Twickenham who had fought four unsuccessful by-elections before beating Churchill at Manchester in 1908 and had been a persistent persecutor of the Liberal government in 1914/15 but who, despite a knighthood for raising a battalion of the Middlesex regiment during the war, had not at fifty-five yet held serious office.

75

In addition there were Salisbury's colleagues in the Association of Independent Unionist Peers. There were the critics of Lee's Agricultural policy who concentrated in the House of Lords around Selborne and Lord Clinton.[1] There was Leo Maxse, the editor of the *National Review*, and H. A. Gwynn, the editor of the *Morning Post*. There was St Loe Strachey – Free Trader, ex-Liberal Unionist and editor of *The Spectator* – who, deciding in 1921 that Ireland, unemployment and government spending necessitated a change of government, tried at various times to bring Salisbury and McKenna together and to persuade Grey, McKenna or Churchill to give the lead necessary to effect it.[2] And there was a body of liberal-minded Conservatives who looked respectfully in Salisbury's direction. Despite policy differences between these groups – especially about Protection – Salisbury's importance lay in the confidence felt by all in his intentions.

Sir Richard Cooper was a chemical manufacturer, a member of the firm of William Cooper and Nephews. In 1920 he was forty-six and had been M.P. for Walsall since 1910. When told in 1919 that Lloyd George, Law, Balfour and Barnes would represent Britain at the Peace Conference, he wondered whether 'any of these gentlemen [was] English'.[3] Ampthill's background was Whig: he was Odo Russell's son and Clarendon's grandson. He was Joseph Chamberlain's private secretary at the Colonial Office in the 1890s, then Governor of Madras and, for a time, acting Viceroy of India. He commanded infantry regiments in France during the war and was Indian Labour Corps Adviser at Western GHQ. Maxse but no one else thought he should be Viceroy when Chelmsford retired in 1920.[4] Page Croft was the son of a naval officer who had married into a family of Ware brewers. He went first to Eton, next (after the death of his housemaster) to Shrewsbury and finally to Trinity Hall where he was an oarsman and Volunteer. On leaving Cambridge he joined the family business. As a slightly self-conscious country gentleman, he became an active member of the 'Confederacy' of 'young gentry' Chamberlainites who organised a Protectionist movement against the Hatfield interest in Hertfordshire. At the election of 1906 he stood unsuccessfully against the Conservative Free Trader at Lincoln. In 1910 he won Christ Church as an anti-German whole-hogging Protectionist. In the House of Commons he was a prominent Food Taxer, advocate of

Imperial Preference and friend of Ulster. He was with Castlereagh at Mount Stewart when Ulster prepared for war in 1914. When the Great War broke out, he went to France with his territorial battalion. In 1915, at the age of thirty-four, he was the first territorial to command a brigade in the field.[1]

His military career did not last long. Reports to politicians in England about the conduct of his commanders caused difficulty: in 1916 he returned to the House of Commons. In 1917, along with Cooper, he founded the National party to fill the void left by the 'discrediting of the old party system'. The National party organised public meetings and presented petitions to the Prime Minister. Its programme was the raising of the Conscription age to fifty, the closing of German banks and businesses, the internment of enemy aliens, conscription for Ireland, a guaranteed price for home-grown cereals, protection for British industry and counter air-raids against German towns.[2] It attacked the close links alleged to exist between heads of firms and government departments which gave them contracts. On one occasion its offices in King Street were raided by the police. The National party was respectful about the working classes, 'for if you wish for a patriotic race, you must aim at a contented people, reared under healthy conditions ... and with full scope for advancement'.[3] One of its slogans was 'no restriction in wages in return for no restriction of output'. From time to time it co-operated with the National Democratic Party.

At the Coupon election Croft and Cooper were supported by the ex-Whig Earl of Bessborough, his son Lord Duncannon – Conservative M.P. for Dover – Captain Fitzroy, who later became Speaker, and the seventy-year-old Lord Leith of Fyvie who, after ten years' naval service in the 60s, had spent a good deal of his middle life in the steel industry in the United States. There were twenty-three National party candidates but only Cooper[4] and Croft were returned. From 1918 onwards its leaders found the going difficult. They sought publicity for their views about Honours,[5] Montagu, Dyer, Russian recognition, the Railway Strike of 1919 and Lloyd George's negotiations with Sinn Fein. They received attention from the *Morning Post*, the *National Review* and *The Globe*. Crewdson,[6] Lady Askwith,[7] Colonel Applin, the Temperance Reformer, Earl Bathurst,[8] Lord

77

Leconfield and the seventy-six-year-old Duke of Somerset provided support which was solid rather than powerful.[1] In January 1921 separate existence was abandoned in order to undermine the Coalition from within. In 1922 the National party machinery was revived as the National Constitutional Association which held public meetings at Caxton Hall, Queen's Hall and elsewhere. Croft and Cooper were prominent in the Honours campaign which was waged in the House of Commons in July 1922. But by early 1922 the party had been absorbed into a wider movement of which the Duke of Northumberland was the public symbol and Maxse and Gwynn the most articulate prophets.

Maxse's primary interest was in foreign policy. He was the most persistent of the pre-war enemies of Germany who warned incessantly of the German menace and the need for Britain to be strong in order to resist it. The pre-war *National Review* demanded a modern grasping of the factors of power and purposeful assertion of Imperial strength in a world in which effortless superiority and liberal idealism provided no guarantee of success. In this area in these years Maxse made a particular application of a general dismissal of Radical Cosmopolitanism, Liberal Idealism and Cobdenite Pacifism which had implications outside his chief area of concern.

In Maxse's mind the war supplied justification of his pre-war stand: the Allied victory in 1918 gave an opportunity to rid Europe of the German menace. But, just as Lloyd George and Haldane had underestimated the German threat before the war, so, from the end of the war, the opportunity was missed which victory had given. For Maxse the Peace Treaties, so far from being too harsh, were not harsh enough. His main purpose from 1918 to 1922 was to expose Lloyd George, who had promised to hang the Kaiser and make Germany pay in 1918 only because the election campaign had taught him that the electorate wanted him to,[2] and to ensure that the nation understood the realities of life as Pacifist, Cosmopolitan, Radical, Jewish and Cobdenite forces enabled Germany to restore herself to the centre of the scene. From the Peace Conference through Spa and Genoa to the fall of Lloyd George in 1922 he gave consistent warnings that Lloyd George was doing what he had done in South Africa in 1900, what he had nearly done in 1914 and what, given a free hand, he would choose to do again. The fact that Lloyd George was criticised from other directions for insensitivity to the League of Nations, and at first, for hostility to Germany did not prevent Maxse blaming him for 'the perversity of statesmanship' through which Allied politicians under President Wilson's pressure had thrown away the victorious predominance Foch had achieved in November 1918.[1]

Maxse attacked all the fashionable excuses for avoiding a harsh Peace Treaty. He did not believe in the League of Nations which was a 'front-bench affair hurriedly adopted and recklessly advocated simply and solely to please President Wilson'.[2] He did not trust President Wilson. He believed that Hindenburg and Ludendorf continued to make the running in Germany whoever appeared to and that Prussianism was so strong that it was unnecessary to be kind to Germany in order to prevent her going Bolshevik. Maxse wanted Bolshevism eradicated. He supported Allied intervention in Russia, treated Poland as a bastion and regarded Anglo-French support of Poland as central to European hegemony. Throughout 1920, 1921 and 1922 he attacked Lloyd George for failing to 'f[i]ght for a ... greater France, support ... Poland, sustain ... Bohemia, nourish ... Rumania [and] uphold our allies in Russia'.[3] In all this he was emphatic. Bolshevism was bad in itself and had to be destroyed. But it had to be destroyed also because, unless it was, there would be no way of enabling Russia to resume the rôle she had played as a main line of defence against Germany in the first three years of war.

From Maxse's point of view Lloyd George's foreign policy was fraudulent, but his criticisms were not just directed at Lloyd George. They were directed at the parliamentary Conservative party which, like the rest of the 1918 parliament, consisted of 'yes-men and place-men', and at Conservative ministers who failed to exert power where power should have been exerted. Law bore chief responsibility for being willing to 'take any amount of Radical doctrine' from Lloyd George, but Balfour's cynicism, Curzon's pomposity and Milner's failure to avoid the 'sea-change that overtakes practically everybody who enters the demoralization of Downing Street'[4] all contributed to the situation in which, while 'international Jews' held sway there, the Unionist party had 'ceased to be a fighting machine and ... degenerated into an agency for the multiplication of titled non-entities'.[5]

Maxse had had no faith in Asquith and his Coalition. He had little more in the ability of the Coalition to do the right thing except under urgent public pressure. He disliked both George Barnes and Smuts who were the only non-Conservative members of the War Cabinet. He opposed both the Coupon election and the proposal to amalgamate the Coalition Liberal and Conservative parties in 1920. At the 1918 election he supported Croft's National party against the Conservative 'Big Six' who, under Lloyd George's 'tame lieutenant Mr Law',[1] would permit the establishment of a Lloyd George dictatorship in which prominence would be given to the 'defeatist financiers, international Jews and Labour Pacifists for whom Mr Lloyd George ha[d] always had a weakness'.[2] He represented the Coalition victory at that election as less a victory for Lloyd George than a reflection of the fact that neither Asquith, Runciman, McKenna nor Henderson – 'the catspaw of the Potsdam pacifists' – had any positive attractions to offer. In 1919 and 1920 he wanted the Liberal party reunited so that Conservatives could pull themselves together[3] and thought Lord Robert Cecil should become Labour or Liberal Prime Minister so as to ensure that he would never lead the Conservative party.[4] In 1919 he found an ally in the Duke of Northumberland.

In 1919 Alan, eighth Duke of Northumberland was thirty-nine. He had been brought up as a younger son and became heir to the dukedom after three of his brothers had died. He was in South Africa during the Boer War and in the Egyptian Army from 1907 to 1910. He served in the British Army from 1910 to 1912 and again, as an official eye-witness, during the War. On succeeding his father in 1918, he returned to Alnwick where he was a member of the county council, Lord Lieutenant and President of the Territorial Association. He had never been an M.P., but was involved in the movement for strengthening the national defences before 1914 and published a volume of essays on this subject in 1911. As an owner of mineral rights in coal,[5] he was called before the Sankey Commission where Smillie, Hodges, Tawney, Webb and Money gave him a hard run. He more than held his own and was led by the prominence he received into taking a political lead himself.[6] He took part in a wide range of meetings from 1919 onwards, was prominent in the management of the *Morning Post* Fund and was closely associated with a group of vigilant M.P.s and peers which included Carson, Sydenham, George Balfour, Foxcroft and Sir Charles Yate.[1] His merits as a political leader were not, perhaps, great. By Lloyd George and the Labour Left, he was treated as a mascot, or figure of fun. He became President of the Conservative party's National Union in 1923. In 1924 he bought the *Morning Post*.

Croft, Maxse and Northumberland were leaders of a fragmented movement of opinion whose objectives were similar. The rhetoric of the Northumberland movement was the most lurid. Others might not have said, as Northumberland did,[2] that 'the defeat of direct action represented the failure of one move ... of a great game played by the enemies of this country [in] Moscow ... India ... Egypt ... America ... [and] Ireland [which] in this country ... [is] called Nationalisation'. All would have agreed that their target was the 'sinister forces' which were 'at work for the destruction of the British Empire' and the 'subversive movements which now confront us ... [in] our great industries ... [in] Ireland ... [in] India and [in] Egypt'.[3]

The message was that the movement of subversion in the trades unions, India, Ireland and Egypt were not isolated occurrences but a concerted threat to the British Empire, to law and order and to civilisation itself. This 'International Conspiracy' was the work of 'Russian and Jewish Adventurers whose purpose [was] the abolition of all law, order, morality and religion throughout the world'.[4] De Valera was a Spanish Jew: the Irish 'terror [was] all very like Russia [and] a Red army in Ireland could set up a Soviet and proceed to loot in the best Russo-Jewish style'.[5] This meant that 'the Terror must be broken at any cost' and any attempt to 'settle with murderers'[6] prevented by destroying the belief about the impracticability of suppressing Sinn Fein which was 'sedulously fostered by those who [did] not want to suppress it'.[7] It meant rejecting the Montagu/Chelmsford reforms in India, expelling the two Jews – Montagu and Reading – who were responsible for the Coalition's Indian policy and strengthening the Indian Army as a defence against Communism. It meant withdrawal from Palestine and Mesopotamia where 'Churchill [was] building up [an expensive] new Empire ... under the mandate of that illusory body, the League of Nations'.[8] In Egypt it meant firm paternalism and no more nonsense from Milner who ought to have known better than to 'lend his name to a policy of scuttle'.[1] In Kenya it meant rejecting the idea that 'any British government would give ... the Indian population ... equal franchise with the white man'.[2]

In Europe it meant vigilance against the 'International Jew' who wanted Bolshevism to survive in Russia so as to prevent Russia holding Germany in check. It meant remembering that 'Germany ... – the "spiritual home" of the "International Jew" – ... was the one great Continental power that ha[d] escaped the devastation of war'.[3] It meant a serious effort to get German Reparations which 'the whole bureaucracy was mobilized to obstruct'.[4] It meant realising that Keynes was 'more Wilsonian than Wilson' and 'more German than the Germans'[5] and that 'Treasury officials' were 'hand in glove with the International Jew' who wanted Germany let off lightly 'lest the "money market" be disturbed'.[6] It meant seeing that 'in any war against England, narrow-minded Germans can ... rely on broad-minded Britons to see ... that Germany escapes the legitimate penalties of defeat and is afforded another opportunity of renewing her strength until she is ready to resume the Frightful Adventure'.[7] It meant learning the lesson of the war – 'that the British are a ... great people with a genius ... for war', that 'not for the first time we were taken completely unawares' in 1914 and that 'Responsible Statesmen' had a duty to ensure that 'no such catastrophe could recur'.[8]

At home the movement stood for loyalty to the throne and religion and a diffusion of Carson's honesty, integrity and frankness in dealing with 'the People'. It attacked the high level of domestic taxation made necessary by the war and attributed the refusal to make Germany pay to the desire felt by 'influences around Lloyd George' to tax the British capitalist out of existence.[9] It opposed 'nationalization as defined by the Labour party' for being 'indistinguishable from Communism, Socialism and Bolshevism'.[10] It called for a strong line with the Miners' Federation and the Triple Alliance as 'threads in the web of conspiracy worked from Berlin and Moscow'[11] and insisted that the Labour party was run by Lansbury, Williams and 'other extremists' in order to 'bring British Labour under the control of the Red International', not by 'such comparatively moderate men as Clynes, Thomas and ... Mr Facing-Both-Ways ... Henderson [who] must be either fools or cowards or knaves' and deserved none of the deference accorded them by the Coalition leaders.[1] It pointed the contradictions between what it took to be the objects of trades union members – better pay and conditions – and the political objectives of some of the leaders. It pointed to a contradiction between the Fabian desire for nationalisation as a way of subjecting employers and workmen to bureaucratic control and nationalisation as a cause to be used to effect a political revolution.

The movement was more interested in the 'Protocols' of the Elders of Zion, first published in English in 1920, than in any Protocols connected with the League of Nations which was 'not a whit more Christian than the balance of power'.[2] It had prejudices against Balliol where 'words meant more than deeds', against 'the young lions of the Round Table', against Lee of Fareham's gift of Chequers to the nation because it would cushion Prime Ministers from the effect of taxation and against the appointment to a college history lectureship at Balliol of Namier, a 'clever Zionist Jew ... who had been employed in the War Office during the war', because it was 'exactly' the sort of thing 'the Protocols' predicted.[3] It spoke well of Sir Basil Thomson, director of the Special Branch at Scotland Yard, for his part in checking subversion in industry, Horne until he left the Ministry of Labour, Edward Wood (despite his belief in the League of Nations), Viscount Grey (in relation to Germany), Baldwin, Selborne, Havelock Wilson, and Admiral Sir Reginald Hall, M.P. for the Walton division of Liverpool who, as Director of Naval Intelligence, was 'one of the real "winners of the war"'.[4] Apart from Carson, its idols were Foch, Haig, Beatty, Clemenceau, Lord Roberts and William Hughes, the Australian Labour Prime Minister whom Lloyd George 'froze out' of the Peace Conference 'because' being 'neither a Cosmopolitan nor a Cobdenite' and unimpressed by the League of Nations,[5] his 'views on reparations were unpalatable to the International influences which held the upper hand in Paris'.[6] For Lloyd George and the Coalition condemnation was complete. Lloyd George was 'the Welsh Walpole' and friend of MacDonald who would peddle any opinion and give in to any Labour leader if that would help him stay in power. The Coalition consisted of 'gibbering Mandarins'[7] who had allowed him to negotiate with Bolsheviks, damage the Entente, throw

Egypt to the wolves and keep an open mind about nationalisation. It would make no difference whether Lloyd George or Law was Coalition leader so long as there was the same evasion, equivocation and ignorance of the facts of life which had marred British government for nearly twenty years.

This platform arraigned the politicians who had ruled England since 1906. It was an indictment of the ruling régime – 'The Bourbons of British public life'[1] – by those who had been excluded from it. In this sense it was radical, with the verbal recklessness and ruthless analysis characteristic of movements whose object is to change the climate of opinion. Like the Labour party, the Die Hards were a party of propaganda, claiming a knowledge of the people's wishes denied to 'Mandarin' politicians who had ignored warnings about Britain's defences before 1914 and made democracy consist in 'concealing the truth from the people in the interests of the politicians'.[2] It attacked corruption, whether in the form revealed by the Marconi scandal or in the form taken by the sale of Honours. It attacked conspiracy – not only the International Jewish conspiracy, but also the conspiracy of deceitful silence which prevented Mandarins appealing to the people's 'better natures'.[3] The people's 'better nature' wanted national solidarity and patriotic endeavour of the sort Carson had given Ulster. It wished to have no part in the 'wave of mad Communism – the work of Jew Bolsheviks ... [in which] there [was] not even any pretence now of safeguarding the interests of the working man' and which, if operating in England, would stamp out trades unionism, mock religion, deny liberty, produce 'rule by terror'[4] and create a system in which 'no constituencies [have] to be consulted, no public opinion [has] to be considered and all hostile assemblies [can be] dissolved'.[5] All these feelings were amalgamated in dislike of the League of Nations

the partisans [of which] ... embraced ... all the Mandarins who ridiculed Lord Roberts and applauded Lord Haldane ... all the Whigs who ... declined to take the only steps that could have prevented the war, all the Potsdam party who worked for the betrayal of France in 1914, the Defeatists who sought to lose the war, the Pacifists who continued to bleat for peace when there could be no peace; all the enemies of our friends and friends of our enemies who mean ... to still further whittle away the miserable Peace Treaty – ... [in fact] every man and woman who habitually goes wrong on every great issue.[6]

Lansbury and the *Daily Herald*, Smillie, Hodges and the Miners' Federation were recurrent bogies, but there was no hostility to the working classes which, it was claimed, could certainly be detached from the adventurers by whom they were being corrupted. There was a persistent belief that they would follow if their rightful rulers would speak out instead of running away whenever a Labour leader raised his voice. Lloyd George was blamed for failing to speak out. When he did so he was blamed still more for dishonestly pretending that the working classes were riddled with Bolshevism in order to pose as the first line of resistance to it. The Die Hards saw that unemployment was the 'constant dread of the working man' but they understood its long-term significance as little as the Labour leaders themselves. They blamed it on the 'hotheads of Labour' – that is to say, on Smillie's action as Miners' leader in increasing the price of coal and his refusal to understand that Prosperity depended on Production.[1] In February 1921 Maxse thought the worst might possibly be over.[2]

To Labour's claims to be a governing party, the attitude was best expressed by Northumberland in reviewing Thomas's book *When Labour Rules* in 1920. This volume, described by Northumberland as 'really a religious work' because of its concern with the 'regeneration of mankind', was, he claimed,

the best proof that Labour has no programme at all. The real situation [he went on] is as follows. A considerable number of the Trades Unions have become ... peculiarly corrupt organizations, the result being that organized Labour is placed under the control of demagogues with very little real ability, knowledge or character. These men, by violent speeches, by holding out hopes of social regeneration and redistribution of wealth, get themselves elected to Parliament where they use the Trade Union organization as a political weapon for gaining their own ends. Finding all their ideas unworkable in practice, and having sometimes sufficient honesty not to carry out a policy they know to be disastrous, but not sufficient to admit that they have been deceived, they adopt a middle-course to which the natural vanity of mankind leads them. They persuade themselves that the revolution they have spent their lives in preaching can be brought about by constitutional means and that their dreams can be easily accomplished once they are returned to power. This nominal adherence to constitutional means eases their consciences but does not prevent them toeing the line when the Extremists call the tune. Their would-be moderation gains them the support of the sentimental section of British public opinion and, above all, of those purblind persons who argue that it is unwise to offend leaders who exercise so much influence with Labour. These persons do not perceive that the one hope of salvation is to tell the British working man the truth, to break through this system of mental, moral and physical tyranny of which these leaders are the outcome, to destroy the gigantic imposture through which they hold power and to let a little light filter through to the masses of Labour.[1]

What, then, the movement believed was that the British Legion was better than the TUC, that Haig was a more democratic figure than Smillie and that the working classes, once faced with the truth, were hard-minded and xenophobic enough to respond to these qualities in their rulers. It demanded an end to the 'soft atmosphere of Westminster and Whitehall'[2] and an effort to ensure that the ruling classes gave positive leadership to destroy the subversive growths and alternative authorities embodied in the Scottish, Welsh, Boer and Jewish leaders of the antinomian, pacifist and Liberal movements which threatened England in the future.

Neither Maxse, Northumberland nor Croft mattered much in his own right. They made little impact on the policy thinking of Conservative ministers. Nevertheless, their world-picture reflected important aspects of Die Hard thinking. Their views, expressed at public meetings, in letters to newspapers and in the editorial and contribution columns of the *National Review*, the *Morning Post* and *The Spectator*, were given corporate expressions at dinners and luncheons attended by substantial numbers of politicians. In 1920 and 1921, Carson, Londonderry, Linlithgow, Northumberland, Sumner, Sydenham, Banbury, Foxcroft, Rupert Gwynne, Esmond Harmsworth, Joynson-Hicks, McNeill, Sprot, Finlay, Yate, Denbigh, Ebury, Rees, Sanders, Jellett, Marriott, Terrell, Hall and George Balfour lent their presence at public functions. In the course of 1922 Gretton organised a party in the House of Commons.

Like Croft, Gretton was a brewer – the Chairman of Bass, Ratcliffe and Gretton. Like Banbury, he had railway interests and strong objections to Sir Eric Geddes's bill to amalgamate the railway companies. He seems to have been alienated from the Coalition in the first place by its anxiety to appease the Temperance movement. He criticised the airing given to fusion with the Lloyd George Liberals in February 1920.[3] He renounced the Conservative

Whip in July 1921 when Lloyd George began negotiating with de Valera. At this time he was fifty-four. He had been an M.P. since 1895 but had never held office. He was a Protectionist before the war and was known as a 'man of moderate views' after it.[1] He did not belong to Croft's party, though he sat next to Croft in the House of Commons. He seems neither to have appeared on Northumberland's platforms nor to have used the rhetoric of Northumberland's movement. From time to time he was taken up by Rothermere. He bored the Duke of Devonshire by his persistence.[2] Wolmer found the atmosphere he created 'impossible' and wanted at one point to put Londonderry or Lord Hugh Cecil in his place.[3]

Before the beginning of 1922 Die Hard action in parliament was sporadic. It depended more on individual members than on a unified exertion of energy. Croft made the Honours system one of the centres of his attack. Banbury was chairman of the Select Committee on Estimates. Gretton took Ireland. McNeil gained a reputation as a Jew-baiter.[4] Carson proposed a motion in the Dyer debate in which Joynson-Hicks acted as a teller. Joynson-Hicks made a reputation over Dyer: he became the man who knew more about Indian Army officers' grievances than the Government of India knew itself.[5] The movement's most remarkable success was the creation of the Dyer Fund which collected over £15,000 from small subscriptions in the first three weeks of its existence.[6] The *Morning Post* carried its views into many Conservative homes. From January 1922 until compelled to amalgamate with Salisbury's movement in the House of Lords in July, Gretton managed a House of Commons 'party' of about fifty. This included Croft and Cooper, the Bottomley M.P.s after Bottomley's conviction, Field-Marshal Sir Henry Wilson during his short period as an M.P., most of the M.P.s associated with Northumberland, one regular Irish Unionist – Sir James Craig's elder brother, Charles – and a sprinkling of the 1918 intake among Conservative M.P.s including Oman, Boyd-Carpenter, Hall and Viscount Curzon, the last three of whom had supported the Lloyd George Centre-party idea in 1919.

Finally, among Salisbury's allies in the Conservative party, there was a body of what may most suitably be called higher-thinking Conservatives. By this is meant neither the Association of Independent Unionist Peers nor the whole body of landowners in the House of Commons many of whom supported the Coalition almost to the end, but an articulate and in some cases intellectual group with connections of friendship, relationship and sympathy with all three Cecils. These were not reactionaries in the Gretton/Northumberland sense, but highly educated professional politicians, not all of them landed, who adopted a Disraelian rôle, attached special importance to the avoidance of class conflict and had a particular desire to be in touch with whatever 'progress' could safely be embraced. Birkenhead and Lloyd George also claimed to be concerned for 'progress' but they found Birkenhead's championing of capitalism as objectionable as Lloyd George's system of peerage by payment. Not all were as quick as Salisbury to abandon the Coalition. They were critical of it and disliked its moral tone. But they had no doubt that it would be difficult to remove, and even more difficult to replace: they saw no point in putting themselves out in order to do so.[1] Halifax in retirement[2] mentions Guinness, Hills, Ormsby-Gore, Winterton, Lane-Fox, Hoare, Wolmer and himself as young M.P.s who worked together in 1919/20.[3]

Some of these had been Hughligans: some had belonged to a previous incarnation of Young England which Bledisloe[4] and Christopher Turnor had run before the war when Hills, Lloyd, Sykes, Scott, Hoare, Griffith-Boscawen, Barlow, Astor, Guinness, Ormsby-Gore and Lord Henry Bentinck had used Housing, Education, Public Health and Agriculture to show that Conservatives had a deep interest in working-class welfare.

Of this group Sykes died in 1919. Turnor joined the National Democratic Party and worked with Mansbridge and Tawney on education after the war.[5] From 1918 Lloyd was Governor of Bombay. Griffith-Boscawen became a junior minister in 1916, Astor in 1918, Barlow in 1920, Wood in 1921 and Scott in 1922. Hills was a member of the Committee on Reconstruction. Bledisloe, after a brief period as a junior minister in 1917, emerged from the war an emotional admirer of Lloyd George, developed the deepest distrust of Birkenhead for his open assault on the Labour party in 1920 and actually appeared on the same platform as Lansbury at a meeting of the Vacant Land Cultivation Society.[6] In 1923 he detached himself from Baldwin's government, in which he did not hold office.[1] In early 1924 he nearly joined the Labour party when his policy for Agriculture included redistribution of all estates bigger than 6,000 acres, occupying ownership everywhere and extensive State supervision of cultivation.

Bledisloe's emotional incontinence marked him out but he was not untypical in his pressing sense of class duty. There was an articulated dislike of the unthinking rich. There was great anxiety to consider the class structure in terms of religious duty and a revulsion from Birkenhead's justification in terms of self-interest. There was an instinctive desire to seek out not the radical nation but the Christian one and, through an Anglicanism of modesty and moderation, to provide a national solidarity which Radicalism claimed to provide through shock and conflict. Above all there was a belief that positive action on the part of the right-minded rich would produce a fellow-feeling among right-feeling men everywhere.

Of these politicians the most effective was Edward Wood. In 1920 Wood was thirty-nine. He was a grandson of Gladstone's Halifax and son of the leading High Church layman in the Church of England. He was a Fellow of All Souls: while at Oxford he wrote a life of Keble. As M.P. for Ripon from 1910, he was neither a Free Trader nor a Tariff Reformer but shared a common desire to prove that Conservatives cared about the working classes.[2] He was a vigorous opponent of Welsh Church Disestablishment. During the war he fought in France and Flanders, was a prominent advocate of Conscription and served for a time under Sir Auckland Geddes in the Ministry of National Service. In 1918 he was a strong supporter of stiff treatment for the Germans. As intellectual, landowner and Social Whig, Wood combined opinions which appealed to Die Hards and Cecilians alike: in 1918/19 he and his father were admirers of Lloyd George.[3] His work *The Great Opportunity*, written with George Lloyd in 1918, elaborated the idea that 'religion taught that "Lazarus [was] lying at the gate" ' and that 'the simple affections of daily life ... the responsibility of service ... and the spirit of generous nationalism' demanded a perpetuation of the 'singleness of purpose' which in war united a divided society where before the war 'the holders of wealth and property ... had been tempted to grow careless of the duties inseparable from ownership and ... the less fortunate of their fellow-citizens had turned ... to the easy belief that their own progress could be effected at the expense of other sections of the community'.[1]

Wood, Hartington and his father, the Duke of Devonshire, were Whig by tradition, but their thought-world was self-consciously Disraelian in its dismissal of the Liberal capitalist as a dangerous reactionary and its not always unstated belief in a natural harmony between the gentry or aristocracy on the one hand and the working classes on the other. It would be truer, however, to say they disliked capitalists than that they disliked capitalism. In 1921 Hartington thought the reaction against Lloyd George was 'positively aristocratic'.[2] Nearly all were Anglican. Some were extremely devout. Hills and Wood had Milner's blessing. Devonshire had been a junior minister from 1900 and remained in office when his father resigned in 1903. He was Governor-General of Canada from 1916 to 1922 but refused to take office in the Coalition on returning. On Northcliffe's death he tried to buy *The Times*. From 1920 until 1922 exclusion from office gave Guinness, Hills, Ormsby-Gore, Lane Fox and Hoare free scope to deploy criticism which might not have been deployed if they had had it.

Salisbury's significance lay in the fact that he was not only respected by Gretton, Northumberland, Ampthill, Croft, Cooper, Joynson-Hicks and the lunatic fringe but was in close touch with Selborne, Midleton, Wolmer, Lord Hugh Cecil, Lord Robert Cecil, Steel-Maitland, Hoare, Ormsby-Gore, Hartington, Devonshire, Wood and other Conservatives or Young Englanders who had joined or in principle supported the Coalition. He was in fact a common broker, less liberal than Lord Robert Cecil, less clerical than Lord Hugh Cecil, less militant than the Die Hards but able to imply – what no one supposed he could provide himself – the need for leadership to preside over these and all other elements of established respectability in presenting a modest, humane, decent, uncorrupt, patriotic *Conservative* face to the people. For the fall of the Coalition and the events which followed it, these facts were of great consequence.

V

THE LIBERAL COLLAPSE

'We are asked to believe that there are abstract principles of Liberalism from which the programme of Labour is not essentially different. We reply that there are concrete examples of Liberalism which are so like examples of Reaction, Toryism, Protection and Imperialism that no difference between them is discernible to the naked eye.'

    Daily Herald, leading article, January 27 1920

'Your husband ... is in the singular position that there is not a human being in the country who would be perturbed or annoyed – I had almost said even jealous – if the reins of power were put into his hands. There has never been anything in our history like the unanimity of estimation in which he is held.'

    Strachey to Pamela, Viscountess Grey of Falloden, October 24 1922, Strachey MSS

The crisis Salisbury sensed did not arise from the existence of the Labour party alone. The Labour party had been in existence for twenty years. The Gladstone/MacDonald alliance of 1903 had given Conservatives the chance to smear the Liberal party by association but it had not always seemed necessary to prepare for major resistance. The Labour party was more successful now than it had ever been before, but even that by itself would not have stimulated the alarm which Salisbury felt. Salisbury was alarmed not just because the Labour party was advancing but because none of the forces which ought to have resisted it were organised to do so. The Conservative party was not organised because it had sold itself to Lloyd George. The Liberal party was not organised because Asquith and Lloyd George had destroyed it.

When Lloyd George became Prime Minister in 1916, the only evidence of a Liberal split was the existence of two Liberal Whips and the refusal of some of Asquith's ministers to accept offers from Lloyd George.[1] If Asquith had taken office in 1917, what division there was would have been healed. When Lloyd George arranged to fight an election on a coalition basis at the height of his popularity at the end of 1918, Asquith failed to stop him.[2]

In dividing the Liberal party in order to fight the election in alliance with the Conservatives, Lloyd George's Liberal supporters made some concessions of principle. They accepted House of Lords reform, limited Anti-Dumping legislation, assistance to key industries, a modest measure of Imperial Preference and temporary continuation of governmental support for Empire development within the scope of the Paris Resolutions provided the main normal economic principle was Free Trade on which, since it 'was a matter of no importance practically in the reconstruction period ... one had', Lloyd George thought, 'to make some concessions to one's Conservative allies'. In return for a Prime Minister who 'belonged to us' and whom the Conservatives needed, they expected Conservative acquiescence in a 'very advanced social programme, Housing, Land ... Transportation and so forth' and a liberal range of policies for India and Ireland even if, and perhaps in the hope that, this would lead 'to the discarding of a certain element of the Conservative party'. Some items, like the nationalisation of Railways, the coercion of Ulster and a Capital Levy were excluded from consideration. Others were embodied in the election address issued by the parties to the Coalition. Many depended on verbal assurances from Lloyd George and his ability or willingness, which Fisher doubted, to press Conservative ministers to accept them. On Ireland Lloyd George's programme was ' "Home Rule" excluding the six counties', not Home Rule for the whole of Ireland. But about this, as about other commitments he claimed to have received from the Conservative leaders, some Coalition Liberals had reservations. Fisher thought of resigning. Others would probably have done so if the overwhelming nature of Lloyd George's reputation and the prospect of continued power had not held them back. Montagu's contemporary account is cynical and suspicious: he reflects the suspicions of others. They may not have anticipated Lloyd George's attacks on the Asquitheans and the divisive distribution of coupons. They did not think they were destroying the Liberal party. It is still the case that, so far as policy was concerned, they made their decisions with their eyes open.[1]

The Coalition Liberals did well at the election of 1918. Three Asquithean victories over Conservative candidates at by-elections in early 1919 increased their importance.[2] In the twelve months which followed the end of the war, they were conscious of atmospheric defects in the Conservative part of the Coalition, but none showed any desire to leave, apart from Fisher who was short of money and Seely who joined the opposition Liberals on resigning his under-secretaryship at the Air Board over Air Force reorganisation.[1] There were policy differences over Russia and the treatment given to Germany in the Peace Treaties.[2] Over the taxation of Land Values pre-war differences were revived.[3] Montagu began his running-battle against Lloyd George's Greek policy.[4] Some Coalition Liberals had as much difficulty as lesser Conservatives in approaching Lloyd George. Mond felt he should have been in the Cabinet when it reverted to its pre-war size.[5] Criticism from Conservative back-benchers gave little pleasure. Asquithean accusations that Liberalism was being betrayed gave even less.[6] But it was not until the first Labour successes at the by-elections of late 1919 that general doubts began. For the Coalition Liberals, more than for everyone else, the Spen Valley by-election raised fundamental questions.

The Liberal/Conservative Coalition had been formed in 1915 and reformed in 1916 for the purpose of conducting the war. There was no union of principle to last beyond the defeat of the Central Powers in 1918. In 1918 Coalition Liberalism was less a principle than a result of the accidental fact that personal conflict between Asquith and Lloyd George made co-operation between the two Liberal groups impossible.

The emergence of a Coalition Liberal doctrine, therefore, followed the creation of the party: it did not precede it. In office the Coalition Liberals supported the Indian Cotton Duties, the Plural Voting provisions of the Representation of the People Bill, the conscription of Ireland and (the more extreme only) legislation against Conscientious Objectors. They wanted vigorous prosecution of the war: they were opposed to a negotiated peace settlement. When coupons were distributed in 1918, these considerations were generally decisive.[7] As a basis for post-war policy, however, they were nebulous. In 1918 Coalition Liberals consisted less of politicians who held distinctive opinions about the future than of the supporters of Lloyd George. In the new situation created by the Labour party's advance in 1919, there were no reasons of policy to account for the support given by some Liberals to Lloyd George, or for the opposition of others.

By 1920 many of Lloyd George's first batch of ministerial

dependents had disappeared. Rhondda had died. Devonport was chairman of the Port of London Authority. Sir Albert Stanley had been dismissed. Cawley, Lever, Winfrey and Compton-Rickett had left. Shortt, MacPherson, Addison, Macnamara, Churchill, Fisher, Montagu and Guest were the Coalition Liberals who mattered: Sutherland and Mond very much wanted to matter. Churchill and Guest – both ex-Conservative Free Traders – had something in common with the Conservative leaders, though many of them were not pleased to be reminded. But this was not true of the others, even when there was agreement about policy. In mind and manner Asquith, Grey and Crewe were much more like the Conservative leaders than Shortt, Mond, Addison, Montagu or Macnamara.

At the 1918 election, the Coalition Liberals thought Coalition tolerable because it contained a Labour element.[1] The Labour withdrawals in 1919 and 1920 and the Spen Valley by-election greatly contracted their political base and forced them to discover a raison d'être for themselves. They did not discover it very quickly. Some did not discover it at all. Apart from Churchill, those who did so concluded in much the same way as Lord Robert Cecil that, in the incipient polarisation between a working-class party and a party of resistance, their business was to ensure that the party of resistance should be decent, accommodating, enlightened, advanced and progressive – and, above all, not reactionary.

When Birkenhead and Lloyd George proposed a Conservative/Liberal amalgamation in February 1920, there were two distinct views among Coalition Liberals. Churchill, Guest, Addison and Macnamara were in favour and had support from the New Members' Coalition group which had been formed with Guest's approval[2] in 1919 in order to advance the formation of a Centre party. Many of its leading members were Unionists, including some who became Die Hards in the years that followed.[3] It had close contact with the National Democratic Party and a management committee on which Liberals and Conservatives were represented equally. Though a number of Lloyd George Liberals supported it, including Churchill who addressed it in July, the majority of Liberal ministers and M.P.s had no wish to be swallowed by the Conservative party. They knew that, by the side of the Conservative party, their own hardly existed. Its electoral organisation was negligible: The Wrekin, Paisley and Spen Valley had been major defeats. In the condition of illiberal hostility already shown by some Conservative M.P.s, they expected amalgamation to remove all chance of preserving a Liberal identity.

Preservation of Liberal 'identity' meant keeping open the possibility of reuniting the Liberal party at some convenient moment in the future by emphasising such issues as Proportional Representation, extension of Women's Suffrage, Home Rule for Wales and Scotland and a continuing sympathy for working-class claims which not all Conservatives were expected to support.[1] It meant also a form of 'progress and enlightenment' which centred on the League of Nations, a reasonable Reparations policy and the admission of Germany to the League of Nations in order to keep her out of Bolshevik hands. Though they were supporters of the Coalition and had no wish to demolish it, the Coalition Liberals were not sure that it would last and had no wish to close their options before they needed to. The by-election had provided no encouragement for themselves but they revealed patches of reviving Liberalism which might well spread if the Coalition's unpopularity increased. This possibility was in the minds of many Liberal back-benchers in both Liberal parties in 1920. It continued to be there in some strength throughout 1921 and continued to have a major impact on their thinking.

The decision about amalgamation was taken not, as seems to have been intended,[2] by Lloyd George himself, but by two meetings – one of ministers and one of Coalition Liberal M.P.s. At the meeting of ministers in the third week of March[3] 1920 Lloyd George found his audience reluctant. When he addressed the party meeting a couple of days later, he talked not about amalgamation but about closer co-operation.[4] In April Munro and Churchill were snubbed while attending a meeting of the Scottish Liberal Federation.[5] Other Coalition Liberals were given a similar cold shouldering and virtually excommunicated by the Asquithean Conference at Leamington in May.[6] In late March Asquith and Lloyd George made speeches which put reunion out of the question.[7] Between March and May the Liberal split deepened.[8] It was only then that Lloyd George began half-heartedly to construct a Coalition-Liberal organisation of his own.[9] After a Conservative defeat by an Asquithean Liberal at Louth in June, he raised reunion with Coalition Liberals for the last time. Finding no response, he dropped it definitively.[1]

For the Asquithean Liberals the damage suffered by Lloyd George in 1919 and 1920 was the sweetest music that could be heard. It promised the possibility of recapturing some part of the Liberal vote he had stolen in 1918. It provided the opportunity to repay him for the humiliations to which they had been subjected and the personal set-backs his success had been responsible for. Resentments accumulated in some cases for six or seven years and in all cases since the election of 1918 seemed about to be met.

In 1920 'Asquithean Liberal' did not mean the ministers who had left office with Asquith in 1916. These never acted as a body. Montagu had joined Lloyd George. Haldane had flirted both with Lloyd George and with Labour. McKenna had joined the Midland Bank and lost his seat in 1918: he was politically detached until he developed relations with Salisbury, Crewe and Strachey in 1921 for a Free Trade 'government of affairs' under his own or Derby's leadership to deal with the economic situation.[2] Grey had become chairman of the North Eastern Railway and for a short period Special Ambassador to the United States. In 1920 he intervened over Mesopotamia, made a declaration in favour of Dominion Home Rule for Ireland and offered to talk to Asquith whenever Asquith might want him to.[3] Otherwise he was living in retirement. He apparently thought Lloyd George the best man to deal with industrial crises and did not want to come to live in London.[4] Simon and Runciman had lost their seats at the 1918 election and had not found winnable ones since. Samuel had lost his and saw no hope of anything else so long as the Asquitheans stood for nothing in particular. He went as Special Commissioner to Belgium in 1919 and to Palestine as High Commissioner the following year.[5]

In the 1918 parliament the Asquitheans were few in numbers and pathetic in quality. Among prominent non-Coupon Liberals, only Maclean, F. D. Acland, George Lambert and Wedgwood Benn kept their seats. Lambert, however, was disliked for maintaining relations with the Lloyd George Liberals even after he had been denied the Coupon: he eventually became their parliamentary chairman. Wedgwood Benn declined to become a Whip. In 1920 the most active of the parliamentary Asquitheans was Sir Donald Maclean. Maclean had been an M.P. with one brief break since 1906. He had been a successful Deputy Speaker but had held no political office. He had been a persistent critic of the government's recruiting policies and left the impression of 'having Liberalism in his bones',[1] but he would have been of no consequence if he had not kept his seat in 1918 and persuaded the Asquithean party to preserve its identity at the moment of deepest gloom after the election. He seems in fact to have been a good leader – and better than Asquith when he returned to parliament in February 1920.[2]

In 1920 the Liberal party machine was managed by Maclean, Hudson, Gladstone, Howard and to some extent Pringle who was Maclean's assistant in the House of Commons after he lost his seat at the general election.[3] Howard had been Asquith's parliamentary private secretary when he was first Prime Minister: he was a junior minister and Whip until Asquith resigned in 1916. Hudson was in his early sixties. In his political youth he had helped to draft the Newcastle programme in 1891. He succeeded Schnadhorst as Secretary of the National Liberal Federation in 1893. During the war he worked with the Red Cross but returned to the Liberal party afterwards. He was an intimate of Northcliffe whose wife was close to him and became his wife when Northcliffe died in 1922. Gladstone was the great Gladstone's son. He had helped to fly the Hawarden kite in 1885 and arranged Lib/Lab cooperation as Chief Whip in 1903. His last period as a party manager had ended in 1905 when the Liberal party seemed indestructible. Until he went to South Africa as Governor-General in 1910, Gladstone was Home Secretary. From his return to England in 1914 he held no office until in 1920, at the age of sixty-four, he was persuaded by Maclean to take charge of the party finances. As a political party the Asquithean Liberals were run by these four in consultation with Asquith, Simon intermittently, Runciman from a distance, Crewe, Buckmaster and Cowdray – the head of Weetman, Pearson and one of the party's most generous patrons – who had been given his first experience of office by Lloyd George at the age of sixty-one in January 1917 only to resign in humiliating circumstances in November when Northcliffe publicly announced his refusal to accept Cowdray's office which Cowdray did not know was vacant.

For the Asquitheans the Coupon election of 1918 was a disaster. The by-elections of 1919 and 1920 were not exactly triumphs. At Rusholme in October, at Sutton (Plymouth) in November and at St Albans in December 1919, the Liberal candidate was third. Three seats were won – at Hull, West Leyton and Aberdeenshire – in early 1919 and one in June 1920 in a straight fight at Louth. Louth, however, had no significance since the Coalition candidate was Christopher Turnor who stood as a National Democratic Party candidate with a programme which combined 'Merrie England' paternalism and 'no promises' in an eccentric combination.[1] In February 1920 Paisley gave Asquith twice the vote the Asquithean received in 1918. Runciman and Holmes did well at Edinburgh by-elections in April, though neither was returned. Simon, though beaten by Labour at Spen Valley, had been adopted by a constituency association which supported a Coalition Liberal in 1918: he pushed the Coalition Liberal to the bottom of the poll. There were other minor achievements of this kind. No Asquithean seat was lost until Pringle lost Penistone in March 1921. At Dartford and South Norfolk, as well as at Spen Valley, Lloyd George Liberal M.P.s on death or retirement were replaced by Asquithean candidates. Macnamara was disowned by his Liberal association in Camberwell for speaking against Simon at Spen Valley. Churchill was disowned by the association in Dundee.[2] But all this amounted to very little in the shadow of the fact that the Asquithean Liberals had fewer than thirty seats in parliament to begin with.

The history of Asquithean Liberalism in the immediate post-war years provides an admirable illustration of the dictum that in politics some sorts of merit often go unrewarded. Of its intellectual and journalistic capability there can be no doubt. Most of the best journalism was Asquithean. So were many of the best economists. In Spender, Gardiner, Sharp, Layton, Muir, Cox, Withers, Hirst, to say nothing of Gooch and Gilbert Murray, Asquithean Liberalism had formidable intellectual assets. In Grey it had a formidable political reputation. In Cowdray it had one of the great entrepreneurs of the age. Nor can it be claimed that it was unadaptable. Asquith, it is true, ran in a pre-war mould but the journalism of the *Daily News* and the *Westminster Gazette* was as relevant to the real problems of the post-war world as anything offered by either of the other parties. The slow seepage in the standing of Asquithean Liberalism cannot be explained by asserting a simple correlation between its journalism and its failure.

This is not to say that the Asquithean Liberals did not try, merely that they did not succeed with the opportunities they were offered. They saw in the success of the Anti-Waste campaign both a threat and an opportunity[1]: they adopted some of its policies. Once Disestablishment was accepted, Welsh Church re-endowment was attacked.[2] Coercion in Ireland provided an opportunity to recall Liberals to Liberal principles: under guidance from Buckmaster, Simon and Simon's wife,[3] they tried to take it.[4] Irish atrocities and the 'policy of reprisals [were] the direct negation of Liberalism'[5] and made an Irish settlement urgent for Lloyd George: they did little to improve the credibility of the 'Liberal cause'. Asquith denied that 'there was any antithesis between Liberalism and Labour': he claimed to be 'a Labour member in quite as full and ... true sense as any man who, representing a great Trade Union ... comes to the House of Commons with a Labour mandate'.[6] Economy was a Gladstonian slogan which Asquitheans made a point of using.[7] Its revival was the work not of Asquith, but of Bottomley and Rothermere. The League of Nations became part of the Liberal platform after Lord Robert Cecil had invented it and put it to the test. In 1919/20 the Liberal party invented nothing except Irish atrocities. It waited until others had created, and then tried unsuccessfully to follow.

In other circumstances or in relation to another government, the Asquithean Liberals might have succeeded in becoming an effective grievance party. In relation to the Coalition of 1920/21 and its Labour opponents, they did not. The Liberal members of the Coalition were in charge of the spending ministries: there was no reason to expect a 'Liberal government' to be more 'economical' than they were. They attacked the Coalition Liberals for being instruments of a class government, but any credibility that might be given to Asquith's claim to be a Labour leader had already been given to Lloyd George. Asquith and Grey were the agents of the 'old diplomacy': Asquith was hardly credible as the agent of the new. Whatever dignity Grey kept after his fall in 1916, Asquith could not attract the moral authority Lloyd George had never been supposed to claim.

Nevertheless, in 1921 the Asquithean leaders thought they had a chance. Labour and Anti-Waste had both done at by-elections what the Asquitheans hoped to do themselves but Anti-Waste was a 'crude' freak[1] on which they expected to capitalise. The Labour leaders, with no chance of forming a competent government by themselves, needed Liberal leadership in order to be effective. In this respect the Asquitheans thought they had, in the names and traditions of historic Liberalism, an asset of the greatest power.

They were conscious, however, of three main difficulties – that Asquith was neither effective in the House of Commons nor attractive as a public reputation; that the Parliamentary Liberal Party, with few seats and hardly any members of proved ministerial capability, did not look like an 'alternative government', and that the Labour leaders 'though ready enough [themselves] were powerless' to damp down 'the rank and file feeling against the Liberal party [which] was stronger than against the Tory'. The Labour leaders they knew best – Henderson and Clynes – were willing to discuss co-operation in case the parliamentary system should require it at some point in the future. But they were afraid of their Left or did not want to blunt the Radical impulse of their followers, and would not agree to open co-operation now. They made it plain that they did not intend to treat the Liberals as the major party of opposition and would have to be persuaded by the ballot box if they were to support a Liberal government. In this situation Lord Robert Cecil's approaches in June 1921 were not made less attractive by his insistence that Asquith should be removed.

Asquith's victory at Paisley in 1920 had been a triumph but his conduct in parliament had not. Asquith at sixty-six was a dignified wreck. His wife was an embarrassment.[2] He drank too much, had lost touch with the movement of events and the spirit of the time, had too much contempt for all his rivals[3] and left the impression on unfriendly observers of being a 'somewhat querulous and very old, old man'[4] 'who [had] not budged an inch from his pre-war attitude'.[5] In his last political phase Asquith leaves an impression of one whom events had passed by – an intermittent operator unable to compete with Salisbury and his followers in conservative directions and incapable of the gestures needed to infuse into Liberalism the novelty needed for the new age which the war and the Labour party had brought. Asquith was still an attractive platform speaker. Doubts centred on his failure 'to make any figure in parliament' which may well have arisen from the fact that 'he ha[d] been so long accustomed to a cheering crowd behind him that he simply [could] not get on without it'.[1]

Doubts arose also from two analyses of the future rôle of the Asquithean Liberals in the party system. There was the view that an anti-Lloyd George Centre Coalition should be constructed with such Labour, Conservative and Coalition Liberal leaders as would feel free to join it. There was the view that the best hope of success lay in reunion with the Coalition Liberals, preferably without, but if necessary with, Lloyd George. Either course called Asquith's leadership in question. The first called it in question because nobody could see the point in constructing a broad-based movement against Lloyd George in order to restore an ageing Asquith to the centre of the scene. The second called it in question because it was far from clear that Lloyd George would serve under him.

Of these lines of action the second made no headway in 1920 and 1921. Though many back-benchers, most constituency Liberals and a number of Liberal ministers wanted reunion as an immediate priority for the future, it did not seem possible while Lloyd George Liberal ministers remained part of the Coalition. They showed no sign of leaving it so long as it was a going concern. The more strongly it was attacked, the more difficult they would find it to desert, but the more it was damaged, the stronger the Asquitheans expected to become. The Asquitheans expected only damage from association with Lloyd George.[2] The more critical their attitude to Lloyd George, the more confident they felt of attracting public support even if that meant detaching themselves still further from the Coalition Liberals they were attacking. In the moment of confidence after Paisley, Asquith rejected the kite flown by Lloyd George in favour of Liberal reunion within the Coalition framework: this attitude persisted.[3] In the course of 1920 the division was deepened deliberately. Lloyd George's repeal of the Land Taxes he had imposed in 1910[4] and the Safeguarding of Industries Bill in 1921 were treated as evidences of betrayal.[5] The withdrawal of Agricultural Subsidies was treated as a breach of faith. The government's Dyes Bill showed what a Coalition was capable of. In June 1921, when joint meetings of back-benchers from both groups revealed a striking desire for reunion even if Lloyd George was made leader, the Asquithean leaders made it clear that they were not interested.[1]

The discussions in mid-1921 between Lord Robert Cecil and the Asquithean leaders[2] started with a demand from Cecil for the construction of a new party to embrace Liberals and sympathetic Conservatives. The Liberal leaders convinced Cecil that the dismantling of the Liberal organisation would 'sacrifice a great tradition and organisation and put nothing effective in its place'.[3] Assuming that the Liberal party would remain intact, the question was how best to attract support from progressive Conservatives in the first place and from Labour leaders and voters thereafter.

Cecil wanted to revive Grey because Grey was the politician he admired most. Asquith wanted him in the sense that any support was welcome and made a point of establishing that Grey did not want to lead.[4] Cowdray wanted him as the person most likely to lead an anti-socialist Centre party on a Liberal basis. Although Asquith did not understand this, Maclean and Gladstone wanted him on the ground that Grey, or possibly McKenna, would be a more attractive leader than Asquith and a more positive 'antithesis of Lloyd George'; and was the Liberal most likely to make the country realise that there was an alternative government able to form a broad-based successor to the Coalition if that should ever become possible.[5]

At fifty-nine Grey attracted a very wide range of sympathetic support. He was a Whig, the grandson and heir of Sir George Grey. He had been elected to parliament in 1885, had been Foreign Under-Secretary in Gladstone's last government and was Foreign Secretary for the whole span of the Campbell-Bannerman and Asquith governments. He had been a willing co-operator in the construction of the Asquith/Law Coalition, but left office on the formation of the Lloyd George Coalition in 1916. In his youth he had had a reputation for the mildest form of Whig-style Radicalism. As a comparatively young Foreign Secretary he was one of the few members of the Liberal government who combined an appearance of political capability with a social eminence which had become rarer in the Liberal party as Whigs had left it. He was the model of a Liberal statesman, without radical or reactionary edges, but with an air of Olympian rectitude which his part in the intrigue against Campbell-Bannerman in 1905 and his responsibility for involving Britain in war had not removed.[1]

It is not certain how seriously Grey took the proposal that he should return to public life. His health was poor. In 1920/21 at times he could scarcely read. In early 1922 he nearly died. It was difficult for him to return at any level except a high one. It is far from certain that he was attracted by any except the highest.[2] Asquith was cautious. He took the initiative in talking to Grey[3] but almost certainly sensed a rival.[4] After his first talk with Asquith, Grey consulted Haldane.[5] At his first and second meetings with Cecil and the Liberal leaders, he agreed that the probable failure of negotiations in Ireland made co-operation desirable. Between the second meeting on July 19 and the third on August 10, it seemed likely that the Lloyd George/Valera negotiations would get properly under way. On August 10 Grey complained that his eyesight made it impossible to return to political life and that the opening of negotiations made it unnecessary: he probably meant that successful negotiations would make the Asquithean prospect less promising. Like Lord Robert Cecil he probably felt that an initiative of his own would be better than a response to a call from Asquith. He may also have been uncertain whether he wanted to return to active politics.[6] He pressed Asquith not to send him a public letter the Liberal leaders had already drafted but promised to make a statement of his own at Berwick in October.[7]

From August 1921 the revival of Grey was pursued with something resembling determination. At Berwick on October 10 Grey announced his return to public life. Cecil replied. Cowdray supplied Cecil with money. Cecil and Steel-Maitland primed the newspapers from one side, Maclean, Asquith and Runciman did so from the other. They did not all say the same thing. Asquith emphasised Grey's adhesion to his own leadership, Cecil the importance of Grey as a way of getting rid of Asquith. Maclean laid stress on the fact that nothing had been decided about the leadership in office. Gladstone tried to persuade Asquith that it should be settled in Grey's favour.[8] But the major claim was clear – that the Grey/Cecil/Asquith alliance would offer a non-socialist alternative for voters who did not like the Coalition and would facilitate a Liberal-Conservative/Lib-Lab government after an election, or earlier if the fall of the Coalition or its refusal to fall produced deep division in the Conservative party.

The prospect of a government of this sort before an election was never great. Grey or Clynes might have become Prime Minister if Lloyd George had resigned in November 1921 in protest against Ulster's refusal to concede. Cecil certainly, Grey possibly, anticipated this: it is possible that this is what brought Grey back to public life. But if Lloyd George had resigned rather than resume coercion of Sinn Fein, either Austen Chamberlain would have succeeded him or Law would have resumed the Conservative leadership. With the signature of the Irish Treaty in December 1921, these contigencies ceased even to be speculative possibilities.

From the Asquithean point of view the Irish Treaty was a set-back. It put an end to British 'atrocities', stopped the drain on Lloyd George's reputation as a Liberal statesman, sterilised Ireland as a major subject and brought unemployment, socialism and foreign policy to the centre of the scene.[1] On these subjects the Asquithean Liberals found it difficult to match their rhetoric to the needs of the situation. A conservative rhetoric was inappropriate since the Coalition leaders took up such options in that direction as Salisbury had left. The situation required the Asquitheans to be 'progressive': in the post-war situation it was obvious that Asquith and Grey were conservative by instinct and inclination. Asquith did his best to differentiate Liberal anti-socialism from the 'class cleavage' variety to which the Coalition was supposed to tend,[2] but neither he nor Grey understood the 'progress' of generations later than their own. They took up co-operation and profit-sharing as the Liberal remedy for class conflict and reiterated the Free Trade basis of commercial success. They attacked the Coalition's use of the Honours system and offered Grey's rectitude as a remedy. Buckmaster certainly, Asquith probably, was willing to propose a Capital Levy.[3] Asquith tried to bring Haldane to his side when the Coalition seemed likely to dissolve.[4] Gladstone tried to persuade Burns to stand as a Liberal in Hackney when Bottomley was jailed.[5] Both failed, as did Gladstone's attempts to turn Cecil into a Liberal.

At the beginning of 1922 Grey began to give his politics content.[6] At Edinburgh on January 27 he committed himself to Economy.

Rothermere then suggested an Asquithean/Die Hard/Anti-Waste government under Grey's leadership.[1] Grey did his best to understand the League of Nations: he did not convince those whose sympathies were instinctive.[2] Pacification of Europe and the re-establishment of Germany in the European polity were subjects to which progressive parties had to turn their minds. Asquith and Grey tried to find words for a policy which had this as its object. Grey, however, was an instinctive Francophil[3] with perhaps an eye on Die Hard and Rothermere's Francophilia. What came out was a demand – anathema to progressive opinion – for an Anglo-French alliance to keep the peace. The result was an explosion from Scott against Asquith, an explosion from Asquith against C. P. Scott and a breach between Asquith and the *Manchester Guardian* which Lloyd George did his best to widen.[4]

It is difficult to measure the impact of the Grey/Cecil/Asquith alliance on the course of events in 1922. Maclean, Crewe, Buckmaster and Gladstone were full of confidence. Co-operation with Salisbury,[5] conflict in the Coalition and the Conservative party, and the support they received from Rothermere, supplied justification. Grey they regarded as a major asset. They were sure they could 'come to terms with Labour', looked forward to a Lib/Lab majority after the election and considered the implications of a Labour government resting on Liberal support.[6] Of the Lloyd George Liberals they spoke with confident contempt; they 'had not carried a single measure which could not have been approved by moderate Conservatives' and had condoned 'every sort of folly and wickedness' on the way.[7] When Lloyd George seemed likely to leave the Coalition in March, Gladstone and Maclean made it clear that co-operation was impossible.[8]

Their expectations were not answered. Lord Islington at last joined them but that was the limit of their success.[9] There was no Liberal voting swing at by-elections. The Asquithean decision to stand down no doubt helped Labour to win Clayton and Camberwell North. It did not enable Alexander Walkden to win as Labour candidate at Wolverhampton West, which he had lost in 1918. One seat was gained – by Isaac Foot in Plymouth. The Coalition Liberal was almost defeated in a straight fight at Inverness. General Gough did well in a straight fight in a Conservative Coalition seat at Chertsey. At Cambridge, East Leicester and

East Nottingham, Asquithean candidates polled less than 30% of the vote and a considerably smaller proportion of the possible electorate. Their failure to support the Anti-Waste candidate in the City of London by-election in May cost them Rothermere's approval.

The Grey/Cecil/Asquith alliance indeed had no impact on the electorate. Its sole impact was in closing one avenue that might otherwise have been open to Lloyd George. If Lloyd George had left the Coalition over Ireland in 1921 or Russian recognition in 1922, he would have received a warm welcome from some Asquithean M.P.s and in many parts of the Liberal party. It is difficult to think that the mechanics of reunion would have defeated him for long. Since he did not resign, the question was not put to the test. But one reason why he stayed with the Coalition Conservatives right up to October 1922 was that he did not have the Liberal party in his pocket and was faced not just by Asquith but by the more formidable authority of Grey, whose revival had been invented by Lord Robert Cecil and whose main political purpose right into 1924, long after Cecil had ceased to think of joining the Liberal party, was to keep out Lloyd George.

Although Cecil did not join the Liberal party, he was an architect of Liberal disunity. What he would have done if the Coalition Conservatives had taken the Conservative party to an election on a Coalition ticket in November 1922, it is impossible to know. He would almost certainly have been allied with the Liberal party which Asquith, however, would as certainly have continued to lead.[1] Cecil might have taken Steel-Maitland, Mosley, perhaps Ormsby-Gore and a few others with him. How much more impressive that would have made the Asquitheans is a matter for debate. The election, when it was fought, was fought by a more or less united Conservative party which had gained whatever credit was available by removing Lloyd George from office. The Asquithean Liberals, instead of gaining the seventy or ninety seats they had expected, gained about thirty. How many they would have gained if the attempt to unseat Lloyd George had divided Salisbury and the Die Hards from the body of the Conservative party and if the Die Hards, the Liberals and Lord Robert Cecil had disputed with Clynes and Henderson the opposition to Lloyd George is an open question. Assuming that the Labour party lost something by the fall of the Coalition, the answer is probably: enough to have prevented the Coalition having an absolute majority at an election and to have made it doubtful whether a Lib/Lab government or a Conservative/Liberal Coalition would be formed afterwards.

VI

THE COALITION DILEMMA

'The Prime Minister ... has acted with perfect loyalty towards his Unionist allies. The agreement which he made with my predecessor before appealing to the country he has, since I was chosen leader of the party in the House of Commons, scrupulously observed. He has strengthened the Unionist element in his Cabinet, and in all the difficulties that we have faced, in all the dangers that we have encountered and overcome, never once has any question of principle separated him and his Liberal friends from my Unionist colleagues and myself.'

Austen Chamberlain, speech to Midland Conservative Club at Birmingham, October 13 1922, *Manchester Guardian*, October 14

'Lloyd George had never shown the smallest party bias ... we were at one in thinking that [his] character and habit of mind made him approach any new problem in a spirit of complete detachment from traditional principles and prejudices.'

Balfour recording a conversation with Law at Whittingehame (December 22), December 29 1922, Add. MSS 49693

'I do not like the idea of complete fusion if it can be avoided but I had come to think, as I think you had also, that it was really inevitable if the Coalition were to continue, but it always seems to me to be more important from Lloyd George's point of view than from ours.'

Law to Balfour, March 24 1920, Whittingehame MSS

From one point of view the history of the Lloyd George Coalition from 1919 until the end of 1922 is the history of serious, powerful and determined attempts at a high level of competence to resolve the major problems which the war had left and the Peace Treaties created. More than at any time before or since, the British government was the arbiter of Europe and Lloyd George in European terms was its head. The attempts to make economic sense of the punitive aspects of the Treaty of Versailles and to restore political stability and commercial markets in Central and Eastern Europe were essential to the politics of the civilised world. They were integral to the government of Great Britain and central to the being of every one of its inhabitants. The stabilisation of the German polity, the establishment of a permanent relationship between Germany and France and the restoration of exchange stability were problems with deep roots in Britain's interest as a

commercial more even than as a political power. At the highest level
of statesmanship, there is a history to be written.

In the world context these questions were of immense significance. In the British context their significance was very different.
In British politics they became detached from the world context
to which they belonged to become the battle-cries of conflicting
groups whose objects were to gain, or keep, political power more
even than to settle Europe's problems or improve Britain's place in it.

In this context it was a question not just of the preservation of
particular parties but of the implied threat to the social order.
Part of Lloyd George's attractiveness to Conservatives arose from
the fact that an ex-Radical was well placed to resist it. At the
1918 election national unity and the war spirit blunted its operation. The issues on which Lloyd George won his majority had
very little to do with the class struggle. In one sense they postponed, in another they were deliberately designed to by-pass,
these questions.

The second facet of the social question began to be prominent
during Lloyd George's conflicts with organised trades unionism
in 1919, 1920 and 1921. In part these conflicts were treated as
conventional industrial disputes in which, in theory, government
became involved as umpire rather than participant. In part they
were conducted in the shadow of the belief that there was a threat
to constitutional government which, dangerous in itself, could be
made to yield political dividends greater even than the danger.
Most important of all, the vigorous rhetorical resistance they
produced from Lloyd George, Birkenhead and Churchill gave the
Daily Herald the opportunity to claim that the interests of government were identical with the interests of capitalism, plutocracy,
'moneybags' or 'Big Business', all of which were as offensive to
some Conservatives as they were to Lansbury.

The third phase of the problem began with the arrival of the
Labour party as the leading party of opposition. It was from this
point that the fears held by the political representatives of the
established order about the future were transferred from industrial
subversion and the political potentialities of Direct Action to the
area of party politics in particular. Despite protestations of
innocence from the official Labour leadership, there was a chrono-
logical connection between Direct Action and the first serious

increases in the Labour vote and a distinct continuity in problem which impinged on the minds of the ruling, property-owning and managerial classes, as well as on the more complicated politicians who represented them. Within the framework of a desire to keep the working classes in their political and economic place, there were two views about the attitude to be shown towards them. On the one hand there was the view that the unions and the Labour party should not only be kept in check but should also be reminded, publicly and frequently, that this was what was happening. On the other hand there was a vein of feeling which started from the assumption that the best way to deal with the working-class political consciousness was to avoid affronting it. In both cases there was a desire to be loved by the people, a belief in the ruling classes as the embodiment of moral unity and an unwillingness to will a confrontation if it could be avoided. Throughout 1920, 1921 and 1922 the fears connected with these feelings were increased by the Coalition collapse at by-elections and by the damage done by the Labour advance to the prospects of both of the existing Liberal parties.

For the Liberal party the years 1919 to 1924 were crucial. Lloyd George's conduct in these years is overshadowed by the damage he suffered from the Labour earthquake and the uncertainty he felt about the opportunity which almost certainly existed beforehand to break out of the Coalition and construct a non-socialist Radical party of the Centre. Though not everyone understood this at the time, the chief effect of the Labour advance was to destroy Lloyd George's credibility as a Radical, to weaken the Coalition on which his authority depended and greatly to reduce his ability to compel Conservatives to swallow Radical policies. From this point of view the events of 1920, 1921 and 1922 were an almost continuous capitulation to the wishes of the Conservative party. Though he continuously revolved the possibility of leaving the Coalition on a progressive issue, he at no point did so: at each point at which he thought of doing so, one calculation or another prevented him. In October 1922, having rejected the chances he might have taken, he found himself expelled from office by the determination of the Conservative party's secondary leaders not to allow him to get away without paying the price he had put on Conservative support. The next three chapters will show him debating, hesitating and finally being driven from office without dignity in the attempt to find secure links to bind the Conservative leaders to him.

Once he had decided to go on with Coalition in 1918, Lloyd George's immediate problem was to persuade Conservative ministers to allow enough 'progress' to keep his Liberal followers happy. In 1919 this was not difficult. The Franchise and Education Acts had been an earnest. The election programme promised action about Agriculture, Allotments, India, Housing, Temperance and Education. The Government of India, Land Settlement, Land Acquisition, Housing, Transport, Industrial Courts, Forestry, Welsh Church, Rent Restriction and Electricity Supply Bills were thought to be achievements.[1] Lee and Griffith-Boscawen at the Board of Agriculture, Montagu and Sinha at the India Office, Fisher and Lewis at the Board of Education, Addison and Viscount Astor at the Ministry of Health supplied a range of 'progress' which went far to remove the fears felt by Lloyd George Liberals when they agreed to a Coalition election.[2] Ireland presented difficulties. Sinn Fein violence destroyed any political policy that might have been available. MacPherson, who was ill, was removed in April 1920 after destroying his Liberal credentials by fifteen months of repression. But so long as the high tide of 1918 persisted, Lloyd George exerted a mixture of energy, blackmail and charm to keep a balance between the wings of his government.

This situation could have continued indefinitely if the political scene had not been transformed. It was the Labour victories which produced strain and tension as back-bench and constituency Conservatives came to believe that the Coalition was no longer so impregnable that they need put up with policies they did not care for. It was the Labour advance which convinced Lloyd George that the only role he could play for the moment was as leader of a Birkenhead-style, anti-socialist, anti-Bolshevik defence of private enterprise against the nationalisation he had flirted with in 1918.[3]

In 1920 the central members of the Lloyd George régime were seven Conservative members of the Cabinet, Derby until he left the Paris Embassy in November, Talbot, the Conservative Chief Whip, F. E. Guest, the Coalition Liberal Chief Whip who managed Lloyd George's finances and Sir George Younger, the Scottish brewer-M.P. who was chairman of the Conservative party. Law, Balfour, Long, Birkenhead, Austen Chamberlain and Horne in that order constituted the party's leadership within the Coalition.

In 1919 the size of the Coalition majority and the brilliance of Lloyd George's reputation gave the Cabinet free scope for policy-making virtually without reference to the House of Commons or the Conservative party inside it. Some measures, including measures of importance, were given only the most cursory examination by the House of Commons. There was at this time something resembling a Cabinet dictatorship. Even in the Cabinet some measures – particularly Lee's Agricultural Bill – received minimal attention. The Conservative members of the Cabinet consented freely to the body of the Lee/Fisher/Addison/Montagu legislation[1] which then and later caused difficulty in the Conservative party. In the first eighteen months there was virtually no Conservative disaffection. Junior Conservative ministers were impressed by 'the glamour' of Lloyd George's 'extraordinary personality'.[2] They had no wish to upset the policy of resistance to the trades union assault. They were pleased to have found a Radical who, however devious in method, would take the lead in resisting violent threats to the established order. They supported, and approved, the programme of De-control, some of which occurred before there was Conservative agitation to demand it. There were difficulties: the decision to remove the compulsory powers proposed for the Electricity Commissioners after the House of Lords had objected was one example.[3] Steel-Maitland's resignation was another. But there was nothing which threatened the Coalition's existence.

This situation was radically altered by electoral defeats in the course of 1919. The first three, suffered in March and April by Coalition Conservatives at the hands of Asquithean Liberals, confirmed the impression that the Coalition Liberal support was crucial. Eight out of the next ten by-elections produced striking increases in the Labour vote, culminating in the Labour victory in the Coalition Liberal seat in Spen Valley in January 1920. To Salisbury and Joynson-Hicks, but at this time to them alone, this showed that the Conservative party must free itself from Lloyd George. To Birkenhead, Long and Law it became the occasion for an attempt to effect a permanent connection between the Conservative party, Lloyd George, Lloyd George's Liberal followers and any other Liberals who might be willing to be connected.

As F. E. Smith, Birkenhead had had a rapid rise in a depleted opposition before the war. He had been Attorney-General from December 1916 until the end of the war but was neither a major Conservative leader nor a close adviser of Lloyd George. Both before and after the 1918 election he nailed his colours to Lloyd George, affecting to be a 'Tory democrat', claiming that he would 'sacrifice everything to [Lloyd George's] support', and discerning in Salvidge and the Liverpool Workingmen's Conservative Association a nucleus of '30 Tory seats which [would] follow *you* anywhere'.[1] He was rewarded with the Lord Chancellorship in January 1919. For him more than for most Conservative ministers, the Spen Valley by-election was a threat.

His object in calling for a new party ten days later was to prop up Lloyd George in whom he had invested heavily, provide the 'invertebrate' Coalition with a new raison d'être and restore the credibility it had lost in the previous eighteen months. The new party was not in principle to be different from the two it would replace except that resistance to Socialism would be the centre of its platform. It would contain the same Conservative party as before and the same Lloyd George Liberals. It would contain as many Asquithean Liberals as appreciated the ineffectiveness of their own group standing by itself and would include such members of the Labour party and working-class voters as rejected Direct Action and recognised that Capital was Labour's ally. It was to be based on recognition that the pre-war party cries had ceased to be relevant, that the Labour party did not represent the whole of the working classes and that there was a fundamental division between everyone who wanted to preserve constitutional government and the menacing minority who wanted to replace it. The real political choice was to be presented as a choice between Lloyd George, Churchill and Birkenhead or perhaps Churchill and Birkenhead on the one hand [2] and Smillie on the other: a fusion of parties in a National, Constitutional or People's party would make it clear that this was so. In a series of articles for the *Weekly Dispatch* between January and March 1920, Birkenhead laid out the bases of such a party.[3]

In doing this Birkenhead reflected the wishes of Law, Long and

Balfour.[1] Austen Chamberlain acquiesced, as he had done in 1918,[2] though it is doubtful whether he took much part. It was followed by an attempt by Law and Lloyd George to effect a permanent union between the Coalition Liberals and the Conservative party. This proposal was under consideration from February onwards: in June it was dropped because the Coalition Liberals decided that they did not want it. Sporadic attempts were made thereafter to improve organisational collaboration without, it seems, much effect except in Liverpool where Liberal/Conservative co-operation produced striking results at the municipal elections in October 1920.[3] It was not revived until the middle of 1921.

One consequence of the Labour advance in 1919 was that Coalition Liberals suddenly realised that the Liberals would have to assert themselves if they were not to be squashed between two major parties. Another was the erosion of Conservative confidence in the Coalition. This did not apply so much to the Conservative party in parliament. But it applied on a wide and increasing scale to the Conservative party in the country where Labour successes, so far from suggesting a need to keep hold of 'Liberal progress', stimulated vigilance about socialistic radicalism in the Coalition itself.[4] These doubts were not removed by Lloyd George's sudden attacks on nationalisation as fusion came under consideration. No one believed that fusion would be popular in the Conservative party. No one believed that a Coalition Liberal organisation existed or that Coalition Liberal candidates were very good.[5] At the Birmingham meeting of the National Union in June 1920 – the first Party Conference held by the Conservative party since the war – there was criticism of the Coalition, though it was muted.[6] As Coalition Liberal ministers justified Coalition Liberal achievements against the accusations of betrayal from Asquithean and Labour leaders alike, the tempo of criticism quickened.

In 1920 and early 1921, however, there was no open full-scale assault. No constituency adopted a Conservative candidate against a sitting Conservative Coalitionist. Only a handful adopted Conservatives against sitting Coalition Liberals. At the Birmingham Conference Law's defence of Excess Profits Duty and negotiations in Ireland and Russia aroused no enthusiasm. There were demands for House of Lords Reform, Anti-Dumping and Safeguarding legislation (by Neville Chamberlain), German Reparations (by Maxse) and a declaration, passed by a small majority, of willingness to use a Tariff and have Tariff proposals ready in case of need.[1] The House of Lords played an important part in stimulating a climate of resistance, though it did not always please the Right.[2] Younger added to his disbelief in the competence of the Lloyd George Liberal organisation an equal irritation at the disproportionate allocation of Honours to Lloyd George Liberals.[3] The Licensing Bill attracted widespread criticism, especially in Liverpool.[4] Lee's Agricultural Bills received sharp criticism in the House of Lords. Addison's Health Bill was dismantled by the House of Commons and rejected by the Lords on the second reading. The Food supplementary estimates were given a hard run. Mond's estimates were almost defeated. Montagu's contribution to the Dyer debate produced resentment against him as a symbol of Coalition Liberalism which it is difficult to think he had not earned.[5]

The major assault, however, came not from the Conservative party in the House of Commons but from Northcliffe, Rothermere and Bottomley who made their mark on constituency Conservatives in the South of England at the same time as the Labour party was making its mark in the North. The context of the assault, which Conservatives thought might be extended,[6] was a steady rise in prices until mid-1920, a sharp increase in unemployment thereafter and a feeling, as widespread as the movement it was directed against, that public sentiment had crystallised against the strike principle and the extravagant rhetoric of Direct Action.[7] In relation to the Miners' Strike in late 1920, Lloyd George displayed enough firmness to satisfy the Cabinet.[8] In the course of 1920 taxation and government spending became symbols of a range of policies to which Conservative ministers had assented, often without very much thought.

In the hands of Rothermere and Bottomley, Anti-Waste became a summary for dislike not only of taxation and government spending as displayed in Addison's Housing and Fisher's Educational policies, but also of the Licensing Bill, the general question of liquor control with which Lloyd George had come to be connected and the reputation Lloyd George retained, even after the war, as a spending Chancellor.[9] Austen Chamberlain's 'preference

for the Treasury's Oxford Fabians' as against the leaders of
the banking community, his inability to reduce taxation and his
insistence on the need for a War Wealth Tax to repay some part
of the National Debt 'in a very short space of time' increased the
feeling that financial policy was based on 'false facts and doomed
to produce false results'.[1] This was increased by the Corporation
Tax in the 1920 Budget[2] and by suspicions that some members
of the Cabinet thought it would be electorally useful to tax war
wealth 'not just by a once-for-all tax but by a more general and
permanent levy'[3] which was rejected by the Cabinet in June.[4]
Among landowners Lee's Agricultural Bill was unpopular[5] both
because of the permanent power it would give County Agricultural
Committees and because of the limitations it imposed on the
negotiability of land let to tenants.[6] Only Long objected in
Cabinet. Griffith-Boscawen had difficulty passing it through the
House of Commons where he annoyed Conservative critics by
making his main concessions to criticism from Labour.[7] Even
more difficulty was expected when it reached the House of Lords.[8]
Strong feelings were aroused by the second part of Addison's
Health Bill,[9] the defeat of which in the House of Lords in December 1920 was the work not of Salisbury and Selborne but of 'back-
woodsmen' stimulated by the Harmsworth newspapers.[10]

The government's reaction was the slow withdrawal from
radical positions which characterised Lloyd George's last two
years in office. In 1920 this did not go very far. It affected chiefly
the Health, Housing and Licensing Bills and the constitution of
the Home Affairs Committee of the Cabinet.[11] It affected the
Government of Ireland Bill, which, beginning as an attempt to
give Home Rule to the South, ended by dividing Ireland, as it
turned out, irrevocably. It stimulated in Addison, Montagu,
Sutherland, Mond, perhaps Churchill and to some extent Fisher
the feeling that their policies were being by-passed or their
prospects neglected.[12]

Not all of this feeling was justified. Many of the Liberal conditions accepted by Conservatives in 1918 were honoured. By
1921 neither of the chief Conservative conditions had been. The
House of Lords had not been reformed: despite Younger's
insistence that it should be, only the vaguest assurances had been
given.[13] The King's speech in February 1921 came no nearer than

before to satisfying the National Union.[1] Curzon's statements in May were no improvement.[2] Anti-Dumping legislation – 'the subject that most divide[d] the Coalition'[3] – had not been introduced, though it was about to be. Coalition Liberals dragged their feet over Horne's Dyes Bill which the Asquitheans opposed in the House of Commons. Until October 1921 Allenby in Egypt gave a demonstration of practical Liberalism which gave no pleasure in the Conservative party.[4] Addison was attacked by Conservatives on grounds which applied to all Liberals equally. So far as Housing was concerned, he was criticised by Coalition Liberals as much as by anyone else for putting out contracts in advance of the building industry's ability to execute them, raising costs and prices and failing to build the houses he was supposed to.[5]

A good deal of the Liberal complaint, therefore, was insubstantial in the context of the terms on which the Coalition was established. Nevertheless, Liberals were subjected to unpleasant attacks from the Conservative party. The Agricultural Bills had been so much emasculated by the House of Lords that there was no prospect of an increase in the acreage under cultivation.[6] Lloyd George used this as an excuse for withdrawing the financial guarantees to agriculture when it became necessary to reduce governmental expenditure, but the Coalition Liberals treated the abandonment of State intervention as a defeat for them.[7] There were difficulties about 'dilution' in the building industry – an Anti-Waste topic – over which Mond threatened to resign.[8] There were difficulties about the Continuation School programme, which Lloyd George settled in Cabinet when Lewis threatened to do the same.[9] Coalition Liberals were about to be asked to support the Anti-Dumping Bill which Horne had drafted at the Board of Trade and also the Safeguarding of Industries Act against which some of them voted with the Asquitheans.[10] Over Ireland they were associated with what the Asquitheans stigmatised as brutal and illiberal repression. A meeting of fifty Coalition Liberals gave expression to these feelings in the House of Commons on March 9[11] at the same time as Lincolnshire and Simon held an Asquithean demonstration about Ireland in the National Liberal Club.

Whether other factors besides illness made Law decide to resign in mid-March,[12] it is impossible to establish. Ministers were working under the intensest pressure in late 1920:[1] Law was feeling the strain. Ireland was the one subject about which he was supposed always to have cared, though he did not leave that impression on Carson and Craig in 1917. In 1920 no agreed solution was in sight which would meet his requirement. His requirement – denial of the unity of Ireland – involved a continuation of coercion. He may well have felt that attempts to solve the Irish question, though necessary, would be inconsistent with his past and present preference and would be better resisted, if resistance was necessary, from outside the government than from inside.

Despite Long's resignation because he was ill, Milner's because he was discontented[2] and Derby's refusal to rejoin the government on his return from Paris[3] – all at a moment of maximum gloom in December 1920 – the Coalition's difficulties had not previously seemed insuperable. Law had begun to attract Die Hard criticism.[4] Rothermere and the Rothermere press had attacked him as much as they attacked Chamberlain for Squandermania. He had not had a happy conference at Birmingham the previous June. Nor had he been particularly good at the latest meeting of the Parliamentary Party.[5] On March 3 Griffith-Boscawen had been run out of Dudley by Beaverbrook who was supposed to be Law's closest friend. Immediately afterwards Labour had won Penistone and Kirkcaldy. Northcliffe was treating Derby as an alternative leader. On March 10 Derby announced his election as leader of a newly-formed group of Lancashire and Cheshire Unionist M.P.s with strong views about House of Lords reform and the Anti-Dumping Bill.[6] To Law these can hardly have been serious threats. From Lloyd George's point of view, it was better to have Law committed to anything the Cabinet might decide than to have him ranging loose and free like Derby.

When, therefore, Law announced his resignation, Lloyd George was 'very low' and very suspicious, wanted to talk to Balfour who, however, was in Cannes and thought of resigning.[7] Nor did he enjoy the election of Law's successor. Three Conservative backbenchers asked Lloyd George to become leader himself as a preliminary to forming a National party of the Centre.[8] Joynson-Hicks, Rothermere and Northcliffe tried to promote Birkenhead who thereupon regained enthusiasm for House of Lords reform. Others tried Curzon and Salisbury, and also Derby who regained enthusiasm for fusion.[1] Carson, Long and Balfour rallied to Austen Chamberlain[2] whose election was virtually unanimous. Chamberlain, however, had made himself extremely unpopular as Chancellor of the Exchequer from which many Conservatives were pleased to see him move. Lloyd George had treated him with minimal courtesy in 1917 and 1919. Chamberlain had no special affection for him and had probably been party to plans to replace him during his period of unemployment in 1918.[3] There was no reason to doubt that his election would make a difficult situation more difficult still.[4] His first attempts at leadership were no more impressive.[5] It was a couple of months before Lloyd George was confident that Austen Chamberlain would 'stick to him' whatever Birkenhead and Churchill might do.[6]

The constitution of a new ruling group was carried out in two stages. Lloyd George would probably have preferred Horne as Conservative leader. Horne was sent to succeed Austen Chamberlain at the Treasury, where he became one of Lloyd George's closest advisers. An unwilling Conservative Chief Whip – Lord Edmund Talbot – was sent to Ireland as Lord Lieutenant. His deputy as Chief Whip – Sir Robert Sanders – was passed over at Lloyd George's insistence in favour of Wilson who was equally unwilling.[7] A clean sweep was made of Conservative Whips[8] on the ground, if Sanders was right, that the Whip's office was too Conservative, too powerful and too full of 'gentlemen'.[9] Lloyd George's Chief Whip – F. E. Guest – was closely involved with Birkenhead: he was sent to succeed Churchill at the Air Ministry and was replaced by C. A. McCurdy, 'a particularly bad-mannered fellow ... the reverse of ... Guest'.[10] Addison was removed from the Ministry of Health: Illingworth was removed altogether.[11] Mond replaced them as a statutory Liberal. Lee of Fareham, apparently rather willingly, left the Ministry of Agriculture. Hewart – the best Coalition Liberal debater in the House of Commons – was not allowed to become Lord Chief Justice, despite his desire to do so: he was persuaded to take over the Licensing Bill instead.[12] Baldwin became President of the Board of Trade – politically one of the most difficult seats in the Cabinet.[13] In this reconstruction Churchill gained nothing. Craig and Londonderry both left the government in order to run the government of Northern Ireland.

Between April and December 1921 Lloyd George faced four problems – Ireland, the Anti-Waste movement and the feelings of the Conservative party about it, industrial depression and unemployment, and the threat presented to his continued leadership by Birkenhead and Churchill. Up to the Conservative Conference at Liverpool on November 17, his object was to keep open as many options as possible while ensuring that, if he had to leave office, he should do so in his own time and in a way calculated to leave open the possibility of finding a bridge back into a reunited Liberal party. At the beginning of 1920 Birkenhead's object had been to save Lloyd George and perpetuate the Coalition. In the eighteen months following, as the threat to Lloyd George came as much from Conservative, reactionary and Anti-Waste quarters as from the Labour party, he cast himself for the leading rôle in whatever government might succeed Lloyd George's. In this he was assisted by Churchill who had been disappointed in the April reconstruction and by Beaverbrook whose object seems to have been to install Birkenhead or Law. In January 1921 Birkenhead tried to make Carson Attorney-General when Reading became Viceroy of India.[1] Birkenhead had some sort of arrangement with Joynson-Hicks who thought of proposing him for the party leadership on Law's retirement and made public demands to end the Coalition.[2] When Derby seemed likely to attack him in April Lloyd George persuaded him to undertake a secret, and probably unnecessary, mission to Ireland, disguised as a travelling salesman.[3] The mission was followed by breakfast parties at Derby House where Lloyd George met the Conservative party in relays. In May, when the idea of an Irish truce was rejected, Birkenhead seems to have decided that Austen Chamberlain must be removed and began buttering Law as a consequence.[4]

Between April and the end of June the attack on Lloyd George was to have been made on the ground, among others, that he had no Irish policy. It was to have been brought to a head by urging Addison to stand firm if Lloyd George decided to give way to Die Hard and Anti-Waste pressure to remove him from the Ministry without Portfolio, which he had been given on his removal from the Ministry of Health in April. Addison was as unpopular as Montagu among Die Hards who treated a Ministry without Portfolio as an example of conspicuous 'waste': his

Housing policy was so 'unsound'[1] that his standing was low even among Coalition Liberals. Addison's attempt, perhaps at Churchill's prompting, to make his continued employment an issue of principle between the wings of the Coalition destroyed any help Austen Chamberlain might have offered in keeping him in office. The proof given by the St George's by-election of the middle-class determination to 'insist upon a drastic cut down' enabled Lloyd George to throw an 'unpopular' intriguer to the Conservative party. At the same time he leaked the Birkenhead/Churchill plot to the *Manchester Guardian* and the *Daily Mirror*, and decided on a major drive to reduce government spending.[2]

In July Lloyd George succeeded in opening negotiations with de Valera. A prolonged illness in Wales was followed by Hoare/Winterton/Churchill/Montagu/Beaverbrook/Birkenhead/Ormsby-Gore preparations to remove him if he conceded too much.[3] In face of the possibility of Birkenhead superseding Austen Chamberlain, Lloyd George found unexpected support in the higher reaches of the Conservative party.[4] He destroyed the first plot by abandoning Addison. He destroyed the second by associating Churchill and Birkenhead in the Irish negotiations, by persuading Churchill and Birkenhead not to abandon him once they had been involved and by threatening to resign if they would not support him.

Throughout the first half of 1921 there were innumerable signs of Conservative restlessness. At Hertford and at St George's, Westminster in June Anti-Waste candidates defeated Conservatives in naturally Conservative seats. From the standpoint of the Coalition Liberals the abandonment of Addison was bad: any further capitulation to Anti-Waste would be worse. Coalition Liberals did not doubt the desirability of reducing taxation, but they had no wish to reduce spending on schemes of social improvement. The Hertford and St George's by-elections convinced Younger, Lloyd George and Austen Chamberlain that an attack on government spending was unavoidable. The device of giving Conservative candidates Anti-Waste labels had its effect at elections later in the summer. The appointment of Sir Eric Geddes and a committee of businessmen[5] to recommend extensive cuts in government spending was agreed without opposition in the Cabinet, though there was extensive opposition in the Conservative party to the exclusion of M.P.s from it.[6]

The third and, in real terms, most important of Lloyd George's problems began with the beginning of large-scale unemployment in the summer and autumn of 1920. This, though a problem of lasting consequence for British political life in the next two decades, did not in the first place make his political position more difficult. If anything it made it easier to find slogans and programmes which would unite the Coalition Liberals and the Conservative party. The sharp fall in world prices created problems in dealing with trades unions, but none that had not been present before. The sharp increase in unemployment brought financial and fiscal problems of its own, but it weakened Union power and bargaining capability. If the manifest failure of Capitalism provided objective support to socialist theory in areas where unemployment was largest, the manifest opportunity to reduce prices and costs – including the cost of government spending – provided a ready-made occasion to manufacture a common-sense rhetoric of resistance and national crisis in face of the extravagance of socialist expectations. If, as the Labour leaders claimed, the slump was responsible for the failure of the Triple Alliance and the recession in Labour prospects in mid-1921, there is a real sense in which 'the way the government handled the Coal strike' made Conservatives 'more favourably disposed towards [it] than they ever had been before'[1] and gave plausibility to the demand for a permanent Centre party of resistance to Socialism which Austen Chamberlain came to want in 1922. It cannot be said that Lloyd George took this opportunity but some of the Coalition Liberals saw it.[2]

Finally, in dealing with Ireland, Lloyd George made almost total capitulation to the Conservative, if not to the Ulster, position while using it to restore his credentials as a Liberal. The passage of the Government of Ireland Act in 1920 and the establishment of two parliaments in Southern Ireland and Ulster with a federal relationship had been 'a *pis-aller*' for Conservatives.[3] Its unpopularity had been reduced by the decision of the Ulster leaders to work it and by the fact that Law and Long had supported it. A parliament and government under Craig had been established in Belfast in 1921. Sinn Fein, however, after winning the elections to the Westminster Parliament in 1918, had boycotted it and in the following year established Dail Eireann as a rebel parliament committed to Republican detachment of all Ireland as the centre of its policy. The failure to effect a federal relationship and the continuation of violence in the South intensified Asquithean accusations that Lloyd George had betrayed Liberal principles. The Labour party added its criticism by becoming the second party of Irish conciliation.

From Lloyd George's point of view there were two possible lines of advance, and one that was blocked by the Conservative majority in both Commons and Lords. He could not expect to carry through an agreement with Sinn Fein if that involved military compulsion on Ulster to belong to a Southern-dominated Irish State against her will. He had the power to force an election on such a programme if the King would agree but he would have the Conservative party united against him. It was clear that, on any programme involving the maintenance of Irish Unity against Ulster and even more for a programme which would end coercion, he would have widespread support among all sorts of Liberals – especially if that involved the destruction of the Coalition.

From July until November negotiations were conducted with two possibilities in mind. The first was that, if he could not persuade Sinn Fein to accept the division of Ireland, coercion could be ended by pressurising Ulster to sign away her independence. The second was that, if neither Sinn Fein nor Ulster would give way, his political future could be assured by resigning on an anti-Ulster ticket.[1] At one stage he seems to have thought of coercing Ulster.[2] It is not certain whether he intended to leave office, whether he was blackmailing Conservatives with the threat of a Clynes government which might do well in an election at which a divided Conservative party would do badly[3] or whether he was trying to carry along Birkenhead and Churchill whose importance in a reactionary successor government might not be as great as it had now become in his.[4] In October he was probably blackmailing, and perhaps keeping open a line to a Liberal election platform from which to undercut the Cecil/Grey/Asquith anti-Lloyd George platform which Grey had begun to build at Berwick.[5] In November he may very probably not have been. In October he succeeded with Birkenhead and Churchill. On October 31 he received an overwhelming vote of confidence in the House of Commons against Gretton and Rupert Gwynne.[6]

The Lloyd George/de Valera negotiations began in July 1921. By the beginning of November Lloyd George had brought them to the point at which, with de Valera refusing to take any further part after his visit to London, Griffith had agreed that Ireland would remain in the Commonwealth and recognise the Crown as its head, provided Irish unity was preserved in a single Dominion under an all-Ireland parliament. An all-Ireland parliament sitting in Dublin and elected on a popular constituency meant a Catholic Irish majority. From November 1 Lloyd George was trying with one part of his mind to pressurise the Cabinet and the Conservative party to bring moral compulsion on Ulster to accept it by insisting that Ulster would have to pay British income tax if she remained part of the United Kingdom.

It is possible that Lloyd George came near to persuading the Conservative members of the Cabinet to accept this. It is not clear how much truth there was to his claim that Craig had been willing on November 5 and had become unwilling only when Law made him.[1] Austen Chamberlain claimed that he would never have connived at the forcible coercion of Ulster, but it is less than clear that he objected to moral coercion. Derby favoured moral coercion: so did Birkenhead and Worthington-Evans. Birkenhead, speaking as Cabinet emissary to Salvidge during an emergency visit to Liverpool on the 15th in preparation for the Conservative Party Conference debate two days later, mentioned Dominion Home Rule as the object of Cabinet policy, though without any suggestion of coercion.[2]

In trying to keep Churchill and Birkenhead interested in negotiation, Lloyd George threatened to resign if the negotiations broke down once Griffith agreed to remain in the Commonwealth: in that respect he was threatening them both with a reactionary Conservative government and with a reversion on his own part to a radical position about Ireland as the basis for a Liberal appeal at an election. In persuading Griffith to trust him, he mentioned the possibility of resignation, suggesting in that case that Law would come into office, unwilling to recognise the unity of Ireland and determined, if necessary, to coerce the South by resuming the war. To Law Lloyd George spoke of resignation also, emphasising the difficulty Law would find in forming a reputable government if his programme was war in the South – as in the circumstances it would have to be.[1] It is not clear whether Lloyd George intended to resign, or whether he was using the threat of resignation as a way of keeping all parties party to the negotiations. What is clear is that Law called his bluff.

When Craig saw Law on November 7 or 8, he was encouraged to withdraw any agreement he may have given Lloyd George three days earlier[2] about an all-Ireland parliament.[3] He reverted to the position that Ulster must be independent, adding the assurance Law wanted – that, if independence involved paying British rather than Irish income tax, he would still want it.[4] With these assurances Law decided by November 12 that, unless Lloyd George renounced any intention he may have had of pressurising Ulster to enter a unified Irish State, he would return to politics, fight the government at the Party Conference on November 17 and, if victorious there, would ensure the adoption of Conservative candidates in every constituency where Coalition Liberals were sitting.

In making this decision it is not certain what Law intended. Lloyd George thought he intended to put himself at the head of the Die Hards in order to make himself Prime Minister. It is possible that he expected the Conservative leadership to be defeated at Liverpool and was preparing for the reversion.[5] Certainly the government might have been defeated in the Conference debate on Ireland: the efforts it made to avoid defeat were signal.[6] The victory it won was the work of Salvidge, Derby, Birkenhead and Worthington-Evans, but it was a victory in favour of negotiation against no negotiation, not a victory for a particular solution. There was no support whatever for forcible pressure on Ulster. Salvidge – the person primarily responsible for the government's victory – knew he was supporting a proposal to put Ulster under Dublin. He was, however, no more willing than anyone else to support physical coercion: he had decided to support the government before the Cabinet sent Birkenhead to see him because he thought Northumberland and Gretton were using Ulster as a way of destroying the Coalition.[7] Salisbury left the Conference with high hopes. It is likely that Younger was right to think that 'the prominent inclusion in [his] amendment of ... safeguarding clauses [gave the Prime Minister] a pull over the Sinn Feiners [who] now know the limits beyond which the government does not and cannot go'.[8]

At some point between November 12 and November 23, Lloyd George abandoned immediate Dominion Home Rule, dropped the intention of pressurising Ulster and began the pressurising of the Irish delegation instead. Until the debate on the treaty in the House of Commons on December 15 Law made no public statement. When asked by Salvidge to deny rumours that he disapproved of the negotiations and the Conference resolution, he refused to: he refused equally to make a statement of approval.[1] But he was in touch with Salisbury, Gretton, Craig and Birkenhead and in continuous contact with Lloyd George. The blocking of the route which led to a unified Irish Free State under a Dublin parliament was his work. It was only when this route was blocked that Lloyd George persuaded Griffith and the Irish delegation that the unity of Ireland could best be preserved by accepting division in principle on condition that it was made intolerable in practice by a Boundary Commission to investigate the wishes of the inhabitants of Fermanagh and Tyrone which Lloyd George had invented and assured Craig would present no threat to Ulster. With the acceptance in principle by Griffith and the Irish delegation of the independence of Ulster and the Boundary Commission, the treaty was signed on December 6.

It is not certain what connection existed in Lloyd George's mind in late 1921 between Ireland, Geddes, inflation as a remedy for unemployment and the transformation of the Coalition into a permanent anti-socialist party of the Centre. As the Die Hards, Anti-Waste, the Grey/Cecil/Asquith nexus and the Labour party made themselves felt, the possibilities that were open to him were greatly reduced. The chance of dividing the Labour leaders from their followers was probably strongest after the failure of the Triple Alliance: if he had used Addison as a pretext for leaving the Coalition, he might have found a response in that quarter. 'Addison', however, was not an issue of strength. If Lloyd George had left over Ireland, he would have found a ready response in the Liberal party, though the return of Grey to public life would have made it less enthusiastic and Churchill and other Coalition Liberals might not have followed. The Labour party's reluctance to be involved in alliances with other parties reduced Lloyd George's freedom of action in that direction. Though he and his Coalition Liberal followers used the threat of resignation freely,[2] it is unlikely that he would have gained much from it and probable that he decided some time in August that the next phase of office must be based on the Conservative party.

This meant a perpetuation of the Coalition and something resembling a reciprocal commitment to revive the proposal for amalgamation of parties which had been rejected in 1920. It is not clear how far Coalition Liberals were involved in 1921. Lloyd George, Austen Chamberlain and Birkenhead all made fusionist speeches when the Irish negotiations began: there may well have been a bargain when Birkenhead and Churchill were brought into the Irish negotiations in August. Despite Conservative heart-searching about 'dealing with murderers', there was an extensive desire to 'avoid civil war and a general desire not to break up the Irish Conference'.[1] This issued neither in open renunciation of the commitment to Ulster nor in abandonment of the historic Conservative reluctance to connive at the dismantling of the United Kingdom. At the Liverpool Conference and elsewhere these feelings, when made explicit by Gretton, Northumberland and their followers, were received with the warmth suitable to the fundamental bases of the party. At the same time the Conservative managers, with eyes fixed less on Gretton than on Conservative and public opinion at large, were conscious of the wish to end violence and coercion, a reluctance to support Ulster to the hilt and the divisive effect the Irish question could have on the creation of an anti-socialist front. It would be wrong to suggest a lack of Conservative interest in the fate of Ulster. It would not be wrong to agree with Younger's view that

any intractable attitude on the part of Ulster [would] be bitterly resented. There is a natural fear of the appalling results which may follow a break-down and while there will be no coercion of Ulster if she disagrees, there is a strong feeling that she ought in the interests of the Empire and of Great Britain, to make every reasonable concession to secure a settlement. That feeling was most strongly expressed to me by hundreds of people who were there [i.e. at Liverpool] and there would, I believe, be an absolute revolt against Ulster if she showed any indisposition to move one inch towards an arrangement.[2]

When Lloyd George revived the 'amalgamation of parties' in tying Birkenhead and Churchill to the Irish negotiations, he prob-ably did so as an insurance against Die Hard dissidence[3] and possibly, because Law was saying the same thing.[1] Perhaps in order to tie Salvidge,[2] amalgamation was given a prominent place in Chamberlain's speech at the Liverpool Conference.[3] In the ten months which followed the signature of the treaty, amalgamation or 'fusion' was the central question.

PART II

VII

THE ELECTION KITE OF
JANUARY 1922

'This dirty little Welsh attorney and his C[o] L[ib] sycophants think they
can dictate a policy to the whole Unionist party.'
        Neville Chamberlain to Ida, January 7 1922

With the signature of the Irish Treaty, the leaders of the Coalition
thought they could now talk chiefly about the thing that interested
them most. Ireland, it is clear, interested none of them. By the
time the treaty was signed, they all hoped that Craig would give
in or go away or make some other unspecified disappearance as a
major problem. What they wanted to discuss was resistance to
Socialism. From the beginning of 1922 until the end of 1923,
this was the major question. Other issues were presented as
central – 'Genoa' in March, 'Chanak' in September and 'tranquillity' in October 1922, Germany in mid-1923; but the major
factor in decision and calculation was the Labour threat. In Part II
we shall watch first Lloyd George, then Law and finally Baldwin
wrestling unsuccessfully until, in October 1923, a drastic attempt
was made to meet it by playing 'Protection'.

Between mid-December 1921 and mid-January 1922, there was
a major upheaval in relations between the Coalition and the
Conservative party as Birkenhead's and Lloyd George's attempt
to force an immediate general election was defeated by Austen
Chamberlain, Younger and the body of Conservative M.P.s.
This episode was important for the future of the Coalition, for
Austen Chamberlain's authority as leader and for Birkenhead's
standing in the Conservative party.

On Birkenhead's side it was an attempt to consolidate the gains
he had made as the leading Coalitionist in late 1921, to perpetuate
the alliance between Lloyd George and the Conservative leaders
and to fix the dividing line, as Austen Chamberlain had come to
want it fixed, between Socialism on the one hand and anti-socialist
Constitutionalism on the other. There was no difference between
Birkenhead's objective and Austen Chamberlain's, but it was

Birkenhead who wanted an immediate election and Chamberlain who stopped it.

It was recommended, however, not only by Birkenhead but also by Sutherland and McCurdy who, though influenced by Birkenhead initially, saw advantages from a Liberal point of view – or rather smaller disadvantages – from an election now than from an election later. There was, they thought, no guarantee that the Irish Treaty could be implemented without violence and every possibility that any government would face the same pressure as before to coerce the Free State which the treaty had created. Liberals were unwilling to face the reactionary implications of the Geddes Report. Both Ireland and Geddes could be faced more happily after an election than with an election hanging over them. Trade prospects and the set-backs suffered by the Labour party since the beginning of the slump were advanced to justify an election which might as easily have been advanced against it. It is just possible that Lloyd George was irritated by Grey and the Asquitheans and wanted an excuse to 'have a go'.[1] Most important of all, an immediate election on a Coalition basis would secure support for the Coalition Liberals from a major party organisation which it was unlikely they would have at the next election if they did not get it at this time and in this way.

Coalition Liberals were a serious party in the House of Commons: there were over 130. But they had been elected in 1918 on the back of the Conservative party without any real organisation of their own. Despite announcements that something would be done, virtually nothing had been done since then, except in Manchester, to develop the organisational roots needed for a political party in conditions of universal suffrage. Die Hards had been adopted against sitting Coalition Liberals in fifteen seats. If Sutherland and McCurdy conceived of a Lloyd George-led Conservative/Asquithean/moderate Labour alliance as the ultimate objective of the next years of political activity, they had no illusion about immediate reunion with the Asquitheans who thrived, and hoped to thrive still more, on Lloyd George's unpopularity. They believed therefore that if Lloyd George was to have any large-scale party organisation behind him at the next election, it would have to be a Conservative one and that the tendency to 'movement among the Tories for a break away from the Coalition [would] grow' so that 'if the Tories [were to] split badly between now and [an] election, we [should] lose a lot of Liberal Coalition seats'.[1]

The arguments in favour of holding an election in February 1922 were made to Lloyd George by Birkenhead, and put by Lloyd George to Austen Chamberlain and Churchill as a question to be settled by the four of them. Derby was consulted and was not much in favour, but sent conflicting opinions from Lancashire followers.[2] Younger was not involved in the initial discussions[3] which began after dinner at Birkenhead's house on Monday December 19 in company with Beaverbrook, Macnamara and McCurdy who were in favour and Salvidge who had no definite opinion beyond the unwelcome view that 'if the Coalition wished to continue, they must bring back Bonar Law'.[4] Lloyd George, Birkenhead, Chamberlain and Churchill then met again on December 20 by themselves. Birkenhead was strongly in favour. Lloyd George was probably in favour but did not make it clear. Churchill was unwilling to be committed. Chamberlain did not want an immediate election. He was not sure of winning it: an election in the New Year would leave no time to 'consolidate the Coalition into [the] single party' he had called for at Liverpool in November.[5] He refused to decide until he had consulted the Conservative party.

The consultations he set on foot next day with Younger, Fraser,[6] Sanders, Neville Chamberlain and J. S. Williams, the Chairman of the National Union, were designed to discover whether anti-Coalition Conservatives would stand as Independent Unionists in the event of an immediate election on a Coalition platform, how much an election would be likely to increase Die Hard representation in the House of Commons, how far Conservatives would support Coalition Liberals and whether the prospect for the Coalition would be better at an immediate election or at an election held in anything up to the eighteen months that could elapse before the next election had to take place.[7] In writing to Sanders, Neville Chamberlain and Williams, Chamberlain adopted an attitude of enquiry. He let Younger know that he did not want an immediate election, that Birkenhead and Lloyd George did and that, if Lloyd George and Birkenhead agreed, Lloyd George would use his undoubted power to ask for one.[8]

Chamberlain may, or may not, have been trying to prod Younger into action: this was the effect of his letter. Younger was in Scotland when he received it. He sent Chamberlain a telegram[1] and, later in the day, a letter which explained that Birkenhead – 'looking after No. 1' – wanted an immediate election because continuation of the Coalition would give him the best chance of becoming leader of the party. Younger was prepared to 'smash [Lloyd George's] hopes ... [if] he please[d] to flout us'.[2] He followed this with two letters on the 28th reiterating the difficulty there would be in any case in 'secur[ing] general support ... for the continuation of the present condition of affairs' and declaring that an election was unnecessary in the absence of any pressing crisis, undesirable in view of the economic uncertainty and would be greatly resented in the Conservative party at a time when nothing had been done about the House of Lords.[3]

By the beginning of January Austen Chamberlain knew that the Conservative leaders he had consulted thought an election would be a mistake. Discussion had not been about the future of the Coalition. No one advocated ending it, replacing Lloyd George by a Conservative Prime Minister or fighting the election as an independent party. It was recognised that the Coalition was unpopular, but this was offered as a reason for avoiding an election, not as a reason for breaking it up. Objection was raised to 'fusion' which Neville Chamberlain 'd[id] not know that [he] could accept', though Fraser found that some Area leaders wanted it.[4] But fusion was a reason for delay since it would 'take at least two years and probably longer' and would involve 'throw[ing] off a certain proportion of Coalition Liberals and hard-shell Unionists'.[5] Younger believed that strong government was needed for the difficulties that lay ahead: he expected an election to produce a crop of 'inconvenient promises ... extracted from ... weak-kneed politicians'. He was typical of the others in his belief that no alternative 'majority elected *now* would be more competent to deal with unemployment and industrial questions than the party now in power'.[6]

Those who opposed an immediate election did so for a variety of reasons connected chiefly with unemployment, taxation, government spending, House of Lords reform, the absence of any but tactical reasons for holding an election, the personal unpopularity of Lloyd George, the unwillingness of many Conservatives to stand as Coalitionists and the need to maintain financial confidence at a moment when trade was on the turn.[1] Electors were not expected to be grateful for the Irish or Washington Treaties. The economy was seen to be the problem that required attention: it was thought that nothing would be gained by having an election before a trade recovery had occurred. Some of those who were consulted favoured eventual fusion of the parties. Others did not. All expected the Coalition to continue for some time yet and wanted to make sure that a mistimed election did not give the Labour party its chance.

Up to this point discussion had been confined to the people Chamberlain had chosen. Parliament was not in session. M.P.s in general were not in London. There had been little newspaper speculation. At the beginning of January, however, a stream of obviously inspired newspaper reports suggested that Lloyd George had decided to hold an election. Lloyd George denied that he was responsible[2]: he went to Cannes on December 26 and stayed there for the Cannes Conference until mid-January along with Horne, Churchill and Worthington-Evans. McCurdy and Sutherland, however, used Downing Street to indoctrinate the press in favour of an election while he was away.[3] Whether it was McCurdy on his own, as Sutherland claimed, or on Lloyd George's instructions, whether it was Beaverbrook and Birkenhead under their own steam, as Austen Chamberlain thought,[4] a press campaign to establish the expectation was conducted, first in *The Times* and *Daily News*, then in the *Glasgow Herald*, the *Evening Standard* and leading provincial newspapers, finally by January 3 in most of the leading London papers, including Lloyd George's *Daily Chronicle*.[5]

The campaign, however, boomeranged. Instead of convincing Conservatives that they were about to fight an election whether they wanted to or not, it made them determined not to. Younger was 'overwhelmed with fierce protests'.[6] He 'had a procession of M.P.s' – not all of them Die Hards – to see him declaring that 'if they have to go to the country, they won't stand as Coalitionists but as Independent Unionists'.[7] Austen Chamberlain 'heard of only one Unionist who favoured dissolution and he was a man who was not going to stand again'.[8] Derby, after hesitating, came down against an election 'in view of the overwhelming protests' he had received from Lancashire Conservatives.[1] Younger cannot have disliked these confirmations of his own opinions. They made it easier to show Lloyd George and Sutherland 'that they cannot regard our party or myself as a negligible quantity'.[2] His interviews with the *Evening News* published on January 4 and the Press Association published on January 6, his article in the *Weekly Dispatch* published on January 8, his letter to Conservative Chairmen published on January 11,[3] his speeches at Troon and Ardrossan reported on January 11 and 12 and the attitude of the *Daily Telegraph*, the Northcliffe/Rothermere newspapers and the *Morning Post*[4] established that a major part of the Conservative party would stand no nonsense.

Younger's letter of December 28 had been sent to Lloyd George by Austen Chamberlain. Younger also sent a massive memorandum by Sir Malcolm Fraser as well as a strong letter of his own (together with a copy for ' "FE" ')[5] in which he made it clear that he would 'rather see ... our combination ... [broken up] ... than be in any way involved in ... an indefensible act'.[6] On December 29 Salvidge gave the opinion he had been asked for in Birkenhead's house which was that 'before there was an appeal to the country ... reduced taxation [should be] an accomplished fact'.[7] On January 4 Austen Chamberlain sent Lloyd George a summary of the views he had gathered together with a memorandum from Neville Chamberlain.[8]

On December 31 Fraser suggested that the King need not grant a dissolution at this stage of a parliament's life[9]: on January 6 Austen Chamberlain wrote to Stamfordham to explain that he did not want one.[10] By then Churchill, Greenwood and Lambert, the Coalition Liberal parliamentary Chairman, had all suggested, and McCurdy had told Lloyd George by telegram, that the election should be dropped.[11] By January 5 Lloyd George had decided to defer a decision.[12] On January 9 he telegraphed Chamberlain to suspend judgment.[13] On January 10 he sent a letter complaining of Younger's breach of confidence in publicising McCurdy's memorandum, blamed Unionist ministers for suggesting an election in the first place and insisted that there should be no statement until he returned to England.[14] On January 19 Chamberlain announced publicly that the election was off and said that the House of Lords should be reformed.[1] Two days later Lloyd George said the same.[2]

There are a number of things to notice about this episode. It exposed the weakness of Lloyd George's position and the strength of Younger's: the exposure of Lloyd George was carried out not by Gretton or Salisbury, who kept quiet at this time[3] but by the great body of central M.P.s who had no objection to Coalition and had supported the Irish Treaty. In order to carry what he thought the body of Conservative opinion with him, Younger produced what was virtually a Conservative manifesto in writing to constituency chairman on January 9. He explained what he thought the party wanted, emphasised that there was no reason why it should not get it and claimed that there was no need to have an election until the House of Lords had been reformed and industrial confidence restored. Finally, although Austen Chamberlain 'stood by Younger'[4] when Younger agreed with him about the election, Chamberlain, far from objecting to the continuation of the Coalition, was confirmed in his belief that fusion between the two parties was more desirable than before. Like his Chief Whip he 'took the most serious view of the Conservative revolt'.[5] He was not sure that fusion would be possible. He could not even say that there would be 'any later date than February on which he could guarantee that we could go to the country ... as a Coalition or as a new party with better prospects than ... at present'.[6] But fusion was what he wanted.

VIII

THE PRESERVATION OF
THE COALITION

'What is the prospect if the Coalition breaks up? You then have three parties, all agreeing as to ... fundamental economic and social conditions, but all fighting one another vigorously. Who will profit by our division? Who but the Labour party and the extreme section of that party?'

> Austen Chamberlain to Sir William Madge, January 26 1922, Austen Chamberlain MSS

'There is the Washington Conference establishing peace in the great West. I am looking forward to the Genoa Conference to establish peace in the East. They will be like the two wings of the Angel of Peace hovering over the World (cheers). The trader, the financier and the manufacturer can go forth without fear of hidden traps and perils and destruction. The worker can labour without apprehension and credit can be given and extended and the broken avenues of trade can be repaired, normal life resumed and the World march on to plenty and tranquillity. That is our programme of peace.'

> Lloyd George to Coalition Liberal Conference, January 21 1922, *The Times*, January 23

'The economic position of the world appears so hopelessly confused, and its financial advisers seem so incapable of finding any plan for alleviating our misfortunes ... that I doubt whether Genoa is likely to mark a turning-point in contemporary history.'

> Balfour to Ian Malcolm, January 26 1922, Whittingehame MSS

From the Younger/Lloyd George conflict, different people learnt different lessons. To Die Hards it seemed that a show-down was at hand in which it was their business to make sure that the right side won. Gretton had resigned the Coalition Whip in July 1921 when the Irish negotiations began: McNeill appears to have done so in November.[1] Both helped to master-mind the demonstration at the Liverpool Conference. Along with Ampthill, Hall, Foxcroft, Applin and Croft, Gretton led the rally at Queen's Hall on November 21 in protest against Lloyd George's proposal to 'capitulate to the force of the assassin'.[2] Despite being a Law Lord, Carson made a 'very bitter' speech against the treaty in the House of Lords.[3] On December 16 fifty-eight M.P.s voted against it including forty Conservatives.[4]

The treaty was not the end of the Irish question. De Valera did not accept it. It was not certain that Griffith and Collins would be able to carry it. There was a danger that the Irish election would return either group by 'such a small majority' that they would seek the only excuse for joining forces by making 'common cause against Ulster'.[1] Ulster had to deal with IRA violence internally and the Boundary Commission on Fermanagh and Tyrone about which Lloyd George's first statements after the treaty were alarming.[2] The British government had virtually abandoned the Southern Loyalists in 1920: they had not been forgotten by the Die Hards.[3] British action to protect Ulster, establish the rights of the Southern Loyalists or enforce acceptance of the treaty if it was not ratified by the Free State remained possibilities in Die Hard minds in early 1922. It was strengthened by the outbreak of war between Collins and de Valera.

Nevertheless, although Ulster remained a Die Hard problem, the treaty altered the character of the movement. There was every desire to make sure that Craig was dealt with fairly,[4] but the support Lloyd George received in the Irish debate made it impossible to make Ireland the chief occasion for a challenge to his leadership. The Die Hards would have found occasions of their own if Austen Chamberlain had not presented one himself. None would have been as central as his revival of the plan to amalgamate the two parties to the Coalition.

When first Salisbury and then Joynson-Hicks demanded an end to Coalition in 1920, they received very little support. In 1921 Conservatives who disliked the Coalition doubted whether anti-Coalition feeling was very strong,[5] did not believe that the Conservative party would do well by itself and thought there was ample scope for influencing ministers from inside it.[6] Even Salisbury's brothers, who wanted to get rid of Lloyd George, did not expect to do so at once.

In late 1921 Ireland had been the centre of the Die Hard attack. It had been so because Die Hards identified resistance to Sinn Fein with the defence of civilisation, believed in the Irish Union as the fundamental principle of the Conservative party and thought Lloyd George likely either to concede what de Valera wanted or to force an anti-Ulster election in England in order to get power to make Ulster give it. Even before the treaty was signed, they did not expect to get rid of the government which had disarmed criticism by abandoning Addison and appointing the Geddes Committee.[1] Salisbury and Steel-Maitland had some success with the Executive Committee of the National Union, but Salisbury had not dared propose a no-confidence vote at the party Conference in November. Irish policy was subjected to searching scrutiny: Salisbury thought the Conference did 'nothing to make [him] distrust the good sense of [his] countrymen'.[2] The body of the party, however, accepted the treaty. He had no illusion about success in the immediate future.

The tactics adopted now were rather subtler than before. A 'Conservative Party' was formed in the House of Commons with a Whip of its own – Sir Frederick Banbury – and a process of election to membership.[3] Preparations were made to demand a meeting of the National Union in case fusion was attempted[4] and to apply for a 'legal injunction ... to prevent the Central Office spending ... money on behalf of a party or persons who had given up Unionist principles'.[5] Constituencies were chosen in which sitting Coalition Liberals were to be opposed.[6] It was suggested that Lord Robert Cecil should be got to press the Asquitheans to keep Ulster boiling as a way of shaming Conservatives into doing so themselves.[7] In addition, a statement of 'Conservative principles' was demanded from Balfour and Austen Chamberlain.

The Die Hard leaders did not do this because they thought the principles mattered, though as a matter of fact they thought they did. Nor did they do it as a protest against the claims made by Hewart and Shortt at the Coalition Liberal Conference on behalf of the Liberal character of the Coalition.[8] They did it because 'the only grounds on which ... we can oppose the National Party would be if its manifesto or its policy departs from Conservative principles' and the best way to make fusion impossible was to draw a dividing line between the Lloyd George Liberals who would not be able to accept 'Conservative principles' and Conservatives who on the whole would be.[9]

On January 7 Rothermere paid for a full-page advertisement in *The Times* which praised their principles, attacked the Conservative ministers for sacrificing principles to office and urged support for Gretton.[10] In the *Morning Post* of February 3 Gretton announced that the Irish Treaty had put an end to the Unionist party in its historic form, demanded from 'the leaders of the Conservative party ... a clear declaration ... as to their views of the future of the party' and 'appeal[ed] to all Conservatives in the country who still believe in their principles not to pledge themselves to support any Coalition candidates until the position of the party and its future policy [had been] made clear'.[1] This letter was followed by a request from Gretton for a meeting with Austen Chamberlain,[2] and a similar request to Balfour from Gretton and Hall.[3]

There is no record of the meeting with Balfour, if indeed it took place. The meeting with Chamberlain on February 13 became a confrontation between twenty-nine of the Die Hards on the one hand and Austen Chamberlain, Curzon, Baldwin, Worthington-Evans, Griffith-Boscawen and Wilson on the other.[4] Most of the talking was done by Curzon, Gretton and Austen Chamberlain. Gretton repeated his request for a statement of principles and asked for an assurance that the party would stand by itself at the next election. Chamberlain replied that there would be no Coalition ticket at the next election which the two parties would fight separately: he delivered a warning, both at the meeting and in writing to Gretton a week later, that Gretton was defying all the Unionist members of the Cabinet.[5]

Chamberlain's statement is said to have satisfied Joynson-Hicks: its reference to Joseph Chamberlain's part in creating Liberal Unionism gave no pleasure to Gretton or Banbury.[6] Neither Chamberlain's firmness then nor his speech to the National Unionist Association on February 20/21 altered the Die Hard position. On February 16 a Die Hard communiqué argued that there was 'no half-way house without a compromise of principles' between 'a candidate [being] either a Conservative or not' and that 'genuine Conservative candidates at the next General Election should stand as such and ... not be hampered by an alliance with any other group or groups, Party or Parties'.[7] After Chamberlain's speech on the 20th, Sir William Davison pointed out in a letter to *The Times* that 'what electors really want to know is, in the event of the Conservative party getting a majority, do they intend to form a Conservative government or have a Coalition under Mr Lloyd George?'.[8]

From February 20 onwards the Die Hards were conscious that a counter-attack was being launched – by Chamberlain in public speeches, by Balfour on his return from America, by Coalition supporters in the House of Commons and by praise from Birkenhead which they 'found the hardest blow of all'.[1] Their reaction to Chamberlain's refusal to produce a statement of principles was a statement of 'Conservative and Unionist Principles' signed by sixteen of their leaders and published in *The Times* on March 8.[2] This affirmed the Conservative party's loyalty to the throne and religion, the importance of a Second Chamber and the need to provide firm and unselfish government in Europe. It emphasised its detestation of political murder, its opposition to 'grandiose schemes of reconstruction', its dislike of excessive taxation and its support for stability, progress, 'life, liberty and property' against the Socialism and Communism which threatened the State and the social system.

This statement contained 'little, if anything' to which Austen Chamberlain 'could not put [his] hand'.[3] It was followed by a circular from Salisbury to Conservative constituency chairmen – at addresses supplied by Central Office[4] – in which associations were urged to decide that they would 'support ... no candidate [at the next election] who does not stand upon definite Unionist principles' and will not 'undertake – should the present Coalition government be still in power after the election – ... [to] consider himself under [no] pledge or obligation to support the Coalition except insofar as they are guided by Unionist principles'.[5] Though this again said 'nothing ... to which ... a Conservative and Unionist ... could not ... be ready to subscribe'[6] and was not expected to prevent Liberals joining the Conservative party,[7] it was designed to prevent fusion being effected against the party's wishes.

The impression left by Die Hard correspondence is that they faced an uphill struggle.[8] Even their best friends did not think their merits very great. Their rigidity over Ireland alienated Southern Unionists to whom it was more important to get good terms within the framework of the treaty than to anticipate a hypothetical reconquest of the South. Salisbury was sensitive to being thought 'reactionary'.[9] He emphasised that the Die Hard movement was antagonistic neither to anti-socialist Liberals nor to the body of the working classes[1] and existed only because no government led by Lloyd George could now deliver an anti-socialist majority.[2]

Gretton's willingness to defer to Salisbury was intermittent. He did not want to merge his 'party' in the House of Commons with Salisbury's in the House of Lords.[3] When joint meetings were instituted on April 6,[4] he held them with extreme reluctance. He had no control over Carson who began fishing for Labour support for Ulster in a speech at Brixton in mid-April.[5] He had difficulty with Joynson-Hicks who found it easier to work with Salisbury. Joynson-Hicks's balloted motion of confidence against the government on April 5 was drafted without consultation.[6] In the debate and vote then, and in the debate and vote on the government's Genoa motion on April 3, the Die Hards, though supported by Labour votes, had only about forty Conservatives voting with them.[7]

Under these handicaps the movement got under way. Gretton appointed a Public Relations Officer.[8] Derby's and Devonshire's refusal to join the government were encouraging. In their turn Derby and Devonshire were given encouragement,[9] though it is far from clear that this gave them pleasure.[10] Salisbury renewed relations with Law.[11] On Lloyd George's withdrawal to Criccieth in March, he predicted a return to 'quiet common sense' as the prevailing tone in government and stressed the importance of remaining united as the party detached itself from the 'eccentric genius' to whom it was attached at present.[12] At a luncheon for the Conservative groups in both Houses of Parliament on April 5,[13] his audience was praised for representing 'the permanent and fundamental principles of the party' against what McNeill called 'the boisterous and bumptious Lord Chancellor'. On April 9 Salisbury told the Junior Imperial League that major decisions would soon be upon them.[14]

To Younger the proposal to hold an election had been a shock. It made him intensely suspicious of Birkenhead. It made him concerned that the Die Hards should not be driven out by him and that party unity should be preserved against him. He was determined to 'stand no nonsense from the Prime Minister'.[15] Even now Younger did not want to destroy the Coalition. As much as Birkenhead or Austen Chamberlain he wanted to erect an obstacle in the Labour party's way which he was not sure the Conservative party could succeed in doing by itself. He wanted the Coalition to continue until the Irish Treaty had been passed into law, the House of Lords reformed, the Geddes report given practical effect and the industrial situation improved.[1] But whereas his ocular refraction had allowed him previously to see chiefly the advantages of Coalition, it now allowed him to see chiefly its disadvantages. He knew that a growing number of M.P.s wanted to stand as Conservatives, not Coalitionists at the next election.[2] He knew that prolongation of the Coalition would 'involve a demand for more seats for the Coalition Liberals' which he did not want to provide.[3] He was acutely conscious of the view that the body of the party might 'wither away', support Die Hard candidates or even go over to the Labour party unless given a 'definite object' to work for.[4] At the end of January 1922 he gave notice to Austen Chamberlain that his support for Chamberlain as party leader was conditional on Chamberlain being prepared to 'come out as our Leader and be ready with a policy which would unite all sections of our party' in the event of a second attempt being made to rush an election.[5] On February 22, two days after Chamberlain's assertion of the continuing need for Coalition, Younger announced that Coalition would have eventually to be replaced by 'a sort of co-operation' between the parties.[6]

For Austen Chamberlain the election episode had been distressing and disagreeable. He had not wanted an election: he did not want one for a long time to come. He was a convinced Coalitionist who wanted to 'lead the Unionist party to accept merger in a new party under the lead of the present Prime Minister'.[7] The election dispute had produced 'an immense anti-Coalition reaction in the [Conservative] party'[8] and 'imminent danger of [a] large section of [the] Unionist party joining [the] Ind[ependent] Conservative group'.[9] Chamberlain had consulted Younger in the first place and accepted his advice when it was given. He was conscious, however, of the dignity and responsibility of leadership. He had no wish to see the party chairman dictating the government's policies. He wanted to discourage 'over-emphasis' which would cause division in the party. He 'd[id] not quite understand why Sir George Younger thought it necessary to make the further declaration' to constituency chairmen.[10]

Chamberlain's reaction was to emphasise by speech and correspondence the part played by the Coalition in defeating extreme
Labour policies in 1921[1] and the need to 'steady' the Conservative
party on the 'permanent issue'[2] so as to ensure that 'Conservatives'
understood 'what the effect would be upon the fortunes of their
party and ... the great causes ... in [their] keeping if we broke
up the Coalition, divided the moderate and constitutional forces
into two hostile camps and left the Labour party to draw its profit
from our differences'.[3] The object was to carry the Unionist party
beyond antiquated or insoluble issues like Free Trade, nonconformity or the House of Lords in order to establish the primacy
of 'economic, financial and industrial issues' in the politics of the
future and meet the 'challenge' presented by the Labour party
to 'the basis of our whole economic and industrial system'.[4]
Chamberlain rejected the accusation that 'the Unionist ...
[ministers were] entirely under [Lloyd George's] influence and
[had] no mind of [their] own'.[5] He believed that Conservative
'associations represented a smaller body of electors than ever
before' and that there was 'a greater difference between the[ir]
outlook ... and the young post-war Conservative and Unionist
than at any previous time'. He believed it to be his business to
establish a common feeling between most Liberals and the body
of possible Conservatives[6] and encouraged 'those (and there are
many) who value the co-operation of our Liberal supporters [to]
make their opinions known'.[7]

For this line of policy Chamberlain in one respect was well
equipped. His political training had been as a Radical. He was
twenty-three before the Home Rule split occurred in 1886.
The first twenty years of his political life had been spent as a
Liberal Unionist. Even if, by 1911, he had become extremely
conservative, he remembered – 'no one better'[8] – the difficulties
his father had had with the Conservative party and had infinite
sympathy for Coalition Liberals in the parallel situation now. It
was their business 'to bring to [the Coalition] the largest measure
of Liberal support that they can command': he was happy that they
should 'dwell on their title to the Liberal name and use some arguments and a good many phrases which are distasteful to our ears'.[9]

Nevertheless, there is an atmosphere of beleaguered gloom about
Austen Chamberlain at this time – a sense of 'vicissitudes ... in

the future' which might carry him away from those with whom he had worked earlier in his life.[1] He knew that the Geddes report would alienate those whose interests it assaulted. He received discouraging testimony about the party's attitude to House of Lords reform, unemployment, the level of trade, the development of the Empire, agriculture, the Graeco-Turkish war, India, Egypt, Ulster and even, from the proprietor of the *Daily Telegraph*, the Geddes assault on educational expenditure. In order to play his part convincingly, Chamberlain had to meet Conservative fears. In doing this he was both helped and hindered by Birkenhead.

Birkenhead was the arch-fusionist: he had flown the first kites in 1919 and been the most ardent anti-socialist propagandist in 1920. His attacks on Ca'Canny and 'the policy of organised laziness pursued by bricklayers' and a fortiori by other trades unionists, were designed to unite the forces of resistance and respectability in face of Labour which was 'the real enemy'.[2] Birkenhead had been the initiator of the election moves in December 1921: Chamberlain had prevented the election taking place. Birkenhead thought Lloyd George's capitulation had reduced the viability of fusion. He believed that Law's return to the Conservative leadership was the only thing that was likely to restore it.[3] He thought Younger's influence with Chamberlain disgraceful. He did not see that he had the chance, which Guest and Churchill supposed was there, to replace Chamberlain and provide the 'brilliant' leadership the party needed to keep it in the Coalition.[4]

Birkenhead was ill, irritable and overworked. His eyesight was bad: after a year's abstinence he was suffering from whatever was meant by 'the old trouble'.[5] If Law had been willing, Birkenhead would have wanted Chamberlain to be replaced. But Law refused to rescue the Coalition on innumerable occasions in 1921 and 1922.[6] Whatever Birkenhead may have wanted, he had to make do with Austen Chamberlain. Chamberlain and Birkenhead agreed about policy. It is far from clear that they agreed about the method to be adopted in pursuing it.

Birkenhead's rhetoric was meant to hurt. It was assertive, aggressive, taut, sharp and offensive. Chamberlain had inherited a party which was formally united: he wanted to keep it united. He did not regard his Conservative critics as enemies to be defeated.

At each point at which conflict could occur he did his best to stop
it. At each point at which he was asked to have a confrontation
he refused. He refused to call party meetings because of the tension
they would produce between Die Hards and the rest.[1] He tried
to stop Coalition supporters outside the government making
public declarations which would divide one group from the other.[2]
To anyone who wanted a showdown he returned a soft answer.[3]
He refused to have a showdown with Younger: he probably did
not know about the move to get rid of him. At Oxford on March 3
he came near to producing a Die Hard set of principles, affirming
his belief in

the throne ... parliamentary institutions ... private enterprise and
individual opinion against the socialization of the state ... equity in the
distribution of public burdens and strict maintenance of public faith
with the creditors of the state [and] a fresh guarantee of peace by an
alliance with France and ... Belgium for the defence of our common
interests against unprovoked attack.[4]

Whatever reservations they had about one another, Birkenhead
and Chamberlain worked together in the attempt to keep the
Conservative party behind the Coalition. In providing reassurance,
the House of Lords, 'Geddes', Balfour and arrangements for the
next election were the major weapons.

Defence of the House of Lords had been a major Conservative
platform at the 1910 election. Reform of the House of Lords had
been a major Conservative cause since the Parliament Act had
been passed in 1911. It was prominent in the minds of the unemployed guardians of Conservatism through the years of Coalition. As Labour became the major party of assault, it acquired
added importance as an instrument of constitutional defence.
The Coalition platform at the 1918 election had given a firm
commitment: it was a central issue whenever the National Union
met in 1920, 1921 and 1922. Salisbury, Selborne and the Die Hards
made it one of their chief points of attack.

It was, however, not only failure to reform the House of Lords
which caused conflict within the Coalition. Many Conservatives
thought the linking of Tariff Reform, Ireland and the House of
Lords had been disastrous in 1910 and 1911.[5] Any attempt to
redeem the failure was likely also to divide the two wings of the
Coalition and deepen the division between Salisbury, Selborne

and the Die Hards on the one hand and the Coalition Conservative leaders on the other. The Bryce Commission had reported in 1919. A Cabinet Committee had sat intermittently under Curzon's chairmanship. Nothing, however, had been proposed by way of legislation: it was unlikely that anything that would be proposed would be acceptable generally. One reason why Birkenhead wanted an election in early 1922 was the chance this would give to avoid the question.[1] Austen Chamberlain did not think it interested the majority of the electorate, or even the mass of the Conservative party.[2] Though it was 'absurd' to expect to settle it in the sessions that remained to the 1918 parliament,[3] Chamberlain nevertheless gave it a central place in his Glasgow speech on January 19.[4] Birkenhead mentioned it on February 1.[5] The resolutions of August 1922 were the outcome.

In keeping Conservatives united behind the Coalition, Birkenhead made use of Balfour. Balfour, of course, was a second-best: Law would have been much better. But Balfour still had his uses. He was the great Salisbury's nephew, and had been his right-hand man and provided a ready-made answer to criticisms from Hatfield. As Prime Minister, and in the impossible period immediately afterwards, his reputation had been cracked by Tariff Reform, but he had played a part in constructing both wartime Coalitions and in winning the war. He remained in office after the war and spent late 1921 and early 1922 negotiating the Washington Naval Treaty which was widely regarded as the most successful of post-war treaties for the limitation of armaments. Derby thought him the only Conservative under whom Lloyd George could take office.[6]

Balfour was a confirmed anti-socialist who believed that Socialism had made all other political issues obsolete. He could see no body of anti-socialist competence adequate to supersede the Coalition: he was prepared to support it. While still in Washington he was made the object of special public praise by Lloyd George.[7] On his return he was fêted by the Cabinet and by M.P s from both wings of the Coalition at a gathering at the Hotel Cecil.[8] At the City Carlton Club on March 7 he reiterated the need to continue the Coalition in a carefully publicised speech to which Birkenhead and Austen Chamberlain attached great importance.[9] He was eventually persuaded to go to the House of Lords[10] where the formal Conservative leader, Lansdowne – who was not a fusionist – had virtually retired from active political life and where neither Derby nor, Derby thought, 'anybody else on the [Conservative] side would accept ... Curzon ... as Unionist leader, although he was the leader of the House on behalf of the Coalition'.[1]

In attempting to restore the Coalition to its original standing, Birkenhead and Chamberlain were assisted, finally, by a series of decisions on Lloyd George's part to prefer the Coalition to any other of the directions in which he might have moved. These decisions were made in March 1922.

IX

WITHDRAWAL TO CRICCIETH, MARCH 1922

'At present the Die Hards are watching you as the old reactionaries in Europe watched Napoleon in 1814, fighting the most brilliant campaign of his whole history from a soldier's standpoint but exhausting himself and his army when both needed breathing space for a fresh start.'

Grigg to Lloyd George, March 23 1922

(i)

In 1921/22 Lloyd George was faced with a number of alternatives. He could resign from the Coalition and try to become leader of a reunited Liberal party. He could try to become leader of a constitutional anti-socialist party. He could detach himself from the Coalition in order to take the Coalition Liberals into suspended animation, offering conditional support to a successor Conservative government and hoping to be recalled once that successor had proved itself inadequate. There was nothing in his past to indicate in which direction he would move. In any direction timing was of the essence of the decision. The chief contribution made to his decision by the Die Hards, by Montagu and by Churchill was to make motion of some sort desirable, even if it was also impossible.

In making his choice Lloyd George was affected by the wishes of Coalition Liberals, by judgment about the probable future of the Conservative party, by his view of the intentions of the Asquitheans and by vague long-term calculations about the Labour party. In none of these cases was there static analysis or permanent intention: in each the possibilities varied. In each case calculation was affected by the party implications of the policy issues with which, as Prime Minister, Lloyd George had to deal. In this respect Ireland, India, Genoa, government spending, the House of Lords and Chanak had party purposes quite separate from their substantive significance.

So far as the Coalition Liberals were concerned, Lloyd George's judgment was conditioned by answers to two questions – would the Coalition Liberal ministers and their supporters certainly follow him? how likely was it that any of them would challenge him? Among Coalition Liberal ministers in 1922 there were two views about the desirability of continuing the Coalition or amalgamating with the Conservative party. Of the Liberals who were close to him, McCurdy, Churchill, Guest and Sutherland were the strongest advocates of amalgamation. The strongest criticism came from Mond, Fisher and Hilton Young among ministers, Grigg and J. T. Davies among his secretaries and Montagu among his enemies. All agreed, however, that an enormous body of Liberal opinion was waiting to be tapped and that a genuinely Liberal programme would tap it. In this respect the chief need was to keep the Liberal flag flying by keeping open escape-routes from the Conservative trap into which Lloyd George might be heading, even if in the end he did not have to take them. This was why the Conference to establish a new Coalition Liberal organisation in January was made a 'splendid' justification of the claim, anathema to many Conservatives, that the Coalition was a vehicle of Liberal principles.[1]

In the next three months Lloyd George tried to construct a position from which he could move with dignity in whichever direction he chose. This meant obtaining assurances of support from the Conservative leaders. It meant keeping open the Liberal escape-route. It meant constructing and presenting policies which could be used for either purpose. All three processes went on simultaneously up to the point in late March when he committed himself to persist with Coalition.

In relation to the Coalition Liberals Lloyd George needed, if not a policy, then a range of rhetoric to enable them to rebut the Asquithean claim that they were traitors to their principles. This Sutherland attempted to supply. Before the war Sutherland had been a civil servant in the Local Government Board and a fertile publicist, and had made himself an authority on the Land Question. He had been private secretary to Lloyd George during part of the war and had published a large amount of Coalition-Liberal propaganda and been a Whip since the war. Sutherland was a 'pusher' and a realist: to some Conservatives he was objectionable as a Liberal-on-the-make. In early 1921 he let it be known that Lloyd George had made him a Whip in order to replace Guest as Chief Whip. In March McCurdy became Chief Whip instead. Though both wanted to construct a broad-based Centre party,

F

Sutherland developed criticisms of McCurdy for pressing for an election in January 1922 and running after the Asquitheans when the right tactical approach was to make sure of the Conservative party first.[1] After his disappointment on Guest's removal, he developed an ostentatious independence of Lloyd George which became greater when he married an heiress in July 1921.[2]

In early 1922 Sutherland returned to favour alongside McCurdy as the most articulate exponent of fusion, replacing Kerr as Lloyd George's ideas man when Kerr abandoned politics for religion. His memoranda to Lloyd George in February and March were far-reaching statements of the view that the position Lloyd George should occupy in English politics was as leader of an anti-socialist party consisting of the whole of the two Liberal parties, as much of the Conservative party as would remain with him and such respectable Labour leaders as saw no immediate hope of a Labour government and disliked Direct Action. Sutherland's appointment as Chancellor of the Duchy of Lancaster in April 1922 in the wake of Montagu's resignation was a recognition as much of the fact that Lloyd George had made his decision to continue the Coalition as of any judgment of Sutherland's intrinsic merits.

Like Kerr, Sutherland assumed that 'the permanent mind of Great Britain' was represented by 'National Liberalism or a left central position'.[3] He claimed that it had no interest in the pre-war party slogans and that any major leader must appeal to the body of the English people who did not understand the subtleties of tone and slogan which interested the older party worker. He stated that Lloyd George must 'break through the bourgeoisie crust that the populace associate with Coalition Liberalism', 'assert a broad democratic basis and programme' and 'attack the extremists both in the Labour ... and in the Tory ranks'. It was necessary to counter Labour and Asquithean accusations that the government was the 'particular guardian of the ... rich and ... indifferent to the ... worker' by showing that 'it ha[d] nearly taxed the capitalist out of existence'. Macnamara's part in extending unemployment relief, Lloyd George's part in abolishing conscription and the help he gave in establishing the League of Nations would show that Asquithean claims to exclusive rights in these policies were bogus.

A kindly reference to Mr Bonar Law's restored health ... and the loyal ... work of ... Mr Chamberlain ... might not be out of place ... The people [Sutherland thought] had long perceived the Prime Minister working in the stoke hole of the Ship of State, keeping up steam against tremendous difficulties ... Their minds are ripe to accept a great proclamation from him from the bridge on the need for this same steady relentless pursuit ... of [a] National Policy ... [of] ... Peace, Disarmament, Proper Retrenchment and the Revival of Trade.[1]

These Gladstonian – or Rothermerian – slogans were designed for movement in one direction or the other. A speech at the National Liberal Club on the 21st contained most of them.[2] An interview with C. P. Scott at the same time contained the rest.[3] In the Scott interview Lloyd George promised that he would give a Liberal lead, let the Tories leave the Coalition if they did not like it and carry Wales, Scotland and a good part of Northern England against them if they fought him. Labour, he claimed, 'preferred him to Asquith': his 'sympath[y]' for the 'underdog' gave him the greatest freedom. Free Trade, Scott was assured, was one of the Coalition's principles. The 'peace policy', though 'essentially a Liberal policy ... [was] also ... the policy of the biggest and most enlightened Conservatives' of whom 'Canning, Pitt in his best day, Salisbury [and] Peel' were examples. If the new policy failed and the Coalition broke up, Lloyd George still hoped to take with him on his Liberal travels Austen Chamberlain, Birkenhead[4] and, in a brazen fantasy, Curzon to whom, on his return from America, Balfour was added as being 'practically a Liberal' and 'in foreign policy far more Liberal than Grey'.[5]

Lloyd George's reaction to Younger in January had been to abandon Birkenhead and pretend that he had never wanted an election.[6] The lesson he learnt was that Conservatives were at the parting of the ways. If their leaders did not exert the authority they were supposed to have, then either the Coalition or the Conservative party would fall apart. Lloyd George would not have minded the Conservative party falling apart if that enabled him to carry the major fragment into a new party of the Centre. But Younger had shown that much work would need to be done before Chamberlain and Birkenhead could be certain of exercising the same measure of control over a united party as Law had exercised in more favourable circumstances before he retired.

For Lloyd George this raised problems. To abandon the

Coalition on his own terms and take up a new rôle as leader of Liberal progress was one thing. To be turned out by the Conservative party was quite another. Lloyd George was prepared to consider amalgamation or continued alliance provided the Conservative leaders could lead their party. What was intolerable was not knowing at any time what they would support or how effectively their support could be given. He had wanted an election in January and allowed it to be discussed because Birkenhead convinced him that the Conservative party would accept it. The public demonstration that it would not lent weight to the Asquithean accusation that he was a prisoner of the Tories.

What Lloyd George needed, therefore, was evidence that Chamberlain and Birkenhead were in a position to resist the Die Hards and would do so even if that involved a party split. If Conservatives were always expecting Lloyd George to jump off the Coalition in a Liberal direction, the Coalition Liberals were equally afraid that the Conservative leaders would not persist in supporting Coalition if a party split seemed likely to result. Younger's intervention, what they thought of as Chamberlain's capitulation and the isolation of Birkenhead confirmed these fears. Chamberlain, it is true, reaffirmed his loyalty to the Coalition on January 19. He did so again on February 23. Birkenhead did so two days earlier. But Chamberlain was 'obsessed' with his duty to the Conservative party:[1] he might fail to stand by Lloyd George if Conservative feeling made it undesirable to do so.

February was punctuated by the Die Hard interview with Chamberlain on the reassembly of parliament and the Die Hard demonstration against the second reading of the Irish Bill which, though smaller than expected,[2] mustered sixty votes. The Conservative junior ministers decided as a body to prevent the Irish Boundary Commission claiming power to remove any substantial part of the Six Counties.[3] Between February 19 and 26 there were by-elections at Clayton, North Camberwell and Bodmin in which seats won by Conservatives in 1918 were lost to Labour in the first two cases and to Isaac Foot standing as an Asquithean in the third. After the first of these, on February 22 – the day after Austen Chamberlain had declared that the Coalition would go on until the election – Younger had made his declaration that it would have some time to come to an end.[4]

In the period immediately after January 12, the Coalition Liberals were doubtful about Austen Chamberlain's competence and suspicious of his intentions. He 'fail[ed] to realise the strength of the non-party vote'. He did not know 'the real opinion of the Conservative rank and file in the country'.[1] He had given in too easily to Younger and Fraser whose views were not reflected in the body of their party. The conflicts which divided the Conservative party were seen as the process of 'making open preparation for the demise of the Coalition'. Chamberlain was even suspected of wanting to make himself Prime Minister. It is possible that he hesitated. His speech at Glasgow on January 19, though a Coalitionist speech, said nothing about permanence. But if he thought of removing Lloyd George, he kept his thoughts to himself. It is far more likely that he moved cautiously in January because he wished to reduce conflict by avoiding confrontation.

Chamberlain's speech at Central Hall, Westminster on February 21[2] was made after a public challenge from Gretton, Birkenhead's speech on the 23rd after a public challenge from Younger. Both denied that a purely Conservative government would win an election. Both defended Coalition as the guarantee of stability in face of the threat from Labour. There was, however, a difference between them. Chamberlain established that there would be no Coupon and that there would be two party platforms at the next election. Birkenhead implied that he would leave the Conservative party if it drove the Coalition Liberals out of the Coalition.[3] He gave a warning that 'a statesman of ... world-wide reputation like Mr Lloyd George was very unlikely to submit indefinitely to the ... humiliation and criticism to which at the moment he was exposed'. From Lloyd George's point of view, neither Chamberlain nor Birkenhead went very far.

In particular they promised little hope of policy options suitable for the leader of 'constitutional progress'. They defended the Irish Treaty, gave assurances about the Boundary Commission and recalled Lloyd George's courage in the dark days in March 1918. Lloyd George was presented as the only man who could pacify Europe. Tariffs were mentioned not in terms of principle but as 'a matter of expediency'. Liberals who could join the Conservative party were encouraged to do so: those who could not were encouraged to join Lloyd George. But the policies sketched were negative if considered as contributions to 'progress'. Birkenhead praised Lloyd George as the leader of a strike-breaking government, not as a beacon of sweetness for the future. Chamberlain pointed out that Lloyd George had abandoned the Land Taxes he had imposed in 1910 once he had seen that they were ineffective. Reform of the House of Lords, 'care for the Empire and our national and imperial strength' and understanding that the Geddes report would leave 'no time for new social programmes'[1] did not amount to a platform from which a 'liberal' statesman could claim credit for his concern for 'progress'.

There is not much evidence to show why Lloyd George wrote to Austen Chamberlain on February 27[2] offering his resignation and the withdrawal of the Coalition Liberals from the Coalition. The letter was written at Lympne the day after he had met Poincaré. It is not clear whether he wrote on his own initiative or whether the letter was concerted with Birkenhead. If it was concerted the object would be to let the public know that Lloyd George's retention of office was a deliberate act of Conservative leadership. If it was written by Lloyd George without consultation, it was designed to extract from Birkenhead and Austen Chamberlain more categorical assurances about the next election than they had given so far and to forestall any recurrence of attempts by Churchill and Birkenhead to replace himself and Austen Chamberlain by a triumvirate under Derby's leadership.[3]

The impression of concerted action is strong. At the same time as Lloyd George wrote to Chamberlain Sir Burton Chadwick – one of Birkenhead's followers – was trying to produce immediate fusion.[4] Guest was trying it on Sanders, whom he approached first on February 17. Sanders told Fraser who consulted Younger and Austen Chamberlain.[5] At lunch on February 27 with Younger and Sanders, Guest claimed that if Lloyd George was abandoned by the Conservative party, 'he would certainly drift to the Left and ... [Conservatives] would find [them]selves with *all* other parties united against [them]'. Younger 'did not think the Tories would get a clear majority' by themselves, but did not commit himself to any particular line of action. It is clear, however, that the Coalitionists did not trust him. The morning after Lloyd George's letter was published, Guest called on Sanders a third time.[6]

Guest was Churchill's mouthpiece: he probably came from Birkenhead and Churchill. He came to Sanders because Sanders was a supporter of fusion[1] who resented Wilson being made Chief Whip when Talbot became Lord-Lieutenant of Ireland nearly a year before. He came to him also because, as a man with a grievance who was an 'old Tory', Sanders would have influence in the Conservative party whichever way he chose to exercise it. Guest had three objects – to find out what concessions would enable Conservatives to go on supporting the Coalition, to persuade Sanders to become Conservative Chief Whip and party chairman in place of Younger and to get assurances that, if he did so, he would withdraw support from Conservative M.P.s and candidates who did not approve of the Coalition.[2] Sanders refused to be party to removing Younger who could probably not have been removed. He suggested that Lloyd George should agree now to stand down from the leadership after the next election. He greatly annoyed Guest who, having threatened to tell Lloyd George to resign, came back next day to say that Lloyd George had 'caved in' without getting any concessions in return.[3]

By this time Lloyd George had seen Austen Chamberlain. At Lloyd George's request Chamberlain had consulted the Cabinet Conservatives[4] who all agreed that Lloyd George should stay in office. Chamberlain had shown Lloyd George, and Lloyd George had approved, the draft of a speech he had undertaken to make at the Oxford Carlton Club. This marked an advance in two respects, though Chamberlain publicly denied that an advance was intended.[5] It announced that the two wings of the Coalition would go to the election 'as a government': it announced – what only Birkenhead had said before – that the alliance between Conservatives and Coalition Liberals would continue 'in government and out of government until some question of principle [should] arise – if it does arise – which clearly separates us one from the other'.[6]

Chamberlain treated his Oxford speech as settling matters between Lloyd George and the Conservative party for the foreseeable future which he thought brighter than for some time past.[7] Its policy commitments, however, were nebulous. The chief problem anticipated in the future was resistance to Socialism. There was nothing to suggest a search for 'progress', much to suggest anxiety to appease the Die Hards. Balfour's speech to the City Carlton Club two days later added nothing except Balfour's authority. Birkenhead's description of the Die Hards as 'the salt of the Unionist party and ... higher mouthpiece of what is permanent and fundamental in ... Tory doctrine' did the reverse.[1] The letter Birkenhead drafted next day for Chamberlain's benefit, instructing Younger to circulate Balfour's speech throughout the party, was intended to be a payback for Younger's independence.[2] Montagu's forced resignation on March 9 still further reduced the government's progressive credentials.

Of all the Coalition Liberals Montagu had been closest to Asquith. Asquith had made Montagu's ministerial career: between the two of them, there was peculiar marital intimacy. It was Montagu who urged Asquith to meet criticisms of his conduct of the war by having a coup of his own in October 1915, Montagu who urged Asquith to stay put up to the point at which Balfour abandoned him in 1916, Montagu who urged him to keep Lloyd George in office and prevent the political question becoming a choice between the two of them. When Asquith fell, Montagu changed horses. Lloyd George persuaded Montagu – he may not have found it difficult – that Asquith would be to blame if he did not co-operate once the new government had been established.

Montagu was Under-Secretary for India from 1910 to 1914, entered the Cabinet in 1915 and was Minister of Munitions in the last months of the Asquith Coalition. He was not at first a member of Lloyd George's. Hankey was not allowed to make him Joint Secretary to the Cabinet in January 1917, perhaps because of his connections with McKenna.[3] He was given work on general post-war reconstruction,[4] then, in March 1917, on reconstruction in India.[5] Montagu was the first Liberal reunionist. In early 1917 he tried to stop Asquith forcing a breach with the Lloyd George Liberals. In May he was on the edge of a Reading/Guest/Churchill attempt to bring Asquith, Churchill and McKenna into the government.[6] In July he accepted the post of Minister of Reconstruction. Before he had taken it up, he accepted the India Office when Austen Chamberlain resigned over Mesopotamia. The wound to Asquith was deeper than Montagu's marriage, the rupture for the time total.[7]

In a Cabinet memorandum before there was any question of

becoming India Secretary, Montagu laid out a policy of increased democratic participation for the Indian provinces and the eventual replacement of the central government by a federation of states.[1] On taking over the India Office, he wrote another at Lloyd George's request excluding Home Rule for India or any 'precipitous' action of the sort he had suggested before.[2] Lloyd George wanted this in order to remove Curzon's and Balfour's suspicions, though it is not clear that he thought it safe to let them see it.[3] Montagu nevertheless treated it as a charter for a liberal policy, just as Addison supposed he had a similar brief for work on Reconstruction. During the discussions which preceded the 1918 election, this was confirmed by Lloyd George when Montagu received a pledge that 'the only ... man in the government' who was against his policy would, if necessary, 'be coerced'.[4]

Montagu's India policy was supported not as a demonstration of Liberal principle but because Curzon did not want a confrontation in India. He supported it in Cabinet and helped to ease its progress through both Houses of Parliament. Conservative hostility to Montagu however, was deep, partly because of his policy, partly because he was an intense Jew who made no attempt to conceal his Jewishness,[5] much more because he glossed agreed policies with explanations of his own which went beyond what Conservative ministers expected in a colleague or had approved in Cabinet.[6] In the Dyer debate in July 1920, a doctrinaire manner of force and offensiveness made many Conservatives vote against the government even though they thought its case was good.[7]

Montagu's persistent, paranoid dissatisfaction from 1918 onwards, however, had nothing to do with the reconstruction of Indian government. It arose initially from his failure to be given the posts he had wanted in 1916, from Lloyd George's refusal to allow him a prominent rôle at the Peace Conference and from a departmental determination to make the government tailor its Turkish, Greek, Egyptian, East African and Palestine policies to the susceptibilities of Indian opinion. So long as Lloyd George's position was commanding, Montagu kept criticism within limits. Like other ambitious figures of the second rank, he got little pleasure from Lloyd George's inaccessibility to anyone he did not wish to see[8] and much irritation from his failure to win demarcation disputes with Curzon and Churchill about Turkey, Egypt and East Africa. He was alarmed by Labour in 1918, thought a Capital Levy, Mines Nationalisation and sweeping social reform the only remedy and was increasingly depressed as Anti-Waste blocked the way in that direction.[1] He deplored the Liberal breach at the 1918 election and protested against the Coupon.[2] In February 1920 he failed to persuade Lloyd George to make him Viceroy (with Fisher as India Secretary): Reading – also a Liberal Jew – was Montagu's fourth choice after Austen Chamberlain, Churchill, Llewellyn Smith or the Prince of Wales as figurehead to carry out his policies.[3]

There are hints that Montagu had Asquithean sympathies as early as 1920. Fraser suspected him of voting for the Asquithean Liberal in the Cambridgeshire by-election that year.[4] The week-end of Addison's resignation he was 'not ashamed' to say in public that he was 'bitterly disappointed at the abandonment of the ... government's ... agricultural policy'.[5] He was protected by a built-in belief in Liberal catchwords and a deep-rooted desire, 'common to all men in this century outside Germany, to temper the autocratic nature of ... existing government'.[6] His Cabinet and private memoranda read like an electoral platform prepared against the need. His attacks on the Versailles Treaty because it would force 'Germany [to] throw in her lot with Bolshevism' and his demand for an increased National Debt in order to reduce taxation while running a major social programme reflect a crusading intention to lead the progressive Liberalism of the future. Montagu was involved in steady conflict with Churchill in defence of the rights of Indian settlers in the East African Highlands. In all directions he developed a self-crucifying passion in personal discussion which stimulated conflict without producing support from the Prime Minister.

Montagu's conflict with Churchill in 1921 was conflict about policy which did not reduce their expectation of a joint Liberal future.[7] Neither was loyal to Lloyd George: each sought independent ways beyond him. Churchill's manifest search for Die Hard support in early 1922, however, raised doubts. His policy declaration against equality for Indian immigrants in Kenya at a public dinner on January 27 went some way beyond any decision the Cabinet had made so far.[8] It caused widespread irritation to the government of India, to the India Office and to Montagu who was more completely in the pocket of his officials than most Coalition Liberal ministers. In February Montagu thought he had been given Wood as under-secretary without being consulted before-hand.[1] In the first week of March he discovered that Churchill had made the offer as part of the projected Birkenhead reconstruction.

When, therefore, on March 6 – five days before the Paris Conference and without Cabinet approval – Montagu published a telegram from Reading recording 'the intensity of feeling in India regarding [the] necessity for a revision of the Treaty of Sèvres',[2] he was adding one step to a ladder of discontent he had climbed in the previous three years. He claimed to have done no more than other ministers had done already and believed Lloyd George got rid of him as part of a package deal to perpetuate the Coalition.[3] It is not certain that Lloyd George knew about Churchill's offer. It is certain, as Sanders wrote, that Wood's appointment would have done 'a lot to pacify [the] Die Hards' and in combination with the other changes proposed in the Guest/Birkenhead/Churchill plot would have limited Montagu's control of Indian policy.[4] It probably made him think that he *had* to challenge Lloyd George.

The Saturday after his resignation, Montagu made a 'bitter' speech at Cambridge in which he denounced Lloyd George for capitulating to the Conservative party. It is unlikely that Lloyd George intended to resign before Montagu's speech. He could not do so once he had been pilloried as the enemy of the Liberal progress his resignation would be designed to protect. He cancelled a meeting he had arranged with Liberal ministers[5] and went off under doctor's orders to Criccieth for a fortnight's rest.

(ii)

When Lloyd George left for Criccieth he had gained nothing. There was every expectation that Conservative militancy would increase. He had no policy guarantees for the future. Whatever assurances Chamberlain had given at Oxford about co-operation at the next election had been explained away: it was unlikely that they would be repeated. Lloyd George had committed himself neither to abandon the Coalition nor to persist with it. This silence was encouraging to Conservative critics and deafening to

Coalition Liberals. It provided Northcliffe and *The Times* with a tailor-made opportunity. It gave Gladstone the chance to remind Liberals that 'the Coupon ... was a national sin ... a betrayal of Liberalism and a deliberate wreck of the Liberal party'.[1] It caused Austen Chamberlain great anxiety. The Conservatives had been 'laid out at [Lloyd George's] feet'; he did not understand why Lloyd George 'should delay in accepting the offering'.[2] On March 18 he asked him to 'declare [his] resolution to continue ... the leadership of the Coalition and ... make a suitable answer to Gladstone's provocative manifesto'.[3]

In order to establish himself as leader of a Centre party, Lloyd George needed to be sure of a sizeable body of Conservatives. He needed to have hope of attracting some of the leaders of the Labour party. He needed to be sure not only of the Coalition Liberal party but also of sizeable support from the Asquitheans. He needed a programme flexible enough to vary the details of policy to suit the character of the amalgamation.

There was no reason to expect the Labour leaders to take the initiative. Even when Henderson thought Lloyd George a more possible ally than Asquith, he doubted whether he could be trusted. Hartshorn, Walsh and McGurk, probably Thomas and perhaps Clynes at various moments made co-operative noises about what they would do if Lloyd George took the lead.[4] But they made it plain that he had to take the first step before they would be in a position to help.

In relation to the Conservative party, Lloyd George's doubts were increased by the failure of a demonstration of loyalty arranged by two Conservative Coalitionists – Goulding and Hannon – in the form of a private meeting of Conservative M.P.s in the House of Commons on March 14 at which not only Die Hards but also Pretyman, Lane Fox and other 'old Tories' prevented resolutions of loyalty being passed.[5] They were increased by Derby's[6] and Devonshire's[7] refusal to take Montagu's place, by Winterton's reluctance to accept an under-secretaryship and by Chamberlain's fear that Hoare and Ormsby-Gore would be reluctant too.[8] Lloyd George's attempts to put Baldwin in Montagu's place, like Guest's approaches to Sanders, were probably suggested by instinctive knowledge that 'old Tories' were the men to watch.[9] Chamberlain's refusal to let him do so probably did nothing to reassure him.[10]

Conservative disbelief in Lloyd George grew steadily in early March. It was sustained by the division on the Irish Treaty and by the dismissal of Montagu which, popular in itself, increased the impression of impending collapse and highlighted the fact that Lloyd George's support for Greece was unpopular among Conservatives, many of whom remained as Turcophil after the war as they had been before it. Distaste and disaffection were increased by the Goulding/Hannon meeting which, as ordinary and 'not particularly popular' back-benchers, it was 'a great impertinence' of them to have called.[1]

The force of the feeling aroused against Lloyd George, however, was counter-productive. Northcliffe's and Rothermere's attacks were never welcome to M.P.s: Beaverbrook, Wilson and Greenwood all thought they could be turned to advantage.[2] The unopposed return at the Liverpool by-election became a Coalitionist triumph.[3] At a time when an India Secretary was being looked for, Baldwin stressed the need for Conservative participation if a Coalition was necessary after the next election and pointed out that 'large numbers of Tories in the House of Commons ... never would have been there if they had not got the Lloyd George ticket in 1918'.[4] Derby's refusal to take the India Office was widely known, but Peel, who did not like the Ministry of Transport,[5] allowed himself to be promoted instead. Winterton eventually became his under-secretary, probably on stringent conditions. Montagu's defence of himself was pathetic, Curzon's answer in the House of Lords 'complete and crushing'.[6] Gandhi's arrest had been both planned and dropped while Montagu was India Secretary: he was arrested as soon as he resigned.[7] The impression was left that Allenby had not got his way over Egypt.[8] Chamberlain's postbag, which had previously been filled with denunciations of Coalition, was now supposed to be filled with letters of support.[9] Derby saw that the wind was blowing towards Lloyd George and assured Austen Chamberlain that he had never blown against him.[10] It was suddenly remembered that Long had written a letter to the Goulding/Hannon meeting strongly supporting the Coalition.[11] The Conservative Chief Whip,[12] the chairman who mishandled the meeting[13] and others were persuaded to assure Lloyd George that the meeting was not typical. At Wilson's prompting Greenwood added his impression that the atmosphere had changed.[14]

Austen Chamberlain was sure the meeting had 'no real significance as regards the Coalition or yourself'.[1] One of the wreckers explained that, far from being Die Hards, they aimed 'only at keeping the Conservative Party together and preventing a split at the present moment as ... it would be a bad thing for the Conservative Party now'.[2]

In dealing with the Liberal party Lloyd George faced the greatest difficulties of all. He was faced here with the Asquithean leaders and their confident belief that their own attractiveness would be reduced by associating with Lloyd George. He was faced by Montagu and the restlessness his departure caused among Liberals generally. He was faced by hostility from McKenna[3] and by sharpening criticism from Crewe who treated Montagu's publication of Reading's telegram as prompted 'by the manner in which No. 10 Downing Street ... conducted the system of Cabinet government'.[4] Above all, he was faced by Grey's determination to avoid all connection with him.

Between October 1922 and the end of 1924 Lloyd George's experience with the Liberal party was unhappy: he succeeded neither in establishing control nor in making a real impact. Resignation in March 1922 on an issue of principle before he had been turned out by the Conservative party might well have had a different outcome. It might have made him a more formidable threat than in 1923 to Asquithean control of a reunited party. The reunited party might not have been complete. Some Asquitheans might have joined the Conservative party if Grey had led the way. Others might have joined the Labour party.[5] But a self-moved renunciation of office on a Liberal programme might well have restored Lloyd George to the centre of the scene.

Lloyd George accepted the Labour party as a fact of life: he wanted to lead resistance to it, even while stealing some of its forces from it. A Die Hard rump on his Right would not matter. But anything more impressive would. He needed, therefore, not only to be sure of large parts of the Conservative party of which he was not sure at all. He needed also to be sure of the Coalition Liberals. He was not sure of Mond, Fisher or Hilton Young. He no longer had Montagu. He did not have Churchill.

Churchill entered parliament in 1900 as a Conservative. He became a Liberal during the Tariff Reform conflict in 1904 and was a Liberal minister from 1906 until 1915. In this period he made a succession of reputations, as an advocate of social reform, as a proponent of Home Rule, as the First Lord of the Admiralty who had the Fleet ready for war and as the strategist whose obsession with the Dardanelles helped to bring down the Liberal government in 1915. Churchill was close to Lloyd George before the war. He was Asquith's right-hand man for the first nine months of war. As renegade and offensive advocate of the policies of his new party, Churchill was distrusted by the Conservative party. Law had him removed from the Admiralty when Asquith's Coalition was formed. At first he was excluded from Lloyd George's.

Churchill changed parties at a convenient moment in 1904: he floated to power with the Liberal tide in 1906. Once established as a Liberal minister, he mastered the language and intricacies of Liberal progress. During the Cabinet conflicts about naval expenditure, he thought of returning to the Conservative party. Like Lloyd George he contemplated Coalition in 1910. Like Asquith, Haldane and Grey he was thought of in 1915 as a suitable ally for a broadened Conservative rally against the 'dangerous spirit of class bitterness' which Lloyd George would stimulate when the war was over.[1] He returned to office in 1917.

For Churchill more than for most politicians the war involved a radical reorientation. He had left the Conservative party when Free Trade was a living issue and had been a prominent member of the Liberal government whose teeth were cut on the Welsh Church, the Licensing Laws, National Insurance, Women's Suffrage, Home Rule and the Parliament Act. That government had been swept away in 1915. By the end of 1916 only Lloyd George among its leading members survived in office. From 1915 to 1917 Churchill was out of office. From 1917 to 1919 he was not in the War Cabinet. It was not until 1919, in conditions very different from the conditions of 1915, that he began once more to devote himself to the conspectus of political questions. In the next three years his mind was formed by the Russian revolution, the Labour party, his membership of the Coalition and the absence of a viable Liberal party.

Just as Churchill learnt one new language on leaving the Conservative party in 1904, so now, a man virtually without a party, he began learning another suitable to the conditions of 1920.

Between 1920 and 1922 the rhetoric of progress was abandoned, the rhetoric of resistance was announced. Many problems were dealt with without doctrinal preoccupation; in many cases no doctrine could be invoked. But in early 1922 there emerged from the Liberal Churchill who had fallen in 1915 a Churchill who could not easily be distinguished from a Tory, who had established his detestation of the Russian revolution and who identified himself with a publicly stated contempt for the policies and leaders of the Labour party which became intenser as their popularity grew greater.

More even than Lloyd George, Churchill at this time had no real party affiliation and was deeply mistrusted in both the parties to which he had belonged. He was therefore under no obligation to react to new situations in a rhetoric that was given. The centre of his political life was not a political party but an alliance of affinity, personality and disagreement with Lloyd George, Birkenhead, Beaverbrook and Guest. This group contained no diarist: its letters are inadequate. Its members did not always work with one another; one cannot speak of a working group with permanent intentions. Since, however, they not only calculated in fact but induced calculation in each other, it is reasonable to impute a high degree of calculation even when evidence is lacking. In the first half of 1921 the last three thought seriously of removing Lloyd George. In the second half they were involved in negotiating with Sinn Fein. Direct evidence of Churchill's calculation is difficult to find. It is reasonable to suggest that Churchill was preparing, even during the Irish negotiations, to dispute with Lloyd George the leadership of the Coalition Liberals and to bring into line behind a new Conservative government such Coalition Liberal ministers, M.P.s and electors as would follow him in case Lloyd George resigned.

For this he was equipped by instinct: he equipped himself better by his conduct. He was a Tory by family and early affiliation. He believed, no doubt romantically, in the people. Many of his opinions were either Tory in origin or could be made acceptable to the Conservative party: in some respects they were Die Hard. Lenin as the 'man of shame'[1] and Soviet trades unionists as 'carriers [of] disease'[2] reflected feelings held as deeply as the Duke of Northumberland's. Of all the Coalition leaders, Churchill epitomised most articulately the anti-socialist, anti-Bolshevik element in its make-up.

For this there were four reasons. First because, as Lloyd George said, even if he said it tactically, Churchill was one of the 'few real Tories left'.[1] Secondly because, as a renegade, Churchill had to work hard to re-establish his credentials. Thirdly, because his whole past had made him unpopular in the Conservative party, not least in relation to the 'concessions to Labour' which Conservatives thought they saw in 1919/20.[2] Finally, because his unpopularity showed that he needed the sympathy not just of the Cecilian part of the Conservative party or of 'industrial Conservatism' but of the Conservative party proper and the Die Hard Right. There is no direct evidence from Churchill that he thought this. There are many suggestions that this was so from those who knew him well.[3]

When Milner resigned in February 1921, Churchill became Colonial Secretary in his place. When Law resigned in March, he expected to be Leader of the House of Commons or Chancellor of the Exchequer. Lloyd George could probably not have given either post to a Liberal. He could not have given it to Churchill with whom he doubled his offence by giving him an undersecretary he did not want and for a time would not see.[4] From this point onwards Churchill's attitude to Lloyd George became critical, distant and disagreeable, expressing itself over a range of topics which began towards the beginning of 1922 to form a pattern. Over Ireland, Palestine, Germany and Egypt and over Horne's conduct of the Exchequer, he deployed distinctive criticisms in Cabinet. He led the Cabinet resistance to the Safeguarding of Industries Bill to which he had committed himself in 1918. He seems to have prepared the ground for a quarrel about Greece: in September/October he had a major confrontation about unemployment. Along with Beaverbrook and Birkenhead he tried to unseat Lloyd George and Austen Chamberlain before negotiations with de Valera began: he pressed Addison to do Lloyd George maximum damage in the negotiations which led up to his dismissal. The start of the Irish negotiations in July for a time intensified these efforts.[5] When Lloyd George put an end to the plotting by involving the plotters in negotiation, Churchill's loyalty was thinner than Birkenhead's.[6]

In 1921 Churchill was not notably reactionary. He had been reactionary about Russia and perhaps became so about India.[1] He saw East Africa as a 'white man's country' where Indian immigrants were 'mainly of a very low class of coolies' whom it would be 'revolting to every white man . . . to put on an equality with the Europeans'.[2] A British guarantee of French security as the only foundation of 'Anglo-German relations' left doors open in reactionary directions.[3] He was only a lukewarm supporter of the election proposal in January 1922: he may well have been shaken by the power shown in Conservative quarters against it. He was doubtless involved in Guest's attempts to press Birkenhead to take the lead.

In early 1922 his position hardened sharply. He claimed credit on the Coalition's behalf for the coercion which had made the Irish Treaty possible. He contrasted the 'old-fashioned' Liberalism of Grey and Asquith with the strike-breaking Coalition's capacity to deal with the industrial problems of the present.[4] At the Coalition Liberal Conference on January 20 his references to House of Lords reform were more ambiguous than in the Cabinet Paper he wrote in December.[5] He made a vigorous attack on Socialism, repeated that the socialist party was unfit to govern and reiterated the sanctity of Free Trade.[6] A week later he made his Kenya speech.[7]

In the period immediately following Lloyd George's offer of resignation at the end of February, Churchill's speeches included praise for Lloyd George and the Coalition as defences against the 'iron state regulation', 'crazy doctrines and anti-national sentiments' of Socialism 'which are contrary to the deepest instinct of the human heart'. The need to fulfil Britain's obligations in India and recognise that Irish remedies were inapplicable there was one facet of this image. The demand for the emergence from the Coalition of a 'strong, united, permanent, national party, Liberal, Progressive and Pacific in its outlook' which would give Britain 'five years of public thrift and trade recovery undisturbed by foreign war or domestic tumult' represented it in another.[8]

Churchill was in no position to remove Lloyd George from office. But, as second figure among Coalition Liberals, he was well able to destroy the group if Lloyd George tried to remove it united from the Coalition. His relevance to Lloyd George's calculations in March 1922 was that Lloyd George saw him as a rival who could not shine while he shone and therefore assumed that he could not rely on a united Liberal following. Sassoon, Beaverbrook, Sutherland and Birkenhead had no doubt that, if Lloyd George resigned, Birkenhead would insist on other Liberals being offered office in a new Coalition. They were equally certain that some, including Churchill, would accept.[1]

Though it was far from true, Lloyd George encouraged the belief that he was a free agent in relation to the Conservative party. He did this to some extent out of simple miscalculation, to some extent in order to sustain his own and others' courage; to some extent because he swallowed flattery from ignorant advisers. McCurdy told him that Younger had no following in the Conservative party, that Younger's views were not reflected in constituency associations and that Austen Chamberlain did not know what constituency Conservatives thought.[2] Lloyd George knew that the Coalition Liberal organisation scarcely existed: he was not alone in claiming – Guest, an ex-Tory, claimed this too – that the 'strength of the Tory organization ... [was] nothing like as great as [was] supposed'. McCurdy believed that about 100 Conservative M.P.s would break away if a Centre party were formed: he compounded the possibility of Conservative resistance by claiming that, 'if ... the Conservative dissentients were a powerful body, it would ... improve the position of the new Centre party ... so far as the new electorate is concerned'.[3] There is abundant evidence that in Wales, Northern England and Scotland, where the Liberal party had always been the major force, Conservative M.P.s and candidates thought Coalition the best way of stopping Labour, but there is no reason to believe that McCurdy knew as certainly as he claimed that 100 Conservatives would leave the party.

Guest, Sutherland and McCurdy were Coalitionists because they thought that, as leader of an anti-socialist amalgamation, Lloyd George would be in a strong position to liberalise the Conservative party. The Liberal critics of Coalition were critics because they no longer believed that this was so. No less than the convinced Coalitionists, Mond, Fisher and Young believed that the political division of the future would be between 'the party of organized labour ... on the left ... [and] the party of all the rest on the right'. No less than the others they wanted to ensure that the anti-socialist party was 'liberal [not] ... reactionary' in temper. So far it had been, they thought: until the last month the Liberal element had been the 'leaven in the lump'. Now, however, the position of the Coalition Liberals had become 'humiliating' and 'disagreeable'.[1] The 'reactionary elements in the Conservative party ha[d] pushed the moderate elements, with whom we were working for a common ideal, right off the stage'.[2]

In these circumstances Mond wanted Liberal reunion at once.[3] Fisher thought 'the experiment of a pure Tory government' would teach the Conservative party that it 'could not survive without the Coalition Liberals'. Young believed that 'a temporary separation' would be the quickest way of achieving 'free and voluntary reunion ... of the Liberal and Conservative parties [with] a common policy and ... plan of campaign'.[4] Fisher, and his undersecretary, Herbert Lewis, threatened to resign in January when the Geddes Committee included Education as an area of possible Economy. Fisher and Young now urged Lloyd George to resign. Mond made it clear that he would support him if he did so.

Lloyd George did not do so. In response to Beaverbrook, Greenwood, Sassoon, Sutherland, McCurdy, Chamberlain, Wilson and Horne (who visited him in Wales), he decided that he would stay with the Coalition. With Lloyd George's approval Austen Chamberlain announced in the House of Commons on March 21 that there would be a vote of confidence on April 3.[5] For the programme of the future Lloyd George chose the pacification of Europe.

Pacification of Europe had two faces. It was 'practical' in the sense that it dealt with the real problems faced by an industrial economy working at less than full capacity. It was 'liberal' because it implied resistance to the militarism of France while giving a chance, which Birkenhead had also taken,[6] to criticise Grey and Lord Robert Cecil for thinking that 'the Genoa Conference ought to be left to the League of Nations'.[7] It beat the Labour party at what the Labour leaders had made their own game. It struck the right note with the public as a whole because it dealt not with war but with peace, which Lloyd George claimed had been his objective when he helped to establish the League of Nations.[8] And it was tailored to his 'logical position' as 'the natural leader of the Industrial Conservatives, the Coalition Liberals and the Asquithean Liberals' – that is to say, of the believers in the capacity of the free economic system to provide prosperity and work without resorting to any of the remedies that might be proposed by the enemy on the doorstep.[1]

However, the point in adopting 'the pacification of Europe' was not just to perpetuate the Coalition. Lloyd George let it be known that he adopted it because it could be used to distinguish his own appeal for 'peace, appeasement [and] reconstruction' from the Die Hard doctrines of 'intervention, ascendancy and vengeance'.[2] At each important point over the previous two years he had capitulated to the Conservative party, but he still left the impression that he could square the circle between progressive options in Liberal and Labour directions and the Conservative option he had committed himself to take.[3] This problem recurred over the question of diplomatic recognition of Soviet Russia.

Non-recognition of the 'men of shame' was a prominent part of the Die Hard programme throughout 1920 and 1921. The need to restore Russia and Germany to the comity and trade of nations had become an important part of Labour and Asquithean doctrine during the same period. The object of the Genoa Conference, as Lloyd George conceived it, was to provide a European 'pact of peace [involving] an undertaking by Russia not to attack her neighbours and by Poland and Rumania not to attack Russia'. Since this could not be done without recognising Russia, Lloyd George needed maximum flexibility in this direction. The resolutions of the Cannes Conference had prepared the ground. The Cabinet had discussed them, but had not reached a decisive conclusion. It had not really discussed Genoa before Lloyd George left for Criccieth, but there was no reason to anticipate widespread disagreement.

There was, however, reason to expect objection from Churchill who 'could not remain a member of the government if *de jure* recognition were granted by this country to the Soviet government'.[4] Since 1919 non-recognition had been the most resounding of Churchill's slogans. In 1922 he was not only feared by Lloyd George as the Coalition Liberal who might destroy the Coalition Liberal party: he was feared also by Austen Chamberlain, Horne and Birkenhead as the man who might destroy the Coalition by 'resign[ing] over ... Recognition ... and join[ing] the Die Hards'.[1] This might not have been decisive by itself. It became decisive when Chamberlain was firm and clear[2] and Law let it be known that he would, if necessary, stop Lloyd George forcing the Cabinet to accept the sort of policy the Die Hards would not swallow.[3]

It took a week to show Lloyd George that he was not a free agent. At the beginning of the week 'office ... [was] not worth a struggle apart from what you can accomplish through it': he 'mean[t] to go wherever the policy of European pacification le[d] him'.[4] He threatened to resign if he was not given the opportunity he wanted and looked forward to seeing others defeated by the 'high ... taxation', 'disappointing ... trade' and 'extensive ... unemployment' any government would face over the next few years.[5] He made it clear that the Cabinet would have to choose between Churchill and himself if Churchill insisted in advance on non-recognition.[6] At the same time as Horne was brought into play with Lloyd George, Chamberlain and Birkenhead were set to stop Churchill burning his boats in a speech scheduled for Northampton on March 25. Lloyd George dropped hints about the blame he would distribute for a change of government in face of the 'desperate' trade and industrial situation. He suggested that Mond, Worthington-Evans and perhaps Baldwin be brought into discussion as well as Curzon and Horne, who, he claimed, were already committed by their presence at Cannes in January.[7] In a *Daily Chronicle* report headed 'Criccieth', of which he denied the provenance, it was announced, to Chamberlain's, Birkenhead's and Churchill's annoyance, that 'he would part with his closest political friend rather than abandon this great fundamental issue of politics'.[8]

Churchill did not resign. His speech at Northampton, though anti-Bolshevik, said nothing about Recognition.[9] Austen Chamberlain flattered him in public for his handling of the Irish question.[10] Lloyd George returned from Criccieth 'in a most reasonable mood and offered a solution which [the Cabinet] had no difficulty in accepting'.[11] The decision taken at the first Cabinet after Lloyd George's return was a statement that Britain should not act in isolation, that the Soviet government must accept the Cannes conditions before any advance was made and that, even if they did so, recognition would be 'only such official representation . . . as is necessary for the working of the extended trade facilities'.[1] These terms were 'so stiff' that Sanders did not think the Russians would accept them.[2] Both this decision and the House of Commons statement on April 3 recorded a capitulation engineered by Horne and Austen Chamberlain to the views held on this question by most of the rest of the Cabinet and an abandonment of the position Lloyd George had kept open for himself in case Churchill forced him to resign.[3] The Genoa debate and a successful vote of confidence on April 3 and 5 were the outcome.

X

UNEMPLOYMENT AND THE
LABOUR PARTY

'The truth of all this talk about revolutionary Socialism is this – the
extremist diminishes in his influence, in number and power, in the degree
that he reaches a stage of responsibility.'

> Clynes at luncheon of Imperial Commercial Association,
> January 24 1922, *The Times*, January 25

'I am a Radical, as I was, and as such am in fact as you say, very near to
the position of *one* of the Labour parties ... I detect nothing in Clynes,
whether in his speeches or his conversation, which isn't just ordinary
Radicalism really, and he is not without understanding of economics.
But I cannot see a Clynesian, Fabian, Marxian, Guild Socialist, Communist hotch-potch as a "party" of any kind – however much it may call
itself one.'

> Major Guy Dawnay to Ponsonby, February 27 [1922]

From somewhere in the first half of 1921 the Labour leaders
understood that large-scale unemployment was not likely suddenly
to disappear. From this point onwards failure to reduce unemployment became a chief facet of the attack on Lloyd George. The
decision to take up unemployment did not mean, however, that
they had a cure for it. They insisted that it would not be cured by
'a general reduction in wages with the object of securing a reduction
in prices': they wanted to increase unemployment relief even though
it meant mortgaging the future.[1] They believed, what politicians in
other parties believed also, that, while a limited remedy for unemployment might be found in the economic activity of government, the real remedy was to be found in a sane foreign policy.
Though they gave increasing prominence after April 1921 to the
belief held by many socialists that it was, they did not believe that
the villain of the unemployment situation was Capitalism. They
claimed that the Coalition was a class government. But class
solidarity was a party necessity and an electoral device: it did not
suggest a policy. Policy cohered with it, but policy depended on
analyses deployed by critics who had no wish to attack the social
structure. Unemployment was blamed on the Coalition failure

to apply liberal principles to the Peace Treaties. It was blamed on the legalised robbery of the German worker embodied in the Reparations clauses and reiterated in the Spa Agreement, the effect of which was to increase unemployment in France and Britain as France received coal Reparation from Germany.[1] It was blamed on the policy pursued by the French government of keeping Europe in a condition of instability and militaristic terror and Central Europe in a condition of economic under-development.

Though they nailed the government for its inadequacies, they had nothing to offer in its place beyond the pacification of Europe, the admission of Russia to the comity of nations[2] and resistance to French militancy towards Germany. The Labour leaders attacked Macnamara's Insurance Act of 1922 which increased benefits, because doles were degrading and State doles wasteful and unrewarding.[3] They demanded extensions of existing State, and municipality-controlled, public works in order to make use of the unemployed. There was doubtless, as Clynes claimed, 'never ... a week in the last eighteen months or more in which Labour men in the House of Commons had not brought forth some proposal or demand dealing with the unemployment problem'.[4] There is still no doubt that they did not conceive that any 'remedy' was possible for the existence of substantial, permanent, long-term unemployment except through political action to increase foreign trade.

The extensive deflation after the economic boom increased the number of unemployed, caused financial difficulty to many small unions and greatly weakened union confidence in bargaining with employers. As prices fell wages fell also. Thomas's part in destroying unified trade union action in April 1921 increased suspicion both of the government and of the Labour leaders themselves. It depressed candidates who began to believe they had stepped on a bandwagon that was not going to roll.[5] There seem to have been difficulties about money as private subscribers were hit by the slump. The slump affected union membership: it had little effect on the Labour vote which, except at Louth, remained formidable at most of the by-elections in mid-1921 and increased in importance as Anti-Waste candidates made inroads on the support of its opponents. Anti-Waste had been trumped by the autumn of

1921. But the Younger/Lloyd George conflict in early 1922 suggested a new range of possibilities, including the disruption of the Conservative party, the dissolution of the Coalition and a situation in which two, or even three, Conservative parties, two Liberal parties and Labour would be in something resembling equal competition both in the existing parliament and at a general election.[1]

In a situation of this sort the Labour leaders were of first consequence. Birkenhead from one side, Gladstone and Lord Robert Cecil from the other wanted, if possible, to involve Clynes, Thomas, Henderson, Hartshorn and Walsh in some sort of Centre party coalition if the occasion required it. Thomas was probably approached by Birkenhead: he was certainly flattered by him in public. Hartshorn, Walsh and others sent messages indirectly to Lloyd George. There is no evidence that anyone met, though some trades union leaders made a practice of calling secretly on Lloyd George. There is no evidence that Clynes was involved: his attacks on Birkenhead make it unlikely that he was. Despite Henderson's experience in 1917, Lloyd George was more attractive to many Labour leaders than Asquith was ever likely to become. If he and the Coalition Liberals had detached themselves from the Conservative party, the possibilities might have been great.

Whether they were likely to become more than possibilities would depend on the balance of power in the new House of Commons. There is no reason to suppose that most of the Labour leaders would have agreed to be involved in any sort of Conservative alliance, or could have carried the Labour party with them if they had tried to. Alliance with Lloyd George, however, was a different matter.[2] In 1922 leading members of the Labour party were contemplating possible relations between the parties after the election and attempting to establish the capacity of potential Labour ministers, even though many of them were not yet in the House of Commons.[3] They seem to have been clear that they would not enter a Coalition with the Asquithean Liberals. One possibility was to support the Asquitheans in office if the Asquitheans were the biggest party in the House of Commons. Another was to take office themselves if Labour was bigger, provided the Asquitheans agreed in advance to a four-year programme including the Capital Levy,

176

mines and railway nationalisation and State action to 'prevent . . . unemployment' by 'provid[ing] for the transfer and training of surplus labour' from depressed industries.[1] When attacked by Williams at the Labour Party Conference in June 1922, Webb rejected the idea. The Conference also rejected it. The absolute majority received by the Conservative party at the 1922 election made it irrelevant.

In 1922 Labour rhetoric abandoned none of the destructive positions the Labour party had adopted in the previous four years. But Clynes, under prodding, began to sketch the constructive rôle it would come to play. The agenda it presented for a Labour government in office included a Capital Levy, nationalisation of mines, land and railways, the cancellation of Inter-Allied Debts, the lowering of interest rates on the National Debt and a reduction in the Debt itself, closer relations with the Dominions, self-government for India, the evacuation of Egypt, Palestine and Mesopotamia, reform of the House of Lords and a general reduction in the naval, military and air forces.[2]

Some of these proposals marked off the Labour party from the Asquithean Liberals: from one point of view that is what they were intended to do. Along with differences of policy, however, there were similarities of manner and reasoning: it is difficult to think that these were not deliberate also. More even than in 1919 and 1920, Clynes presented the policies he was proposing as the self-evident conclusions of common sense, surrounding them with no attempt at intellectualisation, no suggestion of conceptual purity, but merely with the claim that everything the Labour party had in mind arose consecutively from the average opinion of the nation.

This had been an important feature of Labour technique before: the Coalition assault on the Labour party in 1921/22 made it essential. The violence of the language employed by Labour candidates and some M.P.s gave the Coalition leaders the chance to attack Labour as the enemy of sane, popular government; the 'scurrility and abuse' of their attack gave Clynes the chance to occupy a position of dignity in return. Labour policy, as its leaders presented it in 1921/22, not only reiterated its refusal to have any connection with the Communist party and its dedication to the interests of those who had given their lives and services in war: it embraced the 'truths' established by political discussion and agitation in the previous two years. The Anti-Waste campaign had been successful: it became 'wasteful' for a government to pay out unproductive doles to idle men whose productive capacities should be utilised to the full.[1] The Geddes Committee was the government's way of meeting the demand for Economy: 'the most loyal and submissive body of workmen could not save a country doomed to the bungling of ministers whose shrieks for national economy now were due to the improvident spending and reckless extravagance ... during the year after the war ended.' Poplar finance indeed, was 'Christian carefulness in comparison with the lavish spending of public money on worthless and wicked objects abroad'[2]: it was 'humbug and hypocrisy to talk about waste in education, housing and social problems when ... expenditure ... on the Army, Navy and Air Forces was ... two and a half times what it was in 1914'.[3]

Churchill and Birkenhead had accused the Labour party of being internally divided, ignorant of human nature and 'unfit to govern'. The Labour party, it was pointed out, had its differences of opinion but none as great as those that divided the parties to the Coalition. Some Labour leaders had had experience of office. They were not less competent than their predecessors: the Civil Service would serve them as smoothly as it had served everyone else.[4] Labour 'was not a detached section of the nation; it came near being the country itself'.[5] The Labour party 'represented brains as well as brawn': it had persons of all classes among its leaders.[6] It did not create class conflict: 'class politics and ... legislation [were] as old as the parliamentary system'.[7] The state of the country 'was not due to the Labour party'.[8] It could not be said of the Labour party, as it could of the Coalition, that it represented 'landowners [and] commercial and professional' interests. The Labour party did not ignore human nature, but it neither assumed that existing nature was permanent nor that any alteration to the detriment of the rich was absurd.[9] It did not suppose that it could 'bully the public'.[10] It was confident that it could convert the public to see that it wanted what Labour wanted – 'unrestricted trade, improved employment, the nationalization of ... railways and mines ... reduced taxation and better houses ... – improvements [which] could not benefit any one section [but] would be a national possession'.[11]

Clynes, in short, was the advocate of such 'change' as common sense would approve and ordinary Radicalism could stomach. There was very little in his platform that it could not stomach. Clynes took up the League of Nations and the Versailles Treaty: he did not, like Grey, sound as though he believed in the French alliance or pre-war diplomacy. Nationalisation '[could] not be assailed on any ground of patriotism ... a great country [was] humiliated' when its land was owned by private persons. National-isation, nevertheless, did not mean expropriation: Labour would not 'dispossess ... by force or take ... property without pay-ment'.[1] Labour did not intend to repudiate the National Debt[2]: it intended to reduce it and ordinary taxation along with it. The Capital Levy was not designed to destroy the middle classes. 'With Labour ... it [was] not ... a principle but a ... device to ... get the country back more speedily to conditions of pre-war finance'. Clynes could not understand why 'men associated with great businesses' did not prefer it to the 'heavy taxation', super-tax and death duties 'they were suffering at the moment'.[3] He did not conceal the existence of industrial bitterness which wage reductions far greater than price reductions had accentuated.[4] He recognised that the trades unions had been given a shaking[5] and attacked those who had given it.[6] But he did this in sorrow more than in anger. He claimed that the Labour party had never provoked, and had often resolved, industrial troubles, and he attacked 'the efforts of the Tory party, supported by most of the government's following, to smash the political organisation of the trades unions by a new act of Parliament'.[7]

Clynes did not claim for the Labour movement merits that it did not have. He recognised that there were 'extremists' in the Labour party and 'a great deal of innocent misunderstanding in the minds of workmen owing to a lack of knowledge of the elementary facts of political economy'. He agreed it was a 'mistake ... to assume ... that ... commercial ... middle-men ... were wasteful and interfering' or that there was 'a mysterious reservoir of wealth into which [workers] could thrust their hands' in order to get 'any wage [they] might desire'.[8] The Labour party, he claimed, understood that entrepreneurs were 'indispensable to trade expansion' which depended on production increasing while costs fell. Merely to reduce wages, however, 'gave no guarantee of lessened prices ... Workers could not be persuaded to make great effort for more production if they feared that thereby they would ... be out of a job'. Businessmen should no longer fear to exert their influence on foreign policy. But 'the commercial mind' must understand that it was 'an inseparable part of the working-class mind that ... the men who maintained industry when they were at work should be substantially helped by industry when they were out of a job'.[1]

These were attempts to show the commercial community that a Labour government would have time 'for every class if each ... would honestly ... seek ... the common welfare'. They mixed national patriotism, respect for monarchy, the evils of Versailles, reductions in armaments, the Covenant of the League of Nations, a united Irish Free State within the Empire, 'Alliance with All' including Russia and Germany and the restoration of full employment in a careful concoction which made Labour plausible and recognisable and the Labour leaders as fully representative of industrial society as the Coalition itself.

Since the general election was not fought against the Coalition, it is impossible to evaluate the estimates given in the course of 1922 of the probable Labour vote at the next election. Politicians of all parties, however, thought that Labour was advancing rapidly. In December 1921 Sir Malcolm Fraser used the phrase 'landslide' of what he thought a distant possibility. At one point in September 1922 Austen Chamberlain mentioned '300 or even a majority of the whole House' unless the Coalition was kept intact.[2] Henderson,[3] Wood,[4] Peel[5] and Lloyd George[6] at various times between February and October all said they expected the Labour party to have between 200 and 250 seats after an election. It was the range of fears associated with these calculations which gave the Die Hard movement the strength it displayed between January and October.

XI

THE DISAPPOINTMENT OF
AUSTEN CHAMBERLAIN

'The danger which threatens comes from Labour ... Those who think
that the Conservative or Unionist Party, standing as such and disavowing
its Liberal allies, could return with a working majority are living in a
fools paradise and, if they persist, may easily involve themselves and the
country in dangers the outcome of which it is hard to predict.'

> Austen Chamberlain to Parker Smith, October 11 1922, Austen
> Chamberlain MSS

'After all [Austen Chamberlain] is only leader in the House of Commons
but, even if he were leader of the Party, it is his first duty to try to preserve
Party unity, and to adopt a policy which he knows perfectly well will rend
us in twain without ... taking steps to ascertain that the great majority
of the Party is behind him would be in my opinion an outrage.'

> Younger to Sanders, September 25 1922

'... the reunion of the Conservative party is due to the wisdom, ability
and splendid unfailing courtesy with which you led and *controlled* your
group.'

> Long of Wraxall to Salisbury, October 24 1922

(i)

With Austen Chamberlain's announcement to the House of
Commons on March 21 that Lloyd George had decided to use
Genoa as the stake on which to claim his next period of power,
the Coalition's position was thought to have improved sharply.
By the beginning of April the Coalition, far from being about to
collapse, seemed a great deal stronger than it had been a fortnight
before. The rout of the Die Hards in the House of Commons
on April 3 and 5 and Austen Chamberlain's brilliant and even
'witty' speech at Joynson-Hicks's expense on the 5th did much to
persuade Conservative ministers that the worst was over.

Austen Chamberlain made no response to suggestions[1] that he
should take Lloyd George's place. He was not certain that he
should press for a positive policy since 'a positive policy [was] apt
to be associated with the spending of large sums of money' which
the government was 'clearly precluded' from doing.[2] He was
willing to address the Executive Committee of the National Union

whenever its members wanted him to: he refused to call a meeting of prominent Conservatives outside the government because Derby and Salvidge, who would both have to be invited, were not speaking to one another. He let it be known that he would stand no nonsense about relations with the Russians.[1] He persuaded Lloyd George to admit Crawford[2] to the Cabinet, of which he had been a member from 1916 to 1919, so as to gild the pill Conservatives would have to swallow with Sutherland's appointment to the Duchy of Lancaster once the motion of confidence was over.

Austen Chamberlain's understanding of the future was that the Labour party had destroyed Liberalism as an independent force and that Liberals would have to choose between Socialism and anti-socialist constitutionalism. He was sure that 'feeling in favour of continuing the Coalition [was] strong ... among [Conservative] members and ... [their] supporters ... in the industrial districts of the North and ... Midlands and in Scotland'.[3] He believed that 'in the course of time the moderate and Imperial-minded Liberals, with whom we have acted since the formation of the Lloyd George ministry, [might] be drawn into the Unionist Party under that name or another just as the old Conservative and Liberal Unionist parties ... became welded into the Unionist party'.[4]

At the level of diplomatic achievement Rapallo was an affront and Genoa a failure: at a political level they contained elements of success. Poincaré insisted on so hard an anti-Russian line that Lloyd George had ample scope to appear reasonable even within the limits imposed on him by the Cabinet. His pleas for the restoration of the European economy were constructive and eloquent: they created an impression of wise, pacific centrality. Lloyd George stood up to Poincaré and dissociated himself from Wrangel. His judgment that fanaticism on all sides in Eastern Europe should be stopped[5] doubtless made others besides the King ' "feel proud to be ... Englishm[e]n" '[6] at a time when Wickham Steed's attacks in *The Times* were obviously 'not those of an Englishman'.[7] Lloyd George did not 'return like Dizzy from Berlin'.[8] It is possible that Genoa 'aroused very little interest in England'.[9] The 'ascendancy of the Prime Minister ... his patience ... courage ... resourcefulness ... [and] the effect which his personality and the stability of our government' had 'in raising the prestige of Great

Britain',[1] however, provided scope for developing the confidence which the Coalition had begun to regain before he went. On his return to England he was met by the Cabinet and fêted as ceremonially as Balfour had been when he returned from Washington in February.

In the two months which followed Lloyd George's return from Genoa the Coalition faced difficulties but none that seemed likely to destroy it. The peace rhetoric continued and was spiced, on a suitable occasion, with Mazzinian 'brotherhood'.[2] The rhetoric of 'combination' and 'co-operation between parties' was enhanced. The rhetoric of Coalition took new life at a Methodist luncheon organised by Sir Kingsley Wood with the claim that Wesley, Whitfield, Lloyd George and the War Dead were responsible for the moral tone which Frenchmen found it difficult to understand in English politics and life.[3] The Budget was a success: taxation was reduced.[4] Derby continued to wobble: his wobbling was increased by a quarrel with Curzon in May. From the Board of Trade Baldwin supported Genoa, predicted an up-turn in trade and 'appealed to members of the Conservative party to maintain in office the government returned in 1918 to see the country through the difficult and trying days of the after-war period'.[5]

In Ireland the treaty was ratified. De Valera proclaimed a Republic but Collins and Griffith did not participate. The government made it plain that, if Collins and Griffith did so, a blockade would be established, the customs seized and military action taken in Dublin and the Southern ports. By June 3 Griffith had detached himself from de Valera. By the end of June it seemed that Griffith and Collins would stand firm. In the Irish debate after the assassination of Sir Henry Wilson, Churchill was very firm indeed.[6]

In these months Northcliffe first over-reached himself, then went mad and finally died soon after the parliamentary session was over. From mid-June until Chanak made him change his mind Rothermere began once more to support the government.[7] On May 16 the government was defeated in the House of Commons on a motion of Lord Robert Cecil about teachers' superannuation.[8] Fisher offered to resign. It was agreed to set up a select committee instead.[9] There were difficulties in Cabinet and parliament about the Canadian Cattle Bill over which Griffith-Boscawen and other under-secretaries thought of resigning.[1] Gilmour threatened to resign from the Whips' office when his advice was rejected about procedure in the House of Commons.[2] Baldwin did the same when Lloyd George seemed likely to defer to Derby's, Churchill's and the Lancashire cotton employers' attempt to reverse the Cabinet's decision to impose an import duty on German Fabric Gloves. Baldwin, however, won this Protectionist battle. Sir William Edge, a Coalition Liberal Whip and M.P. for Bolton, resigned instead.[3] Birkenhead showed little skill in handling the House of Lords: he did nothing about House of Lords reform,[4] which, as Lord Chancellor, it was his business to deal with. After continued prodding from Younger, Selborne and the National Union,[5] Curzon produced a scheme in July.[6] Mond, Fisher and Churchill persuaded the Cabinet to emasculate it: it seemed likely that the Cabinet would reject it.[7] On Montagu's fall Reading came to the top of the Die Hard black-list.[8] Lloyd George prepared a broadside against Indian extremists which he delivered in early August to the accompaniment of a visit by Winterton to Delhi and a proposal, which Reading disliked, to add two *British* members to the Viceroy's Council.[9] Curzon, Birkenhead, Churchill and Lloyd George all had periods of serious illness. There was extensive apprehension in the Conservative party about the exact arrangements under which an election would be fought. But there was no reason to expect the government to disintegrate at once.

Austen Chamberlain, Wilson and the others, therefore, were surprised in mid-July to receive a concerted demand from Conservative junior ministers for consultation about relations between Lloyd George, the Coalition Liberals and the Conservative party at and after the next election. This demand had nothing to do with Genoa or the Near East. It resulted from a change in the Die Hard movement which was to have great significance for the Coalition.

The Die Hards were left operating as a parliamentary group under Gretton, McNeill, Lord Hugh Cecil, Banbury, Joynson-Hicks and Cooper and in the country at large under Gretton, McNeill, Cooper, Carson, Northumberland, Maxse, Sydenham and Ampthill. A 'Conservative Party' had been established in the House of Commons against the possibility that it would eventually become the only party entitled to the name. Londonderry, Craig and, apparently Lord Esher[1] were all involved. Despite McNeill's eloquence, Lord Hugh Cecil's and Banbury's ability and the energy of Joynson-Hicks, it was viewed, however, by the great body of the Parliamentary Party as the work of men who carried little personal weight and would always be opposed to whatever was being done. Salisbury was not technically a member of any of the Die Hard bodies. He did not belong to Gretton's since it operated only in the House of Commons: he did not usually appear on Northumberland's platforms outside. Between Gretton on the one hand and Salisbury and the Association of Independent Unionist Peers on the other, there were differences of tone and manner. The only member of the Salisbury group who was close to Gretton was Selborne's son, Lord Wolmer, who did not think much of him. Gretton was solemn, unsubtle and serious-minded and was vain with the ultimate vanity of believing that he alone was subtle enough to handle the difficulties with which the Conservative party was confronted. Under his leadership the Die Hards did not improve. There were between fifty and sixty of them in the House of Commons[2] but they were not effective. In the Genoa and confidence divisions on April 3 and 5, the turn-out was unimpressive.[3] So inadequate were Die Hards that ministers were encouraged by their weakness and supposed – Birkenhead in particular – that they did not matter.

In late June and early July three events transformed the situation. The first was the assassination of Field-Marshal Sir Henry Wilson by an Irish Republican. Wilson was an Ascendancy Irishman: after a long career as a political soldier he had been picked up by Lloyd George in 1917 as makeweight to Sir William Robertson whom he replaced as C.I.G.S. in early 1918. At the Peace Conference Wilson opposed the creation of the League of Nations. He disliked Lloyd George's dependence on Greece. He was an enthusiastic interventionist in Russia and an advocate of coercion in Ireland. When Lloyd George began negotiating with de Valera in mid-1921, Wilson refused to be present at 'meetings with murderers'. In February 1922 he retired from the army and, at Craig's suggestion, entered the House of Commons as Unionist M.P. for North Down.

From his maiden speech in the week of Montagu's resignation

Wilson stood out as a well-informed critic of Lloyd George, an irreconcilable enemy of Sinn Fein and a formidable accession of strength to the Die Hards, some of whom thought him a possible leader in place of Gretton.[1] During widely publicised visits to Ulster at Craig's request in March and April, he acted as military adviser to the Northern Ireland Cabinet and made speeches attacking Lloyd George for producing chaos and murder in the South.[2] His visit 'created confidence among Loyalists' who thought it showed that Ulster 'meant business'.[3] It was followed by similar speeches in England and a measure of support from the Northcliffe press.[4] His assassination on June 22 was not of first consequence in itself, but on June 26 it produced a vote to reduce the salary of the Chief Secretary for Ireland, Sir Hamar Greenwood, who had not previously been the object of Die Hard hostility. There was no doubt that the vote would be carried. The Coalition ministers voted for it as did most Coalition Liberals and many Conservatives. The Labour party abstained. Out of an anti-Coalition vote of 76 nearly 70 were Conservative M.P.s for non-Irish constituencies, including some who had not previously voted against the government.

The second event was a glaring Honours List and a vote on July 2 in which 242 M.P.s supported a demand for all-party control of the system and an all-party committee to investigate it. Five under-secretaries[5] threatened to resign if it was not met. Salisbury promised to 'refuse to let any legislation through' the Lords until it was. Since it implied criticism of Lloyd George's financial methods, in which some Conservatives were involved as well, the Cabinet took so long to make up its mind that it gained no credit by eventually agreeing.[6]

The third event was that Banbury and others took the leadership of the Die Hard movement out of Gretton's hands and placed it in Salisbury's.[7] It was placed in Salisbury's because Gretton would not co-operate with Salisbury and because Salisbury carried more weight, was more widely experienced and had more effective tone. Even Salisbury was not regarded as a man who could construct a government.[8] But Salisbury was no less willing than Gretton to put up 'Conservative' candidates against Coalitionists whenever the general election might take place.[9] His assumption of the leadership of the 'whole Conservative

and Unionist party' on July 14[1] promised a formidable extension of activity in that direction and marked the most significant
step the Die Hards had taken toward political respectability.

It was in these circumstances that Younger, Derby and the
Chief Whip separately raised the question Chamberlain intended
to leave until after the election – whether, in the event of a Conservative majority at an election, they would be able to have a
Conservative Prime Minister if they wanted to.[2] The discussion
that went on between July 19 and the end of the session in August
was discussion between Conservative members of the government.
Apart from Younger, back-bench M.P.s were not involved: nor,
apart from Derby, were peers outside the government. The
question of abandoning the Coalition was not raised. Assuming
that the Coalition would go on in the immediate future, the
questions were, in what way should an election be conducted?
what should Conservative ministers say about the future of the
Coalition? and whether, in the event of the Conservative majority
at an election in 1923, there should be a Conservative Prime
Minister afterwards.

When Chamberlain met the junior Conservative ministers on
July 19,[3] he was told that, if decisions were not taken soon, 'we
should lose many seats ... the Coalition Liberals would lose still
more and ... many of the Conservatives ... returned would not
support a Liberal Prime Minister'.[4] He was told that, while
nothing should be done to destroy the alliance with the Coalition
Liberals, Lloyd George was so unpopular in London, the Home
Counties, the South, the South-West, the Midlands, Yorkshire
and Liverpool (despite Salvidge), that it was essential to have an
understanding before the election that he would stand down from
being Prime Minister after it. He was told finally that an understanding of this sort was necessary if relations were to be restored
with the Die Hards, whose control of constituency associations
was said to be great and growing. Chamberlain left the impression
that Lloyd George would be willing to give an undertaking. He
promised to ask Conservative members of the Cabinet whether
they agreed.[5] Ten days later he told a second meeting that Lloyd
George agreed, but that 'the Conservative members of the Cabinet
– especially Balfour – did not look kindly on the idea at all'.[6]

This was supposed in Chamberlain's view to 'settle ... the

matter' until the autumn.[1] The junior ministers felt, however, that a mere dictate was not enough and that immediate decisions were needed if Salisbury-backed candidates were not to be adopted against sitting Conservative Coalitionists during the parliamentary recess. Wilson, therefore, insisted on a meeting of all Conservative ministers, which was arranged for August 3. At a meeting of under-secretaries on August 2, Sanders was given authority to speak on their behalf.

At the meeting on August 3 the junior ministers had what they thought a 'silly speech' from Balfour about loyalty and another from Austen Chamberlain in favour of leaving until the holidays were over the decision about the form of approach to be adopted at the election. This gathering received from Birkenhead a 'harangue' about the need to follow the leaders who knew the party's best interests, in the course of which he claimed that the best electioneer in the business was his brother Harold whose advice coincided with his own.[2] Some ministers thought of walking out. Many decided that, whatever else might happen, Birkenhead should never lead the Conservative party and must never be Prime Minister. Criticism of Birkenhead's morals and what is alleged to have been his drunkenness had been common form for many years before.[3] It was from this point that he joined Lloyd George as a major target. Though Sanders pressed for a decision, the meeting ended in annoyed recognition that nothing would be done until parliament reassembled in October. Some ministers went away determined to explain, if asked in their constituencies, that they wanted a Conservative Prime Minister after the election but undecided what to say about the exact procedure to be followed in order to get one.[4]

When the parliamentary session ended in August, therefore, most Conservative junior ministers were concerned chiefly to ensure that the Conservative party should go to the election in one piece. They were not insisting on a purely Conservative government even in the event of an absolute Conservative majority in the new House of Commons. There was no desire to reject the alliance with the Coalition Liberals. They were as much concerned as Austen Chamberlain with that broad range of anti-socialist Liberal opinion which the Coalition had secured for them. But there were now two Conservative parties as well as two Liberal parties. They knew that division would continue so long as Conservatives were expected to be committed in advance to Lloyd George being Prime Minister after the election.

Yet on September 17 the Cabinet decided to fight the next election as a government. On October 19 Lloyd George ceased to be Prime Minister: he took with him out of office not only all the Coalition Liberals but five of the six major Conservatives in his Cabinet, constructing in the process a Cave of an intellectual and political capability greater than that possessed by the Peelites three-quarters of a century before. The essence of the politics of these months is that the second rank of Conservative leaders tried their judgment against Austen Chamberlain and Birkenhead and won, that Salisbury's threats and Salisbury's handling of the Die Hards kept the Die Hards and the body of the Conservative party together and that Lloyd George's success with the Coalition ministers divided the Conservative party not at the Die Hard intersection where division had been expected but at the inter- section between Conservative Coalition ministers on the one hand and the rest of the party on the other. When followed by Law's victory at the election, this meant that the old Conservative party was the most formidable electoral force in the country and the leader in the race to resist Labour. And the fact that division occurred where it did prevented Die Hards standing against official Conservatives which, if they had done so, would almost certainly have prevented the Conservative party winning. Had it lost, it is difficult to know what the outcome would have been. The fact that throughout 1923 the Conservative party continued to act as a united party, whatever the divisions among the leaders, was of major significance for the future and the source of the power exercised by Salisbury, Derby, Curzon and others in the year that followed the downfall of Lloyd George.

(ii)

When Lloyd George decided to stay with the Coalition in March, there was no suggestion of an immediate election. The Coalitionist view was that the Coalition should fight the next election as a government, but in March there was no chance that the Conserva- tive party would agree to do so. Lloyd George was at the peak of his unpopularity among Conservatives: he was extremely unpopular elsewhere. The attacks he suffered in early 1922, however, to some extent rebounded. On returning from Genoa he was in a stronger position than at any time since the previous December. He did not think of an election then, but he had to think of one before the end of 1923. By September he had only the most limited room for manoeuvre: 1923 was unlikely to provide a better opportunity than any there had been so far. The Budget Horne had introduced in May had been highly successful but there would be little scope for reducing taxation in 1923: whatever reduction there was, would do little to pacify the critics of taxation policy. The Coalition had nothing to suggest about unemployment: in the absence of a *triumph* at Genoa, there was nothing of relevance to expect. House of Lords reform and the private member's Trades Union Bill[1] were unlikely to increase harmony.[2] The November meeting of the National Union was likely to be as difficult to manage as the Liverpool meeting a year before. Law knew, and told Lloyd George, that he could break the Coalition if he chose to: he seems to have doubted whether it was possible, or desirable, to save it. A week after his defeat at Baldwin's hands over German Fabric Gloves, Derby spent a week in Lancashire where he found Salisbury more popular than Lloyd George.[3] Derby had no reason to be pleased that Salvidge had replaced him as the most influential Liverpool Coalitionist. At the beginning of September he decided that Lloyd George must be removed.[4] Most important of all in understanding the decision to hold an election was the collapse of Lloyd George's Greek policy in the last week of August.

The policy of making Greece Britain's main ally in the Near East began during the war in face of the need to deal with Turkey: it persisted afterwards as a contribution to stabilising the Near East once the Turkish Empire had been dismantled. Whatever the significance of the Greek policy in the Balkan context, the support given by Lloyd George to the Greek government throughout the post-war period was a facet of the belief that Britain needed a major ally if her power in the Near East was to be effective. Despite persistent criticism from Turcophil Conservatives, it had become the policy of the Coalition. In the course of 1922 Lloyd George, Curzon and Balfour all reiterated their support. On August 3 Lloyd George paid tribute to the military prowess of the Greeks. Their headlong retreat before Mustafa Kemal in late August cast a peculiar light upon his competence.

It was, however, not the collapse of this policy that brought Lloyd George's government to an end. If Lloyd George had accepted defeat, or brushed it under the table, he would probably not have been removed from office. What brought his government to an end was that he treated the Greek defeat as a challenge and carried most of the Cabinet with him. In the three weeks following the Greek retreat, he not only pressed the Greeks to fight back, but made it clear that any further Turkish advances would be resisted. It was this counter-attack and the advantage Lloyd George attempted to snatch from defeat which produced the movement against him at the beginning of October.

The substantive foreign policy decisions were made on policy grounds, not on grounds of electoral calculation. They were made because they needed to be made if the policy which Turkish force had undermined was not to be destroyed. From the point at which it seemed possible that Britain would be involved in war, the policy came to have a domestic political function. The appeal to the Dominions which Churchill and Lloyd George drafted on September 15 certainly had. The decision of September 17 to hold an early election was a consequence.

In the electoral context the significance of the policy was five-fold. It involved the adoption of an issue – 'keep[ing] the Turk out of Europe' – on which it was believed that 'the country would be behind us'.[1] It was a 'Gladstonian policy' – support for Greece – on which, when Liberal claims needed to be raised, Lloyd George could claim to be 'the only Liberal left'.[2] It was, however, not just a defence of Greece against Turkey but a step necessary to maintaining freedom of access to the Straits and handing the Straits over to the League of Nations.[3] It was a question on which, contrary to his normal sympathies, Churchill was as heavily committed as Lloyd George, on which, indeed, he had taken a lead and which he could not use, as he still threatened to use Russian recognition, as a ground for challenging Lloyd George.[4] It was an issue finally on which, while being central to Lloyd George's Liberalism, Lloyd George had with him the leading Conservative Coalitionists. Around September 15 and in the first week of October it seemed possible that Britain would be fighting a major Turkish war. By October 11 the absence of Dominions' support put an end to the immediate crisis. The impact it left was felt through the decision, taken in mid-stream, to hold an election soon in order to make it a leading issue – which became converted, once the issue was dead, into a decision to hold an election without that sort of leading issue.

Chamberlain's speeches to the National Union in February and to the Oxford Carlton Club in March had been taken to imply 'that the party would go to the next General Election, when it came, under its own leaders, on a programme laid down by its leaders and issued over the signature of those leaders only, without prejudice ... to subsequent co-operation ... with any other party or group whose policy was consonant with our own'.[1] These speeches were taken to imply a general permission for Conservatives to stand as Conservatives pure and simple.[2] By September nearly two hundred[3] had told their constituents that they would do so. The feelings these decisions reflected were thought to be more widespread than the decisions themselves. At the beginning of September Wilson took soundings in various parts of the country. These convinced him that the questions Chamberlain had deferred in August should be faced before the National Union meeting in November so as to avoid the danger, in the event of a general election being sprung suddenly, 'of the majority of [Chamberlain's] followers not following but, under the influence of their associations, finding themselves forced into a position which [would] leave [him] as leader of the party in a position in which none of [his] friends and ... colleagues would wish ... or intend [him] to be'.[4] On September 16 Younger told Chamberlain to make Lloyd George hand over the Prime Ministership at once.[5]

The decision to fight an early election was taken at Chequers next day. Chamberlain reported it to only a limited group outside the Cabinet. When Younger, Wilson, Sanders and Fraser were told, their reactions were identical. Younger – at home in Scotland – was 'appalled' at the prospect of going 'again as a government with Lloyd George at our head'.[6] Sanders believed the 'procedure would lead to great resentment among many members of the party besides the Die Hards'.[7] Wilson – like Younger, in Scotland – thought it would be 'very disturb[ing] ... when made public to the Conservative Associations' and would 'mean a definite [party] split' which would produce a situation in which 'many of [his] best friends . . . [would] not be able loyally to follow [Chamberlain] in the course [he] propose[d]'.[1] Younger 'ha[d] lost all confidence both in the government and in the lot who represent us in the Cabinet'[2]: he went to London to see Fraser who had already seen Law.[3] Sanders thought of a mass resignation and suggested a meeting of the Council of the National Union before a final decision was taken.[4] Wilson, having written one letter the day he received Chamberlain's, sent another next day to ask him to keep the decision secret until all ministers had been informed and party dignitaries consulted:[5] he insisted that Sanders, Younger, Fraser and himself do nothing without consulting each other.[6] Though they were scattered – only Fraser was in London – these four thereafter acted together.

It was not at this time clear whether the Cabinet intended to have an election before the annual meeting of the National Union already scheduled for November 15. Either way, November 15 became a crucial date. The immediate object of Fraser, Younger, Sanders and Wilson was to avoid the resentment they expected in the party if a Cabinet decision to hold it before November 15 prevented the National Union expressing an opinion. Younger saw Chamberlain on September 26. He thought they reached agreement which Horne, met casually, welcomed, that no final decision would be taken about an election until all the Unionist ministers had been consulted and the National Union or a special conference called to discuss it.[7] By October 4 Wilson – who had not seen Austen Chamberlain before because both had been out of London – believed that Chamberlain, while backing down on a special conference, had ruled out the idea of an election before the National Union had had a chance to meet, and would in any case consult all the Unionist ministers before any further decision was made.

To Birkenhead and the Coalition ministers this was a direct threat to the Coalition. One reaction was to point out that, if Lloyd George was removed, Churchill and the Coalition Liberals would join Asquith.[8] Another was to suggest that Derby, Balfour or even Law might become Prime Minister with Lloyd George as Lord President of the Council.[9]

Neither Law nor Derby would play the rôles they had been

given. At dinner in Churchill's house on October 10 it was decided that an election should take place as soon as the Turkish situation made it possible.[1] This decision, made by Austen Chamberlain, Birkenhead, Horne, Worthington-Evans and Curzon for the Conservative party, was made in the shadow of the truce in the Near East and in the knowledge that Law's critical letter to *The Times* had marked his re-emergence as a public figure.[2] After Austen Chamberlain's assurances, it was so objectionable to the Younger/Wilson group that it destroyed their confidence in his leadership. They did not actually resign. But Wilson, who had been present in Churchill's house, consulted Law[3] and then told Chamberlain in writing that he would do so if the 'government ... [went] to a general election as a government and our party [was] asked to support the Coalition as it exists today without any opportunity being given by its leaders of expressing its opinion'.[4] Younger said much the same in person.[5]

(iii)

The Coalition was brought down in the eight days which followed. It was brought down by Chamberlain's, Birkenhead's and Balfour's determination to push their critics into a corner and by the refusal of under-secretaries, M.P.s and leading Conservatives to be pushed. This refusal manifested itself in the disparate and at first imperfect working of about six groups whose members all feared that an election in which Salisbury ran Die Hard candidates of his own would produce a chronic party split and intensify the hostility to the Coalition already felt by a wide range of constituency Conservatives. Though some – Wood and Ormsby-Gore are examples – had no predisposition in favour of Coalition and Wood at one stage thought it should end,[6] no one outside the Gretton/Salisbury group was committed to destroying it. Even at this stage most non-Die Hard Conservatives would have found it possible to say that they would join, or support, a Coalition government after an election provided that did not involve advance commitment to Lloyd George as Prime Minister.

Not all M.P.s were active: those who were held varying opinions. There was a Coalitionist group under Sir William Bull. There was Lord Long of Wraxall, whose private secretary Bull had been when Long was an M.P. There was Sir Samuel Hoare. There were what were sometimes known as 'Old Tory' back-benchers of whom Lane Fox, Fitzroy and Pretyman had been consistent supporters of Coalition even when their preference lay elsewhere. There was the group of party functionaries around Younger. There was the Chairman of the Executive Committee of the National Union – Sir Alexander Leith. There were 'two or three' M.P.s, on whose behalf Lord Eustace Percy could not 'pretend to speak', who prompted Salisbury to call a meeting of M.P.s and peers to discuss the situation on October 17.[1] There were the junior ministers and under-secretaries for whom Wood and Sanders were chief spokesmen until Baldwin became so at the latest stage. There were two dissident Cabinet peers – Peel and Curzon – of whom only Curzon expressed effective, if conflicting, opinions. There were the dissident House of Commons ministers – Griffith-Boscawen and Baldwin whose rôle was of first consequence. There was Derby, whose judgment of the situation and accumulated resentments about France, Chanak, Fabric Gloves and Salvidge's promotion as Coalition adviser, made him refuse to rescue Lloyd George.[2] And there was Law and his earpieces, Davidson and Beaverbrook. What happened in these eight days was that resolute action on the part of Chamberlain and Birkenhead provoked resistance among a large number of M.P.s who would have been prepared to support the Coalition provided there was no permanent commitment to Lloyd George as Prime Minister, and that resolute action on the part of Baldwin, Hoare, Amery, Davidson, Sanders and Younger persuaded Law that a majority of reputable Conservatives wished him to help them reject the advice of their official leaders.

The day Chamberlain received Wilson's threat to resign,[3] he had a memorandum from Long summarising the views of the Bull group who had met a couple of days before at Brown's Hotel. In 1920 Long had favoured fusion. In 1921 he had retired from office because of a serious, and as it turned out eventually fatal, illness. As a contender for the leadership in 1911 and a man of great personal standing, he had given Austen Chamberlain much advice during 1922, making it his business to ensure that Chamberlain understood the fears and feelings of the party. His support for the Coalition did not stop him attaching importance to party unity: his regard for Lloyd George's services in the past did not make him reject the idea that Lloyd George might stand down now. In March he suggested that Lloyd George should do so.[1] In early October he made it his business to discover on what basis, if any, the Coalition could be saved with united Conservative support.

Bull's meeting was attended by a dozen or so 'men – representative in their character, of good position in the House of Commons' and 'having no sympathy whatever with the Die Hard movement' who, far from wanting to end the Coalition, approached Long because he shared their view that it should continue: Joynson-Hicks's presence reflected the anxiety they felt to be in touch with the Die Hards. The meeting commissioned Long to talk to Salisbury. He also talked to Gretton and Law before sending Younger – for Chamberlain's information – an account of the conclusion to which the group had come. This was that the Coalition could be saved and party unity preserved only if Lloyd George ceased at once to be Prime Minister.

It is [wrote Long] an awful situation but it seems to me that the course indicated in the letter I wrote on behalf of a great many of our most loyal and moderate men is the only one ... I deplore the necessity for approaching the Prime Minister, as it is suggested that we should do, but I can see no other possible course.[2]

Austen Chamberlain knew that advice of this sort on this sort of question was both respectable and dangerous: he knew that he had to be cautious as well as firm. He knew that similar views were being propagated through the National Union. Resignation was in his mind already.[3] He reacted to Long's memorandum and the Wilson/Younger threats of resignation by threatening to resign himself: he made it clear that, if the party insisted on getting rid of Lloyd George against its leaders' advice, the Coalition would have to be replaced by a purely Conservative government which none of the leaders would join.[4] When Long's memorandum arrived, Chamberlain was writing a speech: he acknowledged it briefly and asked Birkenhead to make sure that Lloyd George did not announce an election when he spoke at Manchester on Saturday.[5] In speaking at Birmingham next day Chamberlain claimed that the Cabinet intended to save Europe from the Turk, the Straits for free navigation and Constantinople from the fate of Smyrna: he repeated his well-known plea to continue the union against Labour as the 'common foe'.[1]

On Saturday Lloyd George re-told the Chanak story which Chamberlain had told the day before. He defended his Liberalism against Gladstone, his understanding of Anglo-French co-operation against Poincaré and the sort of diplomacy he had been conducting against the 'old diplomacy' of Asquith and Grey. He claimed that he had never wanted to become, or to remain, Prime Minister. Welcoming 'the freedom' he might soon receive, he left it uncertain whether he intended 'retirement, service under Balfour or a straight fight for the Premiership'.[2] He left 're-calcitrant Tories'[3] a promise that he would, if removed from office,

watch many things ... I shall watch for instance to see how we are to forgive Germany all the reparations and yet make France love us more than ever. I shall watch how we are to pay the United States of America all that we owe her, forgive every other country everything they owe us, have a better Army and Navy and Air Force; have more houses for everybody whilst at the same time the rents are not to be economic; strengthen your educational system, give more to the unemployed and yet make the taxation of this country lighter and lighter.

I shall watch the men who say that you ought never to subordinate principles to national unity, men who believe in denominational education working with those who think it is an abomination, men who believe in a State Church as essential to the national recognition of religion and others who think it is putting the faith of Christ into bondage, men who believe in Tariff Reform as essential to national prosperity and those who believe that Free Trade is our only guarantee working together without post-poning, without subordinating, without reconciling ... It will be an interesting experiment to see others trying it. That is one of the joys which I have in store for me.[4]

In the wake of the decision of October 10 Birkenhead had decided to hold a dinner in Churchill's house on October 15, the dinner being held there because Churchill was sick. Lloyd George, Curzon, Churchill, Birkenhead and Austen Chamberlain were to attend. It is not certain what significance it was supposed to have when it was arranged: it became a landmark. When Wilson threatened to resign, he and his predecessor as Chief Whip – Fitzalan of Derwent, the Lord-Lieutenant of Ireland – were invited as well.[5] The dinner on Sunday the 15th, and the meeting of ministers scheduled for Monday the 16th, became the next focuses of activity.

Curzon refused to attend the dinner because Lloyd George's Manchester speech was both anti-Turkish and anti-French. Lloyd George and Churchill were present as Coalition Liberals; Fitzalan, Austen Chamberlain, Birkenhead and Wilson were present as Coalition Conservatives.[1] Discussion started from the assumption that a general election would be held soon and that it was necessary to find ways of persuading Conservative M.P.s to accept the accomplished fact. It was decided to call them to a meeting at the Carlton Club on October 19 when they would be asked[2] to agree that Conservatives should fight the election in support of the Coalition – on the understanding that the identity of the Prime Minister and the party complexion of the Cabinet would be left for discussion at a party meeting after the election results were known.

Despite his démarche to Chamberlain at the beginning of the week, Wilson wanted to keep the Coalition together. Like Long,[3] he wanted to be sure that it stayed united even after Lloyd George had left.[4] He supported the idea of a meeting of the parliamentary party and perhaps accepted it as a substitute for the meeting of the National Union, but it is clear that he was unhappy.[5] The choice of a date before November 15 suggests a deliberate decision to by-pass the National Union – a suggestion which is increased by the brisk treatment given its chairman by Austen Chamberlain when he approached him a couple of days later. Chamberlain and Birkenhead almost certainly believed that a meeting of Conservative M.P.s in the uninformed condition they would be in in the middle of the parliamentary recess would be more likely than the National Union to support the official leadership provided the leadership seemed as firm and reasonable as Austen Chamberlain thought he could make it. If the meeting on October 19 had been held four days earlier, Chamberlain and Birkenhead might very well have won.[6] Three sets of events in the four days following the Churchill dinner ensured that they were defeated.

Of these the least important was the decision taken by the Convention of the National Constitutional Association – the old National party – to co-operate with Salisbury in ending the Coalition.[7] Next in order of importance was the attempt made by Sir Alexander Leith to establish the National Union's right to express an opinion. Leith had been chairman of the Executive

Committee of the National Union for about five months. His first act as chairman was to agree that the Coalition should continue and then to object when Chamberlain made a speech which said so.[1] For most of this time he persuaded Chamberlain that he was a loyal supporter, though the Die Hards regarded him as a friend[2] and Salvidge, who really was a Coalitionist, thought him double-faced and told Chamberlain so.[3] If the normal meeting of the National Union has been held on November 15 with no election in between, Leith would have presided. When he asked Austen Chamberlain for a 'round table' discussion between Younger and Central Office officials on the one hand and Conservative Cabinet ministers on the other to provide guidance about the handling of the Conference, Chamberlain refused to see him until after the Carlton Club meeting was over.[4] On the 18th, in retaliation, Leith persuaded the Executive Committee to demand that Younger be empowered to call an immediate conference of the National Union which was objectionable to ministers because they were far from certain that they could control it as effectively as they had controlled it at Liverpool the year before.[5] Leith's resolution, conveyed in a sharp letter from Younger, made Austen Chamberlain offer to resign the party leadership.[6] If the Carlton Club meeting had accepted Chamberlain's advice, the National Union might still have withdrawn support from the Coalition. The National Union's resentment on October 18 undoubtedly damaged Chamberlain both at the immediate point of decision in the Carlton Club and during the unemployment he suffered in the two years following.

The second attempt to influence Chamberlain was made by the Conservative junior ministers. On hearing of the Cabinet's decision on October 10, Wilson summoned them to meet Austen Chamberlain at five o'clock on Monday the 16th.[7] At Chamberlain's insistence Cabinet Ministers were invited as well. At lunch with Wilson, Lloyd-Graeme and others on the 13th, Amery suggested that the junior ministers should meet separately beforehand and asked them all to lunch at the Metropole Hotel on the day of Wilson's meeting.[8] Though Amery had seen Law that morning, he had got nothing out of him beyond a general pessimism about Lloyd George's future. He knew, because Baldwin had told him, that Baldwin and three other ministers were thinking of resigning.[9]

When lunch was over, Amery suggested a formula to allow the two parties to go to the election separately while 'leaving the terms of the Coalition to be settled by the results of the election'. This was thought vague. It was replaced by another to the effect that 'the Unionist Party, while welcoming the co-operation ... of any party with which it may be in substantial agreement ... shall go to the country as an independent party and ... the leader of the Unionist Party shall be prepared to ... form ... a government if the Unionist Party after the election should be the largest party in the House of Commons'.[1]

At the meeting of ministers that evening Austen Chamberlain made his customary plea for unity and proposed that the government should go to the election as a Coalition, with ministers, M.P.s and candidates standing individually as 'Conservatives or Liberals without a Coalition label and leaving the question of the reconstruction of the government quite vague'. Amery, speaking with more vigour than sense,[2] then explained what had been decided at lunch-time. This made Chamberlain ask angrily 'if this was an ultimatum which [the junior ministers] had decided upon before even learning what he had to recommend'. Pollock, Gibbs and Scott explained that 'not only was that not meant but that [they] unreservedly accepted [his] solution'.[3] Birkenhead assured the meeting that there would almost certainly be a new Prime Minister after the election, but some of the junior ministers so much disliked Chamberlain's formula that they met again next morning in Wilson's room at the Treasury.[4] At this meeting they were joined by Baldwin and Griffith-Boscawen.

Griffith-Boscawen became an M.P. in 1892: in his earliest years in the House of Commons he made a corner for himself as a parliamentary Churchman. He was Hicks-Beach's private secretary from 1895 to 1900 and a member of the London County Council from 1900 to 1913. He was part of the Bathurst/Turnor group before the war with a special interest in working-class housing.[5] He was conscious, however, that he did not belong to the territorial aristocracy and was a Tariff Reformer for whom Joseph Chamberlain represented a way through the Conservative party's aristocratic sound-barrier.[6] He had become a junior minister in 1916 and had supported Welsh Church Disestablishment. On succeeding Lee as Minister of Agriculture in 1921, he lost his seat as a result of Beaverbrook's Canadian Cattle campaign. He had had great difficulty since then explaining why the government had reversed its agricultural policy. He was nervous about the electoral situation in general and, probably, about his personal situation in particular. He had come near to resigning over the Canadian Cattle question in April. He disliked Lloyd George's Greek policy, supported the 'genuine Conservative tradition' of reasonable understanding with the Turks and was upset by the prospect of war at the beginning of October.[1] He had had difficulty, but some success, with plans for agricultural relief in the Budget but had been under heavy pressure from the National Farmers' Union to fulfil promises which the government had made over the previous two years. He had seen agriculture shunted out of the way by the Turkish question and had appealed to Lloyd George and Austen Chamberlain for help in retrieving enough of it to keep the agricultural constituencies happy.[2] Proposals for a temporary subsidy had had to be abandoned in favour of rating relief.[3] On October 10, under guidance from the Prime Minister and Horne's financial axe, he watched the Cabinet consign this remnant to oblivion and the problem to a committee.[4] He offered Austen Chamberlain suspended resignation as a consequence, emphasising the damage the decision would do to Coalition support among agricultural M.P.s and in rural seats if there was an election in the immediate future.[5]

Griffith-Boscawen had had extensive experience of difficulty with the electorate which he probably thought was more interested in agriculture than in Greece. He was not part of Lloyd George's Inner Cabinet: it was not likely that he ever would be. He left Chamberlain the impression that he wanted the Coalition to continue and adduced as one reason for not resigning an unwillingness to rock the boat.[6] He had discussed his position with Baldwin and Law, and probably with Curzon. He thought, like others, that farmers no longer believed anything Lloyd George said.[7] He may well have been searching, like Curzon, for a policy issue with which to justify the decision he had already made to knife Lloyd George on grounds of general political credibility.

The material does not enable us to be certain of Baldwin's mood. He had not entered parliament until he was forty-one. He held no office until Law made him his private secretary in 1916.

When Law retired in 1921, Baldwin at fifty-four was still a junior minister. He was saved from resignation by being made President of the Board of Trade but disliked some of the appointments that coincided with his own.[1] He objected to the atmosphere of intrigue surrounding the attempt to have an election in January 1922.[2] He is supposed at that time to have wanted a restored 'Conservative party with Honest Government, Drastic Economy, National Security and No Adventures Abroad'.[3] He may well have been angling for promotion in March and may possibly have known that Austen Chamberlain stopped him.[4] Until mid-July his speeches were those of an enthusiastic Coalitionist.[5] He had an uphill struggle over Fabric Gloves between April and August but eventually got his way. He disliked the Chanak decisions in mid-September but supported them 'because there was no alternative'. By the beginning of his holiday, he was mentally exhausted. In Aix-les-Bains he restored himself by walking. As a result he read no newspapers until September 29. He was so greatly alarmed by what he read then that he returned to London next day believing, if Mrs Baldwin's account is correct, that he was at a critical moment for the development of his career.[6]

In the next ten days he witnessed a renewed wave of sabre-rattling in Cabinet from Churchill and Birkenhead. On October 10 he dissented from the Cabinet's decision to hold the election immediately[7] and thought of resigning at once.[8] He, Griffith-Boscawen, Curzon and Peel began to meet privately in Curzon's house.[9] Strengthened by the belief that all four might resign if an election were called before the party had been consulted,[10] he threw himself into the movement against Lloyd George, declaring that he would resign rather than go on serving under him and that he would in any case never serve under him again. At this point Baldwin acted with emphasis and determination.

With Baldwin's arrival the under-secretaries not only had a leader who was a member of the Cabinet and in touch with Law: they also had a minister who, through Hoare, was about to be in touch with a wider segment of back-bench opinion than anyone had yet consulted. Baldwin did not create the movement against Lloyd George. It did not need to be created. But Baldwin's significance arose from the fact that he played a leading part in amalgamating the various sentiments of Conservative resistance of which his own was a typical and apparently instinctive example.

Sir Samuel Hoare was a young Tariff Reformer when, after being Alfred Lyttleton's private secretary, he had become M.P. for Chelsea in 1910. He had been in military intelligence during the war. He supported military intervention in Russia after it. Along with the two Cecils and Ormsby-Gore, he voted against Welsh Church Disestablishment in 1919.[1] Through his High Church Ecumenical Anglicanism, he had a reputation as an authority on the Greek Orthodox Church. He was in no sense a supporter of the Turks. He had expert knowledge of the Irish question, co-operated with the Die Hards in the early stages of the Irish negotiations in 1921 and was party to Birkenhead's attempt to replace Lloyd George when Lloyd George seemed likely to go too far in appeasing de Valera. He followed Birkenhead, not Gretton, in December and moved the address in support of the Irish Treaty. Hoare was smooth, soothing and took trouble with newspaper proprietors. He had, however, at the age of forty-two not yet been given office. It is not clear at what point he decided that Lloyd George must go. If his narrative – written thirty years later – is to be believed,[2] it was sometime in the summer of 1922.

Hoare's significance was twofold. He was a central Conservative, not a Die Hard. And he was a back-bencher who played tennis regularly with Law and was in touch with Beaverbrook and Davidson. Hoare had long talks with Law on September 28 and on October 8, 12 and 13:[3] he was given the impression that Law saw that something needed to be done but was so doubtful about any particular thing that he was unlikely to take the initiative. Hoare wrote a letter to *The Times* on the 13th or 14th but held it back because Davidson had ceased to believe that Law would make a move.[4] Hoare saw Law for a few minutes on the 14th but found him sceptical. He sent the letter on the 15th: it was published on the 16th. On the 14th he began to canvass in the Carlton Club. He saw Law twice on the 16th and wrote later to say that, if he made a declaration at the meeting on the 19th, he would have a majority of three to one. Younger, when consulted, thought a vote would be very close. Davidson's attempt that evening to bring Hoare and Baldwin together was probably the start of a movement to convince Law that Hoare was right.[5]

Davidson telephoned Hoare on the 16th to suggest that he, Hoare and Baldwin should meet. At the lunch they had together on the 17th, after Baldwin had been to the under-secretaries' meeting, Baldwin repeated that he would never again serve under Lloyd George and telephoned to cancel the joint appearance they were scheduled to make at the opening of the new Port of London Authority building that afternoon.[1] The three of them spent the afternoon picking the names of eighty M.P.s to whom Hoare sent telegrams of invitation for a meeting at his house at five o'clock next day.[2]

There were now two groups prepared to dispute Austen Chamberlain's authority, and Baldwin was the chief link between them. There is no evidence that Austen Chamberlain knew about the Hoare group: if he had known, his attitude in the next two days might have been different. Even without this knowledge, he did his best to accommodate himself to the under-secretaries when he talked to them alone and became obstinate only when he left them to talk to Birkenhead. At their meeting in the Treasury on the 17th, most of the under-secretaries wanted to fight the election as an independent party but were persuaded by Pollock to make one last effort for peace by asking Austen Chamberlain to call an emergency meeting of the National Union in addition to the meeting of M.P.s already called for October 19. The deputation they sent to Chamberlain consisted of two Coalitionists – Gilmour and Pollock – and Wood who wanted the Coalition to end. Next morning Wood was snubbed by Chamberlain for suggesting a formula to allow individual Conservative ministers to declare their unwillingness to serve under Lloyd George after the election.[3] On the evening of the 17th, though Chamberlain gave no undertaking, the three members of the delegation received no impression of incivility.[4] When Amery, as a Birmingham colleague, saw him alone a little later, he repeated his appeal for unity.

At a further meeting next morning the under-secretaries agreed to propose a formula which Amery, Beaverbrook and Younger all seem to have put into circulation – that the Coalition should go on for the moment and the question of reconstruction be left to a party meeting immediately the election was over.[5] Though they did this as a gesture of unity in face of newspaper accounts of party conflict in a situation in which Law was immobile,[6] they seem all to have accepted it. Wilson took it to Austen Chamberlain in Downing Street and telephoned to say that Chamberlain accepted it.[1]

After lunch that day Chamberlain had a long talk with Birkenhead and other Cabinet Ministers.[2] At this time Chamberlain knew of, and had agreed to, the under-secretaries' request, but he did not know that Hoare was holding a back-bench meeting later that afternoon. When the Hoare meeting in its turn sent him a deputation, he found the list of back-benchers on whose behalf it spoke 'astonishing'. What weight he would have attached to it if he had seen it before talking to Birkenhead, it is impossible to know: it is likely that a resolution in more or less identical terms from both the under-secretaries and a large number of the best names among Conservative M.P.s would have made Birkenhead's rhetoric less persuasive. What is certain is that between Birkenhead who 'would not agree to the proposal for consultation after the election'[3] on the one hand and an alarming threat from the Hoare group on the other, Chamberlain left the impression,[4] which later he strongly denied,[5] that he had gone back on his undertaking to leave until after the election a decision about the identity of the Prime Minister and the party constitution of the Cabinet.

The Hoare meeting took place in Hoare's house at five o'clock on the 18th: no Cabinet Ministers were present. According to Hoare's account, seventy-four of the eighty who received invitations accepted them.[6] Hoare had had lunch with Wood who thought that Chamberlain's compromise would be accepted next day.[7] Law had refused that morning to do anything but resign his seat, so Hoare, having no leader to propose, began tentatively, as did Pretyman who followed him. After 'fighting speeches' from Hills and Ormsby-Gore had set the tone for twenty others, it became clear that all of them would prefer to fight the election on an independent basis. They decided to send Pretyman, Hoare and Lane Fox to tell Austen Chamberlain that they wanted 'independent Conservative action, an independent programme and an independent leader'.[8]

Austen Chamberlain could not see them at once, so Hoare telephoned Law to explain what had happened and took Pretyman and Lane Fox to see him. When they arrived they found him in '[so] unusual a state of excitement ... that he almost broke down in talking'. When he saw the list of M.P.s involved, he was 'very greatly impressed' and so far receded from the position he had adopted that morning as to leave it uncertain whether he would appear at the Carlton Club next day.[1]

Pretyman and Lane Fox were senior and reputable back-benchers. Pretyman had resigned junior office in December 1918 in order to devote his time to agricultural questions:[2] having proposed Austen Chamberlain for the leadership in 1921, he expected consideration. When they eventually managed to see him, they found him irritated, angry and very greatly shaken by the list of M.P.s they represented. Chamberlain, who had just seen Law,[3] recited 'at length and with great heat' his version of the case for Coalition: when told by Hoare that they had come to give him information not to argue, he 'answered angrily ... that he regarded the policy approved by our meeting as a direct attack on himself ... and would fight us at the Party meeting'.[4] Pretyman and Lane Fox were greatly annoyed. Hoare went back by himself to Law who was at dinner. He was told that Law had already decided to go to the Carlton Club meeting and to speak at it.[5]

Law did not want to put himself forward for the leadership. It is possible that he did not want it: in any case he could not suddenly resume it. To almost everyone who wrote or came to see him right up to October 18, he was alternately encouraging and pessimistic, gloomy about Lloyd George's prospects and anticipating a long Conservative period in opposition. Many Conservatives were in touch with him including Younger, Fraser, Hoare, Salvidge, Curzon, Salisbury, Long, Derby, Ormsby-Gore, Griffith-Boscawen, Wickham Steed and Amery. Many more watched him closely – including Rothermere and Lloyd George who saw him often.[6] Until late on October 18 none knew what he would do.

Since his resignation in March 1921 Law had been under continual pressure to resume the leadership or rejoin the government.[7] At each critical turn he exercised decisive authority. He refused to help Birkenhead and Beaverbrook against Lloyd George in June 1921.[8] He warned Lloyd George off excessive conciliation in Ireland in November 1921: he did the same over Genoa the following March. He refused the Foreign Secretaryship during the Younger demonstration in January.[9] He refused to stop Balfour's

Debt Settlement note,[1] but told Lloyd George on a number of occasions in the course of 1922 that his Prime Ministership could not last.[2] He claimed to have warned him in mid-September that he should resign while he 'could do so with dignity'.[3] He certainly told Fraser that only he (i.e. Law) or Balfour 'could reunite the Party'.[4]

Though he had decided that Lloyd George would have to be removed, Law needed support if he was to make him. He had no support of consequence, except possibly from Milner who had been helping Griffith-Boscawen with Agriculture and Devonshire who was willing to join the government if Lloyd George ceased to lead it.[5] Law had discussed with Rothermere the possibility of a Rothermere/Law axis against the Coalition if *The Times* could be bought. But both about purchase and about plans for *The Times* thereafter there was no decision until after the Carlton Club meeting, and it is unlikely that Rothermere's support would have been decisive.[6] On the 6th Law saw Derby, who told him that Salvidge was 'Birkenhead's ... mouthpiece' and reflected nothing outside Liverpool, adding that French policy and Lancashire opinion would compel him to resign his party offices unless it was certain that Lloyd George would be removed.[7]

Conscious of this measure of support, Law next day made the same sort of criticism of the government's Near Eastern policy as he had made of its Irish policy the previous December, this time making it in public in a letter to *The Times* after the moment of decision was over and excusing himself to Austen Chamberlain on the ground that it would help Curzon convince Poincaré that English opinion had abandoned Greece.[8] Sometime in the first week of October he refused a proposal that he should form a government in which Lloyd George would take office.[9] On October 9 he promised to disavow the Coalition if it went to an election without consultation. By the 12th he reverted to a mood of total negativity, influenced no doubt by the fear that, even if he removed Lloyd George, there would be no guarantee of a majority at a general election and every possibility of a Lloyd George come-back in a year's time.[10] Milner, Derby and perhaps Devonshire may have seemed reassurance enough for the letter of October 7. The Hoare meeting provided the reassurance he needed to go further.[11]

On the morning of the Hoare meeting, Law said that he would

not attend the Carlton Club meeting but would resign his seat instead.[1] Why he said this, unless in order to strengthen his case, it is difficult to see. Baldwin came to lunch, intending to tell him[2] that agreement had been reached between Chamberlain and the under-secretaries. Sometime after seven o'clock Law saw Lane Fox, Pretyman and Hoare and knew what they represented. He knew that Curzon had given Lloyd George his suspended resignation the day before.[3] When Hoare saw Law at dinner-time, Law had already made up his mind to be present next morning.[4] His decision was doubtless a decision to save the party; it was almost certainly made in the knowledge that the party might well have been saved by Austen Chamberlain's agreement with the under-secretaries, and that the agreement, if accepted, might well make Austen Chamberlain Prime Minister after the election.[5]

Law was not the only person whose action made Chamberlain's arrangement unworkable. That night some of the under-secretaries were thinking of sabotaging it. When Hoare left Law, he telephoned Baldwin to report on the meeting with Chamberlain. He was asked to Baldwin's house, where he found not only Younger, Davidson, Wilson and Mrs Baldwin, but all the under-secretaries and Whips sitting under Baldwin's chairmanship in the dining-room. While answering questions from the under-secretaries, he heard a debate going on between Bridgeman, Tryon and Sanders who 'stood out as whole-hearted opponents' of the Chamberlain plan and a number of others who were in favour of it. Hoare said that he was against it and left the under-secretaries discussing whether to resign.[6]

Later that night Hoare had a telephone call from Beaverbrook to say that Hoare would be 'the first for the lamp-posts' if the Coalition did not end next day.[7] Later still, or early next morning, Hoare drafted a resolution to prevent waverers supporting Austen Chamberlain. He persuaded Pretyman and Lane Fox[8] to accept it, despite Fox's desire to avoid a formal vote, and telephoned Baldwin and Davidson to make sure that Law did not accept a compromise at the meeting.[9] The fact that Hoare's resolution was thought mild when he showed it around the Carlton Club next morning does not alter the evidence he offers that the final dividing line was drawn not by Austen Chamberlain but by himself, Baldwin, Younger, Wilson, Davidson and others.[10]

From October 10 onwards Austen Chamberlain had exercised what he thought of as a leader's authority. He had been rigid, dignified and angry: he had shown neither magic, charm nor warmth. He had made no rings and squared no circles and was probably inhibited by the advantage he would expect to gain from removing Lloyd George. But he had laid down a line and stuck to it as firmly as he could. He had little appreciation of the belief that the Conservative party would do better at an election without Lloyd George and none at all of the Chief Agent's idea, which others shared, that 'if the Conservatives stood against all comers, they would get a clear majority'.[1] He did not share the view that Churchill and other Coalition Liberals would stay whether Lloyd George went or not[2] or that, even if Lloyd George did resign, he would be no threat and would make no headway with the Asquitheans.[3] He did not believe that Lloyd George could resign while he was the object of public attack.[4] He did not anticipate the result of the Newport by-election.[5] None of the alternative Conservative leaders had challenged him openly. He knew that Curzon's accumulated resentments had erupted against Lloyd George but he intuited neither Derby's, Law's nor Griffith-Boscawen's real feelings, perhaps because they did not make them clear.[6] He had no contact with Salisbury, despite long-standing personal and political affinities which Salisbury recognised. The hints dropped by Wilson, Fraser, Younger and Long did not register. Chamberlain thought his decisions were unequivocal and that Wilson accepted them on October 15: he did not suppose Wilson suspected him of abandoning them. He saw only the injustice to Lloyd George, the danger from Labour and the need to keep close links with the Coalition Liberals in order to resist it.[7]

The Carlton Club meeting, originally scheduled for October 18, was switched to October 19 in order to gain the advantage expected from the Newport by-election. The loss of the Newport seat, announced on the night of October 18/19, merely made Chamberlain determined to draw the line as clearly as he could.

The meeting began with the reading of a letter in which Curzon explained his absence on the ground that the meeting was a meeting of M.P.s. It was followed by a long speech from the chair in which Austen Chamberlain outlined his reasons for continuing the Coalition in face of the 'direct challenge ... by quite the second largest party in the State ... to ... those fundamental principles ... which hitherto both the great parties ... have encouraged and upon which our ... national, industrial and commercial greatness is based'. He emphasised that 'in the next Parliament coalition of some sort [would] be necessary' and that it was better to keep the present one than to have another between 'the Labour party and the Wee Frees on terms and for a policy to which we, with our present allies, alike stand resolutely opposed'. The advice he gave on behalf of the majority of the Conservative members of the Cabinet was that they should 'go as a government' with every 'Unionist and Conservative and every Liberal Coalitionist ... stand[ing] under his own party name' in the expectation of an unspecified reconstruction after the election if it was won, but with no advance decision that the Coalition would be abandoned if the Conservative party had a majority.

Baldwin, on behalf of Griffith-Boscawen and himself, then made three points – that 'a fatal mistake was made in agreeing to go to an election without consulting the party', that Lloyd George was a 'dynamic force' who, having destroyed the Liberal party, was doing the same to the Conservative party, and that, so long as he was supported, existing divisions would grow 'until the old Conservative party [was] smashed to atoms and lost in ruins'.

Pretyman and Lane Fox next proposed and seconded the motion Hoare had drafted the night before. They did so in no spirit of hostility to the Prime Minister to whom 'the country owe[d] a deep debt of gratitude'. But, they said, 'the [Conservative] party ... [was] dead in the sense that ... a new electorate [with] no definite allegiance either to the Conservative or to the Liberal party ... [was] looking for a lead' which it was the duty of Conservatives to supply. Their motion in favour of 'fight[ing] the election as an independent party with its own leader and its own programme' was made lest the 'only change of government available to the country was a Socialist government' and because the Labour appeal could not be met without principles which 'it [was] impossible for a Coalition ... to have'. They made it clear that they not only did not wish to proscribe Coalition Liberals but were willing, if necessary, to speak on their behalf.

Law's speech 'in favour of no Coalition' was a masterpiece of caution and understatement. He apologised for leaving Austen Chamberlain in the lurch by his resignation in March 1921 but implied that the present problem was too big for Chamberlain to handle by himself. He claimed that Chamberlain's policy would inevitably mean coalition after the election for 'if ... any Conservative feels that possibly his return is due to the influence of the Prime Minister ... would it not be infinitely more dishonourable [than in 1918] to say to the Prime Minister "After winning the victory, we ask you to retire in favour of Mr. Chamberlain"?' He stressed the failure to consult the party and left the impression, even at this stage, that the question should be submitted to it. He pictured himself as talking at a point of crisis from which, if Chamberlain won, the party would relive the twenty years 'after Peel passed the Corn Bill' and 'the body that [was] cast off' took 'a generation ... to get back to the influence ... the party ought to have'. Dismissing the idea that a Labour government was an immediate possibility, he thought party unity more important than winning the election. It was in any case not the next election that mattered but preparation for a future in which 'if the Conservative party disappears in the way the Liberal party had disappeared and we have simply ... a party composed of everyone who [is] not Labour with Labour as the only alternative, [there] will inevitably ... [be] a Labour government some day'.

After Balfour had defended Austen Chamberlain, Wilson, the Chief Whip, speaking '[he] believe[d] for a certain number of junior ministers', made it clear that he was against him on the ground that his proposals would prevent members of the government telling their constituents that they would refuse to serve under a Liberal Prime Minister in the event of a Conservative majority after the election. This greatly annoyed Chamberlain who decided to bring the question to a head. He gave no encouragement to a motion to defer voting until next day and emphasised, when asked, that votes in favour of the Pretyman motion would 'exclude the possibility of any but a Tory Prime Minister ... if there [was] a Tory majority'. The vote that followed was decisive. The majority was not just a Die Hard majority: nor would it have been significant if it had been. Though only 188 M.P.s voted against Chamberlain, they were a cross section of the governing part of the Conservative party giving notice that, despite a desire to accommodate Coalition Liberals, support for Lloyd George was at an end.[1]

Lloyd George had already decided to resign if the vote went the wrong way. As soon as he had done so the King sent for Law, whose reaction was rather cool. One of Law's first actions after the meeting was to call on Curzon who may have had expectations of his own.[2] At first he refused to see the King until he had been elected party leader in Austen Chamberlain's place. Next day at a meeting attended by Derby, Salisbury, Esmond Harmsworth, Gretton and Amery, Curzon conveyed Law's wish to know what they thought about Ireland and Protection. When Amery, as leading Protectionist, explained that the election must be 'run ... on one issue – a change of government ... – which should not be confused by putting Tariff Reform as such in the forefront', he was added to Salisbury, Derby and Curzon who went to ask Law to accept nomination at a party meeting on the 23rd.[3] On the 23rd Law became Prime Minister.

XII

THE SHUNNING OF LLOYD GEORGE

'I was a convinced Coalitionist until the country got out of its troubles but that has been brought to an end by the action of the Conservatives themselves. The alternative therefore is the re-creation of the Liberal Party on a policy which will attract moderate Labour and Progressive Conservatives.'

Lloyd George to C. P. Scott, December 14 1922

'Lloyd George is a great danger to the country. We can recover if the appalling conditions are well handled but if Lloyd George were to return to power ... or to ... influence England's policy ... things would get worse. Hence whilst my opinion is all for reunion, I consider, if reunion involved in any way our acceptance of Lloyd George, that we cannot afford to pay such a price.'

Lord Cowdray to Lord Beauchamp, December 30 1922, Add. MSS 46474

'We all want party unity. What we do not want is a "deal". What has happened in the past had been delicately alluded to as "bygones". We want no bygones in our future.'

Lady Violet Bonham-Carter, president of the Womens' National Liberal Federation at Buxton, May 30 1923 in *Manchester Guardian*, June 2

(i)

Between April 1921 and October 1922 Lloyd George had tried on a number of possible hats. To Austen Chamberlain he had been the loyal Coalitionist who wanted to convert the Coalition into a permanent party. To C. P. Scott he was the loyal Radical who had never forgotten the fate of Joseph Chamberlain – 'a mangled soul' – and wanted only to restore radical Liberalism to the centre of the scene.[1] To Conservatives he was the Radical who had sacrificed his Radicalism for the nation's good and would give it free play if deprived of the power he had enjoyed since 1916. To Coalition Liberals he was the cunning tactician who wanted to fight an election as Coalition leader because the Die Hards, the Labour party and the Asquithean Liberals would use the majority the election would give them to bungle the attempt they would have to make to construct a government to replace him.[2]

How far Lloyd George believed this, whether he believed any of it, it is difficult to say. He considered the progressive alternative in late 1921: the decision to hold an election in early 1922 involved its rejection. Younger's assault made him reconsider it in March: his view of Montagu and Churchill made him reject it. It was probably his first preference. The renewal of Coalition was a second best with openings in either of two directions. If the body of the Conservative party supported the Coalition and won an election with an absolute majority, he probably thought there was a chance of remaining Prime Minister. If the Coalition parties had no absolute majority after the election, he probably anticipated a situation in which Birkenhead, Balfour, Austen Chamberlain, Horne and Churchill under his leadership would carry the body of the Conservative party and the Coalition Liberals into a progressively orientated anti-socialist opposition. In either case he contemplated the destruction of Conservative unity, the end of the existing Conservative party and the construction of a Centre party to replace 'Liberalism' which in October 1922 he repeatedly said was dead.[1]

In one respect Lloyd George's calculations were mistaken. The Conservative party did not split. The Die Hards were not extruded. There was no disgruntled group on the Right gnawing at the Conservative party's self-respect. For the first time since 1920, the Conservative party was united in all Rightward directions. Nevertheless, Lloyd George succeeded in taking Birkenhead, Balfour, Crawford, Lee, Horne, Austen Chamberlain, Scott, Pollock, Gilmour, Mitchell-Thomson, Gibbs, Murray and Worthington-Evans. They met in Downing Street immediately the Carlton Club meeting was over, and again at six o'clock that day to draft a press statement.[2] During the election Birkenhead campaigned for Lloyd George. Horne and Austen Chamberlain appeared on his platforms. Scott and Pollock refused office from Law.

Moreover, there were electoral understandings between Lloyd George's headquarters and the Conservative party. Most of the seats won by Lloyd George Liberals were won because of Conservative acquiescence. Though the heightening of public argument between Law, Birkenhead and Lloyd George did nothing to increase the chance of alliance after an election, there was reason to anticipate scope for Lloyd George and the Coalition Conservatives as a Peelite group afterwards.[1]

Of Lloyd George's Coalition-Liberal colleagues in office in October 1922, only Churchill had been close to him during Chanak. Apart from Churchill none was party to the decision to hold an election in November. None now deserted him.[2] Most saw their futures closely linked with his and expected him to make the major decisions affecting them. There were varying emphases and preferences. Before the Carlton Club meeting Kellaway, MacPherson, Macnamara and Shortt favoured a Coalition platform at the election because they depended on Conservative votes.[3] At the meeting of Liberal ex-ministers the day Lloyd George resigned, they agreed to 'stand as Liberals *sans phrase*' while 'accept[ing] a programme to which [their] Conservative colleagues [could] subscribe'.[4] Greenwood saw 'no difference in principle between the two wings [of the Coalition] and much regret[ted] that a more determined effort was not made to form a Centre party earlier'.[5] Grigg, en route from being Lloyd George's private secretary to being a parliamentary candidate, felt 'no interest in a Conservative party which panders to the Die Hards and ... would rather not be in politics than sit on the back benches behind any of the men who spoke of the Irish Treaty and those who made it as the Right wing of the Conservative party did'. He tried to persuade the Round Table to support Lloyd George. With a subsidy from Sir Abe Bailey, he made his début at Oldham where he was opposed by Lady Emmott whose Asquithean candidature was prompted by 'bitter party strife and hatred of Lloyd George ... – motives [which] should not be tolerated in English public life'.[6]

On joining the Cabinet in 1921 Mond had recommended himself to Conservatives by his sterling views about Addison and Ireland.[7] But he thought the Geddes Committee would 'scrap ... all our social reforms [and] ... play straight into the hands of the Labour party':[8] his preference, then and since, was for detachment from the Coalition as a prelude to Liberal reunion. In September 1922 he wanted a Fair Rent Court, rating of urban site values, reductions in arms expenditure, Empire development, abandonment of British War Debts, reductions in taxation and deficit financing as the platform for an independent Liberal policy. He saw 'no future in clinging to the Tories': at the time of the Carlton Club meeting he wanted a 'Liberal breakaway' before Conservatives broke away themselves.[1] His resignation letter to Lloyd George did not promise loyalty for the future:[2] at the beginning of the election[3] there was a misunderstanding between them. Mond thought Law's 'administration ... ridiculous and his policy hopeless'.[4] He did not begin to be happy until Lloyd George's first affirmation of a 'Liberal' position at Glasgow on October 28.[5] Even that did not make it clear that, far from being 'lasso[ed]' by Austen Chamberlain into being leader of 'a little Liberal wing of the Tory party', Lloyd George stood 'high and independent and free as the great Leader of the Democratic forces' who was in a position to destroy the Asquithean rump 'if he [could] regain the confidence of the party whose real leader [he was] for practical purposes before the war and whose leader [he] naturally [was] today'.[6] Mond thought the Greek policy attractive to nonconformists.[7] 'There are', he told Lloyd George towards the end of the election,

thousands of working men who left us because they had the idea that we were mixed up with the Conservatives and ... looked on us not unnaturally as allied to hard faced Capitalists and their hereditary enemies ... Any too obvious Union of ourselves with men who still call themselves Conservatives ... only engenders their distrust. The Labour man is simple, unsophisticated and very suspicious. Labour never understood the Coalition and we have to be very careful not to give them any impression of being too clever.[8]

Fisher shared Mond's opinions in March: he abandoned them when the moment for detachment had passed. After the fall of the Coalition, he leaves the impression of wanting chiefly to recommend himself to Conservative ministers.[9] Hilton Young also wanted a Liberal breakaway in March. In the first half of October he wanted an election on a Coalition basis.[10] After October 19 he wanted, like Lord Clwyd, to be 'associated with [Lloyd George] in whatever action [he] may take'.[11] At the election Young stood as a Coalition Liberal in harness with George Roberts, the ex-Labour minister, at Norwich where the absence of a Conservative candidate enabled them to win with Asquithean support.

In early 1922 Churchill had put all his eggs into the Coalition basket. He wanted a secure base in a Liberal/Conservative party

and hoped that Birkenhead or Derby would help him to get it.[1]
However, he had not got it. He was shaken both by events and
by illness:[2] he found it necessary to fight the constituency for
which he sat. Though he joined in attacking the new government
which 'reminded [him] ... of the days of ... George III',[3] he
regretted the gap which grew between Coalition Liberals and the
Conservative party in the course of the election.[4] From hospital
he conducted a campaign 'as a Liberal and Free Trader' alongside
another Coalition Liberal in the two-member seat at Dundee.
He attacked Grey for the rancour shown Lloyd George since Grey
left office in 1916, called on 'Liberals and Conservatives ... to
stand shoulder to shoulder against the Labour and Communist
candidates' and promised to 'co-operate ... with sober minded
and progressive Conservatives ... against the ... attacks ...
about to be levelled ... [both] by the Socialist-Communist forces
[and by the] menace of ... reaction from the opposite quarter'.[5]

Lloyd George's platform at the 1922 election was a continuation
of the Coalition platform he had manufactured in early 1922 with
some of the reactionary planks left out. There was the claim that
he was concerned solely for the national interest and that the
Conservative party had now put party above nation. There was
resolute defence of the Coalition's record and praise for the
Conservatives and Coalition Liberals he wished to carry with
him. He spoke as an advocate of Liberal reunion which would
outbid the Asquithean leaders on their Left by developing relations with selected Labour leaders.[6] He presented himself as an
anti-revolutionary, distinguishing Thomas, Henderson and Clynes
from the revolutionaries by whom they were propelled and leaving
ajar such doors as might be opened for co-operation with them in
the future.

Lloyd George aimed his appeal at Liberal and potential Labour
voters on the one hand and at patriotic Conservatives on the other.
He attacked the Die Hards, Salisbury, Curzon and Anti-Waste:
he attacked the Asquithean Liberals and the body of the Labour
party as well. He claimed credit for the Irish settlement, the
League of Nations and Genoa: he promised European pacification
for the future. He believed that every European state should join
the League of Nations and that Germany should pay no more
reparations than she could bear. Industrial Co-operation and Trade

Credits made occasional appearances but there was nothing about Free Trade. The Graeco-Turkish truce as evidence of his capability as the agent of tranquillity was paradoxical: sow as the claim, made in rebutting Gladstone, that Balfour and Lloyd George were 'Gladstonians' in the Near East. Gladstonian virtue was claimed for Horne and Austen Chamberlain who, as Chancellors of the Exchequer, had insisted on repaying debt, balancing the Budget and enabling the pound 'to look the dollar in the face'[1] when they might have sought popularity by reducing taxation. Birkenhead was said to be a 'democrat', Austen Chamberlain 'a Liberal', Horne 'a Tory with a difference' and Balfour to have 'become a Liberal in his old age like Gladstone'.[2] Lloyd George made private predictions that the Liberal party was dead,[3] was slow to claim purely 'Liberal' credentials[4] and hinted that, if the Coalitionists did not stay with him, he would be forced to swing sharply to the Left.[5] His position was characterised by such ambiguous affirmations as that

I have been ... and am still ... in favour of all men who believe in the existing fabric of society, who believe in the principle upon which our prosperity has been built – free, private enterprise – of men who are opposed to revolutionary proposals and who are equally opposed to reactionary proposals because, believe me, they are only the reverse of the same medal, acting together for the purpose of bearing the country through the gigantic difficulties which have been left as an inheritance by the war'.[6]

The Coalition Liberals intended at first to fight seats only where they were likely to win. They did not intend to stand against Conservatives from whom they hoped for co-operation. They took few initiatives in standing against Asquithean Liberals: thirty Asquitheans were put up against them.[7] In a number of constituencies Conservative associations adopted candidates of their own volition in seats where Central Office had agreed that Coalition Liberals should not be opposed. When Central Office approved thirty-five of these candidatures, Fisher – and Churchill rather unwillingly – were deputed to choose fifteen Conservative constituencies in which to adopt Coalition Liberals.[8] Younger retaliated by compelling half-a-dozen Coalition Liberals to withdraw.[9] As the election developed Lloyd George not only felt obliged to criticise Law: he discovered that the Conservative

leaders had become less willing than at first to co-operate electorally and were more willing than before to threaten a limited
measure of co-operation with the Asquitheans.[1]

As a result of the election forty-four Coalition Liberals lost
their seats, including half-a-dozen ex-ministers. Just over fifty
Coalition Liberals were returned, eight in seats which had not
been theirs in 1918. Of the seats won, nineteen were in Scotland
or Wales and three in Bristol: there were none in London, Liverpool, Edinburgh or Glasgow. In Birmingham no Coalition Liberal
stood: in Manchester the united Liberal parties put up six candidates, all of whom were defeated. Four Coalition Liberals were
returned unopposed. In Norwich they held both seats with twice
the vote of the two Labour candidates they were standing against.
In six other seats they had majorities of over 10,000, all but one in
straight fights with Labour. In about twenty of the seats they did
not win they came within sight of winning. But not only did they
have no five-figure majority in any other constituency: they had
no other majority of more than 5,000. In fourteen seats they had
majorities of less than 1,000; and all this despite the fact that, in
all but six of their seats, they had no Conservative standing
against them.

At the beginning of the election Guest hoped for a hundred
seats in order to hold the balance in the new parliament.[2] Lloyd
George predicted fifty once the campaign was under way.[3] But
fifty seats held very largely 'on Tory votes' provided no basis
either for reunion on tough terms or for new departures.[4] Election day 1922 marked the end of the period introduced by Sutherland's heralding of Lloyd George as 'leader of industrial society'.

In the course of the election the alliance between Lloyd George
and the Coalition Conservatives was cemented by euphoric
electioneering, by public ovations and by the belief, unexpected
in hard-minded operators, that merit would be rewarded.[5]
Beaverbrook and his papers were against them. So at first was
Rothermere. But Rothermere quarrelled with Law as soon as
Law took office: Esmond Harmsworth refused office and appeared
on Lloyd George's platform. Harmsworth had no Conservatives
against him in the Isle of Thanet but Erskine, the second member
of the Harmsworth party, was opposed at St George's, Westminster by Wilson, the Conservative Chief Whip, whom he

defeated decisively. Rothermere was in touch with Lloyd George:[1] the *Daily Mail* gave prominence to Lloyd George, to the Chamberlainites and to the Asquithean Liberals.[2] In company with Birkenhead, Rothermere plotted to trip up the new government as he had the last. The expectation that an opening would occur to revive the Coalition was strengthened by the general contempt for the quality of the new ministers and by rumours that Law would retire after a year in office, which continued to be his personal intention even after he abandoned it officially on becoming Prime Minister.[3]

The main fact in the new parliament, however, was not these expectations but the damage the Conservative majority did to them. The damage was considerable. Before the election the Chamberlainites hoped that they and the Coalition Liberals between them would hold a balance in the new parliament. Thereafter they hoped only to regain control of the Conservative party when the inadequacy of Law's government ensured its downfall. Though they maintained friendly relations with Lloyd George,[4] there is no sign between October 1922 and mid-1923 that they revived the idea of joining the Liberal party. Birkenhead and Austen Chamberlain tried to establish governments of their own choice in May and December 1923. But on each occasion it was Derby, Birkenhead, Curzon, Balfour or Asquith they thought of as Prime Minister, not Lloyd George. In May Worthington-Evans joined Baldwin's government. In June Austen Chamberlain made it clear that he would do so if offered reasonable office.[5] Balfour helped to smooth the change from Law to Baldwin: he hinted that he was willing to join Baldwin's government. There is evidence that he pressed Coalition Conservatives to join Law's government when it was being formed.[6] Whatever Lloyd George may have said, the idea of a Lloyd George Coalition disappeared as a practical proposition before the end of 1922 and could not be revived so long as neither Lloyd George nor the Chamberlainites controlled a party on which to base it.

For Churchill the downfall of the Coalition, defeat at Dundee and illness provided a cumulative shock. He spent part of the winter at Cannes, thinking of Law wrestling with unemployment. On returning to England he emerged once more without seat or constituency as advocate of a supra-party alliance to resist 'the ceaseless advance and ... victorious enforcement of the levelling and withering doctrines of Socialism'.[1]

At his début at the Aldwych Club on May 4 1923 he faced all ways and left all options open. Lloyd George 'with his ardent popular sympathies' was, he thought, a shade impatient in his desire for social reform, but his Manchester speech a week earlier had 'the clear purpose of rallying the greatest number of persons of all classes ... to the defence of the existing constitution'. Churchill 'could not follow Asquith' in thinking it 'disgraceful for any Liberal to co-operate with any Conservative'. The Asquithean machine, nevertheless, was run by 'cool-headed lawyers ... [who] ha[d] been more friendly to the Conservative government than ... the followers of Lloyd George or the [Chamberlainite] Conservatives'. The government 'had not yet succeeded in ... developing those qualities of initiative, inspiration and conviction which they no doubt possessed and ... were probably keeping in reserve'. Under the 'solitary ... ascendancy of the Prime Minister, [however] ... they ha[d] ... promised ... not to raise any of the old flags of political controversy' and had shown that no issue of principle divided them from Asquith and Grey. Churchill did not attack the Die Hards. He accepted the erosions of Free Trade effected by the Coalition. In both respects he marked himself off from Lloyd George, who had announced at Manchester that the Paris Resolutions, the McKenna duties and the Safeguarding of Industries Act were no longer desirable.

So long as the Coalitionists seemed likely to hold a balance in the new parliament, Lloyd George, while doing nothing about reunion himself, blamed the Asquitheans for making corrupt electoral alliances with Salisbury and the Die Hards before the Carlton Club meeting[2] and with Younger afterwards, and for intending to keep Law's government in office in the event of deadlock after the election.[3] Once the election was over, one of his objects was to attach himself to a reunited Liberal party so as to succeed Asquith and Grey or whoever might lead the Asquithean Liberals after them.

In doing this he had two major disadvantages. He had fifty Coalition Liberal M.P.s instead of the hundred or so he had had before, and he had virtually no Coalition Liberal organisation in the country. He had enemies not only among the leading Asquitheans but also amongst Asquitheans of the second rank like Pringle whom he refused to make Chief Whip in 1916[1] and who '[could] not forgive [him] for keeping him out of the House for four years'.[2] On the other hand he had a newspaper – the *Daily Chronicle* – whose financial position was not likely to be restored by giving the Thistle to one of its largest shareholders as his last act as Prime Minister.[3] He had, or was thought to have, a great deal of money. He had admirers in the middle and lower ranks of Asquithean Liberal M.P.s, a considerable following among Asquithean Liberals in the country and one of the Asquithean Whips – J. M. Hogge – who lost confidence in Asquith before the collapse of the Coalition and tried to act as a linkman with Lloyd George. Above all Lloyd George had a friend, supporter and possible intermediary in C. P. Scott who disliked Coalition, had no time for Asquith[4] and wanted Lloyd George to emerge as Radical leader of the reunited party which throughout the previous eighteen months he had told Lloyd George it was his destiny to reconstitute.

Although Lloyd George wanted reunion, he did not know how to go about getting it. Initial attempts at joint entertainment were not successful.[5] Lloyd George might formally have accepted Asquith's leadership at the same time as the Coalition Liberals applied for the Asquithean Whip. After talking to Lloyd George one Liberal M.P. announced that Lloyd George would do this. Lloyd George denied it:[6] it is unlikely that he ever intended it. He was not willing to accept the primacy of Asquith who had 'no positive policy'[7] and was 'no longer a popular name by reason of his failure in the war'.[8] If reunion was to be achieved, account had to be taken of the equality of standing he claimed for the Coalition Liberals, of his refusal to accept the 'part often proffered to [him] of ... traitor to Liberalism' and of the importance of the contribution made by Coalition Liberalism to the development of a Liberal position about Ireland, the franchise, temperance, land reform and disarmament.[9] He was 'not prepared to repulse any advances towards reunion on the part of Liberals who may wish to act with him'.[10] He favoured consultation with 'rank-and-file opinion'[11] which he supposed he could handle more easily than he could the leaders. He was willing to wait until the Asquitheans recognised this.

From one point of view Lloyd George was in a position to wait. He really wanted reunion. Most Liberals, inside and outside parliament, wanted it too. The Asquithean leaders did not want it and Lloyd George knew it.[1] They wanted to restore relations with the body of Coalition Liberal M.P.s and with Coalition Liberals in the country. They offered the Asquithean Whip to any Coalition Liberal M.P. who 'definitely decided to join our party and work with us and vote in opposition to the government in the House of Commons'.[2] But they wanted to avoid treating Lloyd George as an equal. Whenever Lloyd George made advances they took avoiding action. They made it plain, without saying so, that they did not want reunion with him. This meant that, in urging reunion on them, Lloyd George reflected the body of party feeling. It meant also that, despite his 'betrayal' in 1918 and the relations he maintained with the Chamberlainites, he could contrast his own concern for party interests with the pettiness, carping and personal spite shown him by Asquith, Grey and their followers.[3]

On the other hand, the need to establish equality involved keeping his own group separate, which it was not always easy to do. Even in the House of Commons, where proximity induced tension between the groups,[4] the Lloyd George Liberals had few common policies, not much common voting and a strong belief, which Mond held most strongly, that reunion was urgent. Most Lloyd George Liberal seats had been won on Tory votes with small majorities. In the course of the 1922 parliament about half-a-dozen Lloyd George Liberals joined the Asquitheans. In the party organisation maintenance of identity was more difficult still. In Wales, for example, Coalition Liberals were better organised than anywhere apart from Bristol: at the election they operated independently of the Asquitheans and in places stood against them. Throughout 1922 there had been constant pressure for reunion from within the Lloyd George organisation. In early 1923 it seemed likely that reunion would be effected from below if Lloyd George did not succeed in effecting it on his own terms from above.[5]

Between November 1922 and April 1923 Lloyd George prepared his positions for the opportunity that never came. Fisher, McCurdy, Macnamara, Mond and Hilton Young met as an informal Shadow Cabinet at his house at Churt and elsewhere. In addition he had around him in varying degrees of intimacy Greenwood, Hogge, McLaren, Shakespeare, McCurdy, Grigg, Cope and Seebohm Rowntree, as well as Lords Clwyd, Aberconway, Beauchamp, St Davids, Dalziel, Colebrook, Chesterfield, Gorell and Riddell. With C. P. Scott Lloyd George's relations were probably closer than at any time since the beginning of the war.

In the six months after the election Lloyd George did little to provide a policy. He made a small splash about agriculture.[1] He proposed a Genoa-type policy of progress and peace in Europe,[2] attacked Poincaré[3] and affected sympathy for Law when Law found Poincaré as impossible on Reparations and the Ruhr as Lloyd George had been criticised for finding him on nearly everything else.[4] He found the American Debt terms 'very stiff'.[5] He was unmoved by Proportional Representation, the second ballot, the alternative vote and other mechanical means of arresting the Liberal decline which Scott urged upon him.[6] His chief positive contributions were to suggest privately that Law should make an 'Agadir speech' for Poincaré's benefit to establish that Britain's views could not be ignored,[7] and to fix on 'the Land' as the subject 'on [which] the Tories would be bound to make a stand and you would have a real battle with an unanswerable case'.[8] It was not until the failure of his first serious drive for reunion at the end of April that he laid out a full-scale programme of his own.

Lloyd George's conception of the Liberal party's future was that it should be democratic and progressive but anti-socialist, anti-revolutionary and anti-Die Hard. He knew that a vast new electorate had been created by the Reform Act of 1918. Like Austen Chamberlain he was conscious of the challenge, and chance, given by the fact that there were 'millions of electors ... who [were] not attached to any political party'. He saw no reason why 'Liberalism' should not 'attach these people to its flag' by attracting all shades of opinion between the Die Hards on the Right and the revolutionary socialists on the Left. This was why it was necessary to pretend that Law's government was a Die Hard government, which it was not. This was why he distinguished between 'Labour' which was not the enemy and 'the revolutionary elements in the Labour party' which were.[9] This was why many Labour M.P.s in the new House of Commons thought it desirable to renew the attacks on Lloyd George which they had got used to making while electioneering against the Coalition.[1] This was one reason why Lloyd George spent so much time with Mrs Snowden in 1923.[2]

This, of course, was roughly the policy of the Asquithean Liberals with the difference in their case that the Conservatives to whom they looked for support were the enemies not the friends of Lloyd George. They had, however, given Lloyd George a brush-off in late 1922. There was every sign that they intended to go on doing so in 1923. It is not certain whether it was the increase in the Labour vote at the Whitechapel and Mitcham by-elections in February and March or the personal set-back he suffered with the election of Grey to the leadership of the Liberal peers which made Lloyd George discover that reunion was urgent.[3] He may have been attempting to put the Asquitheans in the wrong.[4] He may have wanted to show that Grey, who had been supported by many peers as an aid to unity, was a symbol of the Asquithean leadership which was opposed to it.[5] He may, as he claimed,[6] have been genuinely alarmed by the Labour party's performance in these elections. In any case, the Willesden by-election[7] on the one hand and Whitechapel and Mitcham[8] on the other provided objective comment which the Liberal leaders could not explain away.

On March 8 Scott, who happened to be in London for dinner with Lady Astor, was summoned to lunch by Lloyd George to meet Hogge and Major Entwistle, a young Asquithean barrister who was M.P. for South-West Hull. Scott was told that Hogge and Entwistle had devised a scheme for reunion to be made public by an exchange of letters between Lloyd George and Entwistle, and that an informal meeting of reunionists from both wings of the Liberal party which had been arranged for that afternoon would be followed by another, more formal, meeting on Monday.[9] These meetings[10] received a frosty welcome from the Asquithean leaders. According to Lloyd George they 'cajoled or even bullied' the Asquithean parliamentary party into opposing the scheme.[11] Asquith made a discouraging speech at Cambridge. On March 14 Scott produced a 'helpful' leader. In a speech that evening Lloyd George made a belligerent demand for a distinctive Liberal policy and programme and a serious attempt to meet the party's desire for reunion by means of 'consultation, discussion between the Whips [and] conferences as to the best means of bringing before the House of Commons matters of common concern to Liberals'.[1] On March 20 the reunionists decided to ask Asquith and Lloyd George to establish a permanent consultative committee on which both would sit with Simon and Mond.[2] The Asquithean leaders once more did their best to stall. Fisher, hearing that they were doing so, called on Asquith and was told that the plan for a meeting between Asquith and Lloyd George was 'premature'.[3] In the third week of March Asquith persuaded a meeting of the Asquithean parliamentary party to reject it unanimously.[4]

From this point on Lloyd George emphasised that 'Liberalism [was] done for as a national driving force' if reunion was not achieved and blamed the Asquitheans for failing to achieve it.[5] On March 25 he decided that his followers would not accept the Asquithean Whip.[6] On April 6 he devised a new programme but decided not to publish it.[7] On April 24 he told the chairman of the reunited Liberals in Manchester that he would make no more speeches about reunion for the present in view of the nagging which went on whenever he did so.[8] When invited to address the Manchester Liberal party on April 29, he spelt out the first of the massive programmes with which his twenty years in opposition were to be punctuated.

With this speech Lloyd George ceased to be the liberal defender of the *status quo* and reached out to become the radical 'champion ... of the weak against the strong'. A call for the rejection of the 'McKenna duties, the Paris Resolutions and the Safeguarding of Industries Act' provided symbolic assurance of his return to the Liberal party. The 'overthrow' of 'the tyranny of the sword', 'co-operation between Capital and Labour', 'utiliz[ing] ... the soil ... for the people' and 'fair play for the underdog' suggested a revived range of Liberal positions. The elimination of 'class favouritism' to produce 'educational opportunities ... for the development of the brain and intellect of the best ... without regard to origin'; a housing policy 'not merely [to] complete the deficiency in the number of houses ... but [to] eradicate slumdom out of British civilization'; a lament, to be investigated later, for 'the waste' the community suffered 'in ... coal supplies' and an attack on the 'waste produced by alcohol in the health and strength and the happiness of the people' completed a programme whose purpose was 'to remedy the evils of modern industrialism' and establish Lloyd George as the only 'safe' politician who could beat the Labour party at its own game.

This programme was tailored to put Lloyd George in the van of Liberal reunion and to stimulate a constituency demand to open the Liberal party to his leadership. It aimed to undercut the Labour party's working-class appeal by promising at least as much as the Labour leaders had promised themselves and to make it possible to attach some Labour leaders to him when Liberal unity had been achieved. It was an attempt to sell 'our liberties' to the poor and to distinguish the Liberal concern for the amelioration of society from the 'fascist' temper of Law's Die Hard supporters in one direction and from 'Socialism [which] would enslave Labour for its own benefit' in the other. It reminded the Asquithean leaders that 'Liberalism [was] not a proprietary medicine sold in bottles with only one label in shops duly licensed and by agents properly authorized' but was something 'broader ... wider' about whose future 'we have a right to express our views'.[1]

The Manchester speech produced a renewal of constituency demands for reunion.[2] It was followed by a similar speech the night Baldwin became Prime Minister.[3] The impetus was sustained in the months following by homilies on the Empire as the Protector of Humanity,[4] the Churches and International Peace,[5] the Churches' duty to the League of Nations,[6] the need for Right to replace Force in political life,[7] the 'Vision of the new Home' which Humanity expected[8] and other persuasive versions of the claim that 'a new temper' needed to be 'created', 'pride [to be] enshrined in the Conscience of Man ... [and] the light lit on the Mercy Seat in the heart of man' if 'Humanity' was to 'leap forward' and men really to believe 'that the Galilean ha[d] conquered'.[9]

When Lloyd George crossed the Atlantic for a well-publicised lecture tour in September, Liberal reunion had made little progress at the top. It was complete in Manchester. In Wales it had been more or less completed by St Davids on behalf of Lloyd George's Welsh National Council and Ellis Davies, the head of the

Asquithean Welsh Liberal Federation.[1] Acland had fought the Tiverton by-election as candidate of a united party and won a seat which was Conservative the previous November. Lloyd George had made clear which side of the divide he stood on so far as Protection was concerned. He continued to claim contact with Austen Chamberlain who, he continued to claim, was a Liberal,[2] and to suggest that a government as Die Hard as Baldwin's would push progressive Conservatives towards himself. He laid claims to lead any movement there might be for Radical progress. He had shown that, if Lord Gladstone would not have him, he could stay at Hawarden with Henry Gladstone instead.[3] But, whatever his more sanguine followers may have hoped,[4] the prospect was unpromising. Apart from his own the newspapers were not helpful.[5] He had no bait except his name with which to attract either 'progressive Conservatives' or the sort of 'moderate Labour leaders' for whom he was fishing. He had lost one parliamentary follower to the Conservative party.[6] The Asquithean leaders had made it clear that, so far as they were concerned, there was nothing doing.

(ii)

From the parting of the ways in 1920, the Asquithean Liberals had tried to become the focus of opposition to the Coalition. They had not succeeded: Anti-Waste on the one hand, the Labour party on the other had done as well as they had. But they welcomed the crumbling of Lloyd George's reputation. They approved of the Conservative party's decision to bring down the Coalition. They expected that no one would get a clear majority at an election and that the Liberal party would be 'the core or nucleus of any new administration' to be formed after it.[7] They convinced themselves that Lloyd George was no longer a Liberal and could not be allowed to return to the Liberal party. They were spared the decision to support Law's government by Law's decision to fight an election as soon as he came into office. During the election campaign they made it clear that they did not want the Coalition restored[8] and hoped for a result which would remove all scope for initiative from Lloyd George.

At the election of 1922 the only formal arrangements between the Lloyd George and Asquithean Liberals were in Manchester and Salford, where the Coalition Liberals approached the Asquitheans after being rejected by the Conservative party.[1] Between the two Liberal parties in general there was no warmth. There was some heat and, at a national level, no co-operation. Gladstone and Maclean made public attacks on Lloyd George as soon as it seemed likely that he would be leaving office. There was backbiting between Lloyd George and Grey[2] and also between Churchill and Grey who thought the fall of the Coalition had taken 'something that was not wholesome out of the political atmosphere'.[3] Grey failed to respond enthusiastically to the announcement, made in his presence at the Free Trade Hall, Manchester, that the Asquithean and Lloyd George Liberals would be fighting the election in Manchester together.[4] Lloyd George seems to have given public encouragement to Maclean's Conservative opponent in Glasgow. Lloyd George appeared on the platforms of Coalition Conservatives: they appeared on his.

Like the Labour party, the Asquithean Liberals fought the 1922 election at a disadvantage. Until Lloyd George fell, they had conducted a personal campaign against him. At by-elections this had not been successful, but, if the election had been fought against the Coalition, they might have attracted support from Conservatives who would not vote for Lloyd George, were not Die Hards and could not face the Labour party. By the time the election came, the situation had changed: 'the suicide of the Coalition ... took much of the punch out of the fight'.[5] Lord Robert Cecil and McKenna supported Law. So did all the Conservatives who had criticised the Coalition in the previous two years. Despite argument between Birkenhead and the leading members of the government, the united front presented by the Conservative party was impressive.

Moreover, the Liberal leaders, far from changing their tactics, acted as though the Coalition had not fallen. They blamed 'both wings' of the Coalition 'for its misdeeds' and claimed credit for the warning they had given in 1918 that the 'specious appeal' put forward by Law and Lloyd George meant the 'abandonment of principle and the substitution of autocratic for parliamentary government'. It was the Asquithean party which had exposed the 'disastrous and costly adventures in Russia ... and Mesopotamia', the Coalition's brutality in Ireland and the 'ill conceived ... breach ... in our Free Trade system ... which ha[d] hampered our industrial recovery during the last four years'. They claimed, in the well-worn phrases of their manifesto, to stand for private enterprise, for 'economy' instead of 'waste', for 'the well-being of the community as a whole above the interests of any particular section or class' and for 'the simple truth ... that great and necessary schemes of social reform, involving large outlay of public money, cannot be realized ... until Peace has been established by a foreign policy ... conceived in the spirit of the League of Nations and National Finance ... placed upon sure foundations by a course of rigorous economy'.

Simon believed that McKenna's support for Law would have no effect since 'most ... voters ... realized that Bonar Law ... as a chief spokesman for the last government, insist[ed] that further economies were impossible'. He believed voters were feeling that the 'Liberals had stuck to their guns and ... fought for the same things ... in the wilderness' as they were fighting for now the election had started.[1] Grey felt the strongest objection to Lloyd George taking foreign policy out of Foreign Office hands[2] and wanted it removed from party politics where it had been put for the first time in thirty years. He drew a line 'between those who think it ... a crime against the nation to destroy th[e] Coalition ... and those who think it would be a crime ... to re-establish it'.[3] Though Grey expressed a half-hearted preference for a Liberal government, he did not expect one to emerge. What he expected was a continuation of Law's government to provide a chance to construct a 'new alternative to Conservatism'.[4] He caused considerable distress by praising Baldwin and 'infinitely prefer[ring] a straight Conservative government to a return to the old Coalition'.[5]

Maclean thought 'public life' would be 'all the better' for Law's absolute majority.[6] Asquith 'gloat[ed] ... with satisfaction ... over the corpses [left] ... on the battlefield' by the massacre of Lloyd George Liberals,[7] but the election of 1922 was hardly a triumph for them. Asquith doubled his following in the House of Commons. But he was eclipsed not only by Law but also by the Labour party which made large inroads on potential Liberal support and was once more the chief party of opposition. Five

Asquithean candidates out of six were defeated, including Maclean, Runciman and Howard. Asquith had a few more followers than Lloyd George, but the Labour party had twenty more than the two Liberal parties put together.

Moreover, the Conservative majority – a decisive condemnation of the Coalition – freed Lloyd George from commitment to the Coalition Conservatives. His freedom presented a threat to Asquithean control of historic Liberalism. The fact that Lloyd George was no longer tied by Conservative allies meant that Asquith was no longer its only guardian. The threat of assistance from Lloyd George disturbed Asquith's immediate followers.[1]

The objection felt by the Asquithean leaders was not just based on anger at past wrongs. It was based on personal and political calculation and on fears about the future. It was based on the belief that reunion meant an attempt to restore Lloyd George to a position of authority in the Liberal party with the danger that he would use his money as a 'bait ... to catch' Asquithean M.P.s in order to make a bid for the leadership when Asquith's age made a change inevitable.[2] In this sense their caution about reunion in 1922/3 was a facet of a simple struggle for power: they thought their own prospects would be poor if Lloyd George returned in strength. This consideration can hardly have applied to Asquith. It may not have applied to Maclean. It probably did not apply in any simple sense to Grey, though any prospect Grey may have had as leader of a Liberal-based, anti-Lloyd George, anti-socialist government of the Centre would have been reduced by Lloyd George's return to the Liberal party. But it applied to Runciman, Crewe, Simon, Cowdray and Buckmaster. It applied most of all to Gladstone who, since January 1922, had been 'the only person in the official Liberal ranks who ha[d] punched Lloyd George without intermission'.[3] Gladstone saw more clearly than anyone else that there would be a demand for 'new men' and a clean sweep if reunion was allowed to happen. He made continued co-operation conditional on an understanding that his retirement would not be negotiable as an instrument of reunion.[4]

It was, however, not just personal fear that stimulated resistance to Lloyd George. There was also a belief that Lloyd George's arrival would do the Liberal party positive damage. This was partly a matter of conduct – what Grey thought of as 'a difference of moral approach'. Partly, it was a consequence of the view that Lloyd George wanted to betray the Liberal party in 1910, did so in 1916 and 1918 and would do so again if the Chamberlainite connection seemed as helpful to him as it was objectionable to Liberals who had kept the Liberal organisation intact since Asquith fell.[1] To Gladstone it was Lloyd George's domestic entourage that made him unacceptable as a colleague. To Simon it was that Lloyd George was 'done' as a political figure.[2] There was a feeling that Lloyd George distrusted the League of Nations, which Liberals had made one of the centres of their creed, and that his return would attract the wrong sort of Conservative, deter the right sort and drive some Liberals into the Labour party.[3] There was the judgment, which some Conservatives shared, that, with Lloyd George back in the Liberal party, the Liberals would attract all the hostility they thought he had earned for the Coalition between 1920 and 1922. And there were the linked convictions that Law's government was inherently inferior, that a government of the Right could not last and that a unique combination of Grey's dignity, Asquith's experience and vague genuflections towards ordered progress would enable them to capture the same measure of Labour support as Gladstone had captured by negotiation between 1903 and 1905.

How far the Asquitheans wanted to co-operate with the Labour party, how far they wanted to undercut it, how far they developed relations in order to undercut Lloyd George is uncertain. In 1923 there was a certain amount of contact with the Labour leaders. The closer the contact, the clearer the contrast became between socialist progress and the unwillingness of the Liberal leaders to consider 'a big shifting of taxation from the mass to the wealthy'.[4] Nevertheless, in an open situation where few landmarks were secure, detachment from Lloyd George, from the Conservative Coalitionists and from the Conservative party itself seemed the course most likely to be rewarded when Law outstayed his welcome.

When Lloyd George began putting out feelers in late 1922 the Asquithean leaders had, however, to tread carefully. They could not afford to offend the body of the party which was supposed to want reunion more than it wanted anything else.[5] They could not easily reject reunionist advances from staunch Liberals with whom they had no quarrel. They did not deny that there were 'quite good Liberals' among Lloyd George's supporters with whom they would be happy to work, even if they had not yet got very far in dealing with them.[1] Nor did they deny that the party organisation was 'rotten from top to bottom' and needed renovating from the top.[2] But there was 'no suggestion of a big, energetic, generous Liberal movement which would sweep the whole party together and make all artificial divisions and names meaningless'.[3]

Although they stopped short of open denunciation, the Asquithean leaders used all the weapons of resistance they could find. The party conference at Buxton was packed and managed in order to produce the results that were required.[4] Mrs Asquith refused to meet Lloyd George: a distribution of pencilled notes emphasised her detestation. Asquith's 'limitations as a leader' were no less marked than in 1921, but his continued leadership now became a necessary barrier against Lloyd George.[5] Maclean took care to attack the record of the Coalition;[6] Simon did the same.[7] Grey's blindness, the intermittent nature of his attention and his instinct for the Conservative party had been depressing. He played the League of Nations, but not in a way which convinced Scott that he had been converted. His taste for Economy and a Muslim foreign policy did little to differentiate him from a Conservative. It was not until Simon prodded him in the middle of the election that he had spelt out the policy changes – in Mesopotamia, for example – which would make Economy possible.[8]

In a party whose policy preferences were hostile to France and became more so with the invasion of the Ruhr, Grey was deviant. He thought France deserved reparation for America's withdrawal from the post-war settlement. On this he was unwilling to compromise, even if compromise might help the party.[9] There was nothing Radical about Grey's mind or speeches: rumours that he was about to follow Novar and McKenna into the Conservative party had that measure of plausibility.[10] He had extensive experience of foreign policy, however, at a moment at which foreign policy was crucial. With the invasion of the Ruhr, Maclean 'press[ed] on him that Destiny – Providence – God, I prefer to say, call[ed] him to a lofty world duty'. Haldane tried to stop him but Maclean persuaded him to lead the Liberal peers if he should be elected, and succeeded in fixing the election.[1]

The leadership of the Liberal party in the House of Lords was important. Birkenhead had appointed himself leader of the opposition peers immediately the general election was over. Lloyd George claimed to have a hundred followers.[2] With Birkenhead in a position of prominence, Lloyd George would be well placed in the event of an unscheduled change of government. Lloyd George tried to prevent Grey becoming leader and to establish that a nominee of his own would be deputy if Grey did so. In doing this Lloyd George operated through Lord Beauchamp.

Though both sides of his family had wobbled in the middle and late nineteenth century, Beauchamp had started life as a Conservative. After being Mayor of Worcester at twenty-five, he had an unsuccessful period in his late twenties as governor of New South Wales. He was one of the Free Traders who joined the Liberal party during Balfour's ministry. During the Liberal government of 1906, Beauchamp and his wife – a Grosvenor – made Halkyn House a major social centre. Beauchamp rose from being Captain of the Gentlemen of Arms in 1905 to the Lord Presidency of the Council on Morley's resignation at the beginning of the war. His usefulness, and office, ended with the admission of real Conservatives to the Coalition of 1915: he had been out of office since. He now set out, at the age of fifty, to reconstruct his political career, fell victim to Lloyd George's charms[3] and annoyed the Asquithean leaders by proposing that the Lloyd George peers should nominate Grey's deputy if Grey became leader. Beauchamp's use of entertainment as an instrument of reconciliation was unimpressive. He had, Crewe thought, 'no capacity to attach people to himself' and was aiming too obviously to lead the House of Lords when Grey withdrew.[4] In 1923 he was not successful.[5]

Between November 1922 and October 1923, then, there were two separate Liberal parties, each claiming to be the guardian of the true tradition, each accusing the other of betraying it. There was co-operation at constituency level and in some cases at by-elections informally between the party headquarters. There were recurrent demands for reunion from leaders at constituency and area level.[1] At each point at which a desire for reunion was expressed by back-benchers, by constituency Liberals or by Lloyd George, the Asquithean leaders paid lip-service but nothing more. At Cambridge in March Asquith refused to take special steps to bring it about. In April he declined invitations to address the reunited Manchester branch of the League of Young Liberals[2] and a Leeds Liberal Federation lunch with Lloyd George which Lloyd George had already accepted.[3] At Bournemouth in early May and at the Asquithean party conference, he attacked the ambiguity of the Coalition Liberal voting record in the House of Commons and pointed out 'that a substantial percentage of the [Lloyd George] Liberals in the House of Commons owe[d] their seats to Tory ... votes'. He claimed that 'there [were] many stages ... in the long road which separates individualism from Communism ... [and] not a few of those who fight in the Labour camp ... ha[d] ideals ... and even ... purposes which [were] of Liberal origin'. He replied to Lloyd George's Manchester speech by repeating that 'reunion mean[t] ... reunion of Liberals for the Liberal purposes and politics' which had grown out of the pre-war assault on low wages, bad housing and 'the evils of the land system' into a contemporary programme of industrial partnership, public motivation and worker security, adding, in words which could be applied to Grey as much as to Churchill and Lloyd George at whom they were aimed, that he 'would take no part ... in any adventure' designed to give reality to the 'phantom ... of a Central party in which Liberals and moderate Conservatives should unite and present a solid phalanx against revolution on the one flank and reaction on the other'.[4] When Baldwin became Prime Minister Grey praised his 'integrity of purpose', did not think that 'in the Liberal party there was hostility to the Labour party as such' and feared that the 'difficulties in the way of re-union' about which the party would have to 'go slow' – were 'founded on a deep moral feeling ... and it was no use pretending that they did not exist'.[5]

The policy of resistance did not exclude consultation between Asquith and Lloyd George about day-to-day tactics in the House of Commons. But it was designed to achieve reunion without the obligation to allow Lloyd George to return to the 'counsels of the party'. This line of policy was strengthened by the appointment of Vivian Phillips as Chief Whip.[1] It was continued right up to the point at which Lloyd George returned from America in November. By himself Lloyd George could not have done very much about it.

XIII

THE INADEQUACY OF BONAR LAW

'If Bonar Law gets a majority, we shall have five years of reaction.'
> Lloyd George talking to C. P. Scott, C. P. Scott diary, October
> 23 1922

'I think perhaps it would be useful if I repeat again to you the words which I used in the first speech when I became leader of our party [in 1911] ... "No government of which I am a member will ever be a government of reaction ..." That was my view then: ... it is my view today, and if I thought the Unionist party was, or would ever become, a party of that kind, I would not be a member of it.'
> Bonar Law at Public Baths, Old Kent Road, November 7 1922,
> *Daily Telegraph*, November 8

'They are, of course, a purely Conservative administration, but they have promised, I believe quite honestly, not to raise any of the old flags of fierce political controversy. Free Trade is not to be interfered with. Nothing is to be done which goes farther against Free Trade than the McKenna Tariff, the Paris resolutions of Mr Asquith and Mr Runciman or the Safeguarding of Industries Act of the late government. The protective taxation of food which broke up the Conservative government of 1900, which caused many secessions from the Conservative party and which was for so many years a furious battle-cry, has ceased to figure in any programme. The attempts to restore the veto of the House of Lords and to repeal the Parliament Act have been relegated to a remote, hypothetical and nebulous futurity. The Home Rule settlement, which is marching on its path, is being ... loyally and skilfully carried out by this Unionist and Die Hard administration ... Practically all the controversies about the franchise have been settled in a Liberal and Radical sense. As for taxation there is no great country in the world where it is raised on a more democratic basis, nor is there any government which today makes more severe demands upon the direct tax-payer and upon the owners of property than this high Tory government.

None of these facts can be disputed: and in the face of them I ask "where are the great crucial questions that separate Mr Asquith and Viscount Grey on the one hand from Mr Bonar Law and Lord Curzon on the other?" '
> Churchill at Aldwych Club, May 4 1923, *The Times*, May 5

At first sight the Carlton Club meeting of October 19 1922 looked like a victory for the Die Hards. In the months which followed, Lloyd George, Birkenhead and MacDonald claimed that the

237

Conservative Party was sunk in the most deplorable reaction. Historians may be excused who have supposed that it was.

However, just as the movement against the Coalition had not been effective until first Salisbury and then a wide range of central Conservatives had joined it, so now the Die Hard movement was weakened by Salisbury and these central Conservatives joining Law's government.

Law had some things in common with the Die Hards. He was opposed to Lloyd George's policy in the Near East. He had been critical of the Genoa exercise so far as it involved direct dealing with Lenin. He had been one of the most aggressive of Ulster's supporters at many relevant moments in the previous twelve years. He had, however, been a loyal supporter of Lloyd George's government until his retirement in March 1921: he had made no move to dissociate himself from its policies in India and Egypt. He had favoured a Capital Levy during and at the end of the war and had had persistently to explain to the House of Commons why Economy could not be effected.[1] He had been responsible for the only serious attempt to amalgamate the Conservative party with the Lloyd George Liberals in 1920. He had supported the Irish Treaty in December 1921 and had no intention now of taking steps to abrogate it. Before he retired in 1921, Law had attracted Die Hard criticism: if he had not left office then, he might well have suffered the fate of Austen Chamberlain. One of the major planks in the Die Hard platform had been reform of the House of Lords: Law said nothing in the earliest stages about that. It did not appear in his election manifesto in 1922. It appeared in his election speeches late in the day after urgent prompting and without commitment. It is unlikely that he had any greater interest than Birkenhead in taking this 'last chance of stabilizing the constitution' and removing the opportunity, opened by the Parliament Act of 1911, to an extreme Labour government of producing circumstances in which 'the Soviet system would ... be ... established ... constitutionally'.[2]

It is true that Law's government included a number of ministers who had been close to Salisbury in 1922. Salisbury was Lord President of the Council, a member of the Cabinet and chairman of the Committee of Imperial Defence. After some hesitation[3] McNeill was offered the Foreign Under-Secretaryship and, in

Curzon's absence, became chief Foreign Office spokesman in the House of Commons. Londonderry was offered office, but refused in order to concentrate on membership of the Northern Ireland Cabinet.[1] Office was offered to Milner who refused also.[2] Joynson-Hicks let it be known that he would refuse an under-secretaryship: he became Secretary to the Department of Overseas Trade. Wood and Devonshire joined the Cabinet. Hoare became Air Minister outside the Cabinet.

Of these, however, Joynson-Hicks was the only Die Hard: there were no Die Hards in the Cabinet. Hogg and Inskip had their first experience of office as Attorney- and Solicitor-General respectively. Hills, Buckley, Guinness, Ormsby-Gore, Boyd-Carpenter, Jackson, King, Ashley, Wolmer, Linlithgow, Lane Fox and the Duke of Sutherland all became junior ministers for the first time. Apart from Wolmer, Linlithgow and Boyd-Carpenter, none was a Die Hard. Cave, Home Secretary from 1916 to 1919, was made Lord Chancellor instead of Salisbury's distinguished Die Hard candidate, Lord Sumner, whom Lloyd George had taken to the Peace Conference as a guarantee of financial rectitude.[3] Gretton's offer to succeed Younger in December was not accepted:[4] he seems not to have been offered a peerage.

Lord Robert Cecil, it is true, was offered nothing. Nor was his collaborator, Steel-Maitland, who received an indeterminate offer and an assurance of admiration which was probably all he wanted in view of the risk involved in leaving a directorship of Rio Tinto for a government that might not last.[5] McKenna, however, was offered the Exchequer,[6] while Novar, the new Scottish Secretary, was a Liberal until he joined the Cabinet and had been thought of as a Coalition Liberal replacement for Montagu in March.[7] The Cabinet included Montague-Barlow, Lloyd George's under-secretary at the Ministry of Labour, who claimed that he would have voted with Austen Chamberlain on October 19 if he had been in England, though he 'did not believe ... in a Centre party'.[8] Apart from Cave, Novar and Barlow, every member of Law's Cabinet had detached himself from Lloyd George in the previous twelve months or taken positive steps to bring an end to the Coalition. But Viscount Curzon, Lord Hugh Cecil, Gretton, Banbury, Midleton, Selborne and Salisbury's private secretary, Lord Erskine, were all left out, despite Salisbury's attempt to ensure that they were included.[1] Charles Craig was offered a Household post, which he declined after talking to Carson.[2] Salisbury failed to make policy conditions on joining the Cabinet, let alone the conditions Gretton wanted.[3] So far from imagining that they had gained control, the Die Hards were deeply suspicious. On Carson's advice they decided to keep their organisation in existence against the need that might arise when the government faced the problem of restoring order to the whole of Ireland.[4]

Before the election Law did not know that he would win it. He knew that, if he did not get an absolute majority, there would be tough bargaining with the Chamberlainites. He probably thought that he might have to co-operate with Asquith unless Asquith and the Labour party were strong enough between them to form a government of their own: his government was almost certainly designed to ensure that co-operation would be possible. Co-operation would not necessarily mean Coalition. But the fact that Law had ridden to power on the crest of one wave of anti-Coalition feeling did not remove the need to attract anti-socialist Liberals, whether of the Coalition-Liberal variety in order to weaken the Chamberlainite/Lloyd George axis or 'of the McKenna type as, in Derby's words, 'in fighting Communism we shall want all the help we can get'.[5] In the event Law received a majority big enough for independence but not so big that the Die Hards would be a threat.[6] The Die Hards had been so successful that they had nothing left to do. Their leader was in office. They did not believe that anything effective could be done about Ireland for the moment.[7] They could, therefore, safely be ignored. Until his government suffered a major crisis of confidence in early 1923, Law ignored them.

Law took office in conditions of great uncertainty. Once he had done so, it became necessary to conduct government, create an atmosphere and have a policy at the same time as he decided to hold a general election. The decision to hold an immediate election was not inevitable.[8] It was taken as a result of the time-table implied by the prior decision to honour the Irish Treaty by having a special session to pass the necessary legislation before December 6.[9]

This, the first major decision taken by Law as Prime Minister, caused much smaller difficulty than might have been expected. As in November 1921 there was a strong desire in most parts of the Conservative party to play down the Irish question and there was now no feeling that the government would inevitably be double-faced. Salisbury played the game.[1] McNeill allowed himself to be used to persuade the *Morning Post* to support the Treaty.[2] Gretton may have wanted an excuse to drop the Irish question in order to play a part in the new régime: he may really have believed that 'if the British government accept[ed] the fact of a Republic in Southern Ireland and allow[ed] chaos to continue, ... [the] attempt ... to establish a government ... on Soviet lines ... [would] enforce [British] intervention [to which] the majority in Southern Ireland wo[uld] consent when distress and misery ha[d] gone sufficiently far'.[3] Either way he took the view that the Treaty should not be abandoned.

Of Law's tasks the creation of an atmosphere was the most important. It was also the one in which most originality could be displayed. Not that the originality was exciting, or designed to be. On the contrary, it was designed to be as unexciting as possible in order to impress upon the public mind a contrast between the brassy, vulgar, assertiveness of Lloyd George and Birkenhead and the decent sobriety of the government which had succeeded them. In the eight months of Law's Prime Ministership, the official leaders of the Conservative party gave expression to what can best be described as a mood of pessimistic anti-intellectualism. Provoked by Birkenhead's arrogance towards themselves, by Lloyd George's degrading versatility and by the 'smartness' of the Birkenhead/Lloyd George set-up, they retaliated by offering a mood which was anti-political in the sense that the promises of politicians were devalued and efforts made to establish consonance with what they took to be particularly English qualities of 'honesty, simplicity and balance'.[4] 'Modesty'[5] was opposed to cleverness. The 'hard-headed Scotsman ... frank, honourable and free' now 'at the head of affairs' was contrasted with his predecessor – the 'brilliant person' who had been 'apt to act on the spur of the moment and [to be] a little devious in his political ways'.[6]

Law, Baldwin and Younger began the election campaign uncertain whether they would have an absolute majority at the end of it and needing, therefore, to keep open the possibility of alliance in office with either Lloyd George and the Coalitionists or with Asquith, Grey and the Asquitheans. Law also wanted to restore the unity of the Conservative party: he began therefore by avoiding criticism of Lloyd George. The campaign, however, developed a momentum of its own once Birkenhead and Lloyd George had given it a push. Whether because he calculated that attack was necessary or because he was 'sick as a dog in contemplating the wreck he ha[d] caused by his stupid attitude',[1] Birkenhead developed a heat and sharpness in campaigning which compelled the Conservative leaders to return his compliments.

During the fall of the Coalition, one objective the Conservative rebels had not achieved was to carry Coalition-Liberal ministers with them. When the operation was complete, the Conservative managers began by intending to persuade as many constituency associations as possible to support sitting Lloyd George Liberals. As friction developed between the Conservative leaders and the Lloyd George/Birkenhead group, and as Lloyd George extended the battle against the Conservative party, it became more difficult to ensure that this was done. Younger stopped the battle spreading by threatening to withdraw all support from the Lloyd George Liberals: the Lloyd George Liberals took the hint.[2] At the same time Younger developed arrangements with the Asquitheans. The atmospheric affinity between Grey and most of the Conservative leaders was closer than between them and the Lloyd George/Chamberlainite combination. It is probable that Law really was, as he said, '*very* sorry' about Maclean's defeat at the hands of a Conservative to whom Lloyd George gave, or sent, a message of support.[3]

The decisions to create this atmosphere had three main sources. They reflected feelings which were held genuinely by politicians in rural seats or with rural connections, and the circles in which they moved. They were a development from the rhetoric and image presented by some of these leaders in the past. And they were a response to what they took to be the condition of public feeling. All three operated in proportions which it is difficult to measure. No one who reads the letters written by Conservative politicians to one another in the two years between the disintegration of Lloyd George's reputation in 1920 and his fall in 1922 can doubt that some of them – not only in the Salisbury

circle – disliked and to a certain extent feared the atmosphere
which Austen Chamberlain, Birkenhead, Lloyd George and
Churchill had been creating. They disliked it because political
aggression, verbal disingenuousness, unfulfilled promises, exces-
sively good living and open enjoyment of the use of power abroad
in circumstances which might lead to war were hostile to the
atmosphere they wished to create. They feared it because corruption in the rectitude of the governing authority, deliberate
affronts to the working classes and the philosophy of self-seeking
propagated by Birkenhead would stimulate among the working
classes a reciprocal hostility to the ruling classes which they already
thought was dangerous.

Salisbury had not brought down the Coalition single-handed.
Nor did he run Law's government. But between 1920 and 1922
he reflected feelings to which Baldwin especially, and Law to some
extent, instinctively responded and to which they found it easier
to respond when they had nothing else to offer. The self-consciously
'English' characteristic of the image was Baldwin's, and perhaps
Davidson's, contribution. The assertion that the Russian
situation was the work of 'first-class brains' and the claim that
government by second-rate brains, who happened by a happy
accident sometimes to have had Firsts, was a tranquillising and
unifying factor in the nation's life began to acquire in these
months something resembling the status of cult. Law leaves the
impression of having few articulated convictions even about
Ireland, but it is clear that he knew, and wished to respond to the
fact that the movement by which he had been brought to power
had had as its object to purify the tone of English politics.

The image of simple, unpolitical honesty, even when it had to be
adopted by suppressing what Law actually said,[1] was a reaction
against Birkenhead and Lloyd George. It came to be the first line of
defence against the Labour party. Socialism and 'Communism'
were the objects of attack. It became the object of the 'English
party' to stimulate resistance to the corrupting cleverness with
which alien and alienated minds had imposed themselves upon the
great mass of good-hearted Englishmen. A process of indoctrination was demanded at all levels of the national life in order to
clear out the gains Socialism had made already: the Conservative
party was presented as a spearhead in the assault. Instead, however,

of aggressive attacks on trades union leaders with which Lloyd George and Birkenhead had approached the public, the target now became not so much trades unions as the 'intellectuals' who were misleading the working classes and destroying the natural unity of the English scene. During and immediately after the election, Law refused to receive unofficial deputations of un-employed workers.[1] In December, however, he received one in Glasgow, where his own constituency was situated: despite attempts by Lansbury and others to pretend that he was deter-mined to drive the unemployed to revolution,[2] it is likely that he wished merely to contrast his own desire to return to 'ordinary methods of government'[3] with the personal rule characteristic of the previous government.[4] It is certainly the case that the Clyde-siders were a good deal more respectful of him than they had been of Lloyd George.[5]

A negative mood, though adequate to the circumstances of November 1922, was not thought adequate as a basis for the future. The election gave the Labour party over four million votes and doubled its representation in the House of Commons. Law had an absolute majority of 79, which he had not expected to have, and the prospect, if he wanted it, of five years undisturbed in office. Even allowing for Law's pessimism, however, the outlook seems not to have been bright. It was not only the Labour party that was feared. There was also the danger that the two Liberal wings might reunite to provide a progressive liberal bulwark against Socialism.

Law claimed in public that he wanted the Liberal party re-united and restored to its original place in the party system.[6] Apart from a talk to C. P. Scott, which is not evidence of intention, there is no evidence from private conversation that Law welcomed the restoration of the Liberal party. The most that can be said is that he may really have believed that 'Labour was ... at the top of the wave' from which it would 'decline' if the Liberal party could win back the intelligentsia and present a united front now that the Coalition was finished.[7]

The Liberal belief that the Conservative party could provide only reactionary resistance to Socialism was not fact but mythology: neither the Asquithean Liberals nor Lloyd George at this stage had any constructive policy of their own. But as the session of 1922/23 got under way and the government's public standing dropped, the Conservative leaders felt increasingly obliged to establish that they could challenge and beat on its own ground any anti-socialist bloc which might emerge from either section of the Liberal party.

The second threat came from the ex-Coalition ministers. In this respect the danger was twofold. On the one hand there was the danger, of which Law was acutely conscious, that the government would be so incompetent that it would be turned out by the Conservative party.[1] On the other, there was the danger that the consequence of a governmental collapse would be a further advance in the Labour vote at a general election or a Lloyd George/Austen Chamberlain/Birkenhead or Austen Chamberlain/Birkenhead/Derby government, thereafter. The exact nature of the possibilities envisaged varied from week to week. There was little prospect of any startling success in foreign policy, either at Lausanne or in relation to France,[2] not much expectation of any immediate reduction in the level of unemployment and only the most speculative hope that the government would be credible enough, whenever it fought an election in the future, to provide the best alternative to Socialism.

The problem, then, was to govern competently and consolidate Conservative leadership of the anti-socialist forces without appearing reactionary in the process. This involved attempts to restore Conservative unity by restoring relations, so far as they could be, with the Chamberlainites. On both sides there was a desire not to destroy the Conservative party organisation. In telling Salvidge on October 18 that he would oppose Austen Chamberlain next day, Law did not suppose he could 'rule the country with the sort of people that will be left after the break to-morrow', explained that he 'must have' Chamberlain and Birkenhead back 'at the first possible opportunity' and asked Salvidge to 'tell them not to let it be protracted by unnecessary bitterness'.[3] The morning after the Carlton Club meeting Birkenhead told Salvidge that, as leader of Orange Liverpool, he should rally to the new leader. On October 19 Balfour was extremely angry. Immediately after Law's election as leader, however, he was party to an attempt to persuade Ullswater to join the government as Colonial Secretary in order to repeat in Ireland the success he had had in producing an agreed scheme for electoral reform in preparation for the Reform Bill of 1918.[1] In December Balfour agreed to go to Geneva in the coming session to carry on the work he had done in office on the Austrian Treaty.[2] At the end of the year Law paid him a visit at Whittingehame.

Law did his best to extend the range of his government in Liberal directions. In spite of refusing the Exchequer, McKenna advised Law freely and saw him often.[3] Grey also saw him regularly, if only to play bridge.[4] Novar was a Liberal Imperialist who had once been Rosebery's secretary. After six years as Governor-General of Australia, he had been out of politics since he returned to England in 1920. He was, however, a friend of Long and a well-known figure in Scotland. His appointment as Secretary for Scotland was a symbol of the fact that in Scotland the Liberal party was the natural party of resistance. In November 1922 the Paris Embassy was given to Crewe who had been a minister in all Liberal governments between 1892 and December 1916 and part of the Asquithean leadership since.

These, however, were minor gains: though Law was better placed to do so than anyone else, he succeeded neither in significantly extending the range of his government in Liberal directions nor in healing the breach in the Conservative party. The rebuffs he received from Worthington-Evans, and from Horne the night Griffith-Boscawen was defeated at Mitcham,[5] reflected the widespread belief that the government would disintegrate as soon as Law's health compelled him to leave it.

Law's failure to make headway in either direction did nothing to improve the security of his position: his health did nothing to guarantee permanent security for the group which had destroyed the Coalition in the first place. Law's health, Birkenhead's alliance with Rothermere and Beaverbrook's and Rothermere's attacks[6] all provided elements of danger. Since the Chamberlainites would not play, special pains had to be taken with the Die Hards. The promotion of Joynson-Hicks, Hall's appointment as Chief Agent on Fraser's retirement and two distributions of under-secretaryships[7] as a result of ministerial defeats at by-elections in March 1923[8] were part of an attempt to 'break up the Die Hards' or to ensure that they had no respectable leaders.[9] They may also have been an attempt to keep close to them in case Law's retirement precipitated a Chamberlainite coup. The transfer of Younger from the party chairmanship[1] to the treasurer-ship to remove the confusion caused by Farquhar's donation of Conservative funds to Lloyd George was a recognition of the importance the Die Hards attached to keeping party funds in party hands.

The second problem Law faced was to provide long-term guide-lines in establishing an attractive policy. This was connected with his third task – of conducting day-to-day administration without damaging his government's reputation for competence and rectitude or making a long-term policy incredible. In both these problems Law faced considerable difficulty, the extent of which was concealed by his resignation in May and Baldwin's more obvious failure later in the year to deal with the problems he had left.

In the first place, it was not clear what, if any, alternative could be offered to the positive policies put forward by the Labour party. This problem, though it existed at the election of 1922, was greatly increased by MacDonald's return to the House of Commons, by his election as leader of the Parliamentary Labour Party and by the greatly increased Labour vote, which in itself increased the plausibility of the Labour party. In searching for a plausible alternative, Law was chained to some extent by his immediate past. One of the chief sources of discontent with the Coalition government had been the high level of taxation and government spending. From the beginning of the Law government, and more especially after the election of 1922, Baldwin and Law committed themselves to a cautiously hedged promise to reduce both.[2] Baldwin made some reductions in his Budget in April 1923[3] by keeping a close check on other ministers.[4] These reductions were smaller than the reductions Horne had made in his Budget in May 1922 and, even so, had been made possible less by anything the new government had done than by the organised assault on govern-ment spending of which the Geddes Committee had been the spearhead. Reductions in government spending continued to be a prominent feature of the government's commitment, but it was by no means certain that it would be possible to fulfil them. Law evidently wanted to pursue policies which 'sounded like private enterprise',[5] but he made it clear in January 1923 that there would have to be subsidies for housing and it was far from certain that he would be willing to encourage a cut-back anywhere else.[6]

Again, agriculture presented problems. As leaders of a government whose existence had been made possible by a change of allegiance on the part, especially, of agricultural M.P.s, Baldwin and Law felt obliged to do something for agriculture. The two commitments – to reduce government spending and taxation and to satisfy agriculture – conflicted, and the conflict was resolved, again negatively, by declarations that any assistance that might be given to agriculture would be given in the form not of subsidies but of improved credit facilities and reform of the rating laws. This did nothing to pacify Selborne, Pretyman, the NFU and the agricultural lobby.[1] To judge from his speeches, Baldwin did not expect quick results from rating reform. One way of reducing taxation, however, was to tax imports. It is likely that Baldwin was thinking about this range of options as an insurance against his inability to fulfil promises about taxation and agriculture in a situation in which industrial depression would reduce the yield of existing levels of taxation in the future.

The difficulty about Protection as a basis for positive policy was that it was certain to divide the Conservative party. The Coalition had not been brought down by Protectionists alone or on Protectionist grounds. Baldwin, Law, Neville Chamberlain, Amery, Bridgeman and Gretton were convinced Protectionists but Salisbury, Derby and Devonshire were not. There had been conflict, even in the Lloyd George Cabinet, between Derby and Baldwin about Safeguarding. Law was more willing than anyone else among the new leaders of the party to contemplate immediate Protection.[2] The decision to avoid Protection at the 1922 election was taken in view of the fact, which even Amery recognised, that any insistence on 'putting Tariff Reform in the forefront of official policy' would loosen the ties which bound together the Conservative enemies of Coalition.[3] The pledge given by Law during the election[4] not to make any fundamental change in the fiscal system of the country during the new parliament, which might last until 1927, was designed to encourage support from the 'very large number of prominent men engaged in business who belonged all their life to the Liberal party', but who had 'declared to [him] personally that at present, whatever happens in the future ... the best chance of restoring confidence and stability is by returning a Unionist Government'.[5]

248

In this respect McKenna led the way both by public statements and by appearing on a Conservative platform in the City of London.[1] Baldwin flattered neither the Conservative Coalitionists nor the Asquitheans. But the comparative absence of Die Hards from the government and Law's election speeches left no doubt that stability, tranquillity and an absence of positive commitment in nearly all directions were designed to attract as wide a range of anti-socialist *voters* as Austen Chamberlain had hoped to attract by formal Coalition, while making it possible for individual supporters of the Coalition-Conservative, Coalition-Liberal and Asquithean groups to vote for him, appear on his platforms or join his government.

In early 1924 when Protection had been tried and found wanting, the Conservative party committed itself to a combination of anti-socialism and limited but positive social reform in place of the mixture of anti-socialism and positive Protection it had offered at the election of 1923. In late 1922 it was common ground that anti-socialism was not enough by itself to ensure permanent Conservative leadership of anti-socialist sentiment. If it be asked why Law added neither Protection nor any very strong social reform emphasis to the Conservative platform, the answer must be that, though the first would have cohered with the commitment to reduce taxation, it would have destroyed the government, and that the second would have conflicted with the taxation commitment itself.

In appreciating the atmosphere which Law was trying to create, one must be conscious, finally, of the restraints imposed, and the opportunities given, by the needs of policy. Political atmosphere was not created in a vacuum: it went on within a framework of practicability. But the framework of practicability did not provide the atmosphere. A course of action was presented as desirable according to the atmospheric preferences of the politician concerned. There was no need to present criticism of Lloyd George's Greek policy as the difference between a policy and manner suitable to war and a policy and manner suitable to peace.[2] It was not essential to turn Birkenhead's sarcasm at the limited experience of the new ministers into something resembling a claim that they 'stood for youth'. Nor was it obligatory for Baldwin to present the payment of the American debt, on which the Die Hards had always insisted, as an action which, whatever its political and financial point, 'must [in addition] add moral ... weight'.[1]

When Law's retirement was first mentioned in April 1923 the government was doing as badly as the Coalition at its worst. Its by-election performance had been uniquely bad.[2] The Labour party had been as good as in its period of maximum success in 1920/21. In fighting the Mitcham by-election after losing his seat at the general election, Griffith-Boscawen, without consulting the Cabinet, had committed it not to de-control housing in 1924, and lost the by-election notwithstanding.[3] There has been serious Cabinet conflict between Curzon and anyone else who tried to speak about foreign policy.[4] There had been a marked want of cordiality, expressed in many parts of the Cabinet and issuing in threats of resignation from Derby and Devonshire, towards Law's negative pessimism and his 'uncompromising', 'autocratic' and 'dictatorial' tendency seriously to limit Cabinet discussion.[5] The Ruhr had been occupied and relations with France deteriorated more than at any time under Lloyd George.[6] The government had actually been defeated on one occasion in the House of Commons.[7] When Law announced that his doctors had advised him to take an immediate holiday in order to decide whether to continue as Prime Minister, it was certain that a Chamberlainite coup was on the way.[8]

XIV

THE ARRIVAL OF MR BALDWIN

'There is nothing to be said against Horne ... Personally I do not
see ... any objection to Worthington-Evans ... But I do not agree with
you about Austen Chamberlain. He is a very old friend of mine and I
like him very much, but he is identified in the public mind not unreason-
ably with the abandonment of principle and the disintegration of Conservatism which was ... one of the main reasons of the fall of the late
government.'

> Salisbury to Stamfordham, May 23 1923, Geo. V K1853/24

'Lord Balfour ... more than once ... stressed the need ... for reunion
for the sake of the very existence of the Conservative party and mentioned
Mr Austen Chamberlain, Sir Robert Horne and Sir L. Worthington-
Evans – he did not refer to Lord Birkenhead.'

> Stamfordham to the King, n.d. but May 21 or 22 1923, Geo. V
> K1853/10

'Mr Baldwin said he could not continue to be Chancellor of the Exchequer
as well as Prime Minister and would try to secure the return of Sir
Robert Horne for that office. If Lord Curzon resigned [from the Foreign
Office], he should then hope to induce Mr Austen Chamberlain to
return to the Party to fill that office, failing him perhaps Lord Robert
Cecil.'

> Stamfordham memo dated May 22 1923, Geo. V K1853/17

(i)

For leading Conservatives in the Coalition the Carlton Club
meeting had been an affront. Their advice had been rejected. It
had been rejected in public. They had been turned out of office.
Most of them had not been offered office in the new government
which they would in any case not have joined. And all this had
been done to them by men who, apart from Curzon and Law,
they thought as inexperienced as they were second-rate. Law was
ambitious enough to want to be Prime Minister 'even for three
weeks'. Curzon had double-crossed them. The opportunity to
use Lloyd George to create a powerful party of resistance to
Labour had been lost: there was no guarantee that it would recur.
They believed there was a danger that Lloyd George would yield
to the 'clamour' the Labour party was supposed, quite wrongly,
to be making in order to get him.[1]

At the Carlton Club meeting 88 M.P.s supported Austen Chamberlain. Thirteen of his ministerial supporters signed a declaration the same afternoon objecting to the ingratitude being shown to Lloyd George, dissociating themselves from the government they expected to be formed and raising a banner for Coalition and what was taken to be 'a Centre party[1] in the future'.[2] Of these thirteen[3] Lord Lee of Fareham knew he could expect no quarter from the Conservative party under Law's leadership, had an unbalanced regard for Lloyd George's personality and acknowledge no leader but Lloyd George himself.[4] He was, however, a figure of no weight and, as it turned out, no future except as chairman of commissions beginning with the Royal Commission on the Civil Service in India to which he was consigned early in 1923. Crawford was a representative of prevailing Scottish Coalitionism: he withdrew from active politics, as it turned out, for good. Pollock refused requests, transmitted by Beaverbrook on Law's behalf, that he should become Lord Chancellor: he was rewarded and put out of action by being made Master of the Rolls in late 1923. Gilmour decided that his regard for Lloyd George should not divide him from the body of the party: he continued to act as Scottish Whip during the election.[5] Scott kept feet in both camps. He stayed close to Birkenhead but by the end of March was clear that there should be no Cave.[6] G. A. Gibbs – Long's son-in-law – who had been Treasurer of the Household since April 1921 appeared on Coalitionist platforms during the election but resumed office on November 6 and was made a Privy Councilllor in 1923. Mitchell-Thomson lost his seat at the election and did not return to parliament until December 1923. Among the junior signatories Elliot and Thomson were restored to office early in the New Year.

In Birkenhead's case, the fall of the Coalition induced a mixture of temper and contempt which he made no attempt to conceal from the public. He deputised for Lloyd George at Bristol when Lloyd George was ill,[7] spoke for McCurdy in Northampton and exerted himself on Kellaway's behalf in Bedford.[8] He attacked the 'forces of reaction',[9] which had engineered the coup and praised Lloyd George – 'the most distinguished living Englishman' – throughout.[10] He sneered at the government for having five Secretaries of State in the House of Lords.[11] As the campaign developed, he attacked Law with whom at first he commiserated for having to confront 'first-class problems' with a Cabinet of 'second-class brains'.[1] Earlier in the year Younger had been the 'cabin boy' who 'tried to seize the helm ... when the tempest raged and the captain was on the bridge'. Now 'no man ha[d] been in such grave physical danger ... since the day th[e] proverbial bullfrog swelled itself up in rivalry with the bull until it burst'.[2] Griffith-Boscawen's transition from the Ministry of Agriculture under Lloyd George to the Ministry of Health under Law showed that there was hope for 'a country which possesse[d] statesmen able to adapt themselves so quickly to ... new surroundings'. Wilson's conversion from being Austen Chamberlain's Chief Whip to being his executioner was 'swifter than any known in secular or sacred history since Saul of Tarsus changed his name'.[3] Birkenhead claimed to have refused the Lord Chancellorship: he is supposed to have said that the only thing he would accept from Law was the Archbishopric of Canterbury.[4] He had a brawl in Liverpool with Derby which greatly annoyed Salvidge and lasted until after the election when Birkenhead, who needed allies, sent first Chilcott and then Churchill to patch it up.[5]

Like Balfour, Horne did not expect Law to get an absolute majority. He expected him to tire quickly of leading a government of incompetents: he looked forward to circumstances in which the difficulty of conducting a minority government in face of an augmented Labour party would make him propose to restore the Coalition. Horne maintained relations with him, while reiterating his support for Lloyd George and appearing on a joint platform in Glasgow.[6] Worthington-Evans toed the Birkenhead line, but was anxious not to be left stranded in the event of the government succeeding. When the election was over, his contribution to discussion was that any Chamberlainite who was offered office should take it.[7]

To Austen Chamberlain the situation contained political and personal aspects of the most disagreeable kind. He had been moved by the responsibility he felt in the last fifteen months of Coalition to construct an anti-socialist party and to ensure that Lloyd George, far from edging towards Labour, would lead resistance to it. Lloyd George had been cast off in circumstances that were as disreputable personally as they were dangerous politically. Chamberlain had been betrayed, as he thought, both by Curzon who 'did promise to go with' the Coalition in Churchill's house and by his own Chief Whip on October 19: for the second time in his career Law had got in his way.[1] The Central Office decision to leave to constituency associations the power to support or oppose Lloyd George Liberals where no Conservative was standing was regarded by the Chamberlainites as a blow to them.[2] Chamberlain's bitterness was not reduced by his inability to prevent Neville Chamberlain taking office which made it difficult to prevent minor Coalitionists doing the same.[3] It was increased by a general party desire, of which Long was a prominent proponent, that even those who had supported the Coalition should recognise that it was finished.[4]

It was intensified by the government's comparative success in the first session of parliament[5] and by the series of Die Hard promotions among which Hall's appointment as Chief Agent was a particularly 'serious offence'.[6] Chamberlain declined the chairmanship of the Royal Commission on the Civil Service in India before Lee accepted it.[7] He did little to encourage Balfour to help the government at the League of Nations.[8] Five months observing it in office taught him that it was not 'second rate' but 'fourth rate' and that the Ministers of Labour and Agriculture had 'no brains'.[9] In chewing over what he took to be the end of his career, Chamberlain had no grudge against Baldwin who 'always showed a strong dislike to the continuation of the Coalition over another election'.[10] To Law Chamberlain's hostility persisted so strongly that it was generally assumed, and Chamberlain stated, that he felt that 'Bonar Law [had] behaved [so] badly to him ... that he could not serve under him'.[11]

Between the fall of the Coalition and the announcement of the election results on November 16, the Chamberlainites hoped that Law would fail to get an absolute majority.[12] His success in getting one did nothing to reconcile Austen Chamberlain to him. The Chamberlainite objective in the next six months was to maintain the strongest group possible in order to take advantage of any opportunity that might arise to destroy Law's government in the future.

As in the last six months of the Coalition, so now Birkenhead was the driving force: on this occasion his expectations were rather different. The restoration of Lloyd George may have been a long-term objective. In the situation created by Law's majority, the primary need was to present the Chamberlainites as alternative leaders of the Conservative party. In doing this he had a number of weapons of which the first was the resentment felt by Austen Chamberlain at the treatment to which he had been subjected. He had the regard in which a good number of Conservative M.P.s continued to hold both Austen Chamberlain and the idea of a Centre party. He had support from a number of peers: in the absence of a Liberal, he did his best to establish himself as opposition leader in the House of Lords. Along with Chamberlain, he had a bodyguard of close supporters including Chilcott, Sassoon and Oliver Locker-Lampson. Until December 1922 he had an office and secretariat under J. C. W. Reith who was introduced by Sir William Bull after Reith had failed to persuade Clynes to give him an entry into Labour politics. The group had a good deal of money – some of it probably from Lloyd George – which Bull made Reith responsible for using. Among ex-ministers Horne, Pollock and Scott were most closely involved. So were Thomson and Walter Elliot until offered office by Law.[1]

Birkenhead thought he had about fifty supporters in the new House of Commons, but it is far from certain that he had.[2] Of the back-benchers who supported Austen Chamberlain on October 19[3] almost half had retired or been defeated: a handful had joined the government. On November 30 sixty M.P.s and peers sat down with Austen Chamberlain to hear a speech from Birkenhead and a letter from Balfour. Balfour, however, had decided, once Law got his majority, that the Gifford Lectures were more important than the autumn session.[4] Despite pressing requests, he neither came from Scotland for the meeting nor did more in his letter than praise Austen Chamberlain for his conduct in the last twelve months.[5] At the dinner Austen Chamberlain repeated his rejection of the view that the two non-socialist parties could forever 'alternate gracefully ... one retiring when tired and giving way to the other'. He announced that the Conservative Coalitionists and the Lloyd George Liberals had paid their debts to one another and that his own group would probably support the Law government provided it was 'true to [the] Unionist ... tradition ... of being the party of moderate constitutional social reform and progress'. He added that the existence of an absolute Conservative majority – which he found 'surprising' – provided no guarantee that four-and-a-half million socialist voters would be beaten at the next election unless special efforts were taken to bring Liberals and Conservatives together.[1] On March 22 1923 another dinner-demonstration was held in Birkenhead's house with Balfour present.[2]

The third thing Birkenhead had, or supposed he had, was widespread support for a Liberal/Conservative alliance among constituency Conservatives and others in many parts of England – especially in Lancashire, West Scotland, Liverpool, Bristol and Birmingham. Most of this support was in no way personal to Birkenhead as the reaction against him when he attacked Derby in Liverpool during the election campaign showed. Even if it existed, it did not make itself effective in the House of Commons.

Fourthly, Birkenhead had his considerable capacity as a journalist and the support given, and platform provided, by the Rothermere newspapers. This may not have done Birkenhead good with Conservative M.P.s: at almost every point at which Rothermere played a hand, it provoked some measure of reaction against him in the House of Commons. Nor was Rothermere's support constant. It had been given freely to the enemies of the Coalition but, until Chanak, was not in principle hostile to Lloyd George and sprang from no instinctive liking for the Conservative party. Esmond Harmsworth had been offered junior office by Law but declined when Law refused to promise immediate withdrawal from Mesopotamia.[3] With Law's refusal to give guarantees about Mesopotamia or to promise Rothermere an earldom, Rothermere went once more into opposition, involving signed attacks by Rothermere himself and a licence to Birkenhead to write freely in the *Daily Mail* which Rothermere acquired on Northcliffe's death.

In late 1922 Beaverbrook and Rothermere made business agreements which gave each shares in some of the newspapers of the other. This made little immediate difference. In January Rothermere refused to meet Law on the ground that they disagreed about Reparations, Palestine and Mesopotamia.[4] In early 1923 Birkenhead and Rothermere spent time abroad together. It is not certain which of them first decided that the new government would not last long. Nor is it clear that Lloyd George and Austen Chamberlain took Birkenhead's advice to 'avoid selecting issues for attacking the government which would not have Rothermere's full support'.[1] In April Birkenhead and Rothermere quarrelled. Urged on by Beaverbrook at the time of Law's illness, Rothermere then swung sharply towards the government, supporting it over Baldwin's Budget and offering, if Law would 'place himself in my hands', to win him the next election and 'hand him down to posterity ... as one of the most successful Prime Ministers in history'.[2] It is difficult to estimate the impact of newspaper criticism on that government's reputation. Rothermere had some effect on the Mitcham by-election in March when an Independent Conservative, financed by Oliver Locker-Lampson and supported by the Rothermere press, put an end to Griffith-Boscawen's career.[3] But it is unlikely that his Rothermere connection did Birkenhead good with parliamentary Conservatives, few of whom were likely to be amused by the contemptuous treatment he gave Bridgeman's hesitations about Divorce Law reform or by his description of Salisbury and Selborne as the 'Dolly sisters' of the movement for House of Lords reform.[4]

Finally, Birkenhead was assisted by the government's lack of success in matters of policy and its positive failure at by-elections. The Chamberlainites missed none of their opportunities to emphasise the illusory nature of the claim that Law and Curzon would be better than Curzon and Lloyd George at dealing with the French.[5] During the Mitcham by-election Austen Chamberlain criticised the government's proposals for decontrol of rents which, in Labour hands, contributed to Griffith-Boscawen's panic and defeat.[6] Though the impression left by the Cabinet of being politically underprivileged arose less from its record than from the inexperience and intellectual poverty[7] of its members, the electoral record was striking. The loss of Conservative seats at Willesden, Mitcham and Edge Hill – two of them to Labour – greatly reduced the government's credibility as the leader of anti-socialist resistance. It lent weight to Austen Chamberlain's claim that, since 'the larger part ... of the electorate belong[ed] to no party', something needed to be done if 'a firm, stable and consistent policy' was to be possible.[8] It confirmed his belief that faced ... with an attack upon the whole social order ... it [would be] madness ... by our divisions [to] lay ourselves and our country open as a prey to the Socialistic and subversive doctrines which the Labour party [were] preaching with great enthusiasm ... passion ... success and a far larger measure of acceptance than I for one care to see or like to acknowledge.[1]

In the course of March and April 1923 the conjunction of by-election results, accidental defeat in the House of Commons[2] and rumours about Law's retirement convinced Birkenhead that a serious opening was about to occur:[3] he actually referred, ironically, at a public meeting on April 11, to the possibility that the government's 'last word' had been spoken.[4] Birkenhead was not the only person who thought this. Davidson, Amery, Younger and others in the Law/Baldwin circle thought so too. Younger's speeches in April 1923[5] were suddenly and sharply critical of the critics of the government.

(ii)

Law first mentioned resignation to the Cabinet on April 26. He then went away to see whether a 'complete rest' would make it unnecessary.[6] On May 8 he broke off his cruise at Genoa and went to Aix-les-Bains. There he was so ill that he moved to Paris where Beaverbrook and Horder, his doctor, came to see him. By May 18 Law, not knowing that he had less than six months to live,[7] decided to return to London in order to resign. Amery happened that day to stop off in Paris on his way to a Swiss holiday. Calling to see Davidson and his wife, he was told what Law intended. Since neither Law nor Amery knew that Law was dying, Amery and the two Davidsons went through the motions of persuading him to stay in office until the end of the summer in order to ensure a smooth transition to a successor. Next day Law returned to London with Beaverbrook and offered his resignation.[8]

When Law offered his resignation, he did so on grounds of extreme ill-health in anticipation of an imminent operation. Either he or his family asked that he should not be consulted about a successor. He was in any case uncertain what he would say and welcomed Crewe's advice when he saw him in Paris that he was under no obligation to say anything.[9] It is reasonably certain what

Law wanted. It is clear that he neither wanted Austen Chamberlain nor believed that the party would swallow him as leader.[1] Beaverbrook thought he *wanted* Baldwin but would nominate Curzon if he nominated anyone.[2] Amery, a suspect witness, and Salisbury, who had no partiality for Baldwin, both record conversations with Law. Amery found him 'on the whole leaning towards Baldwin ... but inclined to doubt the possibility of displacing Curzon against his will'.[3] Salisbury thought him 'disinclined to pass over Curzon'.[4] It is probable that he did not favour Curzon with whom he had had difficult moments in the last six months:[5] on the 20th he told Baldwin that he did not see how Curzon could be avoided.[6] The same day his son-in-law, Sir Frederick Sykes, and Waterhouse, his private secretary, visited the King at Aldershot with his letter of resignation. The anti-Curzon memorandum Waterhouse left with Stamfordham on that occasion was the work of Waterhouse, Davidson and perhaps Amery.[7] Though Waterhouse may well have told Stamfordham that it reported Law's opinions, it was intended to be an account, drawn up at Stamfordham's request, of what Davidson would be thinking if he were a backbencher. It is possible that neither Law nor Sykes knew about it. It is not certain that it misrepresented Law's view.

When the King received Law's letter he asked Sykes and Waterhouse to ask Law who should advise him.[8] Law, when told, thought first of Neville Chamberlain but then asked Salisbury to come to London with an opinion.[9] The King also sent Stamfordham to London. On the day in question, however – Whit Sunday – hardly anybody was there. According to the account Derby was given over a week later,[10] the King decided on his own initiative during Sunday that he would have to send for Baldwin. When Stamfordham telephoned that Curzon was the obvious choice, he was told to take no further action until the King arrived in London.

At this time the only advice the King had had had come through Waterhouse. It is not clear that the King was as certain at this point as he afterwards claimed:[11] Stamfordham's consultations continued next day. After the telephone conversation with the King, however, Stamfordham seems to have been searching less for guidance than for assurance that Baldwin, if appointed, would not deepen the party split which Stamfordham wanted ended.

The decision to send for Baldwin had almost certainly been made by seven o'clock on Monday evening.[1]

On Monday Stamfordham saw Sir George Murray, the ex-Permanent Secretary to the Treasury, at 10 a.m. At noon he saw Salisbury who had already seen Law and Davidson.[2] He was caught at his front door against his will by Bridgeman and Amery just before lunch, and went for a short walk with them.[3] He had two conversations with Balfour who travelled supine in a car from Sheringham suffering from phlebitis – the first at 3 p.m., the second rather later, after he had seen others whose names we do not have.[4] Balfour, who saw Davidson before Stamfordham's visit,[5] recommended Baldwin: Murray and Salisbury wanted Curzon. After his Monday meeting with Stamfordham, Salisbury saw Bridgeman and Amery and had lunch with Amery.[6] Bridgeman and Amery left Salisbury the impression that Stamfordham had asked the three of them to consult.[7] In fact Stamfordham neither wished to see Amery and Bridgeman[8] to whom he attached no weight, nor asked them to consult Salisbury.[9] It is certain that Stamfordham was annoyed by their attempts at manipulation and greatly resented their view that party reunion could not be accomplished, and should not for the moment be attempted.

Salisbury, nevertheless, after lunching with Amery wrote Stamfordham a note to say that he 'quite agree[d] ... that any reunion with the Unionist Coalition ministers who resigned [the previous October] was out of the question'.[10] In view of Stamfordham's uncertainty about Law's opinion, Salisbury wrote a second time early next morning to emphasise its importance and offered to find out from the Law family exactly what it was.[11]

By this time the King had decided that Curzon should be called to London to hear that he would not be Prime Minister and had told Stamfordham to see Baldwin at half-past ten in preparation for an audience later in the day. At his interview with Baldwin Stamfordham rather made it a condition that Baldwin should keep Curzon as Foreign Secretary. Baldwin agreed, provided Curzon was willing.[12] Baldwin, as we have noted, had been chosen the day before: only decisive unanimity against him would have changed the choice. Stamfordham had not yet seen Jackson whom he visited at midday, but Baldwin knew from the morning interview with Stamfordham that he would become Prime

Minister that afternoon.[1] It testifies to the ubiquity of Waterhouse's presence but not on this occasion to his importance that, on receiving Salisbury's letter in the morning, Stamfordham sent for Waterhouse who told him that Law had authorised him to say that 'on the whole he should advise [the King] to send for Baldwin'.[2]

As senior member of the Cabinet in experience of office and public service Curzon expected to succeed. The summons sent by Stamfordham, his construction of a Cabinet during the railway journey from Montacute to London and his hysterical reaction when told that Baldwin was being asked to form a government have often been described.[3] There is, however, a little more to be said.

As soon as it was certain that Law would resign, Waterhouse and Davidson from one side, Amery and Bridgeman from another swung into action. Amery may have helped to draft the Davidson memorandum[4] but there is half a hint that his help was not welcome. Davidson came to London as soon as it was known that Law would have to resign. Baldwin arrived in London the same day and dined with Davidson that evening.[5] Bridgeman was in London by May 21.

Baldwin was in close touch with Jackson: Davidson and Waterhouse may, or may not, have acted in collusion.[6] Baldwin, however, organised no contingent of ministers to urge his claim: since parliament was not sitting, few M.P.s were available for the purpose. According to his own account, Baldwin saw no ministers apart from Bridgeman and Amery.[7] He seems to have made no attempt to attract Chamberlainite support. What Baldwin did was to wait and see. He was consulted by Davidson before the Waterhouse memorandum was drafted.[8] He showed willingness to serve under Curzon if a Curzon Cabinet was formed. At what he probably thought the crucial interview with Stamfordham on Tuesday morning he showed willingness to keep Curzon at the Foreign Office if he became Prime Minister.

In his attitude to Curzon, Baldwin was typical of this group. They were aiming to stop Curzon becoming Prime Minister, not just because they thought Baldwin preferable but because Baldwin was an obstacle in the way of a general re-admission of the Chamberlainites. They emphasised their personal willingness to serve under Curzon if he formed a government, while recalling the objections that would come from the body of the party if

Curzon was chosen or the Chamberlainites admitted. They knew that their own position would be weak if the Chamberlainites were admitted as a body. They were even more aware that Horne in office might insist on Curzon admitting not only the Chamberlainites but also Churchill whose presence would be a symbol of the decision to relegate Protection to the distant future.[1] They thought Derby had it in mind to form a government of his own:[2] pains were taken, by Jackson among others, to carry him along.[3] They may have feared that Curzon would resign if Baldwin was appointed[4] and form a focus for an alternative government to include the Chamberlainites, Derby and even Salisbury.[5] How far they thought the body of the party objected: how far they used the body of the party to reflect their own unwillingness to be pushed down the Cabinet hierarchy it is impossible to tell. What is certain is that they wanted Curzon to be offered the Prime Ministership only if it was clear that he would have to refuse it.

It is far from certain that any of this activity, except the Waterhouse intervention, affected the King's decision. The King decided to send for Baldwin before most of it began: if it was effective, it was so chiefly in persuading Salisbury to make clear his objection to reunion. There is no evidence that the Chamberlainites were any more effective.

At the same time as the anti-Chamberlainites set to work, Austen Chamberlain, Birkenhead, Worthington-Evans, Sassoon, Horne and Oliver Locker-Lampson decided to ensure that Derby or, when Derby refused, Curzon should become Prime Minister at the head of a reunited party which would treat them as a united body for negotiation, appointment and re-admission. Curzon was a *pis-aller*: he had earned particular hatred for the part he played in ending the Coalition. Nevertheless, one reason for his confidence when he arrived at Stamfordham's house after his journey from Somerset was that he knew that the Chamberlainites would not serve under anyone else except Derby who had refused to take the lead and that Austen Chamberlain 'now realised the truth about Lord Curzon's conduct [the previous] October'.[6] Curzon may not have known that Salisbury also preferred him: if he did know, the fact that Salisbury regarded Curzon not as a bridge towards reunion with the Chamberlainites but as an obstacle in their way would not necessarily have reduced Curzon's confidence that he alone could reunite the party. The questions that have to be asked are therefore: why did Balfour urge the King not to send for Curzon who was supposed to be able to bring back the Chamberlainites whose ally Balfour was supposed to be? Why did he urge the King to send for Baldwin for whom the Chamberlainites had the greatest contempt?

Stamfordham's chief object was to ensure that whoever was appointed would reunite the party. With the King the decisive factors were the objections the Labour party would raise to Curzon's absence in the House of Lords where Labour had virtually no supporters, his temperamental inability to manage a Cabinet and the fact that the weightiest advice he received – from Balfour and, so far as he knew, from Law – was in favour of Baldwin. There is no sign that the King knew anything about Chamberlainite support for Curzon,[1] or indeed that it crystallised until after he had made his decision. Birkenhead did not take steps, as he did the following December,[2] to make sure that the King knew what his group thought. So far as the King was concerned, there can have been no problem except the personal problem of letting Curzon down lightly. When one finds him claiming a week later that there was,[3] one wonders whether he was cushioning the blow to Derby's hopes as tactfully as Curzon's had been cushioned already.[4]

When Law offered his resignation, the Chamberlainites were scattered, Austen Chamberlain in particular being in the South of France. Those who happened to be near London had decided to meet before the resignation was announced because they knew that Law was ill and thought 'the position was likely to develop quickly' if it developed at all. Horne, Locker-Lampson, Sassoon and Worthington-Evans met Birkenhead around May 15. On the basis of hints which Birkenhead claimed to have had from Derby, they decided that Derby was the man to secure the 'support of a united and unpledged party'.[5] Locker-Lampson was commissioned to visit Austen Chamberlain in the South of France. Sassoon was sent to Paris in order to canvass Beaverbrook who was there with Law and had already given attention to the Derby question. Someone – not necessarily Locker-Lampson – got in touch with Austen Chamberlain, though it is not clear what Chamberlain said. Sassoon established contact with Beaverbrook, who agreed on his own and Rothermere's behalf that Derby should be told to be Prime Minister. On May 20 Sassoon went in person to tell Derby that Beaverbrook, Rothermere and the Chamberlainites would support nobody else and that the potential ministers involved would not serve under any other leader.[1]

At this point Derby, according to his diary, was first cautious and then reluctant, and finally, when Sassoon had gone, wrote him a letter of refusal. He refused to support Curzon because 'brilliant as he was, he must have a restraining hand over him', but refused to take the initiative to become Prime Minister himself. He announced his willingness 'to serve under Stanley Baldwin'. While willing to press Baldwin to offer office to Austen Chamberlain and Horne, he would 'not say that [he] would not ... serve under Stanley Baldwin' or even that he 'would not serve unless Austen Chamberlain also agreed to serve'.[2] In talking and writing to Sassoon,[3] Derby may merely have been making sure that, in the event of Baldwin becoming Prime Minister, Baldwin would have no reason to turn a rival out of office. In circumstances we have examined already, Amery spent the week-end at the house of Rupert Gwynne where Horne, a fellow-guest, left Amery the impression that Derby had already formed his Cabinet. It is not clear that Horne and Derby met during this week-end or immediately after it. Horne, however, was impressed by the confidence shown by Gwynne and Amery 'who bet him that they would win the next election'. Derby may have had other evidence that Baldwin's was the winning side.[4]

When Sassoon had had Derby's answer in person on Sunday, Locker-Lampson saw Balfour. Balfour repeated what he had told Stamfordham – that the present government should continue without disturbance from the Chamberlainites.[5] Locker-Lampson then tried to see Derby, but was not allowed to. Birkenhead telegraphed from Paris to ask for an interview. Derby refused this too and arranged to see Beaverbrook and Jackson instead. There is no record of Derby's conversation with Beaverbrook. In the course of the Jackson conversation on the morning of the 22nd, Derby and Jackson agreed that Bridgeman and Amery were right in thinking that 'Curzon as Prime Minister would split the party' and that the only possible peer was Derby. They decided nevertheless that Baldwin would be the 'right man' and Derby offered to persuade Horne and Austen Chamberlain to join a Baldwin government.[1]

Despite the uncharacteristic decisiveness displayed, at any rate in his diary, it is possible that Derby was trying to keep in with both sides. At his meeting with Jackson both recognised that Curzon, once sent for by the King, might be supported by 'a lot of people who do not agree to [him] being Prime Minister' but there may have been the implication that Curzon would fail to form a government in which case it might be Derby rather than Baldwin who would try next. Derby's diary records his anxiety to keep in touch with Amery and Bridgeman. He told Jackson that he 'resented' newspaper claims that he was 'indispensable to ... the reunion of the party'.[2] It is possible that Derby's professions of support for Baldwin, both in person and in his diary, were designed to anticipate the 'accus[ation] of having refused in order to get the premiership'.[3]

Whatever Derby was trying to do he convinced the Chamberlainites that they could not rely on him. On receiving his negatives on Sunday and Monday morning, Sassoon called a meeting which Horne, Locker-Lampson and Worthington-Evans attended.[4] They decided that they wanted a Curzon Cabinet and telegraphed Austen Chamberlain to break off his holiday and go to Paris.[5] They decided that Austen Chamberlain and others should join even if Birkenhead 'who for the moment would not be accepted were left out'.[6] Horne then went to Scotland at the same time as Birkenhead returned to London. The same ground was covered next morning by Birkenhead, Locker-Lampson and Worthington-Evans with the result that Locker-Lampson talked to Curzon between his arrival in London and his interview with Stamford-ham. When Curzon saw Stamfordham, therefore, he had just been told that, though Austen Chamberlain would not be available for a Baldwin government, he and 'the ex-ministers would serve under [Curzon] if thereby unity could be obtained'.[7]

Unfortunately for the Chamberlainites this intervention came too late to make any difference, if indeed it would have made a difference without a direct approach to Stamfordham or the King. The King had received no advice from the Chamberlainites: the nearest approach to Chamberlainite advice came from Balfour. Balfour, however, when asked by Stamfordham who should replace Law, had pointed to Baldwin as the repository of party feeling and mentioned the difficulty of having a Prime Minister in the House of Lords.[1] The difficulty in having a Prime Minister in the House of Lords was that the Labour party would make it a centre of attack, 'though [Balfour] did not mention this' in talking to Stamfordham.[2] It has normally been assumed that Balfour's reasons centred on Curzon's inability in the last four years of his life to handle his colleagues or show anything resembling a patient front in negotiation abroad. These, doubtless, were considerations which weighed with the King. What has to be asked is whether additional considerations weighed with Balfour – whether he advised the King to send for Baldwin not because he was the better candidate, but because he was the worse?

In Salvidge's diary for April 1923,[3] Birkenhead is reported to have told Salvidge that, in the event of Law's early resignation, the King should send for Baldwin, whom the Die Hards would insist on, because, however 'serious' a 'joke' a Baldwin Prime Ministership would be, 'Balfour took the view, and Birkenhead believed Austen Chamberlain concurred, that it might be the best way of teaching the Die Hards the lesson which they have apparently not yet learned' – that the essential prerequisite to success was a return to Chamberlainite leadership. The Salvidge account is not the only reference to the existence of this view among the Chamberlainites: Locker-Lampson urged it a couple of days before Baldwin was appointed.[4] The fact that Balfour urged Baldwin on the King while giving a different range of reasons raises the question whether it provides a key to Balfour's action.

The belief that it does implies no inconsistency with Balfour's immediate past. Balfour and the Coalitionists had all developed the strongest aversion to Curzon in October. Balfour was angrier at the fall of the Coalition than anyone else.[5] Its fall did not alter his belief that a union of the best brains from the non-socialist parties was needed to carry the constitution through the socialist assault. Until Law got a majority at the 1922 election, Balfour expected to be at the centre of negotiation after the election between Law, Lloyd George and the Chamberlainites.[6] There is no reason to doubt that Balfour would use whatever method he thought best to achieve his objective or that, if he expected a short Baldwin government to convince Conservatives that they had been mistaken in October 1922, he would have thought it worth the inconvenience. What he is supposed to have predicted in fact happened: the Baldwin government of 1923 ended in electoral ignominy and, very nearly, in eclipse for Baldwin. Yet Balfour did nothing to remove Baldwin in December 1923. Whatever Salvidge may have been told by Birkenhead, it is unlikely that he was intending to do so in May.

Balfour, indeed, was in no position to make long-term calculations of this sort, and there is no reason to imagine that he did. In 1923 he was a cloistered seventy-five. October 1922 had taught him that he knew very little about party feeling: the election showed him that he did not understand the country's. He had given, and may even have offered, Law help in the months following the election: he may well have felt that a Baldwin Prime Ministership was inevitable. He offered to join Baldwin's government once Baldwin began to form it[1] and wrote a public letter of support.[2] He asked Stamfordham to let Baldwin know that he had recommended him once it was clear that Baldwin would be appointed.[3] Birkenhead tended to claim that Balfour was in his pocket, but Balfour's words to Birkenhead in April, if they were ever uttered, may well have been a way of telling Birkenhead that Baldwin would *have* to be Prime Minister. Balfour's advice to the King was important and may have been decisive. In giving it he mentioned the importance of reunion with Horne, Worthington-Evans and Austen Chamberlain: he did not mention Birkenhead. The more closely Balfour's actions are examined, the more likely it seems that he was playing both sides and backing all horses and that the advice to the King in May to send for Baldwin and the advice to Birkenhead in April that Baldwin should be sent for were dual facets of the desire he shared with Derby to receive the respect which comes from swimming with the middle of whatever stream is flowing.

(iii)

On May 22, then, the King asked Baldwin to form a government. Baldwin agreed to do so, and at once asked all the resigning Cabinet ministers to remain. By May 25 they had all agreed to do so. Baldwin brought into the Cabinet from posts outside it Hoare and Joynson-Hicks who had both been architects of Lloyd George's and Austen Chamberlain's downfall the previous October. Davidson became Chancellor of the Duchy of Lancaster. On receiving Horne's refusal on the 25th, Baldwin brought into the Cabinet from total unemployment Lord Robert Cecil whose hostility to Lloyd George had been the longest-lived among all effective politicians. The question of the Chamberlainites remained.

The Chamberlainite candidates for major office were Birkenhead, Worthington-Evans, Horne, Pollock, Scott and Austen Chamberlain. None of these was consulted by Baldwin before May 24, by which time he had filled all the major offices except the Exchequer. By the time he began negotiating with them, he probably knew that Balfour had recommended that he should become Prime Minister. Curzon had been bribed into acquiescence by being pressed to keep the Foreign Office, for which there were other candidates in case he resigned. Derby had agreed to stay in office and probably told Baldwin when he saw him that he had promised the Chamberlainites to press for offers of office to Horne and Chamberlain. He offered, or was asked, to go to Paris, to intercede with Austen Chamberlain who had waited there 'in order that he might not seem to be sitting on the doorstep'.[1] Derby did not actually go since Baldwin telegraphed Austen Chamberlain on the 25th to come to see him instead.[2] By this time Austen Chamberlain was already on his way home and Horne had refused Baldwin's offer of the Exchequer.[3]

Horne had three reasons for refusing. He thought the government should be killed; he could not afford to leave secure employment for the uncertain prospect offered by a Baldwin government; Baldwin made it clear after some hesitation that he did not intend to include Birkenhead or Austen Chamberlain.[4] On Horne's refusal McKenna had been asked and made a conditional form of acceptance which was made public the morning after Chamberlain received Baldwin's summons. Curzon's popularity was almost as negligible as Birkenhead's: but it was unnecessary to alienate him by offering Austen Chamberlain the Foreign Office instead. The same did not apply to the Exchequer which Chamberlain had first held from 1903 to 1905. He had held it again with no great distinction, it is true, much unpopularity and initial reluctance[5] between 1919 and 1921, but he had come to enjoy it and had not been pleased to leave it. It was the one office that was obviously vacant. Yet Baldwin did not offer it. Of all the people to whom he could have offered it, McKenna was, from Chamberlain's point of view, almost certainly the most objectionable.

It is probable that Baldwin wanted Horne to join the government. He wanted him because he was financially competent and his adhesion would weaken the Chamberlainites. It is possible that he wanted Worthington-Evans for the same reason, though he told Neville Chamberlain the opposite:[1] it is likely that Worthington-Evans was eventually admitted because Horne had refused. But he wanted to avoid invasion from a powerful body of ex-ministers who would push out existing ministers – themselves Baldwin's supporters – and create a powerful block within the Cabinet with special significance by reason of its connection with Lloyd George. There is no evidence that Baldwin followed up the hint Derby dropped about Balfour's willingness to join. Birkenhead was 'hated and despised': his reputation and conduct in the past year made it easy to avoid him.[2] Austen Chamberlain attracted a similar measure of disapproval, not least because of his association with Birkenhead.[3] Despite what he said to Neville Chamberlain it is likely that Baldwin did not want Austen Chamberlain either: he was probably fishing to get Neville Chamberlain to say what he thought – that Salisbury was right in believing it 'futile' to bring him back for the moment.[4] It is almost certain that Austen Chamberlain would have been offered office only if Curzon's resignation had made it necessary to forestall an alliance between them.

As soon as they knew that Baldwin had been appointed, the Chamberlainites had to decide whether to join him if they were given the opportunity. Horne and Birkenhead agreed not to do so. Despite fears that the government might not turn out to be a failure,[5] Horne did as he had promised: Birkenhead went to Paris to persuade Chamberlain that he should refuse too. At the same time Worthington-Evans sent Austen Chamberlain an agitated note to say that he, Scott and Pollock would like to feel free to accept any offer Baldwin might make even if Chamberlain, Birkenhead and Horne did not.[6] Though Chamberlain sent a telegram of acquiescence which he later used as proof of goodwill towards Baldwin,[7] he sent it under the impression that negotiations would be conducted with the ex-ministers as a body even if in the end he and Birkenhead did not join, and before Baldwin had given Cabinet appointments to Hoare, Joynson-Hicks and Lord Robert Cecil. The letter he sent on May 24 apparently strengthening his acquiescence did not mean that he wanted his followers to take office.[1]

When Austen Chamberlain reached England, he knew that Horne had been approached, as he thought, behind his back. He knew that the Exchequer had been more or less accepted by McKenna whom he greatly disliked. Worthington-Evans had told him that he would be offered the Washington Embassy.[2] He thought that three of his supporters wanted to desert him, not as a prelude to his eventual return, but in order to co-operate with the people who had thrown him out seven months before. He had had no serious word from Baldwin. He could see that he was not only not being treated as the leader of a group but was positively being ignored.[3] In these circumstances he was probably in no mood to accept office which it seemed unlikely was available.

Baldwin had already said[4] that Chamberlain should be offered the Privy Seal as an unacceptable token designed solely to establish that he might return to office later. By the time Chamberlain arrived at Chequers even the Privy Seal had gone. What he found was that Baldwin put him on probation 'like a naughty boy'[5] against the possibility of office in the future, coupling this, as Worthington-Evans had predicted, with an offer of the embassy in Washington. When Austen Chamberlain reminded Baldwin that he had in the past been offered

both the Paris Embassy and the Viceroyalty of India, even though at the time he was in office and no-one could have said it was given him to cover up a failure, Baldwin had the simplicity to reply that as he [Baldwin] was a comparatively young man and now blocked the way, he thought [Chamberlain] might like to take something outside politics.[6]

In the short run Baldwin's 'suggestions that [Austen Chamberlain could] be bribed to good behaviour or bought off by a lucrative appointment [were] galling to a proud man'.[7] Retailing the conversation to Neville Chamberlain a week later, he became 'very emotional, shouting loudly and banging the table with the greatest violence ... evidently writhing under the humiliation he had undergone'.[8] In the long run Baldwin's 'blundering' conversation convinced him that, though Baldwin would be grateful for support now, he would be less grateful if support were delayed until the future, that the longer opposition was maintained, the less likely it would be that support would be needed and that there was a point beyond which even a weak government would not go in bringing back errant leaders.[1]

Baldwin may not have intended to irritate Austen Chamberlain: to that extent there was probably inadvertence more than cunning. He had had a lecture from Stamfordham about the importance of doing something about reunion: he probably felt obliged to go through the motions. On the other hand, he felt no pressing desire to have Austen Chamberlain in office. He did not want to put others out in order to get him and had no intention of precipitating resignations especially if, as Neville Chamberlain thought, they 'would carry with them a section of the party and thus perpetuate disunion'.[2] What he probably wanted was less to unite all elements in the Conservative party than to ensure that one source of danger to himself and his government would be neutralised, partly by detaching two of the Chamberlainites – Horne and Worthington-Evans, though in the event only the less important one came – and partly by suggesting to their formal leader who, he suspected, had been involved in the plot to make Derby Prime Minister,[3] that he was a declining asset and had better capitulate completely. This pattern was to be repeated six months later.

PART III

XV

BALDWIN'S NEED FOR A PLATFORM

'We've got to settle Europe.'
> Baldwin talking to Thomas Jones, *Whitehall Diary*, May 28 1923

'He said he had been a good deal criticized for not taking more decided action sooner ... It was forgotten that he had been only three months in office and other Prime Ministers had not been called upon to take such swift decisions.'
> Baldwin talking to C. P. Scott, C. P. Scott diary, October 26/27 1923

'A Prime Minister who decides on a complete reversal of fiscal policy would have naturally mentioned it, one would have thought, to a Free Trade colleague who had joined his government on the faith of the Bonar pledge. Remember I passed an afternoon with him at Talloires, that he had more than an hour's conversation with me on my return and that I saw him frequently besides ...

Meanwhile others were in the secret. A candidate who applied to the Central Office for a seat in July was asked whether he would support a Protectionist policy. The matter was formally discussed and treated as settled at a meeting on October 11 at the Central Office and indeed before the Cabinet was told of the matter, a lady I met at lunch referred casually to the adoption by the government of a Protectionist policy ... yet ... the first I heard of it was a casual announcement – not on the Agenda – to the Cabinet two days before the Plymouth speech.'
> Lord Robert Cecil to Davidson, November 15 1923 (copy), Add. MSS 51080

(i)

In the first two sections of this book, we have followed the invention of the idea that Lloyd George's function should be to lead resistance to Socialism. We have watched this conception crumble. We have watched Law's efforts to put something in its place and have noted that Law's failure was concealed by his retirement and death. We now follow Baldwin's attempts to do the same from the first summer of brisk self-confidence when he thought success would come more easily than it did through the Protectionist disaster of December 1923 to the final upland of undoctrinaire resistance from which, once planted in mid-1924, the Conservative party has never really moved. In understanding Baldwin's conduct between May 1923 and October 1924, it is necessary to concentrate in the first place on the interlude from October 1923 to February 1924 when Protection and agricultural subsidies were first adopted and then abandoned as the chief elements in official Conservative policy.

Baldwin became Prime Minister on May 22 1923. On August 14 it became clear that McKenna would not be joining the government. On August 27 Neville Chamberlain became Chancellor of the Exchequer. At some point between August 27 and October 8 Baldwin decided to adopt a general tariff – Protection – as the Conservative party's policy and to fight an election within the next twelve months to ask for power to make it effective. From about October 11 onwards, he, Neville Chamberlain, Lloyd-Graeme and Amery, together with Hewins in a private and secret office, prepared the details. On October 23 the Cabinet was told of Baldwin's decision, which was made public in the course of a speech to the annual conference of the National Union in Plymouth two days later. On November 13 the Cabinet was told that the King had agreed to a general election which would be held on December 6.

At the election the Conservative party lost nearly ninety seats. The Liberal and Labour parties gained between forty and fifty each. Baldwin, having gone through the motions of offering to resign the Prime Ministership and the party leadership, decided by December 10 to do nothing until he was defeated in the House of Commons. This happened on January 21 1924 when the Liberal and Labour parties carried a Labour vote of censure. MacDonald then took office with Liberal support. By February 11, with Baldwin still leading the Conservative party, Protection and agricultural subsidies had been replaced by a combination of social reform and anti-socialism as the front-runners in official Conservative policy. The question that has to be asked is: what significance had this Protectionist interlude for the development of Baldwin's position?

In answering it we must remember Baldwin entered politics in 1906 when progressive Conservatives naturally believed 'that the time [was] ... ripe for ending that era of unrestricted competition which ha[d] brought so much suffering to the working classes of these islands'.[1] Protection had been part of his background during the whole of his time in parliament. It was the positive alternative to any constructive policy proposed by other political parties, as well as being a symbol of a powerful Midland Industrial presence. It had been the answer to the Liberal party before the war. From some points of view it was the natural answer to the socialist claim that the Labour party alone had positive policies for the twentieth century.

The fact that this was so in general would not mean that it need be so at any moment in particular. Even if he picked up Protection from Cunningham at Trinity, Baldwin seems to have had no zeal in the pursuit.[1] Before the war he was not a 'whole-hogger', but a Midland industrialist with some experience of foreign dumping[2] who absorbed Protection as part of official Conservative policy. He fought a running battle with Derby in the last six months of the Lloyd George government over the application of the Safeguarding of Industries Act but accepted Law's pledge against Protection in November 1922. He can have had no doubt about the divisive effect a systematically Protectionist platform would have on any government that proposed it.

It is true that Law and Baldwin explained on a number of occasions between October 1922 and mid-1923 that Protection and agricultural subsidies were impossible only because the predominantly urban electorate would not swallow them. Sound finance, debt reduction, reductions in government spending and limitation of governmental intervention made it impossible to consider returning to the policy Lloyd George had abandoned under pressure from Anti-Waste in 1921 – of directly subsidising agricultural production. Protective duties for agriculture were equally out of the question. Agriculture could not be covered by the Safeguarding of Industries Acts: 'it [was] impossible', Law had said, that 'agriculture [should] be supported by the State'. Rural education, credit facilities, price adjustments and rating reform were promised freely at the election of 1922 in order to help 'agriculture help itself'. A committee was set up to enquire into the causes of the agricultural depression. When it reported, Sanders, the Minister of Agriculture, had to stop Law restoring Wages' Boards which farmers did not want unless prices were guaranteed by subsidy.[3] Despite pressure to reduce new legislation to a minimum,[4] legislation was passed in 1922/3 to fulfil the promises made before the 1922 election.[5] But about subsidies, as about Protection, the negative position was unequivocal.

The government's refusal to propose 'Protection' or agricultural subsidies did not mean that farmers received no relief and domestic industry no protection. The Sanders measures included a substantial measure of rate abatement on agricultural land and a tax on imported barley, about which there was difficulty in Cabinet.[1] The Safeguarding of Industries Act and the McKenna duties provided substantial protection for a number of British industries. Either could have been extended in late 1923. There was discussion at Cabinet and in Cabinet Committee in the Law government and in the first five months of Baldwin's about the possibility of doing this. On the first occasion, when Amery wanted silk and lace added to the McKenna duties, Derby and Devonshire threatened to resign.[2] When Lloyd-Graeme proposed extra McKenna duties on silk, lace, tyres and possibly woollens in August, Lord Robert Cecil objected. Baldwin suggested delay – in Amery's view because McKenna might not be pleased to find a decision of this sort made for him in the event of his becoming Chancellor, probably also because he did not want this sort of disagreement in Cabinet while McKenna was making up his mind. There is no sign that Amery's Protectionist letter to Baldwin next day had any impact.[3] But it is likely that, if McKenna had joined the government, further McKenna duties would have been proposed which Derby and Lord Robert Cecil would have had to stomach. Joynson-Hicks believed that all the practical effects which Baldwin wanted could have been achieved by protection without the name.[4]

It is possible that the Imperial and Economic Conference, due to meet on October 1, necessitated a change of policy. Or it may be that the sterling statement of Protectionist Imperialism made by Bruce, the Australian Prime Minister,[5] and the unexpected advances towards Imperial Preference made by Smuts[6] merely made it easier to adopt a policy which was adopted for other reasons. Much of the Conference was conducted behind closed doors without publicity. At one stage Baldwin regarded it as an embarrassment he would have preferred to put off – presumably until he had rid himself of his 'ignorance about the Empire'.[7] The impression that he did not welcome it is strong.[8] The Conference adjourned for a time on October 10 to enable the British delegation to decide how far it could go and what relationship there could be between a Tariff Reform campaign in England and its proposals at the Conference.[1] Bruce and Mackenzie King were present at the Chequers week-ends of October 13/14 and 20/21 when Baldwin discussed the Protectionist platform with Amery, Lloyd-Graeme, Davidson, Neville Chamberlain and others.[2] But virtually nothing that the Conference decided was outside the scope of the Law pledge.[3] Apart from Lord Robert Cecil most members of Baldwin's Cabinet were as willing to accept a measure of Imperial Preference[4] as to extend the McKenna duties,[5] provided the ostensible object was not protection of the home market. It is even possible that the Cabinet would have accepted agricultural subsidies to offset taxation on imported food if they had been presented as necessities on military, agricultural or unemployment grounds.[6] The Conference imposed no binding need to raise the Protection question apart from the criticism Baldwin might expect from the Chamberlainites or Rothermere and the demoralisation he might fear in the Conservative party if he had nothing to say in Imperial directions at a moment when his European policies had not succeeded.[7]

What needs to be explained, therefore, is not why Baldwin wanted to protect domestic industry and agriculture and extend Imperial Preference, but why he decided to do in October 1923 what he and Law had refused to do before, despite their long-term preferences and commitments, when he could have persuaded the Cabinet to accept most of what he wanted so long as he did not call it Protection. In order to explain this, we must examine the treatment he received as Prime Minister from the Labour party, the Asquithean Liberals, Lloyd George, Rothermere, Beaverbrook and the Chamberlainites.

The Chamberlainites had been shaken by the election of 1922, divided by acceptances of office in the course of 1923 and reduced to a rump by the detachment of Balfour and Lloyd George. In 1923 Chamberlainite criticism meant criticism from Birkenhead and Austen Chamberlain. Before Birkenhead quarrelled with Rothermere in April and after they were reconciled in June or July, it meant criticism from Rothermere. When Baldwin succeeded Law, it meant criticism from Beaverbrook and his newspapers. Criticism from these quarters assumed that the Law and Baldwin governments were so weak that they would eventually be destroyed by the magnitude of the events with which they had to deal and by their inability to carry Liberals along with them.[1]

Not all the Chamberlainites prognosticated as confidently as Birkenhead. Horne and Austen Chamberlain hardly did so at all. When Rothermere prognosticated, he did so with journalistic energy, but his front changed so regularly that he did not leave the impression that his judgment had been considered. Beaverbrook's objectives were not consistent: he was jealous that with Baldwin he no longer had the access he had had to Law, however small his effective influence had been with him. Rothermere and Beaverbrook had both helped to destroy the Coalition. Rothermere had no desire to restore it: from June onwards he seems to have wanted the Conservative party reunited under Austen Chamberlain. In August he began to support Lloyd George.[2] Davidson was not the only person who found the extension of the Beaverbrook/Rothermere alliance 'sinister'.[3] On October 13 it became public property that the two of them had carved up Sir Edward Hulton's newspaper empire in anticipation of Hulton's death.[4]

The assault developed by these critics was made along a number of lines. A certain amount was heard about the government's failure to reform the House of Lords and deal with the political levy which had been a Die Hard issue towards the end of the Coalition.[5] Rothermere supported the Admiralty in the battle it fought for control of the naval arm of the Air Force, criticising Hoare with whom his relations had previously been good.[6] The government's weakness towards Turkey was criticised, though this criticism, repeated nevertheless, became less reasonable with the signature of the Lausanne Treaty which in many respects gave the Turks much less than they expected. The continued existence of a high level of unemployment was expected to defeat any government: Birkenhead and Chamberlain did not mention it, no doubt because it had defeated the Coalition. The main attack dealt with the government's failure in Europe.

In this respect the French occupation of the Ruhr was central. It stimulated an optimistic desire to pay back the Coalition's 'idealistic' critics by showing that the new government was less successful than Lloyd George in controlling French militarism. Die Hard Francophilia had played a part in destroying the Coalition: Law and Baldwin had promised better Anglo-French relations once Lloyd George was removed. Curzon's attempts to bully Poincaré into defining the purpose of occupation stimulated the claim that Anglo-French relations were worse than under Lloyd George.

These criticisms were made in the knowledge that Derby – the Chamberlainite Trojan horse – agreed. They were made in the belief that the occupation of the Ruhr was part of a major crisis and likely to carry the country 'into very deep water'[1] which no government as inexperienced as Baldwin's could handle successfully.[2] Even at its kindest, criticism was designed to show that the government had no idea what to do if bullying failed and that a German recovery would damage British prosperity.[3] At its worst the departure from Law's policy was 'sheer madness'[4] which would 'lead to war with France in 5 or 7 years'.[5] The British note to France and Belgium on August 11 had destroyed the Entente Cordiale which had been 'made ... [by] King Edward the Peacemaker ... twenty years ago'.[6] Its presentation, and Poincaré's reply, revealed Baldwin 'not as a hard, shrewd businessman but as a particularly emotional sentimentalist' with special support 'among the lesser lights of Radicalism, the minor ornaments of the Labour party and those curious products of our public life who seem to be at heart more German than the Germans'.[7] These criticisms continued until Birkenhead went to America.

Lloyd George's criticisms were not of first consequence in themselves. From Baldwin's point of view, criticism from that quarter was in some respects a source of strength. The importance of Lloyd George came from the cumulative similarities between his attacks and the attacks made by Birkenhead, MacDonald and Asquith.

From Lloyd George there were attacks on the French occupation of the Ruhr[8] and on Poincaré himself.[9] There was criticism of the government's failure to handle Poincaré, control Turkey or pacify Europe.[10] There was the claim that 'the government [had] come into office with the express policy of greater friendship with France' but had reached the point at which the Entente had been disrupted, the Ruhr occupied and Britain no longer consulted.[11] There was the assertion that Europe was more like an armed camp than before the war and that Britain was being 'snubbed out'. On

September 8 in his last speech before leaving for Canada, Lloyd George told the Welsh National Liberal Federation that the combination of tranquillity, fuller employment, a fair Turkish treaty and restoration of the French alliance which Law had promised at the last election had been destroyed by the government's capitulation to the Die Hards who were making reasonable government impossible, and necessitated the revival of Liberalism and 'a State based on liberty, duty, right, sympathy and brotherhood'.[1]

At the election of 1922 the Asquithean leaders, while competing with the Conservative party for the anti-Coalition vote, had given Law a comparatively easy run. When they attacked him their attacks reflected the necessities forced on them by the need to affirm a Liberal identity.

Grey, on the other hand, was not so readily inhibited. He had returned to public life less as a Liberal than in a national context. In the event of deadlock in the new House of Commons, his prospects were good, and so, perhaps, were his expectations. Grey had begun by leaving the impression that he wanted the Conservative government to stay in office. He was persuaded to make it clear that, unlike McKenna, he positively wanted a Liberal government.[2] But he thought a majority Liberal government an impossibility and left the impression of feeling a strong affinity with the new Conservative leaders.

In the next nine months Grey's position shifted. Even during the election he had kept lines open to Haldane for co-operation in constructing a new alternative to the Conservative party.[3] As a revived Lloyd George/Conservative Coalition became less possible and the excuse for a Cecil/Grey resistance less plausible, the need to emphasise the Asquithean affinity with the Conservatives receded. It became less necessary to build up the affinity against a renewal of Coalition and more necessary, from a Liberal point of view, to present the Conservative government as a Die Hard government to which the Liberal party could become the party of resistance. With Lloyd George's first major attempt to effect reunion by storm in his Manchester speech of April 29, these necessities began to press.

Grey's progress was not uniform, nor was it willing or enthusiastic.

Neither he nor Asquith wanted a change of government. The longer Law or Baldwin stayed in office, the less scope Lloyd George would have for joint action with Birkenhead. Asquith's opinion of Law had always been low, but his relations with Baldwin began to develop in early 1923.[1] Runciman dropped hints of admiration for the 'soundness' of Baldwin's Budget in April, adding that his father, who controlled the Runciman purse-strings, felt the same.[2] McKenna's flirtation with Baldwin and Novar's membership of his Cabinet showed that Baldwin was willing to take trouble to get Liberal support. When Smillie stood at, and won, the Morpeth by-election in June, he was opposed by an Asquithean standing with Conservative support where there had been three candidates in 1922. It seems likely that Baldwin was as much admired in Asquithean quarters in the summer of 1923 as he was by the Webbs in the summer of 1924.[3]

An indictment, nevertheless, had to be developed. It was developed by Asquith vigorously, and by Grey reluctantly, from a position slightly Left of Centre. It was designed to pre-empt the position Lloyd George might think of adopting on their Left and to show that Liberals had responsible versions to offer of some of the attitudes which Labour claimed to have made its own. They reiterated their objection to any proposal for a Coalition-style Centre party and repeated the claims they had made before about Liberal responsibility for the rise of Labour. In stigmatising the government as a prisoner of the Die Hards, they attacked four sorts of defect in its conduct.

As soon as Baldwin succeeded Law, Asquith denounced the new government's confirmation of the Irish Indemnity Bill and the arrests and deportations without trial initiated before it came to power.[4] He highlighted back-bench Conservative demands to reduce the powers given to trades unions by the Liberal Acts of 1871, 1906 and 1913. He compared the positive Liberal policy of industrial co-operation and worker security with the absence of positive proposals from the government. He contrasted the Liberal desire for 'public advantage' with the pursuit of private profit and gave prominence to the Liberal proposals for the taxation of land values which Lloyd George had passed as Chancellor under Asquith and abandoned as Prime Minister.[5] Most important of all, using foreign policy to distinguish the

Liberal party from the Conservative Right, he pressed hard at the government's most vulnerable point.

Where foreign policy was concerned, Asquith needed to square a number of circles. 'Keeping open negotiations with Russia' supplied one instrument: the League of Nations supplied another. Party sentiment was anti-French, as Lloyd George knew when he attacked Poincaré, but Grey's sympathy for France put an outright attack on France out of the question. An anti-French position on Reparations, therefore, was adopted without being spelt out as such, the conflict between the demand for appeasement of Germany and Grey's position in relation to France being resolved by assuming that a League of Nations' guarantee of French security and German membership of the League would go a long way towards reconciling the Germans.[1] The League of Nations, and Germany's admission to it, thus became the centre of Liberal foreign policy. In Simon's hands the transformation of the 'hopes of 1919' into the 'sombre disillusionments of 1923' was connected with the fact that it was not in the League of Nations but in

the Supreme Council [i.e. of the Allies] that the real influence over Allied action ha[d] continued to rest ... The interests of democracies [Simon wrote] are one ... A real League to enforce peace, under which the democracies of the world renounce in advance [the] barbarous recourse to armed strife, lay aside the constant temptation which is offered by vast preparations for war and limit their armed forces to contingents which ... operate as international police would change the whole current of history. A world-wide movement for peace as the only tolerable basis for the life of ordinary men and women may yet prove the salvation of mankind.[2]

Mussolini's occupation of Corfu provided the occasion for a major declaration from Grey in favour of the League of Nations.[3] In Asquith's first speech of the winter campaign,[4] the League had a major place. Between September 28 and October 24, however, he began a public campaign to revivify the Asquithean organisation in the course of which Free Trade was brought to the fore and any attempt Baldwin might make to develop a Protectionist position was condemned in advance to the crushing rejection Protection was said to have received in 1906.[5] The hints at a Protectionist platform given by the newspapers and the Australian Prime

Minister before and during the Imperial Conference received total condemnation. Even Imperial Preference was subjected to such ridicule as Asquith had available.

These declarations of war, made before Baldwin said anything about Protection, were designed to destroy in advance whatever initiative he might take. They were intended to pinpoint the ambiguities the Asquitheans expected to emerge in the Free Trade position Lloyd George had adopted at Manchester in April and to use the opportunity offered by McKenna's withdrawal and Neville Chamberlain's appointment to attract the essentially liberal opinion which McKenna, Lord Robert Cecil and Novar symbolised among Baldwin's colleagues and supporters.

In October 1923, therefore, the Asquithean Liberals were offering Free Trade, the League of Nations and industrial co-operation as the basis of Liberal policy at the same time as they claimed that Liberal reunion was progressing without special safeguards for Lloyd George's position. It is not clear how far Asquith and Grey thought reunion could be completed without Lloyd George: it is certain that Free Trade and the League of Nations were designed to impede his return. There had been blotches on the Liberal flag in by-elections at Leeds Central, Berwick-on-Tweed and Mitcham. But seats gained by a united Liberal association at Willesden East in March, at Anglesey in April and at Tiverton in June gave the Asquithean leaders better ground for optimism than at any time in the last eight years. Their success from one angle looked doubly important when combined with the Labour attack on Baldwin from the other.

(ii)

The fall of the Coalition took the Labour leaders by surprise: it induced pessimism and presented a problem.[1] Having made Lloyd George the major target for attack, they needed another. The Conservative party supplied it. They had attacked Lloyd George for failing to keep his promises:[2] they attacked Law for failing to have promises to keep.[3] Lloyd George was now 'a comic turn – ... [a] mountain of ... froth and generalities'.[4] It became the central point in Labour propaganda that he had been brought down by 'the largest Rolls-Royce gathering ever known'[5] and that 'the Tory party [would] gather [around itself] all the interests from oil to beer which ... see in Labour the dread menace of a just government concerned with ... the life of the whole people and not with the material interests of a few'.[1] The Labour leaders foresaw a 'profiteers'' world as Safeguarding extended out into general Protection.[2] Derby at the War Office would advocate a military alliance with the French.[3] McKenna's support for Law was the 'money power' of the 'City of London' looking after its own.[4] The housing problem would not be solved by men 'whose only difficulty was in choosing for the season which of [their] numerous houses [to] use'.[5] The large number of peers in the new Cabinet and the 'unbroken outpouring of misrepresentation' anticipated from the 'millionaire press' showed that the country was 'faced by the danger of a government frankly class, frankly reactionary, frankly committed to subordinate life and human interest to material possessions'.[6]

The Labour manifesto, when it was published on October 25, had a poor reception amongst political leaders: even the friends of Labour thought it abandoned some of the high ground from which they thought the campaign could most easily be conducted.[7] Nevertheless, the ground taken by the leaders was high. 'We are', Clynes claimed, 'not prejudiced ... we will readily give up ... the Capital Levy' if other parties 'find a better way to clear off the burden of the National Debt'.[8] The moral initiative was claimed, and also the intellectual: Labour candidates 'included ... men who stood high in literature, in art, in law and science and ... who ... had won a reputation in other than Labour quarters'.[9] Moral disreputability was attributed to Labour's opponents. It was attached to their 'treating [the workers] no better than animals in relation to conditions of ... housing and unemployment'[10] and to their inability to grasp the need for pacification through alliances not just with one State or another but with all. It was attached to their reluctance to establish political relations with Russia. It was attached to the contradiction between Law's approval of the Capital Levy in 1917 and the Conservative party's attack on it now[11] and to its willingness to destroy the constitution where class interests needed to be defended. MacDonald wrote on November 4:

So far as the government is concerned, no elector has any excuse for mistaking its intention. It is to make the financier more powerful ... to use the evils done by the war to increase the power of material wealth ...

to develop a policy of protection of the kind which Mr Chamberlain advocated from 1902 onwards ... to return to secret diplomacy ... [and] to do what it likes on social questions. Its election funds come from sold honours: its leader in 'tranquillity' is the man who committed the Unionist party to civil war against Parliament rather than give Ireland Home Rule. Truly [it would be] a revolutionary government were it to get a majority.[1]

At the election of 1922 the Labour party geared its appeal to the poor and public-spirited against the selfish and the rich. It stood for 'the value of life as against property'.[2] It appealed to war weariness against the chauvinism of France and to the sanity, moderation and common sense 'of the plain man and woman'[3] against positive action from the Right. It distinguished itself from the Liberal party, which opposed the Capital Levy: it made it clear that the object of the Capital Levy was 'to increase the spending power of forty millions, even if three hundred thousand were the poorer for it'.[4] By constant harping on the connection between the Capital Levy, foreign policy, nationalisation, the level of employment and the National Debt, it suggested a community of interest not just within the working classes but between shopkeepers, businessmen, 'brain-workers' and the whole body of 'the lower-middle class who suffer from grinding Income Tax'[5] against the reactionary revolution by which they were threatened.[6]

At the 1922 election Labour lost about twenty of the seats it won in 1918 and gained over seventy. But it kept only three[7] of the fourteen seats it had won at by-elections since. It established a major base in Glasgow and other parts of Scotland where an 'avalanche' of 'blind ... hatred' produced 'revolt against the parties which failed to find a way out of the misery' of Scottish housing.[8] In South Wales, Northumberland and Durham it consolidated a hold which had begun to be established before. In London and Sheffield it did well. But it did badly in agricultural seats, even where it had done well in 1918. Despite formidable majorities in many of the industrial and mining areas over which it had gained control, it fulfilled none of the expectations raised in 1921/22 of a broad-based, supra-class party dedicated to the altruistic reformation of British society.

This did not mean that the Labour party did not benefit from the election. It benefited greatly. It was strengthened by the return of nearly all the pacifists whom the war and the Coupon election had removed in 1918. There were only ten Fabians,[1] but, apart from Pethick-Lawrence, it included the whole of the Executive of the Union of Democratic Control. Many of the missing ILP leaders returned also. In the new parliament MacDonald, Snowden, Trevelyan, Morel, Ponsonby, Webb, Buxton, Wedgwood, Lees-Smith and Wallhead provided an intellectual leadership which had not existed in the old.

On the re-assembly of parliament Clynes was replaced as chairman of the Parliamentary Labour Party. MacDonald was elected in his place because some trades unionists failed to vote and the intellectual, ILP, socialist and non-trades union elements decided to support him. MacDonald had taken political refuge in Scotland during the war where the Clydesiders were his closest friends, but he was not expected to pursue the policies of the Left which supported him because 'they had not yet a man of their own to put forward or sufficient strength to gain an independent success'. His election was seen as a victory of 'the Socialist and political elements' over the Coalition-conscious, 'bureaucratic' trades union leadership for which the more intelligent Labour leaders felt great contempt while out of parliament between 1918 and 1922.[2]

Nevertheless, what MacDonald and the other Labour leaders said in the next twelve months was a continuation of what had been said by Clynes, Thomas, Henderson and Webb in the three years before. There was the same denial that the Labour party was connected with Bolshevism,[3] the same claim that the Labour party had 'principles and policies which ... will serve the interests of the nation far better than those professed by the gentlemen on the benches opposite to us'.[4] The Glasgow ILP was heavily represented in the new parliament. MacDonald dissociated himself from its attacks on Asquith and criticised its willingness to disrupt parliamentary procedure, the cumbersome nature of which he defended in the *New Leader* at the end of the first session.[5] He presented the 'hatred and struggle' its members claimed to have brought with them from the Labour movement outside[6] as a 'generous warmth of righteous indignation'.[7] Labour policy was not, he claimed, 'impracticable'. Nor was it 'at war with private enterprise' which had long since ceased to be the only source of education, roads, police, Army, Navy and so on. The problems of British society which 'combine[d] individual ... initiative with social legislation' could best be solved 'by careful and well-thought out experiments [to] find a wider civic life and greater social power'.[1]

MacDonald and Thomas both claimed that the government was not doing enough to provide work.[2] They criticised Law for refusing to see a deputation of unemployed. But they also said that 'mob law' must be resisted and that unemployed marchers who assembled in Downing Street in November were guilty of 'sheer advertisement'.[3] MacDonald spoke for 'men who had faced death ... in the mines and workshops and ... seen their industrial comrades maimed and killed'.[4] He spoke also for the war dead whose sacrifice would best be remembered by pursuing in foreign policy 'those principles and that peace for which they had laid down their lives'.[5] He stressed the importance of the new opportunity to make parliament an instrument of policy,[6] the Labour party's ability to take it and its determination, even when it knew it would be defeated, to insist on discussions of principle before defeat took place.[7] The impression of competence was heightened by his ability to command a leading place in parliament.[8] The impression of centrality was heightened by deliberate criticism of Clydesider hatred.

The election of 1922 had exposed the weakness of the Liberal party.[9] MacDonald was determined to destroy it and replace it by Labour which had grown because its 'ideas ... were right', because it was the party of 'principle ... progress and ... vision' and because it was 'the heir of all the Liberal opinion that was hammered out before it'. It was, MacDonald claimed, 'the heir ... of the thought, of the moral achievements, of the ideals and of the conditions that the Radical party ... the Liberal party and the non-conformist movement had made possible', and it had come 'not to destroy but to fulfil'.[10]

For MacDonald the disruption of the Coalition was both a hindrance and a help. On the one hand it increased the plausibility of Lloyd George's claim to be a leader of the Left and made imminent an assault by him on the loyalty of the Labour leaders to their movement. On the other it made the Conservative government an easier target to attack. Whereas Lloyd George's government, even after the removal of Clynes, Walsh, Roberts, Addison and Montagu, still claimed progressive sympathies, the new government made few claims of this sort. From November 1922 onwards, MacDonald's chief claim was that the national choice was between reactionary Conservatism and the progressive Labour party – 'the alternative government of the future',[1] which would need all the discipline the reactionary parties had used in parliament in the past.[2]

Just as Salisbury had wanted to keep Birkenhead out of the Conservative leadership because he stimulated class bitterness by provoking open conflict between the Haves and the Have-nots which the Have-nots, if driven to unified action, would win, so MacDonald, from a similar position of controlled extremism in his own party, gave practical expression to the parallel belief that bare assertion of Have-not demands would deny the Labour party all hope of power for a generation. Have-not demands were made, but they were covered with moral merit and made on behalf of everyone except 'the rich'.[3] ' "Black-coated people" ' were encouraged to welcome the Capital Levy.[4] De-control of middle-class housing – an issue at the 1923 by-elections – showed that 'there was nothing the government were more afraid of and ... there was nothing more natural than a junction between the Labour party and the middle classes'.[5]

Whereas Clynes tended to defend a sane Capitalism against capitalistic excesses, MacDonald's emphasis was on Socialism as the real embodiment of the claims Capitalism's apologists had made for the operation of their system. There was about MacDonald's rhetoric at this time a great deal of the tone of Mill, Green, Gladstone and Cobden – a sense of the connections between a pacific, as opposed to a dynastic, foreign policy, a consistent rejection of the practice and theory of Bolshevism and repeated reminders of claims that

the Fabian Society's economics ha[d] always been avowedly Jevonian and anti-Marxist, and that the ILP founded itself on a social ethic which was religious in inspiration and ha[d] always declined to associate itself with the Marxian view of the class war, economic determinism and the revolutionary conclusions which Bolshevism claims to be its most characteristic application of Marxism.[6]

Socialism, indeed, was quite different from Marxism. It was not against Capital.[1] It meant 'Capital and Labour ... co-ordinated in a unified way, Labour using Capital and contributing to the well-being of the community'.[2] Nationalisation meant seeing that 'as men got ... nearer the status of self-determined, civilised, human being, ... willing ... production would have to ... replace ... forced ... production'.[3] Socialism also meant 'cycling' and 'singing': 'the Socialist movement must remain a purely mechanical and hard economic thing unless it was inspired by good music'.[4] Although the 'modern methods of stunt propaganda' practised by 'gentlemen who wrote on Bolshevism for pantry girls and stock-brokers', made it difficult to make the position understood, Socialism rested on 'reason' for its justification and on legality for its accomplishment.[5] The Labour party 'propose[d] to do nothing without a ... majority':[6] when it did things it would use the Civil Service. There was 'no body of service more magnificent ... wonderful [and] essential than the ... Civil Service'. When, at a 'time not ... far distant', the Labour party formed a government, the Civil Service 'from Sir John Anderson down to the humblest member' would give 'as whole-hearted a service as was ever given to any government'.[7]

The political target – reactionary Conservatism – having been chosen, it remained to find something to say about it. The obvious thing, which MacDonald began to say during the election – was that it was 'law-abiding only in so far as it suits its own purpose' – was, in other words, 'a Fascismo with respect for nothing but its own will ... imagin[ing] that it stands with Society against a crowd of Goths who have come from the steppes to upset things'.[8] Another accusation was that 'in the Tory party morality comes after grab ... it was the party that said "If you get something, keep it" '.[9] A third accusation, in relation to ex-Servicemen's pensions, was that 'since 1919 [the] great patriots who ... drank the health of the men who were ... in the trenches had rather forgotten ... about them'.[10] A fourth was that the Conservative party had no policy for house-building, did not see that house-building could help to relieve unemployment[11] and only reversed its policy about Rent Control when the Labour party pointed out that De-control would hit the middle classes.[12] A fifth was that its doctrinaire hatred of Russia closed an avenue for British trade which ought to be opened.[1] A sixth was that it was led by 'passion' rather than 'reason' and had no foreign policy: a seventh that the State insurance principle was not an adequate remedy for unemployment, that it was bad to give money without a return and that 'those who said it was impossible to turn dole receivers into serviceable wage-earners ... [should] make way for those who claimed ... they could'.[2]

MacDonald did not become Labour leader because of his interest in foreign policy. Foreign policy nevertheless became a central concern.[3] With the French invasion of the Ruhr and France's attempt 'to secure the destruction of the economic life of Germany'[4] he and Snowden in particular were on home ground. What they said throughout 1923 was that there had 'never before [been] a trade depression and widespread unemployment which was so directly attributable to a political cause'[5] and that unemployment had been intensified by the government's policy on Reparations and the Ruhr.[6] France had been the 'most militaristic country in Europe [for] 50 years before ... 1914': French militarism, French vengeance and French belittling of the League of Nations all stood in the way of restoring international goodwill on which the renewal of international trade depended. The invasion of the Ruhr meant that Europe was 'armed to the teeth'. Meanwhile Britain was doing nothing.

About the remedy MacDonald did not commit himself. He asked that parliament be recalled a fortnight after the invasion of the Ruhr.[7] He urged France to seek security through a democratically enlarged League of Nations.[8] But in the early months at least, he recognised the difficulties. He knew that 'for the moment nothing could be done to stop the ... occupation' which had to be accepted as 'the failure of the League of Nations'. In these circumstances the Asquithean demand to bring the matter before the League was 'fruitless'. What was occurring was the 'breakdown of Versailles'. What was needed was 'reconsideration of the Versailles and other Treaties' and a major effort to ensure that the League was 'reconstructed and made representative and then ... used for conciliation and arbitration'.[9]

These criticisms of the League of Nations distinguished the Labour party from the Liberals: they also reflected the UDC feeling that the existing League was a conspiracy and the League of Nations Union a fraud which had ostracised the Labour party pacifists in their period of major unpopularity.[1] If they were expressed in terms that were rhetorical rather than practical, there can be no doubting the suitability of a rhetoric which concentrated on 'removal of apprehension and fear' and 'security [as] the fruit of moral conduct', treated 'the evil of armaments' as the source from which 'every fear is nourished' and characterised 'a League . . . of Nations obedient to the will of victors . . . [as] a poor guarantee of the security which nations [were] nervously seeking'.[2]

These lines of attack were developed by MacDonald before Law's retirement. They were not radically changed by Baldwin's arrival. Baldwin, it is true, was more alert than Law to the needs of the situation. He was a stronger opponent of Lloyd George. His policy was 'not that of his back-benches and his Die Hards': he might even become an 'enfant terrible' to the Conservative party.[3] But in other respects there was only development of existing lines of argument. McKenna's 'apostasy' showed that the ranks of reaction were being aligned. It showed that the Liberal party was 'a decaying survival'[4] and that the liberal mission would have to be pursued through 'the only party which has zeal and inspiration to fight for . . . progress'.[5]

What MacDonald was saying, therefore, when the House of Commons went into recess on August 2 was that the government had to face up to these problems. He was saying that the government would find it difficult to face up to them because of its reactionary back-benches and that its ability to do so would be a crucial test of its capability. He was saying that the attempt to whip up anti-socialist feeling without putting anything constructive in its place showed that the Conservative party was the class-dominated party of reaction. He apologised for his own wild men in parliament. He stressed that the Labour party was not a Red Plot and did not want a Red Terror. He emphasised that it was on the contrary a steady, reforming party whose object was to soften the harshness of existing society and, through a combination of social service and hostility to militarism, to provide policies suitable for the age in which it was living. It is difficult to know what impact MacDonald's writings and speeches had on opinion at large. They had an impact on Asquith. There is no doubt that they had an impact on Baldwin.

(iii)

In May Baldwin's first task had been to establish his government: extension of its range of support could involve movement in either of two directions. It could involve embracing individual Chamberlainites if they would join. It could involve embracing such Liberals as were suitable and available, provided they would abandon their Liberal affiliation. Accessions from either direction would strengthen a weak government and reduce the ability of any non-socialist alternative to benefit from the difficulties it would face in the years immediately ahead. But because Baldwin's personal following was weak even within the Baldwin government, the accessions had not to be too strong to upset the balance. Baldwin's régime at its widest consisted of Bridgeman, Baird, Davidson and Jackson. Amery would have formed part of it if Baldwin had not been anxious to keep him at arm's length. He had given Joynson-Hicks and Hoare the chance to be Cabinet Ministers. Sanders, though scarcely a powerful minister, seems to have had no doubts about Baldwin: the same was probably true of Peel and Barlow. But Neville Chamberlain and Lloyd-Graeme thought originally of a Curzon government: Chamberlain did not begin to be close to Baldwin until he became Chancellor of the Exchequer. Salisbury, Derby, Cave, Curzon, Devonshire, Wood, Worthington-Evans, Lord Robert Cecil and Novar felt no special loyalty. Baldwin had the advantage of actually being Prime Minister: suspicions and rivalries in the Cabinet made con-certed action against him unlikely so long as he did nothing foolish. But an organised admission of Chamberlainites under Balfour and Austen Chamberlain in a situation in which Bald-win had not established himself would put him in considerable danger.

Baldwin's position, however, though weak, was not so weak that he had no cards to play. One card was that he meant different things to different groups and used the ambiguity of his position to the full. He needed successes of his own to establish himself as a self-moved leader but, even without these and perhaps because he was without them, was in a better position to balance each group off against the others. Derby and Curzon were in a state of constant tension. In relation to Salisbury and his followers,

Baldwin's strength was that he was a barrier against Birkenhead. One point of his repeated protestations in favour of party unity was that the Chamberlainites would be more likely to abandon opposition if they thought Baldwin wanted to admit them in the end.

In forming his government Baldwin had covered himself in progressive directions with Lord Robert Cecil and in Die Hard ones with Salisbury and Joynson-Hicks. His first attempt to extend himself with the Chamberlainites failed when Horne refused the Exchequer on May 25: Baldwin then tried the second by offering Worthington-Evans the Post Office. Worthington-Evans, though in some respect a catch, was not much of a catch. The offer of the Exchequer to McKenna was an attempt to extend in a Liberal direction where a radical past and financial experience made a happy combination with the McKenna duties which had gone as near as a Liberal could go towards Protection. McKenna's commitments were not in fact Protectionist. The proposal to appoint him, like the appointment of Lord Robert Cecil, aroused suspicion in Protectionist quarters:[1] the most that could be claimed was that he was much changed about Free Trade and might help the government 'in getting round the corner early'.[2] His expertise was less fiscal than financial. Baldwin probably wanted him because he expected a Dawes-style conference in 1923 to establish the government by repeating over Reparations and the Ruhr the success he had had in negotiating the settlement of the American Debt.[3] McKenna's appointment, like the hopes Baldwin expressed for Grigg and Hilton Young,[4] the angling he did for Grey and, perhaps, a favour to Runciman in July warned the Chamberlainites that, if they would not play, he would construct the anti-socialist front they wanted without them.[5]

McKenna made acceptance of the Exchequer conditional on his health improving and a safe seat being found in the City of London: he may have wanted to see how the Franco-German position developed. Banbury refused to give McKenna his seat: by mid-August it was clear that no seat could be found. It was clear also that the Franco-German situation had not reached a point at which his knowledge would be helpful. With the announcement on August 14 that he was not fit to take office,[6] Baldwin had failed to extend himself in either direction. He then offered the Exchequer to Neville Chamberlain who at first refused and then agreed to take it.[1]

In 1920 Neville Chamberlain was fifty-four. He was educated at Rugby and at Mason College, Birmingham. Austen Chamberlain had been trained to be the family's politician: until he joined Birmingham City Council at the age of forty-two Neville Chamberlain played no major part in politics. His first step in national politics was at the top – as Director-General of National Service in Lloyd George's first government immediately after the end of a year as Lord Mayor of Birmingham. He was removed after less than a year in office, convinced that Lloyd George had double-crossed him. He entered parliament in 1918, was an early enemy of Lloyd George and one of the first Conservatives actively to wish an end to the Coalition. Chamberlain had none of the misplaced dignity of Austen Chamberlain, had an acuter and more accurate intelligence and had developed a strong capacity for loathing. In 1921/22 he was inhibited by Austen Chamberlain's support for Lloyd George. He disliked the Die Hards and tried to run Steel-Maitland out of Birmingham when Steel-Maitland attacked Austen Chamberlain's leadership.[2] But his loathing of Lloyd George and his entourage – especially the Geddes brothers – was intense.

Neville Chamberlain was out of England when the Coalition fell. He did not expect it to fall, did not think much of the government that succeeded it[3] and did not expect it to survive. Nevertheless, he joined it as Postmaster-General. In the months following the election, he dissociated himself from Austen Chamberlain's wilder excesses.[4] Law took pains with him, but he was not at first in the Cabinet and was used as a disposable pawn until given his chance with Horne's refusal to take the Ministry of Health when Griffith-Boscawen had to leave it. Neville Chamberlain's first political success came in his four months as Minister of Health. Between March and August 1923 he dissipated the gloom in which Griffith-Boscawen had left the Conservative party, establishing an intellectual predominance in the House of Commons on Housing about which Conservatives felt naked and vulnerable and he was sure no one would contradict him because he 'h[e]ld the key position'[5] and knew best what was politically possible.[6] Most of what is known as 'Wheatley's Housing policy' was his, apart from the finance. The combination of private enterprise building, limited local authority support and individual ownership was eminently presentable within the framework of Conservative assumptions.

When Law retired, Neville Chamberlain expected Curzon to succeed.[1] He had no special enthusiasm for Baldwin and may just possibly have taken Lloyd-Graeme seriously when told to be Prime Minister himself.[2] He probably hoped to be Chancellor of the Exchequer:[3] he did not like the appointment of McKenna.[4] His reluctance to accept the Chancellorship in August, if reluctance it was, may have arisen from unwillingness to offend Austen Chamberlain, a feeling that he 'never could understand finance' or reluctance to court the odium which Chancellors faced for 'put[ting] a spoke into other people's wheels'.[5] From Baldwin's point of view he was a better choice than Worthington-Evans, who did not believe in sound finance, was a more permanent prospect than Wood whose father – a peer – was eighty-four and had greater momentum than Lloyd-Graeme.[6] He was the one member of the new government who had been a success in matters about which the Labour party was taking the lead and, though a Protectionist, was not Amery who wanted very much to be Chancellor.[7] Also, he happened to be a Chamberlain at a time when Austen Chamberlain had cut himself off, when Derby was threatening to resign and when Birkenhead was attacking the government's desertion of the French and the Lausanne Treaty as 'the biggest give-away in English history'.

On succeeding Law, Baldwin had not proposed any striking departure from his policies. His first step was to declare his 'love' for 'the man' and to emphasise the continuity between them.[8] Others thought Baldwin 'more cheerful and robust ... a better judge of men' and more capable of providing practical ideas.[9] But the climate he wished to create depended, as Law's had, on the claim that, by contrast with Lloyd George and Birkenhead he was 'honest to the verge of simplicity',[10] had none of the marks of 'genius' and had 'never yet known a good workman who could talk ... [or] a good talker who was a good workman'.[11] References to Disraeli as defender of the Constitution, the Empire and 'the welfare of our people, whether industrial or agricultural',[12] claims that he, Baldwin, had the merits of the 'thoroughly capable businessman'[1] and the constantly repeated emphasis on the connection between the European problem, the Imperial opportunity and the solution of the unemployment question represented no striking departure from the line Law had used to distinguish his government from the Coalition.

Baldwin highlighted the moral merits of private enterprise. The primary task of government was presented as provision of opportunities for individual initiative to make its way in the world and, through 'economy ... debt reduction ... sound, prudent and careful finance' to maintain the 'credit ... which carried us through the French wars of one hundred years ago and ... must ... always carry us so long as we ... hope to keep our place ... industrially, commercially and financially ... in the front of the nations of the world'.[2] Baldwin believed in the intimacy of the connection he described between British prosperity, the responsibility to rescue Europe from 'collapse' and the avoidance of 'social reactions among our people that may be beyond the power of all statesmanship to cope with'.[3]

In MacDonald's hands Socialism was a central, constructive programme extending out from known positions on foreign policy towards a claim to solve the unemployment problem. The Capital Levy had become a persuasive threat. So long as it seemed possible to go on reducing governmental expenditure from a high wartime level, every Chancellor could feel free, if necessary, to reduce taxation. This form of relief had now come to an end. As Neville Chamberlain explained in his earliest speeches as Chancellor: 'you will be foolish to count upon further remissions of taxation in the near future': 'unless we cut down our expenditure still further, we shall be faced with a deficit in our Budget which can only be met by increased taxation'.[4]

This meant that, in addition to being able to do nothing about unemployment except by 'pacifying Europe' which would create as many economic problems as it would solve, there was not much prospect of domestic popularity unless new sources of revenue could be found. In June 1923 Davidson seems to have been preparing a plan for universal old age pensions.[5] In introducing his Budget in 1923 Baldwin committed himself to reduce the level of the National Debt, but proposed to do this by refusing to remit taxation. In a situation in which the taxation of income could not be reduced and the National Debt had to be, the claim that a Capital Levy would facilitate both operations had the cogency in political terms of something approaching the unanswerable.

Far from denying the appeal of the Capital Levy in the 'business-like' form in which MacDonald presented it, Baldwin warned Conservatives that 'it was no good meeting propaganda about [it] by merely saying it is a form of robbery'. It was in fact 'not ... a form of robbery' and 'nobody would believe you when you said it'. Capital Levy was a 'legitimate form of taxation': people were more likely to vote against it if they could 'be made to believe that [it] was ... stupid ... than if you think you have succeeded in convincing them that it is immoral'.[1] Baldwin wanted to be a 'healer', to beat off the challenge of 'class war ... by the hardness of our heads and the largeness of our hearts'.[2] He displayed an acute sense of the fillip which unemployment had given MacDonald's appeal and the damage which threatened the existing order from 'grumbl[ing]' on the part of the 'more fortunate members of the community ... when the government has to spend the tax payers' money in ... trying to help men through this time of stress'. Baldwin had 'never had any fear about the character of our people' which unemployment would 'test ... as much as the war tested it'. But unemployment made it necessary to buttress hostility to Socialism by diffusing accurate economic information, having a positive economic policy and exhorting industry to develop large-scale plans for capital investment.[3]

It is necessary to emphasise Baldwin's sense of the possibilities inherent in MacDonald's rhetoric because one easily supposes that his eyes were fixed solely on Lloyd George. They were fixed on Lloyd George as a short-term tactical danger. But they were fixed on MacDonald as the long-term strategic one. Baldwin was as conscious as Austen Chamberlain of the existence of a new electorate which had no fixed party loyalties. His speeches in the summer of 1923 were reminiscent in their calculated centrality of the positions of Rothermere, Bottomley, Salisbury, Lord Robert Cecil and Lloyd George immediately before Genoa. They drew attention to 'one of the most vigorous and sustained propaganda ... that ha[d] ever appeared in this country'[4] and proposed a nation-wide campaign to halt it. But they were sensitive to the attractiveness of MacDonald's appeal. They did not deny that the Labour party 'strive[s] ... genuinely for the uplifting of the masses of this country'. They claimed that, if Disraeli had become Prime Minister 'in the plentitude of his own strength', he would have found solutions for the 'many problems which were growing up all unseen under the eyes of the statesmen of the régime of laissez-faire'. They recognised that, though the Conservative party was 'the first to offer a serious contribution to the amelioration of ... the working-classes', it had 'lagged behind' since Disraeli died. They urged 'both sides in industry to be slow to assert ... their rights ... quick to assert ... their duties and ... willing ... to forgo the little bit of what they think might be due to them rather than run the risk of driving a single man or woman to the ranks of the unemployed'.[1]

In 1922/23 the positive remedy for unemployment suggested by leaders of all parties was not primarily a domestic remedy. Asquith, Lloyd George and MacDonald were all committed to a basically Free Trade position. The domestic remedies they suggested were either Utopian, that is to say, Socialism, or unemployment insurance, which was a palliative. Lloyd George had thought of abandoning Free Trade when he went to America: he had not done so. Law and Baldwin had avoided Protection because of the difficulty it would cause in the Conservative party. It was assumed that the only available remedy for unemployment lay in a foreign policy which would stop the French creating economic dislocation in Germany and central Europe. Baldwin's main object from May to October 1923 was to establish himself by achieving the same sort of success in pacifying Europe as Lloyd George had hoped for at Geneva a year before.

From October 1922 until October 1923 there was continuing friction within the Law and Baldwin Cabinets about the conduct of foreign, Imperial and defence policy. There was a three-cornered struggle between the Admiralty, War Office and Air Force about the future of the Naval Air Arm. Over the American Debt settlement, Derby, Devonshire, Baldwin, Cave and Law all contemplated resignation. Dissension was increased by Lord Robert Cecil's dual rôle as Cabinet Minister and leading figure at the League of Nations which was unpopular in the Conservative party and had critics in the Cabinet. Salisbury had no great opinion of it until Lord Robert Cecil persuaded him that he ought to. Curzon was scarcely its friend. McNeill and Amery were its declared enemies. In the course of 1923 they were encouraged by its impotence in face of Mussolini's occupation of Corfu where it was thought that Poincaré used *French* influence to persuade Mussolini to let the League down lightly. Lord Robert Cecil's attempt to commit the British government to a Treaty of Mutual Guarantee without Cabinet consultation brought the League question to a head.[1]

The Mesopotamia mandate had been the object of continuous criticism in Die Hard and Anti-Waste quarters and from pro-Muslims who disliked it as the basis for an anti-Turkish policy in the Middle East. Law, however, made no commitment to withdraw at the 1922 election: he reiterated his refusal to be committed immediately afterwards. The Coalition had made, but not ratified, a Treaty with King Feisal. The Iraq sub-committee of the Cabinet, the Cabinet and eventually parliament itself saw a prolonged struggle between McNeill, Lloyd-Graeme and Novar, who advanced financial reasons for honouring an unspoken commitment to reject the Treaty, and Curzon, Derby and Amery who wanted to ignore the cost – 'mere base millions' as Curzon put it[2] – maintain a British presence and ratify the Treaty.[3] Derby, Curzon and Amery won the day Law announced that he was going on his final cruise.

These, however, were minor matters on which ministers flexed their muscles. The major cause of conflict was Curzon and Curzon's handling of the French.

One Conservative criticism of Lloyd George before October 1922 was that his dishonesty had destroyed the Anglo-French alliance: one of Law's chief claims at the 1922 election was that he would restore it. Restoration of the alliance was not merely a Die Hard position: it had much support in the Conservative party at large. In some quarters it was taken to be compatible with extending the influence of the League of Nations: in others, it was thought to be the political reality of which the League was the illusory sham. There were currents – in the City of London in particular – which were friendly to Germany. But support for the Entente distinguished the Conservative party from its rivals, which was why Birkenhead made a point of claiming that the government had abandoned it.

The claim that the Entente had been abandoned was false. Law's policy was based on the belief that nothing would be gained by an open showdown with the French, that an Anglo-French showdown would exacerbate Franco-German relations and that any showdown would delay trade recovery indefinitely. There was no dispute about Germany's ability to pay indemnity and reparation: the question was as to the amount. The Law government was clear that France would be restrained only if she was sure of British support, and that support should usually be forthcoming. On this basis Law claimed credit in December for dissuading Poincaré from action against Germany.[1]

With the occupation of the Ruhr in January 1923, this policy had been shown to be ineffective. It was not abandoned. The British government neither approved nor denounced the occupation. But even France's strongest supporters were alarmed. Passive resistance in the Ruhr, assisted as it was said to be by the German government, provoked French attempts at suppression, with a consequent increase in tension in the British zone of occupation. There was a danger that inflation and financial collapse would destroy the German state as French occupation increased Franco-German tension. By the time Baldwin became Prime Minister, there was no sign either of a settlement or of a French withdrawal.

It was this, and a simple desire to have a success, rather than any sentimentality about Germany[2] that made Baldwin anxious to produce conditions in which the French left the Ruhr and a Reparations settlement was made. Baldwin signalised his appointment by a friendly message to the French people. He did not, however, expect immediate success and thought chiefly of establishing agreement with Belgium and Italy as a preliminary to seeing Poincaré himself.[3] On July 4 a predominantly Francophil Cabinet, knowing that the French were becoming obstinate but believing that the contraction of trade made a European settlement 'vital', decided 'to take a definite line' even if the French resisted.[4] By the end of July it seemed that the Italian government certainly, and the Belgian government really, agreed.[5]

From the point of decision on July 4 the Ruhr and Reparations questions were less a problem of policy than a problem of manner.

So much indeed were they problems of manner that almost everything turned on the drafting of notes to the French and German governments. Curzon had been left a free hand in negotiating the Turkish Treaty. When his attention turned to Western Europe, he was no more successful than under Lloyd George in persuading Cabinet ministers to avoid independent statements about foreign policy.[1]

The Cabinet's difficulty was that it wanted to modify French intransigence towards Germany while remaining popular in the Conservative party many of whose members did not. Poincaré was supposed to represent French feeling about Germany. Curzon's relations with Poincaré had been poor under Lloyd George: they were no better under Law and Baldwin.[2] Curzon's despatches were criticised in Cabinet: the redrafting which Baldwin and Curzon were asked to undertake, was designed to remove sarcasm and hectoring at the expense of France. This happened, for example, on May 7[3] and July 12.[4] It happened again on August 9 when they were asked to redraft a Curzon note to France and to send the new draft to the leading Francophils – Derby and Amery, on holiday at Evian and Chamonix respectively.[5]

Amery probably carried little weight, but Derby's position was peculiar. He was the last ambassador in Paris and had made friendships there which he continued to renew. Birkenhead had twice told him that he should be Prime Minister: it is possible that he thought he could be. In October 1922 he had asked Law for non-departmental office and roving commissions on foreign policy, but had been pushed into the War Office instead. He was politically jealous, and perhaps socially contemptuous, of Curzon: his opening shot in the new Cabinet was to criticise him for failing to invite the United States to Lausanne. He agreed to the change of policy on July 4, but had no confidence in Curzon's ability to execute it. After talking to Amery at Evian he suggested changes in the Curzon note: when he discovered that it had been done before his comments reached London, he sent Baldwin a general attack on Curzon and threatened to resign if the hint that Britain would act independently of France over Reparations was meant to reflect a settled purpose.[6] On August 23 he was in London to see Baldwin, who explained that the reference to separate action by Britain was bluff and agreed that Curzon was the worst Foreign

Secretary the country had ever had.[1] Derby replied that Baldwin must meet Poincaré. A week later, on hearing that Curzon had asked to see Poincaré, he wrote to say that Baldwin must go himself.[2]

It is not certain that Baldwin took Derby's resignation seriously, though his resignation would have strengthened the Chamberlainites and Baldwin might well have liked to put Grey in Curzon's place.[3] However, he visited Poincaré on September 19 and claimed to have restored relations without abandoning anything of importance.[4] Whatever improvement had been achieved, there was a prospect of Cabinet conflict, opposition criticism and a recurrence of bad relations in the future. By mid-October Baldwin seems to have renewed his initial mistrust of Poincaré.[5] He may well have thought the time had come for the Cabinet and the country to think, and talk, about something else.

Thirdly, one must see Baldwin's adoption of Protection as a way of removing Die Hard mistrust of his foreign policy and to establish himself as a distinctive party leader. For both purposes Protection was suitable. The one truth that had been established in the Conservative party by the beginning of the war was that Protection was desirable. Many Die Hards were as Protectionist as they were pro-French: they were as likely to respond to a Protectionist programme as Birkenhead hoped they would be to an anti-German one. Protection was not a subject about which the Chamberlainites were enthusiastic: it was a subject on which Derby, Salisbury and Lord Robert Cecil had nothing in common with the Die Hards. Gretton may, or may not, have told Baldwin on his return from France that, 'as the Die Hards had made him, so they could un-make him'. He may or may not have 'rattled' Baldwin by 'demand[ing] Protection' in as many words.[6] He certainly sent a letter on July 30 in which 103 M.P.s asked for a party discussion of Imperial Preference and the Economic Conference.[7] There is much reason to suggest a feeling on Baldwin's part that the best way of establishing himself in relation to these forces was to assert a position of his own which would be acceptable to the body of the party and would divide Salisbury, Derby and Lord Robert Cecil from it.[8]

Finally, in explaining Baldwin's decision to adopt Protection, one must ask: did Baldwin intend to drive the two wings of the

Liberal party together in order to detach Lloyd George from the Chamberlainites and to strengthen the Liberal party in relation to MacDonald? In other words, did he want to produce a situation in which Asquith and Lloyd George on the one hand disputed with MacDonald on the other for the progressive vote, while the Conservative party was strengthened in its own hold on its own vote by restoring party unity? The doctrine that it was the Liberal party's business to provide a safe alternative government existed in the higher reaches of the Conservative party both in late 1922 and afterwards. Baldwin expressed it in talking to the King in October 1923.[1] The fact that he adopted a Protectionist rather than an Imperial platform lends weight to the view that it played a part in calculation.[2]

Its usefulness as an explanation of the decision is reduced, however, by the fact that Davidson said the opposite to Thomas Jones,[3] that Baldwin's Swansea speech was highly critical of the Liberal party and that the Liberal leaders themselves were conscious that they were being assaulted with particular vigour. It also conflicts with the possibility that Lloyd George might, even after his return from America, have tried to outbid Baldwin in Protectionist directions.

It may be that Lloyd George would have found it difficult to do after Baldwin's speech on October 25 what he might have done effectively beforehand. But Beaverbrook was not the only person who thought that Lloyd George had room to manoeuvre on November 9. Austen Chamberlain thought that Baldwin had destroyed his own policy. Mond, Grigg, Greenwood and Churchill all thought it worthwhile to send messages to the *Majestic* to make sure that Lloyd George did nothing they did not want. What would have happened if Lloyd George had made a major declaration on November 9 it is difficult to know. The Chamberlainites might have followed him, but it is not certain that they would have made much difference. One reason why Lloyd George stuck to Free Trade was probably the feeling, which Austen Chamberlain had already, that Coalition Conservatism did not have very much future.

Nevertheless, the effect of Baldwin's decision was to drive Asquith and Lloyd George together in order to face an election they would have much preferred to face later. Baldwin almost certainly calculated that this would happen. In this respect there was a difference between the decisions of October 11, 23 and 25 to adopt Protection which may have been designed in part to assist Liberal unity, and the decision to hold an immediate election which may well have been designed to catch the Liberals before they were ready.

The more closely one examines the possibilities in the light of the evidence, the more difficult it is to attribute exact calculation to the decision to adopt Protection as distinct from the decision to fight an election in November. The Protection commitment stands out as a bold risk, a display of authority by an inexperienced but self-confident political leader who had settled the American Debt question, become Prime Minister after a comparatively brief ministerial career and thought, perhaps, that he knew how to handle Poincaré. It was an attempt to meet the accusation that he had no policy, to pursue the only policy he could think of and to use the best method he knew, before the Labour party used it itself,[1] to appeal to the sympathy of the Conservative party and prove to the working classes that Conservatives had a positive policy – the protection of the indigenous industries of the country in a situation in which 'as Europe recovered, our position must get worse in competition with European cheap labour and low exchanges and ... we could not face the winter of 1924/25 without a change in our fiscal system'.[2] At Plymouth he promised a cruiser programme, at Swansea a programme of railway orders from the LMS and at Cardiff similar promises of detailed employment for the future. Whether he had in mind the party conference of 1923, the electoral situation of 1923/24 or the unemployment situation of 1924/25, there is no reason to doubt the truth of the political character revealed in a letter written to Arthur Ponsonby by Trevelyan – an old friend of Baldwin – a week after he became Prime Minister.

I think Baldwin is an improvement upon Bonar Law. I had a talk with him yesterday when he was surprisingly frank. Of course he knows my views well. The things he said were as follows.

That he was going to try and settle Europe, though he failed and failed again. That he had hopes of avoiding the breach with Russia. That he regarded the stabilizing of the German mark as of the first importance, though it might lead to an irresistible Protectionist outcry here. That the

French papers were receiving him well but that he didn't know how long that would go on. That he was trying to get McKenna to help him for the sake of dealing with Europe. That it wasn't worth being P.M. except to do something of the kind. Very frank and well intentioned![1]

XVI

SALISBURY'S REVOLT

'Liberals and Labour are against Tariffs. The two together will have a majority of several millions, but there is the possibility that you may have a majority in Parliament representing a minority of the population . . . If you ask Mr Baldwin at this moment if he expected a majority of the voters to vote for Tariff Reform, he would say "No" for he is an honest man. He will not say it in public – he is not quite honest enough for that. But he knows it.'

Lloyd George at Leeds, November 27 (or 26) 1923,
Manchester Guardian, November 28

(i)

The decision to adopt Protection was made by Baldwin. It is not certain exactly when. In late September Amery thought something was on the way.[1] Unless he was being discreet in talking to Amery, Neville Chamberlain expected no abrogation of the Law pledge on October 1.[2] He spent the night of October 5/6 with Baldwin at Chequers where Baldwin talked vaguely about discussing fiscal policy when he spoke to the party conference on the 25th.[3] In a speech at Stirling on October 6 Younger hinted that there would probably have to be 'some fundamental change in the country's fiscal system'.[4] On the 8th Amery and Jackson were both told that a change was imminent: Jackson, much to his annoyance, was asked by Baldwin whether 'he would be ready for an election in November' if it became necessary to go in for general protection.[5] On the 10th Bruce, the Australian Prime Minister, had a meeting with Amery, Neville Chamberlain and Lloyd-Graeme to decide which Commonwealth imports could be given preferential treatment.[6] Baldwin made a strongly Imperial speech at the Guildhall on October 12.[7] Baldwin, Amery and Lloyd-Graeme spent the week-end together at Chequers on October 13/14 and Davidson came for lunch on the Sunday. It was decided then that Baldwin should announce at the party conference at Plymouth on October 25 a 'whole-hearted policy of Protection and Preference' but should do nothing to produce an immediate general election: in the period between the Plymouth speech and the end of the year further McKenna duties would be imposed within the framework of the Law pledge and the election postponed 'until after the middle of January' so that 'the country [would have] a chance of understanding what it [was] all about'.[1]

The Cabinet Baldwin inherited with some modification from Law was not Protectionist. Derby, Salisbury and Devonshire were Conservative Free Traders, two of whom had already shown that they would resign without very much scruple if the circumstances were right. Novar was a Liberal Imperialist. Curzon was nominally a Protectionist but wanted to be left alone at the Foreign Office where Baldwin probably did not want to leave him. In Law's Cabinet it had been felt that that decisions were taken by the Prime Minister without adequate consultation. With the example of the Cabinet overruling Law over the American Debt, there was no reason why Baldwin should expect to be more successful in imposing a policy which only four Cabinet Ministers can be said to have wanted and which at least half the Cabinet was known to dislike.

At the time of the Chequers meeting Protection had not been discussed in Cabinet. It was not discussed for another ten days, and even then was sprung on the Cabinet without being put on the agenda. By the time Baldwin explained it to the Cabinet on October 23, Hewins had been set up in a private office to give Baldwin Protectionist advice untainted by Treasury doctrine.[2] The editor of *The Times* had been told, though he thought 'Baldwin's policy and plans too immature for immediate action'.[3] Rothermere and Beaverbrook had been talked to by Jackson and Davidson and had promised support, provided there were no import duties on meat or wheat.[4] Baldwin had told Bridgeman and, also, apparently, Sir Eric Geddes and Joynson-Hicks. Bridgeman had warned him that 'if he made such a speech, an election campaign would begin the next day': he suggested putting it off until an agricultural policy had been prepared and the Central Office was ready with Protectionist literature.[5] Jackson had told Sanders, who wanted a wheat subsidy to match the tariff on manufactures.[6] Hall had told Gretton who thought the policy should have been announced as 'a National policy' at the Imperial Conference, not at a 'party meeting ... as the echo of an appeal for votes'.[1] Somebody – probably Gretton – had told Lord Long of Wraxali.[2]

In addition Neville Chamberlain had told Austen Chamberlain and his sister Hilda: Hilda or Austen Chamberlain told their sister Ida.[3] Baldwin had told Derby, and also Salisbury. Austen Chamberlain had decided that 'if Baldwin came out full-blooded at Plymouth' he would 'publicly abandon all criticism of other matters'.[4] Neville Chamberlain did his best to persuade him that this was what was intended but had to make it clear that there would be no taxation on imported food, even though he claimed that Baldwin wanted it.[5] Derby grumbled, but agreed to give support in the context of a 'comprehensive scheme of Empire settlement' because he thought this would restore relations with Rothermere: he insisted – not necessarily to Baldwin – that Birkenhead should be brought into the Cabinet to help sell Protection to Lancashire Conservatives against their interests and inclinations.[6] Salisbury explained that 'a regular Protectionist tariff ... might be rather awkward for [him] and possibly still more awkward' for Lord Robert Cecil. He refused to commit himself until the two of them had talked.[7]

Baldwin had begun by wanting to have an immediate election. He had then swung right round the other way. At Chequers during the week-end of October 20, in the company of Davidson, Bruce, McKenzie King, Ormsby-Gore and Neville Chamberlain, he 'had quite abandoned the idea of an early election ... no longer thought it practicable to advocate food taxes but had it in mind to say he had concluded that a general tariff was necessary to meet unemployment'. Neville Chamberlain's proposal to put McKenna duties on twelve new articles and abandon the general election was sunk by Lloyd-Graeme – at this point one of the most relentless Protectionists – on the ground that he 'could not find such articles'.[8]

When the plan was announced at the Cabinet on October 23 Curzon and Lord Robert Cecil objected – Curzon because an upheaval would disrupt his foreign policy, Lord Robert Cecil by reason of his known Free Trade views and 'the ... Liberal support [he had got] in his constituency by pledging himself to Free Trade at the last election'. The discussion in general, however, was less about the substance of policy than about 'the desirability in which all concurred of a statement being so framed as to avoid our being pushed into a general election this autumn'. No one thought of resignation except Lord Robert Cecil who had been at war with Curzon over the League of Nations.[1] The policy decision and the intention to announce it at Plymouth two days later were accepted after brief discussion. It was thought that after the announcement, time would be needed for the electorate – particularly the women – to establish the dishonesty of the claim, which was expected from the Liberal and Labour parties, that taxation was to be imposed on imported food.[2] When the Cabinet was over, Wood and Lord Robert Cecil from the one side, Amery, Hoare and Neville Chamberlain from the other met in committee to work out details.[3]

When they had slept on the commitment of principle which Baldwin had explained on October 23, Cabinet Ministers became extremely alarmed. Neville Chamberlain had already pressed him to avoid calling an immediate election.[4] Joynson-Hicks had suggested ways of getting economic results without either a 'general tariff ... [which] would frighten a great many people' or a general election which would be needed if a general tariff was proposed.[5] Devonshire, Novar, Bridgeman, Cave and Gretton now wrote to say that he should do nothing to renounce the Law pledge since that would produce an electioneering atmosphere.[6] Gretton was not in the Cabinet: Baldwin avoided seeing him.[7] He and Bridgeman were both Protectionists: Joynson-Hicks was 'in full sympathy' with the content of Baldwin's proposals.[8] Cave had no objection to a Protectionist policy: he shared Smuts's opinion that 'in the midst of a world crisis ... it [was] undesirable to throw ... this great apple of discord' before the country at a general election.[9] Their warnings were prudential. Devonshire's and Novar's objections were fundamental. They were shared by Salisbury, Lord Robert Cecil and Derby, whatever grudging assent Derby had given beforehand.

Neville Chamberlain's letters leave the impression that this concentrated assault compelled Baldwin to make a vaguer speech at Plymouth than his preliminary soundings had encouraged him to think suitable.[10] The Plymouth speech mentioned neither an immediate general election nor specific policy proposals. It included a long analysis of the difficulties in the way of solving the unemployment problem and emphasised the differences between the pre-war and post-war economic situations. It promised attention to the consultations which were going on with the leaders of the agricultural industry and implied an attempt to give them what they wanted. Two-thirds of the way through, Baldwin announced that he had 'come to the conclusion that the only way of fighting [the unemployment] question [was] by protecting the home market' but gave no indication of the timing, scope or degree of the protection he proposed. Baldwin and Neville Chamberlain were both extremely nervous before the speech was delivered. Amery, who travelled with Baldwin's party to hear it, was probably right to think that Baldwin had succeeded in launching his protection campaign 'without doing so in a form which would precipitate a general election'.[1]

From October 25 onwards, therefore, Free Traders amongst ministers and M.P.s were expecting to prepare themselves for a gradual change of front and to work out the best way of justifying proposals they had previously opposed. They expected to reach agreement among themselves and with Baldwin in Cabinet about the exact form Protection would take. The Cabinet expected to have time to devise an adequate agricultural policy, which had not been discussed at the Cabinet on October 23. They wanted to establish in the public mind – what Joynson-Hicks and McNeill had emphasised in speeches[2] – that there would be no taxation on imported food and that there were complications surrounding the phrase 'raw material'.[3] As the Duke of Devonshire wrote to Baldwin on October 24, 'I fail to see how the ... proposals ... will to any appreciable extent relieve unemployment during the coming months';[4] so delay seemed reasonable. Bridgeman with tactical and Die Hard considerations in mind, Novar from a viewpoint of doctrinal doubt made the same point.[5]

Salisbury and Lord Robert Cecil then began searching for positions. During informal discussion at the end of a Cabinet meeting on the 29th, Salisbury announced that 'he meant to give a score of different reasons why we could not go to the country for some years'.[6] Lord Robert Cecil told Baldwin that he would have to discuss his position with his constituents in case the policy he was expected to support was not one he could decently carry around Hertfordshire villages: he asked whether, if he went on as a minister, he might be found 'a less exacting constituency'.[1] He then gave resignation four days' rather bad-tempered thought,[2] deciding eventually to test his belief that membership of the Cabinet had not destroyed his power to help the League of Nations.[3] After consulting Salisbury he decided to offer support for Baldwin's 'tariff nonsense if [Baldwin would] adopt a vigorous League [of Nations] policy' in return.[4] These views were embodied in a long memorandum. In this, after explaining Britain's economic difficulties in terms of 'the collapse of [European] credit ... and the uncertainties of governmental indebtedness', he claimed that the root of the matter was nothing that a Tariff policy would solve but 'international suspicion' which would only be set 'at rest' by a 'League policy'. Provided Baldwin would commit himself to withdraw support from all international organisations except the League of Nations, he undertook to suppress the doubts he felt about Protection.[5]

These machiavellian soul-searchings were carried on in the belief that there would be no election until the New Year, and that all the proposals would be carefully considered by the Cabinet and scrupulously explained to the public. Baldwin had given no hint to any Cabinet Minister that he was thinking of holding an election at once, if indeed he was. The committee which was set up to manage the Protection campaign was not expecting an immediate election.[6] Amery and Lloyd-Graeme even thought of delaying the election until after the Budget in April so that 'the public would realize that any concession we had given on tea or income tax would have to be undone if a government came in that was not prepared to have the revenue tariff'.[7] There is no indication from anywhere in Baldwin's circle at this time that anyone had an immediate election in mind.[8] Neither the Plymouth speech nor Baldwin's theoretical exposition of Protection at Swansea on October 30 suggested that he had either. Derby thought his speech at Manchester on November 2 must necessarily produce an election, but Baldwin neither made this clear himself nor discussed the possibility when he stayed with Derby at Knowsley.[9] As late as November 5 Wood received no indication in talking to Baldwin that Baldwin was thinking of an immediate election, though Wood himself 'on the supposition that the dates would permit of our meeting Parliament for effective discussion of his proposals on and after November 13 ... [suggested that Baldwin] should not exclude from his mind the possibility of a December election'.[1]

The Conservative Free Traders were therefore greatly shaken when they discovered on November 6 that Baldwin had warned the King that he might ask for an election at once. It is not certain how they found this out. Salisbury claimed that Devonshire had heard 'from the "highest quarter" i.e. the King'.[2] The King certainly thought of refusing Baldwin a dissolution when told that he might ask for it: he had probably been searching for other opinions. Whatever the channel, Salisbury was extremely upset. He asked for help from Lloyd-Graeme who did not see that they could 'bind the Prime Minister to fix the date of the election'.[3] After seeing Baldwin on the evening of the 6th, Salisbury called Devonshire, Novar, Lord Robert Cecil and Wood to his house on the morning of the 7th. Wood felt no particular objection 'to the tariff proposals per se' but all five, 'object[ing] to the method by which [the question] was being handled ... agreed to write a letter to the Prime Minister deprecating a December election'.[4]

The grounds they gave included the fear that the election might 'result in handing over the fortunes of this Country to the Socialist party' at a time when 'the critical condition of Europe renders the continuation of a stable government in Great Britain of the utmost importance',[5] reluctance to adopt anything like a '"tricky" policy' by 'attempt[ing] to snatch a verdict from the country before they really understand what it is they are asked to decide upon'[6] and the danger, if the policy seemed to be 'tricky' even though it was not, that it would be 'tactically unsuccessful'.[7] Salisbury pointed out that 'there was no real opportunity for the Cabinet to consider the policy before it was published' and added that, since 'none of us know precisely even the broad outlines of the plan ... [he could] not promise to accept the ultimate scheme unreservedly'. A couple of days before[8] Wood had suggested a December election: in abandoning December he was eating his own words. He leaves the impression that the real objection they all felt was that they had not been consulted.

By the time the Cabinet met next on November 9, Younger had written from Scotland to say that delay was essential.[9] Curzon, Salisbury and Lord Robert Cecil wanted to put off an election as

long as possible.[1] Wood really agreed but, assuming a long delay
was impossible, preferred January to December because that
would give time to work out a policy for agriculture.[2] Amery
repeated his desire to delay until after the Budget. A number of
House of Commons ministers, however, wanted to dissolve at
once.[3] The impression left by Baldwin was that he did not wish to
say anything[4] because he had already made up his mind.[5] The
impression that Baldwin's mind was made up was strengthened
in the next twenty-four hours. Hall, Jackson, Joynson-Hicks and
Worthington-Evans all wanted an immediate election, though
Maclachlan 'had not evidence enough to make a prediction' about
the result.[6] The final decision was probably made at a meeting
attended by Baldwin, Lloyd-Graeme, Monsell, Amery and
Worthington-Evans on the evening of the 11th. At a Cabinet
committee on the morning of the 12th Bridgeman explained that
the agricultural policy would have to be ready by that evening.
Salisbury was told by Curzon at lunch the same day that 'he was
sure ... immediate dissolution was decided'. Wood was told by
Thomas Jones that evening that he was starting to draft the
King's speech for the dissolution. Baldwin had received the King's
agreement that afternoon. In announcing it to the Cabinet next
morning, he seems both to have made the dubious claim that
Law approved and to have avoided mentioning that the King did
not.[7]

By the time the Salisbury group heard of this decision, which
was offensive in itself, they heard rumours of another which was
more offensive still. They had received no reply to the letters
they wrote to Baldwin on November 7 and 8. They had been
confronted at the Cabinet on the 9th with an insulting reticence
on Baldwin's part and a general feeling that the election might be
held at once. On the 13th, they had discovered that it would be.
They were now confronted with the threat of Birkenhead and
Austen Chamberlain joining the Cabinet.

(ii)

Austen Chamberlain had been much put out by Baldwin's handling
of him in May: his reaction had been to prepare himself for
capitulation. Worthington-Evans had discredited himself by
grabbing the meagre office he had been offered: Chamberlain did

not intend to repeat his mistake. He did not expect McKenna to find a safe Conservative seat. He thought it likely that Horne would accept the Chancellorship when McKenna refused it. He thought Horne might make acceptance conditional on Chamberlain being offered office as well. In a long letter to Birkenhead on May 31 Austen Chamberlain laid bare his pain, deployed his doubt and made clear his desire to accept any offer Baldwin might make even if Birkenhead was not included.[1]

Chamberlain was searching for comfort. He did not get it. Birkenhead showed gratitude for 'the closest political association [he had] ever formed', suggested that 'the mere fact of ... joining [the government] may ... be regarded as an admission that the decision of the Carlton Club was right' and reminded Chamberlain that, if he did so, 'men hopelessly inferior to [him]self ... much younger ... [and] some ... politically ... [his] avowed and bitter enemies ... [would] be in control of the government'. Birkenhead continued to believe that 'the result of the next election must be unfavourable to the Unionist party' and that the Chamberlainites would be strongly placed to resume negotiation with others from whom, 'in the existing circumstances, we do not disagree upon any important public questions'. He held up 'the history and influence of the Peelites' as worthy of 'careful study'.[2]

It is not clear that Chamberlain shared these expectations or, really, that Birkenhead did either. But[3] Chamberlain was inordinately sensitive to imputations of self-seeking. His sarcasm at McKenna's expense during the Report Stage of the Finance Bill on July 3[4] was designed 'to show that he was not hankering for office'.[5] When told by Warren Fisher next day to join the government and 'rule its policy' in collaboration with McKenna and Baldwin, he replied that he 'profoundly distrusted and disliked McKenna [who was] the last person [he] would seek for an ally' and that he 'had deliberately made [his] speech of the afternoon before in order to prevent any offer being made'.[6] His belief that McKenna would not swallow Imperial Preference makes it difficult to take at its face value his promise that a Cabinet decision 'to take up ... Imperial Preference ... would naturally bring him in support ... and separate him from others with whom he [was] at present associated'.[7]

It is just possible that Birkenhead expected Austen Chamberlain's prospects to be improved if Rothermere backed a 'reconstruction of which [Chamberlain was] to be the head'.[1] It is as likely that he needed to believe it because Austen Chamberlain might otherwise be tempted by Baldwin to leave Birkenhead in the lurch. Whatever his motive, he found it difficult to keep Chamberlain up to the mark.[2] When he left for Canada and the United States on August 18, he cannot have been very confident. Like Lloyd George, Birkenhead was out of England when Baldwin made his speech at Plymouth.

While Birkenhead was abroad, most of the excuses Austen Chamberlain offered for objecting to the government were removed by McKenna's withdrawal from the Treasury and Neville Chamberlain's appointment in his place. In this sense he was in greater difficulty than when his grievances had been real ones.[3] The adoption of Protection made his position more difficult still. He was torn between resentment against a government which had been founded on his own humiliation, a feeling – crucial to self-respect – that he could not help it unless it took special pains to meet his wishes and the belief that he could salve his conscience by promising to support it if it proposed a range of Protection he probably believed it could not propose. What Chamberlain really wanted, of course, was not Protection, but Coalition-style resistance to Socialism. His father's legacy, however, made it difficult to attack a Protectionist programme unless he could claim either that it was inadequate or that Baldwin did not mean it. He prepared the ground for attack beforehand.[4] It was not until Birkenhead returned that he developed its implications in public. In his first speech after Birkenhead's return – which was his first public comment on Baldwin's proposals – his message was that, although he would support Baldwin if, as he 'hope[d] and th[ought] ... [he] was declaring a great policy, [he spoke] at the ... moment with some ... difficulty for I am puzzled ... to know exactly what his meaning was'.[5]

Between October 29 and November 12, when Birkenhead and Chamberlain called on Baldwin in Downing Street, there were extensive calculations on the Chamberlainite circuit which had to be resolved before Chamberlain and Birkenhead would negotiate with Baldwin. These concerned their relations with Lloyd George.

In office Lloyd George had not been a doctrinaire Free Trader. On the other hand he had gone further than ever before at Manchester on April 29 towards becoming one. When a Ruhr settlement became, briefly, a possibility in July, he saw, like Baldwin, that the next phase in the German problem would be fierce German competition which the high level of British production costs would make it difficult to deal with.[1] It is, however, by no means clear that it was Protection that Lloyd George would have proposed as a remedy. Horne saw him before he went to Canada: the idea then was a programme of 'active intervention by the state both to develop our resources and to extend our markets'.[2] It was this rather than Protection that Lloyd George meant in discussion with McCurdy about 'proposals for the modification of our fiscal system' more radical than was implied by the McKenna duties and the Safeguarding of Industries Act.[3]

It is possible that Baldwin adopted Protection in order to forestall Lloyd George in these directions: certainly Horne thought he had done so.[4] But it is unlikely that Lloyd George persisted with the intention he had thrown out in September. According to the information he received in Canada and the United States, much of the Imperial Conference had gone on 'behind closed doors' and had made little impact on the public mind.[5] In any case Baldwin's Plymouth speech, however weak in content,[6] had closed the option. Baldwin's decision to confuse 'Imperial Preference with Insular Protection'[7] was 'disastrous' for Imperially-minded Liberal Coalitionists: it made it difficult for Lloyd George to think of following or outbidding him. The mere mention of Protection made it impossible for Horne, and difficult even for Austen Chamberlain, to make that an occasion for breaking up the Conservative party.[8] Like Birkenhead, both were Protectionists: neither could really attack Baldwin for adopting Protection, even though it might separate them from Churchill and Lloyd George and delay the reconstruction of an anti-socialist alliance.[9]

As Lloyd George considered the matter in the *Majestic* on the voyage home, it is difficult to see what choice was open to him. Eight months later Greenwood claimed to have gone on board when the ship docked to persuade him to come out as a Protectionist in support of Baldwin. Lloyd George is supposed to have replied that 'he [wouldn't] help Baldwin who [had] knifed [him]' the year before. He is supposed to have added that Baldwin's policy was right and that he would have supported it if it had been proposed by 'Austen [Chamberlain] or Horne or one of the fellows that stood by [him]'.[1] Horne, however, had said nothing, and had probably decided already that he would support Baldwin. Chamberlain, so far as he had said anything, had done the same. Churchill objected to the idea of abandoning Free Trade when told about it in the summer. If Lloyd George had done so, he would have moved off in the opposite direction. Lloyd George had no reason to be impressed by Beaverbrook and Birkenhead.

In his new rôle as Rothermere's ally, Beaverbrook had considerable newspaper power. He had helped to defeat Griffith-Boscawen at the Dudley by-election in March 1921. He had run one, perhaps two, Conservative candidates against Coalition Liberals in 1922. He had been close to Law for over ten years and had been particularly close in 1922/23. But he had not had very much influence over him and was detested for the influence he was supposed to have had. He could not guarantee a Conservative accession to Lloyd George and would almost certainly produce a considerable counter-reaction. Austen Chamberlain disliked him. In the Conservative party he was as unpopular as Birkenhead.

It is possible that a Lloyd George/Imperial/Protectionist declaration on November 9 would have strengthened the hands of the anti-protectionists in the Cabinet to the point of resignation, with the consequent fall of Baldwin and the creation of a Free Trade/Salisbury/Asquith Centre party government. It is more likely that Baldwin would have covered himself with his Free Traders by interpreting the contentless commitment he had made at Plymouth in an even less Protectionist direction than he eventually did. In any case the advice Lloyd George received in favour of the Imperial/Protectionist commitment seems to have come from no one except Beaverbrook, Birkenhead and perhaps Greenwood. He received equally pressing advice in other directions from Churchill.[2] Grigg,[3] Mond,[4] McCurdy, Edge, Sutherland and Macnamara.[5]

Lloyd George received also from Mond the news that Asquith had agreed to immediate reunion and was willing to meet him.[6] At his press conference in the Palm Court of the *Majestic* on

November 9, Lloyd George 'adhere[d] exactly to the position [he] took up in Manchester in April last' and declared war against Baldwin for 'insult[ing] ... the intelligence of the nation [by] feed[ing] starving industries ... the mildewed straw of the last century with every grain of statesmanship ... beaten out of it'.[1] This was followed by a journey to London, by dinner at Mond's house in Lowndes Square and by a Mond visit to Asquith at Sutton Courtenay to arrange a meeting. By November 13, the day after the election was announced, Lloyd George and Asquith had agreed to fight the election in harness.[2] On November 15 Fisher appeared alongside Asquith as Lloyd George's substitute at a reunion meeting at Queen's Hall.[3] On November 17 Lloyd George opened his 'great Free Trade campaign' in support of McCurdy in Northampton.[4] At Paisley on November 24 Lloyd George and Asquith shared a common platform for the first time since Asquith left office in 1916.[5]

The week-end after Lloyd George's return from America, Beaverbrook, Austen Chamberlain, Lloyd George, Churchill and Birkenhead met at Beaverbrook's house. They decided that, since nothing better could be expected for the moment, the Chamberlainites should return to the Conservative party and support Baldwin on an Empire Free Trade basis while Churchill and Lloyd George made Free Trade noises as Liberals so as to be able to link up on an Imperial Preference/Empire Free Trade position when Baldwin lost the election.[6]

In relation to Baldwin, Austen Chamberlain had half-opened the door before the Plymouth speech but had half-closed it again in the ten days following the Swansea speech. When Baldwin received the letters from the Salisbury group on the 7th or 8th of November he asked to see Birkenhead. He did not ask to see Austen Chamberlain on the principle, no doubt, that concerted approaches were undesirable. Neville Chamberlain, however, when told that Birkenhead was coming, insisted that Austen Chamberlain should be asked too.[7] During a visit on the morning of the 12th, Birkenhead said the same.

Later in the day Birkenhead came back with Austen Chamberlain who asked for an import duty on meat and wheat as a *quid pro quo* for his support and insisted on guarantees of office for Gilmour, Scott, Crawford and Locker-Lampson, the Privy Seal for himself and the Lord Chancellorship for Birkenhead. It is not clear whether Chamberlain made these conditions because he thought they could be met, because they would make Baldwin's position more difficult or because he wanted to establish that he would not return unless his influence was manifest.[1] Baldwin made no commitment about import duties and ruled out the Lord Chancellorship. At this meeting he did not agree to invite the Chamberlainites to return to office. At a second meeting after he had received the King's agreement to a general election, however, he called in Birkenhead and Austen Chamberlain to pacify Derby when Derby called with resignation in mind to protest against the calling of an election. After they had left he told Derby that they would be joining the Cabinet.[2]

Baldwin's object in beginning these negotiations could have been threefold. They could have been designed to prevent Birkenhead and Austen Chamberlain committing themselves to Lloyd George. They could have been designed to appease Derby who thought him a 'damned idiot' for wanting an election, and to detach him from the Salisbury group with which he had begun to work.[3] They could have been designed to show the Salisbury group how vulnerable it was. Derby believed that at Knowsley a fortnight before he had made Birkenhead's return to office a condition of his own support for Protection in Lancashire.[4] Baldwin, however, did nothing to encourage serious conversation during his stay at Knowsley and had no discussion with Derby about the timing of the election:[5] he had done nothing since. Derby may or may not have urged party reunion at Knowsley on November 2/3: he certainly told Jackson that Birkenhead was indispensable for a Protection election in Lancashire. There is no Derby letter of complaint to Baldwin recording his objection to an immediate election, but there are letters of complaint from Derby to Jackson,[6] Salisbury and Lord Robert Cecil from November 9 onwards.[7] It is unlikely that Baldwin did not know what Derby thought and probable that the approach to Birkenhead was designed, from that point of view, to satisfy Derby that he would not suffer from Birkenhead's tongue on his doorstep at the next election as he had at the last.

This, no doubt, was one element in Baldwin's decision, but not probably a very strong one.[8] Derby had made the condition, if he had made it at all, a fortnight before: nothing had been done in the meantime. Derby had no brief for Austen Chamberlain, but he probably wanted Birkenhead in the Cabinet or wished it to be thought by Birkenhead that he did. He did not press for Birkenhead very strongly. Perhaps in deference to Salisbury and Lord Robert Cecil, whom he met before he called on Baldwin on November 12,[1] he told Saunders that he 'did not ... at all ... like' the idea of Birkenhead in office.[2] He was working closely with Devonshire: their joint intention on the morning of the 13th was to resign. Derby did not resign but he lost his temper in talking to Baldwin before the Cabinet at which the election was announced. His objection at this point, however, was partly to the adoption of Protection and partly to the calling of an election. It was not until plain speaking from Birkenhead at lunchtime that Derby telephoned Devonshire and wrote Baldwin a letter in which he alleged that Baldwin had gone back on his undertaking to admit Birkenhead and threatened to fight the election with Birkenhead from outside the government if he could not do so from inside.[3] It is likely that Derby's enthusiasm for Birkenhead varied with Birkenhead's presence and that he was trying chiefly to keep lines open to all interested parties as a demonstration of his own indispensability.

From August until the end of October[4] Birkenhead was engaged in a transatlantic speaking tour in the course of which he made himself prominent by denouncing Woodrow Wilson. He then returned to England in time to deliver his Rectoral address at Glasgow University on November 7. This was a statement that the world was and always would be full of strife; that idealism was dangerous and the claims made on behalf of the League of Nations fantastic; that Christ did not really intend 'him who was assaulted to turn the other cheek ... or him who was rich to ... give ... his possessions to the poor'; that 'politically, economically and philosophically the motive of self-interest not only is but must ... and ought to be the mainspring of human conduct'; and that, since 'the world continues to offer glittering prizes to those who have stout hearts and sharp swords ... it is for us who, in our history have proved ourselves a martial ... people ... to maintain in our own hands the adequate means for our own protection and ... to march with heads erect and bright eyes along the road of our imperial destiny'.[1] When Birkenhead was approached by Baldwin on the 7th or 8th, he did not respond immediately. He refused Baldwin's invitation to call on the 9th[2] – the day of Lloyd George's return to England. It was not until he had spent the weekend at Cherkley with Beaverbrook, Churchill, Austen Chamberlain and Lloyd George that he accepted.

From Birkenhead's point of view the five-day gap between Baldwin's approach and their actual meeting was almost certainly significant. But for Baldwin the significant days were the 7th or 8th, when threats of resignation arrived from Salisbury, Devonshire, Novar, Wood and Lord Robert Cecil. Feelers had already been put out to persuade Austen Chamberlain to replace Curzon in the event of Curzon resigning;[3] it is plausible to suggest that Baldwin began negotiating not because he particularly wanted Birkenhead and Austen Chamberlain in the Cabinet or had been pressed by Derby to take them, but because he wished to let the Salisbury group know that if they resigned, he would switch horses.

When Baldwin told Derby on November 12 that Chamberlain and Birkenhead were about to join the government, he asked him to tell Devonshire but not to tell Salisbury.[4] Derby seems not to have mentioned it, though he was in close touch with Salisbury during the next two days.[5] Newspaper reports nevertheless did. It is not clear whether these reports came from Baldwin through Davidson or from Birkenhead himself. Wherever they came from, they produced a considerable sense of outrage. Davidson's wife thought Birkenhead's return would 'offend all decent people'. Amery later recalled 'M.P.s' wives' complaining that Birkenhead was morally intolerable.[6] At the time his 'instinct ... harden[ed] against submission to FE's and Austen's demands especially if you can keep Derby and the rest of the Cabinet together'.[7] McNeill thought Birkenhead's 'proceedings *since* Bonar took office [had] alienated people even more than anything that happened during the election, and his abominable Rectoral address the other day had put the lid on it'.[8] Sanders thought 'the Ulster men ... would not take the Whip if he was in the government'.[9] Derby claimed to be 'delighted' but thought there would be opposition from Salisbury, Curzon and Bridgeman.[10] Ormsby-Gore and Elliot seem to have threatened to resign.[11] Wood had thought of resigning because of the secrecy with which dissolution had been surrounded. The new affront convinced Salisbury, Novar and Devonshire that the time had come to resign 'partly on general grounds, partly because they were convinced that the Prime Minister wanted to get rid of them to make room for Austen Chamberlain and Birkenhead'.[1] Wood was now more cautious 'in view of the ... danger of breaking the party on the eve of an election'.[2] He visited Baldwin on the evening of the 13th 'and asked him whether he wished to get rid of Salisbury and company'. On being told that Baldwin 'certainly did not' he pointed out that 'he was proceeding very much as if he did and that, if he wished to keep them ... he should see Salisbury [and] explain his position'.[3]

That evening Baldwin had a 'none too friendly' talk with Birkenhead.[4] He also sent Sidney Herbert, his private secretary, to call on Salisbury with a letter. In this Baldwin, 'proud of his team' and prepared to 'blame [him]self horribly if we could not face the election as a united family', told Salisbury 'that it would be a real grief to [him] if [he] were to resign'.[5] Davidson wrote to Lord Robert Cecil, assuring him of Baldwin's 'genuine affection' and recording his 'gratitude for the support [Lord Robert] and [his] brother had given ... in a difficult situation'; he excused his letter on the ground that he 'could not bear knowing what was in his mind that you should think Stanley capable of doubtful dealing with you'.[6] Early next morning Salisbury and Baldwin had a 'very friendly interview' in Baldwin's room in the House of Commons at which they discussed the draft of a letter the Salisbury group proposed to send Baldwin.[7] Baldwin received this letter later in the day[8] and again saw Salisbury 'who was not unfavourably impressed'. Baldwin promised to examine the letter with Lloyd-Graeme and Neville Chamberlain and to incorporate parts of it in his dissolution speech in the House of Commons next day. Wood made a point of seeing Lloyd-Graeme and Neville Chamberlain to tell them 'exactly how the Prime Minister should state his policy if he wanted to keep the dissentients'. When Salisbury saw Baldwin next morning, the letter was returned with Baldwin's annotations and an undertaking to consult more extensively in the future.[9]

Novar woke up that morning intending to tell Salisbury to

resign and create the nucleus of a Free Trade wing of the party.[1] The previous evening Lord Robert Cecil had drafted an indictment of the 'secrecy and intrigue' with which he supposed the introduction of Protection to have been surrounded, adding a blast against Northumberland's recent election to the Chairmanship of the National Union and the welcome proposed to Birkenhead after his Rectoral address – both of them blows, in his view, at the League of Nations.[2] He did not, however, send it, deciding instead to send another which simply asked Baldwin to recommend him for a peerage.[3] Freed by Baldwin's agreement from the need to face his constituents and conscious, doubtless, that he could not work with the Asquith/Grey Liberals now that Lloyd George had joined them, he agreed that Baldwin's annotations would enable them all to stay in office.[4]

On the 14th Baldwin received from Davidson and Herbert a memorandum reporting that Hall, Jackson and Hacking – 'a great friend of Derby and a Lancashire member' – all thought the return of Birkenhead before the election would 'have a most serious effect . . . on the party [and] the electorate – especially the women', and that 'your good name and high reputation . . . one of the greatest assets among the non-party electors . . . would suffer a most serious blow if you were to come to terms'.[5] At the same time Chamberlain and Birkenhead, knowing that their return was under attack, decided that they would withdraw and wrote to Baldwin to say that they would support him at the election notwithstanding. In Baldwin's replies, which were cooler versions of a Davidson draft, he repeated the idea which had annoyed Austen Chamberlain in May – that, so long as they helped at the election, they would be brought into the government whenever that should be possible afterwards.[6]

Baldwin, then, had obtained assurances of good conduct from Birkenhead and Austen Chamberlain. He had committed the party to an emasculated form of Protection and had kept the Cabinet united. The question remains, why did he rush the election?

For this there are four credible sorts of explanation. The first is suggested by the fact that the Conservative Chief Whip believed that the government would be defeated in the House of Commons by a Liberal/Labour/Conservative Free Trade vote if the House of Commons was not dissolved at once. There is no independent confirmation that he was right: there is not much evidence that this weighed with Baldwin. Baldwin called in Monsell to explain this to Derby when Derby objected to an immediate election,[1] but that does not by itself establish that it was a major factor. One junior minister from Liverpool, Colonel Buckley, resigned when the election was announced because he could not support Protection.[2] The strength of opposition to Protection fluctuated: the strength of opposition in any particular circumstances could not be predicted. A Liberal/Labour anti-Protectionist motion would have attracted enough Conservative Free Trade votes to produce a major party split. It was not certain that the government would have been defeated or that opposition from Free Trade M.P.s was designed to do more than to ensure they kept their seats in Free Trade constituencies.[3] But the potential opposition was large: this is probably why Conservatives co-operated with the Labour Whips to closure the debate without consulting the Liberals.[4] If Derby, Salisbury, Devonshire, Wood, Novar and Lord Robert Cecil had resigned, the Free Trade movement might have been impressive. It is not clear what would have followed defeat or resignations on this scale. It is difficult to believe that Salisbury and Derby could have co-operated with the sort of Liberal party Asquith had decided to lead. But Baldwin can hardly have wanted to fight a general election with a divided party. Since the King was not pleased at being asked for a dissolution so soon after the last one, it is not certain that he would have got it. He might well have had to resign instead. The damage this would have done to his own following and to the Conservative party was avoided by a dissolution.

The second factor – which probably mattered more than the first – was Baldwin's belief that the Liberal party, though well on the way to reunion, was not yet ready to fight a general election. There is no evidence that Baldwin thought this. This is what a number of Liberals thought he thought.[5] It is not incompatible with the view that Baldwin raised Protection in order to separate Lloyd George from the Coalition Conservatives: in a sense it is strengthened if we accept the view that he did. Whether we accept that view or not, it was obviously better to fight an election before

Asquith and Lloyd George had constructed a united programme than afterwards.

Thirdly, it seems reasonable to assume that Baldwin thought he would win the election. At the election his chief agent, Sir Reginald Hall, lost a seat he had won in 1922 by a majority of 10,000. Davidson lost Hemel Hempstead where he had had a majority of 6,000. It is possible that Baldwin's immediate followers put about the view that the election would be won when in fact, not being certain whether it would be or not, they needed to persuade others that it should be held. After the election Younger claimed that Hall and Jackson had not been in favour of the election. But there is abundant evidence that they thought they would win handsomely. Two separate Central Office estimates confirm what Baldwin is reported to have told Stamfordham on the eve of the election – that 'they had been through all constituencies with a toothcomb and were sure of a majority of 30 over Labour and Liberals'.[1]

What calculation this could have been based on is not clear – hardly the by-election or municipal election results of 1923. At the municipal elections there were extensive Labour gains. At parliamentary by-elections three seats had been lost. The only increases in the Conservative vote were in straight fights with Labour at Darlington and Rutland where there had been three candidates in 1922. At the two by-elections closest to the decision to ask for an election,[2] the Conservative party did well and the Labour party – especially at Yeovil – rather badly. The intermittent Liberal improvement may have suggested that the Liberal party was at last catching up with Labour. It may have been thought that, with the two progressive parties more evenly matched than before, the Conservative party could not fail to win.

In retrospect the election results make these calculations seem fantastic. Yet there were as good reasons for making them as for making others. If Protection was calculated to drive away some sorts of Conservative voter, the ambiguity of the Liberal attitude towards Labour was calculated to hold them back. At the 1922 election nearly every Coalition Liberal seat had been won with Conservative support: a handful of Asquithean Liberal seats had been won because Conservatives did not stand. The Conservative party already had an absolute majority of over seventy. Baldwin would have been right to think that both Liberal groups – and especially the Lloyd George Liberals – would lose more than they would gain by disrupting these arrangements. This is what happened. Four Asquithean losses can be attributed to Conservative interventions where there had been none in 1922.[1] The Lloyd George Liberals, deprived of Conservative support, did extremely badly.

Finally there is the question of the relationship between Baldwin on the one hand and Amery and Neville Chamberlain on the other. In November 1924 Sir Auckland Geddes told Derby that when he stayed the week-end at Chequers with Baldwin on October 27/28 1923, he found him determined to go slow on Protection and avoid an immediate election. When asked by Derby why Baldwin had changed his mind, Geddes replied that Amery 'might have had something to do with it' and that Neville Chamberlain, in speeches at Plymouth and Preston had gone so much further than Baldwin himself that Baldwin had either to abandon Chamberlain or have an election at once.[2]

So far as Amery was concerned, Geddes overestimated his importance. Until November 11 Amery did not want an election before the Budget. He supported an immediate election on November 11 only because he had been defeated in his real preference.[3] Amery wanted to fight the election on a 'principle': he constantly urged Baldwin to go further than he wanted to, or went, in his public speeches, especially about taxing imported food.[4] Even on bread and butcher's meat he wanted to avoid 'any pledge that would absolutely preclude [him] from imposing any conceivable duty'.[5] Amery went to some trouble to remove the misconception he supposed *The Times* to be encouraging that the 'declaration' Baldwin had made at Manchester 'about meat and wheat' was meant 'to cover the whole range of foodstuffs'.[6] Baldwin did nothing to remove this misconception, which *The Times* had probably got from someone in his circle. The point, however, is that, since Amery's plans were more extensive than anyone else's, they necessitated the longest possible preparation before an election began.

Nor did Neville Chamberlain do much that reduced Baldwin's freedom. It is true that he made more positive claims for Protection

and spelt out the policy in greater detail than Baldwin.[1] But
Neville Chamberlain shared Baldwin's nervousness about the step
he was taking. In the earliest stage he was thinking that nothing
would be done until another Imperial Conference had been called.[2]
He said nothing to which the Cabinet had not agreed in principle
on October 23, except about the general tariff on manufactured
imports and in relation to the Advisory Committee.[3] His views
about the timing of an election included nothing which had not
been said at that meeting.[4] Neville Chamberlain liked neither the
vagueness of Baldwin's position nor the pretence he had been
forced to adopt that 'our tariff [was] a revenue tariff with special
duties for special cases instead of a protection tariff'.[5] It may be
that he went further than Baldwin wished in giving Austen
Chamberlain public assurances that Baldwin had not destroyed
his policy by his reservations. It may be that the dismissive
certainty displayed in his speeches once the plunge had been
taken had an adverse effect on Free Trade acquiescence in the
Cabinet. This is not particularly likely. What is much more likely
is that MacDonald's reaction to the Plymouth speech – the playing
of the Capital Levy against Protection – was expected by Baldwin
to push anti-socialist Free Traders towards the Conservative party
in spite of Protection,[6] and that Asquith's uninventive reassertion
of a Free Trade policy which no government had followed since
the war, was thought to be so seriously out of tune with the
public mind that an election could safely be undertaken at
once.

Whatever Baldwin expected, the election was a disaster. In
Lancashire and Wales – and probably elsewhere – Protection was
so much disliked, not only by electors but by Conservatives themselves, that one must speak of the election being fought by a
divided party. The failure to do anything substantial for agriculture
enabled Liberals to present themselves as the alternative governing
party in some agricultural seats. The lack of positive interest in
Protection, and its food-tax connotations, produced Liberal gains
in Lancashire and Liberal M.P.s elsewhere in seats which had
been Conservative for forty years. At the same time as the Liberal
party restored itself at the expense of the Conservative party,
Labour made further inroads in industrial areas and in areas of
possible Liberal support. The result was that the adoption of

Protection, designed to prove that there was a Conservative answer to Labour and unemployment, greatly increased Labour strength in the House of Commons. When 258 Conservatives found themselves faced by 191 Labour and 159 Liberal M.P.s in the new parliament, it was clear that Baldwin had produced a major catastrophe from which no comfort could be drawn.[1]

XVII

THE DEFEAT OF BIRKENHEAD

'Be of good cheer, Greatheart. What are our difficulties to theirs? We shall do them all in yet. Bless you.'
     Amery to Baldwin, December 7 1923 (telegram)

'I have no doubt you are feeling a bit disappointed as I am, but you will not have lost a single real friend and as for the quidnuncs and grouses of the Clubs, be damned to them.'
     Bridgeman to Baldwin, December 8 1923

'. . . we have to beat Socialism, Lloyd George, the press magnates and getterbits like Derby and Birkenhead. We can do it . . . but it will require patience and deliberation.'
     Ormsby-Gore to Davidson, December 9 1923, James, p. 190

The election had been held on Baldwin's responsibility. Having failed in a major exercise of power, he could see that his leadership would be called in question. When he arrived in London he was told by Jackson and Younger that he should resign both the Prime Ministership and the party leadership and consult the Cabinet meeting scheduled for Tuesday before advising the King about a successor. In the course of an interview with Stamfordham on Saturday the 8th, he denied that Labour would join a Lib/Lab Coalition of which Lloyd George was a member and did not respond to the suggestion that Austen Chamberlain might be asked to form a government. He implied that he expected a Liberal/Conservative Coalition, by which he meant a Coalition between himself and Asquith with Asquith as Prime Minister, 'although there again Mr Lloyd George might be a difficulty'. He explained that he was going to Chequers and asked for the week-end to consult his colleagues before deciding whether to resign.[1] By the time he returned on Monday morning, he had become the indispensable barrier against Birkenhead and the Chamberlainites.

To the Chamberlainites Baldwin's defeat seemed to be the opportunity for which Birkenhead had been waiting since the fall of the Coalition. It showed – what they had almost ceased to believe – that Birkenhead had been right to predict that so foolish a government would destroy itself if the supreme minds left it free to do so. Austen Chamberlain and Birkenhead had hardly left it 'free to do so'. But by mid-November they had come to believe that events had so far passed them by that they would have to join the government if Baldwin would let them. Even then they had not received office. But they supported Baldwin at the election – Birkenhead contemptuously, Chamberlain resentfully[1] – because Baldwin, however stupid, was in control.

The election result made it clear that these latest calculations were mistaken. Protection had 'united the Liberal party' which 'no Liberal could do'.[2] The election had brought closer the formation of a Labour government which both the Coalition and the destruction of the Coalition had been designed to prevent, but there was 'no fear of any Die Hards opposing a Coalition now that they see what they have brought us'.[3] There was a better chance than there had been in May to replace the men who had destroyed the Coalition. Between Saturday December 8, when he first heard that Baldwin might resign, and Tuesday December 11, when Balfour put an end to the attempt to make him, Birkenhead did his best to take it. In these four days of active lobbying, Birkenhead tried to ensure that the King should send for Balfour, Derby, Austen Chamberlain, Asquith, Grey or himself in order to construct a Liberal/Conservative Coalition to keep out MacDonald.

In attempting to restore himself to the centre of the scene, Birkenhead had the advantage of knowing that Austen Chamberlain thought it 'in harmony with the traditions of the great Constitutional Party that we should offer no vexatious opposition to any moderate government which [could] be formed ... to resist fundamental changes ... ruinous to the industrial, social and economic constitution of the country'.[4] He knew that Derby wanted to get rid of Baldwin in view of the 'disaster' to which 'our great leader' had led 'us', and thought the King might give Birkenhead, Austen Chamberlain (or perhaps Derby himself?) the chance 'to see if [they] could not come to an agreement with Lloyd George for a Coalition government'.[5] Fortified in this way, Birkenhead sent Oliver Locker-Lampson to Stamfordham on Monday morning to explain on his own and Austen Chamberlain's behalf that Baldwin should be succeeded not by MacDonald but by Austen Chamberlain, Balfour or himself.[6]

In doing this Birkenhead probably thought he could rely on Balfour. This was the impression Locker-Lampson gave Stamfordham. At lunch on December 10 Birkenhead told Derby that 'the King was going to send for Balfour to ask his advice and Balfour was going to advise that Austen Chamberlain should be sent for'.[1] Austen Chamberlain arrived after lunch 'and confirmed this, having got his information through Locker-Lampson' who, in fact, had got it wrong.[2] Chamberlain also claimed to have had 'a communication' from Asquith 'to say that they could not under any circumstances support Baldwin', but in the event of a Balfour/Austen Chamberlain government[3] 'would give a benevolent support to them and prevent Ramsay MacDonald forming a government'. Joynson-Hicks and Worthington-Evans, who came in after lunch, were much impressed. They agreed to 'try and persuade Baldwin to accept this'.[4]

Derby's advice to Stamfordham that afternoon that the King should 'accept Baldwin's resignation and send for Mr Austen Chamberlain' assumed that what Birkenhead and Austen Chamberlain had told him was true. When he saw Derby Stamfordham made it clear that it was not, adding that the King 'felt that Mr Baldwin should ... meet Parliament as Prime Minister'.[5] Despite this, Derby went back to Birkenhead who persuaded him that Stamfordham was wrong.[6] Derby then wrote a letter forecasting his resignation[7] and a memorandum in preparation for the Cabinet next morning in which, in language like that used by Locker-Lampson at Buckingham Palace that morning, he argued that a MacDonald government, if allowed to take office, would introduce a 'budget which ... would destroy everybody in this country who had got anything to lose ... and ... be an attractive programme for those who have nothing'. In arguing that the government should resign 'and the Prime Minister recommend that Lord Balfour be sent for'[8] Derby probably thought he was majesterially advocating a course which events were taking already.

That evening Derby had a verbal message from Balfour[9] which made him 'suspicious of the afternoon's conversation'.[10] On calling next morning he was told emphatically that Baldwin should stay in office until he was defeated in the House of Commons. He found that the expectation Birkenhead had led him to entertain could not be realised. He came suddenly to understand that the movement against Baldwin was not strong enough to justify him in supporting it. He went back to the War Office where Worthington-Evans and Joynson-Hicks came to see him, 'the latter ... in a state of great indignation as, after our conversation of yesterday ... Birkenhead had gone down to the Carlton Club and detailed the whole of it'. All three saw that they had been 'misled' and that Balfour had made a Balfour government impossible. They decided 'to put [their] views before the Cabinet but to agree to the proposal ... that Baldwin should meet Parliament'.[1]

Birkenhead was certainly capable of trying to move events in the direction he wanted by suggesting that they were moving there already. But on this occasion there is not much evidence that he did. He was right on Saturday to believe that Baldwin was thinking of resigning. The fact that by Monday morning Baldwin had been persuaded not to resign and that the King had decided not to let him does not mean that Birkenhead knew this. It is unlikely that he did, particularly as Stamfordham was unwilling to say much during his interview with Locker-Lampson.[2] Again, although Locker-Lampson's claim that he spoke for Balfour as well as the other Chamberlainites was a parenthetic claim which Stamfordham noted as such,[3] it is certain that Balfour was in touch with Birkenhead at the time. Balfour's reaction when he saw Stamfordham on Saturday morning was the same as Birkenhead's. While skirting the possibility of forming a government himself, he reminded Stamfordham how much he regretted the fall of the Coalition, suggested that 'the King would naturally turn to someone else in the Party to form a new Administration in the event of Mr Baldwin's resignation' and promised to stay near London in case the King should want to see him.[4] It is reasonable, therefore, to suggest not that Birkenhead misled Derby, Joynson-Hicks and Worthington-Evans but that Balfour changed his mind. Since Balfour's change of mind ensured that Derby, Worthington-Evans and Joynson-Hicks changed theirs and since Balfour's view may have weighed with others, we must ask why he changed it.

Balfour had had a nasty experience in October 1922. Like Derby's standing in respect of his reputation as a magnate, Balfour's standing as an elder statesman could not bear open contradiction. He had been contradicted and had not enjoyed the experience. His advice to the King in May in favour of Baldwin had been important, but he had not been offered office, despite the offer he had allowed Derby to make on his behalf. He probably wanted respect and admiration as much as he wanted office. There is no doubt that he wanted, like Derby, to move with the movement of events and was unwilling to be found on the limb he had been found on the previous October.

Moreover, the situation as Balfour saw it when talking to Stamfordham on Saturday was altered by the probability that Baldwin would stay in office. This resulted from a coincidence between the interests of the Protectionist ministers and the fears felt by almost everyone else at the consequences of resignation. These fears were stimulated by the announcement of the Birkenhead plot in the evening newspapers on Saturday which convinced Amery, Bridgeman and Neville Chamberlain that they were in danger and created a widespread feeling that Birkenhead must be resisted.

When Bridgeman arrived in London after the election Jackson told him that Baldwin had decided to resign.[1] Bridgeman told Amery.[2] Bridgeman and Amery wrote to and telephoned Baldwin.[3] Bridgeman, Amery, Davidson, Baird and Neville Chamberlain were invited to Chequers on Sunday December 9. This gathering was a gathering of the politicians who would be 'throw[n] out on the street[4] ... if [Baldwin] threw up the sponge'[5] and left them 'without a leader ... at the mercy of all the intriguers'.[6] Resignation would leave to the King the responsibility for choosing a Prime Minister: they were not certain that he would choose MacDonald if Baldwin resigned.[7] The one thing about which they were certain was that Baldwin's resignation would create a fluid situation in which Balfour, Austen Chamberlain, Derby, Worthington-Evans, Joynson-Hicks,[8] Lloyd-Graeme,[9] Beaverbrook, Birkenhead and Rothermere would have a better chance of constructing a Coalition with the Liberal party. They pressed him to stay in office until he was beaten in the House of Commons.

Secondly, the Salisbury group reacted helpfully. Salisbury had followed the election from Cannes. The extent of Protection, the position of the Chamberlainites and Salisbury's influence depended on the result:[10] during the election he told Baldwin how much he admired his 'courage and moderation'.[1] At this time Salisbury expected a Coalition if Baldwin was defeated:[2] he probably changed his mind as soon as he saw what sort of coalition it might be. Wolmer was 'not prepared to follow any leader except Stanley Baldwin'.[3] Lord Hugh Cecil was clear that Baldwin 'ought to be made to stay': he was 'the great obstacle in the way of [the] plot to restore the old coalition' and, 'tho' a bad leader ... [was] no worse than Austen [Chamberlain] or that empty roulette-ball, Derby' who were 'hypnotised by Lloyd George'.[4]

It is true that Lord Robert Cecil wanted Baldwin to leave office at once. But h e wanted this because he was trying to restore relations with the Asquitheans in the hope of the Grey Premiership which he had tried to bring about in 1921 and had not ceased to lament since.[5] From his point of view Protection had made Baldwin a standing provocation to Liberals, 'an Aunt Sally' against whom the Labour and Liberal parties might unite and an obstacle to permanent union between Conservatives and Asquitheans which Cecil thought could take place once the Conservative party was in opposition. Cecil would have preferred Salisbury, Devonshire or himself to preside over the process but even he realised that this was impossible. He did not think of Horne or Neville Chamberlain. Since the only alternative leader of requisite experience in the House of Commons was Austen Chamberlain, he preferred Baldwin to remain.[6] Cecil was proof against coalition with Birkenhead and Lloyd George whom he regarded, along with 'the Labour extremists[7] ... as the most dangerous enemies' of the League of Nations.[8] If he forgot that a Coalition situation could not certainly be avoided in the event of Baldwin resigning before being defeated in the House of Commons, he would have agreed with Amery, Bridgeman and Neville Chamberlain that nothing should be done to reverse the victory that had been won at the Carlton Club a year before.

Thirdly, it is clear that Younger changed his mind. Younger's view of Baldwin's conduct of the election was unprintable.[9] On Friday the 7th he persuaded Jackson that Baldwin should resign. On Saturday morning he told him that the Conservative Party had done well with 140 M.P.s 'in 1909 against a united Liberal and Irish party', would have innumerable opportunities in a bad winter 'with 260 against one rent by internal differences',[10] and should go at once into opposition. Younger, however, had no desire to be involved in a Birkenhead plot, still less a Lloyd George government. When the Birkenhead plot was revealed on Saturday evening, he at once said publicly that Baldwin would probably stay in office, though 'he did not know ... whether the Unionist party would carry on under [him] ... or another Prime Minister with some sort of agreement with one of the other parties'.[1] He began next day to prepare for a McKenna-led coalition of his own.

Finally, a note by Balfour and a memorandum by Stamfordham establish that the King had made up his mind to see Baldwin before Baldwin next met the Cabinet and to tell him that

if he wishe[d] to resign, the King [would] refuse on the grounds that he is still the head of the largest party in the House of Commons and, for every reason, constitutional and otherwise, it would be right ... for the government to meet Parliament and leave it to the representatives of the people to decide whether or no they will support the government.[2]

When the King saw Balfour at six o'clock on Sunday evening Balfour, according to his own account, remarked that this 'seemed to [him] to be perfectly constitutional', adding that 'in spite of the fiasco of the election, Mr Baldwin was ... more ... popular with his party ... than any possible substitute' and 'in these circumstances it was very important that he should not resign the leadership'.[3] According to Stamfordham, Balfour 'said that in his opinion that would be quite a constitutional course for the King to adopt but raised the question whether, if Mr Baldwin ceased to be the head of the Conservative party, he could still remain Prime Minister. [The King] was inclined to think that such a contingency ... should not affect the Sovereign's choice': he asked Balfour whether

in the event of Mr Baldwin's resignation, it would be possible for Mr Austen Chamberlain or Sir Robert Horne to form a government. Lord Balfour was uncertain and rather doubtful about the former, to whom he is personally much attached but who has played his cards badly with the party since the break-up of the Coalition. The latter would, in Lord Balfour's estimation, be out of the question, as he is now head of Baldwin and Company, receiving probably a salary of £5,000 a year and he is a poor man ... Lord Balfour went on to suggest Mr Neville Chamberlain as a possible leader'.[4]

It is not clear whether the King insisted on Baldwin staying in office in order to avoid an anti-socialist coalition[1] or whether he did so in the hope of avoiding a MacDonald government. Stamfordham probably preferred 'Coalition under an elder statesman [like] Balfour, Asquith, Derby [or] Grey':[2] it is probable that he and the King were buying time to face an unwelcome situation. When combined with Baldwin's decision to stay put, the King's decision put an end to any chance of an immediate change of government. In these circumstances one can see why Balfour persuaded Derby to change his mind. One can see why he told Birkenhead to lay off. One can see why the Cabinet on December 11 was 'unanimous'[3] in support of Baldwin's decision to stay in office.

The failure of the immediate 'intrigue'[4] did not, however, dispose of the question of an anti-socialist Coalition when parliament reassembled. By those who wanted no change, Baldwin's leadership, in office or opposition, was treated as settled.[5] Bridgeman and Amery – and Neville Chamberlain[6] and Baldwin after the Chequers week-end – were determined that there should be no attempt to construct a coalition with the Asquith/Grey Liberals, no agreement to stay in office with Asquithean support and no step to relieve Liberals of the responsibility they should be made to bear if the Labour party was allowed to form a government. Baldwin had 'the confidence of nine-tenths of [the Conservative] party'. The 'clean fight' he had 'fought' had 'appealed to all white men and even [to] those who may have thought it unwise to fight on that issue or at that time'.[7] A Coalition would split the Conservative party. A Unionist government 'hanging on by sufferance from the Liberal party' would be 'overwhelmed' at the next election.[8] A Liberal government under Asquith, Grey and Lloyd George might hold an election after an attractive Budget and get a majority as a consequence. The ideal arrangement would be for Asquith to allow Labour to take office 'too weak to do much harm but not too weak to get discredited'[9] so that Liberals would constantly be faced with 'the necessity of supporting Labour which is bound to mean their eventual break-up and disappearance as a party'.[10]

Those who held these views differed from Rothermere and Birkenhead in their analysis of the present and the choice they made of things to anticipate in the future. On December 10 Rothermere from the South of France authorised Beaverbrook to offer Horne newspaper support in removing Baldwin which Horne refused. Throughout December and the first half of January Rothermere's newspapers ran a brisk campaign to keep Labour out of office.[1] For Birkenhead the assumption that there must 'inevitably' be a 'Socialist government in four weeks' was 'the most astonishing ... irrational and cowardly assumption which experienced politicians ha[d] ever made'. It meant that the enemies of Coalition were handing the country over to the Labour party which, after a short period playing along with the Liberals, would produce a redistributive Budget as a prelude to electoral landslide at the expense of both parties in industrial areas.[2]

Limited, indeed, in their prognostications by the need to avoid the Coalition which Birkenhead needed to justify, Baldwin's friends saw chiefly that Liberal support for MacDonald would confront Liberals with so fundamental a choice that a large number of Liberals of the right sort would flee to the Conservative party as a consequence. Forced though they were to believe this by the necessities of their personal situation, there can be no doubt that the enemies of Coalition at this point wanted as a major priority to force Liberals to take sides.

When Baldwin told the King on December 10 that he would not be resigning, 'the King suggested that ... Mr Baldwin ... might be able to approach Mr Asquith with a view to ascertaining what, if any, co-operation the government might receive from the Liberals'.[3] Baldwin promised to ask the Cabinet on the 11th. When the Cabinet confirmed Baldwin's decision to stay in office, Stamfordham repeated the King's question.[4] On December 10 Balfour also suggested that Baldwin should approach Asquith.[5] In writing to Birkenhead next day, Balfour told him that the Conservative party would not accept Austen Chamberlain as leader, even if Asquith insisted on the removal of Baldwin as the price of Liberal co-operation. His view was, however, that the 'grave national danger' presented by the financial and 'electoral consequences' which might follow a Labour government required Asquith to support a Baldwin government, however 'stupid ... [and] unsuccessful' Asquith supposed Baldwin to be.[6] He was surprised and annoyed when Asquith refused.[7]

It is unlikely that Baldwin intended to make arrangements with Asquith or with any other Liberal leader at any time after December 8. Certainly he took no step to do so. It was, however, not just Baldwin but also Asquith who put a working arrangement out of the question.

XVIII

THE LIBERAL MISCALCULATION

'When the Liberals took the very foolish course of turning us out to put the Socialists in, I was much relieved. If they had kept us in at the end of a tether, they could have prevented us from carrying out any effective measures, and chosen their own moment for turning us out with little to show to our credit, and making very advantageous ground for their own appeal to the country ... The result of the next election might well have been to secure for the Liberal party the triumph which their shortsighted action eventually gave to us.'
Bridgeman diary for 1924, p. 103

'It ... would seem that the immediate future is now settled: that Baldwin is to resign and Ramsay to come in. I doubt whether either of them is right. Baldwin could easily have snapped his fingers at a no-confidence amendment and announced that, as leader of the largest section of the House, he had better moral authority than anyone else to carry on the King's Government until he was absolutely blocked. And Ramsay might well have declined to start the first Labour Government under impossible Parliamentary conditions.'
Asquith to Pringle, January 10 1924, Asquith MSS

'Surely the right solution is for the Liberal Party to disappear by one section of it gradually joining with and diluting the Labour Party and the other section coming into line with us.'
Amery to Geoffrey Dawson, January 9 1924, The Times Archive

(i)

To Liberals, and to the Asquithean Liberals in particular, the election results of 1923 provided the first serious hope they had seen since 1916 for the restoration and renewed authority of a united party. Through the first ten months of 1923, both Liberal groups had expected to find their natural allies outside the Liberal party. Neither assumed that any authority Liberals might exercise in future would necessarily be exercised in a united party or a Liberal government. Lloyd George's relations with Austen Chamberlain and Birkenhead on the one side and with Mrs Snowden on the other indicate the range of options he was keeping open or opening up. Grey's approval of Conservative hostility to Lloyd George indicated one line of advance in another. The

341

possibility of an Austen Chamberlain/Birkenhead/Lloyd George Coalition diminished rapidly. The likelihood of a Conservative/ Asquithean alliance was never great so long as the Conservative party had a majority in the House of Commons. But reunion, when it came after November 9, was a shotgun marriage which Lloyd George entered because his potential allies in the Conservative party had nothing to offer and he had nothing better in prospect. There was an element of paradox and unreality that any co-operation should have taken place at the 1923 election between the Asquitheans, whose sympathies lay with the anti-Lloyd George Conservatives, and Lloyd George whose Conservative followers had been defeated by them in October 1922.

In negotiating with Lloyd George the Asquithean leaders had two disadvantages. Their own organisation had very little money, very little prospect of raising any and the likelihood that they might soon have to fight their third election in two years. On the other hand, they had three advantages – a larger share of the Parliamentary Party, a more effective party organisation and the fact that they were sitting tenants of the name and machinery of organised Liberalism. In negotiating for a place among the Liberal leaders Lloyd George had three assets – 'big money' the exact extent of which was unknown, his reputation which, however, was declining and the belief held by the Asquithean leaders that Liberal reunion was wanted so much by rank-and-file Liberals of both wings that there could be no public repetition of the undermining tactics adopted by Grey and Asquith after the election of 1922.[1]

The Asquitheans did not know how they would deal with the extravagance of the Lloyd George organisation, but the essential point was that Lloyd George was thought to have a great deal of money while they had very little – and certainly not enough to go on spending the £50,000 p.a. they had been spending since 1918.[2] In 1923, when they wanted more than anything else to keep Lloyd George at arm's length, they were conscious that his fund rested on 'the proceeds of corruption' and could not be 'accept[ed] even if it were offered'.[3] Once they had been saddled with Lloyd George whether they liked it or not, they came to see that his wealth was so much bigger than anything they had that they were willing to negotiate with him in order to lay their hands on it.

The period between November 1923 and October 1924 from their point of view was a prolonged attempt to get financial backing from Lloyd George without allowing him any real share in running the party or any opportunity to establish a claim to become leader when Asquith died or retired in the future.

At the time of reunion on November 13, Lloyd George promised financial support, though there is no record of the extent of his commitment. Gladstone was responsible for collecting whatever contribution Lloyd George was expected to make: Sir Alfred Cope was responsible for giving it. Mond, Maclean and others agreed on a contribution of £100,000 from the Lloyd George wing and £50,000 from the Asquitheans for payment of candidates' expenses. Lloyd George's headquarters seem, however, to have paid expenses direct to their own candidates on a lavish and non-accountable scale. By November 30 Gladstone had received £30,000, but had the greatest difficulty in persuading Cope to visit or talk to him. When at last Cope did so on the 30th, he was told that another £70,000 at least was expected, to which he replied that he had no authority to make decisions while the Trustees were away.[1]

It was not until the election results established the strength of Asquith's position that the attempt to get hold of Lloyd George's money began in earnest. On December 19 there were preliminary discussions between Phillips and Howard for the Asquitheans and Guest and Sir William Edge as representatives of Lloyd George. Maclean, however, refused to permit negotiation with Guest and Edge, despite Guest's part in collecting the Lloyd George fund, because he knew that Guest and Churchill were trying to negotiate joint entry into the Conservative party.[2] Since he did not trust Asquith to be sharp enough with Lloyd George, he asked that he should negotiate with Mond, Fisher, Illingworth or Young. Negotiations were conducted thereafter by J. T. Davies on Lloyd George's behalf and by Hudson and Maclean on behalf of Asquith.[3]

Lloyd George's method of negotiation was to make decisions himself or empower his negotiators to decide for him about proposals he wanted to accept and to insist on referring proposals he disliked to his Trustees. This may have been a Lloyd George trick: it may, as Gladstone thought, have been that Lloyd George was not a free agent because 'Guest kn[e]w too much' and insisted on holding back so long as a Centre party was a possibility.[1]

Not many decisions were accepted by both sides to the negotiation. At an early stage Gladstone wanted a pooling of the two funds with responsibility for expenditure vested in the Asquithean Liberal headquarters. Lloyd George claimed he had no power to agree to this.[2] When Maclean saw Lloyd George on January 10, he rejected a periodic contribution which could be withdrawn at will because it would put the Asquitheans 'completely at Lloyd George's mercy'. As the price for letting Lloyd George into 'the inner counsels of the party', he asked for a capital endowment – 'capitalization of . . . between £40,000 and £50,000' and '£200,000 for the election' – but was told that Guest and Illingworth, who were now the Trustees, would agree only to a contributory scheme.[3] Maclean consulted the rest of the Asquithean leaders who all agreed that a contributory scheme was impossible.[4] On January 16 Maclean told Lloyd George who replied that there was no basis for agreement. To Lloyd George's suggestion of a joint committee of the two wings to organise the next election, Maclean replied that a capital sum was essential if co-operation was to continue.[5] Six days later Maclean and Lloyd George met once more at Lloyd George's request, Maclean repeating that a capital sum was the only basis for amalgamation. When Lloyd George refused to alter his position, it was agreed that the two organisations should carry on separately, with whatever measure of non-financial co-operation was possible between them.[6]

It is not certain how much money Lloyd George had at this time. At one point Maclean and Gladstone thought he had £2,000,000: at another a very great deal less. J. T. Davies led them to suppose that only £200,000 could be made available immediately. The Abingdon Street headquarters cost Lloyd George a great deal of money: his decision to close them, taken suddenly in the fortnight following Baldwin's re-election to the Conservative leadership, made Gladstone and Maclean suppose that he was about to give way.[7] Since, however, the Asquithean headquarters immediately took over responsibility for Lloyd George candidates at considerable expense without any contribution from Lloyd George, this merely made the Asquithean financial position worse than before.[8] When Maclean asked Lloyd George for money immediately to support candidates in preparation for the general election, he was referred to J. T. Davies who promised to consult Lloyd George's bankers.[1] Three weeks later Davies explained that Lloyd George could afford the amount Maclean wanted,[2] but was consulted so little by the Asquithean managers that he would not make a contribution until he was consulted more.[3] On July 1 when Maclean and Hudson called on Lloyd George, they were told that he was willing to *promise* £100,000 for a general election costing £200,000 but would not do so in writing, and would not accept Maclean's proposal for a joint pooling of £30,000[4] unless the Asquithean organisation was improved.[5]

Throughout these negotiations Maclean was in close touch with Gladstone who had ultimate responsibility for the party's finances. Between Gladstone and Lloyd George there was long-standing hostility which made direct negotiation impossible. By early July, believing that Lloyd George did not mean to hand over any money at all, Gladstone decided to have a public showdown by announcing that he would authorise no further expenditure on candidates until Lloyd George produced £100,000. It was not until late September that Lloyd George, after several passages of nastiness at Gladstone's expense, eventually agreed to do so on condition that a joint committee investigated party administration. He was denied the prospect of Gladstone's withdrawal only by the arrival of a general election in October.

(ii)

The Liberals fought the 1923 election as the party of common sense and established right. They had a programme, but not a spectacular one:[6] despite occasional exaggeration by Lloyd George, they did not think they needed more.[7] They needed only to establish that Protection would raise food prices and that Nationalization and the Capital Levy would damage the working of the economic system.[8] In this nothing distinguished Lloyd George from Asquith and Grey. Asquith promised to abolish the McKenna duties if he found himself in office.[9] Grey made a reasoned case against Protection, distinguished Baldwin's support for the League of Nations from Birkenhead's desire to limit it and offered the League's machinery as the only remedy for Europe's troubles.[10] The 'deep and sincere grief' Lloyd George had felt at separation from Asquith was replaced by 'real and sincere joy that we ... find ourselves fighting ... the same battle side by side'. Pre-war Liberalism had produced a system of old age pensions, health insurance and protection against unemployment without parallel in any country in the world:[1] it would be as successful in the future. The details of the future were left to look after themselves: the radicalism of April 29 for the moment was abandoned. In its place were negative claims that Free Trade was the ground-work of British 'commercial and financial ... supremacy in years gone by', that it was not clear where the agricultural subsidy was coming from,[2] that some industries would be ruined by a tariff on imported raw materials,[3] that the government's pledges against Food Taxes were worthless[4] and that the Conservative party, deeply divided as it was,[5] had not made it clear that it understood the purpose and implications of Baldwin's policy.

At the general election of 1923 the reunited Liberal party lost 40 of the seats which returned Liberal M.P.s in November 1922. It gained about 80 seats including a dozen from Labour and about 70 in constituencies which Conservatives had won the year before. 19 of these gains were in Lancashire and Cheshire, including 5 in Manchester: there were 14 in Somerset, Devon, Dorset, Cornwall and Wiltshire. In the new House of Commons there were 23 Liberal M.P.s for these last five counties, 28 for Lancashire and Cheshire, 23 for Scotland and only 13 for Wales.

These results were a 'triumph for Asquith'.[6] Of the 40 or so Liberal seats which Liberals lost in 1923, nearly 30 had been held by followers of Lloyd George. Two-thirds had been won in 1922 because the Conservative party put up no candidate: in 18 of them the presence of Conservative candidates in 1923 ensured defeat. Of the 70 or so Liberal gains, not more than 15 at the most generous estimate can be said to have been won in constituencies which were fought by Lloyd George Liberals in 1922. On no reasonable calculation can Lloyd George be said to have had more than 30 personal followers in the new House of Commons out of a Liberal party of 159.

Moreover, reunion, the election results and the possibility of a Liberal government increased Asquith's importance. Asquith was no longer the disputed leader of a divided party. He was undisputed leader of a united party who might in some circum-

346

stances become Prime Minister and could justly claim that the Conservative party was as deeply divided as the Liberal party had been until mid-November. Whatever tensions might be expected in the future, reunion had been effected without concession to Lloyd George. This was understood by Lloyd George's followers, and by no one better than Mond who, in the course of 1923, had became the most important Lloyd George Liberal. At the election Mond lost his seat. In the New Year he went to visit Reading in India. It was to Asquith, not Lloyd George that he wrote asking to be given the Exchequer in the event of an Asquith government being formed while he was away.[1]

The election results induced in Liberal minds a euphoric belief that Liberalism was now strong and would grow stronger. It induced the illusion that Liberals were the arbiters of English politics and that the ideology of 'Free Trade' as the 'Middle Way' between Protection and the Capital Levy could become the basis for a commanding Central party to span the area between the Conservative Right and the Labour Left.

Not everyone expressed this idea in the same way. Lloyd George thought 'the Liberals alone had really increased their majority'.[2] Kerr, in England for a visit, saw the election as 'the first signs of a better feeling in Europe' after the 'great crimes' of the previous government.[3] Gladstone was surprised to discover that there was 'a mighty lot of Toryism still in the country'.[4] Trevelyan Thomson of Middlesbrough 'ha[d] visions of greater triumphs in the cause of sane progress in the near future'.[5] Few went as far as Grigg who believed that 'Conservatives must understand that the leadership [against Labour] has passed from them to the Liberals and must gracefully adapt themselves to that situation'.[6]

To the Asquithean leaders the new situation presented problems. They had to decide what treatment to give Lloyd George. They had to decide how to treat Baldwin and MacDonald. Some of the Asquitheans – Beauchamp and Runciman in particular – decided on a thorough burying of the hatchet,[7] but Lloyd George was still treated by Asquith's closest followers as a menace to be kept at arm's length. Reunion had strengthened Liberal prospects, but the prospect of a Lloyd George invasion continued to fill them with the deepest gloom.

In the month following the election, much play was made in Chamberlainite circles with Asquith's name as the possible leader of a Liberal/Conservative Coalition or as the linchpin of an arrangement to ensure that the Labour party was kept out of office if Baldwin resigned. There is no evidence that Asquith was party to this. Throughout the election the Asquitheans attacked 'Socialism', but their most peculiar irony was reserved for Protection, Baldwin and the Conservative party. Simon's comment on the election results was that they showed that 'the country [would] have nothing to do with Protection, ... that [it was] Baldwin's leadership [that ha[d] ... led [the government] into trouble' and that 'the last thing' wanted by 'the keen Liberals of the North' was 'a compromise with the Tories'.[1] If Asquith thought seriously of a Liberal/Conservative arrangement to put himself or keep the Conservative party in office, he did so in order to ensure the removal of Baldwin. In any case Asquith did nothing himself. On returning from Paisley on December 7, he said merely that 'the Trick election' was over and that 'one of the most discreditable adventures in the whole of British history' had produced a situation in which 'Free Trade [was] safe'.[2] On December 8 he told the *Sunday Times* that he had nothing to say. On December 9 he was said by Lloyd George to be 'decidedly against forming a government'.[3] It is not certain what he would have done if Baldwin had resigned on December 8, 9 or 10. It was not until Baldwin told him that the Cabinet had decided to meet parliament that he told the *Yorkshire Evening News* that there was 'needless to say ... no foundation for these foolish inventions' the newspaper had heard about his alleged desire to have a Coalition with the Conservative party.[4]

Definitive rejection of immediate Liberal/Conservative Coalition did not, however, relieve the Liberals of the need to take an attitude towards the questions: would they take office? if they would not, which of the two larger parties would they allow to do so instead? It did not relieve them of the need to take an attitude, though Asquith went some way in speaking to the National Liberal Club on December 18 towards affecting to abandon responsibility, attempting to create the impression that it had become clear, by some means which did not involve him, that the Labour party would take office and that the risk in putting a minority government into office, though extremely small, was not one that could be laid at the Liberal party's door.

Nevertheless, the decision to defeat Baldwin and let MacDonald take office once parliament assembled was taken deliberately.[1] Grey and Runciman seem to have been unenthusiastic.[2] Lloyd George claimed later to have insisted that co-operation with MacDonald must be wholehearted or not undertaken at all: he claimed to have cured Asquith and Simon of the feeling that they should first co-operate with the Labour party to put Baldwin out and should then, after a brief period of Labour rule, co-operate with the Conservative party to put themselves in.[3] Lloyd George may well have persuaded Asquith to consider the possibility that a Labour government might last for a considerable time: he did not remove the feeling that a Liberal-supported Labour government might be a prelude to a Liberal government before the new parliament was dissolved.

A number of calculations were involved here. It was desirable to co-operate with Labour in turning out Baldwin because of the widespread feeling that he had so discredited the Conservative party that the Liberals had a major chance to become the party of respectable progress. This, as much as Liberal anger at 'the unpardonable folly of the election',[4] explains Asquith's contempt for the government's 'unbroken ... record of impotence and humiliation' and his refusal to 'move a finger to continue or to connive at a prolongation of [its] disastrous stewardship'.[5] A Liberal/Conservative arrangement or Coalition, on the other hand, would produce dangers of its own. There was no guarantee that Asquith would be Prime Minister. Grey had frequently been mentioned by Conservatives as a Liberal under whom they would work. A Lloyd George/Conservative alliance was a conceivable threat:[6] there was much to be said for keeping Lloyd George where he was. The Asquithean Liberals had had one experience of the impact of Coalition on the Liberal party: the Lloyd George Liberals had had another. Both knew that Conservatives would be grasping in acquiring command within a Coalition and ruthless in ending it, and would be as dishonest in snatching cheap advantages as they had been in November.[7] In addition, there was the feeling that a Labour government should be put into office because 'a compact between Liberals and Conservatives to keep

Labour out' would leave the impression that the Liberal party wished to identify itself with a Conservative attempt to deny to the working-class party the fruits of electoral success. This feeling might have existed in any case: it was stimulated by Rothermere's war against the Labour party.[1] Asquith, Grey, Mond and Maclean – to say nothing of Lloyd George – almost certainly felt that, although the Liberal party's destiny was to be the anti-socialist party of the future, it had both to establish that the Conservative party was the party of reactionary anti-socialism and to detach itself from the unreasoning hostility they expected some Conservatives to show towards a Labour government.

There can be very little doubt that Asquith allowed MacDonald to take office not just in order to establish that the Liberal party was not a party of bourgeois reaction, but because he expected first to hold the balance in the House of Commons and then to turn out MacDonald and come into office himself whenever Labour incompetence made MacDonald's overthrow convenient to the Liberal party. Liberals did not fear the Labour party. They thought of it as a propaganda party rather than a party of government.[2] They believed that the conflicting nature of its commitments would become apparent once it tried to govern.[3] They expected conflict to drive back into the Liberal party many of the Liberals who had gone over while Asquith was in eclipse.[4] Asquith did not believe that Haldane would join a Labour government.[5] Nor did he believe he had an extreme Left in his own party. He expected conflict in the Parliamentary Labour Party, not amongst Liberals:[6] he made this mistake because he was thinking statically, not realising the pulling power the Labour party would have once it had established that it could govern. He proposed to sit on the Opposition, not the government, benches when Labour was in office, and to take care to remove the suspicion that he was conniving at the establishment of 'Socialism'. He intended to support MacDonald only so long as MacDonald introduced measures which did not conflict with Liberal policy: if a Labour government was ever to be tried, he thought, 'it could hardly be tried under safer conditions'.[7] He showed no sense of the dangers involved and had no intimation of Liberal doom. Doom, however, was not to be put off by incantatory resolutions against Protection and Socialism passed by the Liberal Parliamentary Party the day

MacDonald became Prime Minister.[1] Nor was it much affected by Grey's claim that the Liberal party had allowed MacDonald to take office not in order to 'give Labour a chance' but so that the Conservative party should 'think ... things over ... and come ... before the country on some future occasion as a party which had learned by experience of the past'.[2]

In all this Asquith was taking a greater risk than he knew. One contingency he had to guard against was that MacDonald would remain in office until his electoral prospects justified an election on a low-taxation Budget with both the 'bourgeois' parties against him. Asquith's speech of December 18 was designed to close this avenue by asserting the King's right to refuse a Prime Minister a dissolution.[3] This speech, however, caused alarm in the Royal Household, where the King also was trying to avoid responsibility for taking the lead against Labour. There the judgment that the King had the right to refuse MacDonald a dissolution seemed 'premature'. Stamfordham consulted Cave and Balfour and had a search made without success, for historical precedents. Asquith and MacDonald probably did not know that this was done. It is unlikely that Asquith's subsequent conduct would have been the same if he had known that the conclusion reached by the King was that, since there were no precedents, 'I must use my own judgment', as he did the following October.[4]

There is much we do not know about Lloyd George between December 8 and January 21. We do not know whether he was a party to Birkenhead's plot, whether he was certain from the start that the Liberal party should support MacDonald[5] or whether he still hoped to take part in an anti-socialist Coalition under his own or someone else's leadership. If Birkenhead thought of constructing a Coalition under Asquith who had fought the 1923 election on a Free Trade basis, Lloyd George's attacks on Protection would not by themselves have made a Lloyd George Coalition impossible. His attacks on Die-Hardism made him unacceptable to the Salisbury wing of the Conservative party, but that wing would have nothing to do with him in any case. The vigour of his attacks on 'Socialist intellectuals' kept open all the possibilities he needed in Birkenhead's direction. If, as he claimed,[6] he tried to persuade Asquith that Labour could not just be put in for a short time in order to be replaced by a Liberal/Conservative Coalition, he may have done so because he wanted to make sure that his rôle as Coalitionist was not stolen by Asquith who would have a far wider range of Conservative support than Lloyd George. It is not certain at exactly what point Lloyd George decided that he had no future along a Coalitionist line. By the last week in December, and probably at the end of the first week, he adopted the line that Lib/Lab co-operation must be 'complete and ... concerted' if there was to be a chance to 'reap a full harvest of Radical reforms'.[1]

From the beginning of 1924, therefore, Lloyd George displayed once more his radical plumage. He prepared to convert the Liberal and Labour parties into a massive unit which, beginning with Electricity and Railways nationalisation where nationalisation was 'natural' and possible but leaving the mines where it would be difficult,[2] would be a more effective Radical party than either Asquith or MacDonald could be expected to lead by themselves. This phase of extreme Radical hopefulness lasted until a Labour candidate was adopted against him in the Carnarvon boroughs in March.

In these months Lloyd George, while supporting Asquith's leadership in public, criticised Grey, Gladstone and the 'higher reaches' of the Liberal party for being crypto-Conservative. They had, he claimed, no understanding of the needs and nature of genuine Radicalism which would find nothing to satisfy itself in a MacDonald government. Genuine Radicalism demanded bold, active policies to cut below the appeal made to the working classes by the inert conjunction of a Marx-sodden socialist intelligentsia and innately conservative trades unionists. Lloyd George's conversation was punctuated with praise of Thomas,[3] doubts about the Labour ministers' ability to direct civil servants in a radical direction and uncertainty about MacDonald's ability to think radically at all. The 'idea', in Mrs Snowden's words, was 'the union of all the Radical forces for common ends'.[4]

In early February Lloyd George wondered how 'Liberals [could] go on continuously [supporting] Labour with no share in the government',[5] thought Henderson or any 'moderate Labour man' who stood at the Burnley by-election should be left unopposed and was preparing to anticipate a situation in which, when MacDonald's Left 'bec[a]me clamorous', MacDonald would need further Liberal infusions in order to hold it down.[1] MacDonald, he is recorded as saying, was 'not a man of action'.[2] There was no danger that a MacDonald government would go 'too ... far'. MacDonald would not take risks unless Liberals made him. If he failed 'through lack of courage and initiative' he would drag down the Liberal party 'which had put [him] in office and kept [him] there'.[3]

This rôle did not last long. It was in any case difficult to play it. It was only a few months since Lloyd George had been allied with the Chamberlainites. He had some support among Labour leaders but was disliked and distrusted not only by the leaders of the Conservative party but by large sections of the Labour party as well. The discourtesy he received from the Clydesiders in the 1922 parliament was renewed in 1924. By MacDonald, Henderson and so on, he was regarded as a rival, not a friend: nothing now would do them more good than his eclipse. Lloyd George could not detach himself from the Liberal leadership which, in order to be credible, had at times to be hostile to Labour in a way which his potential Labour allies disliked.[4]

At the same time as MacDonald's government eased itself into office, it made clear its refusal to owe public debts to the Liberal party. The Labour leaders depended on Liberal support to remain in office and had to avoid contentious questions if they were to have time to prove their respectability. But they were aiming to replace the Liberal party, not to be controlled by it. They were willing to accommodate Liberal politicians who wanted to join the Labour party but they wanted neither open Liberal patronage, invasion from Lloyd George nor the internal conflict which a Lloyd George invasion would bring. If MacDonald did not at this early stage frame motions and choose policy positions in order deliberately to divide the Liberal party, he gave Lloyd George as frosty a welcome as Asquith, Gladstone and Maclean had done the year before.

This might not have discouraged Lloyd George in his Radical reincarnation if MacDonald's government had been a failure, or if Liberal opposition had been a success. In fact neither condition obtained. The Liberal party backed down as rapidly as it asserted itself over Poplar.[5] Over the Sudan and the Naval Estimates its performance was 'heart-rending'.[6] Some Lloyd George Liberals

– few in number but formidable in experience – did not share Lloyd George's yearning for the Labour Left:[1] the most prominent among the Liberals of the Left had no yearning for Lloyd George. Pringle and Kenworthy wanted to lead the Radical Left: they did so in aggressive independence of him. The by-election at Burnley was one of Henderson's rare electoral triumphs. The proof it gave that in some constituencies the Liberal party was an obstacle to Labour advance strengthened the belief that the Liberal party was the enemy. By the end of February MacDonald had already occupied the position Lloyd George wanted as 'national leader of the Left'.[2] It seemed likely that he would take many more Radicals with him at the next election.

The establishment of MacDonald's position completed the damage Lloyd George had suffered from the Labour party since the beginning of 1920. It was now clear that he would attract no support in Labour quarters so long as the Labour party was a going concern. There was no sign that it had reached its electoral peak, and no doubt in the Parliamentary Labour Party that opportunities existed to display a governing capability. In one sense there was no less hostility among the Asquithean leaders than there had been before November 13: there was more in the sense that Pringle was a great deal closer to Asquith than he had been previously.

From the beginning of March 1924, therefore, Lloyd George began once more to shift. He excused the Liberals for putting Baldwin out of office, but emphasised more clearly than before that he did not support 'Socialism'. The Conservative party was blamed for keeping the Labour party in office, as it had by support-ing it in the Cruiser division. MacDonald was reminded that government was more difficult than opposition and that the com-promises of office made his opposition propaganda ridiculous. Lloyd George played no part in Churchill's by-election in the Abbey division of Westminster, but he watched it closely, and perhaps suspiciously, as an attempt to restore the Coalition Liberalism he had abandoned the previous November.[3] It was the decision of the Carnarvon Labour party to put up Alfred Zimmern, once an admirer and now Professor of International Relations at Aberystwyth, which convinced Lloyd George that he should do the same.

The Abbey division was untypical of the body of the electorate, but the Abbey election demonstrated the strength of anti-socialist Liberalism and the weakness of the Liberal party itself. It was followed by a catastrophe for Sir John Pratt[1] standing as a Liberal at Kelvingrove in May, a lost seat for C. B. Fry at Oxford in June and an irrelevant and small Liberal vote at Lewes in July. These results were offset by a sizeable vote for Sir Richard Winfrey[2] at Holland-with-Boston and by Mond's retention of Carmarthen in August. But in early April Lloyd George began using Churchill to renew contact with Balfour and Birkenhead. He continued right up to the time of the general election to hope for a renewal of the 1922/23 position at or after the election.[3]

How seriously Lloyd George took these expectations is not clear: perhaps not very seriously. He was not taken very seriously himself. The amount of newspaper attention he received in the summer of 1924, except in his own papers, was small. His aim was to attract to himself rather than to the Liberal party a wide range of followers who would support him whatever he might do after an election was over, but he could not consider an open arrangement with the Conservative Coalitionists since there was no guarantee that they would make the running in the Conservative party. The Liberals he wanted to lead were not just ex-Coalition Imperial Preference Liberals whose popular strength he probably thought was small, but the great body of anti-socialist radicals who would sheer off open alliance with the Conservative party. It is the paradox inherent in his situation – that he was preparing to carry anti-Conservative anti-socialist Radicals into a Coalition Conservative alliance without telling them – which explains the contradiction, more apparent in 1924 than ever before, between his private negotiations and the repeated public claim that the country needed Liberalism, the parent of free speech, conscience and free trade, and a massive policy of State ownership of land and control of education in order to liberate the popular energies the great captains of industry needed if Britain was to be equipped not so much to redistribute wealth as to create it.[4]

In 1924 Lloyd George did not discover the propaganda possibilities of unemployment, perhaps because unemployment had begun while he was Prime Minister. He had no policy for the urban wage-earner because that would not please the urban employer.

He had policies for Electricity and Coal. He set up a Land Committee which had not completed its report by the time of the general election.[1] Land was a recurrent Lloyd George topic before the war and one on which the Labour party had not succeeded in becoming the spearhead of discontent. Official Liberal policy included limited proposals to grant credit facilities to farmers and to ensure the proper working of the land. Lloyd George's involved expropriating all landowners except the cultivating owners of freeholds in order to effect a redistribution in favour of the landless labourer[2] and a programme of State-directed rural education.

How far Lloyd George supposed he could take this in public in the Liberal party, how far he really expected to create a peasant Liberal party is not certain. What is certain is that Mond thought it led Lloyd George to something resembling agrarian Socialism. Mond was one of the great capitalists of the age and a Free Trader who wanted Liberals to avoid any taint of Socialism while carrying the working classes with them. He did not apply capitalist freedom to the rights of property in land, but his criticism of Lloyd George's Land policy and the more general irritation he showed with Lloyd George about organisational questions in 1924[3] arose from the fear that erosions of property rights in Land might be a prelude to similar erosions elsewhere. Lloyd George hinted that a quarrel would do Mond no good while sitting for a Welsh seat. To a man who had sung 'Land of My Fathers' with other Welsh M.P.s in the House of Commons lobby after Welsh Church Disestablishment,[4] this was a threat. September 1924, nevertheless, for Mond marked a parting of the ways which could only have been reversed by a major Liberal achievement at the general election.

Once the Liberal party had made its decision not to be involved in Coalition, it had to decide what policy and platform it would adopt, and on what basis it would support, or criticise, a Labour government. In this there was much euphoria and some constructive thinking, of which Ramsay Muir's Summer Schools were a not contemptible example. The election of 1923 had been fought by the Liberal party on two planks, and virtually two planks only – the League of Nations and Free Trade. There had been a wide range of policy proposals designed to look like a social reform programme, but these were neither as startling nor as expensive as the Labour party's. The League of Nations had supporters in all parties. The Free Trade emphasis paid dividends at the election. The difficulty now was that Protection was dead as a front-runner in the Conservative party and that Capital Levy and Nationalisation had suffered similar treatment at the hands of the Labour party. This might not have mattered if the Liberal party had been able to be sceptical about bogus schemes to establish social equality. Though the Conservative party could do so with an ease which the Protectionist interlude had increased, this was not a thing which Liberals could do. It would be wrong to imply a contrast between a Liberal party which needed 'crises' and 'remedies' in order to have what its members thought political respectability and a Conservative party which did not. It is still the case that Free Trade, which had been presented as the conservative position at the 1923 election, could not be generalised for precisely the reason that the anti-intellectual, intellectually conservative position had already been pre-empted by the Conservative party and rejected by Liberals.

This meant that Liberalism needed to be progressive. It needed to be constructive. It needed to be broad enough to attract not only the liberal-minded Conservatives who had brought down the Coalition but also the 'decent young' who believed that Labour was the heir to the Liberal party's progressive past. The Liberal programme included the taxation of urban land values, state acquisition of mineral rights and royalties in coal and an extension of State pension schemes. It was presented by Asquith in the context of a permanent concern for education. There was, however, no great emphasis. Whereas Lloyd George might have seemed credible in this rôle if he had been allowed to exert himself, Grey, Cowdray, Buckmaster, Beauchamp, Maclean, Simon, Runciman, Vivian Phillips and Asquith at seventy-two hardly had that sort of credibility. Despite Pringle and Kenworthy, they did not sustain the claim that the Liberal party was more effectively radical than the government to which Haldane had given his support. Allowing for all scepticism about the importance of political programmes in determining elections, it is difficult to avoid the conclusion that the Liberal performance at the election of 1924 was affected by the impression it left of mindless conservatism in a situation in which the Conservative party was its natural representative.

There can be very little doubt that the decision to put Labour into office inflicted a deep wound on the Liberal electorate. At the 1923 election the Liberal leaders had been as strongly anti-socialist as they had been anti-Conservative. Their first act in the new parliament – the removal of Baldwin – was consistent with this, but the second – the enthronement of MacDonald – was not. The enthronement of MacDonald left a devastating impression which was increased by Churchill's open dissent. It was increased still more by failure to act as a united party in parliament and by the publicity given to parliamentary debates in which Liberals were found voting and speaking on both sides.

Asquith expected office to divide the Labour party: some Liberals thought they saw this happening once the Labour government began. Lloyd George's Radical swing was designed to prepare for the possibility. So were Pringle's attempts to create situations in which the Labour and Conservative parties would vote together in the parliamentary lobbies.

These efforts underestimated MacDonald's control, the Labour party's unwillingness to split and the effectiveness of Conservative tactics which were designed to polarise differences where Liberal divisions would result. Grey's resignation of the Asquithean leadership in the House of Lords was a personal rather than a policy decision,[1] but it was a symbol of what was to happen at the general election a month later. The damage done to the Labour party by the Russian Treaty, the Campbell case and the Zinovieff letter was small compared to the damage done to the Liberal party which had put it into power. Despite striking attacks by Lloyd George and Asquith on all three grounds, many voters who voted Liberal in 1923 because they disliked both Socialism and Protection refused in 1924 to support the party which had given Labour its first real chance of power.

XIX

THE POLITICS OF THE
FIRST LABOUR GOVERNMENT

'They have shown the country that they have the capacity to govern in an equal degree with the other Parties in the House ... and, considering their lack of experience, ... have acquitted themselves with credit in the House of Commons ... The Labour Government have also shown the country that patriotism is not the monopoly of any single class or party. Finally, they can justly claim that they have left the international situation in a more favourable position than that which they inherited. They have in fact demonstrated that they, no less than any other party, recognise their duties and responsibilities, and have done much to dispel the fantastic and extravagant belief which at one time found expression that they were nothing but a band of irresponsible revolutionaries intent on wreckage and destruction.'

> MacDonald to the King, October 10 1924, Geo. V K 1958/26

'On Wednesday the twenty ministers designate, in their best suits ... went to Buckingham Palace to be sworn in; having been previously drilled by Hankey. Four of them came back to our weekly M.P.s' lunch to meet the Swedish Minister – a great pal of ours. Uncle Arthur [Henderson] was bursting with childish joy over his H[ome] O[ffice] seals in the red leather box which he handed round the company; Sidney was chuckling over a hitch in the solemn ceremony in which he had been right and Hankey wrong; they were all laughing over Wheatley – the revolutionary – going down on both knees and actually kissing the King's hand ... Altogether we were a jolly party – all laughing at the joke of Labour in office.'

> Beatrice Webb, Diaries 1924–32, January 19 1924 (misdated), p. 2

'MacDonald's idea is to show how respectable they are.'

> Noel Buxton, Minister of Agriculture in the Labour government, talking to the outgoing Minister of Agriculture, Sir Robert Sanders, Bayford diary, January 23 1924

(i)

Throughout its period of office the Labour government of 1924 was subject to tactical exercises which had scarcely anything to do with immediate policy objectives. MacDonald expected to accomplish nothing, except perhaps abroad. The leaders of the

359

two other parties were searching for ways out of the deadlock in which they had been put by the election of 1923. Baldwin's personal position was so weak that he had virtually no scope for initiative; the nearest he came to taking the initiative was the decision to give MacDonald a fair run. The fact that MacDonald had no majority of his own meant that there were limits to what he could do, whatever the Labour party might want to do. Neither Asquith nor Baldwin used their positions of strength[1] to make him achieve policy objectives which would be of general benefit to the nation. What each tried to do was produce, or wait for, a situation in which he would be in a better position than before to conduct government, win an election or provide leadership in whatever political rôle seemed most appropriate.

MacDonald's intention was to make the Labour party a responsible instrument of radical thinking and to remain leader of a united party in the process. Though he made it plain at all relevant moments until the Russian Treaty demonstration in August that he did not intend to be driven by his Left, he needed to avoid a showdown in which the Left might be driven from the party. For the rest his objective was to achieve such advances as were open to him within the framework of conventional politics and to convince anyone who might wish to know that Socialism meant men of business pursuing the half-measures constitutive of radical progress as England knew it.

In choosing this line rather than any other MacDonald was acting in one of the contexts his life had established. This was not just the Coalition context in which he co-operated with Gladstone in 1903, considered Coalition with Lloyd George in 1910 and 1914 and would have supported a Lansdowne Coalition in April 1918,[2] but also the context from which he had suffered since his opposition to the war. Apart from a brief period in 1917/18, MacDonald had been friendless in respectable quarters since 1914. He had been the object of extensive newspaper abuse. An ex-pacifist had turned him out of his seat at the Coupon election. Bottomley and a naval V.C. had pursued him with his birth certificate when he stood and lost at Woolwich in 1921. In 1921/22 he was depressed both by his own situation and by the Labour party's performance. He despised and distrusted the Labour leadership in the House of Commons, which he thought missed all the opportunities he might have taken. Snowden had deserted the ILP: along with his wife he seemed to be deserting the Labour party. MacDonald knew that some Labour leaders did not want UDC representatives in the House of Commons, that Henderson and the trades union leaders were suspicious of the ILP and that the Webbs had no enthusiasm for him.[1] He thought that Webb, Henderson and Clynes expected to make the running and form the first Labour Cabinet. At fifty-five he was probably conscious that his powers would find no adequate opening if they were not given an opening soon.

When his opportunity came in November 1922, he had taken it. But criticism and abuse had been revived. From December 6 1923 a large segment of the popular press had treated him in much the way he had been treated from 1914 to 1921. In MacDonald's make-up there was a strong will, much vanity, great ability and an inability either to admit error or to suffer folly. The political situation provided real reasons for trying to show that the malice, incompetence and revolutionary intentions attributed to Labour were attributed falsely.

Baldwin expected to win the election of 1923: MacDonald did not expect him to lose it. Baldwin did not intend to create a situation in which a Labour government became an immediate possibility: MacDonald did not anticipate the problems which would follow from it.[2] But, just as the Conservative leaders saw in the situation Baldwin had produced an opportunity to destroy the Liberal party, so MacDonald, once recovered from the shock, welcomed the opportunity to show that the Labour party was the true heir to radical Liberalism. There are hints, not very reliable, immediately after the election, that MacDonald was thinking of constructing a Coalition with the Asquithean Liberals.[3] Since Labour feelings were stronger against the Liberals than against the Tories,[4] it is unlikely that he thought this seriously. On December 8 he arrived in London, made no public declaration of intention and left the impression on his immediate followers that he wished the leaders of other parties to speak before he did.[5] On December 10 at dinner in Webb's house with Henderson, Clynes, Thomas, Snowden and the Webbs he agreed to take any opportunity he might be given to take office himself. By the 13th of the month the National Executive of the Labour Party, the Executive Committee of the Parliamentary Party and a joint TUC and Party Executive Committee had decided that the party should take no part in a Coalition but should form a government if that became possible.[1] MacDonald approached Haldane on the 11th. By December 12 the idea of Coalition, if it had been taken seriously, had been abandoned.[2]

About the desirability of taking office, there was general agreement except among the Clydesiders.[3] Apart from Smillie who did not want a Labour government until the next Parliament but one, all prominent Labour leaders in the end agreed, realising the 'calamitous ... effect on public opinion ... and on the Party itself ... if, when it was offered office, it flatly refused to accept the responsibility'.[4] The decision to take office if Baldwin was defeated in the House of Commons and the decision to co-operate with Asquith in defeating him therefore produced, they were not the result of large-scale expectations about the Party's future. These calculations stemmed, nevertheless, from the same estimate of the objective situation as Baldwin's and were directed at producing a similar outcome. They were based on the assumption that the two-party system was natural and desirable and would shortly be restored,[5] and that the Liberal party was really dead, had been revived by Baldwin's foolishness and would now die completely. Except in Manchester Labour had expelled it from its areas of strength north of the Trent. It had survived in the South-West because Labour had allowed it to.[6] Labour's task now was 'to consolidate political issues in two camps divided on principle'.[7]

Though this meant that the death of Liberalism must be made unmistakable, it does not seem to have been thought impossible that it should be. It was thought, on the contrary, that the Liberal party would die because it was the party of 'fratricidal' strife and because the real political division lay between the Conservative and Labour parties. Many Liberals were really Conservatives. Liberal tactics were unscrupulous. Some of the 'dirtiest hitting in the election' was the work of Liberals, but the only Liberal *idea* was Free Trade.[8] Free Trade was Labour policy as much as it was Liberal policy, but Labour

Free Trade was part of a well-balanced contribution to the positive tasks of the twentieth century. The Liberal party presented Free Trade as an antiquated shibboleth. It did nothing to conceal the fact that about the only issues that mattered – unemployment and foreign policy – the Liberal party had had no original idea for thirty years.

These assumptions, vaguely rooted in Labour thinking and propaganda before and during the election, become firm assumptions afterwards. They were combined with a defensive feeling that, although the Labour party was spontaneously in touch with a larger segment of public feeling, Labour needed governmental experience if it was to attract the respect which Asquith and Grey still seemed to attract. All trades union leaders were used to conducting political business at a high level. A few had held office during the war. But the feeling was as widespread in the Labour party as it was among Liberals that the Labour party had distinguished itself so far as a party of propaganda, not as a party of government. A successful period of office would show that it could govern, provide attractions for Liberals it wished to suborn, enhance its status in relation to the Liberals it was attempting to replace and help to produce a split in the Liberal party.[1]

In order to take the opportunities which office would offer, it was necessary to prevent the formation of an anti-Labour Coalition and to remove the impression, which the Rothermere and Liberal newspapers were attempting to leave, that a Labour government would not behave constitutionally. In the five weeks before the return of parliament on January 15, MacDonald and the Labour leaders did their best to leave the impression that, if given the opportunity to govern, they would do so not because of 'office ... prestige or emoluments'[2] or the benefits the Labour party was falsely expected to gain,[3] but because the Labour party, as a 'party of principle',[4] felt obliged 'to give constitutional effect to the duty of carrying on the King's government'.[5] The public statements of MacDonald, Clynes, Snowden and Thomas were models of propriety, suggesting a sympathetic understanding for the 'difficulties of employers',[6] a Christian pursuit of moral perfection,[7] a concern for the national credit,[8] a standard of financial rectitude of which Gladstone would have approved and a consonance with the war dead who did not lay down their lives

for 'petty passions' but so that Britain might be 'purified and ...
justice ... done among the nations of Europe'.[1] It was not Labour,
they claimed, that was damaging the country's standing and its
financial credit,[2] but the anti-socialist press which seemed to
neither know nor care what blows its baseless accusations were
striking at Britain's reputation abroad.[3] The Labour party had
become 'an enduring factor of the political life of the country and
was well on the way to become the dominating force in Parliament'.[4]
It was a barrier against revolutionary change. Any attempt to
'wangle a situation' in order to deny Labour the chance to govern
would intensify militancy and do great damage to constitutional
government. 'I would appeal to the nation very seriously and
solemnly', said MacDonald at Elgin, 'not only for the forms of the
Constitution but for the spirit of the Constitution ... [and] for
fair play [and] honest and gentlemanly dealing in politics'.[5]

In choosing a Prime Minister, the King and Stamfordham were
of first consequence. MacDonald knew this. MacDonald was
neither a Privy Councillor nor an ex-Minister: this seems to have
inhibited communication. After a visit to London immediately
the election was over, he spent the end of December in Scotland.
In his absence Thomas[6] acted as intermediary in assuring
Stamfordham that MacDonald would form a government if
asked to, would introduce 'no extreme legislation or ... violent
administrative changes' and would not '*play* ... up to the Clyde
division'. On the telephone on December 28 and in person in
Stamfordham's house on January 1,[7] he committed MacDonald
to accept the outgoing government's Budget and to let the King
keep all his Household officers so long as they did not 'antagonise
the government'. Instead of a Capital Levy about which 'nothing
would be attempted', he promised a Royal Commission 'composed
of the very best men of all parties ... to consider the best means of
dealing with the National Debt'. A MacDonald government would
do its best 'to abolish the Dole which was exercising a ... per-
nicious ... effect ... notably among the young, who were
growing up to dislike work and to live upon the State', and would
raise loans to guarantee the interest on investment capital made
available for projects involving extensive employment of labour.
There would have to be plain speaking to the French, and Russia
would be recognised. But ministers would use the existing Civil

Service machinery in office. There would be no tampering with discipline in the Army. There was no truth in press predictions that trades unionism would be introduced into the armed forces.[1]

If Derby's letters to the King and the letter columns of *The Times* were typical, the King received hysterical demands from many quarters[2] that he should not let Labour take office. He was disturbed by the speeches of Clydesider M.P.s who neither wanted a Labour government on sufferance nor minced words about the lack of cordiality between themselves and the Court. Between December 6 and 19 Stamfordham investigated the possibility of Coalition. The King's decision to make Baldwin stay in office was probably taken in order to avoid choosing between Asquith and MacDonald. The decision to allow MacDonald to take office in January if Baldwin was defeated was taken in view of Asquith's decision that he should do so.

Once the King decided that MacDonald would have to form a government, he did his best to treat him as one man of the world would treat another. During MacDonald's period of office, relations between the King and the Prime Minister developed cordially. On both sides this cordiality reflected a genuine interest. The King was a reactionary with strong anti-socialist instincts and a real dislike for many aspects of the modern world. But he was anxious to avoid conflict between the Crown and a powerful segment of popular opinion. He felt a special obligation to maintain the integrity of the police and the armed forces and some personal measure of responsibility for India. He disliked the 'filthy rags of newspapers'[3] and doubtless wanted to dissociate himself from too close an identification with Big Business on the pattern of the Birkenhead/Rothermere movement. He was both firm and anxious. Both he and Stamfordham emphasised that 'His Majesty ... was not in the least alarmed ... at the prospect of a Labour government ... never doubted their loyalty or patriotism and felt that the best interests of the country would be the primary aim of their policy'.[4]

MacDonald had every reason to reciprocate the tactical cordiality of a contemporary. In MacDonald's make-up there was a Victorian pride in achievement and an obvious enjoyment of respectability and power achieved after years of struggle. It may well have been true, as the sourer members of his party thought, that having 'no woman' he was not to be trusted with the rich, and that 'only gentlemen [were] proof against the blandishments of Court and Society'.[1] This feeling of 'arrival' was not confined to MacDonald. Dalton, Wedgwood, Haldane and Beatrice Webb testify to the excitement caused among the families of some Labour leaders by their imminent presence at Court and by the invitations they received from the owners of large houses; it is easy to believe that the chief interest in the higher reaches of the Labour party was in catching a glimpse of a world of which its members had previously known nothing. Yet in the longest haul MacDonald had as good reason as Disraeli had had sixty years before for getting on to the right side of the King and 'Society' and as strong a desire to assure both the King and the public that he would conduct government as other Prime Ministers had conducted it, whatever content he might insert into it.

In taking office MacDonald hoped to keep it for a long time. The longer, he seems to have supposed, the better the opportunity to show that the Labour party need not attract the fear and hostility which Rothermere and Birkenhead had attempted to arouse. How long he could remain in office would depend on the Liberal and Conservative leaders and on the willingness of the Liberal and Conservative parties to support him with votes in the House of Commons. He may or may not have said of the Red Flag that it was 'the funeral dirge of our movement'. He may, or may not, have believed that 'the Capital Levy lost us fifty seats'. He may, or may not, have been pleased when Mrs George Keppell – 'a lady, very famous in her day' – told him that 'she sympathized with Labour very much and agreed with all the party's policy except Capital Levy'.[2] What is certain is that his decision to dash for respectability explains why he did not ask for dissolution in order to fight an election on a contentious issue arising from the Budget. Had the Conservative party behaved more militantly, he might perhaps have thought it worth his while to do so. Had he been without a militant Left, he might have thought it helpful. It was probably the prominence of the Left which made him prefer the advantages to be gained from a long period of office to the dangers to be faced at an election in which the newspapers would give prominence to Smillie, Kirkwood, Maxton, Buchanan and Campbell Stephen.

In constructing a Cabinet, MacDonald aimed to produce a combination competent enough to command confidence, respectable enough to dispose of the accusation that the Labour party was revolutionary and comprehensive enough to include anyone who might be dangerous outside. It was clear that office would have to be offered to some 'revolutionary' names especially among the miners, even if not necessarily in positions of importance. This made it doubly important to provide reassurance in other directions. Reassurance meant disappointing claims arising from long service to the Labour movement, particularly when intellectual vigour was lacking.[1] It was the difficulty he would face in the Labour party if it was known that outsiders were being given places that accounts for the secrecy he imposed on the course of Cabinet construction. It was the desire to avoid open dependence on the Liberal party which involved MacDonald in negotiation to attract politicians who, while reflecting the same range of opinions as Asquith, were demonstrably not Asquitheans.[2]

In this MacDonald found Haldane as valuable as Lord Robert Cecil had found Grey in 1921/22. Haldane had been Asquith's closest political friend and, as War Minister, one of the successes of the 1908 Cabinet. Asquith, however, had failed to rescue him when he was driven from office in 1915. He played no part in the Asquith or Lloyd George Coalitions, detached himself from the Liberal party and emerged after the war as the Olympian proponent of Administrative and Educational Reform and the renovation of the mines. The Spen Valley by-election in January 1920 made him demand a Lib/Lab alliance of the Centre.[3] At the Paisley by-election he stated that he would have voted for Asquith if he had had a vote, but gave an interview in the course of the campaign which implied the opposite.[4] He resisted Asquith's advance when Grey re-entered public life in 1921 and tried to dissuade Grey from conducting himself as a member of the Liberal party. While still declaring himself a Liberal and hoping for a Lloyd George Radical party in the future, Haldane came increasingly to support Labour politicians. He would probably have liked some sort of alliance with Grey, or even Lloyd George if he had abandoned his Conservative connection,[5] but the 1922 election taught him that the Liberal party had had its day. He appeared on carefully selected Labour platforms at the elections of 1922 and 1923[6] on the ground that only the Labour party had a genuine concern for education.

Unlike other Liberals Haldane did not regard the 1923 election as a Liberal victory. He did not exclude a Lib/Lab fusion as the basis for a party of progress in the future: this was still in his mind the day after the election results were declared.[1] When he urged Baldwin to stay in office to govern by general agreement in the House of Commons,[2] he may well have thought this the best way of developing a non-socialist progressive alternative in opposition to him.[3] By way of response Cave urged Haldane to support a MacDonald government if one was formed.[4] A week later, on Baldwin's instructions, he was briefed by Hankey, the Cabinet Secretary, so that he could become chairman of the Committee of Imperial Defence if MacDonald asked him to. He was pressed by Hankey to the point of being told 'I think meaning it' that Hankey 'would rather work ... under me than under any man alive'.[5] Haldane did not respond to MacDonald's first offer of office on December 11.[6] It was not until Baldwin made it clear that he would be leaving office that Haldane agreed in principle to help. Even then it was not clear that MacDonald felt strong enough to use him.[7] On December 24 Haldane laid out the conditions on which he would take office – his occupancy of the chairmanship of the Committee of Imperial Defence, a definite policy and some money for Education and an attempt to reform the machinery of government. On December 29 – before MacDonald visited Cloan for the second time – he did not know whether MacDonald would be able to sell him to the Labour party.[8] Nor was he certain before MacDonald came to see him on January 11.[9] It seems clear that MacDonald handled Haldane very skilfully.[10]

Haldane was important because of his past because, although an ex-Liberal, he was not an Asquithean and because he brought with him a number of non-Labour dignitaries who would probably not have joined without him. Buxton, Wedgwood, Arnold, Ponsonby and Trevelyan had all been Liberal M.P.s. Haldane and the non-party members were essential as further demonstrations of continuity. Apart from Bledisloe, however, none of the non-Labour candidates for office approached by MacDonald were followers of Lloyd George. His connection with Lloyd George, and newspaper pictures of him walking with Baldwin at Astley during the election, may explain why Thomas Jones, though a Fabian, did not get the call he may have half expected.[1] In 1924 there were three Labour peers. MacDonald did not fill up, as Henderson suggested, with retired trades unionists. Nor did he use Sir Leo Chiozza Money who thereupon became an enemy of the government. Instead he made peers of Arnold, Thomson and Muir McKenzie, and gave minor office to Earl de la Warr – a Conscientious Objector during the war who at twenty-three had not long ceased to be an undergraduate. Even if MacDonald had had greater confidence in the administrative ability of the Labour M.P.s[2] he would have had fundamental reasons for showing that Sankey, Chelmsford,[3] Bradbury,[4] Meston,[5] Muir McKenzie,[6] Bledisloe and Parmoor[7] regarded the Labour party as a suitable heir to one of the great political traditions.

Some who were thought of were not appointed. Despite the importance of the Sankey Commission, Sankey in the end was kept in store for the future.[8] Bradbury, if indeed he was approached,[9] and Meston, whom Montagu had thought a possible India Under-Secretary in 1920[10] both declined for reasons which we do not have. Bledisloe refused because he was 'not a Socialist', but thought of joining the Labour party when Birkenhead and other 'Cave Men' seemed likely to return to prominence in the Conservative party. He was held back by Lord Robert Cecil to whom MacDonald apologised for failing to keep him in office as minister responsible for the League of Nations.[11] Chelmsford was a lifelong Conservative. He was appointed, on Haldane's recommendation,[12] because, as an ex-Viceroy, he would be strong enough to stop Admiralty opinion upsetting the government in parliament: he gave MacDonald no satisfaction. Parmoor – although a 'faddist' – was a lifelong Conservative, Churchman and believer in 'Christian methods' in government who made a reputation in the 1895 parliament by defending employers' rights in relation to Workmen's Compensation, and in 1908 was the chief Anglican obstacle in the way of Archbishop Davidson's attempt to reach a compromise with Runciman over the Church Schools question.[13] It is an indication of the importance MacDonald attached to this range of opinion that he had four ex-Liberals, an ex-Conservative and two Conservatives in his Cabinet and invited at least two other Conservatives to join it.

Even where the Labour movement was concerned, choices were made with an eye to reassurance or on the principle that specialists should be given posts about which they knew little.[1] Despite strong claims, Bertrand Russell's brother was excluded because of his matrimonial history.[2] Apart from Wheatley, who became Minister of Health after refusing an under-secretaryship, the Cabinet contained no prominent advocate of Direct Action.[3] Hodges was a Civil Lord of the Admiralty, Shinwell Secretary for Mines and John Muir, a Clydesider, parliamentary secretary to the Pensions Ministry. None, however, had power to make major decisions and Shinwell, already singled out as the most responsible Clydesider in parliament, made it his first object in office to 'inspire confidence ... on both sides of the [Coal] industry',[4] Morel was violently anti-French and anathema to genuine believers in the League of Nations:[5] he was also ill. He was given neither the Foreign Office, which he obviously hoped for, nor anything else. Ministers who had belonged to the General Council of the Union of Democratic Control and other similar bodies were expected to resign from them.[6] Lansbury was offered office outside the Cabinet late in the day after Henderson had asked for him: he refused, as he was probably meant to.[7] So did Smillie. So also did Neil Maclean who gave up a whipship on being denied promotion.[8] Wallhead whose parliamentary manner was sour was offered nothing.[9] Jowett became first Commissioner of Works because 'he was not equal to anything else'.[10] Noel Buxton was sent to the Board of Agriculture where he felt 'like a fish out of water'.[11] The India Office went not to Josiah Wedgwood, who had strong views and had been sharp with MacDonald,[12] but to Sir Sydney Olivier.

Olivier was one of the leading Fabians in the 1880s. As a civil servant from 1882 until 1920, he had been Governor of Jamaica, Permanent Secretary to the Board of Agriculture and Assistant Comptroller and Auditor. On retiring he had been chairman of the Labour party's Enquiry into the Prison System. He was the only minister who aroused real antagonism. He had considerable difficulty with Wedgwood who had wanted his job and resented the fact that he was nearly left out of the Cabinet altogether.[13] Olivier's Indian positions were probably not as advanced as Montagu's. He committed himself at one point to the view that

Reading suffered the 'racial defect' of being 'always out for a deal' and was therefore 'apt to give away more than he meant'.[1]

It was not affinity but probably fear that made MacDonald gear Snowden to a major task. Thomas was given the Colonial Office in order to deal with Ireland, which was delicate and to keep the Dominions happy. Walsh, the War Minister, had been a junior minister in the Lloyd George Coalition and had lost a son – Captain Walsh – during the war. Derby had 'known him all [his] life' as a 'straightforward little miner [who would] work most harmoniously with the soldiers'.[2] He completed the impression left by Chelmsford at the Admiralty, Thomson – an ex-Conservative and ex-Brigadier – at the Air Ministry and Haldane as chairman of the Committee of Imperial Defence. Even the Air Under-Secretary – Leach, who was a pacifist – was appointed not for that reason but because Thomson 'wanted a business man to help him deal with the important contracts that had to be made'.[3]

Wheatley represented the only group which objected to the Labour party taking office in a minority: his appointment to the Ministry of Health was neutralised in some respects by first Webb's, and then Snowden's, appointment as Chairman of the Housing and Unemployment Committee and by Haldane's chairmanship of the Home Affairs Committee of the Cabinet. Webb 'wished [he] knew what could be done at the Board of Trade'.[4] Trevelyan received a favourable reception as president of the Board of Education where he revived a thirty-year-old plan for renovating elementary schools and laid down a programme of expansion for secondary education which subsequent governments continued.[5] On paper Thomas, Hodges and Gosling constituted a formidable contingent from the Triple Alliance. But Gosling was a hard-worked sixty-three with a weak heart.[6] Thomas had already demonstrated his flexibility. In the case of Hodges, whose reputation as a militant leader had been dented by Black Friday, office provided a foot on an official ladder which, despite inadequacy and cantankerousness in office,[7] reached its final resting-place a few years later as permanent member of the Central Electricity Authority.

The Labour government of 1924, therefore, was not a crusade but a consistent continuation in an intellectual version of the line taken by Clynes, Webb, Thomas and Henderson since the Labour party had first seen the chance to occupy office in 1920. It held office for nine months.

(ii)

Between December 8 and January 22 MacDonald and the Labour party had been subjected to a campaign of vilification. From the announcement of the names of the Cabinet Ministers on January 22, the steam disappeared.[1] From January 22 until the end of February, the government played itself in. By the end of February its opponents were thinking that it showed 'day by day at question time' that the new ministers took 'practically the same view of things as the late Capitalist government'[2] with only such safe variations as any Radical-Liberal government might have been expected to produce.

Maxton and the Clydesiders, Lansbury and the *Daily Herald*, Brailsford, Wise, Brockway and the *New Leader*[3] criticised MacDonald for betraying Labour principles. Pringle, Masterman and other Liberals attacked him for having no principles to betray. The ILP group in parliament, taken over by Maxton, deployed criticism over a wide front. Smillie became chairman of the Parliamentary Party's Liaison Committee, offering the view that the government should 'deal drastically and fundamentally with [some] of the great Social evils' and, if defeated in the House of Commons, as they would be, should have an election from which they 'would be returned to real power as well as office'.[4] Two Whips were ill, including the Chief Whip, who was in fact dying: from the start there were 'unhappily prevalent intrigues' in the Parliamentary Party. One of its earliest meetings protested against the presence of Conservatives in the Cabinet and the appointment of the Scottish Law officers neither of whom belonged to the Labour party.[5] When MacDonald was compelled by administrative fact to back down on ex-Ranker officers' pensions about which he had made much during the election, there was prolonged difficulty in the House of Commons.[6] The Parliamentary Party was strongly in favour of Coal Nationalisation:[7] it made clear its dislike of Buxton's failure to specify a minimum wage in his Agricultural Wages Bill.[8] In deciding whether to give governmental support to private members' bills proposed by Labour back-benchers, the Cabinet displayed considerable caution. Over

Widows' Pensions, Local Option, Liquor Control, Proportional Representation, Divorce Law reform, M.P.s' salaries and Free Railway Vouchers, it sat on the fence. Over a private member's motion to limit the use of the death penalty for military offences, it first stalled and then stood firm.[1] Though it bowed to the point of establishing a Committee of Enquiry into the cases of policemen and prison warders dismissed after the Liverpool police strike in 1919, it persisted in its initial decision that they should not be reinstated.[2]

MacDonald established early mastery over the Cabinet and the House of Commons. The Cabinet stressed the confidentiality of its discussions and its collective responsibility in relation to outside bodies like the newspapers and the TUC.[3] There were neither resignations nor, except from Parmoor, threats of resignation: there were no ministerial changes.[4] Henderson, Haldane, Snowden and Webb (or perhaps Mrs Webb) objected to MacDonald's secrecy and aloofness. C. P. Scott thought him too much at ease in Zion.[5] Lord Robert Cecil thought that 'overwork' had produced 'a very bad attack of swollen head'. MacDonald was ready to blame colleagues, the Cabinet, the party or the governmental machine when things went wrong: the blame he tried to lay on Thomas Jones over the Campbell case was not unique.[6] He was not only overworked but at times was both arrogant and irritable. He would have agreed with Webb that Smillie was 'impossible' as a parliamentary politician. Towards the end of September he actually said that a Labour majority after the election would be 'a grave misfortune as the Party (not the Cabinet!) was not "fit to govern"'.[7]

After initial bungling, he kept a tight rein on the Cabinet. Haldane ran the Committee of Imperial Defence as a private empire in which neither MacDonald nor the Cabinet interfered.[8] The Home Affairs Committee – criticised in opposition for being an inner ring – was retained after exhaustive discussion. Wheatley was criticised for disregarding 'Cabinet responsibility', especially in relation to his unilateral action in withdrawing Mond's Poplar order. After having been put down by Webb over Housing Finance, he conducted Housing policy without regard to Webb's overlordship.[9] The fiasco over the Evictions Bill, which was approved by the Cabinet and presented to parliament in an unworkable form, was a result of Wheatley's pushing and the failure of a depleted meeting of the Home Affairs Committee to examine it properly. The public discredit attaching to the government produced a tightening up of procedure and the emergence of Thomas Jones from the routine obscurity to which he had been pushed when Baldwin left office.[1] Snowden and Chelmsford had departmental disagreements of the sort which occurred in all governments. So did Snowden and Trevelyan and Snowden and MacDonald.[2]

In Cabinet the talking was done chiefly by MacDonald, Haldane, Thomas, Wheatley, Shaw, Snowden and Trevelyan. In spite of Wedgwood there seem to have been no cliques, few quarrels and no wrangling.[3] Those who were effective were so by reason of their knowledge and authority. Snowden impressed civil servants and the House of Commons by his grasp of material fact: he exerted iron control over proposals that government spending should be increased. He was responsible for reducing the level of the Housing subsidy proposed by Wheatley and Webb. It was under pressure from him that the Cabinet refused to authorise Exchequer grants to Parish Councils in needy areas in Scotland on the ground, which Adamson pressed the Cabinet to ignore, that they had already been refused in England.[4] At the end of May Snowden became the chairman of a new Unemployment Committee to replace the Housing and Unemployment Committee of which Webb had been chairman since the government was formed.[5] His Budget contained no increase in taxation, made various reductions in Indirect Taxation and abolished the thrift rules for old age pensioners[6] in a way which caused distress on the Labour back benches.[7]

In its first few months in office the government carried out the policies which MacDonald had authorised before Baldwin resigned. The Capital Levy was postponed. An early decision was made to appoint a committee of businessmen to examine the National Debt. Webb was originally asked to be Minister of Labour.[8] He became President of the Board of Trade and, as Chairman of the Cabinet Committee on Housing and Unemployment, had supervisory control of unemployment policy. Much capital had been invested in the claim that a Labour government was uniquely qualified to deal with unemployment. The outcome was a statement that 'the most helpful solution of the unemployment problem lies in the re-establishment of normal peaceful conditions throughout the world',[1] the adoption of dilution in the building industry to which the Labour party had led resistance during and after the war, and an increase in the amount to be spent through the Trade Facilities, Export Credits, Trunk Road, Empire Development, Housing, Drainage and Afforestation programmes all of which had been inherited. The collapse of Shaw's reputation as Minister of Labour and the replacement of Webb by Snowden as unemployment overlord at the end of May reflected widespread criticism of the negligible character of these achievements.[2]

If it be asked what was new about the government's policies, the answer is that very little was new. Adamson's bill to give women the vote at twenty-one was introduced as a private member's bill, but taken up by the government. The gap in the receipt of unemployment insurance was abolished.[3] There was an increase in weekly benefit. Unemployment insurance was extended to juveniles. A decision was taken to find out whether agricultural labourers wished to be included in the Unemployment Insurance Scheme.[4] There was no bill to nationalise the mines and there was a decision that it was inexpedient to introduce one, but a Coal Mines (Washing and Drying Accommodation) Bill was presented instead on the ground that it would be 'excellent propaganda and arouse controversy', and Shinwell prepared a nationalisation bill of his own which MacDonald agreed to proposing in 1925.[5] The Hours of Industrial Employment Bill was scarcely an innovation. Even so it caused difficulty as an undesirable interference with the working of industry.[6] Railway nationalisation was ignored. The first steps were taken to give the Electricity Commissioners the powers of compulsion the House of Lords had removed when the Electricity Bill was passed in 1919, but this was no more than a restoration of proposals which had been made by the Coalition.[7] Buxton's statement of Agricultural policy in early February involved a strengthening of County Agricultural Committees, a plea for agricultural co-operatives on the line of the Linlithgow Report,[8] a restoration of Wages Boards which Law had tried to restore the year before and a declaration that 'neither protective duties nor subsidies' could be applied to agriculture which 'must be conducted on an economic basis without artificial supports from the public purse'.[1] The second reading of the Agricultural Wages Bill was opposed by the Conservative party which did not oppose the need for machinery of some sort. It received the Royal Assent after being amended by the House of Lords.[2]

It is true that the level of housing subsidy was increased and that Wheatley provided rented houses where Neville Chamberlain had concentrated on providing houses for sale. But it was decided that the 'eradication of slumdom', over which much rhetoric had been spilt, could be effected with the powers local authorities had already.[3] Wheatley's housing policies were a continuation of Neville Chamberlain's: his chief contribution was to increase the level of subsidy so as to put new houses within the means of workers whom mortgage arrangements could not convert into house-owners.

A number of decisions were made whose object was to demonstrate the government's liberal credentials. The abandonment of the Protectionist decisions of the Imperial and Economic Conference was one example:[4] the termination of the McKenna duties was another. So was the reversal of the Baldwin government's decision to impose a 33% duty on imported lace. On March 17 the Cabinet instructed Wheatley to negotiate an agreed all-party measure of Poor Law Reform on the basis of the Maclean Committee report. Eventually it appointed a committee of its own.[5] The Budget gave considerable pleasure in Liberal directions. The bill to restore to the Land Valuation Office the power to collect information which had been removed from it in 1923 was a reminder that a Labour government could undo the damage Lloyd George had done to his own creation.[6] The reduction of the cruiser programme recalled 1910/11. The decision to destroy government surplus arms and ammunition instead of selling them to foreign states reflected a position of which Lord Robert Cecil had attempted to make something in 1919/20. The abandonment of the decision to build a major naval base at Singapore[7] was presented as the outcome of 'a policy of international co-operation through a strengthened and enlarged League of Nations, the settlement of disputes by conciliation and judicial arbitration and the creation of conditions [to facilitate] ... comprehensive agreement on limitation of armaments'.[1] The use of force to control the political situation in Bengal was cushioned by the claim that force was to be used not in order to 'deal with political movements, however troublesome' but very strictly to prevent bloodshed and violence.[2] Over the Ulster Boundary Commission a judicious posturing did not conceal unwillingness to force the question to an issue.[3]

Moreover, many decisions followed logically from decisions made by previous governments. For example, the Cabinet adhered to the Imperial and Economic Conference's decisions about emigration.[4] It reaffirmed the obligation, which Churchill had defined in 1922, to keep a close watch on Indian immigration into Kenya, salving its conscience with the claim that it would do this to any 'influx of immigrants of whatever class, race, nationality or character as may be likely to be prejudicial to the economic interests of the natives'.[5] The Lausanne Treaty, like the level of Air Force expenditure, was 'an inheritance ... which it was impossible to amend at the present time'.[6] A decision was made to limit Britain's commitment in the Dardanelles if that should be possible, but the Lausanne Treaty was to be accepted whether approaches to other signatories bore fruit or not. The Iraq Treaty was proposed for ratification because the previous government had given an undertaking, though the Cabinet would probably have abandoned the Mandate if the Iraq Constituent Assembly had failed to ratify the Treaty.[7] The policy of resisting Egyptian claims to direct rule in the Sudan was continued. Consideration was given to Egypt's desire to be rid of the British presence in Cairo,[8] but it was stated at the Cabinet of May 1 [9] that 'the safety of the Suez Canal ... must be guaranteed effectively in some shape or form'. The London Traffic Bill was accepted with minor modifications in face of widespread objection from London Labour M.P.s.[10] The conflict which occurred in the Baldwin Cabinet between Amery and Lloyd-Graeme over the sale of the government stake in the Dye-stuffs Corporation was repeated in the new Cabinet. Despite an undertaking from McKenna that the Corporation would never be sold to a foreign firm, the Cabinet rejected Webb's proposal to sell it and decided to examine its working instead.[11] There was strong criticism of the League of Nations Treaty of Mutual Assistance which the Cabinet rejected.[12]

The compromise arranged by Neville Chamberlain as Postmaster-General in the Law Cabinet[1] to maintain direct government control of the Dominion side of Wireless Telegraphy was finalised. The new government arranged with Marconi for the construction of a Dominion-linked Telegraph service on government contract in the expectation that Marconi would run the telegraphic services with foreign countries under a system of licensed private enterprise.[2]

In addition there were symbols, tokens and promises of action for the future which showed the direction the Labour party wished to take without having to do much about taking it. These included the delay imposed on the sale of government factories at Gretna and Chepstow[3] and the continuation of the Agricultural Rates Act until a major enquiry could be conducted into Valuation and Rating.[4] There was a decision, made after consultation with Scottish Labour and Liberal members, to investigate devolution to which both MacDonald and the Scottish Labour party had been strongly committed in 1919.[5] There was the removal of the barrier erected in Downing Street on Law's instructions the year before to keep out the unemployed.[6] There were bills to prevent profiteering from the construction of new roads and to prevent unreasonable profits in the building industry, and there were threats to penalise profiteering as a result of food shortages during the dock strike.[7] There was the decision, whilst 'work[ing] towards Dominion Home Rule in India, ... thoroughly [to] explore' the situation 'before taking any next step' and to use ministers' contacts with Nationalist leaders to urge them 'not to put pressure on the government to take ill-considered or premature action'.

When the government was being formed, the Dockers, the Locomotive Engineers and the Amalgamated Society of Engineers all seemed likely to strike.[8] There were dock, rail, bus and tram strikes and a continuation of serious disputes in the coal, building and shipbuilding industries. MacDonald's chief concern was to ensure that there should be no coal stoppage and that, if other stoppages occurred, there should be no conflict between strikers and troops. Shinwell, who was criticised because he was not a miner, thought he was given the Mines Secretaryship in order to prevent a strike.[9] Wedgwood was Civil Commissioner in charge of preparations against strikes in key industries. Shaw and Thomas played a major part in negotiating with trades union leaders: Haldane and MacDonald negotiated with employers. Much attention was given to the problem of unofficial strikes: on each relevant occasion the Cabinet decided that it should deal only with official trades union leaders. In general the Cabinet conducted itself as any Cabinet would have done, without partiality for one side or the other, and, in MacDonald's case at least, with considerable annoyance at the 'worries' that would be 'increased', the 'prospects' that would be 'spoilt' and the 'beastly hard luck' the government would suffer if strikes proliferated.[1]

The government's greatest success was in foreign policy, where the success was personal to MacDonald. Policy was conducted by him and Ponsonby, with the machinery of the Foreign Office, in more or less complete detachment from the Cabinet.[2] The Cabinet was told from time to time what was happening about relations with Germany and France. Snowden was closely involved in the London Conference and highly critical of MacDonald's conduct of it.[3] But there was none of the scrutiny Olivier suffered from Wedgwood over Indian policy and, except from Snowden, none of the persistent heckling which Curzon suffered from preceding Cabinets. The London Conference was the sort of milestone Lloyd George expected to reach at Genoa in 1922 and the sort of success Baldwin hoped for in 1923. The prominence given to the negotiations which led up to it was great: the blanket put on concurrent treaty negotiations with Russia was considerable.[4] The London Conference showed MacDonald as the presiding practitioner of a liberal foreign policy which he hoped to make the basis for a renewed period of power.[5] The prominence given to the Russian Treaty was forced on him by the Parliamentary Labour Party when negotiations had broken down in early August. The Treaty, the bungling of the prosecution of the *Workers' Weekly* and the Zinovieff letter pushed MacDonald into a corner he had not intended to inhabit.

Except in this latest phase, then, the government governed as though it was an ordinary progressive government. It gave satisfaction in several parts of the Civil Service and in one respect to the Archbishop of Canterbury.[6] At the CID meeting when the Channel Tunnel was rejected, all four living ex-Prime Ministers were present. Allen expected a wide-ranging Economic General

Staff to construct 'an economic Domesday Book which would show precisely how the great industries are being run [and] draw up the order in which the various industries would be nationalized'.[1] What happened was that a Conservative, Churchman and Freemason who had been a pre-war Master Cutler[2] was appointed to head a Committee on Industry and Trade which was meant to include McKenna, while MacDonald was asked to set up a committee for forward economic thinking with Thomas Jones as secretary.[3]

Morel spent much time reminding Ponsonby and MacDonald that they were supposed to believe in democratic control of foreign policy. MacDonald began paradoxically by recognising the Soviet Union without consulting the Cabinet, let alone parliament.[4] Ponsonby had no wish to be told, working at his desk 'from 10 a.m. till 11 p.m.', that he and MacDonald were 'betraying the cause'.[5] MacDonald made it plain that he could not 'straighten up the mess of Europe in six or seven weeks' and was not going to be run by 'a blethering lot of impractical talkers'.[6] He resented Morel's criticisms in the *New Leader:* on protesting to Brailsford, the Editor, he 'got such a reply as closed everything'.[7] He made clear his dislike of the *Daily Herald* which was 'doing much damage abroad' and 'fast becoming a Communist organ'. Lansbury in his turn, finding 'MacDonald ... more an adept at intrigue and word-twisting and word-spinning than even Lloyd George himself', prepared himself for a future in which he could recall the government's insistence on being 'so very satisfactory to our opponents on the armament side of things and so very unsatisfactory to the poor devils on whose votes people like me got into Parliament'.[8]

Between MacDonald and Baldwin a sympathy developed which was buttressed by political need. MacDonald was put into office not only by Asquith and Lloyd George but also by the decision Baldwin had taken that he should be. He was kept there not only by Asquith and the Liberals but by Baldwin and the Conservative Shadow Cabinet. Since MacDonald wanted to stay in office for as long as possible, it was essential to be on good terms with the Conservative leaders. Baldwin did not want to put MacDonald out so long as there was a chance of a Liberal/Conservative alliance: he was happy to keep MacDonald in office as a way of denying Asquith and Birkenhead the opportunity for which they were waiting. The desire to replace the Liberal party as the leading radical party imposed brakes on what MacDonald thought it desirable to do in office: the prospect of the reversion of a large Liberal vote prevented him doing what Derby and Birkenhead had said he would do. On at least half a dozen occasions in the 1924 parliament, MacDonald was saved from defeat by Conservative support. When MacDonald asked the King for a general election in October 1924, he did so because he had been pushed by his Left into a position he had wanted to avoid, and because both the Cabinet and the Conservative leaders had decided that they were ready to strike the death-blow at the Liberals whom the body of the Labour party probably hated more than at any time before.[1]

XX

BALDWIN'S TRIUMPH

'I suppose it would be impossible to get Baldwin to accept an Earldom with the insurance that in the next unionist Cabinet he should have office. He would, no doubt, be a capital Colonial Minister.'

Strachey to Younger, December 28 1923, Strachey MSS

'Baldwin ... is apparently determined neither to give a Conservative party meeting the opportunity of choosing another leader who might secure Liberal support or ... to offer Conservative support himself to a Liberal government.'

Grigg to Bailey, January 3 1924, Grigg MSS

'... the safest as well as the correct, constitutional course is for Baldwin to face Parliament and be beaten. The King would then presumably send for Ramsay MacDonald, who would be unable to govern without Liberal support and would therefore (if he undertook the task at all) gain some experience of administration with his wings clipped. I do not favour this plan with any notion of scoring off the Opposition, but simply because I feel it is the only way in which you will ultimately arrive at a strong, reasonable constitutional party...'

Dawson to Lord Robert Cecil, December 8 1923, Wrench, p. 224

(i)

Despite the loss of nearly a hundred seats, Baldwin still led the largest party in the House of Commons which was returned at the election of 1923. The conditions in which MacDonald was the person most likely to form a government were created first by Baldwin's decision not to resign because of the scope that would leave for the Chamberlainites and Coalition and then by Asquith's decision not to support a continuation of Conservative government. Asquith and his followers on the one hand, Baldwin and his on the other did not make their decisions out of a feeling that MacDonald had a right to govern which, as leader of the second party in the House of Commons, he manifestly had not. They made their decisions because they supposed that a MacDonald government would provide tactical advantages for themselves and restore personal fortunes while giving MacDonald no opportunity to do serious damage to the social order. Asquith miscalculated.

The Liberal collapse of October 1924 was the outcome. The question we have to ask is: to what extent was Baldwin responsible for the fact that he succeeded where Asquith failed?

The election result did great damage to Baldwin's authority in the highest reaches of the Conservative party. Baldwin put on a brave face but he had made a major error. He was a 'mug' – 'a beloved man but wanting', a 'poor creature' who had thrown away his opportunities.[1] He neither was in a position to give a lead in the months following the election nor attempted to do so. For most of 1924 Baldwin was in danger of dismissal. For much of the year his leadership was negative. Whether out of shyness, inadequacy or instinctive political sense, his contribution to the electoral victory of 1924 was negative leadership in respect of four major topics – the identity of the next Conservative leader, the abandonment of Protection, the expansion of the Conservative/Liberal alliance and the destruction of the Liberal party. It was only in relation to Ireland, the Chamberlainites, party rhetoric, party organisation and the timing of the 1924 election that Baldwin's leadership can be said to have had momentum of its own in determining the events which established his predominance.

The question of an approach to Asquith or of immediate resignation had been disposed of by December 11. Asquith's speech on December 19 indicated a joint Lib/Lab vote to turn out the government when parliament reassembled on January 15 and a Labour government supported by Liberal votes thereafter. It was not, however, decisive and could not be so until parliament reassembled. The questions of Coalition in the new parliament and of Baldwin's future as Conservative leader remained. The first was resolved by mid-January. The second was not resolved until meetings of the Parliamentary Party and defeated candidates on February 11 and of the National Union on February 12.

The ease with which Baldwin was confirmed in the leadership did not mean that there was no desire to get rid of him. There was no lack of desire and no lack of reason to support it. Derby, Younger, Lloyd-Graeme, Hoare, Lord Robert Cecil, Worthington-Evans, Joynson-Hicks and Balfour, to say nothing of Austen Chamberlain, Birkenhead, Horne, Rothermere, Beaverbrook and Strachey, at various times all said publicly or in private that he should go. The difficulty in getting rid of him, and the main reason for his survival, was that the Beaverbrook/Rothermere attacks produced a revulsion in his favour, that no one in his Cabinet would make the first move against him[1] and that there were so many conflicting objectives that, want someone as many leading Conservatives might, 'there [was] no-one'.[2]

Among the original architects of Lloyd George's downfall, and even among those who wanted Baldwin to stay in office on December 8, there were two views about the future. Derby wanted to keep out MacDonald more than he wanted anything else. Lloyd-Graeme came to agree with him. Banbury had been a Die Hard: at this stage he favoured an anti-socialist coalition under Asquith. Ullswater, the ex-Speaker, who had been suggested as a possible Prime Minister in 1918, was mentioned as head of a government of 'the eminent'.[3] Joynson-Hicks had been a member of the Cabinet as Financial Secretary to the Treasury while Baldwin kept the Exchequer for his first three months as Prime Minister: he was probably put out by Neville Chamberlain's appointment to the Exchequer in August.[4] His first brief experience of office encouraged him to think of emulating Baldwin's swift rise to the leadership. He may have discussed the possibility with Salisbury: he certainly told Derby. It seems likely that he looked forward to leading the party into an anti-socialist coalition under Asquith, Balfour or Birkenhead with whom he revived the alliance which had been in abeyance since 1921.[5] When Younger told Baldwin to go on December 8, he also was hoping for an Asquith government. At Strachey's suggestion, he next revived the idea of a McKenna-led 'Ministry of Affairs' and reached an understanding with McKenna on the 11th. When Stamfordham refused to have anything to do with it, he kept it in play as a long-stop the King could use in case MacDonald asked for a dissolution once he was in office.[6]

Baldwin, Hoare, Amery, Bridgeman, Wood, Cave, Salisbury, Lord Hugh Cecil, Geoffrey Dawson, H. A. Gwynn, Ormsby-Gore and McNeill were all opposed to Baldwin resigning immediately the election was over.[7] Apart possibly from Hoare, they all continued to oppose his withdrawal thereafter. But they were confronted with the view that the Conservative party should be agreeable to Asquith and Grey and that some sort of Coalition with them was desirable in order to prevent a Coalition being formed on a Lloyd George/Birkenhead basis instead. The desire to encourage Liberals to join the Conservative party was common to nearly all the Conservative leaders. It was felt by Neville Chamberlain, Bridgeman and Amery as much as by Lord Robert Cecil, Salisbury and Younger. What distinguished the first group was its desire to maintain a Protection and Imperial platform in order to destroy the Liberal party and attract Liberals of the second rank, and its unwillingness to attract Asquith or Grey who were Free Traders and were feared as rivals to Baldwin.[1]

Younger, Lloyd-Graeme, Joynson-Hicks, Hoare and Lord Robert Cecil had not previously had much in common. They now agreed that Baldwin had passed the point at which he could be the agent of union with the Liberals. Protection was a delicate question for the Asquitheans: Baldwin had not treated it delicately. He had sprung an election on them before they were ready for it and had allowed a Conservative to stand against Asquith at Paisley. The combination of the policy, the method of raising it, the militant way in which Amery and Neville Chamberlain had pushed it and the smell of failure had destroyed the Asquithean desire – marked in 1923 – to keep Baldwin in office.[2] It had made Asquith 'so bitter against the Conservative party ... and even more personally bitter against Baldwin' that 'he would [not] come to our party and ask us for help'.[3] It made it difficult to think that Baldwin could build a bridge across which Grey, Asquith, Gladstone or even McKenna would move into the Conservative party or into a Conservative/Liberal union at some point in the not far distant future.

In principle this did not conflict with the view taken of the Liberal party's future by Birkenhead, Horne, Balfour, Austen Chamberlain and Worthington-Evans. In both cases the idea was to facilitate union with the Asquith/Grey Liberals by removing Baldwin and dismantling Protection. In both cases the object was to do for the twentieth century what Salisbury, Hartington and Joseph Chamberlain had done for the end of the nineteenth. Neither insisted that Liberals should join the Conservative party in its present form. Either was compatible with the public demand for an arrangement to keep Labour out of office.[4] But, though both had the same objective, each sought it at the expense of the other, Younger, Salisbury and Lord Robert Cecil wanting to keep close to the Asquitheans in order to avoid Birkenhead, Lloyd George and the Old Coalition,[1] Birkenhead wanting to keep close to them in order to involve Churchill or Lloyd George[2] in a Conservative/Liberal alliance under Asquith's or Grey's leadership. Birkenhead regarded Churchill as the most significant Liberal for the future. Between December 8 and 11 he had been willing to settle for Asquith because Asquith, until he allowed MacDonald to take office, was the way to Churchill and Lloyd George and a restoration of the Coalition which Asquith, Younger, Salisbury and Lord Robert Cecil had done their best to destroy.

Before December 18 Conservatives who wanted to avoid a Liberal/Conservative Coalition wanted Baldwin to remain leader because that was the best way of avoiding it. Between Asquith's rejection of Coalition then and the reassembly of parliament in January, no acceptable successor emerged. A number of names were mentioned – by themselves or by others. Joynson-Hicks was run by Rothermere for a time and probably had a small following in the House of Commons: he carried no weight among his equals.[3] Lord Robert Cecil was clear that he could not lead the Conservative party: it is clear that he would not have minded doing so. He would have welcomed Salisbury or Devonshire, neither of whom had illusions about themselves.[4] Birkenhead was out of the question. No one seems to have mentioned Curzon. Neville Chamberlain was mentioned as a possibility by Balfour in December.[5] He had the advantage of being a link between Austen Chamberlain and the rest of the party but had been so uncompromising a Protectionist that it is difficult to believe that Balfour suggested him seriously. Balfour would have been acceptable both to Birkenhead and to Salisbury. He might at any time have had the leadership pressed upon him, though his absence in the House of Lords during the first Labour government would have made difficult what his preferences probably made undesirable.

Younger's first scheme – to make McKenna Prime Minister – assumed that the King would take the initiative: the King would take no initiative against the Labour party. His second – to put Asquith in office instead of MacDonald – depended on the King demanding from MacDonald formal assurances of Liberal support which Younger thought MacDonald could not get. This plan foundered on the same obstacle.[1] In Younger's view the only men who had the authority necessary to replace Baldwin had ruled themselves out of consideration – Balfour who was ill, deaf and probably unwilling; Austen Chamberlain against whom feeling was 'more bitter than against [Birkenhead] ... because [his] speeches in the House had always been made to help Lloyd George rather than [his own] party';[2] Horne because he was absent in America, had only been six years in the House of Commons and could probably not afford to return to full-time politics unless he was certain of being Prime Minister.[3]

Though flags were raised in favour of an arrangement with the Liberal party at Baldwin's expense, Baldwin's leadership ceased to be a matter of dispute, then, not because of any special merits he was supposed to have but because there was no one to replace him. Baldwin did nothing to prevent himself being replaced except to stay put in the country. He stayed put from about December 20 until summoned by Neville Chamberlain at the end of the first week in January.[4] On returning he looked 'much more worn out than when he went away'[5] and found it difficult to talk to anyone except Davidson who, 'though straight and honest was a fool and a bad counsellor'[6] and the object of an unsuccessful removal operation by Sir Warren Fisher.[7] Baldwin appeared depressed, impenetrable and indecisive.[8] It was really Chamberlain, Bridgeman and Jackson who made the decisions to call a Cabinet in the first week of January and a party meeting and National Union conference for February 11 and 12.[9]

Parliament reassembled on January 15. The government lost a Labour vote of confidence on the 21st and resigned on the 22nd. For a time thereafter Baldwin continued to leave the impression that his leadership was an open question or that he would ask for a vote of confidence from the Parliamentary Party.[10] As February 11 approached, this intention receded. At the Shadow Cabinet on February 7 he accepted Austen Chamberlain's suggestion that he should take the chair on the 11th. At the meeting on the 11th he did so and, after a hesitant start, made a successful speech. The Shadow Cabinet on February 7 and the two meetings of February 11 and 12 saw the return of Chamberlainites and the reuniting of the party under Baldwin's leadership. They also marked the abandonment of Protection as the front-runner in Conservative policy.

(ii)

In the ten days after the general election, the Conservative leaders had made a number of basic judgments about the future. Whether they were made as rationalisations of the need to keep Baldwin in office or out of dispassionate calculation, they produced a range of secondary attitudes as a consequence. The election results, as nearly all leading Conservatives read them, gave hope of union of some sort in the future between anti-socialist Liberals and the body of the Conservative party. Whether the procedure envisaged involved immediate Coalition or long-term union, whether it involved the Liberal leaders in a body or the destruction of the Liberal party in order to embrace second-rank Liberal politicians individually and Liberal voters en masse, no one doubted that this was so. Though many Liberals thought otherwise, all Conservatives agreed that Liberals would have in the coming months to make up their minds whether to join the Labour party or assist a constitutional, Conservative party in resisting it. Between Amery, Neville Chamberlain and Bridgeman, Salisbury, Cecil and Devonshire, Derby, Birkenhead and Austen Chamberlain, there was no disagreement about the prospect. Disagreement centred on the impact this should have on the future of Protection.

The decision to play Protection had been made and elaborated by Baldwin in consultation with Davidson, Neville Chamberlain, Lloyd-Graeme, Bridgeman and Amery, and, so far as the election itself was concerned, with Worthington-Evans in addition. The election result put an end to the existence of this group. Lloyd-Graeme and Worthington-Evans interested themselves in Hoare's and Derby's attempts to have a change of leader.[1] Hoare, Lloyd-Graeme, Worthington-Evans and Joynson-Hicks all came to believe that, Protection having been rejected, Baldwin should go, so that some other Conservative – they were not sure who – should attempt to regain the leadership of anti-socialist Constitutionalism.

The defections of Lloyd-Graeme, Joynson-Hicks and Hoare were important. None was a Free Trader. All had helped to defeat Austen Chamberlain in October 1922. Despite their Protectionism, they now thought Protection so dangerous a topic that they were willing to ditch its advocate.

This meant that Protection had only three leading supporters – Bridgeman, Neville Chamberlain and Amery, who continued to believe that an effective anti-socialist platform must combine Protection and Imperial Preference with a constructive programme of social reform. Amery wanted Baldwin to go out of office on a Protectionist programme laid down by the Milner Committee so that whoever succeeded would bear the odium of deciding whether to accept the pledges given to the Imperial Economic Conference.[1] When a Labour government became a certainty, he was even more emphatic, envisaging a situation in which heavy dumping of Ruhr steel 'and grave unemployment' followed by a Lib/Lab quarrel about Protection would compel Labour to put a Conservative government into office in order to introduce it.[2]

Neither Bridgeman nor Neville Chamberlain went as far as Amery but they shared his general line of thinking. They did not object to Liberals joining the Conservative party, but they were particularly concerned to avoid an organised invasion which would reduce their standing, break up 'our party for the benefit of a mugwump combination quite incapable of affording an effective alternative to socialism'[3] and 'dilute ... the true national philosophy ... with the ditchwater of Liberalism' which was 'disastrous in itself and the origin and breeding ground of social discontent and of the revolutionary spirit'.[4]

Just, therefore, as the timing of the Protection election in 1923 had been interpreted by the Salisbury group as a symbol of its own insignificance, so the retention of Protection afterwards became a symbol of *their* importance for Amery, Bridgeman and Neville Chamberlain. But, just as Baldwin played Birkenhead and Austen Chamberlain in November when Salisbury seemed likely to leave him and dropped Austen Chamberlain and Birkenhead when the Salisbury group agreed to stay, so now he shifted away from the Amery/Bridgeman/Neville Chamberlain group to which he had committed himself the previous September. Though he did this slowly and without any appearance of decision, he did it because there was no other way of retaining the leadership.

There was no other way because everyone of consequence apart from these three regarded them as 'extremists'[5] and agreed that the Protectionist policy had to be dismantled. Salisbury and his group had not wanted it in the first place. They wanted it abandoned in order to accommodate Liberals who would not follow Asquith in supporting MacDonald.[1] Derby had opposed it also; he was working himself into a resigning frame of mind in the event of Protection remaining.[2] Hoare and Lloyd-Graeme abandoned it.[3] Winterton abandoned it when Peel persuaded him to.[4] At the Cabinet on the King's dissolution speech on December 18, Amery, Bridgeman and Neville Chamberlain asked that it be kept intact. Curzon was in favour of dropping it. Hoare wanted to stress the McKenna duties and the Safeguarding of Industries Act instead.[5] Cave suggested a formula to keep it in as unprovocative a form as possible: nearly everyone was willing to retain the decisions of the Imperial Economic Conference. The decision was put off until after Christmas[6] when the Cabinet agreed to drop the election programme and decided to propose that parliament should adopt the Imperial resolutions of the Imperial and Economic Conference and a number of measures of social legislation.[7]

In this connection the admission of the Chamberlainites to the Shadow Cabinet on February 7 was important. Between December 8 and 19 the Chamberlainites had failed to push Baldwin out of office. Birkenhead had demanded a Liberal/Conservative Coalition,[8] but nothing had happened. As the vote of confidence approached, Birkenhead decided that he would get nowhere by waiting for Asquith.[9] On January 18 he asked Derby to tell Jackson that, if Baldwin was proposed again as leader of the party, he and Austen Chamberlain were prepared to support him and Chamberlain 'would be ready to propose him'.[10] Three days later Austen Chamberlain told Neville Chamberlain that he and Horne would not sit on the Opposition front bench unless they and Birkenhead were brought into 'the party's counsels'.[11]

At a meeting of the Commons members of the Shadow Cabinet the day the government resigned, Neville Chamberlain repeated what Austen Chamberlain had said the day before. Joynson-Hicks repeated what Birkenhead had told Derby. Wood was against allowing the Chamberlainites to return, partly because they wanted a Centre party, much more because of Birkenhead's 'moral character'.[12] Salisbury, whom Neville Chamberlain met next day at dinner, was no more enthusiastic than Wood, though he would not discuss Birkenhead's morals.[13] At the meeting of

Commons ex-ministers on the 24th, the same objection was raised and the suggestion made that Austen Chamberlain should be invited without Birkenhead.[1] It was decided, however, that Baldwin should first see Salisbury and then send invitations to all the Chamberlainites.[2]

Whether he tried to or not, Baldwin did not see Salisbury. Instead he sent a letter recording the meeting's decision, remarking that 'some of us hated the idea of receiving FE in full communion' but making it clear that, with Curzon's and Cave's agreement, Birkenhead and Austen Chamberlain would be returning.[3] Salisbury conveyed the contents of this letter to Novar, Lord Robert Cecil and Devonshire: Baldwin's private secretary conveyed them to Ormsby-Gore. They produced a recurrence of the moral outrage of the previous November on the well-known grounds of Birkenhead's 'moral habits', his Rectoral address and the damage his reputation would do the party among women, the clergy and all idealists.[4]

From about January 25 until February 3 Neville Chamberlain was abroad.[5] By the time he came back, all that Baldwin had done about the Chamberlainites was to think apprehensively of asking Austen Chamberlain to lunch at the Athenaeum. Neville Chamberlain insisted that both of them should dine at home with him and told Baldwin how to handle the dinner. The same day Baldwin had a long talk with Balfour whose preference was probably for change of leader:[6] they told each other that Baldwin must remain leader[7] and Birkenhead be included in any reconciliation that was made. Neville Chamberlain eased the way by suggesting that, if Birkenhead and Austen Chamberlain returned, Austen Chamberlain would 'think he ha[d] discharged his obligations of loyalty' to Birkenhead 'and the link which ... [bound] them would disappear'.[8]

At dinner in Neville Chamberlain's house on February 6 Baldwin, on Neville Chamberlain's instructions, explained firmly and clearly that he had decided to ask the Chamberlainites to join the Shadow Cabinet next day and to appear on the official platform on the 11th. Austen Chamberlain then suggested that Baldwin need not submit himself for re-election at the party meeting. In an atmosphere of 'increasing cordiality', Austen Chamberlain urged Baldwin to revert to the pre-Plymouth position on tariffs and spoke freely about Birkenhead's loyalty. Baldwin testified that he 'ha[d] always found [Neville Chamberlain] a rock'. Both had a laugh at the expense of Lord Robert Cecil.[1]

After what Baldwin had 'said privately about Birkenhead',[2] the decision to bring him back was a surprise. Baldwin evidently did not know what to say about it to Salisbury. After his original letter, he said nothing. Until Neville Chamberlain made him write a letter on the morning of the Shadow Cabinet, he did not tell Salisbury that all the Chamberlainites would be present.[3]

Birkenhead and Austen Chamberlain had not changed their minds about Baldwin. They had no more confidence in his ability or his future than they had had before. They offered to support him because they felt they had a better chance to manage, and replace, him by burrowing from within. When Austen Chamberlain asked the Shadow Cabinet to let Baldwin take the chair at the party meeting instead of throwing the leadership open to election, he was merely starting a new phase in Birkenhead's attempt to restore the position he had lost in October 1922.

From the return of the Chamberlainites, nevertheless, Baldwin expected advantages. It would remove whatever threat remained to his leadership. It would strengthen his hand in abandoning Protection, which the Chamberlainites had no more desire to keep than they had had to raise it in 1923. It would free him from dependence on the Salisbury group which had been tiresome before the election and whose power ended when Salisbury came to the Shadow Cabinet on February 7 in spite of Baldwin's letter.[4] It would lessen the chance of the Chamberlainites constructing a Liberal/Conservative Coalition in the event of the MacDonald government collapsing.

These expectations were not fulfilled. Until the 1924 election Baldwin was not certain of returning to office when MacDonald's government went out. Churchill, Birkenhead and others were preparing to put Balfour or Churchill in his place at the next turning-point whenever that might come.[5] Rothermere's hatred was so intense that he was thinking of supporting Henderson at the Burnley by-election the day the Chamberlainites joined the Shadow Cabinet and later had approaches made to MacDonald for an Economy drive to reduce Arms expenditure:[6] he refused to contribute to Conservative party funds in preparation for the general election.[1] Beaverbrook was in the same frame of mind. At the 1923 election Birkenhead and Austen Chamberlain prevented him putting up whole-hogging Protectionists against the Conservative party.[2] Even so he refused to give direct financial support, offering to support two needy candidates who were 'sound Imperialists instead'.[3] In 1924 he refused again because Younger would not arrange for him to support anti-Baldwin candidates.[4] He made his newspapers play down the Zinovieff letter because it would ruin the Liberal party, make Liberals vote Conservative and play into Baldwin's hands.[5]

By January 4 the Milner Committee was wound up.[6] On January 9 the Cabinet modified the draft of the King's speech and gave it to Curzon and Amery for revision.[7] On the 11th it was accepted in a version which satisfied Neville Chamberlain[8] but left Amery aggrieved because he thought that Protection had been dropped.[9] Throughout these discussions Baldwin said virtually nothing at the Cabinet meetings at which it was discussed[10] and took little or no part in the drafting. He listened to the views of others and did his best to allow a position to emerge. His speech in the confidence debate, like the King's speech itself, emasculated the policy and left it uncertain whether the general tariff would be kept or dropped.[11]

In preparing for his speeches to the party meeting and the National Union Baldwin was more self-effacing still. To Neville Chamberlain's, Amery's and Bridgeman's attempts to get him to offer a re-affirmation of Protection, he was silent.[12] He kept his distance from Amery who was not allowed to play a prominent part in the confidence debate.[13] He gave no encouragement to Neville Chamberlain who stopped offering advice when he found it was not taken.[14] At the Shadow Cabinet on February 7 – the first attended by the Chamberlainites[15] – he handed over the talking to Austen Chamberlain and allowed him to lay down a line of policy like that followed by Law at the 1922 election.[16] Apart from Amery and Bridgeman, no one said anything against it. Neville Chamberlain stopped a Hoare move to make this 'a decision not only for the immediate present but one to bind ourselves with at the next election'. Birkenhead was 'deeply ... moved' by Amery's monologue on Protection as the only positive stick with which to beat the Labour party, but 'took the line that there were too many great causes besides Protection bound up with our party which would sink with it'. Derby read out an anti-Baldwin and anti-Protectionist resolution from a Lancashire Conservative meeting which Salvidge had engineered[1] and announced that 'while he proposed to get them to drop the first part, he should support the second'. Curzon made a reproachful speech but explained that Baldwin would be 'forgiven' if

the unpleasant subject were dropped. Balfour urged the maximum of vagueness and in answer to [Amery] suggested that, if Protection and preference were once carried, there [would be] nothing left to put up against Socialism. Finally Baldwin summed up by saying 'I think I see what the general opinion is. I shall have to do some skilful tight-rope-walking on Monday for which my figure is not very well-suited'.[2]

The meeting of the Parliamentary Party and defeated ex-M.P.s at the Hotel Cecil on February 11 began with a half-hearted singing of 'He is a jolly good fellow' and ended with a motion of confidence from Balfour. Baldwin, 'tired and nervous' at first, warmed up as he went along. In a speech which Wood had a hand in drafting, he made his chief point the decision not to resubmit the general tariff to the electorate unless there was evidence that the electorate would be likely to change its mind.[3] At the National Union meeting next day he gave a more successful rendering of the same theme.[4]

The third stage in the development of negative leadership was accomplished at the Abbey by-election in March 1924 where Churchill, standing as an Independent Anti-Socialist, against the Conservative, Liberal and Labour candidates, polled almost as well as the Conservative and left the Asquithean Liberal at the bottom of the poll with 291 votes.

To Churchill the adoption of Protection and the election of 1923 were as great a shock as Lloyd George's resignation in 1922. In returning to politics in May his position had faced more ways than one, but it led most readily towards a broad-based Conservative/Liberal coalition of all the talents available to fight MacDonald. Churchill had not expected Baldwin to introduce Protection or shorten his term of office.[5] The adoption of Protection, and the election itself, forced him to treat the reunited Liberal party as the basis for the anti-socialist party of the future. Asquithean headquarters prevented him being adopted in the Cathcart division of Glasgow.[1] He was eventually adopted in Leicester West which Labour had won in 1922 on a minority vote against Asquithean and Lloyd George Liberals without a Conservative standing, and where the broad-based supra-party anti-socialist platform of his choice would have been logical if Protection had not intervened. The fight for Liberalism and Free Trade was not successful. On election day 1923 Churchill still had no seat in the House of Commons.

Between election day 1923 and the defeat of the government on January 21 1924 Churchill wanted Asquith to take office with Conservative support as soon as Baldwin was turned out. He wanted relations to develop between the Liberal and Conservative parties under a new Conservative leader and feared that 'if the Liberals [kept] the Socialists in office ... the Conservative party [would] gradually gain in strength by the reaction caused in the country [and would] be [so] sure they can win 60 or 70 seats [that] all chance of procuring their acquiescence in a Liberal government w[ould] have passed away'.[2] There was no reason why Asquith should take Churchill's views seriously. His decision to put MacDonald in office strained Churchill's links with the Liberal party. The decision to keep him there almost broke them.[3] Guest supported him.[4] Birkenhead encouraged him to return to the Conservative party. Horne told him that his future lay in leading it.[5] Derby believed Birkenhead supported Baldwin in January 1924 because Baldwin could be got rid of when the time came to make way for Churchill.[6]

It seems unlikely that Churchill intended at this time to join the Conservative party. What he intended was to construct a Liberal group which would be treated as an independent body in forming the next anti-socialist government. There is a hint that he had caught on to Birkenhead's idea of Thomas as a Centre-party figure.[7] Using Grigg as intermediary,[8] Churchill tried to take Grey with him. Grey had already been singled out as a possible seceder if Asquith put MacDonald into office. He had been at pains to distinguish the Liberal party from the Labour party,[9] and had encouraged Grigg to build up an Imperial Preference group in the Liberal party as a nucleus for alliance with anti-Baldwinian Conservatives if Baldwin refused to give up the leadership.[10] When Churchill appealed, Grey left the impression that he was tempted. He thought, however, that the attempt to detach a Liberal group was premature and seems to have been positively optimistic about the prospects for foreign policy in MacDonald's hands.[1] He refused to give public encouragement to anyone who would not stand as a Liberal.[2]

Churchill's original intention was to persuade the Abbey Conservative Association to adopt him as an Independent.[3] When the association refused either to give him special consideration[4] or to adopt him, adopting the son of the late member – General Nicholson – instead, he was persuaded by, among other 'admiring friends', Oliver Locker-Lampson,[5] to stand as an 'Independent and Anti-Socialist' without Conservative support.

In doing this Churchill was both blazing a trail and acting in desperation. He had been out of parliament for eighteen months. As the most pronouncedly anti-socialist of all the Liberal leaders, he had little hope of winning a Liberal seat without Conservative support. No one else had done what he was doing. He was blamed both for doing it when he did and for endangering the scope for others by risking a premature defeat.[6] If he had done badly, as he might have done even in a promising constituency, he would have looked ridiculous. Jackson left the impression of welcoming the idea, while emphasising that the constituency association must be free to choose.[7] Birkenhead welcomed it strongly. So did a number of Conservative back-benchers who thought his 'brilliant oratory' would put backbone into Baldwin's relations with the government.[8]

Neville Chamberlain had no such feeling. Chamberlain had played a leading part in arranging the return of Austen Chamberlain. He had raised no very strong objection to emasculating Protection. Austen Chamberlain had replaced him as deputy leader but had been so much more effective than Baldwin once he returned to the Shadow Cabinet that Neville Chamberlain was thinking of him then – and increasingly throughout the summer – as the next Prime Minister.[9] Churchill, however, was a different matter. He was 'intensely unpopular in the country' and was 'profoundly mistrusted by the working classes especially the women'.[10] He was a dogmatic Free Trader; his return might be a prelude to the return of Lloyd George which would divide the Conservative party irrevocably.[11] Chamberlain did not share

Baldwin's complaisant attitude to Churchill's candidature.[1] On March 5 he told Baldwin that a letter of support must be sent to the official Conservative at once. He was not pleased to be told a few days later that it had not been because Jackson was trying to get Churchill to withdraw. He insisted on Churchill being given a time limit, which appears to have expired on March 16.[2]

Amery mattered less than Neville Chamberlain and was more generally disliked. He had not got very far with Lloyd George. He did not get much further with Law. He did not get the Exchequer for which he asked in 1922. He did not get it when it was vacant in 1923. Nor did he get the Colonial Office. Throughout the summer of 1923 Baldwin had given him the sort of brush-off he had had previously from Lloyd George. In October he had been taken up along with Protection. By November 14 Protection had been whittled away for Salisbury's benefit. After the election Amery wanted Baldwin to remain leader and invite defeat in a blaze of positive Protectionism in the new parliament. This had not happened. The Protectionist element in the King's Speech was even thinner than in the Baldwin/Salisbury letter of November 14.

For Amery Protection was an affirmation that the Conservative party intended 'to live its own Life and have its own constructive policy'.[3] In his view 'a Conservative party which [was] not preferentialist and protectionist [was] an abortion ... just the old Coalition with a reduced and weakened personnel'.[4] The return of the Chamberlainites promised to spread the infection.[5] He thought of resigning from the Shadow Cabinet in order to form a Protectionist pressure group[6] and wrote a public letter of dissent when the general tariff was abandoned in February.[7] He then began to organise a successor to the Tariff Reform League.[8]

Amery expected the arrival of a notorious Free Trader to erode still further any possible Protectionist commitment in the future. He saw Churchill as a formidable and unscrupulous rival and the next step in a major effort by Birkenhead to get rid of Baldwin. He offered to speak, and urged others to speak, against him.[9] When asked by Baldwin whether Churchill should stand in Abbey, he said he should not.[10] When told by his brother-in-law, Greenwood, that the premature nature of Churchill's candidature would make it more difficult for constitutional Liberals to move over in a body, he thought it a 'case of true to type and Winston will desert his Liberal colleagues with the same swift decision that led him to climb over the railings at Pretoria and escape without Haldane and Le Mesurier twenty-five years ago'.[1]

Austen Chamberlain had not originally wanted Churchill to stand.[2] At a meeting of ex-ministers on March 6 he agreed that Baldwin would have to send the Conservative candidate a letter of support. He made it clear, however, that he wanted Churchill to win and got 'angry and excited ... and threatened to speak for Churchill' if Amery and Neville Chamberlain spoke for Nicholson.[3] Amery reiterated his intention of speaking for Nicholson unless there was a general ban on ministers speaking: he discovered next day that Hogg who 'was not even an ex-Cabinet minister' had been told by the Whips that he should not appear on Nicholson's platform.[4] Amery got nothing out of Baldwin except distaste for the subject and a warning that, if Amery insisted on speaking at the election, 'it would bust up the whole party'.[5] Next morning he and Neville Chamberlain received letters from the Association Chairmen to say that their meetings had been cancelled in view of the decision that no ex-Cabinet Minister should speak. They would not have been pleased if they had known that Baldwin persuaded MacDonald at the same time to get the Cabinet to affirm the convention that ex-Cabinet Ministers would not speak at by-elections.[6]

Amery and Neville Chamberlain believed that the decision to cancel their meetings had been made without reciprocal renunciation by Churchill's supporters. Since they thought, and Chamberlain told Baldwin, that 'it was all part of a general scheme to oust him from the leadership',[7] they found it difficult to understand Baldwin's 'hesitation and uncertainty'.[8] Neville Chamberlain, however, did nothing. In the next six days, Amery told Baldwin half a dozen times that *he* would send a letter of support to Nicholson unless Baldwin sent one soon. He was not satisfied by the impression Baldwin left that he preferred Jackson to get Churchill to withdraw from the election on the understanding that he would be adopted in St George's, Westminster as soon as possible afterwards. On March 14, since no letter had been sent by Baldwin, Amery sent Nicholson a letter for publication in *The Times* next morning.[9]

Late that night Baldwin, returning to Downing Street, found a letter of support from Balfour to Churchill which Balfour, who was leaving for Cannes next morning, left it to Baldwin to send or withhold as he wished. He was driven at once to Balfour's house, talked with him until after midnight and persuaded him that the letter should not be sent on the ground he had already used to Amery that, if it went, 'it would break up the party'.[1] When, therefore, Baldwin saw Amery's letter in *The Times* next morning, he was compelled, both by Balfour and by Austen Chamberlain angrily on the telephone from Sussex, to send the Balfour letter as well as a letter of his own in support of Nicholson.[2]

Churchill's defeat at the Abbey election[3] was a defeat only for himself – and only of the most temporary sort. He had demolished the claim that the Asquithean Liberals were the party of the future. Lloyd George had wound up his Coalition-Liberal organisation some months before: Churchill had shown the way to creating a substitute under his own leadership which he claimed might win fifty seats at the next election.[4] Churchill had not yet appeared on a Conservative platform: he did this at Liverpool on May 7 under guidance from Salvidge, who responded to extreme cold-shouldering from Conservative Central Office and a vendetta against him in Liverpool by encouraging a more vigorously anti-socialist platform than Baldwin probably wanted.[5]

It is doubtful whether Lord Robert Cecil approved of Churchill the more because of his defence of Free Trade.[6] Amery and Chamberlain objected to encouraging a Churchill-led Liberal group even more than they objected to Churchill himself. There was doubt about Churchill's ability to bring Liberal constituency associations with him and grumbling about the seat-concessions Conservatives would have to make.[7] Baldwin had made friendly noises about Churchill to Austen Chamberlain during the election,[8] but he had not supported him and could have abandoned him, if he had failed. Now that the movement had been established, Baldwin allowed Jackson to give it a measure of support.[9]

(iii)

From the decision to restore the Chamberlainites to the Shadow Cabinet, other decisions followed. Salisbury, Amery and Neville Chamberlain found their influence diminished. Hall was replaced by a new Chief Agent after Baldwin had got someone else to tell Hall that he was no longer needed.[1] Continuing attempts were made, without success, to create a watertight Trust for party funds.[2] Unsuccessful efforts were made – by Jackson – to raise money to buy the *Morning Post*.[3] A decision to establish a Shadow Secretariat under Amery and Lloyd-Graeme was made as soon as the party went out of office:[4] the 'free hand'[5] Amery thought he was given may well have been designed to make up for the rejection of his advice elsewhere. Departmental responsibilities were allocated to the House of Commons front bench. 'The Commons Standing Conference'[6] had Neville Chamberlain and Horne in charge of Finance, Austen Chamberlain in charge of Overseas questions and Amery, Worthington-Evans, Hoare, Wood, Tryon, Lloyd-Graeme, Bridgeman, Joynson-Hicks, Winterton and McNeill in charge of the various departments.[7] Though Salisbury was left the impression that peers would be asked to attend when matters affecting their previous departments were discussed, this did not happen even to Curzon and Lord Robert Cecil.[8] All ex-ministers were members of the 'Leader's Conference' which met from time to time as a Shadow Cabinet.[9] But it is clear that Baldwin did not much like his 'ready-made Cabinet with too many peers':[10] detailed day-to-day policy in the House of Commons was conducted to Salisbury's annoyance without much consultation with him.[11] Baldwin seems to have spent much time with Joynson-Hicks[12] who thought it 'his chief duty ... to stick by Baldwin and get him out of the mess ... he would get into by every speech he made'.[13] His ambition to be leader may have seemed as great a danger to Baldwin as Joynson-Hicks thought it was himself.

Baldwin's defects as an opposition leader did nothing to improve the security of his position. Austen Chamberlain played straight once he rejoined the front bench, but Neville Chamberlain's reaction to being out of favour was to think of Austen Chamberlain or himself as possible successors.[14] Birkenhead continued to criticise the 'imbecility' of Baldwin's leadership; his attempts to butter up Amery and Salisbury[15] on the rebound from Baldwin were accompanied by articles in the *Sunday Express* at the same time as Beaverbrook and Rothermere subjected Baldwin to highly personal attacks.[16] Baldwin was extremely annoyed.[17] He gave a

newspaper interview, reported in *The People* on May 18, in which
he was supposed to have said that Beaverbrook and Rothermere
were 'both men I would not have in my house' and that 'Lord
Birkenhead, if his health does not give way, will be a liability to
the Party'.[1] The reporter concerned was doubtless as 'untrust-
worthy' as Austen Chamberlain believed and 'had' no doubt
'been warned off Downing Street as long ago as Bonar Law's time'.[2]
It is clear that Baldwin, whether innocently or not, said a good
many unfriendly things about Birkenhead and remained silent
while the reporter said others that were more unfriendly still.[3]

The decision to encourage Liberal accessions did not in Baldwin's
mind involve Coalition. Later in the year he considered Coalition
between himself and Asquith if the election results made it
necessary, but, except in these circumstances, Coalition was what
he wanted to avoid.[4] He wanted to avoid it both in the form
envisaged by the Chamberlainites and in the form – under Grey
if the MacDonald government fell – which Lord Robert Cecil
decided was even more important than in 1921 once it became
clear that the Liberal party would not survive and his version of
the Hatfield influence would not be paramount in the Conservative
party.[5] Baldwin wanted to destroy the Liberal party and to accommodate Liberals its destruction would render homeless. At the
same time he wanted to build up the Labour party, or at any rate
to curb the Conservative party's desire to attack it.[6] Whether
because he wished to deprive MacDonald of an excuse for holding
an election on a tough Labour ticket or because they had a common
interest in destroying the Liberal party, the impression he left of
having 'formed himself into a "Mutual Admiration Society"'
with him was accurate.[7]

The corollary of the decision to accommodate anti-socialist
Liberals was the construction of a rhetoric and programme to
make accommodation possible. This involved from one point of
view the suppression of Amery and in some respects of Neville
Chamberlain, and insistence that they should not commit the
party to Protectionist policies to which Liberals would not wish
to be committed. On the other hand 'accommodation' necessitated
a series of careful statements about the McKenna duties and the
Safeguarding of Industries Act. The abandonment of Protection at
party meetings on February 11 and 12 had been sufficient for the

Shadow Cabinet. More formal statements were needed if Liberal accessions were to be thought of. 'Facilitation' was both a limiting factor, demonstrating that a Liberal was renouncing the Liberal party, and concessionary in the sense that the Conservative party was changing its policy in order to accommodate Liberals. The degree of accommodation envisaged varied, however, with the view taken of the Conservative party's future. Austen Chamberlain and Hoare were active from January 1924 in providing terms loose enough to accommodate any Liberal who would declare himself an anti-socialist. The reform and stability rhetoric and programme of their choice[1] was designed to by-pass the contentions raised by consideration of the McKenna duties, Safeguarding of Industries, Protection and so on. In Austen Chamberlain's mind, if not in Hoare's, the object was to bring in any Liberal who might be likely to dissent from the Liberal party's support for Labour – even including Asquith himself.

This also was Baldwin's attitude – with the difference that in practice he was much less forthcoming than Austen Chamberlain. Baldwin was as willing as Chamberlain to abandon Protection when he found that no one of consequence wanted to keep it: he was as willing to accommodate the Churchill/Guest contingent if that could be done without exertion or inconvenience. It is not clear, however, that he and Jackson worked very hard to find Churchill a seat.[2] Baldwin imposed strict conditions on Liberal adhesion in general. Asquith's attack not only on Protection but also on the McKenna duties, Safeguarding and the Paris Resolutions in the Protection debate on June 18 was designed to draw the line from his side. It provided an opportunity for Baldwin to do the same.[3] After negotiation with Austen Chamberlain, Churchill and Hoare which culminated in a four-sided dinner-party at Hoare's house in July, Baldwin was told by the others what form of words he should use. Chamberlain expected his speech at Lowestoft to be a clarion call to anti-socialist Liberals. In fact it not only attacked Lloyd George and made the McKenna duties and Safeguarding conditions of co-operation, but made of the Conservative party's belief in Imperial Preference the occasion for an appeal to Imperially-minded Labour members[4] to come over too.[5]

Baldwin realised the importance of going through the motions of Liberal accommodation. He – or Jackson – was contemplating a limited and secret 1922-style arrangement with the Asquitheans for agreed withdrawals as between the parties. He was willing within limits to accommodate the Churchill group. He may even have allowed Jackson to make arrangements to prevent constituency associations opposing Asquith, Simon and Lloyd George.[1] But Baldwin did not want Lloyd George. He wanted neither open Coalition nor a Coalitionist deluge. He probably wanted what Law got in 1922 – a situation in which large numbers of Liberals were dependent on Conservative support.

Within this framework Baldwin's object in 1924 was to avoid contentious issues and present a reassuring face to anyone who might wish to prevent a recurrence of the Labour government for which Asquith would be held responsible. He did his best to avoid Shadow Cabinet discussion of Amery's and Neville Chamberlain's Fair Trade Union for Safeguarding British Work and Wages: when compelled by Neville Chamberlain to have a discussion, he did his best to avoid the issue.[2] In the Preference debate on June 18 – the 'grand occasion' – for which Amery had been waiting, Lloyd-Graeme, Tryon, Baldwin and Austen Chamberlain spoke instead of Amery, who was told that Baldwin, 'though genuinely sorry ... had been talked into it' by Austen Chamberlain.[3] In relation to Ireland also Baldwin took pains to avoid a situation in which conflict could damage the anti-socialist front.

When the Irish Treaty was signed in 1921, Baldwin had supported it, not just silently as a Cabinet Minister might but in an anti-Die Hard newspaper article as a harbinger of the 'way to peace'.[4] The treaty, however, fell short of a settlement. It left the exact boundary between Ulster and the Free State to be settled by a Boundary Commission which was not given exact terms of reference. The ratification of the treaty by both parliament and the Oireachtas of the Irish Free State left the Boundary Commission question outstanding.

The Boundary Commission, as envisaged by Article 12 of the treaty, was designed to consist of three members, one to be nominated by the Irish Free State, one by the British government and one by the government of Northern Ireland. The Northern Ireland government, however, had not been party to the treaty:

its leaders had had the strongest suspicion of the Boundary Commission clause. They were determined from the start that they would have nothing to do with it unless it was clear that only minor frontier rectifications would be admissible. Throughout 1923 they declined to concede anything. As a result the Labour government decided to ask the Judicial Committee of the Privy Council to decide whether the Commission could operate without Ulster's consent. On receiving the decision that it could not, the government decided to introduce a new bill to empower the British government to appoint an Ulster representative.

The government did this because it had no wish to face coercion of the Free State if it occupied Fermanagh and Tyrone. It did it also, no doubt, as an aspect of its attempt to behave in a liberal and progressive way. At the same time there was a marked reluctance to bring the Irish question to the boil and considerable fear of the damage to be expected to the government's reputation if it failed to keep down the temperature. Both Thomas and MacDonald went to great lengths to maintain relations with Craig and Cosgrave. In this they had much in common with Baldwin.

The Labour leaders did not think of Ireland as a good election issue for themselves: Baldwin did not think it a good issue for him. Though it is unlikely that the Labour leaders would have played it in this way, Baldwin feared the prospect of an election arising from a situation in which the government's bill, passed with Liberal support, had been thrown out by the Conservative majority in the House of Lords in deference to Ulster's wishes.

No less than the Coalitionists themselves, Law and Baldwin had rejected House of Lords reform. It found no place in the 1922 and 1923 election manifestoes. Law mentioned it during the 1922 campaign, but he did nothing about it in office. With the arrival of a major Labour party in the House of Commons, there was every reason for avoiding a challenge on a question which combined both Ireland and the House of Lords.[1] Baldwin did his best to avoid it. Despite an assurance to Selborne about the House of Lords in April[2] and a public statement in defence of Ulster in early August,[3] he took pains to persuade Craig to accept the bill on the understanding that the government would appoint a suitable Ulster representative – i.e. Carson[4] – to the Commission. After extensive negotiation with Carson, Wood, Salisbury and Guinness, he pressed Churchill, Balfour and Birkenhead to press Lloyd George to acquiesce on condition that he would not be opposed by the Conservative party in the Carnarvon boroughs at the next election. A memorandum written by Birkenhead when Lord Chancellor, limiting the Commission's powers, became the occasion and excuse for Ulster's acquiescence.[1]

(iv)

In the course of 1924 it came to 'seem likely that events [would] shortly place the Conservative party ... in the position ... of being the only effective opponent of Socialism'.[2] In these circumstances the essay-writers among Conservative leaders began to search for something to say which was not just a defence of wealth and property and did not merely repeat Birkenhead's demand to 'resist Socialism or perish',[3] but made a serious attempt to meet 'the necessity' they 'enormously [felt] of trying to illumine [their] practice with some glow of faith'.[4]

The first to start was Sir Samuel Hoare. In the month following the 1923 election, Hoare put into circulation his variant of the idea that the business of the Conservative party was to combine social and agricultural reform and a 'position as the party of stability with as broad and easy a bridge as possible' both for the Chamberlainites to whom he talked much and for all other sorts of possible adherent as well.[5] This was, Austen Chamberlain told him, the opinion he had held since 1920 in view of the need, induced by Asquith's support for MacDonald, 'to smash the Liberal party two thirds of [which was] already Labour in all but name'.[6]

Hoare's formulation, though bare, was typical. So was Wood's pamphlet on *Conservative Beliefs* in which the instincts of reverence, independence and comradeship were offered as the basis of a Conservatism which had it 'in its power to make an appeal nobler and more potent than any other party' provided 'its disciples should take the trouble to reflect upon the origins and implications of their beliefs and ... be willing to preach their Gospel with energy and conviction'.

The Conservative who took the problem most seriously was Neville Chamberlain. Throughout 1921 and 1922 his dislike of

Lloyd George was supplemented by a fear that none of the Coalition Conservatives had any constructive policy to offer either in office or at an election.[1] In 1922 his suggestions included a miscellaneous programme of taxation rearrangement, Colonial Preference, rating relief for agriculture, Poor Law reform, the secret ballot, the political levy and the legitimisation of children of unmarried parents – all of which were 'constructive without involving heavy expenditure'.[2]

In 1922, however, Neville Chamberlain did not matter much. It was not until his success with housing in 1923 that his period as a policy-maker began. He was close to Baldwin during the Protection period, had much to do with the conduct of foreign policy[3] and was sorry to see Protection go in early 1924. Despite being out of favour, he contributed much to the 'social reform programme' which was offered at the 1924 election. He wrote *Aims and Principles*.[4] He set up a committee on municipal reform of which Hoare was made chairman[5] and another to examine the 'superficial' proposals Lloyd George had made about the use of Power.[6] He seems to have offered Monsell and Jackson a new version of the policy for Agriculture.[7] He shared the contempt, common in the Baldwin Shadow Cabinet, for the 'insufferably conceited' Liberals whom it was desirable to destroy.[8]

The decision to be the party of resistance to Socialism did not, paradoxically, produce much animus against the Labour party. The Labour party was assumed to be the natural opposition – the embodiment of a possible view of social and political duty which should be treated with the respect due to a real faith by which people could be moved. It was for the Liberal party – its variety, its insincerity and its tendency to run away – that the real animus was reserved. The desire to destroy the Liberal party had been a cloak for immediate political purposes immediately after the election, but it was not merely tactical. There was a genuine dislike of Liberal superciliousness which many of Baldwin's colleagues had inherited from the period of party conflict between 1906 and 1914. These feelings issued in reluctance to make special arrangements to accommodate anti-socialist Liberals and a judgment that they could be left to join the Conservative party if they wanted to. It issued also in a feeling that there was a measure of affinity between the Conservative party, properly led and presented, and the higher purposes pursued by the Labour party. These feelings would not perhaps have come to the surface if the Liberal party had not looked ready for demolition. There can be no mistaking the desire felt by Wood, Neville Chamberlain, Lord Robert Cecil, Ormsby-Gore and, indeed, Amery to convince themselves that they were more sympathetic than Liberals could be to the only major political force which had emerged since the war.

The intention was not just to be the party of resistance but to show sensitivity to part of the atmosphere which Labour had created. This did not invariably mean making a point of accepting trades unionism as a necessary part of the scene, though it usually did mean that, and in the case, for example, of Barlow included the belief that there ought to be more trades unionism not less.[1] The playing of the national interest was, indeed, a contentless Disraelian conception which enabled its proponents to be as pragmatic as they wished or the situation demanded. It almost always involved an attempt to emphasise what was thought of as the party's higher idealism and to show that a party whose purpose was to protect the nation's existing institutions was neither a society for the reduction of income tax nor solely interested in the power politics celebrated in Birkenhead's Rectoral address, but had policies and sympathies as comprehensive as those offered by the Labour party without being marred by Socialism's dangerous concern with class conflict.[2]

Baldwin's rhetoric in 1924 contained the same warnings against abusing the Labour party as he had given in 1923,[3] but there were differences. It was in fact a reversion to the stability rhetoric of November 1922 with the addition that on this occasion Baldwin made a virtue of necessity by claiming as evidence of his unpolitical honesty the fact that he had first consulted the people about Protection and then, when they did not like it, had abandoned it.[4] He stressed the contrast between himself and the other two parties by playing national defence and Imperial unity, combining them with the claim that, in Singapore and India, and in relation to naval expenditure, the Conservative party alone would refuse to allow 'any weakening ... of the defensive forces of the Empire'.[5]

In case a Die Hard Imperialism should be too much to bear, Baldwin 'ha[d] to see that the heart of the nation ... the key of the empire' was educated 'to bring out the brains of the country [and] use them for the benefit of our race and of mankind'. He claimed for the Conservative party a sense of the 'unselfish service and devotion' which moved men to 'raise the standard of life ... and ideals' in a Europe through whose 'despair and materialism ... a new life [was] bursting'.[1] The picture of 'thousands of girls and young women tramping ... the streets to ... work' during a bus strike suggested that 'sympathy ... for their fellow-men and fellow-women and ... for themselves ... last of all' was a lesson that strikers had to learn.[2] Peace and understanding in industry,[3] Shakespeare's 'magic' as 'redolent of the English soul ... and people',[4] honour, uprightness and perseverance as the gifts of the English race,[5] the responsibility of youth, the loss of the lost generation and the need in the new one for 'a breath of new life ... the spirit of service ... clear brains and clean and sound bodies'[6] constituted the essence of the higher atmosphere which the Unionist party was trying to create. At a Non-Conformist Unionist League luncheon organised by Sir Kingsley Wood, Baldwin competed with Austen Chamberlain in adopting the mantle of their 'non-conformist ancestors'. Now that traditional Liberalism was dead he offered 'a natural haven of rest' for the 'independent and sturdy individualism' of ex-Liberal nonconformists who had seen 'religion' and 'civilization ... bending and cracking ... in the Western world' and knew that 'whatever we may have done in the past, today and for the future all men of religious spirit, whatever they may call themselves, must cling together to hold fast what they have' in the fight against 'Socialism as expressed by the extreme wing of the Labour party'.[7]

Baldwin, no doubt instinctively, avoided extravagance of language. In respect of the 'dangers of socialism' he could do so because Conservative newspapers and many of his followers were extravagant on his behalf. He could pitch his appeal at a level of positive idealism because others had already established the suspicion that 'Socialism' was 'a threat', socialists unpatriotic and the Labour party an instrument of revolutionary Bolshevism. His speeches, anti-political in temper[8] and deliberately lacking in positive programme, made up the positive education of the nation's imagination which he offered in place of the cynicism of Lloyd George, the deadness of Asquith and the 'impracticability' of

Socialism. With the addition of Campbell, Zinovieff and the Russian question, they became the basis for electoral propaganda at the general election in October.

The decision to destroy the Liberal party involved decisions at certain points that the Labour party should be kept in office even when the Liberals refused to support it. There was a genuine attempt to ensure that government was conducted responsibly. There was a desire to leave the public the impression that the Labour party was as competent as a Liberal government would be. There was a belief that collectivist Liberals were more likely to form their own connections with Labour if it was clear that the Liberal party could not turn MacDonald out at will. There was a feeling that the best way to prevent a Labour victory at the next election would be by giving it enough rope to hang itself. At each point at which the Labour government was treated with consideration, one or more of these feelings operated. Cave urging Haldane on December 11 to join MacDonald was one example. The evening Hankey spent at Haldane's house on Baldwin's instructions unveiling defence policy a week later was another. Amery's desire to make it clear in advance that the Conservative party would not turn out the Labour party in order to put Asquith in, the belief that Conservatives had a common interest with Labour in breaking up the Liberal party and the absolute refusal to consider taking office again if MacDonald was turned out, were further aspects of the general policy. Its purpose of course was to build up the Labour government in order to knock it down. In October 1924 it was knocked down very hard indeed. But there can be no mistaking Baldwin's desire to demonstrate to MacDonald his willingness to treat him as he would treat any other party leader and to afford him such assistance as would help him destroy the Liberal party, blunt the sharp edge of Labour policy and prevent the government collapsing before Baldwin was in a position to prevent a Coalition succeeding.[1]

Asquith's attack on Wheatley in the course of the Popular debate on February 13 was taken by Conservatives as an indication that Asquith and Lloyd George expected to turn out MacDonald and take office at once.[2] Horne tried to persuade the Conservative front bench to let them do this. The Conservative front bench decided to let it be known that they 'had not the slightest intention of supporting a Liberal government and would ... sooner have Ramsay MacDonald than Asquith'.[1] Asquith thereupon made a humiliating change of front both because his party insisted and because his electoral prospects were so bad that he could not afford to turn out MacDonald unless he could be certain of forming a government of his own. This pattern was repeated. No effort was spared in criticising the government when it made proposals Conservatives did not like. No hesitation was shown in voting against it when divisions were pressed. But MacDonald found the Conservatives very friendly: despite Amery's fisticuffs with Buchanan, his followers experienced from Conservatives little of the rancorous heckling to which Masterman, for example, amongst Liberals subjected some of the less literate Labour ministers.[2]

On February 21, for example, the Conservatives had intended to mount an attack on the 50% reduction the government proposed in the naval programme Amery had announced before he left office in January. They would have mounted the attack if they had not been forestalled by Pringle's and Kenworthy's assault from the Liberal benches on the ground that the programme, so far from being too small, was too big. MacDonald, 'listened [to by] his followers in absolute stillness, not disapproving, but ... very much impressed by his domination of the situation ... gave Pringle a good dressing down' and was supported by Amery who 'regrett[ed] that the programme had been so much cut down'. The Liberals, however, refused to let the matter drop. When the division occurred, 'practically the whole Labour party and a score of Liberals went into one Lobby [with the Conservative party] and seventy Liberals and two or three Labour men into the other'.[3]

The government was defeated for the first time on March 13, though the Conservative party once more helped it to win a division against Liberal opposition that evening.[4] During discussion of the naval estimates, the Conservative party opposed the government's policy but supported the government in a division over the proposal to cut back the Singapore base on March 18.[5]

It is not clear at what point the Conservative leaders decided that it no longer mattered whether MacDonald was defeated. In the early months the Baldwin circle positively wanted to keep the government in office lest a Coalition or Asquith government should succeed if it fell.[1] Baldwin wanted to avoid a change of government over the Budget: he had more general reasons for not wanting the government to fall before the end of the summer session. He worked during the recess to ensure that Ireland did not become an issue: in this he succeeded. But the Campbell case supplied one of the best occasions he could expect for defeating the government: on the return of parliament in October he took it. The Asquitheans made the same judgment and decided to press the Campbell case as well, realising too late that the government intended to go out of office on this question and proposed, on being defeated, to dissolve parliament instead of resigning. Baldwin had no intention of allowing a change of government without an election. It required only careful parliamentary manoeuvring and certain Royal decisions to ensure that the Liberal party did not escape the election none of its members wanted.[2]

CONCLUSION: THE SIGNIFICANCE OF THE POLITICAL STRUGGLE

'In the beauty of the earth, decking itself anew with leaf and flower, we see the symbol of our own movement. Within our common life there are forces creating for all a world at once beautiful and happy. May Day calls to the people of every nation to unite and be glad that there is promise in life.

This year still, May Day finds millions, at home and abroad, unhappy, oppressed, fearful. At the same time, it brings with it the knowledge that, just as the hard crust of the earth is breaking and opening, so, throughout the world, the old evil order of distrust, hate, division, is being attacked by the new order of co-operation and service. The truth of Socialism is waking the people to a realisation that it is their common work that can alone enrich and glorify the earth ... Labour is marching on.'

MacDonald, May Day message 1924, *Daily Herald*, May 1

'What I want to impress upon you is that, with this enormous new and young electorate, a knowledge of which no party can yet be said to possess, the tendency will be for them to go to the party which offers them an attractive case, put with great persuasion and with great enthusiasm – to the party which, as far as possible, can save them the trouble of thinking.'

Baldwin at National Unionist Association Annual Dinner, Hotel Cecil, June 29 1923, *The Times*, June 30

'What a wonderful place this old country is.'

G. R. Lane-Fox to Baldwin, October 31 1924 on the election results

In the twenty chapters of this book we have watched the process of polarisation as it developed between 1920 and 1924. We have watched Lloyd George being toppled by the Conservative sense that he could not stave off, damp down or bamboozle the sentiment out of which the Labour movement had been made. We have watched the struggle for the succession. We have seen Derby attempting to strike but never succeeding. We have watched Grey wishing to strike but never summoning the courage to do so. We have watched vain efforts being made by Lord Robert Cecil, Birkenhead, Churchill, Austen Chamberlain and Joynson-Hicks.

413

We have watched Balfour coming to terms with the twentieth century and have seen Birkenhead being in succession hated as a disreputable tyrant and ostracised as a nasty smell. What we have seen we have seen in the context of an overwhelming agreement amongst all non-socialist leaders that the major problem of the future was to provide leadership and create conditions in which the existing social order could be preserved.

With the election of 1924 polarisation was complete. The Labour party lost 40 seats. Over 400 Conservatives were returned and only 40 Liberals. This was a triumph for Baldwin. It gave him a parliamentary majority of over 200 which he had won without compromising himself with any of his enemies. It left him 'the dispenser of patronage'[1] and source of power and free to do exactly as he liked.

The government he constructed was almost as broad-based as the Coalition. Devonshire paid for inadequacy in office and Free Trade intransigence, Derby for trying to strike down Baldwin without the ability to do so. Like Novar, Barlow and Sanders, their ministerial careers were ended for good. There was irony, or perhaps malice; Baldwin 'forgetting' to tell Horne – what he had promised Austen Chamberlain – that as Minister of Labour Horne would have the same salary as when Chancellor of the Exchequer;[2] Lord Robert Cecil being offered, and taking, the second post at the Foreign Office under Austen Chamberlain. Horne and Crawford refused what they were offered. It is possible that Balfour was offered nothing because of a 'sense of gaucherie and inferiority' which Baldwin felt in his presence 'especially since the meeting at the Carlton Club'.[3]

Curzon at last was removed from the Foreign Office and replaced by Austen Chamberlain. Birkenhead was put into cold storage at the India Office. Austen Chamberlain, Birkenhead, Gilmour and Worthington-Evans were included from one side along with Neville Chamberlain, Hoare, Joynson-Hicks, Bridgeman, Salisbury and Amery from the other. In Churchill there was an ex-Liberal Chancellor of the Exchequer after McKenna, also an ex-Liberal, had refused it. Steel-Maitland, who had thought of becoming a Liberal in 1921, became Minister of Labour. If the Liberal contingent was smaller than it would have been under Lloyd George, it established that Baldwin, once powerful enough to do so, would attempt to command all the forces Lloyd George had tried to lead from 1920 onwards.

It is often implied, and Baldwin said, that his relations with the Chamberlainites were determined by fear of Lloyd George. Hatred was probably more prominent than fear but to some extent no doubt this was true. By mid-1923, however, Lloyd George mattered extremely little. It is simpler to assume that Baldwin wanted the Chamberlainites back in 1924 not just because of the danger if they were left out but because they were people he knew he could handle and with whom he hoped therefore to feel at ease.

Baldwin was a Midland iron-master who thought his ' "social circumstances made him a better judge of popular opinion" ' than anyone ' "born" ', like Salisbury, ' "in the purple" '.[1] He had no spontaneous sympathy for Derby, Curzon, Devonshire and Balfour who were relics of the aristocratic Conservatism which Joseph Chamberlain had destroyed. These were the people who suffered most when Baldwin won in 1924. They would have suffered earlier if the Chamberlainites had been willing to take Baldwin as their man. Baldwin could not have restored the Chamberlainites to office if he had wanted to in 1923: he did not want to because he did not trust them to support him if he did. It was not until he emerged as a dominating figure in November 1924 that he did so in a government which, in spite of the presence of Wood, Percy and the two Cecils in a Cabinet of ' "middle-class monsters" ' and ' "pure party politicians" ',[2] gave smaller scope than previous Conservative governments to the hierarchy which the great Salisbury had left.

With the formation of the 1924 government we reach the point at which the politics of resistance envisaged by so many politicians since 1920 had been established in viable party form. The question that has to be asked is: What significance had the resistance platform for the purposes of the politicians who used it?

To some readers it will seem that no problem exists – that resistance was a natural reaction to the threat presented by the Labour party. This is an attractive view which rests on the assumption that the Conservative leaders disliked or distrusted the Labour party and regarded it as their chief business to do it down; and this in an important sense was true of many of their followers, even if it was not quite true of them.

In some respects, of course, resistance was the major factor and the obvious objective. Many of the eight million voters who voted Conservative in 1924 doubtless did so because they had been persuaded that MacDonald was a Communist and the Labour party a Bolshevik conspiracy. Much of the propaganda with which the Conservative party approached the electorate matched in the extremity of its accusations the most extreme accusations levelled by Direct Action at the society it was attacking.

In presenting it as an adequate characterisation of resistance, however, there are a number of difficulties. It does not explain the greater dislike which some Conservatives had for the Liberal party. It does not take account of the sympathy between Baldwin and MacDonald. It does not encompass the repeated objections raised by leading Conservatives to Birkenhead's and Austen Chamberlain's claim that 'Labour was the common foe'. It does not embrace a muddled ambiguity towards the Labour question of which Derby provides an illustration.

Derby is worth consideration because he exposes in a raw and obvious way the factors which operated in the minds of political leaders. In the early 1920s Derby was one of the richest men in England. He was both a rural and an urban landowner. He was a great figure, probably the greatest figure, in Lancashire. He was a Conservative whose prominence in the Conservative party was a less significant part of his public position than his racehorses, his houses and his possessions. He knew everything and everybody in Lancashire and in some moods affected to embody all their various opinions.

Like many men of comparable position, Derby wanted the outward marks of political success which had not been satisfied by membership of every Conservative government since 1895. Lloyd George made him War Minister in December 1916: his appointment to the Paris embassy in 1918 was a mark of inadequacy in that rôle. He was a supporter of the Coalition at the Coupon election and played a part in selling Lloyd George to the Conservative party when Lloyd George's stock was at its peak. When Derby returned to England in 1920, Lloyd George's reputation was cracking. He refused office then. He refused it again in March 1922 on the ground that 'he thought he could be of more use to [Lloyd George] outside', though Beaverbrook, who knew him well thought he refused because Northcliffe told him to.[1] At various points in the next few years, Derby saw a boundless future for himself. He was one of the leading movers in the events which brought the Coalition to an end.

When Law took office Derby did not get what he wanted. Birkenhead tried to persuade him that he was the answer to the nation's prayers but he did nothing to prevent Baldwin becoming Prime Minister. It was not until Protection was adopted that he began to treat Baldwin as though he was Lloyd George. For Derby December 6 1923 was a moment of truth.

Derby's attitude to Labour had not previously been hysterical. His attitude to trades unions and individual Labour leaders had been as genial and accommodating as the King's from much the same social temper and for much the same sort of reason. He knew some of the Labour leaders at first hand and regarded them as part of the Lancashire scene. He knew what the working classes had done in the war. He had played a moderating part during the Coal disputes in 1921. With a Labour government imminent in 1923 he lost his head. Under prompting from Birkenhead, who once more tempted him with the Prime Ministership, he made the outburst we examined in chapter XVII in which all the worst fears entertained by any property-owner at the possibility of a Labour government were laid out at length.

Derby did not do this because it represented his settled view, not least because he had no settled view. He was, as Austen Chamberlain said of Curzon, 'not a man to go tiger-shooting with'. We know what happened to his promise to fight 'for all I am worth'[2] against the election in November 1923. Throughout the years discussed in this book, anxiety to be Prime Minister blunted the effect of constant purpose. His outburst was made because he thought Baldwin was finished and could be finished off if Derby embodied the widespread desire to avoid a Labour government. Three months later he agreed that its period of office had done the Labour party damage. This is not what he said at the time. The major question is whether the accommodation offered by the normal Derby or the hysteria of this moment reveal his real state of mind, and any answer must take account of the fact that he held a variety of opinions and gave prominence to each according to their relevance to the tactical situation.

In this, however, he was not unusual. Each politician entertained a variety of opinions which became practical commitments in the light of the possibilities including an instinct for the possibilities for himself or the various sorts of national unity to which he or his party might come to be committed. The Conservative action against Lloyd George in 1922 was an attempt to rescue the Conservative party from disintegration. It was also a revolt against a tone and manner. But the tone and manner had been accepted so long as they were successful electorally and were questioned only when they ceased to be. Even then, revolt did not succeed easily. It would probably not have succeeded at all if Salisbury, Hoare, Hills, Ormsby-Gore and Davidson had not been capable of office and been freed by involuntary officelessness to express feelings which they would not have expressed so clearly otherwise, and if Baldwin, Curzon, Peel, Griffith-Boscawen, Younger, Bridgeman, Sanders, Amery and others had not had reasons for feeling that their prospects were being neglected and their opinions ignored and that the ship in which they were sailing was sinking visibly.

The same is true even where purpose was not infirm nor vanity dominant. Salisbury's revolt before 1922 was a claim that the old Conservative party knew more about the working classes than the sort of people Lloyd George had involved in government: it is difficult to believe that it would have been made if Salisbury had been given office since 1916. His revolt against Baldwin in 1923 was a reaction to the memories Protection aroused among Cecils and a similar assertion about the relationship between the electorate and the Conservative party. It was also a result of the feeling that the régime Salisbury had helped to establish was giving too little attention to his views. The development of Baldwin's hatred of Lloyd George, again, is best explained by assuming that he nearly retired in 1921 because he was too old to get anywhere, did not think, until the middle of 1922, that he ever would and did not decide until September that the best way to get on was to allow his 'real feelings' about Lloyd George to be expressed. Situational compulsions of this sort, manifest in the cases of Neville Chamberlian, Amery, Gladstone, MacDonald and Asquith, and which even Maxton may be found accepting as a fact of life, stand proxy for more general imputations.[1]

The point about them, however, is not just that they were factors which affected the relations between politicians, but that they were the chief reason for the five-year delay that occurred in the establishment of a party of resistance. The need for such a party had been generally understood by the beginning of 1920: the next four years is a record of failure in establishing it. Lloyd George's, Law's and Birkenhead's attempt failed in 1920 because Coalition Liberals and Conservatives would not support one another. Law's failed in 1922/23 because the Law government and the Chamberlainites would not work together. Baldwin failed in the summer of 1923 because neither Grey, McKenna nor the Chamberlainites thought he would survive. The Chamberlainites failed after the Protection election because Baldwin's Conservatives hated Birkenhead, and Asquith and Grey refused to support him. In early 1924 Austen Chamberlain expected the Conservative party to be in opposition for the rest of his working life. If the Labour Left had not forced MacDonald into a corner in August, MacDonald could have gone on governing until he found a favourable moment for an election. There is no reason to think that Labour would have done particularly badly, some reason to think that the Liberals would have done better than they did and a possibility that Baldwin would not have done well enough to be relieved of the Chamberlainite threat.

In this respect it is important to avoid assuming, as a permanent factor in these years, that the Liberal party was doomed. Between 1919 and 1922 the Asquitheans tried to act as an alternative party of opposition: almost anything might have happened if there had been two Conservative parties at the 1922 election. In 1922/23 not only Liberals but some Conservatives believed that Liberals could regain from Labour the position Labour had gained from them. At the end of 1923 it was thought that the Liberal party might replace the Conservative party as, indeed, it might have done if Baldwin had allowed Asquith to take office. Even if the Conservative party was the strongest force at each election, a Liberal government in office in 1924 or at any time in a prolonged 1924 parliament might have made a significant difference both to the Liberal vote at a general election and the

Liberal party's standing in relation to the Chamberlainites afterwards.

One must not be misled by the consistency of Conservative success in 1918, 1924 and 1931. In 1918 only a small proportion of the electorate voted: there had been no Conservative victory since 1900. Between 1919 and 1924 advances and recessions in the votes obtained by all parties at elections and by-elections made prediction difficult. Between 1926 and 1931 there were five years of uncertainty rendered acute by the enfranchisement of younger women. Throughout this period there were increases in the electoral rolls which carried the voting electorate from 10 million in 1918 to 22 million in 1929. There were complicated electoral effects connected with the large number of three-cornered constituency contests, the slow development of the voting habit among the women who had received the vote in 1918 and the enormous and unpredictable variations caused by the three-party system. At each election each major party, apart from the Liberal party in in 1924, polled more votes than at the election before. In 1918 and 1931 the Conservative party was part of a Coalition. At no election except in 1931 did it obtain more than half the actual vote. It was never supported by more than half the qualified electorate.

Moreover, electoral statistics by themselves explain nothing. They do not explain the power of the Liberal party which, despite the loss in 1924 of more than a quarter of the votes polled in 1923, obtained more votes in 1929 than ever before or since. Nor do they explain its decline, which was a more contingent matter than the statistics suggest and was not contained in the pre-war situation. In the pre-war Liberal party there were many Trojan horses. The war destroyed many beliefs and some of the persuasiveness of organised nonconformity. If, however, there had been no division at the top, there is no reason to suppose that the trimming leadership given by Asquith or Lloyd George could not have continued indefinitely. There would have been serious conflict. The atmosphere would have changed. There would have been leftward shifts. Some Liberals would have left when they occurred. But what destroyed the Liberal party was not the inevitability of the Labour predominance in an enlarged electorate but a combination of the loss of Ireland in 1918, the timing of general elections, splits among the leaders, depression in the Liberal party at large, the will of the Conservative party and the energy, ruthlessness and intelligence of Labour propaganda.

What Labour did between 1919 and 1924 was to create an atmosphere which no politician could ignore. What the Conservative leaders did was to respond, not resentfully like the Liberal party towards a prodigal son, but with a coolness which implied reasonable disagreement about the best way to achieve objectives which were held in common.

This was only one possible reaction. More vigorous reactions were demanded, and given, by Conservative newspapers, by Birkenhead and by parts of the Conservative machine. Baldwin's wish to be a 'healer' has been attributed to his insight into the justice of Labour claims and to his desire to restore the sympathy supposed to have existed in the late nineteenth century between the Conservative party and the working classes. These factors doubtless operated. His language in 1923 suggests that they did. They have, nevertheless, to be seen in the context of the personal need to differentiate his own position from Birkenhead's, just as the need to let Labour take office in 1924 arose from a desire to destroy the power of Birkenhead, Rothermere and Lloyd George. Emotional antipathy, personal calculation, social criticism and tactical nobbling (of a leading Die Hard) all figure equally in the declaration at his nadir in December 1923 that 'I will never draw down the blinds until I am a political corpse, but if I become one, it will [be] by an honest blow delivered in open fight and not by a syphilitic dagger from a syndicated press'.[1]

Baldwin did not succeed as 'a man of the highest character' until the election of 1924. What his victory then showed was that his function was to tie together the moral, industrial, agrarian, libertarian, Anglican and nonconformist bodies of resistance in a not yet fully demagogic combination of naïveté, decency and understatement. In the *Daily Telegraph* and *Morning Post* (with reservations) and in *The Times* under Dawson and J. J. Astor, he had atmospheric allies. In large parts of the provincial press he had followers who were prepared to adopt his tone. In Bridgeman, Wood, Hoare, Salisbury and Joynson-Hicks, he was sustained by the only body of leading politicians in English public life for whom prayer was a reality. In a number of his ministers there were strong touches of schoolboy enthusiasm and the Buchanesque rhetoric of nationality along with a low-keyed energy which resented the pitch and tension of Birkenhead, Churchill and Lloyd George and the unpleasant impression they created of wanting to do something positive with power. If Baldwin ever wanted to do anything positive with power, December 1923 seems to have cured him. Thereafter at the same time as a rural social order was passing,[1] he invented a mindless rural persona which, through a new image of pipe-smoking simplicity, aimed to lessen the distance from an electorate whose voting practice at last had shown that 'at core ... the working man [was] sound'.[2] He peddled a modest morality which, even if not 'the old England of the villages ... getting a bit of its own back for once',[3] made a point of distinguishing its own reputation from the reputations attributed, rightly or wrongly, to Rothermere the 'lecher', Northcliffe the syphilitic, Derby the pantaloon, Birkenhead the drunk, Beaverbrook the adventurer, Horne the 'Scotch cad', commercial traveller and smooth ladies' man, Salvidge the 'Tammany boss' with his hand in the till[4] and the moral and political indecency of Lloyd George. In an English context Horne, Lloyd George, Birkenhead and Beaverbrook were emancipated nonconformists. None of the others had much open, conventional religion. Whether tactically or as absolute judgment Baldwin – a near ordinand – thought they suffered defects of character as 'radical' as the 'defect' of political 'character' Beaverbrook discerned in him.[5] The moral quality of the lives of Baldwin's friends may turn out on investigation to be less impeccable than it seems. The 'intriguers' they defeated thought they were as 'unscrupulous' as they thought them.[6] There can still be no doubting the intention of the nervous imagination with which the 'real pen' in Kipling's family[7] approached the task of governing a nation in which a million men had died and $8\frac{1}{2}$ million women had got the vote since Birkenhead's sword had first been sharpened.

About the working-class problem, Baldwin's feelings were mixed. In this he was typical of many Conservatives. Conservatives who felt as he did did not welcome the demonstrations of working-class independence with which they were confronted. They would have been happier not to have to give them a welcome. In 1922 they half hoped that the Liberal party would replace Labour.

But the election of 1922 taught them that Labour was an existing force which could not be obliterated. Thereafter they wanted chiefly to persuade its leaders to avoid the destruction which Liberals had threatened between 1909 and 1914 and Labour between 1919 and 1921.

Resistance to Socialism, therefore, was accompanied by feelings which varied in intensity and from group to group, that resistance was not only not enough by itself, but could only be effective if concealed. Among most of the Conservative leaders dealt with in this book, there was the strongest desire to find something to say which did not just involve resistance to working-class demands and which would save the Conservative party being branded as the instrument of the rich against the poor. This was a desire to talk about something – almost anything – apart from the function the party had to perform. What Lord Robert Cecil thought could be done by the League of Nations and industrial co-operation, Salisbury presented as an assumed cohesion of decency between the gentry and the working classes. Among the Die Hards the problem was solved by social and national solidarity. In 1922/23 Law and Baldwin tried 'straightforwardness', 'tranquillity' and 'commonsense': in October 1923 Baldwin tried Protection. When Protection failed he tried an undogmatic average opinion at the election of 1924. At various points in other hands, 'Coalition', 'Lloyd George', 'a Ministry of Affairs', 'Empire', 'McKenna', 'Grey', Zinovieff and the *Workers' Weekly* were used to conceal concern with the real problem.

What made possible the blurring of Conservative 'resistance to Socialism' was the belief that the trades union leaders were paper tigers. This sprang from a belief among those who had dealings with them between 1918 and 1921 that they were as likely to lose control of the strike situations they had helped to create as that they would deliberately use them to damage the political structure. It would be wrong to imply an understanding between government and the trades union leaders which enabled each to adopt public postures for their followers' benefit. It would be equally wrong to ignore Baldwin's view that the miners' leaders were 'a particularly stupid lot',[1] Sanders's belief that Clynes, Brace and Thomas were out for a deal[2] or the ideas expressed variously by Geddes, Bridgeman and Horne that the Labour leaders were divided, that

Hartshorn hated Smillie and wanted his job,[1] that what Thomas wanted was the limelight,[2] that most workers who threatened to strike did so in order 'to bluff the government'[3] or that union funds were too limited for a prolonged strike.[4] According to Davidson, Baldwin liked Hodges because he understood the practical difficulties in the way of the Socialism he preached in public.[5] Hodges is said to have been 'very reckless during the coal dispute in ... enjoyment of luxuries' and to have occupied Lord Howard de Walden's box at the 1921 Derby.[6] During the war Thomas was lent a cottage on the Astors' estate at Cliveden.[7] In 1919 he introduced a private member's bill to enable W. W. Astor to renounce the peerage he had just inherited. In 1920 or 1921 he was given the use of Derby's box at Epsom for Derby Day.[8] His relations with Lord Churchill, the chairman of the Railway Companies' Association,[9] were probably a factor in ensuring NUR support for the Railway Companies' amalgamation movement.[10] George Barnes, Will Crooks and others were all recipients of benefits to which Conservatives subscribed.

It was recognised that there were clever men among the trades union leaders. Smillie was one.[11] So was Thomas. So also was Brace – Neville Chamberlain's 'big sleek cat'[12] – who, at Bridgeman's instigation, was given 'the goal of the Labour leader' – a permanent and pensionable post in the Ministry of Labour[13] from which, when Shinwell arrived as Secretary for Mines in 1924, he exuded extensive disapproval.[14] By contrast with the employers' representatives – especially in the Coal Industry – they were thought both reasonable and well-prepared.[15] Sometimes they got away with more than was desirable, particularly when Lloyd George intervened. Bridgeman's first doubts about him began when he intervened behind Horne's back in 1919 to produce concessions 'to save Thomas' face' in ending the rail strike when 'it ought to have been made quite plain' to the railwaymen that they would gain nothing from striking.[16] But even when more could have been done to keep them in check, there was a feeling that their cleverness was not dangerous, – that many of them could be bought, argued or charmed into conformity. Austen Chamberlain's understanding of Black Friday was that 'the strikes were settled only by the leaders assuming a responsibility beyond their mandate and overriding the decision of the miners' ballot'. The conclusion he drew was Conservative demands for obligatory secret ballots before strikes were misplaced because the leaders were more 'practical' than their followers.[1]

The process of self-persuasion coloured the attitude of the Conservative leaders to the political side of the Labour movement even before Black Friday showed that they were right. Clynes was thought a moderate, if slightly underprivileged, little man with a genuine vein of quiet eloquence who usually 'got rattled directly he was questioned'.[2] Adamson in the House of Commons seemed 'like an ox, heavy, stupid, pathetic, lurching about without vivacity, humour or sense'.[3] Experience at first hand in office showed that Barnes – a Scottish Episcopalian – was 'an old-fashioned and very cautious Scottish Whig',[4] that Hodge was a very fat, 'rampaging and most patriotic Tory working man' who had been turned down for military service because he was too old[5] and that many of the leaders of the Labour party were distinguished from Tories 'only by the name'.[6]

At first sight the impression left by the Labour leaders in the 1922 parliament was rather different. Neither Snowden nor MacDonald was attractive personally. Neither had been 'patriotic'. Both were too clever to be patronised. Lady Astor, it is true, asked Clynes, Thomas and Snowden to dinner to meet the King – a contrast to her attitude to Charles Palmer, Bottomley's M.P. for The Wrekin, whom she had described in 1920, admittedly under provocation, as 'a little cad from the slums'.[7] Law complimented the Clydesiders as fellow Glaswegians. Baldwin sat with them in the Tea-Room.[8] Walter Elliot, also a Scottish member, spoke of Maxton as 'one of the most sympathetic and finest characters' in the House of Commons.[9] Neville Chamberlain, who had no Clydesiders in Birmingham, thought this rather 'sloshy': even he believed Ammon when told how pleased the Labour benches were to see him putting Jack Jones in his place.[10] There is other evidence of co-operation and cordiality between MacDonald, Henderson and the Conservative leaders and a marked failure to identify Law and Baldwin as the class enemy.[11]

There was, however, not much co-operation. The prevailing feeling was that the Clydesiders were parliamentary bores. One Conservative member caused a major disturbance in 1923 by making anti-semitic noises about Shinwell whose 'cool ironical manner . . . goad[ed] the Conservatives to fury'.[1] Amery had a fight with Buchanan on the floor of the House. Kirkwood, under the impression that he was 'following the example of Disraeli and Gladstone', made a practice of 'yell[ing] . . . violently' at Neville Chamberlain about the condition of the Glasgow slums.[2] Chamberlain had great contempt for Labour ignorance: he used 'sob stuff' in public to get 'tears running down the cheeks' of a Labour man like Wallhead 'who always lap[ped] it up'.[3] He thought his Housing Bill so far knocked the stuffing out of them that, in its later stages, they 'merely poured out sob stuff' where originally they had 'yell[ed] that they were being insulted'.[4]

By 1924 the situation was much what it had been in 1921 with the difference that it was not only the patriotic Labour leader like Walsh or a bankrupt has-been like Tillett[5] who provided reassurance but MacDonald himself. The belief persisted that a wedge should be driven between the 'steady . . . patriotic . . . conservative trades unionist' and 'the Socialist visionary with a foreign, international, anti-British point of view'.[6] But, in the climate created by four years of pacifist and League of Nations propaganda, it was felt in some quarters that Labour's tone was preferable to the tone of Birkenhead and the syndicated press,[7] and that MacDonald had 'high ideals' which were closer than anything Birkenhead taught to 'the lessons which [Bledisloe] (like many others brought up in a like domestic atmosphere) learnt as a child at [his] mother's knee'.[8] Before MacDonald became Prime Minister Lee of Fareham's chief interest was in 'observing what influence Chequers [might] have upon . . . MacDonald and his colleagues' as he had expected 'it [would] do *them* more good than it would do to a Tory or Liberal Prime Minister who [was] accustomed to such surroundings and influences'.[9]

Once Labour was in office, the government seemed very little different from anything that had gone before. Wheatley was impressive as a parliamentarian but Neville Chamberlain's experience of his handling of the Housing Bill was that his 'abilities' were 'very limited and. . . he [was] by no means quick in picking up new ideas'.[10] Lord Eustace Percy said much the same: he thought 'both MacDonald and Snowden shared with Churchill the impatience of the self-educated man with formal school education'.[11] To Strachey MacDonald seemed 'a model of good breeding in Premiers'.[1] His speeches, admittedly to his face, were 'admirable ... fearless ... clear ... [and] worthy in every way of a British Prime Minister'.[2] His preface to *Socialism* and his dismissal of 'bookish associations of "Socialism" '[3] showed that he was an opportunist like everyone else.

In conversation the day Wheatley's Eviction Bill was withdrawn, Neville Chamberlain found MacDonald 'a strange man [with] ... much that is attractive about him'. He was greatly pleased to be told that MacDonald 'knew' Conservatives would be 'ready to help' in cases of 'real hardship' and was much impressed when he ended the conversation 'by exclaiming "if we could only work with you!" ' Even if he was put out when MacDonald told a meeting of Labour women next day that the bill's defeat showed that Tories were 'callously indifferent to the sufferings of tenants' he was probably as much relieved to find that MacDonald's practice did not square with his preaching as he had been when convincing himself that they had common ideals.[4] His opinion of the scandal over the £30,000 MacDonald received from the proprietor of McVitie and Price for whom he arranged a knighthood was that he 'should stay in [office] a bit longer'.[5]

At a primitive level the Conservative leaders had many instincts in common with some aspects of Labour thinking. There was the same affectation of dislike for the millionaire press. There was the same distaste for the ostentation of wealth. There was the same concern with decency and virtue and a belief, derived from Disraeli, the Church of England and 'gentry politics' in some cases and from Joseph Chamberlain, municipal Socialism and the Penny Bank in the rest that the rich had a duty to be kind to the poor within the limits of existing inequality. Many examples could be adduced. None illustrates this better than Austen Chamberlain – the symbol of articulate anti-Socialism – who was 'at a loss to say ... why anyone who lives in [West Birmingham] slums should not be a Socialist, a Communist or a Red Revolutionary'.[6]

The variety of feelings and calculations behind the belief that Labour leaders knew their place, had hearts of gold or feet of clay and were practically innocuous is best understood through the record Neville Chamberlain made of a conversation with Wood the day before Churchill lost Abbey and 'we breath[ed] again'. Wood had been dining with Hilton Young who, he said, was very anxious to attach himself to our party. He had said to Hilton Young that the three-party system was breaking down and that the alternatives for us were an arrangement with certain Liberals or with the more moderate Labour men. This put Hilton Young into a panic and he asked how it was possible that we and Labour could join. I then asked, what put this idea in Edward Wood's mind, adding that I myself felt much more sympathy with Labour with than Libs. He said Haden Guest had ... asked whether he [Wood] had written a certain article which recently appeared in *The Times* under his name in which he had identified Conservative principles with certain human instincts, Comradeship, Independence and Reverence. Haden Guest said he wondered why Conservatives had not said something of the kind before. We did not care much for your opposition so long as you were identified with reaction but if you are going to talk like this you are becoming dangerous. And there is not much between us but Liberals could never adopt such ideas. This bears out something said a little while before by Kirkwood ... to Baldwin one day when they happened to meet. I liked your speech (on unemployment) said Kirkwood, I think you are coming nearer to us and we ought to get together on Protection!

Edward Wood and I then got more confidential on our relations with Liberals and he admitted that he had viewed Winston Churchill's alliance with considerable misgiving. To get 30 more supporters might seem attractive but (1) it would drive a wedge under our Protection door which would make it harder to open (2) it would mean more difficulty in any rapprochement with Labour. Of course I cordially agreed. I said I was against any alliance or working arrangement with Liberals. If they wanted to come in with us, let them join our party. Winston Churchill could only handicap us in the country. In the House he would be a power but his line would be an attack on the Socialists which could only drive the moderates into the arms of the extremists. Edward Wood agreed and added that he feared Winston Churchill would play a part similar to that of Carson in the old days – one of embitterment between those who might have otherwise worked together for the good of the country. I find Edward Wood the most sympathetic of all my colleagues'.[1]

These judgments reflected a mixture of attitudes – optimism about the future, confidence in the goodness of the people, a determination to rub the Liberal party in the dirt and recognition that the fundamental governing duties in the society Wood and Chamberlain wished to rule were to exercise power responsibly, subordinate words to their practical purpose and ensure that careless, exuberant, heart-felt rhetoric was subordinated to the primary task of reconciling all classes and all bodies of potential alienation to the politico-social structure from which they derived their authority.

Whether these judgments were made because Labour had arrived and it was useless to argue with a steam-roller, or because the Labour party was an easy party to beat, there can be no doubt that they reflected very little fear. Whatever may have been felt by Conservative voters, or even by back-benchers, the leaders' desire both to take out the steam in 1923/24 and, if necessary, to stamp down the leaders in 1921 and 1926 reflected the feeling that it was safe to do so because industrial conflict had become a major cause of national contention largely through the Coalition's tendency both to stir it up and to play up to it.

What, then, was the impact of Labour? Between 1919 and 1922 Labour showed Conservatives that Lloyd George could be destroyed. It enabled the second rank of Conservative ministers to overturn their leaders and then use Labour to corner the leaders they had overturned. The consonance between the interests of Labour which wanted to destroy the Liberal party and the Conservative leaders who wanted to destroy Birkenhead continued. What would have happened if the Labour leaders had not been tempted by the tactical possibilities, it is difficult to say. But they were tempted: in the situation they created, Baldwin, Neville Chamberlain, Wood, Amery and the rest knew that Labour had made it possible for them to arrive. Knowledge of this fact meant that they used one language in private and two different ones in public and that, beneath the level of public conflict, the reality of high politics as we leave it was a tension of connivance between MacDonald who was compelled by his situation to mean no harm and Baldwin whose situation compelled him to feel confident that no harm would be done. Whether harm was done and who, if anyone, was being conned, are questions to which later investigation may provide an answer.

THE ACTORS

(Ages in 1920)

(These notes are designed to be of use in understanding the narrative: they do not normally cover careers after 1920. Where an actor has a biography in the text he is omitted from this Appendix.)

ADAMSON, William (57). M.P. since 1910. General Secretary Fife, Kinross and Clackmannan Miners' Association. Chairman of Parliamentary Labour Party 1917–21. Said to have been the only really boring speaker at meetings of the 1924 Cabinet.

ADDISON, Christopher (51). M.P. (Lib) since 1910. Ed. Trinity College, Harrogate and St Bart's Hospital. Sometime Professor of Anatomy and author of medical text books. 1914–16 junior minister. 1916–17 Minister of Munitions. 1917–19 Minister of Reconstruction. 1919– President of Local Government Board and Minister of Health.

AMERY, Leopold Charles M. S. (47). M.P. since 1911. Son of Indian Forestry officer. Ed. Harrow and Balliol (Fellow of All Souls). Ex-private secretary to L. H. Courtney. 1899–1909 editorial staff of *The Times* including period in South African war. 1913 member of Marconi Committee. 1914–16 war service in Flanders and Balkans. 1917–18 Assistant Secretary to War Cabinet etc. Married Hamar Greenwood's sister. Sir Edward Marsh could not bear to think 'of going in to Amery when he rings the bell'.

ARNOLD, Sydney (42). M.P. (Lib) since 1912. Solicitor. Experience as P.P.S. Resigned seat at Penistone in 1921.

ASQUITH, Herbert Henry (68). M.P. (Lib) 1886–1918. Ed. City of London and Balliol. Barrister. 1892–95 Home Secretary. 1905–8 Chancellor of the Exchequer. 1908–16 Prime Minister. 1908– Leader of Liberal party.

ASTOR, John Jacob (34). M.P. (Cons) 1922– . Ed. Eton and New College, Oxford. Proprietor of *The Times* 1922– .

ASTOR, Waldorf (41). M.P. (Cons) 1911–19. Ed. Eton and New College. 1914–17 Army. 1918 P.P.S. to Lloyd George. 1918–21 junior minister.

BAIRD, Sir John (46). M.P. (Cons) since 1910. Ed. Eton and Oxford. Diplomatic Service etc. Army service in 1914–18 war (D.S.O. 1915).

BALFOUR, Arthur James (72). M.P. (Cons) since 1874. Ed. Eton and Trinity College, Cambridge. 1878–80 P.P.S. to Lord Salisbury. In office 1885, 1886–92, 1895–1902. 1902–5 Prime Minister. 1902–11 Leader of the Conservative party. 1915–16 1st Lord of the Admiralty. 1916–19 Foreign Secretary. 1919– Lord President of the Council.

BANBURY, Sir Frederick George (70). M.P. (Cons) since 1892. Ed. Winchester. Chairman, Great Northern Railway.

BARLOW, Sir Anderson Montague- (52). M.P. (Cons) since 1910. Ed. Repton and King's College, Cambridge. Ex-barrister and owner of Sotheby's.

BARNES, George Nicholl (61). M.P. (Lab) since 1906. 1896–1906 General Secretary of Amalgamated Society of Engineers. 1916–17 Minister of Pensions. 1917–20 Minister without Portfolio. 1917 and 1919 member of War Cabinet.

BAYFORD (see Sanders, Sir Robert)

BEAVERBROOK, William Max Aitken, 1st Baron (41). M.P. (Cons) 1910–17. Ed. public school, Newcastle, New Brunswick. February–November 1918 Chancellor of Duchy of Lancaster.

BENN, W. Wedgwood (43). M.P. (Lib) since 1906. Ed. Petit Lycée Condorcet, Paris and University College, London. 1910–15 Junior Whip.

BETTERTON, Henry Bucknall (48). M.P. (Cons) since 1918. Ed. Rugby and Christ Church.

BEVIN, Ernest (39). National Organization of Dockers' Union since 1910.

BIRKENHEAD, Frederick Edwin Smith, 1st Baron (48). M.P. (Cons) 1906–19. Ed. Birkenhead School and Wadham (Fellow of Merton). Barrister. 1915 Solicitor-General. 1915–19 Attorney-General. 1919– Lord Chancellor.

BLEDISLOE, Charles Bathurst, 1st Baron (53). M.P. (Cons) since 1910. Ed. Sherborne, Eton, University College, Oxford and Royal Agricultural College, Cirencester. 1916–17 junior minister.

BRACE, William (55). M.P. (Lab) since 1906. Ed. Board school. President of South Wales Miners' Federation. 1915–19 Under-Secretary at the Home Office.

BRADBURY, Sir John Swanwick (48). 1913– . Joint Permanent Under-Secretary at the Treasury.

BRIDGEMAN, William Clive (56). M.P. since 1906. Ed. Eton and Trinity College, Oxford. 1889–92 secretary to Lord Knutsford. 1895–97 private secretary to Hicks-Beach. 1911–15 Junior Whip. 1915– junior office.

BUCHANAN, George (30). Ed. elementary school, Glasgow. Member of United Patternmakers' Society. 1918– member of Glasgow City Council.

BUCKLEY, Albert (43). M.P. (Cons) since 1918. Ed. Merchant Taylors and Aldenham. Wool-broker. Served in South African and Great Wars.

BUCKMASTER, Stanley Owen Buckmaster, 1st Baron (50). M.P. (Lib) 1906–10, 1911–15. Ed. Aldenham and Christ Church (Student). 1913–15 Solicitor-General. 1915–16 Lord Chancellor.

BULL, Sir William James (57). M.P. (Cons) since 1900. Ed. St Mary's Academy. Solicitor and Company Director. 1892–1901 member of L.C.C. 1902 P.P.S. to Walter Long. 1916 member of Speaker's Reform Bill Conference.

BUXTON, Charles Roden (45). M.P. (Lib) 1910–18. Ed. Harrow and Trinity College, Cambridge. Private secretary to father, Sir T. F. Buxton. 1902–10 Principal of Morley College. Author.

BUXTON, Noel Edward (51). M.P. (Lib) 1905–6, 1910–18. Ed. Harrow and Trinity College, Cambridge. A.D.C. to his father. Served Whitechapel Board of Guardians. Author.

CARSON, Sir Edward Henry (66). M.P. (Cons) since 1892. Ed. Portarlington and T.C.D. 1892 Solicitor-General, Ireland. 1900–6 Solicitor-General. 1915 Attorney-General. 1916–17 1st Lord of Admiralty. 1917–18 Minister without Portfolio.

CAVE, George, 1st Viscount (64). M.P. (Cons) 1906–18. Ed. Merchant Taylors and St John's College, Oxford. 1915–16 Solicitor-General. 1916–19 Home Secretary.

CECIL, Lord Hugh Richard Heathcote (51). M.P. (Cons) 1910– . Ed. Eton and University College, Oxford (Fellow of Hertford).

CECIL, Lord Robert (56). M.P. (Cons) 1906–10, 1911– . Ed. Eton and University College, Oxford. K.C. 1899. 1915–16 junior minister. 1916–18 Minister of Blockade, Foreign Under-Secretary. 1919 British delegate to League of Nations Economic Peace Conference. Author.

CHADWICK, Sir Robert Burton (51). M.P. (Cons) 1918– . Ed. Birkenhead School. Shipowner. Member of Government Committees.

CHAMBERLAIN, (Joseph) Austen (57). M.P. (Unionist) since 1892. Ed. Rugby and Trinity College, Cambridge. 1895–1903 junior office. 1903–5 Chancellor of the Exchequer. 1915–17 India Secretary. 1918–19 War Cabinet. 1919– Chancellor of the Exchequer.

CHELMSFORD, Frederic John Napier Thesiger, 3rd Baron (52). Ed. Winchester and Magdalen College, Oxford (Fellow of All Souls). 1900–5 London School Board and L.C.C. 1905–9 Governor of Queensland. 1909–13 Governor of New South Wales. 1916– Viceroy of India.

CHILCOTT, H. Warden (49). M.P. (Cons) 1918– . Company director (building).

CLYNES, John Robert (51). M.P. (Lab) since 1906. Ed. elementary schools, cotton-worker. President of National Union of General Workers. 1917–19 junior office.

COPE, Alfred (38). 1919–20 2nd Secretary, Ministry of Pensions. 1920–22 Clerk of Privy Council (Ireland). 1922–24 General Secretary, National Liberal Organization.

CRAIG, Sir James (49). M.P. (Unionist) since 1906. Ed. Merchiston Castle. 1916–18 Household office. 1919– junior office.

CRAWFORD, D. A. E. Lindsay, 27th Earl of (49). M.P. (Cons) 1895–1913. Ed. Eton and Magdalen College, Oxford. 1903–5 junior office. 1911–12 Conservative Chief Whip. 1916 Minister of Agriculture. 1916–19 Lord Privy Seal. 1919– Chancellor of Duchy of Lancaster.

CURZON, Francis R. H. Penn Curzon, Viscount (36). M.P. (Cons) 1918. Naval service in Great War.

CURZON, George Nathaniel, 1st Earl (61). M.P. (Cons) 1886–98. Ed. Eton and Balliol. 1891–92 and 1895–98 junior office. 1899–1905 Viceroy of India. 1915–16 Lord Privy Seal. 1916 President of Air Board. 1916–19 Lord President of Council. 1919– Foreign Secretary. Author.

DALTON, Edward Hugh J. N. (33). Economist. Ed. Eton, King's College, Cambridge. As son of Canon of Windsor, talked from time to time to Stamfordham. Despite a number of by-elections, no seat before 1924.

DALZIEL, Sir James Henry (52). M.P. (Lib) 1892– . Proprietor of *Reynolds News*. Helped Lloyd George to control the *Daily Chronicle*.

ST DAVIDS, John Wynford Philips, 1st Viscount (60). M.P. (Lib) 1888–94 and 1898–1908. Ed. Felsted and Keble College, Oxford.

DAVIDSON, John Colin Campbell (31). M.P. (Cons) 1920– . Ed. Westminster and Pembroke College, Cambridge. 1910 secretary to Marquis of Crewe. 1910–15 private secretary to Lord Harcourt. 1915– private secretary to Bonar Law.

DAVIES, David (40). M.P. (Lib) 1906– . Ed. Merchiston and King's College, Cambridge. Company director, landowner and coal owner.

DAVIES, John Thomas (39). Ed. Bangor Normal College and University of London. 1912– private secretary to Lloyd George.

DEVONSHIRE, Victor C. W. Cavendish, 9th Duke of (52). M.P. (Liberal Unionist) 1891–1908. Ed. Eton and Trinity College, Cambridge. 1900–3 Household office. 1903–5 and 1915–16 junior office. 1911 Conservative Chief Whip in House of Lords. 1916– Governor-General of Canada.

EDGE, William (40). M.P. (Lib) 1916– . Ed. Bolton Grammar School and Middle Temple. Cotton Manufacturer. 1917 P.P.S. to Sir Auckland Geddes. 1919 P.P.S. to Sir Robert Horne. 1919– junior office.

ELLIOT, Walter (32). M.P. (Cons) 1918. Ed. Glasgow Academy and Glasgow University.

EMMOTT, Alfred, 1st Baron (62). M.P. (Lib) 1899–1911. Ed. Grove House, Tottenham. Cotton Spinner.

ERSKINE, James M. M. (57). Ed. Wellington and abroad. J.P. for Sussex. Chairman of Clan Erskine Society Committee.

FISHER, Herbert Albert Laurens (55). M.P. (Lib) 1916– . Ed. Winchester and New College, Oxford, Paris and Göttingen (Fellow and Tutor of New College). 1912–16 Vice-Chancellor of Sheffield University. 1916– President of the Board of Education.

FRASER, Sir Malcolm (42). Ed. Heidelberg College. 1918–19 Deputy Director of Airship Production at Admiralty. Newspaper editor. 1920–   Chief Agent (unpaid) to Conservative Party.

GEDDES, Sir Auckland Campbell (41). Ed. George Watson's College, Edinburgh, Edinburgh University, London Hospital and Freiburg. Ex-Professor of Anatomy. Served in South African War and (1914–16) in Great War. 1916–17 Director of Recruiting (War Office). 1917–19 Minister of National Service. 1918–19 President of Local Government Board. 1919–20 President of the Board of Trade. Neville Chamberlain said he was an 'impostor'.

GEDDES, Sir Eric (44). M.P. (Unionist) 1917–   . Ed. Merchiston, Edinburgh Academy and Oxford Military College. Indian railway official. 1914 Deputy General Manager of North Eastern Railway. 1914–17 various high administrative posts. 1917 1st Lord of Admiralty. 1918–19 War Cabinet. 1919– Ministry of Transport. Had a great liking for decorations and medals.

GILMOUR, Sir John (44). M.P. (Cons) since 1910. Ed. Trinity College, Glenalmond, Edinburgh University and Trinity Hall, Cambridge. 1913–15 and 1919 Unionist Junior Whip. 1921–22 Junior Government Whip.

GLADSTONE, Herbert John, 1st Viscount (66). Son of W. E. Gladstone. M.P. (Lib) 1880–1910. Ed. Eton and University College, Oxford (college lecturer at Keble). P.P.S. to father. 1881, 1885, 1886, 1892–94 junior office. 1894–95 1st Commissioner of Works. 1899–1905 Liberal Chief Whip. 1905–10 Home Secretary. 1910–14 Governor-General of South Africa.

GOSLING, Harry (59). President of Transport Workers' Federation. Thames Waterman. 1898–   Member of L.C.C. Not an M.P. until Whitechapel by-election in 1923.

GREENWOOD, Arthur (40). Ed. secondary school and Victoria University, Manchester. Sometime head of economics department, Huddersfield Technical College and lecturer in economics at Leeds. Author and Labour propagandist.

GREENWOOD, Sir Hamar (50). M.P. (Lib) since 1906. Ed. Canadian school and Toronto University. 1914–16 served in Great War. 1919–20 junior office. 1920–   Chief Secretary for Ireland.

GRIGG, Sir Edward William Maclay (41). Ed. Winchester and New College, Oxford. 1903–5 and 1908–13 editorial staff of *The Times*. 1914– military service on staff and in Commonwealth.

GUEST, Frederick Edward (45). M.P. (Cons) 1910– . Ed. Winchester. Served in South African and Great Wars. 1905– private secretary to Winston Churchill, his cousin, whom he had followed out of Liberal party in 1904. 1917– Coalition Liberal Chief Whip.

GUINNESS, Walter Edward (40). M.P. (Unionist) 1907–17 and 1918– . Ed. Eton. Served in South African and Great Wars. 1907–10 L.C.C. Irish.

GWYNN, H. A. (54). Ed. Swansea Grammar School and abroad. Sometime correspondent for *The Times* and Reuters. War Correspondent (including South Africa). 1911– editor of *Morning Post*.

GYWNNE, Rupert Sackville (47). M.P. (Cons) since 1910. Ed. Shrewsbury and Pembroke College, Cambridge. Died 1924.

HALDANE, Richard Burdon, 1st Viscount (64). M.P. (Lib) 1885–1911. Ed. Edinburgh Academy, Edinburgh University and Göttingen. 1905–12 Secretary for War. 1912–15 Lord Chancellor. Author.

HALL, Rear-Admiral Sir W. Reginald (50). M.P. (Cons) 1919– . Ed. H.M.S. *Britannia* and R.N.C., Greenwich. 1914–19 Director of Naval Intelligence.

HARTINGTON, Marquess of (25). Son of 9th Duke. Contested N.E. Derbyshire in 1918.

HARTSHORN, Vernon (48). M.P. (Lab) since 1918. Officer of South Wales Miners' Federation. Member of Coal Controller's Advisory Committee.

HENDERSON, Arthur (57). M.P. (Lab) 1903–18, 1919– . Ed. St Mary's School, Newcastle-on-Tyne. Apprenticed to Robert Stephenson of Newcastle. Extensive experience of local government in Newcastle, Durham and Darlington. 1908 and 1914–17 Chairman of Parliamentary Labour Party. 1915–16 President of Board of Education. 1916 Minister of Pensions. 1916–17 Member of War Cabinet until resignation.

HEWART, Sir Gordon (50). M.P. (Lib) since 1913. Ed. Manchester Grammar School and University College, Oxford. 1916– Solicitor-General.

HEWINS, W. A. S. (55). M.P. (Unionist) 1912–18. Ed. Wolverhampton Grammar School and Pembroke College, Oxford. 1895–1903 Director of London School of Economics. 1903– Secretary of Tariff Commission. 1917–18 Colonial Under-Secretary. Fought five seats unsuccessfully before 1912 and three after 1918. Follower of Joseph Chamberlain. Tariff Reform economist.

HILLS, John Waller (53). M.P. (Unionist) since 1906. Ed. Eton and Balliol. 1914–16 war service.

HODGE, John (65). M.P. (Lab) since 1906. Ed. Ironworks School, Motherwell and Hutcheonstown Grammar School. 1897–1901 Manchester City Council. President of Iron and Steel Trades' Confederation. 1915 Acting Chairman of Labour Party. 1916 Minister of Labour. 1917–19 Minister of Pensions.

HOGG, Douglas McGarel (48). Ed. Eton and studied sugar-growing in West Indies. Served in South African War. Barrister. K.C. 1917.

HOGGE, James Myles (47). M.P. (Lib) 1912– . Ed. Normal School, Edinburgh and New College, Edinburgh. Social investigator, author and journalist. 1919– joint Asquithean Whip.

HORNE, Sir Robert Stevenson (49). M.P. (Cons) 1918– . Ed. University of Glasgow. Advocate at Scottish bar. K.C. 1910. High-level wartime administrator. 1919–20 Minister of Labour. 1920– President of Board of Trade.

INSKIP, Thomas W. H. (44). M.P. (Cons) 1918– . Ed. Clifton and King's College, Cambridge. K.C. 1914. 1920– Chancellor of Diocese of Truro.

JACKSON, Francis Stanley (50). M.P. (Cons) 1915– . Ed. Harrow and Trinity College, Cambridge. Served in South African and Great Wars. Test cricketer.

JONES, Thomas (50). Ed. Pengam County School, University College, Aberystwyth and Glasgow University. 1909–10 Professor of Economics, Queen's University, Belfast. 1912– Secretary, National Health Insurance Commissioners, Wales. 1917– Assistant Secretary to Cabinet.

JOWETT, F. W. (56). M.P. (Lab) since 1906. Fifteen years on Bradford City Council. Member of I.L.P.

KELLAWAY, Frederick George (50). M.P. (Lib) since 1910. Ed. Bishopston, Bristol. Journalist in Lewisham. Member of Lewisham Board of Guardians. 1916– junior office.

KENWORTHY, Joseph Montague (34). M.P. (Lib) 1919– . Ed. Royal Naval Academy, H.M.S. *Britannia*. 1902–20 Royal Navy (Assistant Chief of Staff, Gibraltar 1918). Heir to Lord Strabolgi.

KERR, Philip Henry (38). Ed. Oratory, Edgbaston and New College, Oxford. Part of Milner circle in South Africa. 1910– editor of *Round Table*. 1916– private secretary to Lloyd George. Lapsed Catholic.

KIRKWOOD, David (38). Ed. Parkhead Public School. Engineer. Member of I.L.P. and Glasgow Trades Council. Deported in 1916.

LAMBERT, George (54). M.P. (Lib) since 1891. Ed. privately. Yeoman farmer in S. Devon. 1905–15 junior office.

LANE-FOX, George Richard (50). M.P. (Cons) since 1906. Ed. Eton and New College, Oxford. 1898– Member of West Riding C.C. Service in France 1915, 1916 and 1917. 1921 Charity Commissioner.

LAW, Andrew Bonar (62). M.P. 1900–6, 1906–10 and 1911– . Ed. Canada and Glasgow High School. 1902–5 junior office. 1911– Leader of Conservative Party. 1915–16 Colonial Secretary. 1916–18 Chancellor of Exchequer. 1919– Lord Privy Seal and Leader of House of Commons.

LEE of Fareham, 1st Baron (52). M.P. (Cons) 1900–18. Ed. Cheltenham and R.M.A., Woolwich. Royal Artillery (retired 1900) including chair at Royal Military College, Canada and military attaché in Washington. 1914–15 Army. 1915–16 various sorts of junior office. 1917–18 Director-General of Food Production. 1919– President of Board (and then First Minister) of Agriculture.

LEES-SMITH, Hastings Bertrand (42). M.P. (Lib) 1910–18. Ed. Aldenham, R.M.A., Woolwich and Queen's College, Oxford. 1907–09 chairman of Executive Committee of Ruskin College. Author.

LEWIS, John Herbert (62). M.P. (Lib) 1892–1905, 1905– . Ed. Montreal University and Exeter College, Oxford. 1905–15 junior office. 1915– Parliamentary Secretary, Board of Education.

LINLITHGOW, John Victor Alexander Hope, 2nd Marquess of (33). Ed. Eton. Large landowner.

LLOYD, Sir George Ambrose (41). M.P. (Cons) 1910– . Served in Great War in Near East etc. 1918–23 Governor of Bombay.

A Birmingham Lloyd who married a Maid of Honour to Queen Alexandra.

LLOYD-GRAEME, Sir Philip (36). M.P. (Cons) 1918– . Ed. Winchester and University College, Oxford. 1908 Bar. 1914–17 Army. 1917– junior office.

LOCKER-LAMPSON, Godfrey L. T. (45). M.P. (Cons) since 1910. Ed. Eton and Trinity College, Cambridge. 1914–16 Army. 1917– P.P.S. Author.

LOCKER-LAMPSON, Oliver Stillingfleet (39). Brother of above. M.P. (Cons) since 1910. Ed. Eton and Trinity College, Cambridge (ed. *Granta*). Hon. Sec. Unionist Working Men's Candidate Society. 1914– Navy.

LONDONDERRY, Charles Stewart H. V.-T.-Stewart, 7th Marquess of (42). M.P. (Cons) 1906–15. 1920– junior office.

LONG, Walter Hume (66). M.P. (Cons) 1880–85, 1885, 1892–1900, 1900–6, 1906–10, 1910–18, 1918– . Ed. Harrow and Christ Church, Oxford. 1886–92 junior office. 1895–1900 President of Board of Agriculture. 1900–5 and 1915–16 President of Local Government Board. 1905 Chief Secretary for Ireland. 1916–18 Colonial Secretary. 1919 1st Lord of Admiralty.

McCURDY, Charles (50). M.P. (Lib) since 1910. Ed. Loughborough Grammar School and Pembroke College, Cambridge. Barrister. 1919–20 junior office. 1920– Minister of Food. Sutherland thought he had spent too long in a lawyer's office to be good at affairs.

McKENNA, Reginald (57). M.P. (Lib) 1895–1918. Ed. King's College, London and Trinity Hall, Cambridge. 1905–7 junior office. 1907–8 President of Board of Education. 1908–11 1st Lord of Admiralty. 1911–15 Home Secretary. 1915–16 Chancellor of the Exchequer.

MACLAY, Sir Joseph Paton (63). 1918 Member of War Cabinet. 1916 Shipping Controller. Shipowner. Liberal.

MACLEAN, Sir Donald (56). M.P. (Lib) 1906–10, 1910– . Ed. Haverfordwest and Carmarthen Grammar Schools. Solicitor.

MACNAMARA, Thomas James (59). Ed. St Thomas's, Exeter and Borough Road Training College for Teachers. School teacher and President of National Union of Teachers. 1892–1907 editor of *The Schoolmaster*. M.P. (Lib) since 1900. 1907–20 junior office. 1920– Minister of Labour.

McNEILL, Ronald (59). M.P. (Cons) 1911–18, 1918– . Ed. Harrow and Christ Church. Barrister. 1900–4 editor of *St James's Gazette* and author. Irish.

MacPHERSON, Ian (40). M.P. (Lib) since 1911. Ed. George Watson's College and University of Edinburgh. 1916–19 junior office. 1919–20 Chief Secretary for Ireland. 1920– Minister of Pensions.

MANN, Tom (64). Farm, pit and engineering worker from age of nine. First Secretary of National Democratic League.

MESTON, James Scorgie, 1st Baron (55). Ed. Aberdeen Grammar School and University, and Balliol, Oxford. 1885– Indian Civil Service (inc. Governor of U.P. and Finance Member of Viceroy's Council). A Liberal.

MIDLETON, W. St John F. Brodrick, 1st Earl of (64). M.P. (Cons) 1880–85 and 1885–1905. 1907–13 L.C.C. alderman. 1886–92, 1895–8 and 1898–1900 junior office. 1900–3 War Secretary. 1903–5 India Secretary.

MILNER, Alfred, 1st Viscount (66). Ed. Germany, King's College, London and Balliol. 1887–89 private secretary to Goschen. 1889–92 Under-Secretary for Finance (Egypt). 1892–97 Chairman of Board of Inland Revenue. 1897–1905 High Commissioner in South Africa. 1916–18 War Cabinet. 1918–19 War Secretary. 1919– Colonial Secretary. 1919– Chairman of Mission to Egypt.

MOND, Sir Alfred Moritz (52). M.P. (Lib) 1906–10, 1910– . Ed. Cheltenham, St John's College, Cambridge and Edinburgh. 1916– First Commissioner of Works. 1905 Managing Director of Brenner, Mond & Co. Coal Interests. Failed Natural Sciences Tripos at Cambridge. Strongly guttural voice with German accent.

MONEY, Sir Leo G. Chiozza (50). M.P. (Lib) 1906– . Economist. 1915–16 P.P.S. to Lloyd George. 1916–19 junior minister.

MONSELL, B. M. Eyres- (39). M.P. (Cons) since 1910. Ed. H.M.S. *Britannia*. 1911–14 Junior Whip. 1914–18 Navy. 1919– Household office. 1923 succeeded Sir Leslie Wilson as Conservative Chief Whip.

MOREL, Edmund Dene (47). Author and publicist. 1904–12 secretary of Congo Reform Association. 1914– secretary of Union of Democratic Control. Labour. Died 1924.

MOSLEY, Oswald Ernald (24). M.P. (Cons) 1918. War service. Married Curzon's daughter.

MUNRO, Robert (52). M.P. (Lib) since 1910. Ed. Aberdeen Grammar School and Edinburgh. 1913–16 junior Scottish office. 1916– Secretary for Scotland.

ORMSBY-GORE, William (35). M.P. (Cons) since 1910. Ed. Eton and New College, Oxford. 1917 P.P.S. to Milner and Assistant Secretary to War Cabinet.

PEEL, William Robert Wellesley, 1st Earl (53). M.P. (Cons) 1900–6, 1909–12. 1917– junior office.

PERCY, Lord Eustace S. Campbell (33). M.P. (Cons) 1921– . Ed. Eton and Christ Church. Retired from Diplomatic Service 1919.

POLLOCK, Sir Ernest (59). M.P. (Cons) since 1910. Ed. Charterhouse and Trinity College, Cambridge. K.C. 1905. 1919– Solicitor-General.

PONSONBY, Arthur Augustus W. H. (49). M.P. (Lib) since 1908. Ed. Eton and Balliol. Son of Queen Victoria's private secretary. 1894–1902 Diplomatic Service. 1905–8 P.P.S. to Campbell-Bannerman.

PRETYMAN, Ernest George (60). M.P. (Cons) 1895–1906, 1908– . Ed. Eton and R.M.A., Woolwich. 1900–5, 1915–18 junior office.

PRINGLE, William Mather Rutherford (46). M.P. (Lib) 1910–18. Ed. Glasgow University. Barrister.

READING, Rufus Daniel Isaacs, 1st Earl of (60). M.P. (Lib) 1904–14. Ed. University College School. 1880 hammered on Stock Exchange. Q.C. 1898. 1910 Solicitor-General. 1910–13 Attorney-General. 1913–21 Lord Chief Justice. 1918–1919 Ambassador to United States. 1921– Viceroy of India.

SALVIDGE, Sir Archibald Tutton James (57). Ed. Liverpool Institute. Brewer. Chairman, Conservative National Union 1913.

SAMUEL, Sir Herbert Louis (50). M.P. (Lib) 1902–18. Ed. University College School and Balliol. 1905–9 junior office. 1909–10 Chancellor of Duchy of Lancaster. 1910–14 and 1915–16 Postmaster-General. 1914–15 President of Local Government Board. 1916 Home Secretary. 1919 High Commissioner to Belgium. 1920– High Commissioner in Palestine.

SANDERS, Sir Robert (53). M.P. (Cons) since 1910. Ed. Harrow and Balliol. Served in Great War. 1895–1907 Master of Hounds. Called to Bar. Ex-member of Somerset County Council. 1919– junior Whip.

SANKEY, Sir John (54). Ed. Lancing and Jesus College, Oxford. K.C. 1909. Chancellor of Diocese of Llandaff. 1914– Judge of the King's Bench. Chairman of Sankey Commission. MacDonald claimed to respond warmly to his mind.

SASSOON, Sir Philip Albert G. D. (32). M.P. (Cons) since 1912.

SCOTT, Alexander MacCallum (46). M.P. (Lib) since 1918. Ed. Polmont Public School, Falkirk High School and Glasgow University. Author and journalist inc. a life of Churchill (1905). Junior Coalition Liberal Whip.

SCOTT, Charles Prestwich (74). M.P. (Lib) 1895–1906. Ed. privately and Corpus Christi College, Oxford. Editor of *Manchester Guardian* since 1872.

SELBORNE, William Waldegrave Palmer, 2nd Earl of (61). M.P. 1885–92 and 1892–95. Ed. Winchester and University College, Oxford. 1895–1900 junior office. 1900–5 1st Lord of Admiralty. 1905–10 High Commissioner for South Africa. 1915–16 President of Board of Agriculture. Married Salisbury's sister. A Liberal Unionist.

SHAW, Thomas (48). M.P. (Lab) since 1918. Elementary school. Weaver. Secretary of Colne Weavers and vice-president of Weavers' Amalgamation.

SHINWELL, Emanuel (36). M.P. (Lab) 1922– . Ed. elementary school, Glasgow. Organiser for Marine Workers' Union.

SHORTT, Edward (58). M.P. (Lib) since 1910. Ed. Durham School and University. Barrister. 1918–19 Chief Secretary for Ireland. 1919– Home Secretary.

SIMON, Sir John Allsebrook (47). M.P. (Lib) 1906–18. Ed. Fettes and Wadham (Fellow of All Souls). 1910–13 Solicitor-General. 1913–15 Attorney-General. 1915–16 Home Secretary.

SNOWDEN, Philip (56). M.P. (Lab) 1906–18. Ed. Board school. 1903–6 and 1917–20 Chairman of I.L.P.

SNOWDEN, Mrs Ethel (39). Wife of Philip Snowden. Ed. Edge Hill College, Liverpool. Fabian, suffragette, temperance worker. Author of *Through Bolshevik Russia*.

STAMFORDHAM, Arthur John Bigge, 1st Baron (71). 1910– private secretary to King George V (as to Queen Victoria). Gunner. Served in Zulu War.

STEED, H. Wickham (49). Ed. Sudbury Grammar School and on Continent. 1914–19 foreign editor of *The Times*. 1919–22 editor.

STRACHEY, John St Loe (60). Ed. Balliol. 1896–8 editor of *Cornhill Magazine*. 1898– editor and proprietor of *The Spectator*.

SUETER, Rear-Admiral Murray F. (48). Navy since 1886. 1915–17 Superintendent of Aircraft Construction (Naval).

TALBOT, Lord Edmund Bernard (né Fitzalan-Howard) (65). M.P. (Cons) since 1894. Ed. Oratory, Edgbaston. 1905 junior office. 1913– Conservative Chief Whip. 1917– Deputy Earl Marshal.

THOMAS, James Henry (47). M.P. (Lab) 1910– . Ed. Board school. General Secretary of National Union of Railwaymen. A Tory working man in opinion.

THOMSON, Christopher Birdwood (45). Ed. Cheltenham and Woolwich. 1894–1919 Army (Brigadier) inc. War Office (1913– 19). 1917 tried to become Conservative candidate. 1919 retired from Army to take up Labour politics. 1920 member of Labour delegation to Ireland. *Daily Herald* military correspondent. Author of *Old Europe's Suicide*.

TREVELYAN, Charles Philips (50). M.P. (Lib) 1899–1918. Ed. Harrow and Trinity College, Cambridge. 1918 joined Labour Party. 1906–8 Charity Commissioner. 1908–14 junior office. Author. Bumptious and tiresome to his seniors when a Liberal. Webb thought him much improved by his period in the wilderness. Welcomed the chance to 'chortle over the funk of the possessing classes'. In 1920 thought the Labour party would not take root until there had been major economic collapse.

TRYON, George Clement (49). M.P. (Cons) since 1910. Ed. Eton and R.M.C., Sandhurst. 1890–1902 and 1914–18 Grenadier Guards. 1919– junior office.

ULLSWATER, James William Lowther, 1st Viscount (created 1921) (65). M.P. (Cons) 1883–85, 1886–1918 and 1918– . Ed. Eton, King's College, London and Trinity College, Cambridge. Barrister. 1891–92 junior office. 1905– Speaker of the House of Commons.

WALLHEAD, Richard Collingham. Ed. elementary school, Romford. Decorator, designer, journalist. 1920 Chairman of I.L.P.

WALSH, Stephen (62). M.P. (Lab) since 1906. Miner and official of Lancashire and Cheshire Miners' Federation. 1917–19 junior office.

WEBB, Beatrice (62). Ed. privately. Authoress. Wife of Sidney Webb.

WEBB, Sidney (61). Ed. Switzerland. Civil Servant. 1892–1910 L.C.C. Author, lecturer, barrister, professor of Public Administration. Founded London School of Economics.

WEDGWOOD, Josiah Clement (48). M.P. (Lib and then Independent) 1906– . Ed. Clifton and R.N.C., Greenwich. Naval architect and engineer. Served in South African and Great Wars. Author. Left the impression once in the Labour party of 'trying to pretend that he [was] not a gentleman'.

WHEATLEY, John (51). 1910–12 Lanark C.C. 1912–22 Glasgow Trades Council. 1920 Leader of Glasgow Rent Strike. Printer.

WOLMER, Roundell Cecil Palmer, Viscount (33). M.P. (Cons) 1910–18 and 1918– . Ed. Winchester and University College, Oxford. 1916–18 P.P.S. to Lord Robert Cecil. Described by Winterton as 'the Christian martyr' as 'he always looks injured'.

WORTHINGTON-EVANS, Sir Laming (52). M.P. (Cons) 1910– . Solicitor. 1916–18 junior office. 1918–19 Minister of Pensions. 1919– Minister without Portfolio. Brusqueness and boisterousness of his manner attributed to his 'not being a university man'.

YOUNG, Edward Hilton (41). M.P. (Lib) 1915– . Ed. Eton and Trinity College, Cambridge. 1911–15 financial editor of *Morning Post*. Wartime Navy (lost arm). 1919– P.P.S. to H. A. L. Fisher. Author and journalist.

YOUNGER, Sir George (69). M.P. (Cons) since 1906. Ed. Edinburgh Academy. Brewer. After service as President of National Union of Conservative Associations in Scotland, became chairman of whole party organisation (1916–).

BIBLIOGRAPHY

I. MANUSCRIPT SOURCES

(* indicates the most important for the subject: † indicates the most fragmentary.)

Where a letter which has been seen in a manuscript collection is also available in published form, I have usually quoted from the manuscript. I have not often thought it necessary to compare the published with the manuscript version. Normally the name by which a manuscript is described is unambiguous. It should be noted, however, that Bayford diary refers to the diary of Sir Robert Sanders, that Cecil MSS refers to the papers of Viscount Cecil of Chelwood and that Webb MSS refers to the papers of Lord and Lady Passfield. 'Neville Chamberlain' or 'Austen Chamberlain' to either 'Hilda' or 'Ida' refers to the letters written by either brother to their half-sisters and preserved with the papers of whichever brother wrote a particular letter. BL refers to the Law MSS, AC to the papers of Austen Chamberlain. Geo. V K refers to the papers of King George V at Windsor.

I have tried in the interests of economy to make footnotes as short as possible and have given references to archive material in as brief a form as is compatible with clarity. No catalogue numbers have been given except when the reference would be ambiguous without. Unless the name of a manuscript collection is added at the end of a reference, the letter will be found in the obvious place amongst the papers of the recipient. Thus Rothermere to Lloyd George, May 7 1922 will be found in the Lloyd George MSS, which therefore are not mentioned in the footnote, but Asquith to Pringle, January 10 1924 is in the Asquith MSS which *are* mentioned.

The collections I have used are the papers of:

† 1st Viscount Alexander of Hillsborough (Churchill College).
1st Lord Altrincham (in possession, and by permission, of Mr John Grigg).
* L. S. Amery, diary (in possession, and by permission, of Rt Hon. Julian Amery, M.P.).

446

* 1st Earl of Oxford and Asquith (Bodleian, Oxford).
* 1st Earl Baldwin (Cambridge University Library).
1st Earl Balfour (British Museum and Whittingehame).
* 1st Lord Bayford (i.e. diary of Sir Robert Sanders in possession of Mr G. D. M. Block and by permission of Hon. Mrs Neville Butler).
1st Lord Beaverbrook (parts of, in Beaverbrook Library).
R. D. Blumenfeld (catalogue in Beaverbrook Library).
1st Viscount Bridgeman, diary (Shropshire County Record Office, by permission of Viscount Bridgeman).
† 1st Baron Carson (Northern Ireland Public Record Office).
* Sir Austen Chamberlain (Birmingham University Library).
* Neville Chamberlain (in possession, and by permission, of Mrs Stephen Lloyd).
* 1st Viscount Cecil of Chelwood (British Museum).
Sir Winston Churchill (Chartwell Trust, C & T Publications).
1st Marquess of Crewe (Cambridge University Library).
† 1st Lord Dalton, diary (London School of Economics).
1st Viscount Davidson (in possession, and by permission, of Viscountess Davidson).
* H. A. L. Fisher, diary (Bodleian, Oxford).
* 1st Viscount Gladstone (British Museum).
Sir E. M. W. Grigg (see Altrincham).
* 1st Viscount Haldane (National Library of Scotland).
† 1st Earl of Halifax (Garrowby, Yorkshire).
† Sir P. J. Hannon (Beaverbrook Library).
Sir Samuel Hoare (see Templewood).
† 1st Lord Kennett (in possession of National Register of Archives, by permission of Lord Kennett).
Lord Keynes (Marshall Library, Cambridge, by permission of Professor the Lord Kahn).
George Lansbury (London School of Economics).
* A. Bonar Law (Beaverbrook Library).
* David Lloyd George (Beaverbrook Library).
† 11th Marquess of Lothian (Scottish Public Record Office).
J. R. MacDonald (by permission of Rt. Hon. Malcolm MacDonald).
1st Viscount Milner (Bodleian, Oxford, by permission of the Warden and Fellows of New College).
Edwin Montagu (Trinity College, Cambridge).

E. D. Morel (London School of Economics).
Gilbert Murray (Bodleian, Oxford).
Lord and Lady Passfield (London School of Economics).
1st Lord Ponsonby (in possession, and by permission, of Lord Ponsonby of Shulbrede).
1st Viscount Quickswood (Hatfield House, by permission of Lord Salisbury).
1st Marquess of Reading (India Office Library).
Royal Archives, Windsor Castle.
* 4th Marquess of Salisbury (Hatfield House, by permission of Lord Salisbury).
† 1st Viscount Samuel (House of Lords Record Office).
Sir Robert Sanders (see Bayford).
Alexander MacCallum Scott, diary (in possession, and by permission, of Mr John MacCallum Scott).
C. P. Scott, diary (British Museum).
1st Viscount Simon (in possession, and by permission, of Lord Simon).
Sir Arthur Steel-Maitland (Scottish Public Record Office).
St Loe Strachey (Beaverbrook Library).
The Times Archive (by permission of the editor).
1st Viscount Templewood (Cambridge University Library).
Sir Charles Trevelyan (Newcastle University Library).
Whittingehame MSS (see Balfour, 1st Earl of).

In addition to these manuscript sources, the Cabinet papers have been used (chiefly Cab. 23).

The author wishes to acknowledge the gracious permission of H.M. the Queen to make use of material from the Royal Archives. He is grateful to the owners of collections for permission to make use of them, and to librarians and archivists for making them available. He is grateful to the staff of the National Register of Archives for answering enquiries.

2. PUBLISHED WORKS

The following published works have been quoted or mentioned in the text. Footnote references to an author's name refer to the work listed under his name in this bibliography.

I have referred throughout to the diary of Lord Derby as Derby diary. This, however, refers not to the manuscript version which

I have not seen, but to the lengthy extracts printed in Randolph Churchill's *Lord Derby: King of Lancashire.*

Allen of Hurtwood [Reginald Clifford Allen, 1st Baron, *Plough my Own Furrow*, compiled by Martin John Gilbert, 1965].

Anderson [Mosa, *Noel-Buxton, A Life*, 1952].

Attlee [Clement Richard Attlee, 1st Earl, *As It Happened*, 1954].

Baldwin [of Bewdley, Arthur Windham Baldwin, 3rd Earl, *My Father, the True Story*, 1955].

Beaverbrook [William Maxwell Aitken, 1st Baron, *The Decline and Fall of Lloyd George*, 1966].

Bell [G.K. A., *Randall Davidson, Archbishop of Canterbury*, 1938].

Bentinck [Lord Henry Cavendish-, *Tory Democracy*, 1918].

Birkenhead [Frederick, 2nd Earl of, *F.E.: F. E. Smith, 1st Earl of Birkenhead*, 1959].

Halifax [*the Life of Lord Halifax*, 1965].

Blackham [Robert James, *Sir Ernest Wild, K.C.*, 1935].

Blake [Robert Norman William, *The Unknown Prime Minister*, 1955].

Blaxland [Gregory, *J. H. Thomas: A Life for Unity*, 1964].

Boyle [Andrew Philip More, *Montagu Norman: a biography*, 1967].

Brockway [Archibald Fenner, 1st Baron Brockway, *Inside the Left*, 1942].

Buxton [Charles Roden, and Buxton, Dorothy Frances, *The World After the War*, 1920].

Callwell [Sir Charles Edward, *Sir Henry Wilson: his Life and Diaries*, 2 vols., 1927].

Campbell-Johnson [Alan, *Viscount Halifax: a Biography*, 1941].

Cecil of Chelwood [Edgar Algernon Robert Gascoyne-Cecil, 1st Viscount Cecil of Chelwood, *All the Way*, 1949].

Churchill [Randolph Frederick Edward Spencer-, *Lord Derby: King of Lancashire*, 1959].

Clarke [P. F., 'British Politics and Blackburn Politics 1900–1910', *Historical Journal*, vol. 12, no. 2].

Cole [Margaret Isabel, *The Story of Fabian Socialism*, 1961].

Collis [Maurice, *Nancy Astor*, 1960].

Croft [Henry Page Croft, 1st Baron, *My Life of Strife*, 1948].

Darroch [G. R. S., *Deeds of the Great Railway*, 1920].

De Bunsen [Victoria Alexandrina, *Charles Roden Buxton: A Memoir*, 1948].

Derby diary, see Churchill.

Elcock [H. J., 'Britain and the Russo-Polish Frontier 1919–1921' in *Historical Journal*, vol. 12, no. 2].

Ervine [St John Greer, *Craigavon: Ulsterman*, 1949].

Fisher [H.A.L., *An Unfinished Autobiography*, 1940].

Fraser [Peter, *Joseph Chamberlain: Radicalism and Empire 1868–1914*, 1966].

Gollin [Alfred Manuel] *The Observer and J. L. Garvin, 1908–1914* [1960].

Proconsul in Politics [1964].

Graubard [S.R., *British Labour and the Russian Revolution 1917–24*, 1956].

Griffith-Boscawen [Sir Arthur Sackville Trevor] *Fourteen Years in Parliament* [1907].

Memoirs [1925].

Gwynn [Howell Arthur, *The Causes of World Unrest, with an introduction by the Editor of the* Morning Post, 1920].

H.H.A. [*Letters from Lord Oxford to A Friend (second series, 1922–27)*, 1934].

Halifax [Edward Frederick Lindley Wood, 1st Earl of, *Fullness of Days*, 1957].

Hoare [Samuel John Gurney Hoare, 1st Viscount Templewood, *Empire of the Air*, 1957].

Hodges [Frank, *Nationalization of the Mines*, 1920].

Iremonger [F.A., *William Temple, Archbishop of Canterbury: His Life and Letters*, 1948].

James [Robert Rhodes, *Memoirs of a Conservative: J. C. C. Davidson's Memoirs and Papers 1910–37*, 1969].

Jones [Thomas, *Whitehall Diary*, vol. I, 1969].

Kilbracken [*Letters of Arthur, Lord Kilbracken G.C.B. and General Sir Alexander Godley G.C.B., K.C.M.G. 1898–1932*, n.d.].

King [Cecil, *Strictly Speaking*, 1969].

Kinnear [Michael, *The British Voter*, 1968].

Kirkwood [David, *My Life of Revolt*, 1935].

Lucy [Sir Henry William, *Memories of Eight Parliaments*, 1908].

McKenna [Stephen, *Reginald McKenna, 1863–1943*, 1948].

Mansbridge [Albert, *Fellow Men: A Gallery of England 1876–1946*, 1948].

Maxse [Leopold James, *Politicians on the Warpath*, 1920].

Middlemas [Robert Keith, *The Clydesiders*, 1965].

Midleton [William St John Fremantle Brodrick, 1st Earl of]
Ireland, Dupe or Heroine [1932].
Records and Reactions 1856–1939 [1939].

Morgan [Kenneth Owen Oriel, *Wales in British Politics*, 1963].

Morrison [of Lambeth, Herbert Stanley Morrison, 1st Baron,
Herbert Morrison: an Autobiography, 1960].

Mosley L[eonard Oswald, *Curzon: The End of an Epoch*, 1960].

Mosley [Sir Oswald Ernald, *My Life*, 1968].

Nicolson [Sir Harold George, *King George V*, 1952].

Percy [of Newcastle, Eustace Sutherland Campbell Percy, 1st
Baron, *Some Memories*, 1958].

Petrie [Sir Charles Alexander, *Life and Letters of Austen Chamberlain*, vol. II, 1939].

Reith [John Charles Walsham Reith, 1st Baron, *Into the Wind*,
1949].

Rhondda [Margaret Haig, Viscountess, *This was my World*, 1933].

Riddell [George Allardice Riddell, 1st Baron, *Lord Riddell's War
Diary*, 1933].

Runciman [Walter, 1st Baron, *Before the Mast and After it*, 1924].

Salvidge [Stanley, *Salvidge of Liverpool*, 1934].

Samuel [Herbert, 1st Viscount, *Memoirs*, 1945].

Shinwell [Emmanuel, *Conflict without Malice*, 1955].

Simon [John Allsebrook Simon, 1st Viscount, *Retrospect*, 1952].

Smillie [Robert, *My Life for Labour*, 1924].

[Snowden] Ethel Snowden [Viscountess, *Through Bolshevik
Russia*, 1920].

Snowden [Philip Snowden, 1st Viscount] *Labour and the National
Finances* [1920].
Labour and the New World [1921].
Autobiography [2 vols., 1934].

Spender [John Alfred, *Weetman Pearson, 1st Viscount Cowdray*,
1930].

Swinton [Philip Cunliffe-Lister, 1st Earl of, *I Remember*, 1948].

Sykes [Sir Frederick, *From Many Angles: an autobiography*,
1942].

Symons [Julian Gustave, *Horatio Bottomley: a biography*, 1955].

Taylor [A. J. P., *Beaverbrook* (not yet published)].

Thomas [James Henry, *When Labour Rules*, 1920].
The History of The Times [vols. IV and V].
Tracey [Herbert, ed., *The Book of the Labour Party*, 3 vols., n.d.].
Trevelyan [Sir Charles Philips, *From Liberalism to Labour*, 1921].
Webb, Beatrice ['s *Diaries 1914–24*, ed Margaret Cole, 1952].
['s *Diaries 1924–32*, ed. Margaret Cole, 1956].
Webb, Sidney ['The First Labour Government' in *Political Quarterly*, 1961, vol. XXXII, pp. 6–34].
Williams, Desmond [ed., *The Irish Struggle 1916–1926*, 1966].
Williams [Robert, *What We Want and Why*, 1922].
Wilson [Trevor, *The Downfall of the Liberal Party*, Fontana edn., 1968].
Wood [Edward] and Lloyd [George, *The Great Opportunity*, 1918].
Wrench [Sir John Evelyn Leslie, *Geoffrey Dawson and Our Times*, 1955].

3. WORKS OF REFERENCE THAT HAVE BEEN USED

Dod ['s *Parliamentary Companion*].
Dictionary of National Biography.
Burke's Peerage, Baronetage and Knightage.
McCalmont's Parliamentary Poll-Book, 7th edition.
British Political Facts 1900–1967 by David Butler and Jennie Freeman.

NOTES

PAGE II
1 Sidney Webb, p. 23.

PAGE 17
1 Montagu to Lloyd George, December 13 1916.

PAGE 18
1 Asquith to Montagu, June 19 (copy), Crewe to Asquith, May 31 1917, Asquith MSS.
2 Fisher, Wimborne, Cawley, Rhondda, Addison, Munro and Albert Stanley.
3 Devonport, Compton-Rickett, Illingworth, Maclay, Mond, Morison and Hewart. There were in addition about twenty Liberal under-secretaries and holders of Household appointments.
4 See Rhondda, pp. 173–238.

PAGE 19
1 C. P. Scott diary, July 29 1921; cf. Smuts to Lloyd George, November 14 1918 for Smuts hoping to bring Asquith and Lloyd George together under Lloyd George's leadership.

PAGE 21
1 Neville Chamberlain to Austen Chamberlain, September 26 1917 and to Ida, January 24 1920 for Neville Chamberlain refusing to speak at The Wrekin because he didn't want to defend Coalition Liberals.
2 Electorate in 1918 = 21 m. Last register (1915) under 1885 Act listed 8 m., but only 6½ m. voted at the first election of 1910 and of those an unusually large number would be dead by 1918. 5½ m. out of 21 m. is probably about right.
3 Montagu memorandum, November 6 1918, Montagu MSS.

PAGE 22
1 Including about twenty-five Conservatives who did not stand as supporters of the Coalition.
2 Cf. Griffith-Boscawen to Law, October 25 1918.

PAGE 23
1 At Cannock.
2 MacCallum Scott diary, February 21 1921.
3 Barnes to Law, July 30 1920.
4 Cf. MacCallum Scott diary, February 21 1922. His firm made Wincarnis.
5 Cf. *Morning Post*, May 27 1920.

PAGE 24

1 Clynes in *Manchester Guardian*, November 15 1918.
2 Clynes at Harrow, November 9 1918, *The Times*, November 11; 'there are few Labour candidates who, if they go to the electorate and declare that they will give no further support to the government, will come back to the House of Commons'.

PAGE 25

1 Snowden to Ponsonby, January 2 1919; Clifford Allen, December 29 1918 in Allen of Hurtwood, p. 127; Dalton diary, December 21 1918.
2 For an account of some of the Labour party's difficulties as an agricultural party see Henry Harben to Trevelyan, March 11 1921.
3 Bothwell and Widnes were both new seats in 1918. Dartford was Labour in 1906.
4 Stockport on the retirement of Wardle in April 1920 and Woolwich East in March 1921, where MacDonald was defeated by a naval V.C., were examples.

PAGE 26

1 E.g. Paisley, Horncastle, Stockport, Barnstaple, Edinburgh, Louth, Ilford, Hemel Hempstead, Midleton, Hereford, Dover, Cardiganshire and East Woolwich.

PAGE 27

1 See Jones, p. 3 and *passim*.

PAGE 28

1 See Thomas, pp. 10–13.
2 Snowden, *Labour and the New World*, pp. 38–9.

PAGE 29

1 See Trevelyan, Buxton and De Bunsen, *passim*.
2 E.g. Ethel Snowden, *passim*.
3 E.g. Pethick-Lawrence and Mary Macarthur.
4 E.g. Tawney and Shaw.
5 De Bunsen, p. 94.
6 G. C. Ammon in *Labour's Dynamic*, reports of Speeches delivered at Labour week, in London, 1922.

PAGE 30

1 E.g. Wedgwood, Dalton and Trevelyan.
2 Quoted in Blaxland, p. 145.
3 Ernest Bevin quoted in *Daily Herald*, January 17 1920.
4 E.g. Lady Ottoline Morrell in Allen of Hurtwood, p. 125.
5 John Robertson, M.P. for Bothwell, quoted in *Daily Herald*, August 4 1919.

PAGE 32
1 Smillie, p. 100.
2 *Ibid.* p. 177.
3 Smillie in *Daily Herald*, October 2 1919.

PAGE 33
1 Cf. MacCallum Scott diary, May 13 1922.
2 Hodges, pp. viii-ix.

PAGE 34
1 *Daily Herald*, January 11 1919.
2 *Daily Herald*, August 14, September 9 and September 11 1919.
3 *Daily Herald*, December 10 1919.
4 *Daily Herald*, March 12 1920. The voting was: for trades union action 1,050,000, against 3,870,000.
5 *Daily Herald*, July 14, *Sunday Pictorial*, July 18 1920. The voting against Thomas's and Cramp's advice was 2,760,000 to 1,636,000.
6 Elcock, pp. 137–64.
7 E.g. Rally in Central Hall, Westminster reported in *Daily Herald*, August 14 1920.
8 E.g. *Daily Herald*, January 12, January 28 and February 24 1921.
9 *Daily Herald*, March 19 1921.
10 *Daily Herald*, April 9 1921.

PAGE 36
1 Seamen's Union to Henderson quoted in *Daily Herald*, August 28 1919.
2 Smillie at TUC in Glasgow in *Daily Herald*, September 9 1919.
3 Tom Mann at Norwich, in *Daily Herald*, September 8 1919.
4 *Daily Herald* leading article, November 21 1919.
5 Lansbury at Albert Hall rally in *Daily Herald*, October 13 1919.
6 *Daily Herald*, May 1 1919.
7 *Daily Herald* leading article, September 8 1919.
8 *Daily Herald* leading article, October 9 1919.
9 Tom Mann in *Daily Herald*, August 18 1919.
10 *Daily Herald*, August 22 1919 and Tom Mann in *Sunday Pictorial*, November 6 1919.

PAGE 37
1 *Daily Herald*, September 22 1919 for national campaign for this purpose.
2 Lansbury in *Daily Herald*, October 4 1919.
3 Williams in *Daily Herald*, October 8 1919.
4 Lansbury in *Daily Herald*, October 4 1919.
5 Williams in *Daily Herald*, October 8 1919.
6 Williams in *Daily Herald*, October 23 1919.

7 Lansbury in *Daily Herald*, October 4 1919.
8 *Daily Herald*, January 5 1921.
9 *Daily Herald*, January 6 1921.
10 *Daily Herald*, January 27 1921.
11 *Daily Herald* leading article, January 3 1921.
12 *Daily Herald*, July 14 1921.

PAGE 38
1 *Daily Herald* leading article, February 17 1921.
2 *Daily Herald*, September 26 1921.
3 *Daily Herald*, February 18 1921.
4 *Daily Herald* leading article, October 20 1921.
5 *Daily Herald*, November 19 1921.
6 Lansbury in *Daily Herald*, January 8 and 13 1921.
7 Williams, p. 14.
8 *Daily Herald*, August 28 1921.
9 *Daily Herald*, August 24 1921.
10 *Daily Herald*, February 28 1921.

PAGE 39
1 Clynes at Higher Production Council luncheon, *The Times*, December 3 1920.
2 Clynes in *Overseas* for October 1919, quoted in *Daily Herald*, October 9.
3 E.g. Clynes at Carlisle in *The Times*, September 8 1919 and at Aberdeen in *Glasgow Herald*, May 25 1919; Thomas at Cardiff in *South Wales News*, December 15 1919 and at Southport in *Yorkshire Post*, May 31 1920.
4 For Clynes being booed see *Sunday Pictorial*, March 9 1920. Thomas was also booed at Sheffield in 1921: see *Sunday Pictorial*, October 2 1921.
5 E.g. Sir Eric Geddes to Lloyd George, January 15 1920. Bridgeman diary, September 2 1920.
6 Cf. Bayford diary, October 18 1920. Jones, p. 158 for Hodges.

PAGE 40
1 Derby to Lloyd George, March 21 1921.
2 Bayford diary, October 21 and November 11 1920.
3 Snowden at Preston in *Manchester Guardian*, March 22 1920.
4 Clynes at Norwich in *Eastern Daily Press*, October 14 1920.
5 The last paragraph 'An Indestructible Faith' in Snowden at Bristol in *Western Daily Press*, January 5 1920 is a good example.
6 Clynes at Carlisle in *The Times*, September 8 1919.
7 Clynes to National Union of General Workers in *Glasgow Herald*, May 25 1920.

PAGE 41

1 Thomas at Browning Hall Brotherhood in *The Times*, February 16 1920.
2 Thomas, Bevin, F. O. Roberts, Naylor, MacDonald and John Hodge all say this in *Daily Herald*, March 29 1920.
3 Clynes at Carlisle in *The Times*, September 8 1919.
4 Clynes at Norwich in *Eastern Daily Press*, October 14 1920. Cf. *Daily Herald*, June 23 1920 saying Ireland dominates the minds of delegates to the annual Labour Party Conference at Scarborough.
5 Clynes at Carlisle in *The Times*, September 8 1919.
6 Clynes at TUC, December 10 1919 in *The Times*, December 11.
7 Clynes at Ilford in *Birmingham Post*, September 18 1920.
8 Snowden at Bristol in *Western Daily Press*, January 5 1920.
9 Cf. Snowden in *Labour and the National Finances*, p. 48.
10 Snowden in *Western Daily Press*, January 5 1920; Clynes in *Labour Leader*, March 31 1921.
11 Thomas to Browning Hall Brotherhood, *The Times*, February 16 1920.
12 Clynes at Norwich in *Eastern Daily Press*, October 14 1920.
13 E.g. Thomas in *Sunday Times*, November 2 1919.

PAGE 42

1 Clynes at Conference of National Union of General Workers in *Glasgow Herald*, May 25 1920.
2 Clynes in *Labour Leader*, March 31 1921.
3 Snowden, *Labour and the National Finances*, pp. 48, 42 and 36–7.
4 E.g. Thomas in *The Star*, June 30 1920; Clynes at the Higher Production Council luncheon in *The Times*, December 3 1920.
5 Sidney to Beatrice Webb, January 13 1921.
6 Sidney to Beatrice Webb, January 10 1921.
7 For Trevelyan see M. P. Price to Trevelyan quoting Trevelyan, October 17 1920; for Henderson see Sidney to Beatrice Webb, January 13 1921.

PAGE 43

1 Thomas at Cardiff in *South Wales News*, December 15 1919.
2 Henderson in *Daily Herald*, March 20 1920.
3 Thomas in *Sunday Times*, May 16 1920.
4 Cf. the following signatories of a letter from ex-Liberal M.P.s urging ex-Liberals to vote against Asquith at Paisley by-election: C. R. Buxton, Joseph King, R. C. Lambert, Lees-Smith, R. S. Outhwaite, Ponsonby, Trevelyan, A. V. Rutherford and Wedgwood (*Daily Herald*, January 27 1920).
5 Clynes in *Labour Leader*, March 31 1921.
6 Thomas at Kettering in *The Times*, January 7 1920.
7 For Maclean's speech see Fisher diary, June 5 1921.
8 Beatrice Webb, June 19 1921, p. 210.

PAGE 46
1 King, p. 57 quoting Stanley Morison, author of *The History of the Times*.

PAGE 47
1 Northcliffe memorandum, January 31 1919, *The History of The Times*, IV, 470.
2 E. Harmsworth to Lloyd George, October 25 1919.

PAGE 48
1 Rothermere to Lloyd George, November 14 1918.
2 Rothermere to Lloyd George, November 14 1918. Cf. Petrie, pp. 104–6.
3 Cecil Harmsworth to Lloyd George, December 2 1918 reporting Rothermere.
4 Riddell, pp. 358 and 366.

PAGE 49
1 Rothermere, 'Is the Coalition Government any longer Necessary?', *Sunday Pictorial*, August 3 1919.
2 Bothwell in Lanarkshire which Labour won from a Conservative Unionist and Swansea East where Labour polled impressively.
3 Rothermere in *Sunday Pictorial*, August 3 1919.
4 Rothermere in *Sunday Pictorial*, August 17 1919.
5 Rothermere in *Sunday Pictorial*, August 17 1919.
6 Rothermere in *Sunday Pictorial*, October 19 1919.

PAGE 50
1 Rothermere in *Sunday Pictorial*, August 3, 17 and 31, September 4, December 7 and 9 1919, January 9 1921.
2 Rothermere in *Sunday Pictorial*, December 7 1919.
3 Rothermere in *Sunday Pictorial*, August 31 1919.
4 Rothermere in *Sunday Pictorial*, August 31 1919.
5 Rothermere in *Sunday Pictorial*, August 3 1919.

PAGE 51
1 Rothermere in *Sunday Pictorial*, August 11, September 12 and October 24 1920.
2 Rothermere in *Sunday Pictorial*, August 3 1919. Cf. Rothermere to Beaverbrook, December 8 for the genuineness of his desire for a Lloyd George lead.
3 Cf. *Sunday Pictorial*, November 23 1919.
4 *National Review*, November 1919, p. 318.
5 Bottomley in *Sunday Illustrated*, August 21 1921.

PAGE 52
1 Symons, pp. 105–7.

PAGE 53
1 For Winnington-Ingram see Iremonger, p. 209.
2 *Sunday Pictorial*, May 4 and May 11 1919.

PAGE 54
1 Bottomley in *Sunday Pictorial*, October 19 1919.
2 Bottomley in *Sunday Pictorial*, May 16 1920.
3 Bottomley in *Sunday Pictorial*, April 17 1921.

PAGE 55
1 All these subjects are taken from Bottomley's articles in the *Sunday Pictorial* in 1919, 1920 and 1921.
2 Rothermere to Beaverbrook, April 1 1920.

PAGE 56
1 *Sunday Pictorial*, December 5 1920. For the Conservative votes see Fraser to Davidson, December 22 1920 (Law MSS) and Bayford diary, December 19 1920.
2 Rothermere to Beaverbrook, March 9 1921.
3 It also had Ernest Outhwaite, theosophist and editor of the *Leeds Mercury* as Secretary and Lady Askwith, wife of Lloyd George's ex-Industrial Commissioner, and Harold Cox, ex-editor of the *Edinburgh Review*, as vice-presidents.
4 *Sunday Pictorial*, July 24 and 31 1921 for a list of candidates including Lord Fermoy, Sir George Makgill, Lord Clanmorris, F. M. B. Fraser (a former Minister of Marine in New Zealand who was defeated by Arthur Henderson at Widnes in 1919 when, standing as a Unionist, he received virtually no platform support from the government: *National Review*, October 1919, p. 170), T. E. Haydon – one of the founders of the Middle Class Union – and a number of retired officers and businessmen.
5 *Sunday Pictorial*, June 5 1921; cf. Younger to Austen Chamberlain, June 10 and Bayford diary, June 19 1921 for the anti-semitism and abuse of newspaper power.
6 Hertford had been held previously by Pemberton Billing who, on resigning, urged electors to abstain.
7 *John Bull*, September 10 and 17 1921.
8 Colonel Windham.

PAGE 57
1 *Sunday Pictorial*, August 2 1921.
2 *John Bull*, August 13, August 27 and September 3 1921.
3 Cf. Bottomley in *John Bull*, September 3 1921.
4 *John Bull*, August 20 1921.
5 *John Bull*, January 29 and July 9 1921.

PAGE 58
1 E.g. *Sunday Pictorial*, December 11 1921.
2 *Sunday Pictorial*, January 22 1922.
3 E.g. Esmond Harmsworth at Ramsgate, March 15 1922, *The Times*, March 16; *Sunday Pictorial*, February 9, March 5 and March 19 1922.
4 Rothermere in *Sunday Pictorial*, June 4 1922.
5 Rothermere in *Sunday Pictorial*, June 4 1922.
6 See below, chapter XI.

PAGE 60
1 Neville Chamberlain to Hilda, February 15 1920.

PAGE 61
1 Lord Robert Cecil to A. J. Balfour, January 15 1906 quoted in Clarke, p. 314.
2 Cecil of Chelwood, p. 111.
3 Cf. Neville Chamberlain to Austen Chamberlain, September 26 1917
4 Lloyd George to Lord Robert Cecil, June 7 1918.
5 Lord Robert Cecil to Lord Hugh Cecil (copy), January 14 1921, Add. MSS 51157.
6 He announced his intention to resign at the time of the general election of 1918 because it was proposed to give effect to the bill which had been passed through the House of Commons in 1913 but remained in office until January 1919 because Balfour needed someone to be in charge of the Foreign Office while he was in Paris. See Morgan, pp. 282 and 283.
7 Lord Robert Cecil to Salisbury, May 18 1921.
8 Lord Robert Cecil to Salisbury, May 18 1921.
9 Lord Robert Cecil article in the *Sunday Pictorial*, May 18 1919.

PAGE 62
1 Lord Robert Cecil to Lloyd George, May 27 1919 (copy), Add. MSS 51076.
2 Lord Robert Cecil to Ormsby-Gore, n.d. 1921 (copy), Add. MSS 51163.
3 Lord Robert Cecil to Lloyd George, May 27 1919.

PAGE 63
1 Lord Robert Cecil to Gertrude Bell (copy), April 11 1921, Add. MSS 51163.
2 Lord Robert Cecil to Lord Hugh Cecil, January 14 1921 (copy), Add. MSS 51157.
3 Lord Robert Cecil to J. G. MacDonald (copy), March 5 1921, Add. MSS 51162.
4 Lord Robert Cecil to Austen Chamberlain, April 27 1921.
5 Lord Robert Cecil to Gilbert Murray, August 26 1921 (1924 written).
6 *Ibid.*

7 Lord Robert Cecil to Gilbert Murray, May 25 1920. For Northumberland see below, chapter IV.
8 Lady Eleanor Cecil to Salisbury, October 10 1920.
9 Lord Robert Cecil to Lord Hugh Cecil, January 14 1921 (copy), Add. MSS 51157.
10 See below, chapter IV.
11 See enclosure in F. E. Guest to Lloyd George, May 10 1919.

PAGE 64
1 Lord Robert Cecil to Salisbury, February 4 1920.
2 The *Daily Herald* of August 5 1919 described him as holding out a hand to the Labour party and to the Independent (i.e. Maclean) Liberals.
3 See below, chapter V.
4 Lord Robert Cecil to Cranborne, April 20 1922, Add. MSS 51087.
5 Lord Robert Cecil to Salisbury, May 18 1921.
6 *Morning Post*, February 10 1920.

PAGE 65
1 Lord Robert Cecil to Clynes, June 11 1920 (copy), Add. MSS 51162.
2 Lord Robert Cecil to Balfour, February 3 1921, Whittingehame MSS.
3 Lord Robert Cecil to Salisbury, May 6 and May 18 1921, Add. MSS 51085 and Hatfield MSS.
4 For a letter, drafted by Cecil and signed by, among others, Buckmaster, Lansdowne, Clynes and C. P. Scott see Gilbert Murray MSS Box GM21. Cf. Lord Robert Cecil to Gilbert Murray, May 25, July 12, 20, 24 and 30 and August 16, 23 and 28 1920.
5 Lord Robert Cecil to Grey, April 12 1921 (not sent), Add. MSS 51073.
6 Cf. Unsigned to Lord Robert Cecil, April 17 1921, Add. MSS 51163.
7 Lord Robert Cecil to Gilbert Murray, July 30 1920.

PAGE 66
1 J. L. Hammond to Gilbert Murray, April 15 1922.
2 Lord Robert Cecil to Gilbert Murray, July 18 1922.
3 Blake, p. 101.
4 See Law MSS 96/4 of February 18 1920.
5 Derby diary, March 16 1922.
6 Cf. Steel-Maitland to Selborne and Selborne to Steel-Maitland, February 23 1920; Selborne to Steel-Maitland, August 17 1920; Salisbury to Steel-Maitland, September 16 1920. Steel-Maitland MSS.
7 Asquith's notes of the meeting of June 29 1921 in Asquith MSS.
8 Steel-Maitland to Lord Robert Cecil enclosing Steel-Maitland to Asquith, both July 29 1921; Steel-Maitland to Lord Robert Cecil, August 5 [1921].

PAGE 67

1 Steel-Maitland to Lord Robert Cecil, August 5 and September 14 1921; Lord Robert Cecil to Spender and Garvin, August 30 1921 (copy), Add. MSS 51163; Lord Robert Cecil to Runciman, September 2 1921 (copy), Add. MSS 51163.

2 Lord Robert Cecil, July 1921, Add. MSS 51075.

3 Lord Robert Cecil to Colonel Heaton-Ellis of Buntingford, October 15 1921 (draft), Add. MSS 51163.

4 Lord Robert Cecil, memorandum to the King, November 11 1921, Add. MSS 51163.

5 Bentinck, pp. 1–3.

PAGE 68

1 Lord Robert Cecil to Steel-Maitland, February 15 1922; see also memo dated February 28 1922 with list of persons to whom it was sent (Steel-Maitland MSS) together with some replies which are also in Add. MSS 51163. There is another list in 'Note of meeting of March 15 1922' (Steel-Maitland MSS). Cf. H. Fletcher to Miss Logan, March 8/15 1922. Derby thought some of the people who attended 'very good fellows': Derby diary, March 16 1922, p. 430.

2 Heaton-Ellis to Lord Robert Cecil, March 31 1922, Steel-Maitland MSS.

3 Lord Robert Cecil to Heaton-Ellis, April 22 1922 (copy), Add. MSS 51075.

4 Lord Robert Cecil's platform, May 1922, Add. MSS 51073; cf. Lord Robert Cecil's draft speech, May 22 1922 in Add. MSS 51073.

5 Austen Chamberlain to Lloyd George, May 16 1922 (telegram), Lloyd George MSS F 7/5/29.

6 Cf. Lady Gwendolen Cecil to Salisbury, April 22 1922.

7 Lord Robert Cecil to Asquith, October 9 1922 (copy), Add. MSS 51073; Asquith to Lord Robert Cecil (copy), October 19 1922, Asquith MSS.

PAGE 69

1 Especially the *Westminster Gazette*; cf. Lord Robert Cecil to Maclean, n.d., Add. MSS 51163.

2 *The Times*, January 10 1922 for announcement that Grey would mark his return to public life by making a major speech at the Liberal demonstration in Central Hall, Westminster on January 23. Cf. Lord Robert Cecil to Gladstone, January 10 1922 (copy), Add. MSS 51163.

3 Mosley, p. 140.

4 Lord Robert Cecil to Gladstone, January 10 1922.

5 E.g. Gladstone to Lord Robert Cecil, July 18, August 8 and September 1 1922.

6 Lord Robert Cecil to Gladstone, July 12 1922 (copy), Add. MSS 51163.

7 The 1918 figures in Warrington were: H. Smith (Co U) 10,403; Sir P. Peacock (Lib) 8,011; I. Brassington (Lab) 5,377; cf. Gladstone to Lord Robert Cecil, August 8 1922.

8 Gladstone to Lord Robert Cecil, September 21 1922.

9 Lord Robert Cecil to Law, March 15 1923; cf. Bayford diary, March 2 1923.

PAGE 70

1 Derby diary, March 16 1922, p. 430.

2 Strachey to McKenna, February 10 1921 (copy), Strachey MSS.

3 Cf. Midleton to Salisbury, February 18 1921 for example of Salisbury being tetchy.

PAGE 71

1 Griffith-Boscawen, *Fourteen Years in Parliament*, pp. 41, 57–8, 107, 116, etc. Lucy, pp. 229–36 refers to his inability to remove 'the paternal tendency to utterance of blazing indiscretions'.

2 Gollin, *The Observer and J. L. Garvin, 1908–1914*, p. 338 and *Proconsul in Politics*, p. 371.

3 Cf. Selborne to Austen Chamberlain, March 18 1918. Austen Chamberlain to Strachey, March 19 1918 for evidence that Austen Chamberlain agreed.

PAGE 72

1 *The Times*, February 24 1920 for the Rent Restriction question.

2 See Morgan, pp. 289–90 for Conservative peers walking out of the final stages of the bill after Archbishop Davidson said it should go through.

3 Salisbury to Balfour, May 15 1918 enclosing a minute signed by Conservative peers – Barrymore, Bedford, Beresford, Buccleuch, Churchill, Colville, Desborough, Forester, Halsbury, Harewood, Jersey, Londonderry, Northumberland, Plymouth, Salisbury, Saltoun, Somerset, Sydenham, Willoughby de Broke – to say that any settlement granting 'any sort of autonomy to Ireland' would make public opinion shrink and destroy the Conservative party.

4 *The Times*, February 10 1919.

5 See e.g. his letter to *The Times*, January 17 1920.

PAGE 73

1 Salisbury to the *The Times*, January 9 and 17 1920.

2 See e.g. a resolution of a 'meeting of members of both Houses dated March 23 1920' and signed by Salisbury, Selborne, Willoughby de Broke, Steel-Maitland and Godfrey Locker-Lampson in Law MSS 96/4.

3 Where the Coalition Liberal polled only 500 fewer votes than the Coalition Conservative.

4 See e.g. Salisbury at National Unionist Association Conference at Birmingham in *The Times*, June 11 1920 and Younger to Law, June 14

1920 reporting Salisbury's speech. For Selborne's warning that he was too early, see Selborne to Salisbury, June 13 1921.

5 Salisbury to *The Times*, June 24 1921.

6 Salisbury to *The Times*, June 20 1921.

PAGE 74

1 Salisbury at the Labour Co-operative Conference, October 27 1920, *The Times*, October 28.

2 Salisbury addressing Primrose League demonstration at Hatfield, *The Times*, July 19 1920.

3 Salisbury to *The Times*, January 17 1920.

4 *Morning Post*, July 16 1920.

5 Strachey to Salisbury, January 27 1921 implies that Bowerman also belonged.

6 See Askwith to Law, W. G. S. Adams and G. H. Roberts, December 1918 and January 1919, Lloyd George MSS F 79/5/1-3.

7 *The Times*, March 15 1921 for a meeting.

8 Midleton to Salisbury, March 22, March 24 and April 4 1921.

9 Newman to Strachey, June 11 1921 for the claim that this was so.

PAGE 75

1 Austen Chamberlain to Lloyd George, June 15 1921.

2 Salisbury to Lord Robert Cecil, May 1 1921.

3 See Midleton, *Records and Reactions 1856-1939*, pp. 247-57 and 271.

4 Griffith-Boscawen, *Fourteen Years in Parliament*, pp. 70-1.

5 Selborne to Lloyd George, May 4 1918, to Law, November 19 1918, and to Steel-Maitland, February 18 and 23 1920 for Selborne using the Executive of National Union for House of Lords reform. Cf. Midleton, *Records and Reactions 1856-1939*, p. 272 for Curzon, Midleton and Selborne agreeing in 1891 that the first to succeed to his father's title should try to remain in the House of Commons.

6 Newman to Strachey, June 11 1921.

7 See *Morning Post*, March 25 1920 for list and annual Convention.

PAGE 76

1 Austen Chamberlain to Lloyd George, July 26 1920.

2 For Salisbury and McKenna see Strachey to McKenna, February 10 1921 and Salisbury to Strachey, February 22 1921. For Churchill, whom Strachey had previously disliked, as financial saviour see Strachey to Churchill, August 1 1921, Strachey MSS.

3 *National Review*, March 1919, p. 3.

4 *National Review*, May 1920, p. 325.

PAGE 77

1 See Croft, pp. 98-110.

2 See e.g. Croft on 'The National Party' in *National Review*, October 1918, pp. 192-6.

3 Croft in *National Review*, October 1918, p. 195.
4 Standing in the end as an Independent Conservative.
5 Cf. Croft's motion in the House of Commons on May 28 1919.
6 NDP member for North Norfolk.
7 Wife of Lloyd George's ex-Industrial Commissioner.
8 Husband of the proprietor of the *Morning Post*.

PAGE 78
1 See *Morning Post*, March 25 1920 for the report of the Second Convention.
2 *National Review*, February 1919, p. 689–90.

PAGE 79
1 *National Review*, May 1919, pp. 298–9.
2 *National Review*, November 1919, p. 285.
3 *National Review*, April 1919, p. 152.
4 *National Review*, October 1919, pp. 175 and 169.
5 *National Review*, July 1919, p. 639.

PAGE 80
1 *National Review*, December 1918.
2 Maxse on 'A Blank Cheque for the Big Six' in *National Review*, October 1918, pp. 230–3.
3 *National Review*, December 1919, p. 604.
4 *National Review*, March 1920, pp. 34–5.
5 Cf. Northumberland in *National Review*, September 1919 that he was 'not a colliery owner'.
6 See *National Review*, July 1919, p. 639 which says that his address to the Junior Constitutional Club on June 12 1919 caused a 'sensation'.

PAGE 81
1 Report of meeting of March 1 1921 in pamphlet entitled *The Conspiracy against the British Empire*.
2 Northumberland to the Midland Branch of the National Union of Manufacturers in the *Morning Post*, June 19 1920.
3 Northumberland in *Morning Post*, April 30 1921.
4 'The Truth about the Strike', address by the Duke of Northumberland at Kensington Town Hall, April 21 1921.
5 Sydenham to Salisbury, August 15 1921.
6 Sydenham to Salisbury, August 15 1921.
7 Northumberland to Strachey, November 5 1921.
8 Joynson-Hicks to *The Times*, June 10 1921.

PAGE 82
1 *National Review*, October 1920.
2 Joynson-Hicks, Sydenham and Townshend to *The Times*, August 1 1921.

3 *National Review*, November 1919, p. 308.
4 Maxse, p. 92.
5 *National Review*, March 1920, p. 6; cf. Maxse, p. 93.
6 *National Review*, November 1919, p. 312.
7 Maxse, p. 94.
8 Maxse, preface to Darroch, pp. x and xi.
9 *National Review*, March 1921, p. 4.
10 Northumberland to Midland Branch of National Union of Manufacturers in *Morning Post*, June 19 1920.
11 *National Review*, May 1921, p. 323.

PAGE 83

1 Northumberland to Strachey, March 14 [1921]. See also Northumberland's speech in answer to Mr Hyndman at a debate arranged by the Social Democratic Federation in the House of Commons June 8 1921 reprinted in *National Review*, July 1921, pp. 617–33 as 'Bolshevism and the Labour Party'.
2 *National Review*, July 1919, p. 656.
3 Sydenham to Strachey, June 15 1921.
4 *National Review*, April 1919, p. 173.
5 *National Review*, June 1921, p. 454.
6 *National Review*, October 1920, p. 178.
7 *National Review*, December 1920, p. 458.

PAGE 84

1 *National Review*, August 1920, p. 717.
2 Maxse, pp. 9 and 11.
3 Gwynn, p. 8.
4 Gwynn, pp. 22–3.
5 *National Review*, October 1920, pp. 146–7.
6 *National Review*, November 1919, pp. 292–3.

PAGE 85

1 Cf. Gwynn, p. 21 and Sir Richard Cooper saying after a National party luncheon in January 1921 that 'Labour [was] ... largely responsible for the disastrous condition of the country', *Daily Herald*, January 20 1921.
2 *National Review*, February 1921, pp. 760–1.

PAGE 86

1 *National Review*, March 1921, p. 44.
2 *National Review*, May 1921, p. 291.
3 Cf. Geddes to Balfour, June 21 1921; *Hansard*, May 30 1921, cols. 660 ff; see also Steel-Maitland to Salisbury, October 17 1921, Gretton to Lloyd George, March 15 1921 and Gretton to Steel-Maitland, February 18 1920.

PAGE 87

1 Salisbury to Steel-Maitland, October 15 1921.
2 Devonshire to Salisbury, September 25 1921.
3 Wolmer to Salisbury, December 27 1921.
4 MacCallum Scott diary, July 12 1920.
5 Joynson-Hicks to Montagu, April 29, Montagu to Joynson-Hicks, April 30 1920; cf. Montagu to Reading, April 17 and October 27 1921 for Ampthill as well. For Montagu being annoyed see Reading MSS Eur E 238/10.
6 *Morning Post*, July 9 1920.

PAGE 88

1 Lord Hugh Cecil to Lord Robert Cecil, January 12 1921 reporting his own and Wood's opinion; cf. Devonshire to Salisbury, September 25 1921.
2 Halifax, p. 85.
3 With Ogilvie, later Director-General of the BBC, as Secretary, Birkenhead, *Halifax*, p. 87. Lloyd-Graeme adds his own name (Swinton, p. 14) for the period between his entry into the House of Commons in 1918 and his first period in office in 1920.
4 Then Sir Charles Bathurst.
5 For Christopher Turnor see Mansbridge, pp. 93–6.
6 *Daily Herald*, May 9 1919.

PAGE 89

1 See *The Times*, August 13 1923.
2 E.g. Campbell-Johnson, p. 69 says he suggested that Balfour should put Old Age Pensions into the Conservative programme in 1910.
3 Campbell-Johnson, p. 87.

PAGE 90

1 Wood and Lloyd, pp. 2, 3, 6, 12 and 13.
2 Hartington to Lord Robert Cecil, April 4 1922.

PAGE 91

1 Montagu to Asquith, January 25 1917 (copy), Montagu MSS and e.g. Samuel, pp. 122–7.
2 Asquith to Lloyd George, November 13 1918 for Asquith requesting a meeting, and Smuts to Lloyd George, November 14 suggesting Asquith as Chancellor of the Exchequer. All Asquith was offered was the Lord Chancellorship which he declined (Blake, pp. 386–7).

PAGE 92

1 Montagu memo, November 6, 7 and 8, 1918, Montagu MSS; cf. Macnamara to Lloyd George, December 1918.
2 Cf. Mond to Lloyd George, March 15 1919; Lloyd George to Birkenhead, March 15 1919 (copy), Lloyd George MSS.

PAGE 93

1 Fisher to Law, June 10 1919. For Seely see *Daily Mail*, November 12 1919.

2 Cf. Montagu to Lloyd George, February 14 1919 and Montagu memo, March 25 1919, Montagu MSS.

3 E.g. Guest to Lloyd George, May 1919, Lloyd George MSS F 21/3/21 on taxation of Land Values.

4 E.g. Montagu to Balfour, June 21 1919, Montagu to Fisher, February 4 and 17 1920, Fisher to Montagu, February 5 1920 for the Liberal party being anti-Turk.

5 Mond to Lloyd George, December 12 1918 and February 11 1919 and n.d. [1919] F 36/6/60.

6 For Lloyd George's reply to Isaac Foot's accusations, see Lloyd George to Isaac Foot, November 12 1919, Lloyd George MSS F 95/1/56.

7 I owe this information to Mr E. David of the University of Bristol.

PAGE 94

1 Montagu memos, November 6, 7 and 8 1918; Macnamara to Lloyd George, December 15 1918.

2 Guest to Lloyd George, July 8 1919.

3 For lists see Guest to Lloyd George, May 10 1919. It was supported by Boyd-Carpenter, Hall and Viscount Curzon as well as by Lloyd-Graeme, Betterton, Inskip and Elliot.

PAGE 95

1 Fisher to Balfour, February 4 1920, Whittingehame MSS; Balfour to Lloyd George, February 9 1920 criticising the fusionist manifesto drafted for Lloyd George's use by H. A. L. Fisher, who, however, did not favour the creation of a Centre party. Cf. H. A. L. Fisher, notes for a speech February 3 1920, Whittingehame MSS.

2 Law to Balfour, March 12 (Whittingehame MSS), Law to Derby, March 16 and March 20 (copies), Law MSS, Derby to Law, March 18, all 1920.

3 Bayford diary, March 21 1920 for full accounts being given in *The Times* and *Glasgow Herald*, despite Lloyd George's ban of secrecy.

4 Law to Balfour, March 24 1920, Law MSS.

5 *Morning Post*, May 1 1920.

6 Bayford diary, May 15 1920 reporting Hewart saying so; cf. *Morning Post*, May 11 1920.

7 Bayford diary, March 31 1920.

8 Bayford diary, May 2 1920.

9 The best summary is in Kinnear, pp. 88–90.

PAGE 96

1 See Beaverbrook, p. 9.

2 For Derby and Crewe see Bayford diary, October 3 1921. For Strachey bringing Salisbury and McKenna together, see Strachey to McKenna,

February 10 1921, Strachey MSS. For 'stabilization rather than deflation' as the policy, see McKenna to Strachey, February 7 and 11 1921.

3 Grey to Asquith, October 20 1920.

4 Lord Hugh Cecil to Lord Robert Cecil, January 12 1921.

5 See e.g. Samuel to Runciman, January 9 1919 in Samuel, p. 132.

PAGE 97

1 C. P. Scott diary, January 29 and October 23 1922; cf. August 9 1921 and May 31 1922 for further evidence of Scott's intellectual affinity with Maclean and his desire to see him leader. For recruiting policy criticism see *Sunday Pictorial*, January 5 1919.

2 Wilson, p. 203.

3 Cf. *Sunday Pictorial*, February 16 1919.

PAGE 98

1 Bayford diary, June 23 1920. See above, chapter IV for Turnor before the war.

2 Wilson, p. 214.

PAGE 99

1 Gladstone to Gilbert Murray, June 20 1921.

2 See Morgan, p. 295 for this as a topic mentioned in the manifesto of the Asquithean Welsh Liberal Federation on its formation in January 1921.

3 C. P. Scott diary, March 8/10 1923 reporting Lady Simon confirming – what Scott had suspected – that it was Simon's wife who made Simon stand out 'for once' over Ireland.

4 Cf. Salvidge to Law, November 10 1920 for an example of Simon in alliance with a Labour candidate in Liverpool over Ireland.

5 Marquis of Lincolnshire's resolution at the National Liberal Club and address by Sir John Simon on March 9 1921.

6 Asquith at the National Liberal Club in *Morning Post*, March 25 1920.

7 E.g. *Morning Post*, June 21 1920.

PAGE 100

1 Asquith memorandum of conversation with Grey, June 29 1921.

2 C. P. Scott diary reporting Maclean and Gladstone, January 17/20 1922.

3 Cf. C. P. Scott diary, August 9 1921 reporting Asquith on Austen Chamberlain and Lloyd George.

4 *Ibid.*

5 Neville Chamberlain to Ida, January 24 1920.

PAGE 101

1 Bayford diary, May 15 1920 quoting Maclean at second hand.

2 Cf. Asquith talking to Dalton, January 29 1922, Dalton diary.

3 Asquith at National Liberal Club in *Morning Post*, March 25 1920.
4 Bayford diary, July 18 1920.
5 Bayford diary, May 13 1921.

PAGE 102
1 For the meetings see John Wallace to McCurdy, June 22 1921 in Lloyd George MSS F 34/4/14; Frances Stevenson diary, June 24 1921 in Beaverbrook, p. 27.
2 See above, chapter III.
3 E.g. Asquith note of conversation on August 4 1921; cf. C. P. Scott diary, August 9 1921 quoting Maclean.
4 C. P. Scott diary recording lunch with Asquith, August 9 1921.
5 C. P. Scott diary, August 9 1921.

PAGE 103
1 Cf. Haldane to E, January 28 [1922] for the public 'falling in love' with Grey, Strachey to Lady Grey, see above, p. 91.
2 Maclean to Gladstone, January 19 1922; cf. Lord Hugh Cecil to Lord Robert Cecil, January 12 1921.
3 Asquith memo of conversation, June 29 1921.
4 Cf. Asquith insisting on Buckmaster being present if Lord Robert Cecil was to be at the meeting, C. P. Scott diary, August 9 1921. Cf. Lord Robert Cecil to Gilbert Murray, April 9 1921 for the view that it was 'the female members' of Asquith's family who would not 'suffer him to abdicate in favour of Grey'.
5 Haldane to E, July 5 1921.
6 Cf. Runciman to Lord Robert Cecil, August 22 1921.
7 Asquith, notes of meetings of July 5, July 19, August 4 (without Grey) and August 10 1921, Asquith MSS. See also Crewe MSS Box C/40.
8 Gladstone to Gilbert Murray, January 18 1922.

PAGE 104
1 See Crewe to Asquith, July 11 1921, Crewe MSS, for Crewe anticipating this.
2 Asquith at National Liberal Club in *Morning Post*, March 25 1920.
3 For Buckmaster see C. P. Scott diary, December 2/5 1921; for Asquith see Dalton diary, January 29 1922.
4 Haldane to Asquith, January 16 and Asquith to Haldane, January 17 1922, Asquith Box 18.
5 Gladstone to Burns, May 30 1922, Add. MSS 46304.
6 Crewe to Gladstone, December 31 1921; Maclean note of January 19 1922 in Add. MSS 46474.

PAGE 105
1 *Sunday Pictorial*, February 19 1922 for the Cabinet to include Grey as Prime Minister, Asquith, McKenna, Milner, Inchcape, Simon, Buckmaster, Maclean, Steel-Maitland, Lord Robert Cecil, Runciman,

Joynson-Hicks, Sir Thomas Polson and Harold Cox with perhaps
Lambert, Hogge and Kenworthy thrown in.
2 C. P. Scott diary, May 31 1922.
3 Haldane to E, January 31 1922.
4 C. P. Scott diary, March 1 and May 31 1922.
5 See e.g. Midleton to Crewe, February 2 and 6 1922.
6 Gladstone talking to C. P. Scott, C. P. Scott diary, January 17/20 1922
and C. P. Scott diary, March 1 1922 quoting Maclean.
7 Buckmaster talking to C. P. Scott, C. P. Scott diary December 2/5
1921.
8 C. P. Scott diary, March 1 1922 quoting Maclean.
9 Islington to Crewe, February 2 1922.

PAGE 106
1 Asquith's delay in replying to Lord Robert Cecil between October 9
and October 19 1922 may indicate a willingness to step down if the
Coalition went on.

PAGE 111
1 Lloyd George to Law, December 29 1919.
2 Cf. Addison's pamphlet *Coalition Liberals and Mr Asquith* in *Verities*,
p. 12, 1920 in Lloyd George MSS F 21/4/3.
3 Neville Chamberlain to Hilda, January 11 and February 15 1920.

PAGE 112
1 In the case of Agriculture because the Cabinet contained no one with
direct knowledge apart from Long, Lloyd George and Balfour who
spent much time at conferences abroad; see Long to Balfour, September
18 1920 and vice versa, September 22 1920, Whittingehame MSS.
2 Bridgeman diary, July 4 1919.
3 See Birkenhead in House of Lords, *Hansard*, December 16 1918, cols.
97–101.

PAGE 113
1 Birkenhead to Lloyd George, November 6 and December 29 1918.
2 See Neville Chamberlain to Hilda, January 18 1920 for Neville Chamberlain believing that Birkenhead and Churchill were thinking of getting
rid of Lloyd George.
3 *Weekly Dispatch*, January 11, January 25, February 1, and March 21
1920.

PAGE 114
1 *The Times* and *Morning Post*, January 31 1920. For Balfour see e.g.
Balfour to Aldenham, March 10 1920 (copy), Whittingehame MSS.
2 Austen Chamberlain to Law, November 11 1918.
3 Salvidge to Law, November 2 1920.
4 Bayford diary, August 1 1920.

5 Younger to Law, June 14, August 12 and December 24 1920, Bayford diary, August 12 1920; for the South Norfolk and Woodbridge by-elections, Sanders to Younger, December 2 1920, Younger to Davidson, December 4 1920, Law MSS.
6 Younger to Law, June 14 1920.

PAGE 115
1 Younger to Law, June 14 1920.
2 See Blackham, p. 112 for an example of its failure to do so over the Aliens Bill in 1919/20.
3 Younger to Law, January 2 1921.
4 Salvidge, who was a brewer, to Law, November 18 1920; cf. Bayford diary, November 21 1920.
5 See Joynson-Hicks to *The Times*, December 16 1920; Bayford diary, December 5 and 18, November 21 1920 and February 27 1921. Bayford diary, July 10 1920 and Long to Law, July 11 1920 show that many Conservatives who voted against the government on Dyer would not have done so but for Montagu's speech, i.e. they thought the government had a reasonable case.
6 Bayford diary, December 18 1920; cf. Fraser to Davidson, December 22 1920, Law MSS 100/1/31.
7 E.g. Baird to Law, October 4 1920.
8 Cf. Bayford diary, October 18 and October 21 1920.
9 Austen Chamberlain to Lloyd, December 31 1920, AC 18/1/16.

PAGE 116
1 Sassoon to Lloyd George, June 2, *Morning Post*, June 4 and Bayford diary June 23, all 1920, for Excess Profits Duty. *Morning Post*, April 20 1920 for the 'drastic' budget of the day before and April 21 for the 'breach of faith' involved in the Excess Profits Duty.
2 Bayford diary, July 18 1920.
3 Younger to Law, May 21 1920.
4 *Morning Post*, June 5 1920; cf. Younger (to Law, July 23 1920) urging the Cabinet to accept amendments to EPD.
5 See Law MSS F 31/2.
6 See articles dated August 23 and 24 1920 by Lord Hindlip – described by Long (Long to Balfour, September 18 1920, Whittingehame MSS) as a hard-headed Worcestershire farmer who had been an Assistant Conservative Whip in the House of Lords.
7 Bayford diary, November 11 1920; cf. Lee to Lloyd George, July 26 1920.
8 Long to Balfour, September 18 1920, Whittingehame MSS.
9 Younger to Law, October 13 1920 quoting *The Times* article of the same date.
10 Bayford diary, December 18 1920.
11 Bayford diary, November 21 1920.

12 For Addison see Addison to Bonar Law, July 27 1920. For Sutherland see Sutherland to Lloyd George, n.d. and April 1 and Lloyd George to Sutherland, April 2 1921, F 22/3/16, 17 etc. Cf. Stevenson diary, April 26 1921 in Beaverbrook, p. 35.

13 Steel-Maitland to Selborne, July 15 1920 (Steel-Maitland MSS) reporting Younger telling the executive committee of the National Union that the government intended to do nothing this year but would introduce a bill in 1921.

PAGE 117
1 Bayford diary, February 20 1921; Younger to Law, February 23 1921.
2 Selborne to Salisbury, May 21 1921.
3 Austen Chamberlain to Lloyd George, March 19 1921.
4 Bayford diary, February 18 1921 for Allenby being rather Liberal; Bayford diary, October 22 1921 for proposal to arrest Zaghloul.
5 Tudor Walters to Lloyd George, February 11 1920.
6 Fisher diary, June 1 1921.
7 Bayford diary, June 19 1921 for announcement of the new policy including Wages Conciliation Boards which Boscawen wanted but not the farmers.
8 Mond to Lloyd George, December 8 1920.
9 Lewis to Lloyd George, December 20 1920 and n.d. 1920, F 32/1/24.
10 Mond to Lloyd George, July 1 1921.
11 See above, chapter III.
12 For resignation see Law to Balfour, March 15 1921, Whittingehame MSS.

PAGE 118
1 Cf. Austen Chamberlain to Sir George Lloyd, December 31 1920, AC 18/1/16.
2 Milner to F. S. Oliver, January 13 1921, Milner MSS; cf. Gollin, *Proconsul in Politics*, pp. 597–8.
3 Derby to Law, December 16 1920 for Derby keeping all ways open by saying he would probably take office in a year.
4 E.g. Wolmer, in addressing his constituency association at Aldershot, saying that Carson should replace Law as Conservative leader, *Morning Post*, August 2 1920.
5 Bayford diary, March 13 1921.
6 Derby to Law, March 10 1921 (two letters).
7 Stamfordham to the King, March 18 1921, Geo. V K 1681/3; Bayford diary, March 20.
8 I.e. G. Hamilton, Norton-Griffiths and Grattan-Doyle; see Bayford diary, March 20 1921.

PAGE 119
1 Beaverbrook, p. 20. Bayford diary, March 20 1921. Derby to Lloyd George, March 21 1921 and to Austen Chamberlain, March 24 1921.

2 Davidson to Law, March 24 1921.

3 Cf. MacCallum Scott diary March 21 1921; Austen Chamberlain to Strachey, March 18 1918.

4 Cf. Derby to Lloyd George, March 21 1921.

5 Cf. Goulding to Law, June 11 1921.

6 Stevenson diary, June 11 1921 in Beaverbrook, p. 58.

7 Talbot to Austen Chamberlain, April n.d. 1921, AC 24/3/96.

8 I.e. including Monsell and George Stanley.

9 See Bayford diary, December 18 1920 for Sanders being told by Younger to expect the succession to Talbot; cf. Bayford diary, March 24 and April 17 1921.

10 Bayford diary, March 24.

11 For Illingworth being 'useless' see Stamfordham to the King, March 18 1921, Geo. V K 1681/3 quoting Lloyd George.

12 Bayford diary, February 20 and February 27 1921. Hewart did not become Lord Chief Justice until March 1922 (see Beaverbrook, pp. 35–6).

13 Cf. Austen Chamberlain to Lloyd George, March 19 1921 for Austen Chamberlain saying that Horne should stay at the Board of Trade because it was the most difficult seat.

PAGE 120

1 Guest to Lloyd George, January 12 1921.

2 E.g. *The Times*, June 10 1921.

3 Bayford diary, May 1 1921 for even Fitzalan of Derwent, the Viceroy, not knowing of it.

4 Beaverbrook to Law, May 5 1921; Beaverbrook to Borden, May 12 1921 in Beaverbrook, p. 263; Birkenhead to Law, June 9 1921.

PAGE 121

1 Mond to Lloyd George, July 1 1921.

2 For the Addison episode see Austen Chamberlain to Lloyd George, June 9 and June 15 (two letters), Lloyd George to Austen Chamberlain, June 9 and 10, Lloyd George to McCurdy, June 14, Lloyd George MSS and McCurdy to Lloyd George, June 17, all 1921; see also Beaverbrook, pp. 72–4.

3 Beaverbrook, pp. 83 ff.; Beaverbrook to Hoare, July 9, Winterton to Hoare, July 11 1921 in Templewood MSS.

4 E.g. Fraser in Bayford diary, July 16 1921.

5 Arrangements were made in July and August: the committee consisted of Sir Eric Geddes, Lords Inchcape and Faringdon, Sir J. Maclay and Sir Guy Granet.

6 Austen Chamberlain to Horne, August 8, Austen Chamberlain MSS; Lloyd George to Austen Chamberlain, August 10 1921.

NOTES TO PAGES 122–125

PAGE 122

1 Selborne to Salisbury, June 13 1921.
2 Kerr to Lloyd George, May 18 and June 23 1921.
3 Austen Chamberlain to Sir George Lloyd, December 31 1920, Austen Chamberlain MSS.

PAGE 123

1 E.g. C. P. Scott diary, October 28/29 1921 reporting Lloyd George.
2 Cf. memorandum of December 29 recording Balfour telling Law on December 22 1922 at Whittingehame, Balfour MSS; cf. Lloyd George talking to C. P. Scott, C. P. Scott diary, October 28/29 1921 and Bayford diary, November 1 1921.
3 Derby to Younger, November 5 1921 in Churchill, p. 422. For Clynes see Bayford diary, November 8 1921. Cf. Croal (editor of the *Scotsman*) to Law, November 14 1921 for danger of an 1886 split in the Conservative party over Ireland.
4 Stevenson diary, October 28 1921 and Churchill to Lloyd George, November 9 1921.
5 For C. P. Scott taking it seriously in talking to Lloyd George see diary, October 28/29 1921.
6 Bayford diary, November 1 and *Hansard*, October 31 1921, cols. 1480–4 (vote 439 to 43).

PAGE 124

1 Stevenson diary, November 6 1921 in Beaverbrook, p. 111.
2 Salvidge, pp. 202–3.

PAGE 125

1 Stevenson diary, November 6 1921, Beaverbrook, p. 110.
2 I.e. on November 5, see Beaverbrook, pp. 111–12; but cf. Ervine, p. 444 for Craig being absolutely adamant on November 5.
3 Stevenson diary, November 6 and November 8 1921, in Beaverbrook, pp. 110–12.
4 Law to Salisbury, December 2 1921; but cf. Ervine, pp. 444–5 for the view that Craig never had any doubts.
5 Cf. Law to Croal, dictated letter of November 12 1921 (copy), enclosed in Croal to Law, December 1 1921. This letter shows that Law hoped to become Prime Minister at this time: it includes the remark that he would not serve under Austen Chamberlain.
6 For Birkenhead's, Salvidge's and Worthington-Evans's efforts see Salvidge diary in chapter 14 of Salvidge; cf. Austen Chamberlain to Neville Chamberlain, November 13 1921. For Derby see Derby to Austen Chamberlain, November 14 1921.
7 See Derby to Austen Chamberlain, November 14 1921 for Salvidge being 'furious with Northumberland for trying to split the party' and being 'quite ready to move the amendment'.
8 Younger to Salvidge, November 23 1921 in Salvidge, p. 216.

PAGE 126
1 Salvidge to Law, November 24 and 25 and November 28 1921.
2 See above, chapter III.

PAGE 127
1 For accounts of the Conference see Younger to Law, November 19, Derby to Lloyd George, November 18 and Salisbury to Law, November 18 1921.
2 Younger to Law, November 19 1921; cf. Croal to Law, November 11 1921 saying very little public support anywhere for supporting Ulster up to the hilt, especially after Sinn Fein had abandoned the Republic.
3 See report in *Birmingham Post*, August 11 1921 of discussion by *Liberal News* of Lloyd George's speech to the Welsh National Liberal Council.

PAGE 128
1 Cf. Storey to Law, August 6 1921 retailing to Law what Law had said to him.
2 Cf. Derby to Lloyd George, November 18 1921 for Derby being more doubtful.
3 For Chamberlain's speech at Liverpool see *The Times*, November 18 1921.

PAGE 132
1 Stevenson diary, January 19 1922 in Beaverbrook, p. 136.

PAGE 133
1 McCurdy to Lloyd George, December 26 1921; see also McCurdy memorandum AC 32/2/8, December 20 1921. Sutherland memorandum AC 32/2/7, December 19 1921.
2 Derby to Lloyd George, December 22 and December 24 1921 (with enclosures).
3 Salvidge, p. 223.
4 Austen Chamberlain to Neville Chamberlain, December 21 1921 and Neville Chamberlain to Austen Chamberlain, December 29 1921, show that Neville Chamberlain was also asked but did not go because he did not expect a political discussion. In Salvidge, pp. 223–5 Salvidge says Worthington-Evans was present but Austen Chamberlain does not mention him: nor are his opinions recorded.
5 Austen Chamberlain to Neville Chamberlain, December 21 1921.
6 For Fraser see Austen Chamberlain to Younger, December 22 1921, Austen Chamberlain MSS.
7 Austen Chamberlain to Neville Chamberlain, December 21, to Sanders, December 22 and to J. S. Williams, December 22, all 1921, Austin Chamberlain MSS.
8 Austen Chamberlain to Younger, December 22 1922, Austen Chamberlain MSS.

PAGE 134

1 Younger to Austen Chamberlain (telegram), December 24 1921.
2 Younger to Austen Chamberlain, December 24 1921.
3 Younger to Austen Chamberlain, December 28 1921 (two letters).
4 Fraser to Austen Chamberlain, December 31 1921.
5 Neville Chamberlain to Austen Chamberlain, December 29 1921.
6 Younger to Austen Chamberlain, December 28 1921.

PAGE 135

1 These views will be found in letters written by various Conservatives to Austen Chamberlain between December 24 1921 and January 6 1922.
2 Lloyd George to Austen Chamberlain, January 10 1922.
3 Croal to Austen Chamberlain, January 7, Davidson to Law January 13, MacCallum Scott diary, January 11 1922 for Sutherland blaming McCurdy.
4 McCurdy to Lloyd George, n.d., January 11 1922, F 35/1/13.
5 See *A Short Diary of a Press Campaign*, AC 32/4/15.
6 Austen Chamberlain to Lloyd George, January 4 1922.
7 Younger to Austen Chamberlain, January 4 1922.
8 Austen Chamberlain to Derby, January 10 1922, Austen Chamberlain MSS.

PAGE 136

1 Derby to Austen Chamberlain, January 11 1922.
2 Younger to Austen Chamberlain, January 9 1922.
3 *Ibid.*
4 Churchill to Lloyd George (telegram), copy, n.d., F 10/2/1.
5 Younger to Austen Chamberlain, January 4 1922. The Fraser memorandum is AC 32/4/1b of December 30 1921.
6 Younger to Lloyd George, January 4 1922.
7 Salvidge to Lloyd George, December 29 1921 in Salvidge, p. 226.
8 Austen Chamberlain to Lloyd George, January 4 1922 enclosing Neville Chamberlain to Austen Chamberlain, December 29 1921.
9 Fraser to Austen Chamberlain, December 31 1922.
10 Austen Chamberlain to Stamfordham, Austen Chamberlain MSS AC 32/2/27.
11 McCurdy to Lloyd George (telegrams), January 5 and 6 1922; Greenwood to Lloyd George, December 29 1921 for the Irish grounds. For Dalziel being alarmed by the spread of the Younger and Northcliffe/Rothermere movements, see Kerr to Lloyd George, January 1922, F 34/2/11.
12 Stamfordham to the King, January 5 1922 quoting J. T. Davies.
13 Lloyd George to J. T. Davies, January 9 1922 (telegram), Lloyd George MSS.
14 Lloyd George to Austen Chamberlain, January 10 1922.

PAGE 137
1 Chamberlain's speech reported in *Glasgow Herald*, January 20 1922.
2 Lloyd George at Coalition Liberal rally, Central Hall, Westminster, January 21 1922, *The Times*, January 23.
3 Cf. Wolmer to Salisbury, December 27 1921.
4 Churchill to Lloyd George (telegram), n.d. quoting Austen Chamberlain, F 10/2/1.
5 McCurdy to Lloyd George, January 10 1922 reporting Wilson and Austen Chamberlain.
6 McCurdy to Lloyd George, January 11 1922 reporting Austen Chamberlain.

PAGE 138
1 For Gretton see above, chapter IV. For McNeill see speech at Canterbury reported in *Sunday Pictorial*, November 13 1921. Archer-Shee, M.P. for Finsbury, also resigned the Whip (before Gretton: see *National Review*, August 1921, p. 747. He was a Catholic: he seems not to have been a Die Hard.)
2 *Morning Post*, November 22 1921.
3 Bayford diary, December 18 1921. See Simon, p. 130 for Carson's flouting of the tradition of judicial temperateness.
4 Among them were George Balfour, Banbury, Boyd-Carpenter, Rupert Gwynne, Lord Hugh Cecil, Page Croft, Viscount Curzon, Sir W. H. Davison, Gretton, Hall, Esmond Harmsworth, McNeill, Oman, Sprot, Wolmer, Yate and a handful of Bottomley's followers. For the division list see *Hansard*, cols. 360 ff.

PAGE 139
1 Craig to Strachey, March 27 1922.
2 See Austen Chamberlain to Law, December 16 1921 enclosing Craig to Austen Chamberlain, December 15 1921.
3 For the Southern Unionist view see Midleton, *Ireland, Dupe or Heroine*, pp. 110–21 and 158–63; cf. Midleton, *Records and Reactions 1856–1939*, p. 271 for Law's ignorance of and indifference to the Southern Protestant Unionists.
4 E.g. Steel-Maitland to Salisbury, December 22 1921, Steel-Maitland MSS.
5 See above, chapter IV.
6 Devonshire to Salisbury, September 25 1921.

PAGE 140
1 Cf. Salisbury saying this to Steel-Maitland, October 5 and 15 1921, Steel-Maitland MSS.
2 Salisbury to Law, November 18 1921.
3 For election see Joynson-Hicks to Steel-Maitland, February 6 1922.
4 Salisbury to Steel-Maitland, Christmas Day 1921.

5 Salisbury to Steel-Maitland, December 21 and 23 1921, and Steel-Maitland to Salisbury, December 22 1921 (copy).
6 McCurdy to Lloyd George, December 26 1921 says this had happened in fifteen cases by the time he was writing.
7 Steel-Maitland to Salisbury, December 22 1921, Steel-Maitland MSS.
8 Cf. Gretton to Salisbury, December 29 1921.
9 Wolmer to Salisbury, December 27 1921.
10 *The Times*, January 7 1922.

PAGE 141
1 *Morning Post*, February 3 1922.
2 Gretton to Austen Chamberlain, February 8 1922.
3 Gretton and Hall to Balfour, February 10 1922, Whittingehame MSS.
4 Birkenhead was absent by mistake. It is not clear why Balfour was absent. For Balfour's agreement see Austen Chamberlain to Gretton, February 21 1922, Austen Chamberlain MSS. See Gretton's memo of February 19 1922 for report of meeting, AC 33/1/11.
5 Austen Chamberlain to Gretton, February 21 1922, Austen Chamberlain MSS.
6 Bayford diary, February 14 1922.
7 *Morning Post*, February 16 1922.
8 *The Times*, February 22 1922.

PAGE 142
1 Bayford diary, March 10 1922.
2 The signatories were Salisbury, Carson, Finlay, the ex-Liberal Unionist and ex-Conservative Lord Chancellor, Londonderry, Linlithgow, Northumberland, Sumner, Sydenham, Gretton, Banbury, Foxcroft, Rupert Gwynne, Esmond Harmsworth, Joynson-Hicks, McNeill and Sprot.
3 Austen Chamberlain to Derby, March 23 1922, Austen Chamberlain MSS.
4 Goodwin to Salisbury, March 21 and March 25 1922.
5 The draft of this letter is at Hatfield.
6 Salisbury to Major Hamilton, April 13 1922 (draft), Hatfield MSS.
7 Salisbury's speech of April 9 1922, *The Times*, April 10.
8 Cf. Gretton to Salisbury, April 18 1922.
9 Salisbury to Law, March 4 1922.

PAGE 143
1 E.g. Salisbury reported in *The Times*, March 14 and April 10 1922.
2 Salisbury to Law, March 4 1922.
3 Wolmer to Salisbury, April 29 1922.
4 See *The Times*, April 6 1922 for report.
5 Cf. Gretton to Salisbury, April 18 1922.
6 *Ibid.*

7 Cf. *Hansard*, April 3, col. 1992, (Genoa) voting 372 to 94, April 5 (Joynson-Hicks, motion), col. 2388, voting 288 to 95.
8 Cf. Hooper to Salisbury, June 9 1922.
9 By e.g. Midleton to Derby, March 18 1922.
10 Midleton to Salisbury, March 30 1922.
11 Salisbury to Law, March 4 1922.
12 Speech to Political Council of Junior Constitutional Club, *The Times*, March 14 1922.
13 *The Times*, April 6 1922 including a list of those present.
14 *The Times*, April 10 1922.
15 Younger to Austen Chamberlain, January 12 1922.

PAGE 144
1 Younger to Austen Chamberlain, January 12 1922.
2 Younger to Austen Chamberlain, January 30 1922.
3 Younger to Salvidge, February 7 1922, AC 32/3/9.
4 E.g. H. M. Imbert-Terry, chairman of Junior Imperial League, to Austen Chamberlain, January 31, Amery to Austen Chamberlain, January 21 and January 26 1922.
5 Younger to Austen Chamberlain, January 30 1922.
6 Younger to Women's Branch of National Unionist Association at Central Hall, Westminster, February 22 1922, *The Times*, February 23.
7 Austen Chamberlain [to Stamfordham], January 6 1922, AC 32/2/27.
8 Austen Chamberlain to Derby, January 12 1922.
9 Austen Chamberlain to Lloyd George (telegram), January 12 1922.
10 Austen Chamberlain to Fraser, January 11 and to Younger, January 11 1922, both Austen Chamberlain MSS.

PAGE 145
1 Austen Chamberlain to Sir William Madge, proprietor of *The People*, January 26 1922, Austen Chamberlain MSS.
2 Austen Chamberlain to Derby, January 12 1922, Austen Chamberlain MSS.
3 Austen Chamberlain to Derby, January 12 1922; cf. Austen Chamberlain to Earl Fitzwilliam, January 12 1922, both Austen Chamberlain MSS.
4 Austen Chamberlain to Madge, January 26 1922, Austen Chamberlain MSS; Chamberlain's speech at Glasgow, January 19 1922, *The Times*, January 20.
5 Austen Chamberlain to Sir Alfred Smithers, January 30 1922, Austen Chamberlain MSS.
6 Austen Chamberlain to Long, March 6 1922, Austen Chamberlain MSS.
7 Austen Chamberlain to Salvidge, February 14 1922, Austen Chamberlain MSS.
8 Austen Chamberlain to Imbert-Terry, February 1 1922, Austen Chamberlain MSS.

9 Austen Chamberlain to Madge, January 26 1922, Austen Chamberlain MSS.

PAGE 146

1 Winterton to Austen Chamberlain, February 17 1922.
2 Birkenhead in *Weekly Dispatch*, July 25 and August 8 1920.
3 McCurdy to Lloyd George, January 11 and 12, F 35/1/14 and 17.
4 Guest to Lloyd George, January 16 1922 reporting Birkenhead. Cf. L. Mosley, p. 216.
5 Bayford diary, February 14 1922.
6 See e.g. his refusal at the time of the election proposal in Beaverbrook, p. 130. It is not clear exactly when he met Lloyd George, i.e. whether before or after Lloyd George had dropped the idea of an election.

PAGE 147

1 Austen Chamberlain to Chilcott, March 16 1922, Austen Chamberlain MSS.
2 Austen Chamberlain to Chadwick, March 6 and to Derby, March 23 1922, both Austen Chamberlain MSS.
3 E.g. Austen Chamberlain to Salvidge, March 18 1922, Austen Chamberlain MSS.
4 Austen Chamberlain speech at Oxford Carlton Club, March 3, *The Times*, March 4.
5 Cf. Fraser, pp. 294–310.

PAGE 148

1 Bayford diary, December 18 1921.
2 Austen Chamberlain to Hope, February 3 1922, Austen Chamberlain MSS.
3 McCurdy in conversation in Stamfordham to the King, January 5 1922 (1921 written), Geo. V K 1761/5; cf. Lloyd George reported in Stamfordham to the King, January 16 1922, Geo. V K 1761/12.
4 *Glasgow Herald*, January 20 1922.
5 *Daily Chronicle*, February 2 1922.
6 Derby to Balfour, March 4 1922, Whittingehame MSS.
7 E.g. Lloyd George's speech, January 21 1922 in *The Times*, January 23.
8 *Daily Chronicle*, February 17 1922 reporting luncheon on the 16th.
9 *The Times*, March 8 1922. For the importance of the speech before it was delivered see Austen Chamberlain to Long and to Chadwick, both March 6 1922, Austen Chamberlain MSS.
10 Balfour to Lloyd George, March 16 1922.

PAGE 149

1 Derby to Austen Chamberlain, January 11 1922.

PAGE 151

1 Guest to Lloyd George, January 20; cf. Amery to Austen Chamberlain, January 21 1922.

481

PAGE 152
1 Sutherland talking to MacCallum Scott in MacCallum Scott diary, January 11, February 6 and February 13 1922.
2 MacCallum Scott diary, July 11 1921, February 9 and 13 1922.
3 Kerr to Lloyd George, January 17 1922.

PAGE 153
1 Sutherland memo, January 2 1922, F 35/1/1, Lloyd George MSS.
2 Lloyd George at Coalition Liberal Conference, January 21 1922, *The Times*, January 23.
3 C. P. Scott diary, January 17/20 1922.
4 C. P. Scott diary, January 17/20 1922.
5 C. P. Scott diary, March 2 1922.
6 Lloyd George to Austen Chamberlain, January 10 1922.

PAGE 154
1 McCurdy to Lloyd George, January 11 1922.
2 Bayford diary, February 18 1922.
3 Bayford diary, February 14 1922.
4 See above, p. 144.

PAGE 155
1 McCurdy to Lloyd George, January 11 1922.
2 *Manchester Guardian*, February 22 1922.
3 *Morning Post*, February 24 1922.

PAGE 156
1 Austen Chamberlain at Central Hall, Westminster, February 21, *Manchester Guardian*, February 22.
2 Lloyd George to Austen Chamberlain, February 27 1922 (copy), F 7/5/6.
3 For one hint of this see L. Mosley, p. 216.
4 Chadwick to Coote, February 27 1922 and to Austen Chamberlain, March 3 1922, both Austen Chamberlain MSS.
5 Bayford diary, February 18 1922.
6 Bayford diary, March 3 1922.

PAGE 157
1 Gretton to Steel-Maitland, February 18 1920; cf. Sanders to Austen Chamberlain, January 2 1922.
2 Bayford diary, March 3 and 7 1922.
3 Bayford diary, March 3 and 7 1922.
4 He had also talked to the chairman of the National Union on February 28 (Austen Chamberlain to Leith, March 7, Austen Chamberlain MSS) and got his agreement, though he received a rousing letter on March 5 about the contents of a speech on March 3.

5 Leith to Austen Chamberlain March 4 and Austen Chamberlain to Leith, March 7 1922, published in slightly altered version soon after, see AC 33/3/35, n.d.

6 Austen Chamberlain memo to Lloyd George, March 18 1922, AC 33/1/66; Austen Chamberlain at the Oxford Carlton Club, March 3, *The Times*, March 4.

7 Austen Chamberlain to Long, March 6 1922, Austen Chamberlain MSS.

PAGE 158

1 Birkenhead, speech at City Carlton Club, March 7 1922, *The Times*, March 8.

2 Cf. AC 33/1/42 of March 8 1922 'not adopted' by Austen Chamberlain.

3 Hankey to Montagu, January 21 1917.

4 Montagu to Asquith, January 25 1917, Montagu MSS.

5 Montagu to Hankey, March 1917, Montagu MSS.

6 Montagu memo, May 10 1917.

7 See Asquith to Montagu, June 19 1917 (draft), Asquith MSS.

PAGE 159

1 Montagu to Hankey, March 31 1917, Montagu MSS.

2 Montagu to Lloyd George, July 17 1917.

3 Montagu memo, July 22 1917.

4 Montagu memos of November 6 and 7 1918.

5 Strachey to Sydenham, August 29 1918, Strachey MSS for a good example.

6 Long to Law, July 11 1920.

7 For an example of Montagu's manner see Montagu to Joynson-Hicks, April 27 1920, Montagu MSS.

8 The Montagu papers contain a large number of letters showing Montagu complaining to Balfour and Austen Chamberlain.

PAGE 160

1 Montagu to Lloyd George, December 16 1918; cf. Jones, p. 103.

2 Montagu to Guest, November 18 1918, Montagu MSS.

3 Montagu to Lloyd George, Lloyd George MSS F 40/3/3, 27 and 38, February to October 1920.

4 See Fraser to Younger, October 11 1920 in Law MSS 99/6/10; but see Montagu to Lloyd George, July 22 1920 for rebuttal of similar suspicion.

5 Montagu to Cambridgeshire Farmer's Union, July 16 1921, *Daily Herald*, July 18.

6 Montagu to Sydenham, September 17 1918, Montagu MSS (not sent).

7 Montagu to Churchill, December 27 1921, Montagu MSS (copy).

8 For all this see Montagu to Churchill, January 27 and 31 and February 1 and 2, Montagu to E. Marsh, January 26 and Churchill to Montagu, February 1, 2 and 8, all 1922, all Montagu MSS.

PAGE 161

1 Montagu to Lloyd George, February 21 1922.

2 Viceroy to Secretary of State, Foreign and Political Department, March 1 1922 in reply to Montagu's request for India's views, Secretary of State to Viceroy, February 15 1922, Montagu MSS.

3 Montagu to Beaverbrook, March 13 1922.

4 Bayford diary, March 10 1922.

5 Lloyd George to Guest and others, March 10 1922, Lloyd George MSS F 93/5/8.

PAGE 162

1 Gladstone to *Yorkshire Evening News*, March 17 1922 in *The Times*, March 18.

2 Grigg to Lloyd George, March 18 1922.

3 Austen Chamberlain to Lloyd George, March 18 1922, AC 33/1/66.

4 Cf. Sutherland memo (Lloyd George MSS F 35/1/39), March 18 1922 reports a conversation between Fildes, Coalition Liberal M.P. for Stockport, and Hartshorn, McGurk and others: it also reports Clynes's and Thomas's views at second-hand. Ernest Evans, M.P. (Lloyd George's parliamentary private secretary from 1918 to 1920) to Lloyd George, March 21 1922 reports Hartshorn saying 'tell the Prime Minister that he knows where he has friends and that if he wants them to do anything he has only to let them know and we will set to work'. C. P. Scott diary (p. 145) has an insertion which reports Henderson saying that certain Labour leaders had been approached. However, this is written on a loose sheet which the British Museum in binding has put in at February 28. There is no reason to doubt the dating, but the insertion does not follow naturally from Scott's text and there is no asterisk as there normally is for these insertions. If the date was in fact February 28, this would merely show that the Labour leaders were approached at the same time as Sanders. Birkenhead's eulogy of Thomas, also mentioned in the insertion, was at the Junior Constitutional Club, February 23 1922, *Morning Post*, February 24.

5 Neville Chamberlain to Ida, March 18 1922; Sassoon to Lloyd George, March 15. See list in Sutherland memos F 35/1/34 and 36, Lloyd George MSS.

6 Derby diary, March 10 and Derby to Lloyd George, March 11 1922 in Churchill, p. 427.

7 Devonshire to Austen Chamberlain, March 16 1922.

8 Austen Chamberlain to Lloyd George, March 20 1922 (draft telegram), Austen Chamberlain MSS.

9 Austen Chamberlain to Lloyd George, March 16 (two), Lloyd George to Austen Chamberlain, March, n.d., Lloyd George MSS F 7/5/13 and March 16, F 7/5/14; cf. Sir William Sutherland's memorandum of March 18 1922, Lloyd George MSS where Baldwin is listed as an 'old Tory'.

10 Austen Chamberlain to Lloyd George, March 17 1922 (two).

PAGE 163

1 Austen Chamberlain to Lloyd George, March 15 1922.
2 Beaverbrook to Lloyd George, March 19 1922.
3 Sir Leslie Scott to Lloyd George, March 17 and 21 1922.
4 Baldwin at Junior Carlton Club, March 17 1922, *Manchester Guardian*, March 18.
5 Peel to Austen Chamberlain, December 21 1921.
6 Austen Chamberlain to Lloyd George, March 15; Sassoon to Lloyd George, March 19 1922.
7 *The Times*, March 11 1922.
8 Austen Chamberlain to Lloyd George, March 15 1922.
9 Austen Chamberlain to Lloyd George, March 18 1922.
10 Derby to Austen Chamberlain, March 22 1922.
11 Wilson to Lloyd George, March 20 1922.
12 *Ibid.*
13 Sir S. Roberts to Lloyd George, March 20 1922.
14 Greenwood to Lloyd George, March 21 1922.

PAGE 164

1 Austen Chamberlain to Lloyd George, March 16 1922.
2 Sutherland memo, F 35/1/36 of March 16 or 17 1922, Lloyd George MSS.
3 For McKenna criticising the government's reparations policy in the City, see Horne to Lloyd George, March 14 1922.
4 Crewe in House of Lords, March 14 1922, *The Times*, March 15.
5 For Asquith saying that some might go Labour, see Dalton diary, January 29 1922.

PAGE 165

1 Lord Hugh Cecil to Lord Robert Cecil, January 10 1915 in Add. MSS 51157.

PAGE 166

1 *Morning Post*, June 15 1920.
2 Churchill to Balfour, September 11 1920, Whittingehame MSS.

PAGE 167

1 Sassoon to Lloyd George, February 13 1922.
2 Cf. Gilmour to Law, March 16 1920 reporting feeling in Glasgow when fusion was under consideration.
3 E.g. Beaverbrook to Lloyd George, March 15 1922; Austen Chamberlain to Lloyd George, March 21 1922; Sassoon to Lloyd George, n.d., F 45/1/8.
4 Halifax, pp. 94–5.
5 See Beaverbrook, pp. 253–9; Bayford diary, May 1 and 13 1921, Lloyd George to Churchill, October 1 1921, Lloyd George MSS F 10/1/1; and Churchill to Lloyd George, October 8 1921.

6 Cf. Lloyd George talking to C. P. Scott, C. P. Scott diary, October 30 1921, and Churchill saying how 'patriotic Birkenhead had been' in conversation with Lord Hugh Cecil in Bayford diary, March 10 1922.

PAGE 168

1 Cf. Montagu to Churchill, October 12 1921. But it is worth noting that Montagu had thought of Churchill as a possible Viceroy in 1920.
2 Montagu to Churchill, October 12 quoting a letter from Churchill, and October 1 1921, rebutting Churchill's opinions.
3 Churchill to Lloyd George, November 28 1921.
4 Churchill at 1920 Club, January 5 1922, *Daily Chronicle*, January 6.
5 Churchill memo on House of Lords, December 7 1921, Lloyd George MSS F 10/1/6.
6 Churchill at Coalition Liberal Conference, January 20 1922, *Daily Chronicle*, January 21.
7 See above, p. 160.
8 Churchill at Loughborough by-election, March 5 1922, *The Times*, March 6; letter to the Dundee Conservative Association, March 11 1922, *Daily Chronicle*, March 13.

PAGE 169

1 Sassoon to Lloyd George, n.d., F 45/1/8; Beaverbrook to Lloyd George, March 13 and 15 1922. Sutherland in MacCallum Scott diary, March 12 1922 says the same.
2 McCurdy to Lloyd George, February 24 1922.
3 McCurdy to Lloyd George, March 4 1922.

PAGE 170

1 H. A. L. Fisher to Lloyd George, March 20 1922 (1920 written).
2 Hilton Young to Grigg, March 23 1922 in Grigg to Lloyd George, March 23 1922.
3 Mond to Lloyd George, March 18 1922.
4 Hilton Young to Grigg, March 23 1922.
5 McCurdy to Lloyd George, March 21 1922.
6 Birkenhead's speech of February 1 1922 to New Members' Coalition Group, *Daily Chronicle*, February 2.
7 Lloyd George to Coalition Liberal Conference, January 21 1922, *The Times*, January 23.
8 'partly the work of my own hands', *ibid.*

PAGE 171

1 Sutherland memo, March 18 1922, F 35/1/39, Lloyd George MSS.
2 Grigg to Lloyd George, March 23 1922 for Grigg hearing that Lloyd George was going to resign if the Cabinet did not give him a free hand at Genoa.
3 For Labour quarters see Lloyd George to Stephenson, Beaverbrook, p. 138.

4 Austen Chamberlain to Lloyd George, March 21 1922 quoting Churchill.

1 Sassoon to Lloyd George, March 24, Austen Chamberlain to Lloyd George, March 21 and 23, Horne to Lloyd George, March 23 and 24, all 1922.
2 Especially in Austen Chamberlain to Lloyd George, March 25 1922.
3 Austen Chamberlain to Lloyd George, March 23 quoting Law in the postscript.
4 Lloyd George to Beaverbrook, March 23 1922.
5 Lloyd George to Austen Chamberlain, March 24 1922.
6 Lloyd George to Austen Chamberlain, March 22 1922.
7 Lloyd George to Austen Chamberlain, March 24 1922.
8 See Miss E. M. Watson to J. T. Davies, March 25 1922, Lloyd George MSS.
9 *The Times*, March 27 1922.
10 Austen Chamberlain at Birmingham, March 31 1922, *The Times*, April 1 1922.
11 Austen Chamberlain to Long, March 29 1922, Austen Chamberlain MSS.

1 Austen Chamberlain to Long, March 29 1922.
2 Bayford diary, March 30 1922.
3 Austen Chamberlain to Long, March 29 and Austen Chamberlain to Derby, March 29 1922, Austen Chamberlain MSS for the settlement being satisfactory; cf. Horne to Lloyd George, March 23 and 24 1922.

1 Clynes in *The Times*, January 21 1921.

1 Clynes at Manchester, May 1 1921, *Liverpool Post*, May 2.
2 E.g. Clynes and others to Lloyd George (telegram), January 5 1922.
3 Clynes in *Newcastle Chronicle*, April 13 1922.
4 Clynes at Manchester, May 1 1921, *Liverpool Post*, May 2.
5 Snowden to Trevelyan, October 27 1921 for some 'of our circle' withdrawing including Lees-Smith.

1 Cf. Arthur Henderson expecting between 200 and 220 Labour M.P.s and 150 Asquitheans, C. P. Scott diary, February 28 1922.
2 Though it is difficult to find direct evidence. For evidence of an indirect sort see Thomas's speech at Derby on May 7 1922, *Manchester*

Guardian, May 8, i.e. hoping for success at Genoa for Lloyd George as an indication of Thomas; Snowden in *Forward*, June 17 1922 and also Snowden not going as a delegate to the Edinburgh Labour Party Conference, Sidney Webb to Beatrice Webb, May 29 1922. Snowden and Mrs Snowden at this time may well have been involved in some sort of Lloyd George arrangement: see also Walsh to Lloyd George, June 21 1921.

3 Cf. Henderson in C. P. Scott diary, February 28 1922 claiming that MacDonald, Shaw, Graham or Dalton at the Foreign Office and Snowden or Webb at the Treasury would provide the basis for a formidable government. See also Henderson's remarks at Labour Party Conference in Edinburgh in *The Times*, June 30 1922.

PAGE 177

1 For Henderson see Henderson talking to C. P. Scott, C. P. Scott diary, February 28 1922. For Webb see Dalton diary, January 29 1922. For Snowden being willing to drop the Capital Levy see Dalton diary, February 13 1922.

2 Clynes in *Daily Dispatch*, April 27, etc., 1922.

PAGE 178

1 Clynes in *Newcastle Chronicle*, April 13 1922.

2 Clynes at Berkhamstead, February 4 1922, *Morning Post*, February 6.

3 Thomas at Trade Union Congress Cardiff, September 8 1921, *Western Mail*, September 9. Clynes at Berkhamstead, February 4 1922, *Morning Post*, February 6.

4 Clynes in *Sunday Illustrated*, June 4 1922.

5 Clynes at luncheon of Imperial Commercial Association, January 24 1922, *The Times*, January 25.

6 Clynes in *Newcastle Chronicle*, March 11 1922.

7 Clynes in *Newcastle Chronicle*, March 11 1922.

8 Clynes at Berkhamstead, February 4 1922, *Morning Post*, February 6.

9 Clynes in *Newcastle Chronicle*, March 11 1922.

10 Clynes in *Daily Dispatch*, April 27 1922.

11 Clynes in *Newcastle Chronicle*, March 11 1922.

PAGE 179

1 *Daily Dispatch*, April 27 1922.

2 *Ibid.*

3 Clynes in *Daily Dispatch*, May 4 1922.

4 E.g. at the 1922 conference of National Federation of General Workers in *Liverpool Post*, August 18 1922.

5 Clynes in *The Times*, September 4 1922.

6 Clynes at congress of National Union of General Workers, June 5 1922, *Birmingham Post*, June 6.

7 Clynes at Berkhamstead, February 4 1922, *Morning Post*, February 6.
8 Clynes at luncheon of Imperial Commercial Association, January 24 1922, *The Times*, January 25.

1 Clynes at luncheon of Imperial Commercial Association, January 24 1922, *The Times*, January 25.
2 Fraser memo, December 30 1921 enclosed in Fraser to Austen Chamberlain, December 31. For Austen Chamberlain see Petrie, p. 196 and Austen Chamberlain to Parker Smith, October 11 1922, Austen Chamberlain MSS.
3 C. P. Scott diary, February 28 1922.
4 Wood memo, 'Thoughts on Some of the Present Discontents of the Conservative Party' in Halifax MSS A 4/410/9 (? July 1922).
5 Peel to Reading, October 11 1922 in MSS Eur E 238/5 for anticipation of an increase in Labour seats of between 80 and 250.
6 C. P. Scott diary, September 15 1922; cf. Salisbury to Law, March 4 1922 for nobody getting a majority.

1 E.g. Long to Austen Chamberlain, March 27 and Derby to Austen Chamberlain, March 28 1922.
2 Austen Chamberlain to Derby, March 29 1922, Austen Chamberlain MSS.

1 E.g. Austen Chamberlain stirring up Curzon to give the Cabinet a consolidated account of Russian espionage in England, Austen Chamberlain to Curzon, May 15 1922, AC 26/3/40.
2 A popular Chief Whip before the war.
3 Austen Chamberlain to Long, April 27 1922, Austen Chamberlain MSS.
4 Austen Chamberlain to Sir George Lloyd, May 18 1922, Austen Chamberlain MSS.
5 Lloyd George, reported in *Manchester Guardian*, May 18 1922.
6 Sassoon to Lloyd George, n.d., F 45/1/14 quoting Lord Esher quoting King George V; cf. H. A. L. Fisher diary, May 20 1922.
7 Wigram to Grigg, May 6 1922; cf. Sassoon to Lloyd George, April 28 [1922] for House of Commons' feeling. For Steed (who had been sent by Northcliffe to Genoa rather against his will) and his reporting, or misreporting, of Lloyd George's threat to destroy the Entente Cordiale see *The History of The Times*, v, 667–75.
8 Wigram to Grigg, May 6 1922.
9 Rothermere to Lloyd George, May 7 1922, Bayford diary, May 16 1922.

PAGE 183

1 Austen Chamberlain to Sir George Lloyd, May 18 1922, Austen Chamberlain MSS.

2 Lloyd George at the Mazzini celebration of the Liga Italiana at Wigmore Hall in *Daily Telegraph*, June 29 1922. For the peace rhetoric see Lloyd George at opening of Criccieth War Memorial, *Sunday Times*, June 4 1922.

3 Lloyd George at luncheon given by Sir Kingsley Wood at Hotel Victoria to inaugurate scheme connected with restoration of Wesley's chapel in the City Road, *Daily Chronicle*, June 21 1921; cf. Lloyd George at Hotel Cecil, *The Times*, May 27 and at Aberystwyth, *Daily Telegraph*, July 20.

4 Horne to Lloyd George, April 27 1922; Bayford diary, May 16 1922; Sassoon to Lloyd George, May 5 1922.

5 Baldwin's speech at Newcastle in *Newcastle Chronicle*, July 13; cf. *Daily Chronicle*, July 6.

6 Austen Chamberlain to Long, May 19 1922, Austen Chamberlain MSS. Cf. Bayford diary, April 12 1922 reports Worthington-Evans saying the government would occupy Dublin and Queenstown and blockade the rest of Southern Ireland if a Republic was proclaimed by de Valera but this obviously refers to de Valera in the Free State government whereas in fact he withdrew in order to proclaim the Republic. Cf. also Bayford diary, May 27 and July 2 1922 and Fitzalan to Law, June 3 1922. Desmond Williams (p. 127) says Churchill and Lloyd George were only dissuaded by Macready from occupying the Four Courts in June the day before Collins did.

7 *The History of the Times*, IV, 691.

8 As a result of what Austen Chamberlain thought 'shameless' but effective lobbying by the primary-school teachers organised in 'a very selfish Trade Union', Austen Chamberlain to Sir George Lloyd, May 18 1922, Austen Chamberlain MSS.

9 Austen Chamberlain to Lloyd George, May 16 (two telegrams) and May 17 (telegram) 1922; cf. Bayford diary, May 27.

PAGE 184

1 Bayford diary, April 12 1922 for asking that it be left to back-benchers; cf. July 15 and 19 1922.

2 Bayford diary, May 27 1922.

3 The references for the German Fabric Glove episode are as follows: Edge to Lloyd George, December 22 1921, February 2 and 10 and July 28, Edge to J. T. Davies, August 11, Baldwin to Lloyd George, July 5, all Lloyd George MSS, Derby to Law, July 16, Derby to Austen Chamberlain, July 21 and Baldwin to Austen Chamberlain, August 11, Bayford diary, April 12, all 1922.

4 Long to Austen Chamberlain, May 18 1922.

5 Cf. Austen Chamberlain to Curzon, May 20, Austen Chamberlain MSS and Younger to Chamberlain, May 10 1922.

6 Bayford diary, July 5 for view that the government didn't want to do anything.

7 Bayford diary, July 15 1922. For the House of Lords question generally see Curzon to Austen Chamberlain, May 24 and Austen Chamberlain to Curzon, May 25, June 14 and June 17.

8 Cf. Strachey to H. A. Gwynn, March 11 1922, Strachey MSS.

9 *The Times*, August 3 1922; cf. Lloyd George to Reading, July 26, Reading to Lloyd George, May 4, July 5, August 31 and September 7.

PAGE 185

1 For Esher see Callwell, II, 327.

2 Austen Chamberlain to Sir George Lloyd, May 18 1922, Austen Chamberlain MSS; cf. Strachey to H. A. Gwynn, March 11 1922, Strachey MSS for need for caution in case everything falls down once any piece of the Coalition structure is removed.

3 The victory on April 3 was 94 against the government to 373 for; on April 5 95 to 288. But on each occasion there were substantial Labour and Asquithean elements in the anti-governmental vote. On April 3 not more than a third were Conservatives; on April 5 about 35 were. Those voting against included Banbury, Lords Hugh and Robert Cecil, Captain C. Craig (with Wilson the only Irish M.P.), Viscount Curzon, Erskine, Gretton, Gwynne, Hall, McNeill, Steel-Maitland, Mosley, Gideon Murray, Pretyman Newman, Nicholson, Oman, Polson, Sueter, Sir Henry Wilson and Wolmer (all voting against in both divisions) and George Balfour, Joynson-Hicks, Ormsby-Gore, Lord Henry Bentinck, Page Croft and Sprot (voting against once).

PAGE 186

1 Cf. Northumberland, Maxse and Esher saying so at luncheon on February 16 (Callwell, II, 327).

2 Craig to Strachey, April 7 1922; cf. Callwell, II, 333–6.

3 Craig to Strachey, March 27 1922.

4 Callwell, II, 337–8.

5 I.e. Tryon, Pease, Wood, Winterton and Bridgeman. In addition Godfrey Locker-Lampson, who was not a minister, said the same.

6 Bayford diary, July 2 1922; Bridgeman diary, pp. 45 and 63 ff.

7 Wolmer to Salisbury, July 5 1922.

8 Derby to Austen Chamberlain, September 9 1922.

9 Wolmer to Salisbury, July 25 1922, Salisbury to Law, September 23 1922 for candidates hoping to stand against Coalition Unionists; cf. Younger to Austen Chamberlain, April 3 1922 for Ulstermen intending to stand against Conservatives who supported the Irish Treaty.

PAGE 187

1 *The Times*, July 15. The phrase is from Finlay (the Die Hard President of the International Court of Justice) to Salisbury, July 18 1922.

2 Bayford diary, July 19 1922.
3 I.e. Amery, Baird, Barlow, Bridgeman, Eyres-Monsell, Gilmour, Sanders, Stanley, Mitchell-Thomson, Murray, Pease, Tryon, Wood, Pollock and Scott. Winterton was absent but wrote a letter (Winterton to Austen Chamberlain, July 19 1922, AC 33/2/10 and 11, 33/2/4).
4 Bayford diary, July 21 1922.
5 AC 33/2/4 for Austen Chamberlain's summary of the views of the meeting.
6 Bayford diary, July 29 1922.

PAGE 188
1 Bayford diary, July 29 1922.
2 Bayford diary, August 4 1922.
3 E.g. General Godley to Lord Kilbracken, January 22 1919, Kilbracken, p. 145; cf. Captain Victor Cecil to Salisbury, October 6 1920.
4 Bayford diary, August 4 1922; Fraser to Sanders, August 7 1922.

PAGE 190
1 For the Trades Union Bill see Austen Chamberlain to Derby, September 7, Austen Chamberlain MSS, Wilson to Austen Chamberlain, AC 33/2/26 September for *not* dropping the bill, and Derby to Austen Chamberlain, September 11, all 1922.
2 Cf. Croal saying the Trades Union Bill might break up the Coalition, Croal to Law, August 25 1922.
3 Derby to Austen Chamberlain, September 9 1922.
4 Derby to Austen Chamberlain, September 1 1922, in Churchill, p. 440.

PAGE 191
1 Lloyd George to Curzon, September 15 1922, Lloyd George MSS.
2 Lloyd George talking to C. P. Scott, C. P. Scott diary, May 31 1922.
3 See e.g. Lloyd George's statement in the *Sunday Chronicle*, September 24 1922; cf. the letter from Grigg in *Western Mail*, September 27 1922.
4 Cf. Churchill to Lloyd George, July 26 1922.

PAGE 192
1 George Cockerill, M.P. to Austen Chamberlain, October 17 1922; but cf. Younger memo of September 26 1922 in Bayford MSS for Austen Chamberlain not realising how far he had gone.
2 Austen Chamberlain to Long, April 27 1922, Austen Chamberlain MSS for going separately to the election but forming part of a Coalition.
3 Wilson to Austen Chamberlain, September 1922 n.d., AC 33/2/26 saying 184 probably.
4 Wilson to Austen Chamberlain, September 19 1922, AC 33/2/26.
5 Younger to Chamberlain, September 16 1922; Petrie, pp. 196–8.

6 Younger to Austen Chamberlain, September 22 1922.
7 Sanders to Younger, September 23 1922, Bayford MSS.

PAGE 193
1 Wilson to Austen Chamberlain, September 21 and 22 1922.
2 Younger to Sanders, September 25 1922, Bayford MSS.
3 Fraser to Sanders, September 22 1922, Bayford MSS.
4 Sanders to Younger, September 23 1922, Bayford MSS.
5 Wilson to Austen Chamberlain, September 22 1922.
6 Wilson to Sanders, September 24 1922, Bayford MSS.
7 Younger memo of interview with Mr Chamberlain on Tuesday September 26 1922, Bayford MSS.
8 Wilson to Younger, October 5 1922, Bayford MSS.
9 For J. T. Davies flying this kite, see Wilson to Younger, October 5 1922, Bayford MSS. See also Beaverbrook, pp. 181–2.

PAGE 194
1 L. Mosley, pp. 237–8; Amery diary, October 10 1922 reporting conversation with Austen Chamberlain. Cf. Wilson to Austen Chamberlain, October 11 1922 for election before the National Union meeting, Petrie, p. 200.
2 Law's letter is in *The Times*, October 7 1922.
3 Wilson to Sanders, October 12 1922, Petrie, pp. 200–1.
4 Wilson to Austen Chamberlain, October 1922, n.d., AC 33/2/43.
5 Austen Chamberlain to Wilson, October 12 1922, Austen Chamberlain MSS. for Younger saying so in person.
6 Amery diary, September 20 1922.

PAGE 195
1 Lord Eustace Percy to Salisbury, October 13 1922; Long of Wraxall to Salisbury, October 16 1922.
2 Beaverbrook, p. 181 says Birkenhead asked him to be Prime Minister with Lloyd George as Lord President on October 9.
3 I.e. Thursday.

PAGE 196
1 Long to Austen Chamberlain, March 27 1922.
2 Long to Austen Chamberlain, October 13 1922; cf. Younger enclosing formal letter forwarded in Younger to Austen Chamberlain, October 12 1922; cf. Joynson-Hicks to Salisbury, October 10 1922.
3 Austen Chamberlain to Long, October 12 1922, Austen Chamberlain MSS.
4 Austen Chamberlain to Wilson, October 12, Amery diary, October 10 1922.
5 Austen Chamberlain to Birkenhead, October 12 1922, Austen Chamberlain MSS.

PAGE 197

1 Austen Chamberlain at Midland Conservative Club, October 13 1922, *Manchester Guardian*, October 14. See Amery diary, October 14 1922 for Amery and Lloyd-Graeme finding 'the common foe' stuff objectionable.

2 Amery diary, October 14 1922.

3 H. A. L. Fisher diary, [October 15] 1922.

4 Lloyd George at Manchester Reform Club, October 14 1922, *Manchester Guardian*, October 16.

5 Austen Chamberlain to Birkenhead, October 12 1922, AC 33/2/45.

PAGE 198

1 L. Mosley, p. 239–40.

2 Chamberlain had thought of a party meeting before the dinner took place: he intended it to provide a platform from which 'to tell them bluntly that they must either follow our advice or do without it': Austen Chamberlain to Birkenhead, October 15 1922, AC 33/2/52.

3 Long to Austen Chamberlain, October 12 1922 urging Austen Chamberlain not to burn his boats on Saturday.

4 Cf. Wilson to Sanders, October 12, Bayford MSS for the danger that Lloyd George would make a breach.

5 Petrie, p. 200.

6 For the Die Hards thinking so, see Cooper to Salisbury, October 9 1922.

7 Croft, October 17 1922 in Croft, p. 163.

PAGE 199

1 Austen Chamberlain to Leith, March 7 1922, Austen Chamberlain MSS; Leith to Austen Chamberlain, March 4 1922.

2 Gretton to Salisbury, October 23 1921.

3 Salvidge to Austen Chamberlain, March 17 1922.

4 Leith to Austen Chamberlain, October 15 and Austen Chamberlain to Leith, October 16 1922.

5 Salvidge diary, October 1922 in Salvidge, p. 237.

6 Hoare, p. 28 quoting Wilson.

7 Wilson to all junior ministers, October 11 1922, Austen Chamberlain MSS, and to Austen Chamberlain, October 11 1922.

8 Amery diary, October 13 1922.

9 Amery diary, October 14 1922.

PAGE 200

1 Amery diary, October 16 1922.

2 Bayford diary, October 19 1922 reports that Amery 'stated own views not very well'; he always spoke with vigour.

3 Amery says that he was surprised at what these three accepted at lunch-time.

4 Amery diary, October 16 1922.
5 See above, chapter IV.
6 Cf. Griffith-Boscawen, *Fourteen Years in Parliament*, pp. 75–7.

PAGE 201
1 Griffith-Boscawen to Austen Chamberlain, October 2 1922, AC 33/2/28.
2 Griffith-Boscawen to Austen Chamberlain, October 6 1922.
3 Griffith-Boscawen to Lloyd George, October 9 1922 and to Austen Chamberlain, October 9 1922.
4 Fisher diary, October 10 1922.
5 Griffith-Boscawen to Austen Chamberlain, October 10 and 12 1922.
6 *Ibid.*
7 Cf. Ormsby-Gore to Law, October 17 1922.

PAGE 202
1 Baldwin to Davidson, March 31 1922 in James, p. 112.
2 Baldwin to Mrs Davidson, January 16 1921 in James, p. 112.
3 Davidson to Law, January 13 1922.
4 For the possibility that he might have done, see his speech in support of Lloyd George and the Coalition reported in the *Manchester Guardian* of March 18 1922, at the point at which an India Secretary was being appointed (see above, pp. 162–3).
5 See above, p. 162.
6 Baldwin, p. 114 quoting Mrs Baldwin's account; Baldwin to Mrs Davidson, September 29 1922 in James, p. 114.
7 Amery diary, October 10 1922 reporting Austen Chamberlain.
8 Amery diary, October 12 1922 reporting Baldwin.
9 L. Mosley, p. 233 quoting Curzon.
10 Amery diary, October 14 1922.

PAGE 203
1 He and Ormsby-Gore were tellers: Morgan, p. 289.
2 It seems to have been based on a diary which we do not have.
3 Hoare, pp. 18–19; Law to Hoare, September 27 1922; Hoare to Godfrey ? October 10 1922, Templewood MSS I 11 and I 12.
4 Davidson in James, p. 120.
5 Hoare, pp. 22–3.

PAGE 204
1 Hoare, p. 24.
2 Hoare, pp. 23–4.
3 Wood to Austen Chamberlain, October 17 1922; Austen Chamberlain memo of October 18 1922, AC 33/2/83.
4 Amery diary, October 17 1922.
5 Amery diary, October 18 1922; Petrie, p. 201. Presumably Beaverbrook did this because Law would not yet play.

6 Cf. Sanders saying to constituents at Bridgewater in public that he wanted a Conservative Prime Minister and would resign on Thursday, Bayford diary, October 19 1922.

PAGE 205

1 Amery diary, October 18 1922.
2 Amery diary, October 18 1922 reporting Oliver Locker-Lampson.
3 Amery diary, October 18 reporting Oliver Locker-Lampson.
4 On one under-secretary who was able to question Hoare later that evening, Amery diary, October 18 1922.
5 Austen Chamberlain to Wilson, November 22 1922.
6 Hoare, p. 26 says seventy-four signed the list of attendance; Bayford diary, October 19 1922 says thirty-five.
7 Hoare, p. 25.
8 Hoare, p. 26.

PAGE 206

1 Hoare, pp. 26–7.
2 E.g. Pretyman to Law, December 20 1918.
3 Petrie, p. 202.
4 Hoare, pp. 26–7.
5 Hoare, p. 28.
6 Stamfordham to King George V, October 19 1922 Geo. V K 1814 for Lloyd George seeing Law on the 18th and being told that the Coalition should stop. For Rothermere see *The History of the Times*, IV, 750.
7 The instances are so numerous that it is unnecessary to list the occasion on which Lloyd George, Dalziel, Fraser, Sanders, Younger, Davidson, Waterhouse, Curzon, Birkenhead and Beaverbrook urged Law to be in touch or to come home and resume active political life.
8 See above, p. 121; cf. Taylor.
9 Beaverbrook, p. 132.

PAGE 207

1 *The History of the Times*, IV, 725.
2 Balfour memorandum of conversation with Law at Whittingehame, December 29 1922, Balfour MSS.
3 C. P. Scott diary, December 6 1922 recording conversation with Law.
4 Fraser to Sanders, September 22 1922, Bayford MSS.
5 Amery diary, October 7 1922 reporting the Duke at dinner at Chatsworth; cf. Amery diary, October 13 1922 for Devonshire being alerted for next week. For Milner see Amery diary, October 12. It is possible that Amery's visit was connected with Devonshire's desire to play a part in buying *The Times*.
6 See *The History of The Times*, IV, 675 and 750 for Rothermere's meetings with Law. Beaverbrook and Devonshire separately were also trying to buy *The Times*; so were Birkenhead and Lloyd George.

7 Fraser to Sanders, October 7 1922 reporting conversation with Derby.

8 Law to Austen Chamberlain, October 7 1922.

9 See above, p. 193.

10 Hoare, p. 20; see *The History of The Times*, IV, 754 reporting one of the things Law told Wickham Steed on October 16; Amery diary, October 13 1922 reporting Law.

11 It would be interesting to know whether a meeting of this sort was in Davidson's mind when Davidson brought Hoare and Baldwin together, and how far Law knew what Davidson was doing.

PAGE 208

1 For draft of letter doing so see Law to Archibald Craig, October 18 1922, Law MSS.

2 Amery diary, October 18 1922 quoting Baldwin.

3 L. Mosley, pp. 242–3 and 245.

4 Cf. James, p. 125 for Davidson's having 'no doubt that by the early evening [Law] had definitely decided to attend'.

5 Cf. Petrie, p. 202 for feeling in the Carlton Club at lunch-time on the 18th that the Coalition had been saved. It is of course possible that, when Austen Chamberlain saw Law later on the afternoon of the 19th, he told him that he had himself found insufficient support for the under-secretaries' plan among his Cabinet colleagues.

6 Hoare, p. 29.

7 Hoare, p. 30.

8 And also Fitzroy who was with Pretyman.

9 Hoare, p. 30.

10 Hoare, p. 31.

PAGE 209

1 Sanders to Wilson, October 8; cf. Amery diary, October 10.

2 Cf. Bayford diary, October 1 1922.

3 Cf. Wilson to Younger, October 5 1922; Sanders to Wilson, October 8 both Bayford MSS.

4 Austen Chamberlain to Parker Smith, October 11 1922, Austen Chamberlain MSS.

5 Austen Chamberlain to Fraser, October 6 1922, Austen Chamberlain MSS.

6 For Curzon see L. Mosley, p. 241–2. Law reassured Austen Chamberlain after his *Times* letter: see Law to Austen Chamberlain, October 7. Cf. Derby to Austen Chamberlain, October 9 1922 which doesn't say that Lloyd George should go now but that he should go after the election.

7 Austen Chamberlain to Parker Smith, October 11 1922.

PAGE 212

1 For the meeting see *The Times*, October 20 1922. For the lists of voters see James, pp. 129–32.

2 L. Mosley, p. 247.
3 Amery diary, October 20 1922.

PAGE 213
1 C. P. Scott diary, October 23 1922 reporting Lloyd George.
2 Fisher diary, October 4 and October 8 1922.

PAGE 214
1 E.g. Lloyd George talking to H. A. L. Fisher, Fisher diary, October 4 1922.
2 Fisher diary, October 19 1922 (two entries).

PAGE 215
1 Cf. Fisher diary, November 1 1922 for Lloyd George hoping Law would get a majority.
2 Munro, the Scottish Secretary from 1916 to 1922, decided in September that he would return to the Bar (Munro to Lloyd George, September 1 1922). He became Lord Justice-Clerk in Scotland, reappearing in office in the 1940/5 and Churchill Caretaker governments as a Liberal-National Lord-in-Waiting.
3 Fisher diary, [October 16] 1922.
4 Fisher diary, October 19 1922.
5 Amery diary, October 15 1922 reporting Sir Hamar Greenwood.
6 Grigg to Lady Astor, October 21 1922 and November 3 1922, Altrincham MSS. Lady Emmott was the wife of Lord Emmott for whom see above, pp. 74–5.
7 Bayford diary, May 13 1921.
8 Mond to Lloyd George, July 1 1921.

PAGE 216
1 Mond, memo, enclosed in D. Thomas to J. T. Davies, September 7 1922 Lloyd George MSS F 37/2/18; Fisher diary, October 16 1922.
2 Mond to Lloyd George, October 20 1922.
3 Mond to Lloyd George, November 5 1922.
4 Mond to Lloyd George, October 29 1922.
5 Lloyd George at Liberal Club, Glasgow, October 28 1922, *Manchester Guardian*, October 29.
6 Mond to Lloyd George, October 29 1922.
7 Mond to Lloyd George, November 5 1922.
8 Mond to Lloyd George, November 12 1922.
9 E.g. Fisher to Law, October 24 1922 and February 27 1923, and to Balfour, July 19 1923, Whittingehame MSS.
10 Fisher diary, October 16 1922.
11 Hilton Young to Lloyd George, October 19 1922; Clwyd to Lloyd George (telegram), October 21 1922.

PAGE 217

1 Churchill to Birkenhead, May 1922 in Birkenhead, pp. 441–2; Derby diary, October 25 1922.
2 I.e. appendicitis.
3 Address to the electors of Dundee in *Daily Telegraph*, November 7 1922.
4 Fisher diary, November 2 1922.
5 Churchill, telegram to president of Dundee Liberal Association in *Daily Mail*, October 23 1922.
6 Fisher diary, October 25 1922.

PAGE 218

1 Lloyd George at Leeds, October 21 1922 in *The Observer*, October 22.
2 C. P. Scott diary, October 23 1922 reporting Lloyd George.
3 Cf. Joan to Edward Lascelles, October 30 1922, Whittingehame MSS. 76.
4 Fisher diary, October 21 1922 reporting journalists at the Leeds meeting noticing that Lloyd George did not call himself a Liberal.
5 Horne in Joan to Edward Lascelles, October 30 1922.
6 Lloyd George at Hotel Victoria, October 25 1922, *The Times*, October 26.
7 Lloyd George talking to C. P. Scott, diary October 23 1922 says thirty Asquitheans against Coalition Liberals, only two vice versa.
8 Fisher diary, November 2 1922 for the number 35. Taylor says Beaverbrook subsidised hardly any except Hall Caine against Guest.
9 Scovell to Miss Stevenson, November 8 1922, Lloyd George MSS.

PAGE 219

1 Herbert Lewis to Lloyd George, November 6 1922 reporting a conversation with Younger.
2 Guest to Lloyd George, n.d., F 22/3/45.
3 Fisher diary, November 1 1922.
4 Clwyd in Fisher diary, November 21 1922.
5 For an example of euphoric, and even alcoholic, electioneering see the account of Birkenhead's, Lloyd George's and Horne's visit to Balfour at Whittingehame during Lloyd George's visit to Scotland in Joan to Edward Lascelles, October 30 1922, Whittingehame MSS.

PAGE 220

1 Fisher diary, November 1 1922.
2 Cf. Rothermere to Simon, October 27 1922.
3 Cf. Steed to Law, October 19 1922; cf. Balfour's memorandum of conversation with Law at Whittingehame, December 29 1922, Balfour MSS for Law sticking to the one-year plan. Cf. Joan to Edward Lascelles, October 30, Whittingehame MSS and Kerr to Lloyd George, November 6 1922. Cf. Grigg to Abe Bailey, November 23, Altrincham

MSS and C. P. Scott diary, December 6 (reporting Lloyd George) on the incompetence of the new government.

4 E.g. Oliver Locker-Lampson to Lloyd George, February 17 1923.
5 See below, chapter XVI.
6 Ullswater to Law, October 23, Balfour memorandum at Whittingehame, December 29 1922.

PAGE 221
1 Churchill speech at Aldwych Club, May 4 1922, *The Times*, May 5.
2 C. P. Scott diary, October 23 1922 reporting Lloyd George. I have seen no evidence that this was so.
3 Lloyd George to C. P. Scott, November 8 1922, Lloyd George MSS.

PAGE 222
1 Lloyd George MSS F 42/11/1–2.
2 C. P. Scott diary, December 6 1922 quoting Lloyd George. It was probably Law who prevented Pringle receiving the Coupon in 1918: see Law to Lloyd George, n.d. 1918, F 30/2/59.
3 Bute to Lloyd George, October 18 and Lloyd George to Bute, October 23 1922, Lloyd George MSS.
4 C. P. Scott diary, October 23 1922.
5 Cf. H. McLaren to Miss Stevenson, December 5 1922 reporting Asquith not encouraging, Fisher diary, December 4 1922 for Mrs Asquith refusing to meet Lloyd George.
6 *Daily Chronicle*, November 29 1922.
7 C. P. Scott diary, December 6 1922.
8 Fisher diary, November 19 1922.
9 C. P. Scott diary, December 6 1922.
10 *Daily Chronicle*, November 29 1922.
11 Lloyd George to George Lambert, November 24 1922, *Daily Chronicle*, November 29.

PAGE 223
1 E.g. Lloyd George to Harold Spender, December 12 1922, Lloyd George MSS.
2 For the very limited success they had see the correspondence between Stephenson and Asquith, June 2, 5 and 9 1923 in *The Times*, June 15 1923.
3 E.g. Lloyd George to C. P. Scott, November 18 and December 14 1922, Lloyd George MSS.
4 E.g. Lloyd George saying 'their seats were a little close to each other so that each disagreeable remark was overheard' (in C. P. Scott diary, December 6 1922).
5 St Davids to Lloyd George, January 29 1923.

PAGE 224

1 Fisher diary, November 25 and December 5 1922; C. P. Scott diary, December 6 1922.
2 Lloyd George at 1920 Club, February 20 1923, *Manchester Guardian*, February 21.
3 Fisher diary, February 19 1923.
4 E.g. Lloyd George article in *Liverpool Post*, January 8 1923.
5 Lloyd George reported in *The Observer*, February 4 1923.
6 C. P. Scott diary, December 6 1922.
7 Thomas Jones to Law, March 29 1923 quoting Lloyd George's message.
8 C. P. Scott diary, December 6 1922 quoting Lloyd George.
9 Lloyd George at National Liberal luncheon, March 14 1923, *Daily Chronicle*, March 15.

PAGE 225

1 For the attacks in the House of Commons see Bayford diary, December 17 1922.
2 Lloyd George MSS G 18/8/2–10; cf. Fisher diary, July 23 1923 for Mrs Snowden spending the week-end at Churt.
3 For Lloyd George's concern at Grey's election see Fisher diary, February 9 1923. For Labour having 'captured Ark of the Covenant' see Fisher diary, February 19 1923.
4 Cf. Lloyd George to Sir William Robertson of Benachie, February 16 1923 for Lloyd George complaining of the 'half-dozen men ... at the top' leading resistance to rank-and-file feelings in favour of unity (Lloyd George MSS G 30/2/10).
5 Cf. St Davids to Lloyd George, January 31 1923 for peers supporting Grey on unity grounds.
6 C. P. Scott diary, March 8/10 1923.
7 In which the Liberal party in a straight fight with Conservatives won a seat which had been Conservative in 1918 and 1922.
8 Mitcham where Labour won a seat which had been Conservative in 1918 and 1922 and Whitechapel where Labour increased its vote.
9 C. P. Scott diary, March 8/10 1923. Lloyd George claimed that seventy people were involved in these meetings, *Daily Chronicle*, March 15 1923.
10 See Lloyd George quoted in *Daily Chronicle*, March 15 1923 for Lloyd George's view.
11 Lloyd George to C. P. Scott, March 15 1923, Lloyd George MSS.

PAGE 226

1 Lloyd George in *Daily Chronicle*, March 15 1923.
2 Fisher diary, March 20 1923.
3 Fisher, March 21 1923.
4 *The Times*, March 23 1922 for this.

5 For Lloyd George statement see *The Times*, March 23 1923.
6 Fisher diary, March 25 1923.
7 Fisher diary, April 6 1923.
8 Lloyd George to Sir Edward Rhodes, April 24 1923, Lloyd George MSS.

PAGE 227
1 Lloyd George at Manchester, *Daily Chronicle*, April 30 1923.
2 E.g. Grigg to Bailey, May 11 1923, Altrincham MSS.
3 Lloyd George at Llanfairfechan, May 22 1923, *Daily Chronicle*, May 23.
4 Lloyd George at City Temple in *Daily Chronicle*, May 10 1923.
5 Lloyd George at Edinburgh in *The Times*, May 28 1923.
6 Lloyd George at Hotel Victoria in *Daily Chronicle*, May 30 1923.
7 Lloyd George at Westbourne Park Chapel, London in *Daily Chronicle*, June 11 1923.
8 Lloyd George at Oxford in *Daily Chronicle*, June 23 1923.
9 Lloyd George at Westbourne Park Chapel, London in *Daily Chronicle*, June 11 1923.

PAGE 228
1 *Manchester Guardian*, July 9 1923; C. P. Scott diary, July 26 1923.
2 C. P. Scott diary, July 26 1923.
3 *South Wales News*, August 11 1923.
4 Grigg to Bailey, April 9 1923, Altrincham MSS.
5 Kilbracken to General Godley, August 18 1923, Kilbracken, p. 200.
6 Captain Arthur Evans, M.P. for Lancaster: see Evans to Lloyd George, July 27 and Lloyd George to Evans, July 30 1923 in *The Times*, August 1.
7 Asquith to Lord Robert Cecil, October 19 1922.
8 Grey at St George's Hall, Bradford, October 24 1922, *The Times* October 25.

PAGE 229
1 Rhodes to Lloyd George, November 6 and Lloyd George to Rhodes, November 8 1922, Lloyd George MSS.
2 E.g. Grey at Bradford, October 24 1922, *The Times*, October 25.
3 Grey at Bradford, October 24, *The Times*, October 25 and at Bedford, November 7 1922, *Manchester Guardian*, November 8.
4 *Manchester Guardian*, November 4; Lloyd George to C. P. Scott, November 8, Lloyd George MSS and C. P. Scott to Lloyd George, November 15 1922.
5 H.H.A., November 17 1922.

PAGE 230
1 Simon to Grey, October 30 1922, Simon MSS.
2 Cf. C. P. Scott to Lloyd George, November 15 1922.

3 Grey at Bradford, October 24 1922, *The Times*, October 25.
4 Haldane to E, November 1 1922 quoting Grey.
5 Grey at Bradford, October 24 1922, *The Times*, October 25. For Runciman being depressed when Grey spoke for him, see C. P. Scott diary, December 6 1922 reporting Lloyd George reporting Runciman.
6 Maclean to Law, November 20 1922.
7 H.H.A., November 17 1922.

PAGE 231
1 The first hint is probably in Gladstone to Maclean, November 24 1922, Add. MSS 46474.
2 Gladstone memo enclosed in Gladstone to Maclean, November 24 1922, Add. MSS 46474; cf. Gladstone talking to Scott in C. P. Scott diary, July 1 1923.
3 Gladstone to Maclean, November 24 1922.
4 Gladstone memo in Gladstone to Maclean, November 24 1922, Add. MSS 46474.

PAGE 232
1 C. P. Scott diary [March 9 1923].
2 C. P. Scott diary, January 28 1923.
3 Cf. Masterman saying he would go out if Lloyd George came back, C. P. Scott diary [March 9 1923].
4 Sidney to Beatrice Webb, February 10 1923 for a dinner attended by McKenna and his wife, Grey, Spender, Brand, MacDonald, Hastings, Snowden and Webb which gave Webb this clear impression.
5 Cf. Maclean to Gladstone, February 28 1923 saying Lloyd George would use the constituency party.

PAGE 233
1 C. P. Scott diary, January 29 1923.
2 Gladstone to Maclean, February 14 1923, Add. MSS 46474. For reorganisation of the Asquithean Liberal national organisation see Gladstone to Maclean, [April or May] 1923 and Gladstone to Maclean, June 13 1923.
3 C. P. Scott diary, January 29 1923.
4 E.g. Gladstone to Maclean April, May 1923, Add. MSS 46474 for the Buxton meeting in May.
5 Gladstone to Maclean, February 14 1922; Maclean to Gladstone, December 31 1922.
6 See Lloyd George to C. P. Scott, December 14 1922, Lloyd George MSS.
7 C. P. Scott diary, November 8/10 1922 reporting Lloyd George.
8 Simon to Grey, October 30 1922, Simon MSS.
9 H.A. Gwynn to Law, March 13 1923 [1921 written] reporting Grey.

10 Almost certainly inaccurate; for denial see *Westminster Gazette*, June 29 and Grigg to Bailey, May 17 1923, Altrincham MSS.

PAGE 234

1 Maclean to Gladstone, January 24 1923.
2 See *Daily Chronicle*, November 29 1922.
3 See Beauchamp to Lloyd George, May 14 1923 asking for Lloyd George's and his wife's autograph.
4 For a report of one of his dinners see Maclean to Gladstone, January 24 1923. See also Crewe to Denman, September 27 1924, Crewe MSS.
5 For the contest for the leadership see Maclean to Gladstone, December 31 1922, January 1, January 12 and January 24 1923; St Davids to Lloyd George, January 31 1923.

PAGE 235

1 E.g. Maclean reporting demands in Scotland, Maclean to Gladstone, March 28 1923; cf. *Yorkshire Post*, April 2 for Leeds; for Manchester see *Westminster Gazette*, April 20 1923.
2 *Manchester Guardian*, April 18 1923.
3 *Yorkshire Post*, April 2 1923. For Lloyd George see Illingworth to Lloyd George, March 29 1923.
4 Asquith at Bournemouth, May 2 1923, *Manchester Guardian*, May 5 and at Buxton, June 1 1922, *Manchester Guardian*, June 2.
5 Grey at National Liberal Federation at Buxton, *The Times*, June 1 1923.

PAGE 236

1 Maclean to Gladstone, December 31 1922 and January 12 1923.

PAGE 238

1 E.g. Jones, p. 88 also says that Law claimed in 1919 to have been in favour of State purchase of the Drink Trade for twenty years.
2 Selborne to Law, November 20 1922; Salisbury to Law, October 28 and 31; cf. Selborne to Salisbury, October 26 1922 for Selborne withdrawing from political life for this reason.
3 Occasioned probably by the fear that he wished to abandon the Irish Treaty.

PAGE 239

1 Londonderry to Strachey, January 3 1923.
2 Gollin, *Proconsul in Politics*, p. 600.
3 Cf. Keynes to Austen Chamberlain, December 20 1919.
4 Cf. Younger to Sanders, December 28 1922 and Bayford diary, January 28 1923.
5 Davidson memo of October 28 (BL 109/1/21); Law to Steel-Maitland, October 29; Steel-Maitland to Davidson, October 27 1922.

6 Derby diary, October 19 1922; cf. McKenna, pp. 318–19.
7 Austen Chamberlain to Lloyd George, March 29 1922.
8 Montague-Barlow to Lloyd George, October 28 1922.

PAGE 240

1 Salisbury to Law, October 21, October 22 (two letters) and October 24 1922.
2 C. Craig to Law, October 20 and October 31 (telegram), Law to C. Craig, October 30 1922, Law MSS.
3 Gretton to Salisbury, October 16 1922.
4 Cf. Gretton to Salisbury, October 16 and Wolmer to Salisbury, October 26 1922.
5 Derby to R. D. Blumenfeld, October 25 1922; cf. Derby at Manchester and Griffith-Boscawen at Taunton both saying that, though the Coalition was dead, 'co-operation remains' (both October 21 1922, *Sunday Pictorial*, October 22).
6 Cf. Neville Chamberlain to Hilda, November 19 1922 for Law saying he would have been afraid of the reactionaries if he had had a majority of a hundred.
7 Cf. Gretton to Salisbury, October 16 1922.
8 Law to Salisbury, October 19 1922, BL 107/4/36 for evidence of uncertainty before that which may, however, have merely been evidence of his reluctance to claim the leadership before he got it.
9 Wigram to Stamfordham, October 20 1922, Geo. V K1814/6 quoting Davidson reporting Law.

PAGE 241

1 Salisbury to Law and Law to Salisbury, November 24 1922.
2 I.e. the Irish Constitution and the Irish Free State (Consequential Provisions) Bills; cf. McNeill to Law, November 20 1922.
3 Gretton to Salisbury, October 16 1922.
4 Qualities said by Davidson to be the public's idea of Bonar Law, James, p. 154.
5 Baldwin at Cardiff, November 1 1922, *Western Mail*, November 2.
6 Younger at Ealing Conservative Association dinner, December 19 1922, *Morning Post*, December 20.

PAGE 242

1 Younger to Derby, November 3 1922, Churchill, p. 467.
2 Younger to Derby, November 3 and November 6 1922, Churchill, pp. 474–5.
3 For 'very sorry' see Stamfordham to King George V, November 17 1922, Geo. V K1814/50; cf. Maclean to Law, November 20 1922.

PAGE 243

1 Cf. Fraser to Law, October 20 1922 for the importance of Law's reputation for honesty and the need to suppress what he said at the

Carlton Club meeting about the 'smashing of the Liberal party' etc. in case 'the average reader who is apt to be stupid might misinterpret [his] avowal of being an opportunist'.

PAGE 244

1 Cf. *The Times*, February 16 1923.
2 *Hansard*, November 23 1922, col. 79.
3 *Hansard*, November 23 1922, col. 64.
4 Bayford diary, November 25 1922; cf. *The Times*, November 22 1922 quoting Waterhouse's letter to the unemployed delegation. Cf. also the demolition of the Garden City and other instruments of personal government.
5 Middlemass, p. 121.
6 E.g. speech at Queen's Hall, London, December 15 1922, *The Times*, December 16.
7 C. P. Scott recording Law in conversation, December 6 1922; cf. Law's speech at Glasgow, December 22 1922, *Glasgow Herald*, December 23 referring again to 1922 as Labour's 'high water-mark'.

PAGE 245

1 Cf. Law talking to Salvidge on October 18 in Salvidge, p. 238.
2 See e.g. Law in C. P. Scott diary, December 6 1922.
3 Law reported in Salvidge, p. 238.

PAGE 246

1 Ullswater to Law, October 23 1922.
2 Law to Balfour, December 16 1922, Law MSS.
3 McKenna advised Law over the American Debt settlement (see Jones, p. 228). Swinton, p. 30 says McKenna played bridge with Law weekly.
4 For Grey see Swinton, p. 30.
5 Neville Chamberlain diary [Account of Unionist Government under Bonar Law], January 26 and March 8 1923.
6 Eg. Rothermere demanding a 'wheat bonus' after Law made it clear that the government would not give one, *Sunday Pictorial*, April 8 1923. Mesopotamia and the American Debt terms were Beaverbrook's target.
7 To C. C. Craig in February and to Rupert Gwynne, Godfrey Locker-Lampson, Betterton, Boyd-Carpenter and Lord Eustace Percy, of whom only Gwynne, Craig and perhaps Boyd-Carpenter had been Die Hards.
8 I.e. one minister, Griffith-Boscawen, and two junior ministers, J. W. Hills at Edge Hill and G. Stanley at Willesden East.
9 Derby to Law, March 9 1923.

PAGE 247

1 From which he had first announced that he would resign in 1919: see Long to Law, December 14 1919.

2 Law talking to a deputation from the Glasgow Trades and Labour Council on December 24 1922 in *Glasgow Herald*, December 26; cf. Baldwin to the Birmingham Jewellers and Silversmiths' Association at Birmingham, February 3 1923, *Birmingham Post*, February 5.
3 *Hansard*, April 16 (1721ff.).
4 E.g. Amery diary, February 21 1923.
5 Neville Chamberlain to Hilda, January 13 1923.
6 Cf. Neville Chamberlain diary, January 26 1923.

PAGE 248
1 For the issues see Law MSS 117/3 etc.
2 Derby diary, October 19 1922, p. 454.
3 Derby diary, October 20 1922; Amery diary, October 20 1922. It is difficult to follow Law's changes of position on this question. On October 19 he frightened Derby by referring to a possible 'point of difference between him and me on the question of Tariffs' (Derby diary, October 19 1922) adding that he was hoping that McKenna would join his government. It is possible that he hoped for support from McKenna in office in urging a Protectionist policy, and felt strong enough, in view of McKenna's possible adhesion, to try this on Derby. McKenna's refusal to join and Amery's positive abandonment of Tariff Reform as an immediate issue may have pushed him in the opposite direction. Amery's argument against an immediate Tariff Reform policy was tactical, either in the sense that it would damage prospects at an election or because he was taking the opportunity to show himself judicious enough about his main political interest to be given the Colonial Office which he particularly wanted. His real opinion seems to have been that the general economic situation made him 'more convinced than ever before of the urgency' of a Tariff Reform policy: Amery diary, October 20 1922. He was particularly anxious that Law should not convert temporary suspension of the Tariff question into permanent rejection of Protection for the future; Amery diary, October 20 1922. This, however, was exactly what Law did: it is probable that he was able to do it because he succeeded in ensuring that Amery did not make a fuss by involving him in drafting the election manifesto on the 23rd, 24th and 25th.
4 Law at Public Baths, Old Kent Road, November 7 1922, *Daily Telegraph*, November 8.
5 Law at Glasgow, November 14 1922, *Glasgow Herald*, November 15.

PAGE 249
1 For report see Cranborne to Salisbury, October 25 1922.
2 Cf. Derby at Bolton, November 4 1922, Churchill, pp. 472–3.

PAGE 250
1 Baldwin at the Birmingham Jewellers' and Silversmiths' dinner, February 3 1923, *Birmingham Post*, February 5.

2 E.g. one minister and two under-secretaries defeated in a batch of by-elections in early March in what had been Conservative seats in 1918 and 1922, i.e. Edge Hill, Mitcham and Willesden East.

3 Salisbury to Law, February 27 and Bayford diary, February 24 1923.

4 E.g. Curzon to Law, April 8 and 9 1923 for this in relation to Joynson-Hicks.

5 For all this see e.g. Amery diary, January 29/31 and February 23, Derby diary, January 30 and Devonshire to Hoare, March 30 1923, Templewood V 1.

6 Sanders claims that Poincaré put off occupying the Ruhr until after Christmas because of Law, Bayford diary, December 17 1922; but see Davidson to Baldwin, January 6 1923, in James, pp. 145–6, for Law failing to stop Poincaré a week before the Ruhr was invaded.

7 Amery diary, April 11 1923.

8 Cf. Talbot to Law, April 16 1923.

PAGE 251

1 Joan to Edward Lascelles, October 30 1922 quoting Balfour, Birkenhead, Horne and Lloyd George, Whittingehame MSS; cf. Austen Chamberlain to Sir George Lloyd, December 7 1922, Austen Chamberlain MSS.

PAGE 252

1 Montague-Barlow to Lloyd George, October 28 1922.

2 For original see AC 33/2/93.

3 To whom, perhaps, should be added the Duke of Atholl, the Lord Chamberlain, who claimed, in writing to Lloyd George after the event, that he would have signed the letter if he had not been told by Gilmour that it was unnecessary to come to London: Atholl to Lloyd George, October 20 1922.

4 For Lee's attempts to advance himself and his independence of the Conservative party see his letters to Lloyd George of December 6 and December 11 1916, April 25, July 16, November 27 and December 30 1918, July 16 and 25 1919 and September 15 1920.

5 Gilmour to Law, October 25 1922.

6 See his speech at Birkenhead's Coalitionist dinner, March 23 1923 in Law MSS 116/2.

7 Birkenhead at Bristol, November 2 1922 in *Western Daily Press*, November 3.

8 *National Review*, December 1922, p. 492.

9 Birkenhead at Hotel Victoria, October 23 1922, *Daily Telegraph*, October 24.

10 E.g. at Colchester, October 26 1922, *The Times*, October 27.

11 *Ibid.*; cf. Fisher diary, October 26 1922.

PAGE 253

1 Birkenhead at Glasgow, October 28 1922, *Daily Chronicle*, October 30.
2 Birkenhead, speech at Junior Constitutional Club, February 23 1922, *Morning Post*, February 24, and at Birmingham, November 11 1922, *The Times*, November 13.
3 Birkenhead at Glasgow, October 28 1922, *Daily Chronicle*, October 30.
4 Joan to Edward Lascelles, October 30 1922, Whittingehame MSS.
5 See Churchill, pp. 466–8 and 480–1.
6 Joan to Edward Lascelles, October 30 1922, Whittingehame MSS; Horne to Law, October 24 1922.
7 Petrie, p. 209.

PAGE 254

1 Derby diary, November 23 1922 recording conversation with Austen Chamberlain. See also Austen Chamberlain to Sir George Lloyd, December 7 1922, Austen Chamberlain MSS.
2 Cf. Joan to Edward Lascelles, October 30 1922, Whittingehame MSS.
3 Petrie, p. 212.
4 Long to Salisbury, October 24 1922.
5 Austen Chamberlain to Balfour, December 19 1922, Austen Chamberlain MSS.
6 Report of Birkenhead's Coalitionist dinner of March 23 1923 in Law MSS 116/2.
7 Neville Chamberlain to Hilda, January 27 1923.
8 Austen Chamberlain to Balfour, March 8 1923, Whittingehame MSS.
9 Austen Chamberlain to Ida, April 22 1923.
10 Austen Chamberlain to Sir George Lloyd, December 7 1922, AC 18/1/35; Petrie, pp. 212–13.
11 Derby diary, November 23 1922; Neville Chamberlain to Ida, February 18 1923.
12 See Balfour to dearest A, October 23 1922, Whittingehame MSS.

PAGE 255

1 Reith, pp. 80–2. Bull gave Reith £15,000 between the beginning of November and the end of December.
2 For a list drawn up by Reith see Reith to Austen Chamberlain, November 17 1922.
3 For list see James, pp. 132–3.
4 Balfour to Burt (Birkenhead's assistant), November 16 1922, Whittingehame MSS W/18.
5 For requests to Balfour to come, see Bull to Balfour, November 24 1922, and Horne to Balfour, November 23 1922, both Whittingehame MSS.

PAGE 256

1 Austen Chamberlain speech at dinner of Conservative Coalitionists, November 30 1922.

2 For a list see BL 116/2.
3 Rothermere to Law, October 21 and 23; Harmsworth to Law, October 24(2) 1922.
4 Rothermere to Beaverbrook, January 22 [1923].

PAGE 257

1 Oliver Locker-Lampson to Austen Chamberlain, February 8 and to Lloyd George, February 17 1923.
2 Rothermere to Beaverbrook, April 26. According to Jones, p. 236 the reconciliation between Rothermere and Law was brought about by Beaverbrook. The Beaverbrook/Rothermere correspondence makes this seem likely.
3 Bayford diary, March 2 1923 quoting Younger and Fraser says that Catterell, the Independent Conservative, was financed by Oliver Locker-Lampson, who was one of Birkenhead's closest followers.
4 For the 'Dolly sisters' see *Hansard* (Lords), March 22 1923, col. 576. For Divorce Law reform see Birkenhead speech of April 11 1923 in *The Times*, April 12; cf. Law to Mrs Seaton-Tiedeman of Divorce Law Reform Union in *Manchester Guardian*, February 19 1922.
5 E.g. Worthington-Evans quoted in Thomas Jones to Law, March 29 1923.
6 Austen Chamberlain to *The Times*, March 2 1923.
7 Cf. Haldane to E, October 25 1922.
8 Austen Chamberlain to *The Times*, March 14 1923.

PAGE 258

1 Austen Chamberlain at Birmingham, March 19 1923, *Birmingham Post*, March 20.
2 Fisher diary, April 10 1923.
3 Cf. Amery diary, April 17 1923.
4 Birkenhead speech of April 11 1923, *The Times*, April 12.
5 E.g. Younger speech of April 17 1923, *Morning Post*, April 18.
6 Amery diary, April 26 and May 2 1923.
7 Taylor.
8 Amery diary, May 18 and 19 1923. I have assumed that the account Amery gives of the attempt to persuade Law to stay in office for the summer must be true; I have no evidence that the Davidsons, or Beaverbrook, with their knowledge of Horder's diagnosis, contemplated any delay in resignation.
9 Taylor.

PAGE 259

1 Blake, pp. 508–9 says that Law used Beaverbrook as an intermediary in order to offer Austen Chamberlain the Lord Privy Seal so that, when he resigned in the autumn, Chamberlain might succeed as Prime Minister and reunite the party. Neville Chamberlain's diary of

April 26 1923 makes it seem unlikely that Beaverbrook represented Law's wishes, or was acting on Law's authority. If the episode was significant, it was as part of the attempt of Birkenhead, Beaverbrook and their friends to ensure the succession for the Chamberlainites in the event of Law retiring by making sure that Austen Chamberlain was in a governing frame of mind.

2 Taylor.

3 Amery diary, May 18 1923.

4 Stamfordham to the King, May 21 1923, reporting Salisbury's view of Law's opinion, Geo. V K 1893/8.

5 Blake, pp. 510–11 and James, p. 147.

6 Blake, p. 518 but cf. Jones, p. 236 for Law telling Jones at tea on the 20th that ' "if the King asked for his advice as to a successor, he would put Baldwin first" '.

7 Blake, p. 520. Jones, pp. 235–6, who was shown it on May 20 by Silvester after it had gone, says that it was written by Davidson, Amery and Waterhouse the night before but Davidson (James, p. 166) does not mention Amery, denies that Waterhouse had anything to do with it and claims to have been dictating it when Waterhouse and Sykes left for Aldershot. It is not easy to accept Lord Davidson's view that 'the real explanation of the mystery of Baldwin being preferred to Curzon ... arose out of the general political situation which in the opinion of those whom the King consulted, precluded a peer from holding the office of Prime Minister'. Nor is it easy to match the manner of the memorandum with Lord Davidson's epistolary style.

8 Blake, p. 518.

9 Blake, p. 518.

10 Derby diary, May 29 1923, p. 503 reporting conversation with the King says that Stamfordham saw Salisbury on the Sunday. Blake, pp. 518–19 says, on Beaverbrook's authority, that Salisbury did not arrive in London until the milk train on Monday morning. It is possible, however, that Stamfordham and Salisbury talked on the telephone.

11 For example Balfour was told by Stamfordham that Law had given no advice (Balfour memo of May 22 1923, Whittingehame MSS).

PAGE 260

1 Dawson diary, May 21 1923 in Wrench, p. 217.

2 Stamfordham to the King, May 21 1923, Geo. V K 1893/8. For Davidson see James, p. 157.

3 Stamfordham memo of May 21 1923, Geo. V K 1853/9.

4 Stamfordham to the King, n.d., Geo. V K 1853/10; cf. Balfour memo of May 22 1923, Whittingehame MSS.

5 James, p. 157.

6 Amery diary, May 21 1923.

7 Salisbury to Stamfordham, May 21 1923, Geo. V K 1853/14.

8 Stamfordham had already turned down Waterhouse's suggestion that he should send for Amery and Bridgeman on the ground that 'he felt

that they would be in favour of Mr Baldwin and their advice would not really be helpful', by which he probably meant that they were opposed to any attempt to bring back the Chamberlainites as a body. Stamfordham to the King, May 21 1923, Geo. V K 1853/9.

9 Cf. note by Stamfordham 'never' on Salisbury to Stamfordham, May 21 1923, Geo. V K 1853/14.

10 Salisbury to Stamfordham, May 21 1923, Geo. V K 1853/14.

11 Salisbury to Stamfordham, May 22 1923, Geo. V K 1853/15.

12 Stamfordham memo, May 22 1923, Geo. V K 1853/17.

PAGE 261

1 Amery diary, May 22 1923.

2 Stamfordham memo, May 22 1923, Geo. V K 1853/17.

3 See e.g. L. Mosley, pp. 269–75.

4 It is odd that there is no reference in Amery's diary to his part in drafting the memorandum, if indeed he did so, though he had a long talk with Baldwin on the night of May 19: Amery diary, May 19 1923.

5 Cf. Jones, p. 235.

6 Lord Davidson denies that they did, James, p. 161.

7 For Baldwin saying he was willing to serve under Curzon on May 20, see Taylor, Amery diary, May 19 and Stamfordham memo, May 22 1923, Geo. V K 1853/17.

8 Blake, p. 522.

PAGE 262

1 Amery diary, May 20 1923.

2 Amery diary, May 21 1923.

3 Amery diary, May 21 1923; Stamfordham reporting Jackson in memo, May 22 1923, Geo. V K 1853/19.

4 Stamfordham to the King, May 22 1923, Geo. V K 1853/18.

5 Dawson to Milner, May 23 1923 for the view that Baldwin would be secretly relieved if Curzon resigned.

6 Stamfordham to the King, May 22 1923, Geo. V K 1853/21 quoting Curzon quoting Oliver Locker-Lampson but not naming him.

PAGE 263

1 Stamfordham first mentioned it on May 22 after his interview with Curzon.

2 See below, chapter XVII.

3 In conversation with Derby, Derby diary, May 29 1923.

4 But see Wrench, p. 218 for the King being upset by Liberal accusations of a Die Hard caucus influencing him: so he may have been anxious on other grounds to establish that he made the decision very early.

5 Worthington-Evans to Austen Chamberlain, May 22 1923.

PAGE 264

1 Beaverbrook to Borden, May 10 1923 quoted in Taylor. Derby diary, May 20/22 1923, p. 502 and Worthington-Evans to Austen Chamberlain, May 22 1923.
2 Derby diary, May 20 1923.
3 We do not have the letter.
4 Amery diary, May 20 and 21 1923.
5 Balfour memo of May 22 1923, Whittingehame MSS.

PAGE 265

1 Derby diary, May 20/22 1923.
2 Jackson talking to Stamfordham, Stamfordham memo of May 22 1923, Geo. V K 1853/19.
3 Worthington-Evans to Austen Chamberlain, May 22 1923.
4 Birkenhead being out of London.
5 Petrie, p. 213.
6 Worthington-Evans to Austen Chamberlain, May 22 1923.
7 Worthington-Evans to Austen Chamberlain, May 22 1923.

PAGE 266

1 Balfour memo of May 22 1923, Whittingehame MSS and Stamfordham to King, n.d., Geo. V K 1850/10.
2 Balfour memo, May 22 1923.
3 Salvidge, p. 252.
4 Worthington-Evans to Austen Chamberlain, May 22 1923.
5 E.g. Salvidge diary, October 1922 in Salvidge, p. 239.
6 Balfour to dearest A, October 23 1922, Whittingehame MSS.

PAGE 267

1 Derby to Baldwin, May 24 1923.
2 Balfour to Jackson, May 26 1923, Whittingehame MSS.
3 Stamfordham to King, May 22 1923, Geo. V K 1853/18.

PAGE 268

1 Neville Chamberlain diary, June 1 1923 reporting Austen Chamberlain. There is nothing in the published version of Derby's diary to show who first suggested that Horne and Austen Chamberlain should be asked to join, or who suggested that Derby might go to Paris to intercede. It may have been Baldwin genuinely searching for ways of bringing them in. It may have been Derby fulfilling obligations. Cf. Derby to Baldwin, May 24 1923.
2 Baldwin to Austen Chamberlain sent as telegram from Curzon to Crewe, May 25 1923, Baldwin MSS.
3 Petrie, pp. 215–16.
4 Austen Chamberlain to Sir George Lloyd, June 8 1923, AC 18/1/30; Petrie, p. 216.
5 Cf. Austen Chamberlain to Ida, January 19 1919.

PAGE 269
1 Neville Chamberlain diary, May 23 1923.
2 Neville Chamberlain to Ida, May 26 1923.
3 *Ibid.*
4 Neville Chamberlain to Austen Chamberlain, April 23 1923; Neville Chamberlain diary, May 23 1923.
5 Worthington-Evans to Austen Chamberlain, May 22 1923.
6 Worthington-Evans to Austen Chamberlain, May 22 1923, the second half of which was written after the news of Baldwin's appointment.
7 Austen Chamberlain to Baldwin, May 29 1923.

PAGE 270
1 Austen Chamberlain to [wife], May 28 1923; cf. Petrie, p. 218 for Worthington-Evans being pitied for being 'so eager for office'.
2 Neville Chamberlain diary, June 1 1923.
3 Petrie, pp. 217–18.
4 Amery diary, May 22 1923 quoting Bridgeman quoting Baldwin.
5 Austen Chamberlain to Birkenhead, May 31 1923, AC 35/2/18.
6 Neville Chamberlain diary, June 1 1923 quoting Austen Chamberlain. Cf. also Petrie, pp. 220–3.
7 Austen Chamberlain to Birkenhead, May 31 1923.
8 Neville Chamberlain diary, June 1 1923.

PAGE 271
1 Austen Chamberlain to Birkenhead, May 31 1923.
2 Neville Chamberlain, June 1 1923.
3 Cf. Austen Chamberlain to Birkenhead, May 31 1923 for Law saying that Baldwin knew this.

PAGE 276
1 Baldwin election address to electors of Kidderminster, January 1 1906, Baldwin MSS.

PAGE 277
1 Jones, p. 262.
2 Cf. Davidson, rather vaguely, in James, p. 187.
3 Baldwin at Worcester, October 28 1922, *Yorkshire Post*, October 30. Law at Public Baths, Old Kent Road, November 7 1922, *Daily Telegraph*, November 8. Law, interview with National Farmers' Union, *The Times*, March 19 1923, *Hansard*, December 5 1922, col. 1684ff. Cf. Bayford diary, April 15 1923 for Law's reaction to report.
4 Bayford diary, January 28 1923.
5 For the legislation see Bayford diary, January 28, March 29, April 22, June 1 and July 15 1923.

PAGE 278
1 Bayford diary, July 29, Amery diary, April 18 1923.
2 Amery diary, March 1, Bayford diary, March 2 1923.

3 Amery diary, August 2 1923.
4 Joynson-Hicks to Baldwin, October 20 1923.
5 Amery diary, October 9, Neville Chamberlain diary, October 10 1923.
6 Amery diary, September 25 1923.
7 Dawson diary, June 17 1923 in Wrench, p. 219.
8 See e.g. the Cabinet's view that any small advances in preference – as, for example, on dried fruits – should not be put into the Budget but should be 'kept in hand for bargaining at the Conference', Amery diary, April 12 1923.

PAGE 279
1 Amery diary, October 10 1923.
2 Jones, p. 305.
3 The conclusions of the Conference in Cmd. 1990 of 1923, *Imperial and Economic Conference.* They include an increase in the Empire preference on figs, raisins, plums, apricots, currants so as to free all from duty, the imposition of a duty on other non-dutiable foreign dried fruit and preserved fruits, raw apples, canned salmon, honey and fruit juices (in order to establish an Empire preference), an undertaking to maintain the present sugar preference for at least ten years and an increase in the tobacco and wine preference. See also Swinton, pp. 32–3.
4 E.g. Derby using McKenna's probable prickliness about Imperial Preference as a reason for not having him as Chancellor of the Exchequer: Derby to Baldwin, July 31 1923.
5 Cf. Neville Chamberlain reported in Amery diary, October 1 1923.
6 Joynson-Hicks to Baldwin, October 20, Salisbury to Baldwin, October 19 1923.
7 See e.g. Neville Chamberlain diary, October 10 1923.

PAGE 280
1 Worthington-Evans to Austen Chamberlain, May 22 1923.
2 Rothermere to Lloyd George, August 30 [1923].
3 Davidson to Strachey, October 15 1923.
4 Taylor.
5 E.g. Birkenhead in *Hansard* (Lords), July 16 1923, col. 1051ff.
6 *Daily Mail*, July 30 1923.

PAGE 281
1 Rothermere to Beaverbrook, July 17 1923.
2 Birkenhead to Austen Chamberlain, July 11 1923.
3 Rothermere in *Sunday Pictorial*, August 5 1923.
4 Rothermere to Beaverbrook, July 19 1923, agreeing with Beaverbrook leading article.
5 Rothermere to Beaverbrook, n.d. 1923 [placed in late June].
6 Rothermere in *Sunday Pictorial*, August 19 1923.

7 Birkenhead in *Daily Mail*, August 11 1923.
8 Lloyd George at Wrexham, August 10 1923, *South Wales News*, August 11.
9 Lloyd George at Bristol, July 25 1923, *Daily Chronicle*, July 26.
10 Lloyd George at Llanfairfechan, May 22 1923, *Daily Chronicle*, May 23.
11 Lloyd George speech reported in *Manchester Guardian*, July 24 1923.

PAGE 282
1 *Daily Chronicle*, September 8 1923.
2 Grey at Finsbury Park Empire, November 4 1922 in *Liverpool Post*, November 6.
3 Haldane to E, November 1 1922.

PAGE 283
1 Asquith to Baldwin, January 31 and June 4 1923.
2 Runciman to Baldwin, April 24 1923.
3 E.g. Mrs Asquith to Dawson, July 15 1923 in Wrench, p. 219.
4 Asquith at Buxton, June 1 1923, *Manchester Guardian*, June 2.
5 Asquith at Buxton, June 1 1923, *Manchester Guardian*, June 2.

PAGE 284
1 Fisher diary, July 17 1923 recording conversation with Grey.
2 Simon, 'Democracy and War' in *Congregational Quarterly*, April 1923.
3 Grey at Falloden, September 6 1923, *Newcastle Chronicle*, September 7.
4 At National Liberal Club, September 27 1923, *Manchester Guardian*, September 28.
5 Asquith at Perth, October 11 1923, *Westminster Gazette*, October 12; at Glasgow, October 12, *Glasgow Herald*, October 13; and at Liverpool (three speeches), October 23, *Liverpool Post*, October 24.

PAGE 285
1 For pessimism see e.g. Beatrice Webb, October 24 1922, p. 226.
2 Clynes at Market Harborough, October 24 1922, *The Times*, October 25.
3 J. H. Thomas at Cardiff, November 4 1922, *South Wales News*, November 6.
4 Clynes at Hucknall, October 30 1922, *Manchester Guardian*, October 31.
5 Clynes at Market Harborough, October 24 1922, *The Times*, October 25.

PAGE 286
1 MacDonald in *New Leader*, October 27 1922.
2 MacDonald in *New Leader*, October 27 1922.
3 MacDonald in *Forward*, November 4 1922.
4 MacDonald in *Forward*, November 4 1922.

5 Clynes at Hucknall, October 30 1922, *Manchester Guardian*, October 31.
6 MacDonald in *Forward*, November 4 1922.
7 I.e. there was too much class conflict and too much attack on private enterprise. See Haldane to E, November 1, Peel to Reading, November 2 1922, Eur E 238/5; cf. Haldane to E, November 14 1922 for Henderson doing damage by bad leadership.
8 Clynes at Hucknall, October 30 1922, *Manchester Guardian*, October 31.
9 Clynes at Hucknall, October 30 1922, *Manchester Guardian*, October 31.
10 Clynes at Miles Platting, November 8 1922, *Daily Herald*, November 9.
11 Clynes to *The Times*, *The Times*, November 2 1922.

PAGE 287
1 MacDonald in *Forward*, November 4 1922.
2 Clynes at Manchester, November 10 1922, *Manchester Guardian*, November 11.
3 MacDonald in *New Leader*, November 10 1922.
4 Trevelyan to Henderson, December 14 1922, Trevelyan MSS.
5 *Ibid.*
6 MacDonald in *New Leader*, November 10 1922.
7 I.e. Bothwell, N. Camberwell and S. E. Southwark.
8 MacCallum Scott diary, November 16 1922.

PAGE 288
1 Cole, p. 193.
2 *Labour Monthly*, January 1923 quoted in *Morning Post*, December 27 1923; MacDonald to Ponsonby, November 1 1921 and June 2 1922; Mrs Snowden talking to C. P. Scott in C. P. Scott diary, March 1 1922 and Monteglas to Ponsonby, June 6 1921 or 1922. See also Snowden, *Autobiography*, ii, 528–32 for the shock in the Labour party at the Parliamentary Party's failure to stimulate a great debate about the Peace Treaty in 1919.
3 Cf. MacDonald at the Aldwych Club, February 21 1923, *The Times*, February 22.
4 MacDonald's message to Labour rally in London, *Daily Herald*, November 23 1922.
5 MacDonald in *New Leader*, December 29 1922.
6 *Labour Monthly*, January 1923 quoted in *Morning Post*, December 27 1922.
7 MacDonald at Port Talbot, January 4 1923, *South Wales News*, January 5.

PAGE 289
1 MacDonald at Port Talbot, January 4 1923, *South Wales News*, January 5.

2 E.g. Thomas in *Sunday Times* interview, December 3 1922.
3 Thomas at Warrington, November 26 1922, *The Times*, November 27; MacDonald in *Forward*, December 2 1922.
4 MacDonald at Port Talbot, January 4 1923, *South Wales News*, January 5.
5 MacDonald to delegation from Aberdeen branch of the British Legion, January 22 1923, *Aberdeen Press and Journal*, January 23.
6 MacDonald in *New Leader*, December 29 1922.
7 E.g. MacDonald in *New Leader*, November 24 1922.
8 E.g. Grigg to Bailey, November 23 1922, Altrincham MSS for MacDonald doing well; cf. Fisher diary, November 23 and December 6 1922.
9 Cf. Seymour Cocks to Mrs Trevelyan, November 24, Trevelyan MSS, Margaret Bondfield to Trevelyan, November 22, Trevelyan to Arthur Henderson, December 14 1922, Trevelyan MSS for 'collapse of North Country Liberalism' as a result of the Capital Levy. It was one of the assured truths among Labour speakers at this time that 'the last election marked the passing of the Liberal party', e.g. George Benson at ILP demonstration at Manchester, January 7 1923, *Manchester Guardian*, January 8.
10 MacDonald at Newport, March 25 1923, *South Wales News*, March 26 and at Cardiff, February 18 1923, *South Wales News*, February 19.

PAGE 290

1 Thomas at Warrington, November 26 1922, *The Times*, November 27.
2 MacDonald in *New Leader*, March 23 1923 criticising Bradford ILP resolution against party discipline in the House of Commons.
3 Cf. MacDonald at Holborn Empire meeting, February 11 1923, *Daily Telegraph*, February 12.
4 MacDonald at Aldwych Club, February 21 1923, *The Times*, February 22.
5 MacDonald at Cardiff, February 18 1923, *South Wales News*, February 19.
6 MacDonald in the *Evening Standard*, February 26 1923, Cf. Thomas attacking Radek and Bolshevist delegates to the Peace Congress of the International Conference of Trades Unions at The Hague, *The Times*, December 16 1922.

PAGE 291

1 MacDonald at Newport, March 25 1923, *South Wales News*, March 26.
2 MacDonald at Holborn Empire, February 11 1923, *Daily Telegraph*, February 12.
3 MacDonald at Aldwych Club, February 21 1923, *The Times*, February 22.
4 MacDonald at ILP's Merrie England fair at Newington Public Hall, March 3 1923, *Daily Telegraph*, March 5.

5 MacDonald at Scottish ILP, January 20 1923, *Glasgow Herald*, January 22; cf. *New Leader*, January 19 1923.

6 MacDonald at Aldwych Club, February 21 1923, *The Times*, February 22.

7 MacDonald to annual dinner of Civil Service Clerical Association, November 29 1922, *Daily Telegraph*, November 30.

8 MacDonald in *New Leader*, January 19 1923.

9 MacDonald at Newport, March 25 1923, *South Wales News*, March 26.

10 MacDonald to Aberdeen branch of British Legion, January 22 1923, *Aberdeen Press and Journal*, January 23.

11 MacDonald at Holborn Empire, February 11 1923, *Daily Telegraph*, February 12.

12 Thomas at Darlington, February 27 1923, *Manchester Guardian*, February 28.

PAGE 292

1 MacDonald at Aberdeen, January 22 1923, *Aberdeen Press and Journal*, January 23.

2 Clynes at Manchester, January 7 1923, *Manchester Guardian*, January 8.

3 E.g. *Daily Herald*, November 22 1922 for MacDonald's statement immediately after his election.

4 Snowden at Cardiff, January 14 1923, *South Wales News*, January 15.

5 Snowden at Cardiff, January 14 1923, *South Wales News*, January 15.

6 MacDonald at Whitechapel baths, February 1 1923, *Manchester Guardian*, February 2.

7 MacDonald to Law, January 29 1923.

8 MacDonald at Holborn Empire, February 11 1923, *Daily Telegraph*, February 12.

9 E.g. at Birmingham on January 27 1923, *Birmingham Post*, January 29 and at Aberdeen, January 22 1923, *Aberdeen Press and Journal*, January 23. Cf. also MacDonald at UDC dinner, March 8, *Manchester Guardian*, March 9 and in *New Leader*, February 23 1923.

PAGE 293

1 MacDonald to Gilbert Murray, July 12 1923.

2 MacDonald in *Daily News*, February 20 1923.

3 MacDonald in *New Leader*, June 1 1923.

4 MacDonald in *Socialist Review*, quoted in *Westminster Gazette*, June 4 1923.

5 MacDonald in *New Leader*, June 1 1923.

PAGE 295

1 Amery diary, May 26 1923.

2 Lloyd-Graeme in Amery diary, May 28 1923.

3 McKenna actually helped Dawes in 1924: see McKenna, p. 319.

4 Dawson memo, June 17 1923 in Wrench, p. 219.

5 Jones, p. 240 records Baldwin seeing Grey on foreign policy questions on June 8. Runciman was appointed to a committee to consider regulations under the Restoration of Order in Ireland Act in July 1923: see Dod 1924, p. 433.
6 McKenna to Baldwin, August 13 1923 for the letter of resignation.

PAGE 296
1 Baldwin to Neville Chamberlain, August 14 and 22 (telegram) 1923.
2 Neville Chamberlain to Hilda, April 8 1922.
3 Neville Chamberlain to Hilda, October 24 and 31 1922.
4 Neville Chamberlain to Ida, March 3 1923.
5 Neville Chamberlain to Ida, March 17 1923.
6 Neville Chamberlain to Ida, April 28 and June 9 1923, for Neville Chamberlain's self-confidence.

PAGE 297
1 Neville Chamberlain to Hilda, May 19 1923.
2 Neville Chamberlain diary, May 19 1923.
3 Cf. his coy question in the privacy of his diary, 'would it go to Amery who has specialized?', Neville Chamberlain diary, May 22 1923.
4 Neville Chamberlain to Ida, May 26 1923.
5 Neville Chamberlain to Ida, May 26 1923, when press reports were tipping him as a possible Chancellor.
6 Neville Chamberlain to Hilda, August 26 1923.
7 Neville Chamberlain to Hilda, August 26 1923.
8 Baldwin at Hotel Cecil, May 28 1923, The Times, May 29.
9 E.g. MacDonald: see above, p. 293; Dawson to N. Rowell, July 20 1923 in Wrench, p. 220; Neville Chamberlain to Ida, May 26 1923.
10 Baldwin at Oxford, June 8 1923, The Times, June 9.
11 Baldwin at Glasgow, July 26 1923, Glasgow Herald, July 27.
12 Speech at party meeting, Hotel Cecil, May 28 1923, The Times, May 29.

PAGE 298
1 Younger at Stirling, October 6 1923, Scotsman, October 8.
2 Mansion House dinner, July 24 1923, The Times, July 25.
3 At Hotel Cecil, May 28 1923, The Times, May 29.
4 At Birmingham, October 13 1923, The Times, October 15 and at Cardiff, November 2 1923, Birmingham Post, November 3.
5 Jones, p. 240.

PAGE 299
1 Baldwin at National Unionist Association, June 29 1923.
2 Baldwin at Edinburgh, July 27 1923, Glasgow Herald, July 28.
3 Baldwin at Glasgow, July 26 1923, Glasgow Herald, July 27.
4 At Hotel Cecil, June 29 1923, The Times, June 30.

PAGE 300
1 Baldwin at Oxford, June 8 1923, *The Times,* June 9 and at Swansea, October 30 1923, *The Times,* October 31.

PAGE 301
1 Amery diary, June 29 and October 2 1923.
2 Curzon quoted in Amery diary, February 22 1923.
3 For the Iraq Committee see Amery diary for December 18 1922 and February 9 and 22, March 1 and April 26 1923; Bayford diary, March 29 1923; and Neville Chamberlain diary, March 28 and May 6 1923.

PAGE 302
1 Bayford diary, December 17 1922.
2 See above, p. 281.
3 Dawson memorandum, June 17 1923 in Wrench, p. 218.
4 Amery diary, July 4, Bayford diary, July 4, Neville Chamberlain to Hilda, June 16 1923.
5 Dawson to N. Rowell, July 20 1923 in Wrench, p. 220.

PAGE 303
1 For Curzon and Amery see Amery diary, July 9, October 4 1923. For Joynson-Hicks see Curzon to Law, April 8 1923. For Curzon telling Derby not to have conversations on his own in Paris, see Derby diary, October 25 1922.
2 See e.g. Neville Chamberlain to Ida, June 24 1923.
3 Amery diary, May 7 1923.
4 Amery diary, July 12, Bayford diary, July 15 1923.
5 Bayford diary, August 10, Derby diary, August 23 1923.
6 Derby to Baldwin, July 31 and Derby diary, August 23 1923.

PAGE 304
1 Derby diary, August 23 1923.
2 Derby to Baldwin, September 1 1923.
3 Jones, pp. 261 and 243.
4 There is a record of the meeting in Baldwin MSS F 1/108. For Neville Chamberlain saying the same thing, see Neville Chamberlain diary, September 24 1923; cf. Amery diary, September 22 1923 and Neville Chamberlain to Ida, June 24 1923.
5 Jones, p. 249.
6 Austen Chamberlain to Hilda, October 31 1923 quoting Baldwin talking to Horne; cf. Jones, p. 244.
7 Cab. 45 of August 2 1923 (Conclusion 10).
8 See Neville Chamberlain diary, October 10 1923 for some of the party implications.

PAGE 305

1 Baldwin, October 12 in Nicolson, p. 380. Law sometimes said that the two Liberal parties ought to join together. Churchill speech of May 4 (*The Times*, May 5) testifies to the existence of the doctrine that a strong Liberal party was desirable. See Steed to Law, October 17 1922 for the same feeling and Herbert Lewis to Lloyd George, November 6 1922 quoting Younger.

2 See Grigg talking in Amery diary, October 26 1923.

3 Jones, p. 261 for Baldwin and Davidson believing that the Liberals would never come together.

PAGE 306

1 See Neville Chamberlain diary, October 10 1923 and Guinness talking to Lord Robert Cecil in Lord Robert Cecil to Salisbury, December 9 1923 for the belief that Labour was thinking of doing so.

2 Baldwin talking to Bridgeman in Bridgeman diary, p. 83.

PAGE 307

1 Trevelyan to Ponsonby, May 30 1923, Trevelyan MSS.

PAGE 308

1 Amery diary, September 20 1923.

2 Amery diary, October 1 1923.

3 Neville Chamberlain diary, October 6 1923.

4 In the *Scotsman*, October 8 1923.

5 Neville Chamberlain to Hilda, October 6 1923: Amery diary, October 8 1923; Neville Chamberlain diary, October 10 1923.

6 E.g. Amery diary, October 13 1923, Neville Chamberlain diary, October 10 1923.

7 *The Times*, October 13 1923.

PAGE 309

1 Amery diary, recording the Chequers meeting, October 14 1923.

2 Jones, p. 252.

3 Dawson diary, December 20 1923 in Wrench, pp. 222-3.

4 Amery diary, October 14 and Bayford diary, October 11 1923.

5 Bridgeman diary, pp. 83-5.

6 Bayford diary, October 11 1923.

PAGE 310

1 Gretton to Baldwin, October 19 1923.

2 Long to Baldwin [October 19 1923]. Gretton because Long uses exactly Gretton's argument about declaring the policy at the Imperial Conference and not at a party meeting.

3 Neville Chamberlain to Hilda, October 21 1923 and to Austen Chamberlain, October 25. Austen Chamberlain to Ida, October 23 and to Neville Chamberlain, October 15 (Petrie, pp. 228-9).

4 Austen Chamberlain to Ida, October 23 1923.
5 Neville Chamberlain to Austen Chamberlain, October 23 1923 and to Hilda, October 21 1923.
6 Derby to Baldwin, October 22 1923; Derby quoted in Amery diary, October 20 1923.
7 Salisbury to Baldwin, October 19 1923.
8 Neville Chamberlain diary, October 26 1923.

PAGE 311

1 Bayford and Amery diaries, October 23 1923; Lord Robert Cecil to Davidson, November 15 1923 (copy), Add. MSS 51080.
2 Amery diary, October 23 1923, Bridgeman diary, pp. 83–5 and Wood, 'Narrative of Some Events Preceding the Dissolution and General Election November/December 1923' in Baldwin MSS say the same as Amery but neither is contemporary, i.e. Bridgeman's diary was written on December 15 1923 and Wood's probably at about the same time. Cf. Neville Chamberlain to Austen Chamberlain, October 23 1923 saying the same before the Cabinet.
3 Bayford and Amery diaries, October 23 1923.
4 Neville Chamberlain to Hilda, October 21 1923.
5 Joynson-Hicks to Baldwin, October 20 1923.
6 Devonshire to Baldwin, October 24 1923; Novar to Baldwin October 24 1923; Bridgeman to Baldwin, October 24 1923.
7 Gretton to Baldwin, October 19 and 24 1923.
8 Joynson-Hicks to Baldwin, October 20 1923.
9 Cave to Baldwin, October 25 1923.
10 Neville Chamberlain to Austen Chamberlain, October 23 and 26 1923.

PAGE 312

1 Neville Chamberlain to Ida, October 26 1923, Amery diary, October 25 1923.
2 Joynson-Hicks at Exeter, October 23 1923, *Manchester Guardian*, October 24; McNeill at Truro, October 23 1923, *Daily Express*, October 24.
3 Derby to Baldwin, October 22 1923.
4 Devonshire to Baldwin, October 24 1923.
5 For opposition among Die Hards see Bridgeman to Baldwin, October 24 1923.
6 Amery diary, October 29 1923.

PAGE 313

1 Lord Robert Cecil to Baldwin, October 29 1923.
2 For the bad temper see Lord Robert Cecil to Salisbury, October 27 1923: 'truly it makes me sick'.

3 Lord Robert Cecil to Salisbury, October 24 1922 and memo dated November 22 1922 (Steel-Maitland MSS) discussing whether membership of the Law government would enable him to forward the League cause.

4 Lord Robert Cecil to Salisbury, October 27 1923.

5 Lord Robert Cecil to Baldwin, October 29 1923 with memorandum.

6 Amery diary, October 31 1923.

7 Amery diary, November 2 1923.

8 Unless we read Admiral Hall's insistence that Amery should not set up a separate Protectionist organisation to stump the country because there would not be time to do so, Amery diary, November 1 1923.

9 Salvidge, p. 253.

PAGE 314

1 Wood, 'Narrative', November 5 1923.

2 Wood, 'Narrative', November 7 1923.

3 Lloyd-Graeme to Salisbury, November 6 1923.

4 Wood, 'Narrative', November 7 1923.

5 Novar to Baldwin, November 8 1923.

6 Lord Robert Cecil to Baldwin, November 7 1923.

7 Salisbury to Baldwin, November 8 1923.

8 Because a January election would conflict with, among other things, 'fox-hunting': Wood to Baldwin, November 8 1923.

9 Younger to Baldwin, November 7 1923.

PAGE 315

1 Bayford diary, November 11 1923.

2 Wood, 'Narrative', November 9 1923, Baldwin MSS.

3 Amery diary, November 9 1923.

4 Wood, 'Narrative', November 9 for Baldwin 'exhibiting a certain reluctance on the date of the dissolution'.

5 Amery diary, November 9 1923; Joynson-Hicks talking to Wood in Wood, 'Narrative', November 11 1923; Neville Chamberlain diary, November 9.

6 Bayford diary, November 11 1923; Neville Chamberlain diary, November 9.

7 Wood, 'Narrative', November 12 and 13 1923; Neville Chamberlain diary, November 12 1923. For the King's note on Baldwin's request for a dissolution see Nicolson, p. 380. For Law not approving, for Law's family being distressed by Baldwin's public claim that he did and for Baldwin mentioning his approval in Cabinet, see Novar to Salisbury, February 19 1924; cf. Sykes, p. 324. I have assumed that Novar's letter refers to this Cabinet.

PAGE 316

1 Austen Chamberlain to [wife], May 28 and to Birkenhead, May 31 1923 (copy), AC 35/2/18.

2 Birkenhead to Austen Chamberlain, June 1 1923.
3 Austen Chamberlain to Birkenhead, June 11 1923 in Birkenhead, p. 484.
4 *Hansard*, July 3, cols. 336–40.
5 Amery diary, July 8 1923 quoting Austen Chamberlain.
6 Austen Chamberlain to Birkenhead, July 6 1923, AC 35/2/22.
7 Amery diary, July 8 1923.

PAGE 317
1 Birkenhead to Austen Chamberlain, August 15 1923.
2 Birkenhead to Austen Chamberlain, July 11 and August 1923.
3 Neville Chamberlain to Hilda, September 2 1923 for Austen Chamberlain's real resentment despite ostensible congratulations to Neville Chamberlain.
4 Austen Chamberlain to Neville Chamberlain, October 15 1923 in Petrie, pp. 228–9; cf. Austen Chamberlain to Hilda, October 3 1923.
5 Austen Chamberlain at Birmingham Conservative Club, October 29 1923, *Birmingham Post*, October 30.

PAGE 318
1 C. P. Scott diary, July 26 1923; cf. Lloyd George at Llandrindod Wells, September 7 1923, *Daily Chronicle*, September 8.
2 Horne talking to MacCallum Scott in MacCallum Scott diary, November 13 1923.
3 McCurdy to Lloyd George, October 12 1923.
4 MacCallum Scott diary, November 13 1923.
5 McCurdy to Lloyd George, October 12 1923.
6 McCurdy to Lloyd George, October 25 1923 telegraphing the contents of the speech to Lloyd George across the Atlantic.
7 Grigg to Lloyd George, November 8 1923.
8 Horne talking to MacCallum Scott, November 13 1923, MacCallum Scott diary.
9 Cf. Horne in MacCallum Scott diary, November 13 1923.

PAGE 319
1 Amery diary, June 18 1924. In reporting this Greenwood was talking to his brother-in-law, Amery, at a time when he was hoping that Amery would help him to join the Conservative Party.
2 Churchill to Lloyd George, November 8 1923.
3 Grigg to Lloyd George, November 8 1923.
4 Fisher diary, November 9 1923.
5 *Daily Chronicle*, November 10 1923 reporting the presence of these four on the train.
6 Fisher diary, November 9 1923.

PAGE 320
1 *Daily Chronicle*, November 10 1923.
2 Fisher diary, November 13 1923 reporting Mond.

3 *The Times*, November 16 1923.
4 *Manchester Guardian*, November 19 1923.
5 *Glasgow Herald*, November 26 1923.
6 Beaverbrook to Rothermere, November 14 1923.
7 Neville Chamberlain diary, November 12 1923.

PAGE 321
1 Petrie, p. 234.
2 Austen Chamberlain to Ida, November 17 1923; Petrie, pp. 232–6 and 237. Bridgeman diary, p. 85 says that Birkenhead and Austen Chamberlain *offered* to join the government. So really does Birkenhead, quoting Derby in Birkenhead, p. 496. Amery to Baldwin, November 9 1923 makes it clear that Baldwin had talked to Amery about 'buying FE' so it is possible that Baldwin raised the question. Cf. Derby to Sir Tresham Lever, November 21 1934 in Churchill, p. 534 for further confirmation of this. On the other hand Neville Chamberlain diary, November 12 1923 reports Austen Chamberlain saying – what the published letters between Austen Chamberlain, Birkenhead and Baldwin on the 14th November imply – that *they* offered. Beaverbrook to Rothermere, November 14 1923 suggests that Baldwin made no offer but implied a promise of office in the future in return for support at the election; so does Petrie, pp. 233–6, Beaverbrook to Rothermere, November 14 1923, Neville Chamberlain diary, November 12 1923. Derby to Sir Tresham Lever, Churchill, p. 534 gives a slightly different account of Derby's action which is not confirmed by his diary for November 12 1923. Cf. Derby to Salisbury, November 12 1923 for resignation.
3 L. Mosley, p. 281; Derby to Lord Robert Cecil, November 10 1923.
4 Derby to Baldwin, November 13 1923.
5 Salvidge, pp. 253–4.
6 Derby to Jackson, November 9 1923, Churchill, p. 530.
7 Derby to Lord Robert Cecil, November 10 and to Salisbury, November 12 1923
8 It is strengthened if we accept Beaverbrook's claim that Baldwin asked Beaverbrook to arrange a meeting with Birkenhead when Beaverbrook saw Baldwin on the 5th, Beaverbrook to Rothermere, November 14 1923.

PAGE 322
1 Derby diary, November 12 1923.
2 Bayford diary, November 16 1923 reporting talk to Derby on Tuesday morning.
3 Derby to Baldwin, November 13 1923 on 'my little outburst'; cf. Neville Chamberlain diary, November 18 1923 for Baldwin and Derby walking up and down before the Cabinet. Derby to Baldwin, November 13 1923. Derby in Birkenhead, p. 498, Petrie, p. 236.
4 Derby in Birkenhead, p. 498.

PAGE 323

1 *Glasgow Herald*, November 8 1923.

2 Birkenhead to Baldwin, November 9 1923. But Beaverbrook to Rothermere, November 14 1923 suggests that Baldwin had in mind an invitation for Birkenhead to call when Beaverbrook saw him on November 5. It is possible, however, that Beaverbrook got it wrong or was exaggerating his own importance. It is worth noting that Neville Chamberlain also believed that Birkenhead was invited because of the imminent danger that he would join Lloyd George if he did not join the government (Neville Chamberlain to Hilda, November 17 1923). In this case, however, it is difficult to see why Baldwin waited until November 7 before he wrote to Birkenhead or why he asked Birkenhead to call, and not Austen Chamberlain.

3 Austen Chamberlain to Ida, n.d., AC 5/1/296.

4 (Derby and Neville Chamberlain diaries, November 12 1923), perhaps in order that Salisbury should be kept in suspense, perhaps also so that he should not know until the election was settled – in which case he would not feel free to resign.

5 E.g. there is nothing in Derby to Salisbury, November 12 1923.

6 Amery diary, November 10 1923, but written in January; see entry for November 8 1923.

7 Amery to Baldwin, November 14 1923.

8 McNeill to Baldwin, November 12 1923; cf. Neville Chamberlain diary, November 18 1923.

9 Bayford diary, November 16 1923.

10 Derby diary, November 12 1923.

11 Neville Chamberlain diary, November 18 1923.

PAGE 324

1 Wood, 'Narrative', November 12 and 13 1923, Baldwin MSS.

2 Wood, 'Narrative', November 13 1923.

3 *Ibid.*

4 Petrie, p. 236.

5 Baldwin to Salisbury, November 13 1923.

6 Davidson to Lord Robert Cecil, November 13 1923.

7 Salisbury to Baldwin, November 14 1923; Wood, 'Narrative', November 14 1923.

8 Enclosed in Salisbury to Baldwin, November 14 1923.

9 Wood, 'Narrative', November 14 1923.

PAGE 325

1 Novar to Salisbury, November 15 1923.

2 Lord Robert Cecil to Baldwin, November 14 1923 (not sent); cf. Lord Robert Cecil to Davidson, November 15 1923 (copy), both Add. MSS 51080.

3 Lord Robert Cecil to Baldwin, November 14 1923 (with note that the answer was a 'verbal yes'), Add. MSS 51080.

4 Wood, 'Narrative', November 15; Salisbury to Baldwin, November 15.
5 Davidson and Sidney Herbert to Baldwin, November 14 1923; cf. Jones, p. 254.
6 Baldwin to Birkenhead and Austen Chamberlain, November 14 1923, Baldwin MSS; Petrie, pp. 237–8.

PAGE 326
1 Derby diary, November 12 1923.
2 Buckley to Baldwin, November 16 1923; cf. Beaverbrook to Rothermere, November ? 1923 for discontent among M.P.s.
3 Cf. Neville Chamberlain to Hilda, November 17 1923.
4 Grigg to Bailey, December 20, Altrincham MSS; Neville Chamberlain to Hilda, November 17 1923. See also Cab. 54 of November 13 1923 for Baldwin and MacDonald co-operating to pass Workmen's Compensation legislation which would expire if not passed before parliament was dissolved.
5 E.g. Simon at Leeds, November 26 1923, *Manchester Guardian*, November 28; cf. Grigg to Bailey, December 20 1923 and Asquith reported in Derby diary, December 17 1923.

PAGE 327
1 Dalton diary, December 26 1923 reporting Stamfordham in conversation. For estimates see Jones, p. 257 where Maclachlan is reported expecting 351 Conservative M.P.s. Bayford diary, December 12 1923 has Sanders expecting the government to keep its majority. *The Times* predicted a majority of 90, the *Morning Post* 120, Neville Chamberlain 70, see Neville Chamberlain to Hilda, December 2 1923. Stamfordham memo of December 8 1923 records Baldwin's surprise at the election result, see Churchill, p. 551. Baldwin MSS D42 and D41 have Central Office estimates of 357 and 333 seats (excluding Ulster). Austen Chamberlain to Ida, November 17 1923 reports Central Office expecting a majority of 27.
2 Rutland and Stamford, and Yeovil.

PAGE 328
1 I.e. Kilmarnock, Belper, Leeds West, and Moray and Nairn.
2 Derby diary, November 14 1924.
3 Amery to Baldwin, November 11 1923.
4 Amery to Baldwin, October 29, November 5 and 8 1923.
5 Amery to Baldwin, October 31 1923.
6 Amery to Baldwin, November 5 1923.

PAGE 329
1 I.e. general tariff on all imported manufactured goods, substantial preference for Dominion imports, no tax on wheat, beef or mutton,

no taxation on food, an election before next winter and the existing departmental committee to be assisted by an Advisory Committee to be named in a few days, Neville Chamberlain at Cardiff, November 2 1923, *Birmingham Post*, November 3.

2 Neville Chamberlain to Ida, October 26 1923 and diary, October 10.

3 See Lord Robert Cecil to Davidson, November 15 1923 (copy), Cecil of Chelwood MSS.

4 Except that he seems to have been willing to think seriously about Strachey's and the *Sunday Times*'s desire to have a referendum on Protection instead of an election: Neville Chamberlain to Baldwin, November 4 1923.

5 Neville Chamberlain to Hilda, November 17 and December 2 1923.

6 E.g. Strachey to Baldwin, November 3 1923.

PAGE 330

1 I have benefited in this chapter and elsewhere from examining a draft of a chapter by Mr C. P. Cook of Nuffield College, Oxford on electoral statistics in 1922 and 1923.

PAGE 331

1 Cf. Jones, p. 250; Stamfordham memo of December 8 1923 in Churchill, p. 551; Dawson to Lord Robert Cecil, December 8 1923 in Wrench, p. 224 for the view that Asquith would not drop Lloyd George and the Conservatives would not serve with him.

PAGE 332

1 Bridgeman diary, p. 85; cf. Lord Robert Cecil to Baldwin, February 1 1924. Neville Chamberlain diary, November 18 1923; cf. Austen Chamberlain to Ida, November 17 1923.

2 Austen Chamberlain to Ida, November 17 1923.

3 Derby to Birkenhead, December 7 1923, Churchill, p. 541.

4 Austen Chamberlain at Birmingham, December 7 1923, *Birmingham Post*, December 8.

5 Derby to Birkenhead, December 7 1923, Churchill, p. 541.

6 Stamfordham memorandum, December 10 1923, Churchill, p. 553.

PAGE 333

1 Derby diary, December 10 1923.

2 Derby diary, December 10 1923.

3 Or possibly Curzon: see Derby to Birkenhead, December 11 1923, Churchill, p. 556.

4 Derby diary, December 10 1923.

5 Stamfordham memo, December 10 1923, Churchill, p. 545.

6 Derby to Birkenhead, December 11 1923, Churchill, p. 556 shows Derby telling Birkenhead he was wrong but this did not prevent him

from writing his letter of resignation. Stamfordham reports Derby saying that Birkenhead was in Derby's house at the time of their interview.

7 Stamfordham to Derby, December 11 1923, Churchill, p. 557 refers to this. We do not have it; it is not clear whether it was written to Stamfordham or to the King.

8 Derby memorandum of December 10 1923, Churchill, p. 546.

9 Stamfordham to Derby, December 11 1923, Churchill, p. 557 records the King's anxiety at hearing of Derby's possible resignation. One wonders whether the message from Balfour to Derby was a response to a Royal request.

10 Derby diary, December 10 1923.

PAGE 334
1 Derby diary, December 11 1923.
2 E.g. 'should have been delighted to see Lord Birkenhead', Stamfordham memo of December 10 1923, Churchill, p. 553.
3 Churchill, p. 553.
4 Stamfordham memo of December 8 1923, Churchill, pp. 549-50.

PAGE 335
1 Bridgeman diary, p. 85.
2 Amery diary, December 8 1923.
3 Bridgeman to Baldwin and Amery to Baldwin, December 8 1923.
4 Amery to Baldwin, December 8 1923.
5 Amery diary, October 8 1923.
6 Bridgeman to Baldwin, December 8 1923.
7 Amery diary, December 9 1923, Bridgeman diary, p. 85.
8 For Joynson-Hicks see Amery diary, December 13 1923.
9 For Lloyd-Graeme see Bayford diary, December 12 1923 and Amery diary, December 13 1923.
10 Salisbury to Lord Robert Cecil, December 5 1923.

PAGE 336
1 Salisbury to Baldwin, December 4 1923.
2 Salisbury to Lord Robert Cecil, December 5 1923.
3 Wolmer to Davidson, December 8 1923, James, pp. 190-1.
4 Lord Hugh Cecil to Salisbury, December 8 1923.
5 Lord Robert Cecil to Gilbert Murray, November 2 1922 and November 16 1923; cf. Lord Robert Cecil to Dawson, December 11 1923, Wrench, p. 224.
6 Lord Robert Cecil to Salisbury, December 9 1923.
7 I.e. Morel: see Lord Robert Cecil to Dawson, December 11 1923 in Wrench, p. 224.
8 Lord Robert Cecil to Salisbury, December 9 1923.

9 See Gladstone to Maclean, January 12 1924, Add. MSS 46474 reporting Younger's view of Baldwin ,'richly larded with strong words' in a conversation at Nice a month later.

10 Younger to Baldwin, December 8 1923.

PAGE 337

1 Younger in *Evening News*, December 8 1923. Cf. Jackson to Davidson, December 9 1923, James, p. 190 shows Jackson saying that Baldwin should stay and it would not be possible to go into opposition, even though it was desirable. For Younger claiming ten days later that he stopped Baldwin resigning on the Sunday see Derby diary, December 17 1923.

2 Stamfordham memo of December 9, Geo. VK 1918/25.

3 Balfour memo of conversation with the King, Sunday December 9 1923, dated December 10, Whittingehame MSS.

4 Stamfordham memo of December 9 1923, Geo. VK 1918/25.

PAGE 338

1 Cf. King agreeing with Dawson's leading article of December 10 1923, Wrench, p. 223.

2 Wrench, p. 223.

3 Derby diary and Amery diary, December 11 1923.

4 Davidson to Hoare, December 11 1923, Templewood MSS.

5 Neville Chamberlain to Hannon, December 11 1923, Hannon MSS Box 17.

6 See Neville Chamberlain diary, December 9 1923 for Neville Chamberlain thinking Baldwin must resign before he went to Chequers.

7 Bridgeman to Baldwin, December 8 1923.

8 Neville Chamberlain diary, December 9 1923.

9 Neville Chamberlain diary, December 9 1923.

10 Amery diary, December 8 1923.

PAGE 339

1 Rothermere to Beaverbrook, December 10 and 11, Rothermere to Horne, n.d. and Beaverbrook to Rothermere, December 11 1923, all Beaverbrook MSS.

2 Birkenhead in *Sunday Times*, December 16 1923.

3 Stamfordham memo of December 10 1923, Churchill, p. 552.

4 Stamfordham memo, December 11 1923, Geo. V K 1918/42.

5 Horne to Baldwin, December 10 1923.

6 Balfour to Birkenhead, December 11 1923, Birkenhead, pp. 554–5.

7 Balfour to Stamfordham, December 17 1923, Geo. V K 1918/29.

PAGE 342

1 Gladstone to Maclean, December 30 1923, Add. MSS 46474.

2 Guest, memorandum of conversation December 19 [1923], Lloyd George MSS.

3 Gladstone talking to C. P. Scott, C. P. Scott diary, July 1 1923.

PAGE 343

1 Gladstone to Maclean, November 30 1923, Add. MSS 46474.
2 Maclean memoranda of January 4, 17 and 22 1924, Add. MSS 46474.
3 Maclean to Gladstone, December 29 1923.

PAGE 344

1 Gladstone to Maclean, January 23 1924 (1923 written), Add. MSS 46474.
2 Maclean to Gladstone, December 29 1923; Gladstone to Maclean, December 30 1923 (copy), Add. MSS 46474.
3 Maclean to Gladstone, January 10 1924.
4 Maclean to Gladstone, January 17 1924.
5 Maclean memorandum, January 17 1924, Add. MSS 46474.
6 Maclean memorandum, January 22 1924, Add. MSS 46474.
7 Cope to Maclean, February 13 1924, Add. MSS 46474.
8 Maclean memorandum, March 5 1924, Add. MSS 46474.

PAGE 345

1 Maclean memorandum, March 5 and report of lunch with Sir J. T. Davies at the Bath Club, March 7 1924, Add. MSS 46474.
2 I.e. £30,000 straight away and £100,000 for the general election.
3 Maclean memorandum, c. July 1924 recording Davies's visit on April 15 1924, Add. MSS 46474.
4 I.e. £20,000 now from Lloyd George, £10,000 from the Asquitheans.
5 Maclean memorandum, c. July 1924 recording meeting of July 1, Add. MSS 46474.
6 Cf. Asquith speech of November 23 1923, *Manchester Guardian*, November 24 for remodelling of Insurance Act, courageous use of national credit, internal transport, development of Imperial resources, Imperial trade and full operation of the Trade Facilities Act.
7 See e.g. Lloyd George at Newcastle, November 26 1923, *Newcastle Chronicle*, November 27.
8 Asquith, December 4 1923, *Manchester Guardian*, December 5.
9 Asquith at Paisley, November 28 1923, *Manchester Guardian*, November 29.
10 Grey at Salisbury, November 27, *Manchester Guardian*, November 28; cf. Grey letter to *Daily Telegraph*, November 30 and Grey at Newcastle, December 5, *Newcastle Chronicle*, December 6, all 1923.

PAGE 346

1 Lloyd George at Paisley, November 24 1923, *Glasgow Herald*, November 26.
2 Asquith at Paisley, November 23 1923, *Manchester Guardian*, November 24.
3 E.g. Fisher at Coventry in Fisher diary, November 22 1923.
4 Asquith at Paisley, December 1 1923, *The Observer*, December 2.

5 Cf. Derby as the 'harpooned walrus' who 'since the Carlton Club had condemned [Free Trade] to death ... must do his duty as sheriff': *Manchester Guardian*, November 29 1923.
6 Gladstone to Maclean, December 30 1923 (copy), Add. MSS 46474.

PAGE 347
1 And claiming that two Liberal M.P.s were willing to resign safe Liberal seats in his favour when the time was ripe: Mond to Asquith, January 2 1924 (on board ship).
2 Fisher diary, December 9 1923.
3 Fisher diary, December 21 1923.
4 Gladstone to Maclean, December 24 1923, Add. MSS 46474.
5 Thomson to Lloyd George, December 10 1923.
6 Grigg to Bailey, December 20 1923, Altrincham MSS.
7 Runciman to Lloyd George, December 8 1923; Beauchamp to Lloyd George, December 13 1923; cf. Runciman, p. 284.

PAGE 348
1 *Sunday Times* interview, December 9 1923.
2 Asquith at Euston, December 7 1923, *Westminster Gazette*, December 8.
3 Fisher diary, December 9 1923.
4 *Morning Post*, December 13 1923.

PAGE 349
1 Cf. Mond to Asquith, January 2 1924: 'strong position you have taken up'.
2 Churchill to Lady Violet Bonham-Carter, January 8 1924 (copy), Chartwell MSS; cf. Lloyd George to C. P. Scott, December 27 1923 for evidence of disagreement.
3 C. P. Scott diary, January 5/6 1924.
4 Stamfordham to the King, December 19 1923 quoting Asquith, Geo. V K1918/67.
5 Asquith at the National Liberal Club, December 18 1923, *The Times*, December 19.
6 For the danger of Lloyd George see Stamfordham to the King, December 19 1923 reporting Asquith, Geo. V K1918/67.
7 Cf. Grigg to Bailey, December 20 1923, Altrincham MSS.

PAGE 350
1 Cf. Grigg to Bailey, December 13 and 20 1923 Altrincham MSS; Gladstone to Maclean, January 12 1924 (copy), Add. MSS 46474.
2 Mond to Asquith, January 2 1924; Gladstone to Maclean, December 24 1923 (copy), Add. MSS 46474.
3 Stamfordham to the King, December 19 1923 quoting Asquith, Geo. V K1918/67.

4 Cf. Mond to Asquith, January 2 1924.

5 Asquith in Stamfordham to the King, December 19 1923, Geo. V K1918/67.

6 Stamfordham to the King, December 19 1923, Geo. V K1918/67, but cf. Stamfordham thinking him wrong: see Stamfordham to Balfour, December 21 1923, Geo. V K1918/70.

7 Asquith to Pringle, January 10 1924, Asquith MSS; Stamfordham to the King, December 19 1924, Geo. V K1918/67 quoting Asquith at National Liberal Club, December 18 1923, *The Times*, December 19.

PAGE 351

1 Fisher diary, January 21 1924.

2 Grey at City of London by-election meeting, January 24 1924, *Daily Telegraph*, January 25.

3 Asquith at National Liberal Club, December 18 1923, *The Times*, December 19.

4 See Geo. V K1918 for the King and Stamfordham scrutinising the *New Leader* for clues as to MacDonald's intentions.

5 Despite Fisher diary entries on December 8 and 9: see above, chapter XVII.

6 C. P. Scott diary, January 5/6 1924.

PAGE 352

1 *Ibid.*

2 Lloyd George in C. P. Scott diary, January 5/6.

3 C. P. Scott diary, January 5/6 1924; Fisher diary, January 6 1924.

4 Mrs Snowden to Lloyd George, February 19 1924.

5 C. P. Scott diary, February 4 1924.

PAGE 353

1 C. P. Scott diary, February 4 1924.

2 *Ibid.*

3 C. P. Scott diary, January 5/6 quoting Lloyd George; cf. Fisher diary, January 26 1924.

4 Cf. Mrs Snowden to Lloyd George, February 19 1924.

5 Grigg to Bailey, February 14 and 28 1924, Altrincham MSS; Fisher diary, February 13 1924.

6 For the division on the Naval Estimates in which Conservatives and Labour supported the government while Liberals were to be found in both lobbies see *Hansard*, March 18 1924, cols. 401–8.

PAGE 354

1 Cf. Hilton Young saying thinking of going Tory, Fisher diary, March 2 1924; cf. Hilton Young to S. Winthrop Young, February 6 1924, Kennett MSS; Neville Chamberlain diary, March 21 1924.

2 Grigg to Bailey, February 28 1924, Altrincham MSS.

3 Grigg to Bailey, March 20 1924, Altrincham MSS.

PAGE 355

1 Grigg to Bailey, March 27 1924, Altrincham MSS.
2 Ex-Coalition junior minister.
3 Grigg to Bailey, March 27 1924, Altrincham MSS for Lloyd George's first thoughts; Churchill to Balfour, April 3 1924, Chartwell MSS for the first feelers; Churchill to Balfour, letter and enclosure of September 1 1924 (Whittingehame MSS) for Lloyd George wanting tacit agreement and his willingness to support the right sort of Unionist government after the election.
4 Lloyd George at Llandrindod Wells, June 14 1924, *Manchester Guardian*, June 16; at Manchester, June 27 1924, *Daily Chronicle*, June 28; at King's Langley, July 12 1924, *Daily Chronicle*, July 14; and at Chesterfield, July 19 1924, *Daily Chronicle*, July 21.

PAGE 356

1 See speech of July 12 1924.
2 See Fisher diary, August 20 1924.
3 Mond to Lloyd George, September 25 and Lloyd George to Mond, September 29 1924, Lloyd George MSS.
4 See MacCallum Scott diary, July 12 1920.

PAGE 358

1 See e.g. Denman to Crewe, September 25 1924.

PAGE 360

1 Asquith thought of doing so: see Asquith to Pringle, January 10 1924, Asquith MSS.
2 MacDonald in *Socialist Review*, April 1918.

PAGE 361

1 E.g. MacDonald to Ponsonby, June 2 1922; Sidney Webb to Beatrice Webb, June 19 1922.
2 MacDonald talking to C. P. Scott, C. P. Scott diary, January 5 1924; cf. Beatrice Webb, January 3 1924, p. 257 for the view that no frontbench Labour leader expected the Labour party to be in a position to form a government. Sidney Webb, however, p. 6, says that, though the election results were predicted, the possibility of a Labour government was not.
3 Cf. Dalton diary, December 8 1923 for Egerton Wake thinking this. Snowden, *Autobiography* II, 594 says MacDonald did not at first wish to take office.
4 E.g. Trevelyan to Ponsonby, December 13 1923.
5 Dalton diary, December 8 1923 quoting Egerton Wake.

PAGE 362

1 Cf. Thomas saying to Stamfordham on January 1 that he and MacDonald had decided to take office if offered the chance immediately

after the election, Stamfordham to the King, January 1 Geo. V K 1918/97. J. S. Middleton to MacDonald, February 20 1924 (enclosure).

2 MacDonald to Trevelyan, December 13 1923 saying that no time had been spent on thinking about Coalition and that they were willing to take office if the opportunity offered.

3 See Wheatley's article 'No Coalition, No Compromise' in *Forward* of December 15 1923 for the view that there might be either an actual Coalition or a Coalition of ideas which would be 'equally treacherous and disastrous'. Wheatley could understand a Labour policy consisting of national control of the banking system, the nationalisation of mines and railways, public ownership of the land and better distribution of public wealth. But a 'colourless, diluted policy' would be rejected 'with contempt' at the next election ' and the people might again turn in desperation to the plausible proposals of a Liberal mountebank'. Cf. Kirkwood's speech at Bridgeton, *The Times*, December 24 predicting that there would be neither a Labour government nor a General Election in the next twelve months.

4 Sidney Webb, pp. 7–8; Arnold to MacDonald, January 4 1924 and Lees-Smith to Trevelyan, n.d. but December 1923, for Arnold and Lees-Smith changing their minds; cf. Beatrice Webb, December 12 1923, p. 255. For Smillie see Smillie to MacDonald, December 20 1923.

5 E.g. Dalton talking to Stamfordham in Dalton diary, December 26 1923.

6 Cf. Trevelyan to Ponsonby, December 13 1923.

7 MacDonald in *New Leader*, December 14 1923.

8 Cf. Wheatley at Glasgow, December 9 1923, *Manchester Guardian*, December 10; MacDonald in *New Leader*, December 14 1923; Dalton to Trevelyan, December 21 1923.

PAGE 363

1 Stamfordham to the King, January 1 1924, Geo. V K 1918/97 reports Thomas saying that a successful period of office would bring the Left Liberals over and send the Right Liberals into the Conservative party; cf. B. Riley to MacDonald, January 23 1924.

2 Thomas at Derby, January 1 1924, *Morning Post*, January 2.

3 MacDonald at Albert Hall, January 8 1924, *Daily Mail*, January 9.

4 MacDonald at Elgin, December 22 1923 in *Manchester Guardian*, December 31 (for accurate version).

5 Thomas at Derby, January 1 1924, *Morning Post*, January 2. See also Blaxland, p. 167 showing MacDonald urging Thomas to tell his 'financial advisers' to take steps to allay fears in the City.

6 Snowden at Newcastle, January 6 1924, *Newcastle Chronicle*, January 7 1924.

7 *Ibid.*

8 Thomas at Derby, January 1 1924.

PAGE 364

1 MacDonald to the Buckie branch of the British Legion, *The Times*, December 28 1923.

2 Thomas at Derby, January 1 1924 and MacDonald at Elgin, *Manchester Guardian*, December 31 1923.

3 Thomas at Derby, January 1 1924.

4 Clynes at Platting, December 7 1924, *Manchester Guardian*, December 8.

5 MacDonald at Elgin, December 22 1923, *Manchester Guardian*, December 31.

6 Blaxland, pp. 165–6, quoting Thomas's son, Sir Leslie Thomas, says that MacDonald visited Thomas on a number of occasions at Thomas's house in Dulwich to discuss the shape of the government. There was also correspondence.

7 Stamfordham to the King, December 28 1923 and January 1 1924, Geo. V K 1918/84 and 97. Thomas showed Stamfordham a letter from MacDonald on January 1.

PAGE 365

1 However, Stamfordham's memorandum of January 10 1924, Geo. V K 1918/89 and 90 records MacDonald saying he had asked for no conditions and hoped the King would ask for none, and had his Cabinet ready.

2 See e.g. Dawson to Chaplin, January 4 1922 Wrench, p. 226. The Royal Archives are only partially opened. It is not possible to know what range of advice the King took, nor what sort of gratuitous advice he was given, about putting Labour into office.

3 Neville Chamberlain to Hilda, June 16 1923 quoting the King.

4 Stamfordham to the King, December 28 1923 and January 1 1924, Geo. V K 1918/84 and 97, reporting conversation with Thomas.

PAGE 366

1 Dalton diary, December 12 1923 quoting Dalton and Josiah Wedgwood talking in a bus.

2 Dalton diary, December 8 1923.

PAGE 367

1 E.g. the attempt to avoid offering office to Henderson and also the fact that there was nothing for John Hodge, who had been a Lloyd George Minister, Sexton, Thorne (see Fisher diary, January 26 1924) or Ben Tillett, whose exclusion caused widespread comment. Tillet had been nasty about 'intellectuals' who were 'lions on the platform' but had been 'rats when the sword was drawn' (TUC Annual Report 1919, pp. 158–9, quoted in Graubard, p. 74). Cf. Blaxland, p. 166 reporting MacDonald and Thomas agreeing that Hodges had a measure of intellectual grip where Lansbury had not. For Lansbury being administratively inadequate see Sidney Webb, p. 13.

2 E.g. Beatrice Webb, pp. 259 and 261–2 for examples of the secrecy; C. P. Scott diary, January 5 1924 for MacDonald objecting to Asquith flaunting the Labour party's dependence, cf. Sidney Webb, pp. 10–11 and 12.

3 *Morning Post*, January 14 1920 and March 6 1920; *Daily Herald*, February 9 1920.

4 Haldane interviewed in *Daily Herald*, February 5 1920.

5 Haldane to E, March 17 1922.

6 Brockway, p. 136 leaves the impression that Haldane sometimes forced himself on unwilling candidates, and used the Webbs as his talent spotter.

PAGE 368

1 Haldane to E, December 7 1923.

2 Haldane to Baldwin, December 8 1923.

3 I have rejected the thought that Haldane might have been suggesting himself for office in a sort of Baldwin-led ministry of national emergency.

4 Haldane to his mother, December 12 1923, Haldane to his mother, January 11 1924 for Cave being 'desperately anxious' that he should join MacDonald's government.

5 Haldane to E, December 19 1923.

6 Haldane to his mother, December 12 1923.

7 Haldane to E, December 19 1923 for MacDonald possibly unwilling to stay at Cloan twice for fear of the press getting hold of it; Haldane to his mother, December 24 for continued uncertainty.

8 Haldane to Sidney Webb, December 29 1923.

9 Haldane to E, January 10 and to his mother, January 11 1924. Haldane to E, January 11 1924 shows Haldane agreeing that afternoon to join the government with Parmoor as Leader of the House of Lords if a government was in fact to be formed.

10 Haldane to E, January 15 1924.

PAGE 369

1 Jones, pp. 255 and 266; Sidney Webb, p. 18.

2 MacDonald to Henderson, December 22 1923, MacDonald MSS.

3 MacDonald to Haldane, Chelmsford to Haldane, January 12 1924 for Haldane acting as intermediary.

4 See below, n. 9.

5 Jones, January 16 1924, p. 263.

6 MacDonald to Haldane, January 12 1924 for Haldane acting as intermediary.

7 Parmoor to Haldane, January 6 1924 for Parmoor not joining until assured of Haldane's approval.

8 See MacDonald to Haldane, January 12 1924 for MacDonald saying how much he warmed to Sankey. Haldane says in his letter to Mrs Sidney Webb on January 25 1925 that Sankey was not appointed

because he had too little experience to lead the House of Lords but that it was intended to promote him judicially.

9 For Bradbury see Grigg to Bailey, January 3 1924, Altrincham MSS; i.e. it is not certain that Bradbury *was* offered anything.

10 Montagu to Lloyd George, August 3 1920.

11 Bledisloe to Lord Robert Cecil, January 30 and 31 1924 and to MacDonald, January 12 1924. MacDonald to Lord Robert Cecil, January 24, Lord Robert Cecil to Salisbury and vice versa, February 1 and Bledisloe to Lord Robert Cecil, February 4 1924.

12 Haldane to Mrs Sidney Webb, January 23 1925.

13 For 1908 see Bell, 1, 538; Parmoor to Salisbury, April 24 1921 for 'application of Christian ethics to the methods of government'. Griffith-Boscawen, *Fourteen Years in Parliament*, p. 125 for Workmen's Compensation.

PAGE 370

1 See Lytton (Governor of Bengal) to Haldane, February 6 1924 for the extent to which official opinion in India was reassured by the 'genius' MacDonald had shown in appointing ministers to posts in which their ignorance would make them innocuous.

2 Sidney Webb, p. 15.

3 Wheatley to MacDonald, December 21 1923, Kirkwood, p. 220.

4 Shinwell, pp. 85-6.

5 Cf. Lord Robert Cecil to Geoffrey Dawson in Wrench, p. 224.

6 Spoor to Morel, February 9 1924.

7 Lansbury to MacDonald, January 18 and to Henderson, January 15 1924, Lansbury MSS.

8 Sidney Webb, p. 14; Smillie to MacDonald, December 20 1923, Maclean to Spoor, January 24 1924, MacDonald MSS.

9 Sidney Webb, p. 18.

10 Sidney Webb, p. 13, quoting MacDonald.

11 Anderson, pp. 105 and 117.

12 Wedgwood to MacDonald, May 14 and 23 1923.

13 Sidney Webb, p. 15.

PAGE 371

1 C. P. Scott diary, March 21 1924.

2 Derby to General Rawlinson, February 19 1924, Churchill, p. 567, Cf. Attlee, p. 61 for Walsh being popular with the Army.

3 Sidney Webb, p. 16.

4 Webb to E. D. Simon, January 28 1924.

5 Percy, p. 94.

6 Morrison, p. 76 for weak heart.

7 Sidney Webb, p. 16.

PAGE 372

1 Sidney Webb, p. 12.

2 Amery diary, February 20 1924.

3 See Brockway, pp. 150–1; Dalton diary, February 4 1924 for MacDonald and *New Leader*.
4 Smillie, p. 307.
5 Spoor (March 21 and July 29), T. Kennedy (July 24) and F. H. Rose (February 14) to MacDonald, 1924. Sidney Webb to Beatrice, February 11 1924.
6 Cab. 20 of March 12 (Conclusion 1), Cab. 32 of May 15 (Conclusion 12) and Cab. 47 of August 5 (Conclusion 1).
7 Shinwell, p. 94.
8 Anderson, p. 119.

PAGE 373
1 Cab. 24 of April 2 (Conclusion 2) for the stalling.
2 Cab. 25 of April 7 (Conclusion 10), Cab. 32 of May 15 (Conclusion 11), Cab. 31 of May 14 (Conclusion 3); cf. Stamfordham memos of April 6 and 8, Geo. V K1937/1 and 5 for the King intervening and H. S. Lindsay to MacDonald, May 26 1924.
3 Cab. 22 of March 26 (Conclusion 9) for the TUC request for bills not yet before parliament being refused; Cab. 38 of June 18 (Conclusion 2) and Cab. 51 of September 29 (Conclusion 5) for irritation at press leakages.
4 Beyond the appointment of Gosling, the Minister of Transport, as Paymaster-General in May as a consequence of the discovery, after the government had been formed, that the Geddes Committee had recommended the downgrading of the Ministry of Transport; MacDonald to Gosling and vice versa, March 3 and 5 1924.
5 E.g. Lord Robert Cecil to Gilbert Murray, June 30 1924, C. P. Scott diary, February 2/3 1924.
6 Jones, pp. 287–98. The despatch about the Herriot discussions is another example. Cf. C. P. Scott diary, July 15 1924 for report of lunch between J. A. Hobson, C. P. Scott and MacDonald.
7 For Smillie see Sidney to Beatrice Webb, April 1 1924. For MacDonald see Beatrice Webb, September 24 1924. Cf. Shinwell, p. 96 and Allen of Hurtwood, p. 180.
8 Haldane to Mrs Webb, January 23 1925.
9 Sidney Webb, p. 21.

PAGE 374
1 The original conclusion is Cab. 22 of March 26 (Conclusion 7). The decision to tighten up and the explanation of the confusion is Cab. 25 of April 7 (Conclusions 4 and 5) and Cab. 27 of April 15 (Conclusion 3).
2 E.g. about the Foreign Office view of the importance of the Yangtse Gunboats, Cab. 39 of July 2 (Conclusion 8).
3 Sidney Webb, p. 19.
4 Cab. 22 of March 26 (Conclusion 4).
5 Cab. 35 of May 30 (Conclusion 10).

6 Cab. 28 of April 29 (Conclusion 1), Cab. 32 of May 15 (Conclusion 1), Cab. 39 of July 2 (Conclusion 11).
7 Cab. 34 of May 27 (Conclusion 4).
8 Beatrice Webb, p. 259 quotes letter delivered on January 1.

PAGE 375
1 Cab. 11 of February 8 (Conclusion 4).
2 Mardy Jones to MacDonald, May 28 1924.
3 Cab. 34 of May 27 (Conclusion 7), Cab. 11 of February 8 (Conclusion 9).
4 Cab. 21 of March 17 (Conclusion 2).
5 Cab. 32 of May 15 (Conclusion 4). Shinwell (September 1) and S. Webb (September 8) to MacDonald.
6 Cab. 36 of June 4 (Conclusion 3).
7 Cab. 44 of July 30 (Conclusion 1).
8 Linlithgow being, of course, a prominent Die Hard.

PAGE 376
1 Cab. 11 of February 8 (Appendix to Conclusion 8).
2 Anderson, p. 119. The bill is in *Bills Public* 1924, 1, 105; the amendments at 1, 123 and 141.
3 Cab. 34 of May 27 (Conclusion 2).
4 Cab. 27 of April 15 (Conclusion 12).
5 Cab. 21 of March 17 (Conclusion 3), Cab. 48 of August 6 (Conclusion 11).
6 Cab. 28 of April 29 (Conclusion 1).
7 Cab. 27 of April 19 (Conclusion 5).

PAGE 377
1 Cab. 18 of March 5 1924 (Appendix to Conclusion 1).
2 Cab. 50 of September 22 (Conclusion 1).
3 See below, pp. 403–5.
4 Cab. 33 of May 21 (Conclusion 2).
5 Cab. 40 of July 9 (Conclusion 13).
6 Chelmsford to Haldane, January 12 1924. Amery diary, January 23 1924 saying that Chelmsford got a guarantee that the Navy would not be reduced and the Air Force would be brought up to the French level. Cab. 10 of February 6 (Conclusions 2 and 6).
7 Cab. 29 of May 1 (Conclusion 2), Cab. 38 of June 18 (Conclusion 1) for the Iraq Constituent Assembly ratifying the treaty.
8 Cab. 31 of May 14 (Conclusion 1), Cab. 51 of September 29 (Conclusion 2).
9 Cab. 29 of May 1 (Conclusion 3).
10 Cab. 17 of February 28 (Conclusion 6).
11 Cab. 47 of August 5 (Conclusion 2); cf. Amery to Baldwin, January 14 1924.
12 Cab. 35 of May 30 (Conclusion 3).

PAGE 378
1 Neville Chamberlain diary, February 28 1923 for compromise between what Baldwin suggested – unrestricted private enterprise, i.e. Marconi – and the government control which the Post Office officials wanted.
2 Cab. 25 of April 7 (Conclusion 9), Cab. 40 of July 9 (Conclusion 12).
3 Cab. 39 of July 2 (Conclusion 22).
4 Cab. 36 of June 4 (Conclusion 6).
5 Cab. 46 of June 4 (Conclusion 2). For earlier commitment see e.g. *Daily Herald*, September 22 1919.
6 Cab. 7 of January 23 (Conclusion 17).
7 See CP 318, Cab. 35 of May 30 (Conclusion 2).
8 Grigg to Bailey, January 3 1924, Altrincham MSS.
9 J. Welsh to MacDonald, January 26 1924 and Shinwell, p. 93.

PAGE 379
1 MacDonald to Cramp, February 4 1924, MacDonald MSS.
2 Sidney Webb, p. 20.
3 Boyle, p. 177.
4 Cf. Steel-Maitland saying this in parliament, *Hansard*, August 6 1924, col. 3058. See Sidney Webb, p. 27.
5 Cf. MacDonald at Aberavon in *Manchester Guardian*, July 5 1924 for MacDonald talking about 'three years of useful work'.
6 Cf. Archbishop saying how good MacDonald was at ecclesiastical patronage in Fisher diary, February 27 1924. Cab 39 of July 2 (Conclusion 19).

PAGE 380
1 Jones, January 19 1924, p. 264.
2 Sir Arthur Balfour, Later Lord Riverdale.
3 Cab. 43 of July 22 (Conclusion 3).
4 Snowden, *Autobiography*, II, 594.
5 Ponsonby to Morel, January 31 1924.
6 MacDonald to Morel, March 18 and to Wake, August 23 1924.
7 MacDonald to Allen in Allen of Hurtwood, p. 180.
8 MacDonald to Middleton, July 28 1924; Lansbury to Beatrice Webb, March 14 1924.

PAGE 381
1 See e.g. MacDonald to Lord Robert Cecil, October 10 1924 and to Tom Richardson, February 29 1924, MacDonald MSS.

PAGE 383
1 E.g. Grigg to Bailey, December 13 1923 and January 3 1924, Altrincham MSS; Mrs Asquith to Strachey, December 18 1923.

PAGE 384
1 Derby diary, December 17 1923.
2 Neville Chamberlain diary, December 18 1923.

3 Hunsden to Baldwin, December 18; Banbury to *The Times*, December. 12 1923. Cf. Birkenhead saying he agreed with Banbury in supporting an Asquith government if Baldwin went out, *Sunday Times*, December 16. Newton to Strachey, December 17, Strachey to Newton, December 18 1923, Strachey MSS, said that Ullswater had 'crossed his mind'. For Ullswater in 1918 see Austen Chamberlain to Strachey, March 19 1918.

4 Snowden, *Autobiography*, II, 590 records him being annoyed at the offer to McKenna.

5 Derby diary, January 23 1924 refers to an earlier conversation which makes it clear that Joynson-Hicks had been thinking on these lines for some time.

6 Strachey to McKenna, December 10, to Younger, December 10, to Stamfordham December 8, 10 (with memorandum) and 12 1923, and Younger to Strachey, n.d., Sunday, all Strachey MSS. For Strachey preferring to put the Liberals in if McKenna turned out to be an impossibility see Strachey to Younger, December 17 1923, Strachey MSS.

7 Bridgeman diary, p. 85; Ormsby-Gore to Davidson, December 9 1923. For McNeill see Bridgeman to Baldwin, December 8 1923; H. A. Gwynn to Baldwin, December 7 1923.

PAGE 385

1 Amery to Baldwin, December 8 1923; see Amery diary of same date for a generally censorious view of the 'born idiots from Austen and FE downwards who are clamouring for us to support an Asquith government which would mean the final break-up of our party'.

2 Lord Robert Cecil to Salisbury, December 9 1923.

3 Derby and Younger talking in Derby diary, December 17 1923; cf. Mrs Asquith to Strachey, December 18 1923 for the assertion that Hall had financed several Labour candidates to defeat Asquitheans.

4 Dawson to Chaplin, January 4 1924, Wrench, p. 226.

PAGE 386

1 Lord Robert Cecil to Salisbury, December 9 1923.

2 Cf. Horne to Lloyd George, January 2 1924 (1923 written).

3 Derby diary, January 23 1924 for Joynson-Hicks telling Derby; cf. Amery diary, January 17 1924.

4 Lord Robert Cecil to Salisbury, December 9 1923.

5 See above, p. 337.

PAGE 387

1 Gladstone to Maclean, January 12 1924, Add. MSS 46474 reporting Younger saying that Stamfordham thought this a good idea.

2 Neville Chamberlain diary, December 18 1923 reporting Derby.

3 Neville Chamberlain diary, December 19 1923 for Horne's business commitments; but cf. Derby saying that he knew Horne would take

it, in Derby diary, December 17 1923. Beaverbrook was told by Horne that he was not interested but that may merely have meant that he did not want support from Beaverbrook: see Beaverbrook to Rothermere, December 11 1923, Beaverbrook MSS.

4 Neville Chamberlain diary, January 5 and to Hilda, January 5 1924.
5 Bridgeman diary, p. 97.
6 Neville Chamberlain diary, January 13 1924 quoting Sir Warren Fisher.
7 Cf. Neville Chamberlain diary, January 13 1924 for Warren Fisher trying to get Neville Chamberlain to persuade Baldwin to get rid of Davidson.
8 Amery diary, January 15 1924; Neville Chamberlain diary, January 18 1924.
9 Neville Chamberlain diary, January 13 and to Hilda, January 5 1924.
10 E.g. Baldwin to Lord Robert Cecil, December 31 1923; Derby diary, January 23/24 1924 expecting Baldwin to resign and stand for re-election; Neville Chamberlain to Ida, December 23 1923 for Neville Chamberlain expecting Baldwin to resign if the party meeting insisted on the dropping of Protection.

PAGE 388
1 Derby diary, December 17 1923.

PAGE 389
1 Amery to Baldwin, December 8 1923.
2 Amery to Baldwin, December 21 1923.
3 Amery to Dawson, January 9 1924, *The Times* Archive.
4 Amery to Baldwin, December 29 1923.
5 The word was Lord Midleton's, Midleton to Salisbury, January 8 1924.

PAGE 390
1 Midleton to Salisbury, January 8, Novar to Salisbury, February 2 and 3, Devonshire to Salisbury, January 30 1924 saying Baldwin should remain Prime Minister so long as Protection doesn't stay.
2 Derby to Salvidge, December 23 1923, Churchill, p. 560.
3 Derby diary, December 17 1923.
4 Winterton to Hoare, December 14 (?24) 1923, Templewood MSS.
5 Neville Chamberlain diary, December 18 1923.
6 Amery diary, December 18, Neville Chamberlain diary, December 18 1923.
7 Bridgeman diary, p. 97.
8 E.g. *Daily Mail*, January 7 1924. *Sunday Times*, December 16 1923 and January 13 1924 for Asquith as the Gladstonian of the older generation. Cf. letter to the *Daily Mail*, January 15 1924.
9 Austen Chamberlain to Ida, January 12 1924; Balfour to Birkenhead, December 11 1923 in Churchill, pp. 554–5.

10 Derby diary, January 23 1924.
11 Neville Chamberlain diary, January 21 and to Hilda, January 24 1924.
12 Neville Chamberlain diary, January 22, Amery diary, January 23 1924.
13 Neville Chamberlain diary, January 24 1924.

PAGE 391
1 Neville Chamberlain diary, January 24 1924.
2 Neville Chamberlain diary, January 24 1924.
3 Baldwin to Salisbury, January 25 1924.
4 Lord Robert Cecil to Baldwin, February 1, Salisbury to Baldwin, January 26, Salisbury to Lord Robert Cecil, January 28 and Ormsby-Gore to Baldwin, January 29, all 1924.
5 Neville Chamberlain to Hilda, January 24 1924.
6 Cf. Grigg to Bailey, February 7 1924.
7 Balfour memo of conversation with Baldwin, February 4 1924, Whittingehame MSS.
8 Amery diary, February 4 1924.

PAGE 392
1 Neville Chamberlain diary, February 6 1924 (date of dinner may be the 5th, i.e. Baldwin to Balfour, February 6, Whittingehame MSS says 'last night'); cf. Petrie, p. 240.
2 Ormsby-Gore to Baldwin, January 29 1924.
3 Neville Chamberlain diary, February 7 1924.
4 Neville Chamberlain diary, February 7 1924.
5 Beaverbrook to Strachey, October 18 1924; Jones, p. 297; Derby diary, January 23 1924.
6 E. Outhwaite to P. Gower, February 19 1924, MacDonald MSS.

PAGE 393
1 Derby diary, February 7 1924; Beaverbrook to Younger, October 29 1924, Beaverbrook MSS.
2 Austen Chamberlain to Ida, November 17 1923.
3 Beaverbrook to Younger, November 26 1923 and vice versa, November 27, both Beaverbrook MSS. At Younger's suggestion he appears to have paid £1,000 for G. S. Rentoul at Lowestoft and £750 for Peter MacDonald at the Isle of Wight (Younger to Beaverbrook, December 12 1923 Beaverbrook MSS).
4 Taylor.
5 Taylor.
6 Baldwin to Milner, January 4 and January 8 1924.
7 Amery diary, January 9 1924.
8 Neville Chamberlain diary, January 13 and to Hilda, January 12 1924.
9 Amery to Baldwin, January 12 1924.

10 E.g. Neville Chamberlain diary, December 18 1923; Bridgeman diary, pp. 97–8.

11 Bayford diary, January 14 1924; cf. Novar to Salisbury, January 17 1924.

12 Neville Chamberlain diary, January 18 1924.

13 Amery diary, January 21 1924.

14 Neville Chamberlain diary, January 18 and to Ida, June 7 1924.

15 I.e. Balfour, Austen Chamberlain, Crawford and Birkenhead. Horne was still in America.

16 For this Cabinet see Amery, Neville Chamberlain and Derby diaries for February 7 and Bridgeman diary, p. 99 (which, however, was written later in the year and has the date wrong).

PAGE 394

1 See Salvidge to Strachey, February 11 1924. Salvidge says the meeting would not accept Buckley's resolution for dropping Protection altogether.

2 See Amery diary, February 10 1924.

3 Amery diary, February 11 1924.

4 Amery diary, February 12 1924.

5 Amery diary, September 29 1923.

PAGE 395

1 MacCallum Scott diary, November 7 1923, pp. 311 and 276ff.

2 Churchill to Lady Violet Bonham-Carter, January 8 1924 (copy), Chartwell MSS.

3 *Ibid.*

4 For Guest see Lloyd George in Maclean's memorandum of January 22 1924, Add. MSS 46474.

5 Horne talking to MacCallum Scott, MacCallum Scott diary, November 13 1923 but one has to remember MacCallum Scott was once an admirer of Churchill and had written a life.

6 Derby diary, January 23 1924.

7 Fisher diary, February 28 1924 reports Churchill saying that Thomas's speech at the Canada Club dinner was ' "Tory Democrat" '. For this see also Neville Chamberlain to Ida, February 16 1924.

8 Grigg to Grey, February 22 1924.

9 See, for example, his speech in the House of Lords rejecting any 'permanent working arrangement' between the Liberal and Labour parties (*Daily News*, January 16 1924).

10 Grigg to Bailey, January 17 1924, Altrincham MSS.

PAGE 396

1 Haldane to his mother, March 19 1924, Haldane MSS quoting Grey at lunch.

2 Grigg to Bailey, February 28 1924, Altrincham MSS; cf. Lord Robert Cecil to Gertrude Bell, February 22 1924, Cecil of Chelwood MSS for Grey failing to do his duty by creating a Liberal/Conservative alliance.
3 Grigg to Bailey, February 28 1924, Altrincham MSS.
4 Neville Chamberlain diary, March 17 1924.
5 *Ibid.*
6 Grigg, Grey and Greenwood all said this.
7 Neville Chamberlain diary, March 17 1924; cf. Amery diary, February 24 for Jackson's support.
8 Neville Chamberlain diary, March 17 1924.
9 Neville Chamberlain to Hilda, February 9 and May 18, and to Ida, February 16 and June 22 1924.
10 Neville Chamberlain diary, March 17 1924.
11 Neville Chamberlain to Hilda, February 23 and March 9 1924.

PAGE 397
1 Amery diary, March 4 and 5 1924.
2 Neville Chamberlain diary, March 17 1924 but it is not clear that the timetable operated or that Churchill really was given the chance to have St George's, Westminster.
3 Amery to Baldwin, December 8 1923.
4 Amery to Baldwin, January 28 1924.
5 Amery diary, February 10 1924 for Amery telling Baldwin so.
6 Amery diary, February 10 1924.
7 Amery diary, February 11 1924.
8 Amery diary, March 3 1924 and *passim* in 1924.
9 Amery diary, March 5 1924.
10 Amery diary, February 24 1924.

PAGE 398
1 Amery diary, February 27 1924.
2 Austen Chamberlain to Churchill, March 3 1924, Chartwell MSS.
3 Amery diary, March 6 1924.
4 Amery diary, March 7 1924.
5 Amery diary, March 7 1924.
6 Amery diary, March 8 1924, Cab. 19 of March 12 1924 (Conclusion 8).
7 Amery diary, March 8 1924.
8 Amery diary, March 8 1924.
9 Amery diary, March 14 1924.

PAGE 399
1 Baldwin to Mrs Davidson, March 20 1924; Balfour to Churchill, March 15 1924, Whittingehame MSS 1.
2 Baldwin to Mrs Davidson, March 20 1924 and Amery diary, March 20 1924.

3 The figures were: Nicholson (C) 8,187; Churchill (Ind Anti-Soc) 8,144; Brockway (Lab) 6,156; Duckers (Lib) 291.
4 Churchill to Balfour, April 3 1924.
5 For cold shouldering in Liverpool and hostility to Baldwin there see Chilcott to Austen Chamberlain, April 2 1924.
6 Churchill to Lord Robert Cecil, March 23 1924.
7 Bayford diary, April 13 1924; Amery diary, April 2 1924.
8 Austen Chamberlain to Churchill, March 3 1924.
9 Amery diary, March 27 1924; cf. Churchill to Balfour, April 3 1924.

PAGE 400
1 Hall to Baldwin, March 17 1924.
2 Younger to Steel-Maitland, March 28 1924.
3 Fitzalan to Balfour, April 21 1924, Whittingehame MSS 24.
4 Amery diary, January 23, 24 and 28 1924.
5 Amery diary, January 25 1924.
6 Storr to Lord Robert Cecil, April 5 1924.
7 For table of responsibilities see Storr to Lord Robert Cecil, April 5 1924.
8 Salisbury to Lord Robert Cecil, April 8 1924.
9 Amery diary, May 1 1924; cf. Storr to Lord Robert Cecil, April 5 1924.
10 Fisher diary, February 18 1924 quoting Baldwin.
11 Wolmer to Salisbury, March 4, Salisbury to Lord Robert Cecil, April 8 1924.
12 Bayford diary, June 24 1924; cf. Neville Chamberlain to Ida, June 7 1924.
13 Derby diary, January 23 1924 quoting Joynson-Hicks.
14 Neville Chamberlain to Hilda, August 17 1924; cf. Austen Chamberlain's rebuke to Chilcott in Chilcott to Austen Chamberlain, April 2 1924.
15 Birkenhead to Salisbury, April 8 1924; cf. Amery diary, May 23 1924.
16 Cf. Strachey to Wood, May 8 1924, Strachey MSS, for complaints about Beaverbrook's attacks.
17 Cf. Baldwin to Strachey, May 9 1924.

PAGE 401
1 *The People*, May 18 1924, p. 1.
2 Memorandum of May 18 1924 by Austen Chamberlain, 'Stanley Baldwin's Interview with *The People* reporter', AC 24/6/3; cf. Jones, p. 280 for no incompatibility between what the reporter reported and what Baldwin really believed.
3 Austen Chamberlain memorandum of May 18.
4 Baldwin at Edinburgh, March 24 1924, *Morning Post*, March 25.
5 Lord Robert Cecil to Salisbury, April 10 and May 17, to Grey, April 10, to Gladstone, April 10 and 22 1924 (April 10 was one of the points at which Cecil expected the government to fall).

6 E.g. Chilcott to Austen Chamberlain saying this on April 2 1924.
7 Chilcott to Austen Chamberlain, April 2 1924.

PAGE 402
1 Cf. Hoare to Austen Chamberlain, January 25 1924.
2 Bayford diary, July 29 1924 for the difficulty in finding Churchill a seat.
3 *Hansard*, June 17 and 18 1924, cols. 1963–2088 and 2153–2266.
4 For the alleged existence of such a group under the guidance of Haden Guest see Amery diary, July 17 1924 and September 19 1924; cf. Neville Chamberlain's conversation with Wood in Neville Chamberlain diary, March 21 1924.
5 Baldwin at Lowestoft, July 16 1924, *Eastern Daily News*, July 17. For the negotiations and Austen Chamberlain's disgust at the Lowestoft speech see Austen Chamberlain to Hoare, July 18, Templewood MSS v I and Austen Chamberlain to Baldwin, July 18 1924; but cf. Baldwin to Austen Chamberlain, July 21 1924 for Baldwin defending his position.

PAGE 403
1 Neville Chamberlain to Hilda, April 5 and August 3 1924; Churchill to Balfour, October 11 1924.
2 E.g. Neville Chamberlain to Ida, June 7, 14 and 22 and July 5 1924, and to Hilda, June 28 1924.
3 Amery diary, June 6, 16, 17 and 18 1924; Amery to Austen Chamberlain, June 12 1924.
4 Baldwin in *Popular Views*, January 1922.

PAGE 404
1 Bayford diary, August 10 1924 for the Irish Boundary Commission question being unwelcome to the Conservative party.
2 Selborne to Salisbury, April 15 and October 14 1924 (for Baldwin's position being worse than Lloyd George's).
3 Baldwin at Hemel Hempstead, August 6 1924 *Morning Post*, August 7.
4 Who was in fact not appointed.

PAGE 405
1 It is not clear whether Baldwin had an arrangement with MacDonald and J. H. Thomas about Ireland. References for all this are: Bayford diary, August 10, Baldwin to Mrs. Davidson, August 21 and 31, Churchill to Balfour, September 1 (Whittingehame MSS), Baldwin to Salisbury, September 2, Baldwin to Wood, September 6, Wood to Baldwin, September 10, Strachey to Carson, September 12 and vice versa and 17 (Strachey MSS), Amery diary, August 3, September 19 and 25, Churchill to Balfour, October 2, memo of King's talk with Birkenhead, August 6, Geo. V K 1949/14 and 15, all 1924.

2 Rt Hon Edward Wood, M.P., 'Conservative Beliefs', reprinted from *The Times*.
3 Birkenhead at Grocers' Hall, March 13 1924, *The Times*, March 14.
4 Wood to Salisbury, February 29 1924.
5 Hoare to Austen Chamberlain, January 25 1924.
6 Austen Chamberlain to Hoare, January 28 1924.

PAGE 406
1 Neville Chamberlain to Hilda, February 4 and March 26 1922.
2 Neville Chamberlain to Ida, April 1 1922.
3 Cf. Neville Chamberlain to Ida, October 26 1923.
4 Neville Chamberlain to Ida, June 22 and to Hilda, June 28 1924.
5 Neville Chamberlain to Hilda, July 12 1924.
6 Neville Chamberlain to Ida, July 17 1924.
7 Neville Chamberlain to Hilda, September 20 1924.
8 Neville Chamberlain to Hilda, July 15 1924.

PAGE 407
1 Montague-Barlow to Salisbury (with enclosure), January 29 1924.
2 Birkenhead, *Halifax*, p. 158 for Wood supporting a Labour backbench motion on Widows' Pensions.
3 E.g. Baldwin at Cambridge in *Cambridge News*, March 1 1924.
4 Baldwin at Edinburgh, March 24 1924, *Morning Post*, March 25.
5 Baldwin at Primrose League demonstration, Albert Hall, May 2 1924, *The Times*, May 3.

PAGE 408
1 Baldwin at Albert Hall to Primrose League, May 2 1924, *The Times*, May 3.
2 Baldwin at Usher Hall, Edinburgh, March 24 1924, *Morning Post*, March 25.
3 Baldwin to Junior Imperial League, May 3 1924, *The Times*, May 5.
4 Baldwin at City of London School, June 13 1924, *The Times*, June 14.
5 Baldwin at Hotel Cecil, May 6 1924, *The Times*, May 7.
6 Baldwin at Cambridge and at City of London School.
7 *The Times*, April 9 1924 reporting speech of April 8 at Hotel Victoria.
8 E.g. Baldwin at sixtieth anniversary dinner of Court 'Stour Valley' of Ancient Order of Foresters, *Birmingham Post*, February 18 1924.

PAGE 409
1 Cf. Neville Chamberlain to Hilda, September 7 and 13 1924.
2 Amery diary, February 13 1924.

PAGE 410
1 Amery diary, February 13 1924.
2 C. P. Scott diary, February 2/3 1924; MacDonald to Richardson, February 29 1924.

3 Amery diary, February 21 1924.
4 Amery diary, March 13 1924.
5 Amery diary, March 18.

PAGE 411
1 Bayford diary, April 13 1924.
2 Amery diary, October 8 1924; Stamfordham memo, October 7 1924, Geo. V K 1958/10, 11 and 13; Swinton, p. 158.

PAGE 414
1 Sir William Tyrell to Baldwin, November 1 1924 reporting Birkenhead, Churchill and Beaverbrook at dinner at Sir Philip Sassoon's.
2 Austen Chamberlain to Baldwin, November 6 1924.
3 Jones, p. 303 quoting Hankey.

PAGE 415
1 For these phrases sticking in Salisbury's mind sixteen years after Baldwin used them to him about the Plymouth speech in 1923, see Salisbury to Lord Robert Cecil, November 1 1939.
2 See Lord Robert Cecil to Irwin (i.e. E. F. L. Wood), December 16 1926, Add. MSS 51084 complaining that Wood and Salisbury were the only members of the 1924 Cabinet to whom Lord Robert Cecil could talk 'with real freedom'.

PAGE 417
1 Sassoon to Lloyd George, March 19 1922.
2 Derby to Lord Robert Cecil, November 10 1923.

PAGE 419
1 For Maxton explaining the tactical advantages to be gained if the Clydesiders attacked the Labour government see Beatrice Webb, February 15 1924.

PAGE 421
1 Baldwin to Carson, December 16 1923.

PAGE 422
1 F. M. L. Thompson, *English Landed Society in the Nineteenth Century* chapter XII.
2 R. M. Holland Martin to Baldwin, November 7 1924.
3 Jones, p. 256.
4 For Horne see Jones, p. 244; for Salvidge see Davidson in James, p. 117.
5 Beaverbrook to Younger, October 29 1924, Beaverbrook MSS.
6 See e.g. Salvidge to Strachey, January 25 1924.
7 See James, p. 173 for Kipling, who was Baldwin's cousin telling Davidson that the 'real pen in our family' was Baldwin's who 'spoke such good English because he had absorbed in his youth the best prose and poetry which the country produced'.

PAGE 423

1 Bayford diary, April 10 1921.

2 See e.g. Bayford diary, October 21 1920 and April 10 1921; Sir Eric Geddes to Lloyd George, January 15 1920 for Thomas co-operating with Geddes.

PAGE 424

1 Bridgeman diary, pp. 50-3.

2 For the limelight see Bayford diary, April 17 1921, p. 3 and also Bridgeman diary, October 18/25 1920.

3 Wigram to Grigg, August 26 1920, Altrincham MSS.

4 Wigram to Grigg, August 26 1920, Altrincham MSS.

5 Davidson quoted in James, p. 106 but Davidson may have been reading back into 1921 opinions which Hodges expressed later in the twenties.

6 MacCallum Scott diary, May 13 1922 reporting a group of Coalition Liberal M.P.s talking about Labour leaders' corruption.

7 Collis, p. 60.

8 Blaxland, p. 152; Halifax, p. 156; Hansard, November 26 1919.

9 Blaxland, p. 151.

10 MacCallum Scott diary May 13 1922. Thomas neither voted nor spoke during the second reading of the bill against which Clynes moved the motion: see Hansard, May 30 1921, col. 732.

11 Bayford diary, April 10 1921.

12 Neville Chamberlain to Hilda, February 15 1920.

13 Bridgeman diary, p. 50.

14 Shinwell, p. 92.

15 Bayford diary, April 10 1921; cf. Austen Chamberlain to Long, April 15 1921. For Sir Allen Smith as a 'cantankerous person' see Neville Chamberlain to Ida, September 15 1923.

16 Bridgeman diary, April 17 1920. For Bridgeman saying the same thing about a possible coal strike see Bridgeman diary, September 2 1920.

PAGE 425

1 Austen Chamberlain to Gilmour, July 7 1921, Austen Chamberlain MSS.

2 Neville Chamberlain to Hilda, April 5 1924.

3 Neville Chamberlain to Hilda, February 15 1920.

4 Griffith-Boscawen, Memoirs, p. 195.

5 Griffith-Boscawen, Memoirs, p. 207 Griffith-Boscawen served under both Barnes and Hodge.

6 Willoughby de Broke in the National Review, 1918.

7 See MacCallum Scott diary, June 22 and October 25 1920.

8 Middlemas, p. 121.

9 Neville Chamberlain to Hilda, June 30 1923.

10 Neville Chamberlain to Hilda, March 24 1923 and Mrs Neville Chamberlain to Hilda, March 10 1923.

11 Cf. Neville Chamberlain to Hilda, November 17 1923 and Williams of Barnburgh, p. 61.

PAGE 426

1 Neville Chamberlain to Hilda, June 30 1923.
2 Neville Chamberlain to Ida, June 24 1923.
3 Neville Chamberlain to Ida, May 12 1923.
4 Neville Chamberlain to Hilda, May 5 1923.
5 For Ben Tillet hinting that he was broke, for Davidson suggesting to Admiral Hall that he should be supported and for Jackson considering 'a special grant of £1,000' see Davidson to Hall, October 19 and Hall to Davidson, October 23 1923 in James, p. 188.
6 Montague-Barlow, short memorandum on policy for Tory party, January 29 1924 enclosed in Barlow to Salisbury, January 29 1924.
7 Ormsby-Gore to Baldwin, January 29 1924.
8 Bledisloe to Lord Robert Cecil, January 30 1924.
9 Lee of Fareham to Reading, January 10 1924, Eur E 238/26.
10 Neville Chamberlain to Ida, July 19 1924.
11 Percy, p. 97. For similar views of Snowden and Clynes in 1918 see Fisher, pp. 110–11 and Bentinck, p. 82.

PAGE 427

1 Strachey to Massingham, January 31 1924, Strachey MSS.
2 Strachey to MacDonald, June 25 1924.
3 MacDonald to ILP Conference at York, April 21 1924, *The Times*, April 22.
4 Neville Chamberlain diary, April 7 and November 5 1924.
5 Neville Chamberlain to Ida, September 13 1924.
6 Austen Chamberlain quoted in Petrie, p. 208.

PAGE 428

1 Neville Chamberlain diary, March 21 1924.

INDEX

Bothwell, 25
Bottomley, Horatio, 12, 65, 87, 99, 104, 115, 299, 360, 425; career, 52–9
Boundary Commission (Ireland), 126, 139, 154–5, 377, 403–5
Bournemouth: Asquithean conference, 235
Bow, 33
Bowerman, C. W., 18
Boyd-Carpenter, W. B., 87, 239, 468, 478, 506
Brace, William, 18, 23, 31, 39, 423, 433
Bradbury, Sir John, baron, 269, 432
Brand, R. H., baron, 503
Bradlaugh, Charles, 52–3
Brailsford, H. N., 35, 372, 380
Bridgeman, W. C., viscount, 2, 208, 257, 323, 387, 418, 423–4, 491, 492; Protection, 248, 311–13, 385, 388–90; successor to Law, 260–1, 264–5; and Baldwin, 294, 335–6, 384, 387, 400, 421
Bright, John, 6, 9, 19
Bristol, 219, 223, 252, 256
British Empire Union, 75
British Legion, 86, 519
British Workers' League, 22
Brockway, A. Fenner, 372
Bromley: by-election, 25
Bruce, Stanley, Viscount Melbourne, 278–9, 284–5, 308, 310
Bryce Commission, 148
Buccleuch, 7th Duke of, 463
Buchanan, George, 366, 410, 426, 433
Buckley, Albert, 239, 326, 432, 546
Buckmaster, S. O., viscount, 17, 97, 99, 104–5, 231, 357, 432, 461, 470
Bull, Sir William, 194–6, 255, 433
Burnley: by-election, 352, 354
Burns, John, 17, 104
Business Government League, 53
Buxton: Liberal conference, 233
Buxton, Charles Roden, 28–9, 43, 370, 433, 457
Buxton, Noel E., baron, Noel-Buxton, 28–9, 43, 288, 368, 370, 372, 375, 433

Camberwell, 25, 98, 105, 154
Cambridge, 76, 105, 160, 225

Campbell, J. R.: case of, 358, 373, 379, 409, 411, 423
Campbell–Bannerman, Sir Henry, 8, 16, 102–3
Canadian Cattle Bill, 183, 201
Cannes conference, 135, 171–2
Canning, George, 153
capital, 36, 40, 42, 46, 51, 53, 73, 88, 113, 122, 174, 226; Labour and, 291
Capital Levy: Labour, 37, 41, 176, 179, 286, 290, 298, 357, 366, 374, 488; Liberals, 92, 104, 160, 287, 345–7, 364, 518; Conservatives, 238, 299
Cardiff, 33
Cardiganshire, 454
Carlton Club meeting, 57, 210–11, 239, 251–2, 388
Carmarthen, 355
Carson, Sir Edward, baron, 8, 21, 81–7, 118–20, 138, 143, 184, 240, 404–5, 428, 433, 478–9
Castlereagh, see Londonderry
Cave, George, viscount, 21, 239, 252, 294, 300, 311, 351, 368, 384, 391, 409, 433
Cawley, Sir F., baron, 94, 453
Cecil, Lady Gwendolen, 71
Cecil, Hugh, baron, Quickswood, 48, 63–5, 71, 87–8, 90, 184–5, 203, 239, 336, 433, 478, 491
Cecil, Robert, Viscount Chelwood, 60–9, 80, 94, 100, 106, 140, 176, 183, 229, 239, 299, 304, 373, 376, 386, 399, 401, 407, 413, 457, 470, 491; career and character, 60–4, 70–1; League of Nations, 62, 65, 68, 99, 170, 300–1, 311–12, 369, 423; and Salisbury, 73, 75, 90, 310, 312, 314, 388, 391; Grey/Cecil/Asquith, 103–6, 123, 126, 282, 325, 336; and Baldwin, 268, 270, 278–9, 283–5, 392, 400, 414; 1923 election, 321–6
Cecil, William, bishop of Exeter, 71
Central Church Committee, 71
Centre Party, 1, 2, 8, 63–5, 87, 94, 101, 110, 118, 122, 151, 162, 169, 214, 231, 235, 239, 252, 255, 319, 344, 367, 390, 395, 468
Chadwick, Sir Robert B., 156, 434
Chalmers, Robert C., baron, 74
Chamberlain, Austen, 8, 71, 115, 124,

Poincaré, Raymond, 156, 182, 197, 207, 224, 281, 284, 301–6
Poland, 34, 36, 50, 79, 171
Pollock, Sir Ernest, Viscount Hanworth, 200, 204, 214, 252, 255, 268–9, 442, 492
Polson, Sir Thomas, 55, 57, 471, 491
Ponsonby, Arthur, baron, 27, 29, 43, 288, 306, 368, 379, 380, 442, 457
Pontefract: by-election, 25
Poor Law, Royal Commission on, 34; Reform, 376
Poplar Board of Guardians, 33, 38, 353, 373
Portsmouth, 45
Pratt, Sir John, 355
Premium Bonds, 55
Pretyman, E. G., 75, 162, 195, 205–8, 210–11, 248, 442
Pringle, W. M. R., 97–8, 222, 354, 357–8, 372, 442
Proportional Representation, 68, 95, 224, 373
Protection, 16, 20, 46–8, 62, 66, 75–6, 87, 115, 131, 147–8, 155, 197, 200, 212, 228, 248, 275–8, 286; as election issue, 295, 297–322, 325–7, 345, 347–8, 350, 358, 376; abandoned, 383, 385–94, 397, 401–2, 407, 417–8, 423, 507
Prothero, R. E., baron, Ernle, 21
Protocols of the Elders of Zion, 83

Radicalism, 2, 7, 15, 179, 352, 355, 358, 367, 376
Rappallo, 182
Reading, Rufus Isaacs, Marquess of, 17, 18, 81, 158, 160–1, 184, 371; India, 120, 347
Reconstruction after War, 71, 88, 159
Rees, Sir J. D., 86
Reform Acts: (1832), 6, 7; (1867 and 1884), 6, 7, 9, 23; (1918), 6, 51, 93, 224, 246
Reith, J. C. W., baron, 255
Rent Control, 291
Reparations, German, 54, 58, 62, 82–3, 95, 115, 175, 197, 217, 224, 256, 281, 284, 292, 295, 302–3
Rhondda, D. A. Thomas, viscount, 17–19, 94, 453
Richardson, Thomas, 27

Riddell, G. A., baron, 19, 224
Ripon, 89
Ritchie, C. T., baron, 71
Roberts, F. S., earl, 83–4
Roberts, G. H., 18, 22–4, 54, 216, 290
Robertson, Sir William, 185
Rochdale, 10
Rosebery, 5th Earl of, 46, 246
Rothermere, Harold Harmsworth, viscount, 1, 12, 36, 54, 60, 87, 99, 115, 136, 140, 153, 163, 183, 279–80, 309–10, 350, 365; career and policy, 45, 47–52; and Law, 118, 206–7, 219–20, 246, 256–7; and Baldwin, 299, 317, 335, 339, 383–6, 392, 400; and Labour, 350, 363, 366, 421–2; see Anti-Waste
Round Table, 66, 83, 215
Rowntree, Seebohm, 224
Ruhr, 224, 233, 250, 280, 292, 295, 302, 389
Rumania, 79, 171
Runciman, Walter, viscount, 17, 21, 48, 66, 80, 97–8, 103, 295, 347, 349, 357, 369, 470; defeats, 98, 231
Rusholme: by-election, 25, 98
Russell, Bertrand, 28–9, 62
Russell, F. S., 2nd Earl, 370
Russell, Odo, 76
Russia, 3, 49, 54, 81, 93, 182, 243, 306; Revolution, 29, 31, 40, 165–6, 169; intervention, 34, 61, 79, 185, 203, 229; recognition, 77, 180, 191, 284, 286; Labour and, 291, 358, 360, 364, 379, 409; see Bolshevism
Rutherford, A. V., 43, 457
Rutland: by-election, 327

Saar, 61
St Albans: by-election, 25
St Davids, Sir John Philipps, viscount, 224, 227
Safeguarding of Industries, 38, 101, 115, 117, 167, 221, 226, 248, 277–8, 318, 390, 401–2
Salford, 229
Salisbury, 3rd Marquess of, 20, 60, 73, 153
Salisbury, 4th Marquess of, 1–3, 48, 63–4, 66, 72–3, 91, 96, 100, 104, 116, 118, 188, 190, 195, 299, 301, 385–8,4 79, 511; career, 60–1, 70–2,